THE MODERNIZATION OF FRENCH JEWRY

The Modernization of French Jewry: Consistory and Community in the Nineteenth Century

Phyllis Cohen Albert

Published by the Brandeis University Press

Distributed by the University Press of New England

Hanover   New Hampshire   1977

Published with the assistance of the
Lucius N. Littauer Foundation and the
Alexander Kohut Memorial Foundation
of the American Academy for Jewish Research

TO THE MEMORY OF MY FATHER

PAUL COHEN ז״ל

WHO HELPED FROM BEGINNING TO END

PREFACE

Like many young and inexperienced scholars I originally set for myself an overambitious goal. Motivated by a double interest in France and in modern Jewish history, and inspired by the paucity of publications on French Jewish history between Napoleon and the Dreyfus Affair, I decided to write a social, institutional, intellectual, and religious history of nineteenth century French Jewry. I soon realized that several works of a more restricted nature must precede a comprehensive study. The present volume, a study of the process of modernization of the French Jewish community during the nineteenth century, is intended to be a central building block in the larger edifice that I still dare to hope I will eventually construct.

This book describes several aspects of the modernization of French Jewry: evolution of the post-emancipatory status of Jews in French law; demographic evolution toward contemporary geographic and occupational distributions; and certain social, institutional, and religious innovations which characterized the final break with traditional society and signaled the irrevocable step into the modern era.

Nineteenth century French Jewry is shown to possess two characteristics which are hallmarks of modern societies. The first is a conscious re-evaluation of traditional values and behavior coupled with a decision to effect deliberate (as opposed to evolutionary) change. The second is a movement toward secularization.

The study emphasizes the consistories, although it is not exclusively about them. Such emphasis seems natural—the consistories were the most comprehensive institutions of the French Jewish community, and were involved directly or indirectly with most aspects of Jewish social, institutional, and ideological evolution. Furthermore, the consistorial archives and the consistorial correspondence found in public archives constitute the largest body of documentation for the study of nineteenth-century French Jewry.

Although the book is concerned with the entire nineteenth century, the focus is on the years between 1830 and 1870. It has been my hypothesis that this period was the formative one for modern French Jewry. Before 1830 the major institutions of French Jewry existed only in embryonic form. The future and stability of the emancipation were far from ensured. By 1870 French Jewry boasted a full network of institutions, all of which interacted with or reacted to the consistory. The emancipation was no longer in question, although antisemitism was a continuing threat. The major ideological arguments had been made, and patterns of behavior had emerged which have remained remarkably stable. The 1871 loss of the eastern provinces as a result of the Franco-Prussian War completed the process by which French Jewry's major concentration had been shifting from Alsace-Lorraine to Paris.

When this work was begun eight years ago the consistory had never been studied systematically. Its archives, which had been utilized for only a few articles and monographs of limited scope, were only beginning to undergo extensive cataloguing and become readily available to scholars. Sections of the archives which had been thought destroyed, or which had been dispersed beyond the French borders, were only beginning to come to light in France, Israel and America.[1] This book is based on an examination of all the consistory archives I could locate and to which I could gain access between 1968 and 1973. Subsequent research in additional depositories has not caused me to modify any of the lines drawn in this book; on the contrary, it has confirmed previous assumptions while supplying additional details and further examples.

In addition to the Jewish archives, I have made use of French national and departmental archives, especially the series for religious groups. Because Judaism was an officially recognized religion in France, its major institutions were quasi-governmental, and the public archives contain extensive correspondence between the Jewish bodies and municipal, departmental, and ministerial authorities. Such documentation sheds light on the social and religious history of France's Jewish community, and is particularly useful in evaluating the nature and tendencies of the consistories. I also relied heavily on the periodicals, books, and pamphlets of the period. Good collections of the rare materials exist at the Bibliothèque Nationale and the Alliance Israélite Universelle in Paris. Some rare pieces are available at Harvard's Houghton Library, and copies of the more readily available periodicals exist in many research and university libraries.

Many people helped me at various stages of this work. I am of course indebted to the scholars whose work preceded mine, but especially to Zosa Szajkowski, whose articles introduced me to the period. Professor Nahum Sarna first alerted me to the presence of consistory documents in the archival collection of the Jewish Theological Seminary library. Dr. Menahem Schmelzer, librarian at the Seminary, graciously facilitated my

1. For further details on the state of the consistorial archives see my articles, "The Archives of the Consistoire Israélite de Bordeaux—1809–1905," in *Revue des Etudes Juives,* CXXXI, 1972, 171–180, and "Consistorial Sources for Nineteenth Century French Jewish History," forthcoming.

consultation of those materials. In France many librarians and archivists assisted and encouraged me, guiding me through the labyrinths of catalogues and uncatalogued materials, and making suggestions for further investigations. I owe a special debt of gratitude to Dr. Gérard Nahon, archivist of the Paris Consistory, who has always been extremely friendly, helpful, efficient and supportive. His interest and encouragement have been of vital importance throughout the years. His invitation to present my initial findings to the Société des Etudes Juives provided my first opportunity to develop the conceptual framework for the study. I am grateful to Dr. Georges Weill, archivist of the central consistory and the Alliance Israélite Universelle; to Mme. Yvonne Levyne, librarian of the Alliance Israélite Universelle, and to her amiable staff; to Dr. Gilbert Cahen, archivist of the Moselle Department; to Dr. François Delpech, of the University of Lyon; to Grand Rabbi Max Warchawski, of Strasbourg; to Professor Simon Schwartzfuchs, of the Central Archives for the History of the Jewish People, in Jerusalem; and to Rabbi Jacky Amar, Cantor Maurice Zerbib and Mr. Emile Léon, of the Bordeaux Consistory. My research was facilitated by the excellent archivists and personnel of the Archives Nationales and the departmental archives of Bas-Rhin, Haut-Rhin, Moselle, Gironde and Seine. The librarians of the Bibliothèque Nationale in Paris were extremely helpful. I would like to thank my friends, Dr. Frances Malino, who paved some French roads for me, and Karl Goldstein, who assisted me with some research and bibliographical problems at the Bibliothèque Nationale.

The distinguished scholars, my teachers, who read the thesis upon which this book is based, offered generously of their time and advice. Professors Alexander Altmann, Rudolph Binion, Nahum Glatzer, Marshall Sklare and Ben Halpern made many useful observations and suggestions, some of which have been incorporated into this book, and some of which have helped me formulate plans for future research. Professor Halpern not only read the thesis in various stages, guided me and prodded me through the awkward first steps of scholarship, and encouraged me by his friendly support; he had a profound influence on my thinking from the time I began studying with him in my early days at Brandeis University.

Bill Earle, who typed several drafts of the manuscript, deciphered the most illegible handwriting, and maintained his cheerfulness and reliability throughout the project.

Acknowledgment is gratefully made to the National Foundation for Jewish Culture, and to its Executive Director, Harry I. Barron, for a grant which financed a large part of this research.

My family was constantly helpful and a source of encouragement. My mother, Ruth Cohen, proofread the entire work at several stages. My sons, David and Michael, helped by sorting papers, drawing maps, proofreading, and letting me work. My husband, Dr. Martin Albert, traveled, read, corrected, discussed, suggested, xeroxed, proofread and much more. Without his belief that this task was worthwhile, it could never have been completed. My daughter, Rachel, who was born during the final stages of revision of the manuscript, put everything into perspective. My father, to whose memory the book is lovingly dedicated, helped from beginning to end.

P.C.A.

Cambridge, Massachusetts
December 1976

CONTENTS

TABLES

MAPS

INTRODUCTION

With the emancipation of the Jews in 1791, France put an official end to the traditional organization and status of the Jewish communities and created the assumption that Jews, freed of their medieval corporate attachments, would be integrated into general society as individuals and citizens. The terms of the emancipation included not only the abandonment of communal autonomy but also the revision of Jewish occupational and geographical distribution. It was expected that Jews would spread themselves throughout the country and be absorbed by the economy in a full range of jobs and professions, and it was especially hoped that they would prove their attachment to France by settling on the land and engaging in the noble, healthy, and fundamental work of agriculture. No attention was given by the young republic and its philosophers to the problem of Jewish institutions.

Most prerevolutionary apologists for the Jews, such as Dohm and Mirabeau,[1] had assumed that political reform and improvement in the status of the Jews would take place with no prejudice to the autonomous structure of the Jewish community, but the Revolution eliminated the option of retaining Jewish autonomy. Thereafter, it was expected that in integrating themselves into France the Jews would give up particularist institutions. In fact, during the early years of the *nouveau régime,* Jews, like Christians, were "integrated" by the destruction of their religious institutions. With the loss of rabbinic jurisdiction and the demise of the *kehilla* (community) structure, the communities lost their ability to collect taxes, and therefore to finance religious, educational, and charitable institutions. Synagogues were pillaged and turned into Temples of Reason to which Jewish schoolmasters conducted their young charges for rationalist patriotic sermons. The Terror finally receded, leaving in its wake the rubble of demolished Jewish institutions, and the question that faced the Jews was the totally new one of whether to rebuild the old institutions or to create others in response to the new expectations and new opportunities. When it was realized that a modern form of the old *kehilla* was not likely to emerge in the impoverished communities, the need for new structures became clear.

The humanist, rationalist philosophy of the Revolution gave

---

1. Christian Dohm, *Ueber die bürgerliche Verbesserung der Juden* (Berlin, 1781); Marquis de Mirabeau, *Sur Moses Mendelssohn, sur la réforme politique des Juifs* (Paris, 1787).

way to the Napoleonic reconciliation with the Church, and interest in religion revived. In 1802 the organizing power of the Catholic Church was marshaled for state use when Napoleon concluded his Concordat with the Pope. In the same year the Protestant sects were given an official government-sponsored hierarchical organization, and the members of these churches were thereby brought under state control. Only the Jews remained beyond the scope of state-organized religion, and Napoleon was not averse to extending this "benefit" to them when they requested it.

Destitute and disorganized, the Jewish communities appealed for governmental intervention and financial aid in the restructuring of their floundering institutions. In response to repeated requests, government representatives, together with selected Jewish leaders, worked out plans for a Jewish consistory, which was instituted in 1808–09 and became the main instrument for effecting reforms in the organizational and cultural structure of French Judaism. State funding, however, was denied until 1831.

The consistory was a quasi-official, hierarchical administration, composed of both rabbis and laymen, which derived all its authority from the government and which was directly responsible to the Ministry of Cults. It was both a religious and an administrative authority, and an internal struggle ensued between the rabbinic and lay factions to determine which of them would dominate in making "religious" decisions. Through a series of legislative and practical gains the laymen obtained control and attempted to use their power to mold a modern Judaism with aesthetically redesigned ceremonies. They introduced sermons, orderliness, pomp, choral music, organs, confirmation ceremonies, temple weddings, ceremonies on the birth of girls, funeral orations and music at the graveside, reforms in the practice of circumcision, and a modern kind of rabbi whose functions were largely pastoral.

From the diversity of several independent Jewries, the consistory sought to unify the French Jews and to convert the *Juif* (Jew) to *l'Israélite français* (the French Israelite). Prior to the Revolution each community—the Sephardim of the Southwest, the Ashkenazim of the Northeast, the Comtadin Jews of the Papal Provinces—had its own particular customs, forms of organization, and relationship to governmental authority. There were no official ties among the several communities and very little similarity in socioeconomic patterns. The consistory's goal of unifying the Jews in a single set of aims, views, and practices was partially a response to the threat of assimilation and partially a means of improving the Jew's image in general society. Insecure in their own emancipated status, consistory members sought to end the embarrassment and potential danger caused by the persistent existence of a group of anachronistic coreligionists. As acculturated Jews, they attempted to protect their own position by implanting in the public mind a new image of the Jew as *l'Israélite français*.

Although nineteenth century Jews generally found it to their advantage to ally themselves with liberalism, which endorsed Jewish emancipation, French Jewish leaders were very conservative. This is partially explained by the fact that the consistory required the support of the authorities, especially in suppressing rival Jewish institutions. Even in its adopted role of protector of the Jewish community, the consistory generally pursued a discreetly conservative approach that made use of political connections and secret petitions to the government, and eschewed publicity and appeals to public opinion. Because of its conservative approach the consistory alienated many of the young liberals of the mid-century, thus paving the way for the founding of the *Alliance Israélite Universelle*.

Because it was unrepresentative of the masses, the consistory was vulnerable to competition from small societies of poor people, who frequently formed mutual aid societies or *minyanim* (prayer meetings). Such societies functioned democratically; in them the poor found meaningful social contacts and leadership, both of which were denied them in consistory institutions.

Outside France the consistory enjoyed a mixed reputation. In its early years it was looked upon as a potential agent of reform and as an international spokesman for Jews; its religious views were sought by Jewish communities elsewhere, and were regarded as authoritative. Thus in 1818 the Copenhagen Jewish community (probably because of reforms in Hamburg) requested that the central consistory pronounce on the permissibility of certain religious reforms, such as omitting the prayers for the Messiah, eliminating Hebrew from the service, introducing family pews, and following Biblical law only, not Talmud.[2] In 1831 Jewish leaders in Mayence, faced with the need to justify to the orthodox their introduction of a choir, requested that the central consistory certify that choral music is permitted in Judaism.[3] In 1837 reformer Michael Creizenach of Frankfurt asked the central consistory to declare that it is permissible to eat peas, beans, lentils, and rice during Passover,[4] and in 1847 the Hamburg Jewish community asked the central consistory to define who is a Jew and to report how the Paris synagogue treats (ritualistically) the uncircumcised son of Jewish parents.[5]

In 1838 Ludwig Philippson, writing in his *Allgemeine Zeitung des Judentums,* judged that the consistory had not fulfilled its promise; although it could have been an effective

2. Draft of the reply by the rabbis of the Paris and central consistories to the Copenhagen community, October 7, 1818, in Arch. JTS. (The French rabbis denied the permissibility of such reforms.)

3. Letter from "le président et préposés du culte israélite à Mayence" to the central consistory, June, 1831, in Arch. P.C., I^{CC} 59.

4. In reporting ironically this request, consistory critic and early reformer Olry Terquem observed that this was a singular request to make of men who ate pork! Tsarphati [Terquem], *Neuvième lettre d'un israélite français à ses coreligionnaires* (Paris, 1837), p. 3.

5. Arch. P.C., I^{CC} 60.

institution, it had in fact only impeded progress. Yet in 1854 Philippson suggested that the central consistory take charge of an international organization that would be created to extend aid to the Jews of the Ottoman Empire, by bringing Turkish Jews to Europe for education and teacher training. Evidently he considered that the consistory was still a viable institution. (Although the consistory agreed to participate in this work, such a project did not materialize until the formation of the *Alliance Israélite Universelle.*)

The proponents of Jewish emancipation in France erroneously believed that legal equality and social integration would be the immediate results of the new order. In fact, however, legal equality was not achieved until the middle of the nineteenth century, as exceptional legislation continued to be enforced until the Jewish oath (*More Judaïco*) was abolished in 1846. Even after that date the communities were pressed to pay prerevolutionary corporate debts, which the Revolution had refused to nationalize, although it had nationalized the debts of other religious corporations.[6] Social integration was even more elusive than legal equality; despite many individual cases of assimilation, large-scale social integration of the Jews never occurred; there was a continual current of anti-Jewish sentiment, which engendered periodic outbursts of slander, discrimination, and even violence.[7]

Nor did the Revolution bring about the geographic and economic integration of the Jewish population. Although Jews spread slowly into areas where they had been prohibited from dwelling during the *ancien régime,* they tended to remain in communities with sizable Jewish populations, and only a tiny fraction of them moved beyond the *départements* where Jews were already living at the beginning of the century. Unlike the rest of French society, the Jews rapidly became an urban population, concentrated in several of the largest French cities. With increased opportunity, Jews sought and obtained education in numbers never before reached, and in higher proportion than was common among the general population. They entered the liberal professions and public careers previously closed to them. Yet the majority of Jews throughout the century continued to be engaged in commercial enterprises, virtually none became farmers, and very large numbers remained indigent. Moreover, despite the rationalism of the intellectuals, the masses of French Jews remained orthodox. It is against this background (described in Part One, below) that we must understand the work of the consistory in asserting itself and attempting to "reform" the French Jews.

6. The official justification for this was that prior to the Revolution the Jews had been a foreign group, not a French corporation.

7. Anti-Jewish riots in Alsace accompanied each revolution, and during the 1850's there were complaints of mob violence directed against Jews. Louis Veuillot and others attacked Jews in the press; lawyers called them "juif" in the courtroom. Some Jews were denied judicial and teaching posts solely on religious grounds.

PART ONE

DEMOGRAPHICAL BACKGROUND

CHAPTER I   POPULATION LEVELS AND

CHANGES IN GEOGRAPHIC DISTRIBUTION

During the course of the nineteenth century, partly as a result of the emancipation and the new legal system governing Jewish organization, and partly as a result of the changing French economy, the demographical patterns of the French Jews were modified. The present chapter deals with four major aspects of the population changes: population levels, changing regional distribution, urbanization, and the ratio of Jews to the total French population.

A. French Jewish Population Levels

When the consistory system was established in 1808–09 the total French Jewish population was approximately 47,000. During the next twenty-five years, under Napoleon and the Bourbon Restoration, it increased rapidly to a total of about 70,000 in 1831. In 1845 the consistory estimated a Jewish population of 86,000. By 1853 it had increased to 89,000, and in 1861 it reached 96,000 (Table I-1). The figure was approaching the 100,000 mark when the loss of Alsace-Lorraine entailed a 45 percent loss to France of its Jewish population. Thus it is clear that the French Jewish population more than doubled from 1808 to 1870 and was subsequently reduced to approximately the level at which it had been at the beginning of the century.[1]

The rapid increase in Jewish population is generally attributed to the favorable effects of the emancipation, although nineteenth century claims that there was much immigration of Jews into France have been disputed by recent scholars, who attribute most of the population growth to natural increase. Only after 1880 was mass immigration from the east an important factor in Jewish population growth.

B. Changing Regional Distribution

The distribution of the Jewish population among the various departments has never paralleled the general population distribution. In 1809 there were eighty-six departments.[2] In one half of them there was not a single Jewish inhabitant. Jews lived only in the other forty-three, in which they numbered between one and more than 16,000 per department. Although the Jews began to spread throughout France they never achieved a typical population distribution. Even in 1861 Jewish population levels by department varied between zero and 25,000.

The nineteenth century saw large increases of Jewish population in some areas and moderate increases elsewhere; in some areas the Jewish population dwindled. Although very few Jews moved into areas previously totally uninhabited by Jews,[3] new Jewish communities began to develop in regions that were contiguous to older Jewish centers, and in which very small numbers of Jews already lived at the beginning of the nineteenth century. Maps I-1 to I-4 show population levels, by department, in 1815, 1841, 1853 and 1861.

In 1809, 99 percent of the total French Jewish population

TABLE I-1.
French-Jewish Population
1808–1861

Year	Jewish Population[a]
1815	46,863
1831	70,000
1845	85,910
1853	89,220
1861	95,881

[a]The 1815 figure is the author's calculation, based on the decree of December 11, 1808, establishing the consistories, and on S. Posener, "Les Juifs sous le premier empire: les statistiques générales," *REJ*, 93 (1932), 197. The 1831 figure is the author's estimate, based on 1831 central consistory estimates, in Robert Anchel, *Notes sur les frais du culte juif en France de 1815 à 1831* (Paris, 1928), p. 43, and the 1845 consistory census, in A.N., F^{19} 11016. The 1845 figure is the central consistory census of that year, in A.N., F^{19} 11016; cf. *U.I.*, 5 (1849), 40. The 1853 figure is the author's calculation, based on the 1853 consistory census, in A.N., F^{19} 11024, and the Jewish population of an additional thirty-four departments reported by the 1851 general census, in *Statistique de la France*, 2ème série, tome 2, p. xxv. The 1861 figure is the author's calculation based on an 1861 consistory table of Jewish population statistics, in A.N., F^{19*} 1821, and the 1861 general census for the departments not counted by the consistory, in *Statistique de la France*, 2ème série, tome 13.

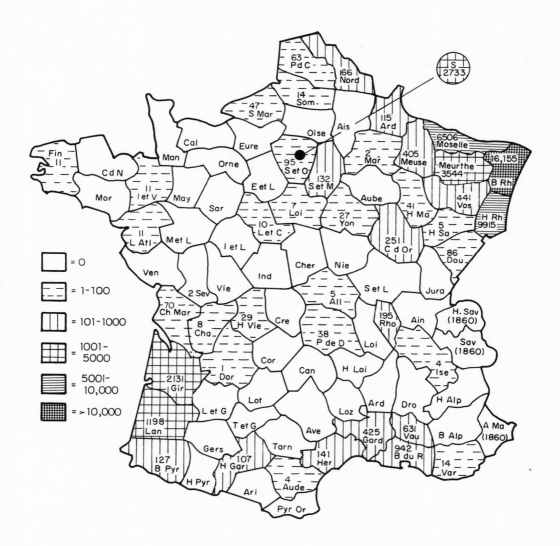

I-1   1815: Jewish Population by Department

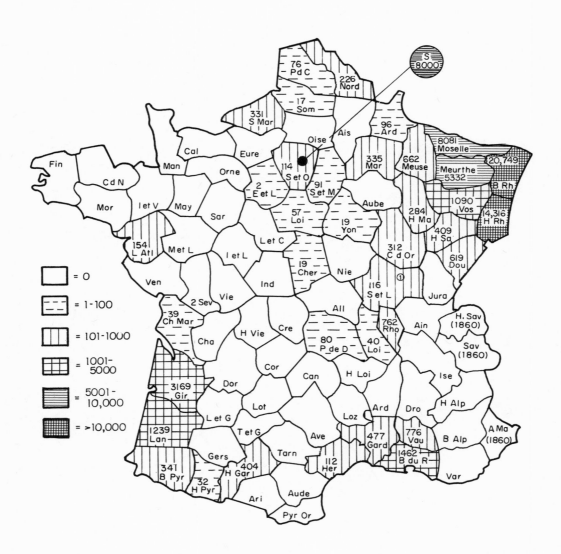

I-2   1841: Jewish Population by Department

I-3   1853: Jewish Population by Department

I-4   1861: Jewish Population by Department

lived within twenty-one of the eighty-seven departments (Map I-5). Gradually the population spread out, and these twenty-one departments housed only 94.5 percent of the Jewish population in 1861. We must count the Jews of an ever-increasing number of departments in order to account for 99 percent of the total Jewish population. In 1841, twenty-seven departments, in 1851, thirty-two departments, and in 1861, thirty-three departments housed 99 percent of the French Jews (Maps I-6 to I-8). Thus, between 1809 and 1861 twelve departments saw the implantation of sizable new Jewish communities. These were departments which already contained a tiny scattered Jewish population prior to 1808. Few Jews ventured into regions that had been totally uninhabited by Jews prior to the establishment of the consistories.[4] Yet some few entirely new Jewish settlements did develop. We shall first describe this small movement of Jews into thirty-eight of the forty-three departments which had no Jews at all in 1808, and then turn our attention to the larger migrations of Jews within the area of original settlement (forty-three departments).

1. Migration of Jews into Departments Which Had No Jews in 1808

As late as 1861 there were six departments in which no Jews resided. Jews were clearly not achieving full geographic integration. Yet a small number of Jews (1034, or 1.08 percent of the total) had, in fact, moved into thirty-eight departments which had no Jewish population in 1808. In twenty-three of them there were only between one and nineteen Jews, or a total Jewish population for these twenty-three departments of 167 (0.10 percent of the total 1861 Jewish population). It was in the remaining fifteen departments that there were Jews located in sufficient concentration (from twenty to 300 people) for us to say that they constituted new communities (Map I-9). In eight of these fifteen departments there were twenty to forty-eight Jews; in five there were forty-nine to sixty; in one there were ninety-six; in one there were 300. In 1861 the Jewish population of all fifteen departments amounted to 867, or 0.98 percent of the total 1861 Jewish population.[5]

We do not know the precise chronology of Jewish population growth in these fifteen departments, because neither the government nor the consistory was able to gather completely accurate data. It is clear from a comparison of the various statistics at our disposal that the consistories were not in contact with many of the small Jewish communities that had developed by the 1850's and 1860's. Thus the only population data that we have for some of these communities are derived from the (usually low) general French census returns, and the earliest set available is that of 1851. In 1853 the Jewish census by the consistories ignored about a thousand Jews in thirty-four

I-5   1815: Jewish Population Distribution

I-6   1841: Jewish Population Distribution

I-7   1851: Jewish Population Distribution

I-8   1861: Jewish Population Distribution

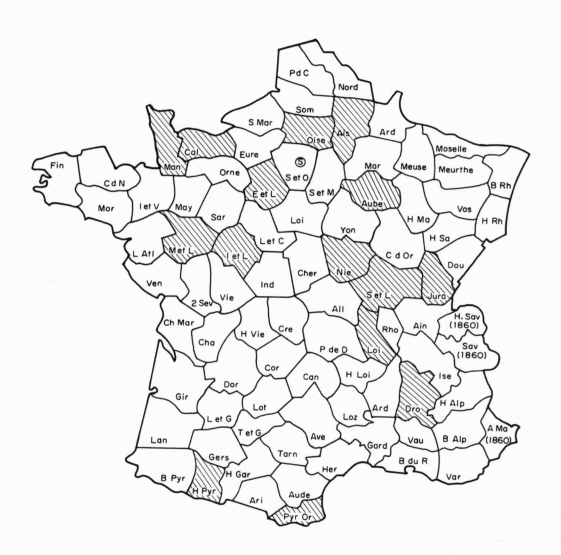

I-9 New Jewish Communities, 1808–1861

departments where the 1851 general census had located them. A similar problem no doubt exists with the 1841 and 1845 consistory censuses, on which we rely. If some day we are able to tap the 1841 and 1846 general census results for the communes of these departments, they may provide a corrective to the consistory's data, and thereby clarify the chronology of the movement of Jews beyond the original Jewish settlement.

*2. Movement into Departments
That Already Had Jews in 1808*

In the "original twenty-one departments," which in 1808 had housed 99 percent of the Jewish population, the number of Jews either remained stable or increased; only that of Gard decreased.[6] The increases ranged from slight in some places to eightfold in the Seine (Paris).

As we have said, new Jewish communities, in areas beyond the original twenty-one departments of major concentration, developed more frequently in the additional twenty-two departments that already had a small Jewish population in 1808, than in the departments with no Jews in 1808. Thus the Jewish population of these twenty-two departments grew from 508 (one percent of the total) in 1808, to 3929 (4 percent of the total) by 1861, an increase of 700 percent. Within these twenty-two departments Jewish population growth had varied considerably. Ten of the departments had a very small Jewish population in 1861 (one to fifty-one Jews, or a total of 221). In the ten departments taken as a group, the Jewish population increase between 1808 and 1861 had been 46.35 percent, although in three of the ten departments the Jewish population had decreased.[7] In the remaining twelve departments (Map I-10), the Jewish population of 1861 ranged from sixty-seven to 842 Jews, or a total of 3708 in the twelve departments. In these twelve departments the increase in Jewish population from 1808 to 1861 was more than 900 percent (Table I-2).

In summary, we show (Table I-3) the growth of the Jewish population between 1808 and 1861 in the twenty-one departments of original concentration and the twenty-two additional departments which had a small Jewish population in 1808. We also show the movement of Jews into thirty-eight departments which had no Jews in 1808.

Within the original departments of Jewish settlement, three main groupings are apparent. In the northeast was the Ashkenazi Jewish community of Alsace-Lorraine, comprising more than three quarters of the 1815 Jewish population. In the south were the Sephardi and Comtadin communities, which accounted for 12 percent of the French Jewish population in 1815. Paris (a mixed community of Ashkenazi, Sephardi, and Comtadin elements) was the third major Jewish center, and held 6 percent of the total Jewish population in 1815.

I-10   Departments Which Together Had 1% of the
Jewish Population in 1808 and 4% in 1861

TABLE I-2.

*Jewish Population Increase
in Twelve Departments, 1808–1861*

Department	Jewish Population 1808	Jewish Population 1861	Amount of Increase	Percent of Increase
Doubs	86	842	756	879
Loire Inférieur	11	159	148	1345
Loiret	7	81	74	1057
Marne	2	446	444	2220
Haute-Marne	41	301	260	634
Pas-de-Calais	63	140	77	122
Puy-de-Dôme	38	350	312	821
Haute-Saône	5	616	611	12,220
Seine-Inférieur	47	464	417	887
Somme	14	81	67	479
Var	14	67	53	379
Haute-Vienne	29	161	132	455
Total	357	3708	3351	911

TABLE I-3.

Changes in Population Distribution, 1808–1861

Location	1808			1861		
	Number of Departments	Jewish Population	Percent of Total Jewish Population	Number of Departments	Jewish Population	Percent of Total Jewish Population
Concentration of original main settlement	21	46,355	99	21	90,108	94.48
Area of original small, scattered Jewish population	22	508	1	22	3,929	4.11
Area with no Jews originally	38	0	0	38	1,034	1.08
	5	0	0	5	0	0
Departments added in 1860	—	—	—	1	0	0
	—	—	—	2	363[a]	0.33[a]
Total	86	46,863	100	89	95,434[b]	100

[a]Mainly in Alpes-Maritimes (Nice). The population there in 1861 was 321 (compared with 303 in 1808).

[b]This total ignores the 447 Jews scattered in unknown regions of the Bayonne consistory. Cf. Table I-1.

3. Alsace-Lorraine

In 1808, 79 percent of the French Jewish population was concentrated in the six departments that had been formed from the old provinces of Alsace and Lorraine,[8] but because of more rapid growth rates in other areas, the ratio of the Jews of Alsace-Lorraine to the total French Jewish population began a steady decline. Thus the percentage of the French Jewish population which lived in Alsace-Lorraine was 71 in 1842, 62 in 1853, and 57 in 1861.[9] By the time the provinces were lost to Germany in 1871, they contained only about 55 percent of the total Jewish population within the old boundaries, and this again decreased when many Jews opted for French citizenship and moved into areas within the new French borders.[10] One may assume that had the war not occurred, the natural decline would have continued, and that by the end of the nineteenth century Alsace-Lorraine would no longer have been the home of the majority of the French Jews. Historically, however, it was the war that gave Paris the majority of the French Jewish population.

It should be stressed that despite the decline in relative importance of Alsace-Lorraine as the residence of the French Jews, the total Jewish population in Alsace-Lorraine increased 46 percent between 1808 and 1861. The rate of increase ranged from a low of 19 percent in Moselle to a high of 246 percent in Vosges. In two of the departments (Meuse and Vosges), the growth rate exceeded that of the total French Jewish population, suggesting that there had been movement into these departments. Comparing the population increase of the two provinces, we find that Lorraine saw a more rapid rate of growth during this period (49 percent) than did Alsace (44 percent).

During the entire nineteenth century some Jews did leave Alsace-Lorraine to go to other parts of France and abroad, especially to Algeria and the United States. The main motivations for emigration were poverty, famine, and epidemics,[11] although an additional factor was undoubtedly anti-Semitism.[12] Until the middle of the century, as we have already shown, the population continued to increase, apparently because the exodus was balanced by a small amount of immigration from Germany and Poland, coupled with a high rate of natural increase. After the midpoint of the nineteenth century, however, the population in the northeastern provinces began to decline. This phenomenon was not restricted to the Jews alone; between 1851 and 1861, according to the general censuses of those years, the total French population in eight northeastern departments decreased by 2.1 percent. During approximately the same period (using the 1853 consistory population statistics and those of 1861) there was a decrease in the Jewish population of 2.6 percent in the same eight departments.[13]

4. Seine

The percentage of the French Jews living in Paris increased in proportion to the decrease in Alsace-Lorraine. Thus these two areas taken together constituted a fairly stable proportion of the Jewish population—85 percent in 1808 and 83 percent in 1861 (Table I-4).

TABLE I-4.
Relative Concentration of Jews in Paris and in Alsace-Lorraine, 1808 to 1861, Showing the Stability of the Concentration in the Combined Areas (Expressed in percentage of the total Jewish population)

Date	Alsace-Lorraine	Seine (Paris)	Combined Total
1808	78.87	5.83	84.70
1841	71.42	11.38	82.90
1853	62.52	20.38	83.00
1861	56.50	26.20	82.70

Although it is true that Paris was growing rapidly at this time, the growth of its Jewish population was far in excess of its general growth rate. Twenty percent of the French Jewish population lived in Paris in 1853, as compared with only 3 percent of the total French population. By 1872 the gap had widened, and the respective percentages had risen to 47 and 5.[14]

5. The South

After Alsace-Lorraine and Paris, the third major Jewish center was in the south. These were mostly "Portuguese" and "Comtadin" Jews. The Portuguese, or Sephardim, were originally from the Iberian peninsula, and were the descendants of those merchants who arrived in Bayonne and Bordeaux as New Christians. Some Ashkenazim lived among them and shared their (Sephardi) institutions. The Comtadin Jews were originally from the area that had been the papal province of Comtat Venaissin (later the department of Vaucluse). There they lived in the "Four Communities" of Avignon, Carpentras, Cavaillon, and L'Isle-sur-Sorgue. Marseille was a mixed community of all three groups of Jews: Ashkenazim, Sephardim, and Comtadin.

The total Jewish population of the nine departments which encompassed the southern communities increased by 46 percent during the period from 1815 to 1861. This reflects mainly the growth of Marseille, in Bouches-du-Rhône (Table I-5). Despite the absolute increase, however, the percentage of the total French Jewish population that resided in these nine departments decreased from 12 percent to 9 percent.

TABLE I-5.

*Increase/Decrease of Jewish Population in Nine Departments
of Sephardi and Comtadin Population, 1815–1861*

Department	1815	1861	Increase/ Decrease
Charente-Inférieur	70	51	–19
Haute-Garonne	107	394	287
Gironde	2131	3000	869
Landes and Basses- Pyrénées[a]	1325	1293	–32
Bouches-du-Rhône	942	2532	1590
Gard	425	375	–50
Hérault	141	171	30
Vaucluse	631	650	19
Total	5772	8466	2694 (46%)

[a]These two departments are taken together to show the evolution of the
population of St. Esprit and Bayonne, without the confusion caused by
the annexation of St. Esprit to Bayonne in 1857.

6. Distribution by Consistory

It is important to look at the size of the Jewish populations
controlled by the various consistories whose tendencies and relative strengths concern us. Upon the creation of the consistories,
Strasbourg controlled the largest population, followed by Colmar, Metz, Nancy, and Paris, in that order. By 1841 Paris had
overtaken both Metz and Nancy and was third in importance by
size. By 1845 Paris had moved into second place, and Nancy
had grown larger than Metz. The order was now Strasbourg,
Paris, Colmar, Nancy, Metz. This order was retained for about
ten years, and sometime prior to 1861 the Paris consistory
moved into first place.

The smallest consistories in 1808 were Bordeaux and Marseille. By 1861 they were still the smallest of the original
consistories, but two new and even smaller consistories had
been created in St. Esprit and Lyon. The decrease of population suffered between 1845 and 1851 by the Bordeaux consistory was due not to a diminution of the population in that area
but to the creation, in 1846, of the St. Esprit consistory.
Similarly, the 1857 creation of the Lyon consistory drew population from the three consistories of Nancy, Colmar, and
Marseille (Table I-6).[15]

C. Urbanization

The French Jewish population was not initially an urban population. Prior to the Revolution, 80 percent of the French Jews

lived in Alsace-Lorraine, where they were prohibited from resid-
ing in the cities. They therefore formed small communities—
generally fewer than 500 people—scattered among several
hundred villages.

TABLE I-6.
Relative Size of Each Consistory District, 1815–1861

	1815		1841		1853		1861	
Consistory	Jewish Popu- lation	Percent of Total Jewish Popu- lation	Jewish Popu- lation	Percent of Total Jewish Popu- lation	Jewish Popu- lation	Percent of Total Jewish Popu- lation	Jewish Popu- lation	Percent of Total Jewish Popu- lation
Bordeaux	3,713	7.92	5,304	7.52	4,042	4.58	3,663	3.82
Colmar	9,920	21.17	14,725	20.94	17,184	19.45	17,335	18.08
Lyon[a]	—	—	—	—	—	—	2,415	2.52
Marseille	2,352	5.02	3,629	5.16	4,612	5.22	4,220	4.40
Metz	6,621	14.13	8,177	11.63	8,075	9.14	7,853	8.19
Nancy	4,517	9.64	7,987	11.36	8,998	10.19	8,752	9.13
Paris	3,585	7.65	9,753	13.87	20,540	23.25	28,507	29.73
St. Esprit- Bayonne[b]	—	—	—	—	2,074	2.35	2,200	2.29
Strasbourg	16,155	34.47	20,749	29.50	22,806	25.82	20,936	21.84

[a] Consistory established in 1857.
[b] Consistory established in 1846.

Immediately after the Revolution and the removal of
previous restrictions, Jews began to move to the cities, both in
Alsace-Lorraine and throughout the country, and quickly
achieved a rate of urbanization considerably higher than that of
the general French population. Thus a study of the Jewish
population distribution during the First Empire has shown that
in all areas with recent Jewish implantations, the Jews were
almost all concentrated in *villes chefs-lieux,* the capital cities of
the several districts (*arrondissements*) within each *département.*
Secondarily, they entered the other cities of the department
and almost always formed an urban population.[16]

The tendency toward urbanization is evidently ascribable to
the economic opportunities of the cities and large towns, although some writers have also cited as a cause the anti-Jewish
attitude prevalent in the smaller settlements.[17] The outstanding
example of the movement toward the cities is the growth of
Paris, which had a small Jewish community of several hundred
in 1789, and which became the center of French Judaism, housing about 40,000 Jews (67 percent of the estimated total of
60,000) in 1880. In the east Jews moved toward established
centers of Jewish population, especially Nancy and Strasbourg;
Metz increased less rapidly.

Although the tendency to move to the cities was less pronounced among the Jews of Alsace-Lorraine than among the
rest of the French Jews, even in Alsace-Lorraine the Jews were

more highly urbanized than the general population.[18] In all of France the Jewish population was much more highly urbanized than the general population, which remained rural throughout the entire nineteenth century.[19] According to the 1851 general census, 45.1 percent of the French Jews lived in the 368 cities that were *chefs-lieux d'arrondissements* (capitals of districts, and generally the largest towns or cities of their *départements*), whereas only 17.9 percent of the total French population lived in the same 368 cities and towns.[20] By 1871 the proportion of the total population that resided in the *villes chefs-lieux* within the old boundaries had risen slightly, to about 20 percent, but the percentage of the Jewish population that lived in *chefs-lieux* had climbed much faster—to 63.2 percent.[21]

Separating the statistics for Alsace-Lorraine from those for the rest of the country, we find that the degree of urbanization of the Jews outside Alsace-Lorraine was considerably higher than the combined figures would suggest. Thus, according to the 1851 census, 24 percent of the Jewish population of Alsace-Lorraine lived in cities that were *chefs-lieux,* but elsewhere 91 percent lived in *chefs-lieux.* By 1871 the degree of urbanization had increased further; 31 percent of the Jewish population of Alsace-Lorraine lived in *villes chefs-lieux,* as did 97 percent of the rest of the Jewish population.

It is possible that the urbanization rates were even higher than the available data indicate; a problem arises from using the criterion of domicile in a *chef-lieu* as an indication of urbanization in Alsace-Lorraine. The pattern of population distribution in that area was more diffuse than elsewhere; the *chefs-lieux,* with some exceptions, were not large cities, and there were many additional small towns and cities that did not have the status of *chef-lieu,* which had Jewish communities.

The Jewish population tended not only toward urbanization, but toward concentration in few areas and in several cities. Thus 35 percent of the French Jewish population of 1841 resided in sixteen cities, all located in the nine departments housing consistories. In 1861 45 percent of the total Jewish population lived in the same sixteen communities (Table I-7).

It is possible to compare relative Jewish and general concentration in the nine cities that housed the largest French Jewish communities (Bordeaux, Colmar, Lyon, Marseille, Metz, Mulhouse, Nancy, Paris, and Strasbourg). Thirty-nine percent of the entire French Jewish population and 5 percent of the general population lived in these nine cities in 1853.[22] In the next eight years Jewish concentration in the nine cities grew more rapidly than did the general concentration. Thus in 1861 they housed 42 percent of the Jewish population and 7 percent of the total population[23] (Table I-8).

The Jewish population of Paris increased more rapidly than that of any other city. In 1811 it was already the largest Jewish community of the country, accounting for 5.8 percent of the total Jewish population. But Metz was a close second with 5.12

TABLE I-7.
Jewish Population in Sixteen Cities, 1841–1861

City[a]	1841 (Total French Jewish Population: 70,324)		1861 (Total French Jewish Population: 95,881)	
	Jewish Population	Percent of Total	Jewish Population	Percent of Total
Bischeim	741	1.05	830	0.87
Bordeaux	3,050	4.34	3,000	3.13
Colmar	611	0.87	1,250	1.30
Haguenau	837	1.19	637	0.66
Hegenheim	845	1.20	841	0.88
Lyon	679	0.97	1,100	1.15
Marseille	1,007	1.43	?	?
Metz	2,232	3.17	2,863	2.99
Mulhouse	800	1.14	1,750	1.83
Nancy	1,100	1.56	1,389	1.45
Paris	8,000	11.36	25,000	26.07
St. Esprit-Bayonne	1,126	1.60	?	?
Soultz	625	0.89	750	0.78
Strasbourg	1,628	2.32	2,229	2.32
Toul	402	0.57	612	0.64
Wintzenheim	806	1.15	803	0.84
Total	24,804	34.82	45,484	44.90

[a] Cities listed are those with a Jewish population of more than 600 in either 1841 or 1861. These sixteen cities are in the nine departments with consistories.

percent, and Bordeaux and Strasbourg followed with 4.55 percent and 3.15 percent respectively. There then ensued a spectacular increase of the Parisian Jewish community at the expense of most of the other cities.

Jews moved toward Paris in greater proportion than did non-Jewish provincials. Paris housed 5.83 percent of the French Jews in 1811, 11.38 percent in 1841, 17.46 percent in 1845, 20.38 percent in 1853, and 26.20 percent in 1861. In the latter year, by comparison, only 4.54 percent of the total French population lived in Paris. By 1880 Paris held approximately 67 percent of the total French Jewish population.

D. The Ratio of Jews to Total Population

From 1811 to 1861 the ratio of the Jewish to the general population increased from 0.16 percent to 0.26 percent

(Table I-9). Even the second figure is very low; at that time the ratio of the world's Jewish population to the entire world population was probably around 0.30 percent, and in Europe since the middle ages it has varied from 0.5 to 6 percent.[24]

Although the overall density of Jews was quite low, it did reach considerably higher proportions in areas of large Jewish population. Thus, on a department level, the density of Jewish population varied from zero to 3.6 percent. In five departments

TABLE I-8

Comparison of Jewish and General
Tendency to Concentrate in Nine Cities, 1811–1861[a]

City	1811 Jewish	1811 General	1853 Jewish	1853 General	1861 Jewish	1861 General
Bordeaux	4.55	0.32	3.96	0.37	3.13	0.44
Colmar	?	0.05	1.40	0.06	1.30	0.06
Lyon	?	0.36	1.24	0.49	1.15	0.85
Marseille	0.94	0.35	1.69	0.56	?[b]	0.70
Metz	5.12	0.14	2.70	0.16	2.99	0.15
Mulhouse	?	?	1.73	0.08	1.83	0.12
Nancy	1.58	0.10	1.57	0.13	1.45	0.13
Paris	5.83	2.14	20.38	2.94	26.07	4.54
Strasbourg	3.15	0.18	2.70	0.21	2.32	0.19

[a] For each city, figures are expressed as percentages, which represent that city's Jewish or general population with respect to the total Jewish or general population of France. Percentages listed are the author's calculations. For 1811: Jewish statistics based on Posener's figures (see Table I-1); general statistics based on *Statistique de la France,* vol. 2, pp. 267–279. For 1853: Jewish statistics based on 1853 consistory population figures (see Table I-1); general statistics based on *Statistique de la France,* vol. 2, pp. 262 ff., 1851 general census. For 1861: Jewish statistics based on 1861 consistory figures (see Table I-1); general statistics based on *Statistique de la France,* vol. 13, pp. 208 ff., 1861 general census.
[b] Figure not available. Probably not lower than in 1853.

TABLE I-9

Ratio of Jews to Total Population, 1811–1861

	1811[a]	1836–41[b]	1861[c]
Total population of France	29,092,734	33,540,910	37,386,313
Total Jewish population of France	46,863	70,324	95,881
Ratio of Jews to total population, expressed in percentage	0.16	0.21	0.26

[a] Jewish statistics: see Table I-1; general statistics: general census of 1811, published in *Statistique de la France.*
[b] Jewish statistics: A.N., F[19] 11024 (1841); general statistics: general census, 1836, published in *Statistique de la France.*
[c] Jewish statistics: see Table I-1; general statistics: general census, 1861, published in *Statistique de la France.*

(Bas-Rhin, Haut-Rhin, Moselle, Meurthe, Seine) the ratio exceeded one percent, with a range of 1.27 to 3.62 percent.[25] (See Appendix A, Table A-15.) In the individual cities Jewish density varied from zero to 8 percent. It was in Toul (Meurthe) that the density reached 8 percent. In three other cities (Colmar, Haguenau, and Metz) it exceeded 5 percent. In Mulhouse it was 3.81 percent, and in Strasbourg it was 3.12 percent. A density greater than 2 percent was achieved only in Bordeaux and in towns located in Alsace-Lorraine (Table I-10).

TABLE I-10

*Percentage of Jews in General
Population of Twelve Cities, 1808–1861*

City	1808–11	1836–41	1851–53	1861
Bayonne			5.51	
Bordeaux	2.27	3.09	2.67	1.84
Colmar		3.83	5.84	5.52
Haguenau			6.57	5.75
Lyon		0.45	0.62	0.35
Marseille	0.43	0.69	0.75	
Metz	5.97	5.22	4.13	5.03
Mulhouse			5.16	3.81
Nancy	2.55	3.50	3.08	2.82
Paris	0.44	0.88	1.71	1.47
Strasbourg	2.81	2.81	3.16	3.12
Toul		5.48	7.19	8.18

A. Occupations

Prior to the Revolution and during the early years of the nineteenth century the primary Jewish occupations were the
lowest levels of trade and banking. Jews were rag dealers,
itinerant peddlers, second-hand dealers, money lenders, and
money changers. Studies by Szajkowski and Catane show that
these occupations remained predominant during the First Empire: "nous les trouvons encore, plus de quinze ans après [la
révolution] adonnés en grand nombre au "petit commerce" qui
était autrefois leur seul gagne-pain possible."[1]

Some wealthier French Jews were involved in wholesale
supply, higher levels of banking, and horse trading. Horse trading earned Metz Jews both a decent living and a degree of
respectability. This was proudly pointed out by the orthodox
Jew Moïse Biding, who printed a reply to the attacks on traditional Judaism and Jews by the reformer Olry Terquem
(Tsarphati). Biding refuted the notion that the Jews needed to
be "regenerated." He argued that as early as the eighteenth century Metz Jews engaged in supplying the government, the
military, and the shopkeepers with wholesale goods. In regard
to the advantage that accrued to France as a result of Jewish
horse traders from Metz, Biding quotes an eighteenth-century
geography by Hosmann: "Les Juifs de Metz font un commerce
de chevaux très-étendu, et très avantageux à la France."[2]

Throughout most of the century, at least until 1870, the
majority of Jews remained in commercial occupations, but
within this broad category there was an upward movement.
Thus there were decreasing concentrations of Jews in *colportage*
(peddling) and *brocantage* (second-hand dealing). Larger numbers of Jews now moved on to the levels of *commerçant* (shop-
keeper), *marchand* (merchant) and *négociant* (wholesaler).[3] The
rapidity of this rise varied with the area, but everywhere the
same trend occurred. In her study of Paris Jewry 1809–1840,
Christine Samson found that 55 percent of the population had
been engaged in *petit commerce* in 1809, as compared with an
average of only 52.6 percent during the period from 1809 to
1840. A slight downward trend was already evident. Moreover,
even within the field of *petit commerce* the trend was away
from *brocantage* and *colportage,* and into shopkeeping. Samson
found those who were still peddlers to be significantly older
than the shopkeepers, thus confirming this trend. In 1840 only

4.7 percent of the Jewish peddlers in Paris had been born after 1800.[4]

Similar trends are indicated in a series of confidential reports submitted by several of the prefects in 1843 in reply to a government request for an evaluation of the effect of emancipation on the Jews. The prefect of the Gironde (Bordeaux) reported that the poorest Jews were still often peddlers, but that others had become craftsmen since the emancipation. The prefects of Bas-Rhin (Strasbourg) and Meurthe (Nancy) also reported continued pursuit of peddling and second-hand dealing, but stressed that there were also cattle dealers, business agents and skilled workers.[5]

In his study of Lyon Jewry, Delpech found the movement away from peddling very striking. Seventy-five percent of the Jewish population of Lyon were peddlers in 1810. By 1830 this had dropped to 50 percent, and by 1860 to 13 percent.[6] Similarly, in the Marseille consistory district in 1809 there were ninety-eight peddlers, but by the end of the nineteenth century their number was reduced to ten.[7] According to an 1853 list of 1684 people required to share the expenses of liquidating the pre-revolutionary Metz debt, 1.5 percent were peddlers. However, such a low figure appears unrepresentative of the national average.[8]

As early as 1825 the tax rolls for ten of the communities under Metz consistory supervision reveal that of the 202 taxpayers listed on these rolls, only twenty-three (or 11 percent) were engaged in peddling and second-hand dealing. In these areas cattle and horse dealing and butchering were the occupations of 126 taxpayers (62 percent).

Cattle and horse dealing by Jews seem to have grown during the first half of the nineteenth century, and to have spread geographically, following the path of the Jewish migrations. Many cattle and horse dealers were located in Paris by the 1860's, as evidenced by the consistory's opening of three new primary schools for the children of rag, cattle, and horse dealers: "à la Villette, pour les marchands de bestiaux alsaciens, rue Poliveau, pour les Juifs fréquentant le marché aux chevaux du quartier Saint Marcel et la Halle aux cuirs, aux Invalides, pour les chiffonniers de Grenelle."[9] Fourteen percent of the Jews listed on the 1853 Metz debt list were engaged in cattle and horse dealing in Paris and in the eastern departments of Ardennes, Meurthe, Meuse, Moselle, and Bas-Rhin. The 1843 Bas-Rhin report on the effect of the emancipation emphasized the extent to which the Jews controlled the cattle and meat trades. "When market day falls on a Jewish holiday," the prefect declared, "it is essential to change it to another day, lest the city go without meat for a week."[10]

From the beginning of the nineteenth century there was always a group of Jews described as *capitalistes*. These people lived on their capital, through returns on investments, property, or loans, and by small- or large-scale banking. During the nineteenth century there was an increase in the size of this group and a trend toward greater affluence within the group. For example, Szajkowski reported one *rentier* in Marseille in 1809 and fifty-four in 1844.[11] As was the case with peddlers, the small money changers and lenders continued to exist well into the middle of the nineteenth century.

The nineteenth century saw a trend toward increased numbers of Jews in the professions, increased diversification of such occupations, and higher incomes. In her study of Parisian Jews, Samson found Jews in the liberal professions by 1809. Between 1809 and 1840 the percentage of Jews engaged in these professions remained stable (3.2 percent); there were, however, greater diversification and considerably higher incomes in 1840. For example, some of those involved in the liberal professions in 1809 were very poor teachers "dont la situation financière ne se distinguait guère de celle des classes populaires mais qui s'en détachaient par un certain prestige de la fonction."[12] By 1840 members of the liberal professions were often in the middle and highest income groupings.

Everywhere there was a continual movement of Jews toward the liberal professions during the first half of the century, although such movement had been earliest in Paris. By 1843 the Prefect of Meurthe was able to stress with pride the effect of the emancipation on the Jews of his department. He specified their gradual entry into legal, medical, and engineering professions.[13]

Virtually no Jews had been skilled craftsmen before the revolution, and their absence from these fields was simultaneously caused and condemned by Christian society. As late as 1825, of 202 taxed Jews from ten communities of the Metz consistory district, only one (0.5 percent) engaged in a craft—that of tailoring. An important issue in the integration of the Jews into French society, from both the Christian and the Jewish viewpoints, was measuring the increase in Jewish *productivité*. *Productivité* denoted manufacturing and handicrafts as opposed to commerce and finance, which were considered inferior by the contemporary work ethic. A rise in *productivité* was considered tantamount to integration, as well as proof of patriotism. Teaching Jews skilled crafts was one of the earliest programs of the consistories, and committees to encourage and place apprentices developed early in the various regions. Published and unpublished reports on the beneficial effects of the emancipation always pointed with pride to the apprentices and craftsmen, and we therefore can trace the development of this class. The government's 1843 request for information on the effect of the emancipation on the integration of the Jews specifically inquired about the proportion of craftsmen in the Jewish population. In the Bas-Rhin this was estimated at 5 percent. In Bordeaux, the crafts exercised by the Jews included joiners, cabinet makers, furniture makers, blacksmiths, locksmiths, bakers, pastry makers, and tailors. In the Nancy district participation in skilled crafts was still very low in 1843. The Châteausalins district of the department reported less than a one percent incidence; Toul reported none. In Sarrebourg 2-3 percent of the Jewish population were estimated to be engaged in agriculture and skilled labor.[14]

Samson found a trend between 1809 and 1840 toward greater participation in the skilled crafts in Paris. Thus, while participation of the Jewish population engaged in *métiers* in 1809 was 28.1 percent, the overall average for the period 1809-40 was 29.6 percent. Moreover, the ages of those involved in crafts in 1840 were lower than those involved in commerce, and there was a greater diversification of skills than there had been at the beginning of the century.[15]

Twenty-three percent of the 1843 Jewish population in Nantes were skilled craftsmen.[16] This is the highest rate that we have noted anywhere. The lowest rate that we calculated was an overall average of 5 percent of the Jews on the 1853 Metz debt list. It would appear that the latter figure is not indicative of the levels of skilled craftsmanship in the total Jewish population.

Although the data on occupational distribution are incomplete, a comparison of several different sources for the years between 1843 and 1866 reveals a high degree of consistency. Assuming that occupations do not change rapidly, it is therefore possible to estimate Jewish occupational distribution for at least the period 1840-70, and probably for 1830-80, within the fields broadly designated as "trades," "production" (industry and handicrafts), "capitalism" (banking, *agents d'affaires, propriétaires, rentiers*), "professionals" (the liberal professions, religious and state functionaries) and "military." We disregard, at this time, the different levels of affluence within the occupational groupings, but they are discussed in the following section. The sources used are Szajkowski's statistics for the Marseille consistory district (1864 and 1866),[17] a list of the professions of twenty-nine of the thirty-one heads of Jewish households in Nantes in 1843, and the 1853 Metz debt tax lists.

Table II-1 shows the occupational distribution of the Jews 1843-66, according to the four sources we described. It shows that trade was the dominant Jewish occupation, accounting for 42-55 percent of Jewish activity. "Production" and "capitalism" were next, although the order is not clear. In the various sources there is a range from slightly more capitalists to twice as many "producers" as capitalists. This seems to reflect local differences. The proportion of Jews engaged in "production" was 10-30 percent; for "capitalism" it was 10-17 percent. Jewish professionals consistently accounted for 7-10 percent of the population. Military service was chosen by very few, and the range that we found was 0-3.5 percent, depending upon the document.

Thus we have seen that during the nineteenth century there was an increasing participation in liberal professions and skilled labor, a greater diversification of such occupations, a rise in "productive" occupations, an improvement in socioeconomic status within the various groups, and a decrease of activity at the lowest levels of commerce. Trade remained the most popular occupation of the Jews, and military office the least popular. All these trends continued steadily throughout the century, until massive immigration from the east, beginning in 1880, changed the demographic picture.[18]

TABLE II-1.
Occupational Distribution of Jews, Described in Broad Categories (Expressed in Percentages), 1843–1866

Occupational Category	Nantes, 1843[a]	Marseille, 1844[b]	Metz, 1853[c]	Marseille, 1866[b]
Trades	42	49	52	55
Production	31	15	15	10
Capitalists	14	10	17	10
Professions	7	7½	10	9
Military	0	>1	3½	>1

[a] Arch. P.C., I[CC] 22.
[b] Szajkowski, *Jews and the French Revolution*, p. 129.
[c] *Liquidation des dettes . . .*

B. Wealth and Class

There are several possible ways of analyzing the class structure of a community. In a recent study of the early nineteenth century Paris Jewish community, Samson followed Daumard's analysis of the Parisian bourgeoisie.[19] The criterion for "bourgeois" designation is that the individual, on his death, left an estate valued at a minimum of 2000 francs. The bourgeoisie is estimated at 16–17 percent in 1840, both for the total Parisian population and for the Parisian Jewish population.[20] Within the category of "bourgeois" there are breakdowns by both occupation and wealth. The three occupation categories used are "business," "liberal professions," and "others." Within each group the person is of the *haute, bonne,* or *moyenne* bourgeoisie, according to the level of wealth.

According to this classification system, all who are not bourgeois belong to the *classe populaire,* which includes many of what is usually called *petit bourgeois*—the struggling shopkeepers with no fortune. The *classe populaire* included about 82 percent of the Parisian Jewish population in the middle of the nineteenth century. These people are further classified into one of three levels: (1) the *couche supérieure,* or those with enough wealth to warrant a declaration of the value of the estate at death (8.3 percent); (2) the *couche moyenne,* those with no declaration of the value of the estate (56 percent); and (3) the *couche indigente,* or those whose death certificates were marked "indigent" (17.3 percent).[21]

In 1840 the Jewish bourgeoisie of Paris was overwhelmingly involved in business. The *bourgeoisie d'affaires* accounted for 10 percent of the total Parisian Jewish population. 3.2 percent were in the liberal professions. Another 3.4 percent were engaged in banking, diplomacy, government, military, and other careers.

Samson found that 6 percent of the *bourgeoisie d'affaires* were of the *haute bourgeoisie,* 24 percent were of the *bonne bourgeoisie,* and 70 percent were of the *moyenne bourgeoisie.* Among those in the liberal professions "many" were of the *bonne bourgeoisie* and "some" were of the *haute bourgeoisie,* but the majority of the professionals, as of the businessmen, were in the lowest group by wealth.

Samson's monographic study, based on the death and estate records of Parisian Jewry for the first half of the nineteenth century, will have to be repeated for several other periods and places before a thorough demographic study of nineteenth century French Jewry can be synthesized. If we attempt to study wealth by using the 1853 Metz debt list the results are unreliable. This list specified the *facultés imposables* of each person on the list. Presumably this is the estimated net worth of the individual. Using the same 2000 franc cut-off point used by Samson to determine bourgeois status, we find that 806, or 48 percent of the 1684 Jews, are above this level. It is immediately clear that this figure is too high to be representative of the population in general. This is due to the fact that only those who could afford to share in the expense of repaying the debt are listed. We have no way of estimating the number of Jews who were indigent and therefore not qualified to appear on the list.

The debt list also reveals that levels of affluence vary enormously (and not unpredictably) with geographic area. The poorest, as a group, were those who were still living in the Moselle (Metz) district; the richest were those currently living in Paris. Many of the "enlightened" Metz Jews had made their way to Paris in the early years of the emancipation and had made their fortunes at the end of the Empire or at the beginning of the Restoration. Their success was due both to their knowledge of French (as compared with the Alsatians, who spoke their own dialect) and to the development of the Parisian bourgeoisie at this period. The early part of the nineteenth century was an opportune time to make a place for oneself in the developing Parisian bourgeoisie; later arrivals were to find the society more closed, and breaking in much more difficult:

La simultanéité entre l'émancipation des Juifs et la restructuration de la bourgeoisie parisienne joua, donc, en faveur des bourgeois juifs qui purent aisément s'intégrer dans un milieu social en pleine transformation.[22]

Among the eleven Parisian Jews cited by Samson as having risen from very humble beginnings to financial success, six were from Metz families. Salomon Halphen arrived from Metz with fifteen francs, and died in 1840 a millionaire. His widow's taxable wealth in 1853 was assessed at 200,000 francs, and she and the rest of Halphen's family were very highly taxed to repay the Metz debt. B. L. Fould, founder of the wealthy banking family that later entered into government, began his career as a shoeshine boy. His taxable wealth in 1853 was 300,000 francs. That of Léon Berr Fould was 350,000 francs and of Louis Fould 150,000. Olry Dupont had been a worker in a jewelry firm before he became one of the richest jewelers of the nineteenth century. He was taxed on the basis of a 20,000 franc fortune in 1853. Michel Lévy, physician, Hayem Bloch, *négociant,* and Prosper Wittersheim, printer, also rose from humble Metz families.[23]

1. Wealth and Occupation

We have attempted to find the correlations between wealth and occupations, on the basis of the 1853 Metz debt list. Estimated wealth on this list ranges between 200 and 500,500 francs. Fortunes of more than 30,000 francs were reported in about twenty cases, many of them held by members of the same families, as in the case of the Fould and Halphen families. The professions of those in the over-30,000-franc assessment category included bankers, *rentiers,* grain auctioneers, notaries, engineers, jewellers, and manufacturers.

The lowest assessments of wealth (200–1000 francs) are made for butchers, cattle dealers, horse dealers, other *marchands,* shopkeepers, peddlers, craftsmen, *rentiers, agents d'affaires,* and religious functionaries. None of these occupations, however, is strictly determinant of wealth, and they are also represented in the next highest group (1000–10,000 francs). Horse dealers are found even in brackets up to 30,000.

Between the lowest and the highest lie two intermediary groups. The first (whose wealth is evaluated at 1000–10,000 francs) comprise the majority of the people on the list. Almost all occupations are found in this group. Manufacturers start at this level, and are found also in all higher categories. The next highest level (10,000–30,000 francs) is comprised mainly of bankers and members of the liberal professions.

It is interesting to compare the Metz debt list findings with the data supplied by ten 1825 Metz tax rolls. On most of the ten lists we analyzed, 20–30 francs are the highest assessments. The individuals we are studying in these tax rolls are mainly small-town traders and laborers. The only professional is a teacher and therefore in a low tax bracket. There are no classes equivalent to the two highest found in the Metz debt list. The only occupational groups found in the over-35-franc bracket are *propriétaires* and cattle dealers. Being a cattle dealer, however, is not of itself an indication of great wealth, as members of this profession are found at all levels.

Aside from those who paid more than 35 francs in taxes, the rest of the taxpayers may be divided into four groups, those taxed at 1-5 francs, 6-10 francs, 11-25 francs, and 26-35 francs. The first two groups corresponded approximately to the lowest class (evaluated at 200-1000 francs) on the debt list. In the first group (1-5 francs) we find the religious functionaries at the bottom of the ladder. Their taxes never exceed 5 francs. Day laborers come next. Their taxes are always under 10 francs. Peddlers, butchers, and cattle dealers also fall into the lowest category, but as we already found to be true from the debt list, these occupations do not strictly determine wealth. Most notably, cattle dealers are found at all tax levels, including the highest (more than 35 francs). Even itinerant peddlers sometimes paid as much as 25 francs. Horse dealers and other merchants (the majority of the population) fall into all the middle income groups, just as they did on the debt list. Table II-2 shows graphically this analysis of the 1825 tax roles.

TABLE II-2
*Taxes Paid to the Metz Consistory
(10 Towns), 1825*

Occupations	1–5 Francs	6–10 Francs	11–25 Francs	26–35 Francs	Over 35 Francs
Bedau	/ / / / /				
Cantor	/ / / / /				
Laborer	/ / / / / / / / / / /				
Peddler	/ / / / / / / / / / / / / / / / / / /				
Butcher	/ /				
Cattle dealer	/ /				
Tailor		/ / / / /			
Teacher		/ / / / /			
Horse dealer		/ / / / / / / / / / / / / / / / / /			
Marchand		/ / / / / / / / / / / / / / / / /			
Propriétaire					/ / / / /

---

2. Social Mobility

A thorough examination of the issue of social mobility remains to be done. Samson's work treats the issue in Paris, and only until 1840. She found that despite the rare and spectacular cases it was uncommon for the professional level or the living standard of the children to exceed that of the parents.[24] In contrast, Roblin, discussing the entire nineteenth-century situation of the Jewish immigrants to Paris, claims that social mobility was very dramatic: "Colporteurs et chiffonniers des petites bourgades des Vosges et des bords du Rhin vont se transformer peu en peu en artisans, en industriels, voire même en capitalistes ou en intellectuels."[25]

Despite these changes of profession, social mobility was minimal. If the numbers of peddlers diminished and their children became craftsmen and shopkeepers, this did not produce much improvement in socioeconomic status among the *classe populaire*. This fact is visible in the high poverty levels that remained through the 1860's. The improvement that did take place between 1809 and 1840 among the Parisian Jewish population was the growth of the bourgeoisie from about 12½ to about 16½ percent.[26] This marked a corresponding decrease in the lower classes. At the same time there was improvement in living standards within the liberal professions—whose proportion to the total Jewish population had, however, remained constant.[27]

3. Poverty

The densest concentration of Jews, even by 1861, was in the region of Alsace-Lorraine, which housed the poorest Jewish communities and suffered chronic economic depression and frequent famine. Throughout the 1850's the Bas-Rhin consistory, considering emigration to be the only solution to the poverty problem, financed a project to send poor Jews to America. In 1868 Léon Werthe, a lawyer of the Haut-Rhin and a local Jewish community leader, estimated that only half of the Alsatian Jewish population (of 35,000–40,000) had an assured livelihood. The other one-half "cherche, et souvent sans trouver, des positions où son expérience l'a fait broncher; elle vit d'incertitudes, se nourrit de déceptions et se perd souvent dans la lutte entre l'honnête et le nécessaire."[28]

In Paris, Jewish poverty remained a problem throughout the century. It had not been solved by 1880 when the large eastern European immigrations compounded the difficulties. Samson estimated that one in five of the Parisian Jewish population in 1840 was indigent. She compared this with an estimated one in 13.4 for the general population in 1844.[29] Whether we should conclude that the Jewish poverty rate was higher than that of the general population is not certain, as the discrepancy in the figures may be due to more than one cause. It is possible that the Jewish charity board was more generous in its inclusion of the working poor on its relief rolls. We have no clear indication, in the case of either the Jewish or the general poor, just what level of need had to be manifested before one received assistance. Furthermore, the French system of public charity was not fully developed in 1840, and many of the needy simply were not helped, or they relied on church charity. Increases in the general welfare rate that were noted between 1833 and 1860 were due more to an expansion of services to cover existing needs than to an increase in poverty:

Il ne faudrait pas conclure de cette augmentation progressive que le paupérisme s'est accru, en France, dans la même proportion. En réalité, par suite de l'ouverture d'un plus grand nombre de bureaux, et surtout par suite de l'accroissement des ressources des bureaux existants, beaucoup d'indigents, qui autrefois étaient entièrement à la charge de la charité privée, ont pu être secourus par la commune.[30]

The 20 percent of the Parisian Jewish population who were on the relief rolls, and the approximately equal number who were marked "indigent" at death, were not the only poor. The statistics published by the *comité de bienfaisance* (charity board) show that more than 50 percent of the burials through the 1860's were paid for by charity.[31] Thus it is clear that many of the *couche moyenne* of the *classe populaire* were able to eke out their existence in life and avoid the stigma of charity, but their families could not afford the extra expense of burial.

Even when the family managed to pay burial expenses it was able in only one half of the cases (less than 20 percent of the Parisian Jewish population) to purchase permanent graves. The other graves (despite the contrary requirements of religious law) were temporary concessions, subject to exhumation after five years. Apparently, then, it was almost exclusively the *bourgeois* (17 percent of the total Parisian Jewish population) who could afford to buy permanent burial plots.

The situation in the rest of the country is very difficult to quantify. The various documents, including the contemporary press, convey the distinct impression of high poverty rates everywhere. Yet, in the absence of charity records for other areas of the country, we cannot be precise.[32]

The class structure within nineteenth century Jewish society is somewhat dismaying to those who like to believe that democracy has always been a characteristic of the synagogue. In fact, however, studies of eighteenth-century French Judaism reveal similar patterns, and we have to go much further back than this to find the traditional democratic mode.[33] Mutual disdain of the rich and the poor, control of the community by an oligarchy, and tax disputes (especially complaints by the poor concerning the tax on kosher meat) were all common during the eighteenth century.

A typical example of disdain for the poor is the letter sent by the Paris consistory to the police prefecture on May 18, 1846, complaining about a "Society for the Aid of Poor [Jewish] Foreigners." The consistory pointed out that this organization was not under the auspices of the consistory, and that the consistory, therefore, could not guarantee the morality of its acts. At a consistory meeting held to draft the letter, the view was generally presented that this society, under the "appearance" of morality, would tend to attract foreigners from all countries to the generosity of Paris, and some of the foreigners might not be "worthy" of this hospitality.[34]

Just as the hostility between classes in nineteenth century France was not new, so was it not complete. Among the Jewish population of Paris, Samson found greater cohesion and less cleavage between classes than in society in general, but also a certain tension or contradiction between Jewish solidarity and class solidarity.

The place where class distinctions hurt the most was in the synagogue. The poor could not forgive the consistory for the high price tag on the good seats. Those without means were relegated to the seats behind the pillars (and in the annex in the schoolrooms for the High Holy Days). Not only could the poor not afford the synagogue, but they could not identify with it. Many of them preferred to pray in small chapels where traditional *minyanim* gathered for prayer. In these small prayer meetings, even the most humble could assume an important position of leadership. Their membership fees guaranteed them religious honors among friends. Here the poor did not feel the contempt of the rich. But private prayer meetings jeopardized the temple budgets and the consistories sought to eliminate them, as we shall see.

The poor objected also to the consistory ruling that weddings must take place in the synagogue. It is not difficult to imagine the embarrassment felt by a poor family when their wedding party arrived for a fifth-class wedding immediately after a rich wedding. They would have to wait and witness all the changes being hastily made in the seats and decorations and lighting. The embellishments were very few for the fifth-class wedding; even the bridal canopy used was different.

In 1844 the Paris consistory decided that there would no longer be different wedding canopies for the different classes of marriage. That was well received and much appreciated by the poor and their defenders. Simon Bloch, conservative leader and editor of the *Univers Israélite*, greeted the change in these terms:

On announce que le consistoire de Paris vient de décider qu'à l'avenir il n'y aura plus qu'un seul dais pour tous les mariages célébrés au temple consistorial. Tous les amis du bien applaudiront à cette sage et libérale mesure, qui ne permettra plus que l'image de la pauvreté soit mise sous les yeux de jeunes époux. C'est l'égalité devant Dieu que le consistoire vient de proclamer en forçant l'orgueil humain à déposer ses vaines prétentions au seuil du sanctuaire.[35]

C. Social Integration

Jews and non-Jews were all very much concerned throughout the nineteenth century with the progress of Jewish integration. By this was usually meant an adaptation to social mores, conformity to general habits of cleanliness and dress, education, and a spread of Jews throughout the general occupational spectrum. Special emphasis was placed on the accession of Jews to skilled crafts and to agriculture, as proof of their "usefulness" and of a real tie to the country (i.e., its land). Social behavior similar to Christians' was expected as a part of integration, and social acceptance by Christians was desired.

If we use the word "integration" to mean "acculturation," we can say that the Jews in many places were well integrated by 1840 and even earlier. In Paris in 1809 seven Jews were studying at *lycées*. A greater proportion of the Jewish population than of the Christians enrolled in such institutions. This was true also of the Jewish enrollment at the prestigious *Ecole Polytechnique* (although not so at the equally prestigious *Ecole Normale*).[36] By 1840 the Jews were fairly well spread throughout many crafts and professions, and were reasonably well adapted socially.

Cultural, social, and occupational integration came more slowly outside the big cities, and especially in the eastern provinces. But Jewish expectations everywhere were the same: Jews could and would be integrated into French society, and in that direction lay their salvation. The reference group was that of the socially and economically successful Jewish individuals in Bordeaux, Marseille, and Paris.

In his study of the Jews of Lyon, Delpech found them "assimilés et installés" from about 1842. The generation coming of age at that period had received a French education and had begun entering the liberal professions.[37] In regard to the Jews of Paris, Samson points out that by 1840 they were integrated in the sense of a social adaptation that admits of a certain amount of ethnic consciousness:

Si l'on entend par "intégration" de l'Israélite une assimilation de toutes les valeurs de la société française et l'oubli de toute appartenance ethnique, il est incontestable qu'une faible minorité, pour ne pas dire l'exception, se soit "intégrée"; si, par contre, l'on comprend par là une adaptation sociale qui admet la conservation de certaines valeurs particulières, une grande partie des Israélites était "intégrée" en 1840 et entrevoyait dans cette solution tout l'avenir du judaïsme.[38]

Roblin's overenthusiastic appraisal of social mobility has already been cited. This scholar estimated that by the middle of the century Jewish writers, professors, and engineers were making a mark for themselves. It took only one generation, Roblin exclaims, to transform Alsatian Talmudists into Sorbonne professors:

déjà les écrivains, les professeurs, les ingénieurs juifs se font
remarquer sous Louis-Philippe et Napoléon III; une génération
a suffi pour transformer les talmudistes alsaciens et
méridionaux en professeurs de Sorbonne, en directeurs de
grands quotidiens, en membres des plus hautes assemblées; la
réussite personelle a été totale dans bien des cas.[39]

Public service is an indication of integration. The nineteenth-century Jew was being watched to see if he rendered service comparable to his Christian neighbor. The 1843 reports that we have already cited mentioned Jews in military service and in public office. The *sous-préfets* of the Châteausalins and Lunéville districts of the Meurthe pointed out that Jews were frequently elected municipal councillors, and that some were members of the National Guard. In the Lunéville district there were many who had entered the military and achieved high ranks. In the Sarrebourg district of the same department the Jews were the first to join the National Guard in 1830 and had remained loyal to the Orleanist government. In Bordeaux a confidential report was prepared by M. Gauthier, the mayor's aide. According to this document, Jews were elected by Christian votes to the Chamber of Commerce, municipal councils, and other organizations.

But it was to the contemporary foreign Jew that the integration of the French Jew seemed the most spectacular. Ludwig Philippson (rabbi of Magdebourg and editor of *Allgemeine Zeitung des Judentums*) visited Paris in 1854 and was struck by the extent of the integration of Jewish leaders and by public support for Jewish institutions. The proud French Jewish press translated his account:

Me voilà devant l'école communale des israélites; à qui appar-
tient cette maison-dans laquelle douze cents enfants juifs
reçoivent gratuitement l'instruction? A la Ville. Qui salarie les
professeurs, fournit les livres, les plumes, le papier? La Ville.
Je regarde la liste des membres du Consistoire israélite. Son
honorable président est colonel, son vice-président, membre de
l'Institut; le grand-rabbin est un élève de l'école rabbinique de
Metz entretenue aux frais de l'Etat; un autre membre est
conseiller de la Cour d'appel et préside en ce moment les
Assises; un autre encore est professeur au Conservatoire.[40]

By the 1840's the Jews had adopted most of the French behavioral norms. Observers often cited changes in Jewish behavior such as a greater regard for personal cleanliness and an appreciation of modern secular education. Jews had begun dressing in the general style (even in the countryside of the eastern provinces). In Paris an entire generation of the young had been raised in French culture, and only the oldest Jews and the newest arrivals spoke Yiddish or Judeo-Alsatian.[41]

Social behavior of the Jews who were considered integrated was very similar to that of the Christians. Gauthier reported that the rich Bordeaux Jews spent their leisure time in the same way as the rest of the wealthy population: walking in the same places, going to the same theaters, etc. It was difficult, he remarked, to tell them apart on the basis of their behavior. But if their time was spent in a way similar to that of the Christians, this did not mean that it was spent together with Christians. Except for the very richest class, Jews were still restricted to socializing within the Jewish milieu.

Several of the reports from the various parts of Meurthe stressed that the private life of the Jews was essentially unchanged, and that although the Jews were accepted in public life they were still not welcome in the social circles of Christian private life.[42] The *sous-préfet* of Toul reported that "malgré leur émancipation ils ont continué à vivre dans l'isolement."

As early as the 1820's Olry Terquem (the polemicist, pamphleteer, and advocate of radical reform who wrote under the pseudonym "Tsarphati") had observed that mixed marriages were desirable as a practical way to obey the Sanhedrin commandment to love the Christians like brothers.[43] By the 1860's and 1870's in Paris about 12 percent of all Jews who married, married Christians.[44]

The integrated Jew had adopted most of the French values while retaining something of his ethnic solidarity. His biggest problem was how to reconcile the two. Delpech notes this problem in Lyon during the 1840's: "Le grand problème pour ces hommes nouveaux est de concilier leur appartenance d'origine et la culture à laquelle ils accèdent."[45] Delpech found that Lyon Jews were frequently writing letters to the local press in order to correct tendentious remarks published by these papers. The Jews were very sensitive and were always anxious to defend and justify Judaism.

The 1843 reports to the ministry comprise a series of direct answers to the question, "What has been the effect of the emancipation on the Jews?" The answers varied from one area to another, but stressed the positive, if limited, effect of the emancipation. The prefect of the Bas-Rhin noted that the Jews had profited from the emancipation, but more so in the cities than in the countryside. Within the department of Meurthe the *sous-préfets* responded in varied ways. That of Lunéville stressed that since the emancipation the barriers have weakened and relationships with the Christians have become more firmly established. Saarebourg agreed that the emancipation had had a good effect, but deplored the fact that it had not caused as much improvement as might have been hoped. The Château-salins *sous-préfet* found that it was really only the rich who had made progress: "En résumé l'émancipation des Juifs a peu modifié leur manière d'être avec les Chrétiens et ce n'est guère que chez les familles riches qu'on recontre quelques progrès à cet égard."[46]

The integration problem posed by the emancipation was largely viewed as one of fusing the Jews into the society in such a way as to eliminate the notion that they constituted a separate people. This meant accomplishing the triple goal of eliminating apparent differences, changing the Jewish self-image and changing the Christian popular conception of the Jews. Olry Terquem wrote in 1836 that integration thus far had been successful only on an individual basis; none of the private successes of individual Jews, he argued, meant anything for the Jews as a group:

La loi peut bien nous appeler "français" sur le papier; mais en réalité, n'étant unis à nos concitoyens par aucun lien de famille, nous formons une caste, une nation distincte, et on n'aime pas de passer pour étranger dans son propre pays, et pour étranger mal famé. C'est pourquoi aussi dès qu'un israélite se distingue dans une carrière quelconque, il s'éloigne, déserte de fait notre culte et vit dans le nihilisme, s'il est permis de s'exprimer ainsi. On honore les individus, quoique Juifs. La masse n'y gagne rien.[47]

Because the general public held strong opinions about honorable and dishonorable occupations, and despised the Jewish concentration in the "dishonorable" ones, integrationist Jews (frequently the "successful" Jews) espoused the same views. One of the dishonorable professions was that of military insurance agent. In 1852 Pierre Lévy, a consistory member in Nancy, published an open letter of complaint concerning the treatment he had received from the consistory's president, Lévylier, when Louis Napoleon visited Nancy. Lévy charged that because he sold military insurance he was prevented by Lévylier from taking part in a public ceremony to which the entire consistory had been invited.

On attendait l'arrivée à Nancy du Président de la République, et ainsi que les autres corps constitués, le Consistoire devait offrir ses hommages au Chef de l'Etat. Les membres du Consistoire sont priés de se rendre chez leur président pour entendre le projet de discours; j'assiste à cette réunion, et nulle observation à mon égard de la part de ces Messieurs; c'était deux jours avant l'arrivée du Prince. Or, le jour même de cette arrivée, et à peine quelques heures avant le moment fixé pour la visite, j'apprends que M. Lévylier, notre président, me fait demander pour une communication. Je me rends à l'invitation, présumant quelque retard de la cérémonie, ou peut-être quelque changement à introduire dans le discours. Pas du tout. M. le président est seul . . . avec M. Picard, l'un de nos collègues. A l'air grave de ces Messieurs, je redoute l'annonce de quelque malheureux événement; l'inquiétude s'empare de moi, et j'attends le mot

*terrible. Jugez de ma surprise quand j'entends M. le président
me faire part de ses scruples . . . de se montrer officiellement en
compagnie d'un agent d'assurance militaire.*[48]

The popular image of the Jew as someone who would buy or
sell anything if the transaction was profitable was expressed in
several of the 1843 reports on the effect of the emancipation. In
the Bas-Rhin the old prejudices had somewhat diminished in the
cities, probably because the education, dress, and outward
manner of the Jews was close to that of the Christians. In the
countryside the old prejudices continued to be strongly held,
and improvement was slight.

The report of the *sous-préfet* of the Châteausalins district
displayed a distinct antipathy to Jews. Although he conceded
that the majority of convicted usurers were Christians, the
official insisted that Jews, with their notorious love of money,
were no less prone to this crime. The fact that the number of
Jewish usurers was decreasing was attributed not to an increase
in morality, but to the recent availability of loans at lower rates
than those asked by the Jews. Jews were naturally lazy, he continued, and did not like manual work. He summed up the
popular feeling by saying that Christians had no confidence in
Jews because of the kinds of occupations they pursued.

The report from the Toul district sounded a similar note. It
reported that the Christians there dealt with the Jews only when
necessary. The *sous-préfet* of Toul charged the Jews with a lack
of nationalism and gratitude toward the country that welcomed
them. He summarized his views:

*Pour relever les juifs, les réhabiliter entièrement, il faudrait une
régénération complète, dans leur religion, leurs moeurs, leurs
habitudes. Je la regarde comme impossible, du moins pour
longtemps encore.*

But such opinions were not unanimously held. The *sous-
préfet* of the Lunéville district claimed that in his district the
Jews (as evidenced by their participation in the National Guard
and in several municipal councils) had been enjoying the high
esteem of the people ever since the revolution.

PART TWO

THE CONSISTORY AND THE COMMUNITY

The consistory was the single most important and comprehensive French Jewish institution of the last century; it was responsible for molding French Judaism throughout the nineteenth century, and, to a large extent, into the twentieth century. Not in any sense a traditional Jewish institution, it was conceived in 1806 and created in 1808–09 in imitation of the administrative organization of the French Protestant sects (which had followed the establishment of Catholicism as the state religion). The Jewish leaders themselves had requested a state-sponsored organization to consolidate the gains of emancipation, and Napoleon had been quick to see the advantage to the state of such a system.

The system was hierarchical. At the top was a central consistory in Paris, composed of three rabbis and two laymen, initially appointed by the government and subsequently self-perpetuating. Its task was surveillance and supervision of all French Jews and especially the rabbis. It was directly responsible to the government through the Ministry of Cults. Next in the chain of command were the local consistories, which comprised one or more *départements,* and sometimes more than one hundred Jewish communities. Whereas previously the basic unit of Jewish institutional life had been the autonomous community, the consistories were now the institutional units of French Jewry. These local consistories governed the communities of their districts, and were in turn responsible to the central consistory. The local consistories, as originally established, consisted of three lay members and one or two rabbis; the members were elected by twenty-five *notables* (the *notabilité*), named by the government from the highest taxpayers and most respected citizens among the Jews in each consistory district. The masses of Jews were disenfranchised, and this often meant that entire communities were unrepresented in the new Jewish institutions. The old community structures, such as mutual aid societies, burial societies, and *minyanim* (small prayer meetings), although not entirely dismantled, lost their legal recognition.

The consistory system was quasi-governmental, viewing itself, and being generally accepted as, a lesser authority in a chain of command that led to the national government at the top. The local consistories were often in direct contact with the officials of the general administration of France: mayors, subprefects, and prefects. They also had direct access to the police prefecture, and cooperated with these public officials on a basis of mutual confidence.

The consistories were originally thirteen in number. Seven of them were located in France proper, and the other six were within the boundaries of the Empire and were lost in 1815. The seven consistories within France were located in Wintzenheim (later Colmar), in Haut-Rhin; Strasbourg, in Bas-Rhin; Nancy, in Meurthe; Metz, in Moselle; Paris, in Seine; Bordeaux, in Gironde; and Marseille, in Bouches-du-Rhône (Maps III-1, III-2). In 1846 an eighth consistory was established, in St. Esprit (Landes), the suburb of Bayonne in which the Jews, long-barred from residence in the city, had established themselves prior to the revolution. In 1857, when St. Esprit was incorporated into the city limits of Bayonne, the name of this consistory was officially changed to "the consistory of Bayonne" (Basses-Pyrénées), and in the same year a ninth consistory was established in the growing Jewish center of Lyon (Rhône) (Map III-3). This was the last consistory to be created until after 1870, when significant demographical changes were caused by the loss of the eastern provinces and the migration of many of the Jews into new areas within the reduced French territory. In 1872, due to these changes, two new consistories were created, in Lille and in Vesoul. In 1881 one more consistory was inaugurated, in Besançon.

During the nineteenth century Algeria came under French rule, and shortly thereafter a consistory system was established for the Jews of that colony. By law of November 9, 1845, the traditional Algerian Jewish authority embodied in the *Beth Din* (religious court), *Mokdem* (government), and *Shaoush* (executive agent)—the entire civil, political, and administrative system—was abolished. It was replaced by three consistories and a rabbinate, which could exercise only "religious" authority.[1] Until 1862 the three Algerian consistories were not linked to those in France. From 1862 to 1867 the consistories of Algeria were under the authority of the central consistory via the intermediary of the Algiers consistory; in 1867 the intermediary was suppressed, and the three Algerian consistories were authorized to name representatives to the central consistory.

The history of the consistory system in Algeria is a reflection of French consistorial aims and ambitions, and an illustration of the growth of the monopolistic character of the consistory. We will not treat it in the present work, as it is in itself a vast subject worthy of separate study.

The history of Judaism in nineteenth-century France must be viewed in light of the Church–State issue in that country between the Revolution and 1905. It is well known that the Revolution engendered an initial outburst of anticlerical activity which saw the destruction of churches and synagogues and the reconsecration of these edifices as "temples of reason." The excesses of the "reign of terror" threw Jewish institutions into turmoil. After Napoleon had made peace with the Catholic

III-1   Consistory Districts, 1808

= Bouches-
du-Rhône
(Marseille)

= Gironde
(Bordeaux)

= Meurthe

= Moselle
(Metz)

= Bas Rhin
(Strasbourg)

= Haut Rhin
(Colmar)

= Seine
(Paris)

III-2   Consistory Districts, 1841

III-3 Consistory Districts, 1857

Legend:

- = Bouches-du-Rhône (Marseille)
- = Gironde (Bordeaux)
- = Meurthe (Nancy)
- = Moselle (Metz)
- = Basses Pyrénées (Bayonne)
- = Bas Rhin (Strasbourg)
- = Haut Rhin (Colmar)
- = Rhône (Lyon)
- = Seine (Paris)

Church through his Concordat with the Pope and had granted recognition to the Protestant sects,[2] the Jewish leaders saw an opportunity to request similar benefits for their own communities. Requests led to negotiations, and Napoleon's attention was fixed on the question of defining the Jews' position vis-à-vis the State.

Napoleon soon realized that a state-imposed centralized organization of the Jewish "cult" would guarantee government supervision and control. Negotiations between Jewish leaders and Napoleon's agents led to the establishment of an official Jewish organization known as the consistory. Although this move elevated Judaism to the rank of an officially recognized religion, state funding was not immediately available, as it was for the several Christian churches. Only in 1831 did Judaism become a state-supported religion, its synagogues being built by the government and its clergy receiving state-paid salaries. A century of Church–State relationship in France came to an end in 1905 with the promulgation of the Law of Separation.

From the early years of the consistory system, there were some—generally critics who expected greater consistory initiative in making reforms—who understood the system's potential power. These people, such as the philanthropist David Singer (who in 1820 published *Des consistoires israélites de France,* a brochure critical of the consistories), and the vitriolic Olry Terquem (mathematician, librarian, first "reformer" among French Jews, and author of many "Lettres Tsarphatiques") attacked the consistories as ineffectual institutions that ignored their responsibility to mold French Judaism and merely offered public office to rich Jews.

Although ultimately the consistories developed very much in the way envisaged earlier by Terquem and Singer, progress in this direction was slow. At first the consistories consolidated their positions in their cities of residence, while leaving relative freedom to the other towns of their districts. No general consensus concerning the role of the consistories emerged for some time after their establishment; eventually the Jewish press provided a forum for reasoned analysis of the Jewish situation. Although some short-lived Jewish journals were published earlier,[3] the Jewish press as a permanent institution dates from 1840, when the *Archives Israélites* was founded by Samuel Cahen (teacher at the Paris consistorial school, author of the official "catechism," *Précis élémentaire,* adopted by the central consistory in 1820, translator and commentator of the Bible). A second journal that remained a permanent institution of the community was the *Univers Israélite,* begun in 1844 by Simon Bloch, secretary to the central consistory, to combat the reformist stand taken by *Archives Israélites.* (Bloch subsequently lost his consistory post for printing his conservative and anti-consistory views.) In the columns of both journals French Judaism and its intimate relationship with the consistory was discussed throughout the century.

In 1844 Bloch published an open letter to the *notables* who were about to elect a new consistory, stressing the significance of the consistory's role in shaping the future of French Judaism:

Ici vous comprenez tous toute la gravité de votre vote. Le consistoire départemental, plus que le consistoire central, exerce une influence directe, immédiate sur la vie religieuse de nos coreligionnaires. Il est plus que le pouvoir exécutif du règlement organique; il en est, pour ainsi dire, l'interprète et le commentateur.[4]

Bloch was not wrong in thus predicting the significance of the consistory. It did eventually define the nature of Judaism throughout the century. Already, issues of a reform versus a conservative view had begun to emerge from private discussions among the privileged elite like Terquem and the consistory members, and made their way into the public eye. In 1839 Abraham Ben Baruch Créhange (dealer in oil lamps, who later became journalist, publisher, one of the founders of the *Alliance Israélite Universelle,* and a consistory member) had led the way in organizing the poor orthodox members of mutual aid societies to combat the growing pressure of the Paris consistory. Créhange achieved limited success in arranging a modus vivendi between the consistory and these independent groups.

Several times during the nineteenth century—beginning with a central consistory project of 1839 to reorganize the consistory system—the question of the adoption, change, or implementation of the laws divided the Jewish population along various lines, most frequently those of rich and poor. In general the rich and the educated favored moderate reforms, strong lay influence, weak rabbinic powers, and increasing centralization of power. The poor tended toward orthodoxy, insisted on what they believed to be the traditional dignity and power of the rabbinate, and urged the popular voice in elections. They were supported in their attitude toward the rabbis by the wealthy Sephardim of Bordeaux, who maintained a traditional respect for the rabbinate. Principled liberals, especially Adolphe Crémieux (lawyer, deputy to the National Assembly, Minister of Justice for the Second and Third Republics, consistory member and president of the *Alliance Israélite*), agreed that Judaism should not have to compromise its religious laws in order to be accepted in modern secular France.

It was not only during the drafting of the laws concerning the consistories that the various factions sought legal justification for their own views. The squabbles extended also to the courtroom, and even to the highest court, where individuals and consistories fought over the enforceable limits of consistorial control over Jews and Jewish institutions.

The pretentions of the consistory to monopolistic control of Jewish institutions were never fully realized. The system did become progressively hierarchical and centralized during the period 1839–62, but the consistory failed to convince the government to impose penalties for violation of the laws defining consistory powers. Recalcitrant individuals and groups, advised by lawyers that there was no force in such legislation, repeatedly challenged consistory power. (As we shall see, such challenges frequently came from traditionalists, for whom the intimacy of the small *minyan* within the mutual aid society could not be replaced by the modern "temple.")

Those in a position to implement the laws concerning Jewish institutions were confused by the lack of clearly defined procedure, and the result was that one arm of the state often forbade what another permitted. Interpretation of the laws by the police prefecture was not uncolored by personal, political, and religious viewpoints, as well as by honest variations in the interpretation given to ambiguous legal provisions.

The consistory system, as noted above, expanded the basic unit of Jewish institutional life from the community to the departmental or district level, but it simultaneously limited administrative obligations to the local district. With regard both to national and international Jewish solidarity, the consistories— although not all individuals—tended toward isolationism. Like-minded administrators in Bordeaux and Metz might join together to fight unwanted Parisian reforms, but these coalitions were political and ephemeral. The response to appeals made from one region to another for aid in various charitable endeavors was frequently one of effusive encouragement, accompanied by regrets about lack of funds. Thus, for example, when the consistory of Strasbourg wrote to ask their colleagues in other districts to support their "amelioration" project (for the economic and educational improvement of the Jews of Bas-Rhin), the Paris and St. Esprit consistories responded that the expenses they bore were too heavy for them to be able to help.[5] Similarly, when the consistory of Marseille sent one hundred fund-raising lottery tickets to Paris, the Paris consistory, after a long discussion about not having any funds for such a purpose, eventually resolved the difficulty by turning the tickets over to the grand rabbi and asking him to sell them.[6]

On an international level and due partly to their insecurity and need to identify strongly with France, and partly to financial difficulties, the consistories often ignored appeals for assistance. The Paris consistory received many requests for financial aid from foreign Jewish communities and generally declined to help. In 1853, for example, the consistory turned down requests for aid from Jewish communities in Italy and Switzerland.[7] There were exceptions to this, such as the aid sent by the Strasbourg consistory to the Moroccan Jews who fled to Oran in 1859. Bordeaux demonstrated certain ties to Sephardi communities elsewhere. Thus in 1853 the Bordeaux consistory contributed one hundred francs toward rebuilding the burned Sephardi synagogue of Hamburg, and offered fifty francs to the

(Ashkenazi) Worms community for the maintenance of the tombs of famous rabbis of the middle ages.[8]

Two major themes dominate the history of the consistory system: the development of lay domination and the trend toward reform. Both tendencies were antitraditional. They sought secularization and socioeconomic integration of French Jews and a modification of Jewish institutions, along the lines of Christian institutions. It is important to remember that the so-called reformers offered no new theological statements and did not construct a new ideological basis for understanding Judaism. Reformers sought outward changes which they regarded as superficial and in harmony with traditional Judaism. Those who advocated such changes were themselves often personally unconcerned with religion. It was not for themselves that they felt the need for reform, but for their less fortunate coreligionists. They thought that the popular image of Judaism, hence of Jews, would improve if Jewish institutions were brought into line with those of Christianity. Thus they placed a premium on secular education and vocational training, and they opposed the traditional view that religious education must take priority over secular training in case of conflict. In seeking to control the rabbinate and in restructuring rabbinic training, Jewish leaders were displaying both an acceptance of the general antireligious and anticlerical attitude of nineteenth-century France and a desire to make the French rabbinate fit the model of the Christian clergy.[9]

Nineteenth century France did not offer a sense of security to its Jews, who nervously watched and analyzed each new regime for its attitude toward religion and Jews. Jewish leaders were frequently anxious to accommodate themselves quietly to the ways of general society and to display no glaring differences or special needs. Thus, for example, the Paris consistory agreed to discard Jewish law as a basis for burial procedures in the Parisian Jewish cemetery. A few insistent liberals, notably Adolphe Crémieux, insisted on the right of French Jews to be accepted with their differences. The ideology of those who rejected assimilation and believed in a compatability of patriotism and a certain degree of ethnic identification was bolstered by the success of the Jewish press and led eventually to the foundation of the *Alliance Israélite Universelle*.

Many of the innovations that were sought, first by reform propagandists and then by the consistories, were of a ceremonial nature: increased orderliness, dignity, and standardization of ceremonies, French sermons in the synagogues, and methodical religious instruction in the schools. When the conservatives opposed such aims, it was not on religious but on social grounds. However, there were also innovations that conservatives rejected on specifically religious grounds. They rejected a girls' choir, an organ for use on the holidays, changes in the circumcision ceremony, reduced Talmudic training of rabbis, elimination of some *piyyutim* (religious poetry introduced into the ritual during the Middle Ages), and temporary paupers' graves.

The Sephardi community included both nonobservant and observant Jews, but both groups were satisfied with the state of religious institutions. The Sephardim tended to be orthodox in their attitude toward religious institutions but modern in conducting an orderly ritual. Because the Spanish and Marrano experience had caused an influence of the church on the Sephardi synagogue ritual, the Sephardim had already implemented many of the reforms that Ashkenazi leaders were advocating: Sermons were preached in the vernacular (Spanish at first, then French); baby girls were presented in the synagogue soon after birth; circumcision was generally performed in the synagogue; the rabbinic role had a long history of being limited to ritual matters; a laxity was allowed in the interpretation of the problem of defining who was a Jew. In regard to the latter, many of the Sephardim were of multireligious families whose members kept crossing the lines from one to another of the religious groups, and since Talmudic prescriptions received less attention among the Sephardim, Jewish status was frequently granted to those who claimed it.

In attempting to modernize Jewish practice, Ashkenazi reformers used this Sephardi model. Reformers also urged the adoption of the Sephardi pronunciation of Hebrew, and the replacement of the Ashkenazi *piyyutim* and chants by the Sephardi ones. Later, attempts at fusion sought to combine the two traditions into a new French ritual, but it was assumed that the Sephardi customs would predominate. The higher socioeconomic status of the Sephardim and their more satisfactory integration may have appeared to the Ashkenazim as evidence of the superiority of Sephardi customs. In any event, it is clear that the Ashkenazim imitated Sephardi behavior in an attempt to achieve Sephardi status. Moreover, the Sephardi ceremonial bore greater outward resemblance to church ceremonies than did traditional Ashkenazi ritual, and, as we have said, Jewish leaders, in their insecurity, felt compelled to imitate church practices in order to be understood by the French.

A reform leader emerged in the person of Adolphe Franck, professor of philosophy at the Sorbonne and the *Collège de France,* member of the *Institut* and vice president of the central consistory. From the time of his election to the central consistory in 1844, Franck embarked upon a program that included improving and modernizing the curriculum of the rabbinic school, moving the school to Paris to enable the students to benefit from the university, and obtaining the appointment of grand rabbis who favored reform of synagogue ritual. In his 1846 questions to the candidates for the post of grand rabbi, Franck appears to have been influenced by the German rabbinic conferences.[10]

Some of the arguments made in the name of reform or conservatism actually cut across these lines, and reflected financial, social, ethnic, or other concerns. For example, the "reformers" wanted strong consistorial control of Jewish institutions, while traditionalists pleaded for greater latitude in forming *minyanim* and in creating religious schools and other institutions. In reality, financial considerations motivated the reformers of the consistory, and social and traditional feelings motivated recalcitrants.

Reform, conservative, modern, traditional, liberal, assimilatory, religious, nonreligious, antireligious—such were the various trends among the French Jews in the middle of the nineteenth century. Our analysis of the consistory, its laws, its tasks, and its tendencies will elaborate upon these trends.

Legislation regulating the "Israelite cult" in the nineteenth century may be divided into four main periods: (1) initial organization: the original "organic law" and some minor modifications of the system (1806–34); (2) revision: the drafting and implementation of the 1844 *ordonnance* (1834–48); (3) crystallization: the effect of the 1848 revolution on the legal status of Judaism, including the introduction of universal suffrage into consistory elections and the counterreaction and drafting of new legislation to restore centralized power (1848–62); and (4) consolidation: after short-term vacillation, the gains of the preceding period are retained (1862–1905).

A. Before 1834: The Period of Initial Organization

A series of legislative acts governing the organization of Catholic and Protestant religious institutions was completed in 1802. One of these laws established a consistory system for the Protestants, and it was subsequent to this organization of a "dissenting" church that Jews began to request state involvement in the ordering of their own internal affairs. They believed that an official organization would remedy the destruction suffered by Jewish institutions during the Revolution and the Reign of Terror. They estimated that government involvement in internal Jewish affairs would be necessary in order to guarantee both Jewish equality and the maintenance of the liberal principles of 1789, upon which Jewish emancipation depended. It is clear, too, that the Jews expected that official organization of their "cult" would imply state aid for their destitute institutions and rabbis; the minutes of the Assembly of Jewish Notables record their unsuccessful bid for state-salaried rabbinic posts.

Many of the Jewish communities, especially in Alsace, had petitioned for an official organization,[1] and Jean Portalis, the Minister of Cults, had designated a commission of Parisian Jews to draw up a proposal for an administrative organization of the Jews.[2] The commission gathered opinions from Jewish communities in the provinces and issued its report in April or May, 1805.

The report emphasized that the Jews themselves solicited "surveillance" by the government, and it suggested that rabbinic power be limited to preaching, reciting prayers for the government, blessing marriages, and pronouncing divorces. It proposed that two rabbis be named in Paris and one in each department with at least 200 Jews. The Emperor would approve their nomination, they would be salaried by the state, and they would take an oath. The departments in which there were rabbis would also have councils comprised of six notables named by the twenty highest taxpayers. The notables would in turn name the rabbis and administer the "cult."[3]

After receiving the commission's suggestions, Portalis prepared a report for the Emperor, but the draft of this report is incomplete and Robert Anchel assumes that it was never sent. It seems, however, that the 1805 commission's proposals were the basis for the subsequent creation of the Jewish consistories.

In 1806 Alsatian Jewish leader Berr Isaac Berr wrote to Abbé Grégoire, a senator in Paris who had been an active supporter of Jewish emancipation, asking him to support a government-sponsored organization of Judaism.[4] In the same year an interesting proposal for a system of organization very much like the consistory system that eventually emerged was formulated by Israel Jacobson (German reformer and philanthropist, and director of the famous school at Seesen) in a letter to Napoleon. Jacobson seems to be speaking of the needs of the German Jews when he outlines his plans for an internal organization:

il faut 1º établir un conseil souverain juif présidé par un patriarche, siégeant en France. 2º diviser toute la communauté en districts, dont chacun aurait un synode particulier, qui, sous la surveillance du Gouvernement Français et du Conseil souverain juif, déciderait de toutes les affaires relatives au culte, nommerait les rabbins. 3º enfin que le dit conseil souverain accorde à chaque juif les dispenses nécessaires, pour le mettre à portée de remplir ses devoirs de citoyen dans tous les pays.[5]

The first ministry report to reach Napoleon was dated August 20, 1806, more than a year after Portalis' report and a month after the convening of the Assembly of Notables.[6] It suggested (1) division of the population into synagogues by districts, (2) government control of the community structure and the rabbis, (3) educating the children for trades (the expense to be borne by the synagogues), and (4) registering all Jews.[7] Three days later, on the 23rd of August, Napoleon replied with instructions for the drafting of a project of organization.[8] Shortly thereafter, three government officials and a nine-man council chosen from the Assembly of Jewish Notables began their work on the definitive project, which was adopted by the entire Assembly on December 10. On December 18 the Emperor ratified the *règlement,* satisfied that the projected consistories "doivent exercer une police sévère sur les rabbins."[9]

We can see, then, that there was a double impetus for the consistory system as it ultimately emerged in the 1806 *règlement.* On the one hand it was a response to requests by Jewish leaders from 1802 to 1805; on the other it was the work of the ministry, which prepared the outline of the project even before the Committee of Nine was appointed from the ranks of the Assembly. When the Committee reported back to the Assembly on the result of its work, and asked for ratification of the *règlement,* it indicated the significant extent of the government's involvement in the project:

Si le culte mosaïque, ses dogmes, ses pratiques eussent été aussi parfaitement connus de l'autorité publique que ceux des autres religions positives, notre concours n'eût point été nécessaire dans ce travail. Bien mieux instruite que nous-mêmes sur ce qui nous convient, cette autorité, dirigée par le désir de notre amélioration, aurait statué sans avoir besoin de nous appeler à Paris. Le règlement dont nous venons de vous donner connaissance, rentre essentiellement dans les motifs qui ont déterminé notre convocation.[10]

The *règlement* approved by the Assembly on December 10, 1806, lay dormant for fifteen months, during which time the Sanhedrin was convened and recessed and the Assembly was reconvened and permanently dissolved, while Napoleon's attention was focused elsewhere. On March 17, 1808, an imperial decree gave the force of law to the project and made certain amplifying modifications of the *règlement.*[11] This decree was to become the first of many French laws to regulate the internal organization of French Jewry with ever-increasing precision. All subsequent laws stem from, modify, or react to this early legislation, and in order to discern the patterns that developed, we must analyze both the initial provisions and the subsequent modifications.

According to the *règlement,* a synagogue and a consistory were to be established in each department with a Jewish population of at least 2000. Departments with fewer than 2000 Jews would be joined to as many contiguous departments as was necessary in order to reach the required population, thus constituting the district for one consistory. The *chef-lieu* (seat) of the consistory would be the city with the largest Jewish population. There would be one consistorial synagogue per department. Private synagogues could only be established upon request of the consistorial synagogue to the government. A decree of 1808, which promulgated the *règlement* specified that private synagogues required approval by the *conseil d'état,* upon the recommendation of the consistorial synagogue, the central consistory, and the prefect of the department. Such requests would have to be justified by the size of the population of the district to be served by the proposed synagogue. The *règlement* provided that private synagogues would be administered by two *notables* and one rabbi, named by *l'autorité compétente.* (This authority is defined in the 1808 decree as the departmental consistory, with the central consistory's approval.)

The meaning of the term "private synagogue" was unclear and led to a debate as to whether it referred to all synagogues throughout the district (other than the consistorial synagogue) or only to additional synagogues in the *chef-lieu.* Most consistories made use of this provision to justify their control of all the synagogues within their districts, but the ambiguity of the law engendered disputes which were only resolved when the 1823 *ordonnance* expressly granted the consistories the right to name the administrators of the various communal synagogues.

According to the *règlement,* the departmental consistories were to be composed of a grand rabbi, an additional rabbi (if one was available), and three other Jews of the city where the consistory sat. This led to confusion about whether the membership of the consistory was to be five in all cases, or only four in the event that a second rabbi could not be named. What in fact happened was that no district named a second rabbi but some of them named a fourth lay member. The 1819 law corrected this confusion by calling for the election of a fifth member in all districts, and noting a preference that the seat be given to a rabbi.

The *règlement* required that a grand rabbi be assigned to each consistorial synagogue. It was not specified whether he was to be the same grand rabbi who was a member of the consistory. In fact, this became the general practice, and it had probably been the intention of the legislation.

In each consistorial district the government was to choose, from among the highest taxpayers and most respected of the Jews, twenty-five *notables* who in turn would elect the consistory members.[12]

A central consistory, composed of three grand rabbis and two lay members, was to be established in Paris.[13] The rabbinic majority on this consistory is to be noted. In fact, the provision for two lay members was a later addition to Napoleon's original concept of a rabbinical council and was due to the ministry's judgment (probably suggested by some of the Jewish *notables* themselves) that the rabbis were not to be trusted and required lay surveillance. It will be demonstrated below that this addition of lay members led eventually, through increasing laicization, to a domination of the lay element not only over the consistorial administrative machinery, but over the entire rabbinate.

Minimum allowable salaries were established by the *règlement,* with the provision that the communities might vote increases. The funds for payment of rabbis' salaries, as well as for other "cultic" purposes, were to be raised by a special tax on the Jewish population. The Jewish expectation that their religious expenses would be assumed by the state (as had been done for the Catholics and Protestants) was thus not fulfilled.

It will be remembered that Napoleon had conceived of the consistories as exercising surveillance over the rabbis. This was the purpose of the following provision in Article 26 of the *règle-*

ment: any rabbi who did not have a post after the establishment of the consistory system and who wanted to remain in the country would be required to sign a formal declaration that he adhered to the decisions of the Sanhedrin.

From 1808, when the March 17th decree put the *règlement* into effect, until 1819, no legislation intervened to modify the consistory system's legal basis. The *ordonnance* of June 29, 1819, was eventually made necessary by three difficulties which arose in the first decade of consistory functioning.

The 1806 *règlement* had prescribed that one central consistory member's term would expire each year, and that the rest of the consistory would elect his successor, he himself being eligible for re-election. The instability of the post was seen by some as incompatible with the dignity and the efficacy of the rabbinate, and it was questioned immediately whether this provision was to apply to the grand rabbis as well as to the lay members.[14] It developed that none of the grand rabbis of the central consistory retired before his death, and the 1819 law subsequently specified that only lay members were subject to the annual *sortie* of a central consistory member.

The second difficulty that had arisen was the question of the election of a second rabbi to the departmental consistories. Nowhere had this been done, and there was confusion as to whether a fourth lay member should be elected instead, in order to bring the total membership to five. A membership of four was found to be undesirable, both because it limited the consistory to a small size and because it was an even number, susceptible of resulting in tied votes. The 1819 *ordonnance* called for the election everywhere of a fifth member, preferably a rabbi.[15]

The third, and undoubtedly major, difficulty that led to the enactment of the 1819 *ordonnance* was that of collecting taxes. Anchel has described this aspect of the consistory experience very well, and we need not repeat his findings.[16] Suffice it to say that the 1819 *ordonnance* attempted to alleviate the difficulties encountered by the consistories in receiving the special Jewish taxes designated for the expenses of the cult.

The 1819 *ordonnance* was the first of several laws to be promulgated as modifications of the original decree in response to consistory demand. The next such law, the *ordonnance* of 1823, responded also to the needs expressed by the consistories. First, it prescribed methods for replacing *notables,* lay members of the consistories, and the grand rabbis of the central consistory. Secondly, it defined certain powers already exercised by the departmental consistories but frequently challenged. Thus, it was specified that the *ministre officiant* (cantor) of the consistorial synagogue, the *shochet* and other religious personnel of the *chef-lieu* were to be named exclusively by the departmental consistories. In the other communities of the district, consistorial authority was to be exercised by the consistory's delegate, the *commissaire surveillant*. (This seems to have eliminated the 1808 provision for central consistory approval of such officers.) It was the *commissaire surveillant's* job to preside over the local commission named by the consistory to elect the rabbis, cantors, and other functionaries of the communities. Through him the consistory would exercise its control of the local budgets and tax collection. The 1823 *ordonnance,* then, is to be understood as the first attempt of the departmental consistories to use legislative means to increase their influence in the communities of their districts.

The third major effect of the 1823 law was the dramatic increase of lay power in the central consistory. From the equilibrium of two rabbis and two laymen,[17] the central consistory was to grow to two rabbis and seven laymen. At the same time it was ruled that prior to making any decision concerning religion, the central consistory would have to obtain the consent of its two grand rabbis. Nevertheless, it will be shown in Chapter 10, where we discuss the lay-rabbinic struggle, that this provision was in fact often disregarded. At the same time, the central consistory received the right to decide which books would be allowed in the Jewish elementary schools, subject only to the condition that the grand rabbis agree.

Further state legislation in 1829 transformed the modern rabbinical school (established by the Metz community in 1821) into an official seminary. This school was to be the only training school for the rabbinate, and it was given the exclusive right to attest to an aspiring rabbi's capacities.

The next important law modifying the consistory system was the act of the July monarchy of January 1831, which put Judaism on the state payroll. This act put an end to the special Jewish tax, which had been the source of many complaints. It is reasonable to assume that another of the prime considerations in soliciting state salaries for the rabbis was the expectation that this would produce tight control over the recipients of the post. In fact, the 1831 law was followed by one of the following year (October 15, 1832), which *did* spell out very detailed requirements for the rabbinate. Earlier the same year, Judaism had received another assurance of its status as an approved "state religion" in the law of June 19, 1832, which provided dispensation from military service for rabbinic students.[18]

The laws and decisions of 1806, 1808, 1819, 1823, 1829, 1831, and 1832 constitute the essential background for an understanding of the further legislative developments of 1844 and 1862. Together, these early laws form a series which established the consistories, provided them with circumscribed powers, ensured their continuity through election, and put the whole system under the control and patronage of the state.

B. 1834–1848: The Period of Revision

1. Prior to 1839

The earliest trace that we find of an attempt to completely reform the organization of the consistory is an entry in the
minutes book of the Paris consistory for October 21, 1834.[19]
On this date the consistory decided to appoint a commission
(composed of Goudchaux Weill, Edmond Halphen, Elie Brandon, Jules Lan, and Polack, secretary to the consistory) to
examine possible ways of revising the *règlement* in accordance
with contemporary needs. It was pointed out that some of the
dispositions of the original *règlement* had lost their force, because of the religious freedom provisions of the 1830 *Charte,*
promulgated upon the accession of the July monarchy: "Chacun
professe sa religion avec une égale liberté, et obtient pour son
culte la même protection" (Article 5).

The minutes do not elaborate further as to which dispositions they had in mind. It is no mere coincidence, however, that
for some time previous to the date of this entry the Paris consistory had been in close contact with the police in an attempt
to have all private prayer meetings closed down. The freedom-
of-religion clause in the 1830 *Charte* was being widely interpreted as implying freedom from consistorial control, and many
small groups had opened prayer meetings.

The history of the regulations governing *associations* and
réunions goes back to the Napoleonic period: Articles 291, 292,
and 294 of the penal code promulgated in 1810 put *associations*
under the control of the government. The code specified that
their meetings had to be government-approved, and it prescribed
certain penalties for infractions. *Réunions,* on the other hand,
were subject only to municipal control. *Associations* were
groups that met frequently or at least at regular intervals. The
assemblées de prières, or *minyanim,* that formed (frequently in
mutual aid societies) were included among such *associations.*
They were registered with the *préfecture de police* and received
an authorization number. The consistory's difficulties in controlling them arose out of the refusal of the *préfecture* to
follow the consistory recommendation in granting such authorization.

After the 1830 *Charte* had proclaimed religious freedom,
people began to challenge interference with their religious practices; struggles for freedom from all control were staged by
sectarian Protestant and Catholic clergy and congregations.
Initially the *Charte* seemed to be in their favor, but at least
seven decisions (from 1836 to 1854) of the *Cour de Cassation*
(Supreme Court) destroyed this impression. The court established that although meetings of official (*reconnus*) cults were
subject to no control, all non-official (*non-reconnus*) religious
groups required permission to meet. For the Jews this included

nonconsistorial prayer meetings, as only consistorial Judaism was *reconnu*. In printing an 1838 court decision to this effect, one of the editors of the collection of jurisprudence (L.-M. Dev) pointed out that the court's interpretation reduced Article 5 of the *Charte* to meaninglessness:

Inutile de revenir ici sur les objections graves que soulève cette solution. Tous les commentaires, toutes les digressions historiques sur l'origine de nos libertés religieuses ou politiques, toute l'habilité dialectique que l'on peut apporter dans cette question complexe, ne feront pas que l'article 5 de la Charte, entendu dans son sens naturel, ne perde toute sa force et ne devienne presqu'un non-sens devant la disposition de l'article 291 du code pénal. [20]

The consistories had been in existence for a quarter of a century when the Orleanist rule began. The 1830 *Charte's* promulgation of religious freedom coincided with the settling of the consistories into a comfortable position as established institutions, jealous of their role as the only legally recognized Jewish institutions in the country. They fully expected to be able to close down all the private prayer meetings that remained. It was the consistories' ambition that all of the Jewish population worship together in the large, official temples which were springing up in the cities of major Jewish population. Both fiscal considerations and a desire to effect religious reforms dictated this aim.

In 1834 the Paris consistory had been unsuccessfully battling the separatist prayer meetings for seventeen months before it decided to call for legislative change. The consistory had repeatedly requested the police to close down such meetings, but it was informed that the Ministry of Cults had ruled that the prohibition of prayer meetings would be in conflict with the religious liberty guaranteed by the *Charte*. [21]

It appears likely that the High Holy Days of 1833 were celebrated in Paris by a large gathering at the private chapel of a teacher named Lipman Lévy Aron Sauphar. [22] In June 1834 the police prefect informed Grand Rabbi Ennery of the Paris consistory that Sauphar had requested permission to hold prayer meetings privately with about eighty people present. [23] From the nature of the questions the prefect asked the grand rabbi, it is clear that the government's liberal position on the interpretation of the *Charte* was as yet unchanged. Before granting the requested permission the prefect merely wanted clarification on two points: (1) Does anything in Judaism prohibit the teaching of religion outside the official temple? and (2) Does Sauphar offer the necessary guarantees of morality and orderliness? After a discussion, during which it was noted that private meetings hurt the temple treasury, the consistory decided to recommend that the prefect not satisfy the request. Sauphar was required to close his chapel. [24] In September the consistory noted that the prayer meetings were continuing, and it requested police intervention.[25] On September 25 the consistory rejected a request by Sauphar for permission to hold prayer meetings.[26]

It is evidently against this background that we must understand the decision of the Paris consistory in October 1834, to establish a commission to study ways of modifying the legislation governing the consistories. The consistory obviously wished to strengthen its power to control the independent prayer meetings. For the three years that followed the establishment of the commission we have no information about any meetings, discussions or actions. However, it seems possible that the "Mémoire sur quelques réformes à faire aux règlements constitutifs du culte israélite en France," dated November 28, 1837, and addressed to the Ministry of Cults by one Baruch Weill, is a reflection of the work of the 1834 commission. Baruch Weill is probably none other than the Goudchaux (Baruch) Weill appointed by the Paris consistory to the 1834 commission. The ministry took note of his proposals, thanking him for his observations.[27]

There may have been a connection between Baruch Weill's proposal to the government and the decision of the central consistory shortly thereafter to name a commission of its own. An entry in the minutes book, dated December 24, 1837, states that a member had proposed the creation of a commission "chargée de revoir les décrêts, ordonnances et règlements régissant notre culte, d'en coordonner les dispositions, de proposer les modifications dont plusieurs dispositions sont susceptibles, en un mot, de mettre cette législation en harmonie avec le progrès et la position actuelle des Israélites en France." The following were named to the commission: Adolphe Crémieux, Ed. Halphen, Myrtil Maas, Ph. Simon, Elie Brandon, Philippe Anspach, Alphonse Cerfberr, Polack.[28] (Crémieux was the guiding force behind the bill, from its inception through the several drafts, and into its final form.) It was apparently this commission that prepared the draft for a new law which the central consistory circulated to the departments in 1839 and which led to heated controversy and eventually, with some changes, to the 1844 *ordonnance*.

Paris was not the only departmental consistory to decide, before 1839, that the Jewish legislation needed a thorough overhauling. Several other departmental consistories, especially those of Metz, Strasbourg, and Nancy, requested the central consistory to draft a measure that would put the Jewish administration "in harmony with the times."[29]

Almost immediately after the central consistory had decided to work for changes in the statutes that governed the consistories, it received a *mémoire* from Noé Noé, teacher and librarian in Bordeaux, urging modifications in the consistorial system through legislative changes.[30] Noé's argument was that the consistory was unsuited for the important task of improving the moral condition of the Jews because it was defective in its original conception. He justified the changes that he requested by the same principle of putting the Jewish organization into "harmony with the times." The 1806 *règlement*, he observed, was a product of times of despotism and military glory; it had been largely fashioned by Napoleon and was not compatible with the contemporary liberalism of the Orleanist monarchy.

The moral regeneration that Noé envisaged had a strong religious foundation, and his version of consistory reform would allow for the independent development of religious leaders. The rabbis would be licensed and appointed to their posts not by the laity but by a "rabbinic college," composed of the two grand rabbis of the central consistory, the grand rabbi of the Paris consistory, and two other Jews, well-versed in rabbinic studies and chosen by the central consistory. Noé's views were typical of the Bordeaux community, which always insisted on the rabbi's independence and dignity, and his authority in religious matters. It is not surprising that Noé also asked for a return to the rule of having two rabbis on the central consistory.

Noé also urged a liberalization of the requirements for membership in the *notabilité*. To be eligible as a *notable* or as a consistory member, Noé suggested, a man should pay at least forty or fifty francs in tax (*cens*) or be a member of one of the liberal professions. The consistory members would thus be named by a larger electorate, composed of all those eligible for membership in the consistory and *notabilité*. Such changes would put an end to the circular practice of the consistories naming the *notables* who in turn named the consistories, and to the absence of all but extremely wealthy businessmen among the ranks of both groups.[31]

Arguing in favor of placing lawyers, teachers, and doctors in the posts of *notable* and consistory member, Noé said that this was the only way that moral regeneration could be carried out. In order to encourage education, teach a love of industry, create useful institutions, and ensure eloquent preaching, it would be necessary to seek energetic and talented men who appreciated these needs. Why, he asked, seek such men only among the restricted *notabilité* of the rich, as prescribed by the 1806 règlement? Why not recruit "ceux qui précisément étudient les hommes et les choses?"[32]

Noé wanted the *notables* to control the consistory, reviewing complaints about the consistory that were brought before it, examining its accounts, and aiding in the inspection of the primary schools. He thus betrayed a skepticism and wariness of the consistory system. The kinds of modifications he envisioned were not always the same kind sought by the consistories. Noé's proposal came at the very time when the question of reform of the organization was ripe, but his proposals were not adopted. Although the project developed by the central consistory the following year included changes to broaden the concept of *notabilité*, its thrust, like that of all nineteenth-century consistory legislative proposals, was for increased lay domination of the rabbinate and increasingly centralized power.

Interestingly, there are two suggestions Noé made which would have augmented consistory power. He wanted the departmental consistories to conduct extensive correspondence with the communities of their districts to gather information on their "moral state." These documents would be used in drafting annual reports to be submitted by the departments to the central consistory. In addition, each consistory would render triennial reports on "les améliorations faites, entreprises, ou en projet; l'état moral et religieux." The consistories, however, were not interested in increasing the volume of their administrative work and correspondence. Funds for such purposes were very limited, and the consistories frequently complained of their financial problems to the central consistory and to the ministry, requesting increases in their allocations. They were not able to supervise closely improvements in the communities that were at great distances from themselves. It will be seen below, in our discussion of "regeneration" as one of the three legislated functions of the consistories, that they often did not take as much initiative in this area as did private individuals (especially those with money for the creation of charitable and educational institutions).

Early in July 1839, the commission that had been appointed by the central consistory on December 24, 1837, completed its work and issued its proposals for a new law to reorganize the consistories.[33] The project was printed and distributed by the central consistory to the departmental consistories for their observations. But before the 1839 draft could become law, there would be five years of protests by rabbis, consistories, individuals, and even a prefect. There would be six drafts plus numerous consistorial amendments of three of these drafts. Why was the issue so controversial?

2. 1839–1848

French Jews in 1839 were deeply divided over the question of whether to introduce changes into the religion. They were equally divided over what constituted changing the religion, and disagreed about what should be considered untouchable. The people that became known as "orthodox" were particularly concerned about the status of the rabbinate, because they rightfully saw the fate of this institution as the key to the kind of Judaism that would be allowed to develop under the aegis of the consistory. Holding to what they conceived as the traditional concept of rabbinic autonomy and unchallenged religious authority, they refused to condone attempts to create a clerical hierarchy, or to establish lay control of the rabbinate. Reformers, on the other hand (none of them rabbis), had been requesting liturgical and practical changes for twenty years. They believed that the way to implement their program was to obtain lay control of the rabbinate and progressive centralization of power in the hands of like-minded reformers in the departmental and central consistories. This was precisely what the orthodox and the rabbis found so frightening in the central consistory's 1839 proposal.

The idea that the laity was to dominate is clear throughout the project. The central consistory was to be composed of one rabbi and seven lay members (Article 6).[34] The choice of the central consistory grand rabbi was to be based on a *concours* (competition) and was to be exercised by a nine-member commission, composed of the president of the central consistory and eight people appointed by the ministry (Article 56). The consistories would have the right to suspend or dismiss the *ministres officiants* (cantors) in their districts, to ask the central consistory to suspend or dismiss the rabbis and assistant rabbis, and to complain to the central consistory about their grand rabbi (Article 16). The central consistory would have the right to dismiss the rabbis and to censure or suspend the grand rabbis. They could ask the minister to dismiss the grand rabbis (Article 25). It is clear that this domination of the rabbinate was sought for the purpose of placing control of the cult firmly into the hands of the laity. Article 24 of the project gave the central consistory the right to decide which books might be used in the schools and which prayerbooks could be used in the temples, but it said nothing of the role of the grand rabbi in this decision. Even more strikingly, it allowed the central consistory to change the ritual and to adjust the length of public prayers:

il [le consistoire central] fait, après avoir pris l'avis des consistoires départementaux, les règlements qu'il juge utiles pour la police générale du culte dans les temples, pour la durée des prières publiques, pour les changements que peut nécessiter le rituel.

It was this article that aroused the anxiety of the orthodox. In a lay-dominated central consistory in which the rabbi's voice counted only as a single vote, laymen would be empowered to introduce significant ritualistic changes.

Additional attempts to centralize power in the hands of the central consistory were included in the bill. The central consistory was to name the director and the teachers of the rabbinic school (a function formerly performed by the Metz consistory) (Article 67). Perhaps the most audacious of the proposals was that preachers, chosen by the central consistory and funded by a special government grant of 5000 francs, would be sent to "carry the holy word and religious and moral instruction" to the Jewish population all over the country (Article 68).

The central consistory insisted, also, on its position at the top of a hierarchical administrative structure. All communications to the ministry would go via it, and require its endorsement (Article 18). Moreover, the central consistory would have the right to censure departmental consistory members, and even to request that the government dismiss them.

The departmental consistories, in their turn, would be assured of total control over the Jewish institutions within their districts. They would administer all funds, name officers of the charities, have exclusive right to license ritual slaughterers (Article 17). (The latter had already been prescribed in the 1823 *ordonnance*.) It should be noted that in the 1839 draft there was still no attempt to control the practice of circumcision. The *shochet*, but not the *mohel*, was to be named by the consistory. (The Bordeaux consistory complained about this, and its observations led to inclusion of the control of the *mohelim* in the 1844 *ordonnance*.) In an effort to assure its authority over prayer meetings, an article stipulated that such meetings were to be authorized by the government only upon the approval of the departmental consistory (Article 63).

Lay control of the rabbinate was not the only trend that alarmed the orthodox. Equally abhorrent to them was the concept of hierarchy within the rabbinate. Although an established fact since the Sanhedrin, this hierarchy was now, for the first time, spelled out. Article 37 of the draft read:

La hiérarchie des ministres du culte est ainsi détérminée:
1⁰ Grand-rabbin, membre du consistoire central
2⁰ sept rabbins consistoriaux, membres des consistoires départementaux
3⁰ rabbins
4⁰ sous-rabbins
5⁰ ministres-officiants

The right of surveillance and censure over the entire rabbinate was to be exercised by the grand rabbi of the central consistory (Article 41). The departmental grand rabbis were granted the same rights within their districts (Article 45).

The three main thrusts of the proposed legislation were, then, lay dominance of the rabbinate, hierarchy, and centralization within the consistory system, and hierarchy within the rabbinate. In addition, the project introduced a significant liberalization in the composition of the *notabilité*. It proposed as electors not just twenty-five government-appointed *notables*, but all the people who fulfilled certain property or professional requirements (Article 28). In this respect, this proposal was similar to that made earlier by Noé Noé.

Six complete drafts of the new *ordonnance* were prepared by the central consistory and the government between 1839 and 1844. In addition to these, the departmental consistories, invited to comment on three of them, prepared numerous extensively revised versions at each stage of the work.[35]

The project had first been communicated to the central

consistory (by the commission that drafted it) in July 1839, but no action seems to have been taken during the summer. In October the central consistory was preparing to communicate copies to the departments when Grand Rabbi Deutz registered a protest against Articles 5 and 24, which dealt with the centralization of power in the central consistory; Article 16, concerning centralization of power at the departmental level; and Articles 45 and 48, which listed the conditions under which a rabbi could be suspended or dismissed and provided that salaries be reduced during suspension. It is less remarkable that Deutz raised objections to these points than that he limited his protests to these articles. In so doing he implicitly accepted much of the tendency toward lay domination (as expressed in Articles 6, 56, and 25) and toward centralization of power (spelled out in Articles 17, 18, 63, 67, and 68). He did not even object to the creation of a hierarchy among the rabbis (Articles 37, 41, and 44).

Crémieux claimed that Deutz's objections should not prevent the central consistory from sending copies to the various departmental consistories. Each member's future right to comment on the adoption of the various articles would remain unprejudiced, and the final discussions and decisions would benefit from the reactions of the departments.[36] In November the copies were in the hands of the departmental consistories. Immediately protests were registered. By February 1840 the central consistory had received observations from all the consistories, some rabbis and grand rabbis, and other individuals. Crémieux was asked to study the replies and to prepare a report summarizing them for the consistory.[37]

In the meantime complaints were being received also at the ministry and at the recently founded periodical, *Archives Israélites*. Perhaps the first two grand rabbis after Deutz to go on record in opposition to the project were Grand Rabbi Gougenheim of Nancy and Grand Rabbi L. M. Lambert of Metz. In November 1839 a protest by Gougenheim and many of the rabbis of his district was circulated. One copy reached the *Archives Israélites*.[38] Lambert published his "Réflexions générales sur un projet d'ordonnance relatif à une nouvelle organisation du culte israélite" on November 26, 1839. He protested both against the project's obvious aim of introducing innovations and its intention "de substituer l'influence des laïcs à l'action des rabbins sur tout ce qui concerne le rite et l'instruction religieuse." His protest was countersigned by Mayer Lazard, *Grand-Rabbin honoraire,* and L. Morhange, *Gradué Grand-Rabbin, Bachelier-ès-Lettres,* and by ninety-five heads of families in Metz.[39]

A short time later the ministry received a copy of this protest together with an additional list of Jews who supported Lambert's views. Complaints from other sources also arrived at the ministry. Marseille's Grand Rabbi M. D. Cahen sent his protest. The prefect of the Moselle reported that the project had caused controversy in Metz,[40] and the grand rabbi of Bordeaux also registered a protest.[41] In March the ministry received a thick document from the community (not to be confused with the consistory) of Strasbourg, consisting of petitions protesting the central consistory project. The complaints were directed especially against Articles 16 and 24, which permitted the suspension of rabbis by laymen, and gave the central consistory the right to make changes in the ritual and the length of prayers. These were the articles that had already evoked the wrath of Deutz. The petitioners argued that the proposed legislation threatened the rabbis' authority and would prevent them from disagreeing with the laymen on religious matters. The petitioners declared that lay control of religion would completely destroy Judaism. Eighty-two communities of the Bas-Rhin (the district controlled by the Strasbourg consistory) adhered to the Strasbourg petition.[42]

The Jewish press publicized the controversy. In 1839 Abraham Ben Baruch Créhange fulminated against the project in his *La Sentinelle Juive*. He, too, understood that the project "n'avait pour le moment d'autre but que de placer l'autorité spirituelle sous la dépendance du pouvoir temporel."[43]

In July and August 1840 the *Archives Israélites* printed Crémieux's April report to the central consistory. It reached the readers before the official communication of the report arrived at the departmental consistories, which did nothing to soothe the already ruffled feelings of the provincial bodies.

In his report, Crémieux insisted on the tentative nature of the original project, which was, he said, conceived only as a working suggestion to elicit comments and opinions from the departmental consistories. In emphasizing the open channels that the central consistory had established for receiving all advice and recommendations, he emphatically blamed those who took public exception to the project's provisions, through printed protests or communications with the ministry. He claimed that these opinions should properly have been forwarded directly to the central consistory, which would have given them serious attention. Grand Rabbi Lambert of Metz came in for special condemnation:

il nous est pénible de dire qu'il a dépassé toutes les limites. Il a tout-à-coup refusé son concours aux délibérations du consistoire dont il est membre; il a lancé dans le public, imprimées à un grand nombre d'exemplaires, les plus virulentes protestations; il a fait réclamer, ou l'on a réclamé en son nom, des signatures à Metz et dans diverses communes de sa circonscription; le tout a été transmis, non au consistoire central dont M. le grand rabbin ne s'est occupé, mais au ministre des cultes, qu'on voulait ainsi armer d'avance, même contre un projet de réforme.

But the views of Lambert, although they had come to the

attention of the central consistory, were not quoted in Crémieux's analysis of the reactions to the 1839 project. Nor were the views of the grand rabbis of Marseille and Nancy, nor those of the sixteen rabbis of the Strasbourg district, nor any of the opinions, both individual and collective, of citizens. Yet the separate opinions of the various consistory members of Marseille and Nancy, which had been forwarded separately, were included in the analysis.

It is evident, we must conclude, that the central consistory was interested in arriving at a concert of opinion exclusively with the lay element of the provincial consistories. Lambert had well understood this when he addressed his protests directly to the ministry, rather than attempt to work through the consistory. The nature of the (albeit "tentative") 1839 project had caused the battle lines to be clearly drawn.

Crémieux reported accurately the views of the departmental consistories.[44] After a long summary of the various reactions to each section of the project, he proposed a modified version. Crémieux maintained much of the thrust of the original project, however, despite the often contrary views expressed by others. Although the consistories of Metz, Colmar, and Nancy, as well as two rabbis[45] and others had requested three grand rabbis on the central consistory, Crémieux retained his version, which allowed for only one (Article 6). He also maintained the provision that a lay committee would choose the grand rabbi by a *concours* (Article 56). Similarly, the stipulation that the departmental consistories could propose the dismissal or suspension of the district's communal rabbis (Article 16) was maintained despite disapproval from the Metz consistory, from Benjamin Gradis (a prolific letter-writer and petitioner, and Bordeaux Jewish leader), and from petitioners in eighty-two communities of the Bas-Rhin. The central consistory retained for itself the right to suspend or dismiss the rabbis and request the ministry to dismiss them. In deference, however, to some of the observations, Crémieux provided that the complaint of the departmental consistory would be a prerequisite to the suspension of a rabbi (Articles 25 and 45).

The only significant concession to the pro-rabbinic faction was the re-drafting of Article 24, which had given the central consistory the right to adjust the length of the prayers and to modify the ritual. Here was the heart of the problem, and the reason for the violence of the public outcry. Traditionalists were astounded that the central consistory could have claimed such sweeping power. Crémieux's new version provided for the concurrence of the majority of the grand rabbis before such decisions could be made by the central consistory, and it added the requirement that the grand rabbi of the central consistory approve books for the schools and prayerbooks for synagogue use.

Despite the revision of Article 24, the bill remained a threat to rabbinic authority. As Benjamin Gradis put it:

*Toute la nouvelle ordonnance n'a qu'un but, c'est de faire
tomber les ministres du culte, sous la dépendance des laïques,
et de cette manière, d'acquérir une action directe sur la religion
à laquelle on ne déguise pas l'intention de faire subir une
transformation complète.*[46]

In addition to lay control, the 1839 bill had proposed a hierarchical structure for the French rabbinate. In their responses the consistories had requested modifications of the hierarchy, but none of them had challenged the basic concept. Crémieux retained it (Articles 37, 41, 44).

The hierarchy within the consistory administration itself emerged less unscathed. Predictably, the departmental consistories had favored their own centralized control over the communities of their districts (Articles 16 and 17), but had rejected the central consistory's attempt at encroaching on departmental autonomy. Crémieux was forced to restore to the Metz consistory the right to propose the nomination of teachers and the director of the rabbinical school (Article 67) and to drop the plan for the central consistory to send preachers throughout the country, a move which was correctly viewed as "missionary" by many critics (Article 68). He also yielded to protests against the draft's stipulation that the central consistory be the only intermediary between the Jews and the Ministry of Cults. Article 18 was revised to permit communication through the prefects as well.

By the time Crémieux's report was published, the Damascus affair had intervened.[47] For almost a year attention was directed elsewhere, and no further action was taken. In August 1841 it was decided that in November, when most of the central consistory members would return to Paris after their summer vacations, a final decision would be made about the new project.[48] In November and December Crémieux presented one after another of the propositions of his new draft to the vote of the central consistory, which adopted all of them by December 26, 1841.[49] Grand Rabbi Deutz was not present, having fallen seriously ill. He died shortly after, and it was not until March 19, 1842, that the central consistory addressed its project to the ministry. In a covering letter the members explained their claim to update the legislation and to abrogate those attributions which were no longer "en harmonie avec l'état actuel des choses." Duties and functions of the consistory, which were no longer exercised, had been removed from the law. They were referring, undoubtedly, to the policing actions required by the 1806 *règlement,* such as reporting indigents and conscripts.[50]

In this second draft the essential elements of centralization and lay domination were retained at the same levels as had been proposed by the Crémieux report two years earlier. In regard to a rabbinical hierarchy, the covering letter argued that allowing the grand rabbis to censure all other rabbis on religious questions would favor "the hierarchy that we seek to establish among the Israelite clergy."[51]

The proposal of March 1842 was transmitted to the departmental consistories by the ministry. The following August Crémieux complained that no decisions had been made, and he tried to stir the ministry into action. On August 27, 1842, Pierre Dessauret, Deputy Director of Cults, wrote that he hoped to receive and analyze the departmental consistories' replies by October.[52] Crémieux was anxious to see the bill through, and wrote again on August 30, asking for an appointment.[53] The sources do not indicate whether he did meet with Dessauret, but it seems unlikely that his request could have been refused, considering his membership in the Chamber of Deputies. Again on November 7, Crémieux asked for an audience to discuss the project.[54] Dessauret replied on the ninth, setting up a late afternoon meeting.[55] On December 12 Crémieux requested still another appointment.[56]

Crémieux's efforts bore fruit when Dessauret recommended to N.-F.-M.-L.-J. Martin, Minister of Cults, on December 21, 1842, that a commission be named to handle the drafting of the new law. The commission was immediately established. It consisted of Dessauret (*"membre de la chambre des députés, conseiller d'état, directeur de l'administration des cultes"*), président; R.-E.-N. Cuvier (*"maître des requêtes au Conseil d'Etat, chef de la section des cultes non-catholiques au ministère des cultes"*); Crémieux (*"membre de la chambre des députés et du consistoire central des Israélites"*); Max Cerfberr (*"membre de la chambre et du consistoire central"*); Marchand Ennery (*"Grand Rabbin du Consistoire Départemental de la circonscription israélite de Paris"*). A week later Edmond Halphen of the Paris consistory was added to the commission.[57]

Again a long delay occurred. On July 11 the commission was called to its first meeting.[58] We have no information, either in the files of the ministry or in the archives of the central consistory, as to what occurred during the meetings of the commission from July through October 1843. On November 2 Dessauret dispatched the commission's bill, which he described as a revision of the central consistory's project of March 10, 1842, to the central consistory.

At this time Crémieux resigned from the central consistory, apparently in protest, although it is not clear whether his protest was directed against the ministry, the central consistory, or Worms de Romilly, the inactive and unpopular president of the central consistory. His letter of resignation has disappeared from the archives, and we have only an allusion to it in the minutes of November 5, 1843.[59] At that time the central consistory resolved to write and request him to reconsider. By November 22 he was once again taking part in their work, although we have no further explanation. On this date he sent a letter thanking the ministry for the new project and promising a reply by the end of the week.[60] The following day Crémieux was elected president of the central consistory, defeating Worms de Romilly, the incumbent.[61]

The central consistory, under Crémieux's leadership, then proceeded to negotiate with the ministry concerning some of the provisions of the November 2, 1843 project: it sought enlarged rabbinic districts, a reduction in the number of rabbis, and an increase in rabbinic salaries. Crémieux, especially, was a persistent champion of higher state allocations.[62] The negotiations led to a new version, which was sent to the *Comité de législation* on January 22, 1844. When A.-F.-A. Vivien, *conseiller d'état,* returned the bill as amended by the legislative committee, he ordered that the draft should be reviewed by the departmental consistories before it could be voted into law. The government's interest in providing satisfaction to the departments was a matter of preserving the consistory system, which was threatening to dissolve.

Tension must have been high between Vivien and Crémieux, because in requesting the departmental consistories' views, Vivien pointed out that although the central consistory claimed to have met the departmental objections to the 1839 project, its claim had not been documented.[63]

Vivien's concerns were not unjustified. When the provincial reactions were studied during March and April, it was found that four of the consistories were still arguing against lay domination of Judaism, centralization of power in the central consistory, and rabbinic hierarchy.

The Metz consistory continued to insist that the number of rabbis on the central consistory be restored to three. The other consistories that objected to lay domination of Judaism centered their attacks on the issue of the central consistory's rights of censure, suspension, and dismissal of the rabbis. The Strasbourg consistory asked that the grounds for suspension of the grand rabbis be specified. The Colmar consistory wanted revocation limited to irreligious or immoral behavior. Nancy pushed for limiting the sanctions to censure and suspension, and eliminating the provision for dismissal of the rabbis. Grand Rabbi Arnaud Aron of Strasbourg sent his own comments, wherein he declared that giving the central consistory complete control over the rabbis was in basic opposition to Judaism.[64]

An additional proposal for the improvement of the rabbis' status was made by the Colmar consistory, which pointed out that communal rabbis were excluded from the list of the *notabilité.*

The dissenting consistories also attacked the centralization of power in the hands of the central consistory. The Strasbourg consistory asked that departmental consistories with more than 10,000 Jewish inhabitants be represented on the central consistory by an additional member. The same consistory asked that the grounds for suspension of departmental consistory lay members by the central consistory be specified. Colmar urged that the local consistories, rather than the central consistory, be allowed to censure the grand rabbis. Likewise, Strasbourg thought that the right to dismiss a cantor belonged with the departmental, not the central, consistory. It also asked that the central consistory be allowed to suspend a communal rabbi only upon the recommendation of the departmental consistory. Colmar wanted the departments to have the right to bring any conflict between themselves and the central consistory to the attention of the ministry.

Finally, the issue of hierarchy within the rabbinate came in for its share of criticism. The Strasbourg consistory and its grand rabbi, Aron, were opposed to allowing the grand rabbi of the central consistory to have the power of censure over all the rabbis of France. Similarly, Strasbourg and Aron opposed granting the departmental grand rabbis the right of censure over the rabbis of their districts. Aron claimed that such provisions were opposed to the principles of Judaism. Aron and three consistories also attacked the notion that the accord of the grand rabbi of the central consistory is sufficient to permit the central consistory to make religious decisions. Strasbourg wanted to require the agreement of all the grand rabbis, a requirement that had been present in the 1840 Crémieux draft. Colmar asked for the same, but added that the grand rabbis should formulate their opinions only after conferring with their district rabbis, thus assuring any future reforms a "true synodal character." Nancy went a step further and asked for the agreement of all the rabbis. It requested the inclusion of an article which would allow the central consistory, upon the request of the majority of the departmental consistories, to solicit from the ministry permission to call a synod, which alone would have competence in religious decisions: "En dehors de cette assemblée aucune décision doctrinale ou dogmatique ne pourra être publiée ou devenir la matière de l'enseignement." But it was Grand Rabbi Aron who was most eloquent in his attack on the innovation of a hierarchy in the French rabbinate:

Et ce qui a été fait, délibéré, consacré, sanctioné par plusieurs générations de rabbins, par des synodes, par des sanhedrins, par des convocations saintes, un seul grand-rabbin n'aurait qu'à souffler dessus, et tout cet édifice tomberait! Et l'oeuvre de plusieurs siècles et de l'immense majorité des docteurs de la loi pourrait être renversée démolie, ruinée de fond en comble par le Grand-Rabbin du Consistoire Central par le fait du pouvoir illimité, grâce à l'espèce d'infaillibilité que proclame le nouveau projet d'organisation! L'infaillibilité, notre Loi ne l'accorde à personne, elle la refuse même aux prophètes, même aux anges!

The remaining three consistories (Paris, Marseille, and Bordeaux) accepted the March 1844 bill essentially as it was. In fact, the members of the Paris consistory feared that the bill's provision for lay control of religious decisions would prove insufficient. They claimed that requiring the grand rabbi's agreement in "religious" decisions would give him too much influence and he might take advantage of it! They suggested that the word "religious" be changed in order to indicate clearly that the rabbi's concurrence was needed only in questions of "dogma."[65]

The reactions had not all been received before April 20, the date on which the ministry forwarded the responses of five consistories (all except Paris and Nancy) to the legislative committee. It is not clear whether the last two were sent on for consideration. On May 2 the bill was deliberated and approved by the *Conseil d'état* with very few corrections on the draft, none of any import.

The central consistory retained its proportion of one rabbi to seven lay members (and more lay members would be added when the number of consistories increased). Central consistory rights of censuring, suspending, and dismissing (or requesting the ministry to dismiss) rabbis, grand rabbis and cantors were all left intact. Nor were the grounds for such disciplinary measures added to the *ordonnance*. The provision, added to an earlier draft, that the agreement of a majority of the grand rabbis be obtained before the central consistory could make any changes in the ritual did not appear in the final version. The only concession made to the rabbinate was the addition of the communal rabbis to the *notabilité*.

Centralization of power in the hands of the central consistory emerged equally intact. Each consistory, regardless of the size of its population, retained its one member "representation" on the central consistory. The reasons for which the central consistory could censure the lay members of the consistories or ask the ministry to dismiss them, or even to dissolve an entire consistory, were left unspecified. The departments were totally unsuccessful in attaining any of the powers confided to the central consistory, nor were they officially granted the right to appeal directly to the ministry in complaining of the central consistory.

Rabbinic hierarchy, too, was retained, despite the loud protests. "Surveillance and admonition" remained the hierarchical right of the higher-placed "clergy" over the lower. And the grand rabbi of the central consistory retained his exclusive voice in the formulating of religious decisions by the central consistory. We can only ask ourselves why Dessauret and Vivien bothered to solicit the views of the provinces.

It is striking that the departmental line-up on the issue falls in the following way: the east versus the south and Paris. The four eastern consistories represented about 67 percent of the French Jewish population, for the most part Ashkenazi and orthodox. They were the opponents of the bill. Bordeaux and Marseille represented Sephardi and Comtadin elements, probably less than 10 percent of the population. Although Bordeaux had previously been protective of its own traditions, uninterested in religious reforms, and consistently respectful of the rabbis' independence, it now favored the structured hierarchical innovations from Paris, which was the growing center of Judaism and already represented about 20 percent of the Jewish population. It was also the only community with large numbers of both Ashkenazim and Sephardim.

The requirement of the new *ordonnance* dissolving the consistories and electing completely new ones met with great interest and enthusiasm. The electorate had been significantly enlarged. Those who had a strong feeling for the religion—either for the maintenance of the status quo or for change—saw how important it was to influence the vote. The September 17th issue of the *Archives Israélites* printed a letter to the editor by a Mr. S. Caton, in which the author observed the significance for French Judaism of the upcoming elections. He regretted that the only conditions of eligibility for the electorate were of a social order, and he suggested that it would be better if electors in religious affairs were religious men:

Jamais l'élection des membres du consistoire n'a excité un si vif intérêt, parce que jamais son influence sur la religion n'a été aussi immense . . . dans l'état actuel des choses, les consistoires, munis de l'immense pouvoir que leur accorde la nouvelle ordonnance royale concernant notre culte, pourront en abuser d'une manière vraiment affligeante pour une très-grande partie des israélites . . . les qualités voulues par la loi, presque toutes prises dans l'ordre social, sont insuffisantes pour constituer un parfait notable dans les affaires religieuses. Pour être mis à la tête des affaires religieuses, il faut encore une autre qualité, une qualité essentielle, indispensable: il faut que le notable soit homme religieux.

C. 1848–1862: The Period of Crystallization

Subsequent legislation did not supplant the 1844 *ordonnance*. As late as 1899 Baugey wrote, "[cette] ordonnance constitue encore aujourd'hui la charte fondamentale de ce culte."[66] In fact, the effect of the 1844 *ordonnance* has persisted to this day, despite the numerous political and legislative changes that have intervened (most notably, perhaps, the 1905 law of separation of church and state).[67]

The democratic revolution of 1848 brought universal suffrage to France, and, after a struggle, to the consistories.[68] When it became apparent to the central consistory that universal suffrage threatened to allow the orthodox majority to control the elections of rabbis and consistories, it began to work for a revision of the 1844 *ordonnance* that would offset the effects of the suffrage. This led, temporarily, to a decree of 1853 concerning the election of rabbis and ultimately to the 1862 decree, the last important legislative modification of the consistory organization.

The period 1848 to 1862, examined from the point of view of the legislation, may be subdivided in the following way: (1) 1848–1853: from the introduction of universal suffrage to the law recapturing the choice of rabbis from the people; (2) 1853–1857: the negotiations between the central consistory and the government that resulted in the 1857 draft for a new law; (3) 1857–1862: the central consistory-government negotiations that culminated in the 1862 decree.

1. 1848–1853

The revolutionary events of February 1848 had immediate repercussions in the Jewish community. The orthodox agitation for better representation had for some time been led by Abraham Ben Baruch Créhange, who later became a founder of the *Alliance Israélite* and a member of the central consistory. Referring to the March 7, 1848 decree which instituted universal suffrage, he asked that the same privilege be extended to the Jewish population in consistory elections. A *Club démocratique des fidèles,* organized by Créhange, grouped the politically revolutionary, religiously orthodox Jews of Paris. They petitioned the provisional government for the dissolution of the Paris consistory and its reconstitution through universal suffrage.[69] When the Paris consistory heard of the petition, it discussed whether to pressure the government to uphold the 1844 *notabilité* system, but finally decided to wait for the government to take action.[70] In *La Vérité* Créhange continued his fight for universal suffrage. He saw the 1848 revolution as a golden opportunity to bring about a return to the traditional democracy of the Jewish community:

Désormais, tout Israélite est notable et tout notable est électeur. . . . Aujourd'hui, notre antique et sainte loi, qui n'a jamais été abrogée et qui ne le sera jamais, est remise en vigeur. Cette loi porte: Vous me serez un royaume de prêtres, tous égaux, vous serez tous saints.[71]

The departmental consistories were uncertain how to handle the question of eligibility, and the central consistory requested instructions from the ministry of cults. By letter of June 7, 1848, Lazare Hippolyte Carnot, Minister of Cults for the provisional government, declared that the 1844 *ordonnance,* which granted suffrage in consistory elections to all Jews on the general elections lists, be interpreted in the light of universal suffrage. The only restriction would be the age requirement of twenty-five years prescribed by the 1844 *ordonnance.*[72]

A central consistory circular of June 12, 1848 informed the departmental consistories of the ministry's ruling and invited the consistories to reexamine the 1844 *ordonnance* in the light of the imposition of universal suffrage and the new political situation to see what changes appeared necessary.[73] We have located the responses to this central consistory circular from the consistories of Nancy, Strasbourg, Metz, and Colmar. The main concern that these four consistories had was with the introduction of universal suffrage into consistory elections. They all agreed that despite the obvious difficulties of implementing such elections, it was necessary to introduce them. Metz and Strasbourg added that it would be possible to improve the representation on the consistories if the number of lay members were increased to six. The members of the Colmar consistory suggested that elections be carried out indirectly, or in two degrees. (This would tend to neutralize the influence of the orthodox masses on the elections.) They justified their proposal, manifestly contradictory of the government's intent, by stating that since these elections were purely "religious" in content, their arrangement on a suitable, indirect, basis would not violate the principle of equality introduced by the revolution.[74]

The balance of the recommendations for a new law dealt with the religious views and aims of the three responding consistories. Strasbourg urged the addition of an article that would call for a rabbinical synod at ten-year intervals, where needed religious reforms could be made in those parts of the religious code that did not touch the dogma. Metz and Nancy took a somewhat more conservative religious position. Metz again requested an increase to three rabbis on the central consistory. Nancy also took the occasion to repeat its protests against lay domination in religious questions, and suggested that the right of censuring rabbis in regard to religious questions be withdrawn from the consistories and delegated exclusively to other rabbis placed higher in the hierarchy.[75]

In July 1848 the Paris consistory members wrote a circular to inform Parisian Jewry of the introduction of universal suffrage. They took advantage of the opportunity to improve their own image by overstating the part they had played in procuring this democratization of the consistory elections:

Le Consistoire Israélite de la circonscription de Paris, pénétré du besoin de mettre les règlements organiques du culte en harmonie avec le grand principe de liberté consacré par la révolution de février 1848, s'est adressé, dans les premiers jours qui ont suivi cette révolution, par l'intermédiaire du Consistoire central, au Ministre des cultes et lui a soumis, particulièrement en ce qui concerne la notabilité, des observations tendant à donner à l'ordonnance du 25 mai 1844 toute l'extension possible.

Le Ministre répondant à la demande du consistoire a déclaré, par dépêche du 7 juin dernier, que le droit d'électeur devait, en effet, être établi sur des bases plus larges que celles qui étaient

fixées par l'ordonnance du 25 mai 1844, précitée, et il a ajouté:
"L'extension du droit électoral en matière politique jusqu'à
ses plus extrêmes limites, implique une extension analogue pour
la notabilité israélite, et par suite se concilie également avec la
lettre et avec l'esprit de l'ordonnance du 25 mai 1844.—*Rien ne*
s'oppose dès lors à ce que les Israélites qui dans l'état actuel des
choses figurent sur les listes électorales, soient également portés
sur la liste des notables de leur culte, pourvu qu'ils soient âgés
de 25 ans accomplis. C'est la seule restriction qui résulte du
rapprochement de l'ordonnance du 25 mai 1844, et du décret
du 7 mars 1848, et je ne vois pas d'inconvénients à ce qu'elle
soit maintenue."[76]

It will be remembered that, despite its claim to the contrary,
the Paris consistory had reacted negatively to the news of a petition for universal suffrage, but had decided to take no action
while awaiting the government's ruling on the issue.

In September 1849 the Minister of Cults informed the central
consistory that he had received many requests for the dissolution of the consistories, their re-election by universal suffrage,
and an increase in the number of consistory members. The
government requested the central consistory's opinion. The
only orthodox member, Michel Hemerdinger (a lawyer who had
been active in the revolution of 1848 and a believer in the need
for Jewish "regeneration"), urged the adoption of both proposals. The liberal majority decided, however, that neither
proposal should be examined alone, but only in connection
with a revision of the entire organic *règlement*.[77] By this formula they meant that a new law must be drafted in order to counteract the effect of universal suffrage.

By November universal suffrage was seventeen months old,
but no elections had taken place. It was time for consistory
elections, because the terms of two departmental consistory
members in each district had expired. In Paris these two members were Bénédict Allegri and Olry Dupont. The other two
laymen on the Paris consistory, Dr. Moïse Cahen and Léopold
Halphen, decided to resign in order to force a total election by
universal suffrage. The central consistory received this news
with dissatisfaction, fearing an orthodox takeover of the consistory system. At a joint meeting with the Paris consistory, the
central consistory argued against the scheme, convincing Cahen
and Halphen to withdraw their resignations. A dissident view
was expressed by Hemerdinger, who expressed his dissatisfaction with Cahen and Halphen; he would have thought more of
them, he said, had they maintained their resolution to withdraw
from the consistory.[78]

The central consistory's tactic was to minimize the impact
that universal suffrage would have on the consistories by postponing the elections as long as possible, and by avoiding any
elections that were not absolutely necessary. The consistory expected that in the interim it would find a way to reconcile the

principle of universal suffrage with consistory goals. Such an analysis is confirmed by a fragment of a letter sent by the ministry to the central consistory on December 15, 1849: "vous [le consistoire central] avez été d'avis qu'il y a lieu d'ajourner tous les changements que le nouveau régime électoral ne rend pas dès à présent absolument indispensable."[79]

The only full election by universal suffrage took place in the first few months of 1850. Because of orthodox successes in the balloting, several individuals and consistories led campaigns to abolish universal suffrage or to render it less significant. Accordingly, a new law in 1853 took the election of the grand rabbis out of the hands of the electorate, and gave it to the departmental consistories, together with twenty-five *notables* chosen by the electorate. Lay members of the consistory, however, continued to be elected by universal suffrage until an 1862 decree reinstituted some restrictions over the electorate. The argument over universal suffrage, then, continued to be debated from 1850 to 1862.

In Bordeaux Benjamin Gradis emphatically opposed universal suffrage (although several years later, as we shall see, he reversed himself and became a champion of democracy, in a frantic effort to maintain local control of community affairs in the face of the central consistory's efforts to consolidate control in its own hands). In 1850 Gradis was arguing against the sudden abandonment of a half century of tradition of *notabilité* in the consistories. The idea of a *notabilité* comprised of everybody shocked him, and he argued that it was a contradiction in terms. The electorate, he suggested in a petition to the ministry, should be limited to those who pay at least thirty francs in annual contributions to consistory institutions and to heads of families who are more than sixty years of age.[80] According to his views, it would endanger the dignity and stability of the religion to subject it to the changing course of political events and to allow the people to make the important and irrevocable decision of naming rabbis. In a letter to the central consistory he added:

Le choix des rabbins surtout dont les fonctions sont à vie et de l'ordre spirituel, ne saurait émaner des masses, qui se laissent trop facilement séduire par les apparences, par ce qui flatte leurs passions, et souvent par le désir immodéré des changements.[81]

Whereas in Ashkenazi communities Jewish leaders were worried about the conservative opinions of the people, Gradis voiced alarm at the desire for change that might be expressed through universal suffrage. Although we have no documentary evidence of any desire for religious reforms within the Bordeaux Jewish population at this time, perhaps Gradis' letter is an indication that some such agitation was in fact occurring. Equally possible, however, is that Gradis feared that the enfranchised people might have sought further democratic reforms in the

Jewish administration. Or he may simply have used the warning of the danger of people seeking change as a tactic to bolster his argument against universal suffrage.

The contrast between the elitist views of Sephardi orthodox leader Gradis and the democratic ones of Ashkenazi orthodox leader Créhange points up an essential difference between the two communities. Orthodoxy in the northern communities belonged to the poor masses and meant traditional Ashkenazi practices, some of which were questioned by educated and integrated Jewish leaders of these communities. Orthodoxy in the south appealed equally to all elements of the community. There was pride in the maintenance of Sephardi traditions and ceremonies, both because they were linked to the more favorable economic and political history of this community and because they were now being imitated by Ashkenazim. The southern communities therefore did not desire many innovations, nor were changes that were made received with the shock and opposition that greeted reforms in Paris or the eastern provinces.

Gradis frequently spoke for himself alone, but on this occasion the consistory was in total agreement with him. In September of the same year (1850) the Bordeaux consistory decided to complain to the central consistory about the use of universal suffrage, and Grand Rabbi Marx drafted a letter asking the central consistory to find another method of election closer to the spirit of the 1806 principle of *notabilité*.[82] In another letter to the central consistory, Benjamin Gradis again condemned the system of universal suffrage and asked for either a return to the original system of *notabilité*, or a reform in the system, such as that he had suggested in his petition (which the ministry of cults had passed on to the central consistory). Gradis insisted that it was dangerous to allow each political change to affect the administrative organization of Judaism. Jewish leaders, he said, must learn to maintain an attachment to the original legal foundations of the cult, as adopted by the Sanhedrin in a unanimous decision.[83]

On November 10, 1850, the central consistory appointed a commission, composed of Colonel Max Cerfberr, president of the central consistory, Grand Rabbi Ennery, Adolphe Franck, vice-president of the central consistory, and Philippe Anspach, to revise the 1844 *ordonnance*.[84] The commission then solicited departmental views on changes that should be introduced. Between November 1850 and January 1851, Paris and Metz forwarded their reports. Probably the other consistories did likewise.[85] Only the Paris reply is extant in the archives, and it enunciates a curious position. In order to counteract the effect of universal suffrage, the Paris members suggested a resurrection of rabbinic independence, not at all characteristic of either their previous or subsequent views: they proposed a method of electing the grand rabbis by rabbinical councils, eliminating all involvement of the laity. To bring the provinces under the tight control of the central consistory, they suggested that communal rabbis be elected by local commissions from a list of four candidates proposed by the central consistory. With the same end in mind, they suggested that the post of *ministre officiant* (cantor) be abolished and replaced by communal rabbis, who would be trained at the consistory-controlled rabbinical school in Metz. (Cantors received no standardized training.) They further proposed restricting the vote to those who rented a place in the temple or contributed to the charity board, which was similar to the proposal already made by Gradis, and to that ultimately incorporated into the 1862 decree: "Le consistoire, en proposant ces modifications a pour but d'écarter des élections consistoriales ceux qui se séparent pour ainsi dire de leur coreligionnaires."[86]

It should be noted that, contrary to the Paris consistory's contention, those who "separated themselves," or were indifferent, did not seek to vote. The people whom the Paris consistory wished to exclude were, rather, the poor, orthodox, mutual aid society members, who would have liked to gain some control of the consistory in order to form it more to their own views.

After the recommendations of the departmental consistories had been received, the commission proceeded to draft a bill for a new law. It was endorsed by the full central consistory on June 11, 1851,[87] but it appears to have been September before this project was communicated for comments to the departments,[88] and January before the reactions were received in Paris.

It is interesting to study the responses of the departmental consistories from the point of view of the three trends discussed in the development of the 1844 *ordonnance:* hierarchy within the rabbinate, hierarchy within the administration, and the question of lay versus religious dominance.[89] On the first point, none of the consistories had any comment. A hierarchical rabbinate had become an accepted institution. Centralization of power in the central consistory, however, was still stubbornly resisted. Strasbourg and Bordeaux asked to retain the right to award the first rabbinic degree, a right which the central consistory now sought for itself alone (and achieved in 1862).

Colmar asked for proportional representation in the central consistory: "d'ailleurs c'est un principe que la législation politique a consacré." Bordeaux further sought to escape the dominating influence of Paris and the east by refusing to accept the replacement of the cantors by assistant rabbis; it pointed out the special needs of the Sephardi ritual and cited the special training that Sephardi cantors received in the south but could not receive in Metz.

The issue of lay domination over the rabbinate was revived also. Most of the consistories took the opportunity to attempt to undo some of the effect of the 1844 *ordonnance.* Bordeaux requested that grand rabbis not be subject to dismissal. Only Paris, with Grand Rabbi Isidor dissenting, approved of the provisions for dismissing grand rabbis. Strasbourg agreed to dismissal only in cases where rabbis had been convicted in French courts. St. Esprit, Strasbourg, and Bordeaux claimed, also, that jurisdiction in religious decisions within the departmental consistory was not clearly defined. They proposed that such jurisdiction be assigned to the consistories, to be exercised only with the approval of their grand rabbis. Colmar went further and claimed that the choice of books of religious instruction could properly be made only by the rabbis, in view of the fact that lay members were not chosen for their religious qualifications. Furthermore, Colmar asked for a return to three rabbis in the central consistory in order to constitute a traditional *beth din*. On the departmental level, Bordeaux was also concerned with the proportion of rabbinic to lay representation in the consistories; it asked for the maintenance of four lay members, rather than the proposed increase to six.

But in 1851 the controversy was no longer limited to these three points. The maintenance of universal suffrage and direct elections were the issues that had led to proposals for new legislation. The central consistory had proposed, very much after the manner of the 1850 Paris suggestion, that suffrage be limited to those who contributed to the expenses of the cult through consistorial, or consistory-approved, institutions. This would have excluded the indigent and members of the mutual aid societies practicing charity only among their own membership. (These societies often constituted the *minyan* for the members, who did not frequent the consistory temple and consequently did not contribute to its expenses.)

Of the departmental replies which are now extant, only those of the Paris consistory and the majority faction in Strasbourg supported the central consistory proposal on restricted suffrage. Bordeaux, Nancy, and a minority of the Strasbourg consistory, although asking that all exclusions be dropped and that suffrage be universal, proposed a two-degree, or indirect, election, as compensation for some of the dangers of universal suffrage. Colmar alone requested the maintenance of universal suffrage and direct elections, pointing out that poverty should not disqualify one from participating in religious institutions.

Another issue that aroused concern in 1851 was whether consistory rights and powers as defined by French law were actually protected by that law. Prior to 1851, organizers of prayer meetings not authorized by the consistory, and *mohelim* and *shochetim* who practiced without consistory permission, had been cited before the *tribunal de simple police,* and punished in accordance with Article 471, paragraph 15 of the penal code.[90] A supreme court decision of February 20, 1851 ruled, however, that violations of the 1844 *ordonnance* defining consistory prerogatives were not punishable by the sanctions of the penal code. According to the decision, the section applied only to state and municipal administrations, as defined by the laws of August 16-24, 1790. This decision, depriving the 1844 *ordonnance* of any penalties for infraction, effectively destroyed the enforceability of consistory authority. The Paris consistory wished to restore its rights by drafting the new law in such a way as to build into it the necessary legal sanctions. The consistory recommended the addition of an article that would specify the applicability of Article 471, paragraph 15:

Cet article aura pour effet de donner une sanction aux dispositions prohibitive concernant notamment les réunions de prières, les mohelim et les schohetim. Autrement la prohibition serait illusoire et l'autorité consistoriale serait méconnue.

Despite a concerted effort by the central consistory, and especially by Adolphe Franck, the sanctions that all the consistories sought were never added to the Jewish legislation. By 1857, largely because of this failure, the consistories stopped pressing for an entirely revised organization and worked toward the much abbreviated 1862 decree.

The convening of rabbinic synods had been authorized by the 1844 *ordonnance,* but none had been called. Strasbourg took the opportunity in 1851 to repeat its suggestion that such synods be convened at ten-year intervals in order to introduce needed reforms. Synodal decisions would be enforced by the central consistory in the same way as Sanhedrin doctrine.

On March 22, 1852, after considering the departmental reactions, the central consistory proposed a new draft to the ministry, requesting speedy referral of the bill to the *Conseil d'état.*[91] The central consistory was forced, however, to recognize that the ministry's legislative wheels were going to turn no faster than they had during the tense 1839–44 period. Adolphe Franck notified the ministry that while waiting for the full reforms to be implemented, the central consistory and departmental consistories would appreciate a special measure regulating the elections of the rabbis and grand rabbis. As a result, a decree of July 9, 1853, recaptured these elections from the hands of the people and returned them to consistory control: departmental grand rabbis would be elected by the local consistory, voting together with twenty-five *notables* chosen by universal suffrage. Communal rabbis were to be named directly by the consistory.

The modifications of 1853 were mere preliminaries to the 1862 decree, which furthered centralization by transferring to the central consistory the right to name departmental grand rabbis.

2. 1853–1957

From the time the 1853 law was enacted, the central consistory was dissatisfied with its provisions, and for the next four years unsuccessfully attempted to have the government pass new legislation to strengthen and expand the centralization of power within French Judaism. These were four years of polemics, which engaged the attention of the French government, the central and departmental consistories, the press, and individuals, but produced no new legislation.

In February 1854 the central consistory met to reexamine the status of its projected new *ordonnance.* Grand Rabbi Salomon Ulmann (the earliest grand rabbi of France to favor religious reform), criticizing the law of July 9, 1853, urged that the central consistory insist on obtaining the right to name departmental grand rabbis directly. Adolphe Franck seconded the proposal and recommended that the central consistory's choice be made from a list of three candidates nominated by the department.[92] In its anxiety to shape the face of French Judaism, the central consistory continued to insist on this provision until it obtained satisfaction with the 1862 decree. By May 1854 the government had not taken any action on the March 22, 1852 project, and the central consistory sent another reminder.[93] In July the ministry responded with its own draft.[94]

It was immediately noted by the central consistory that the government's version was unsatisfactory in two ways: the bill called for direct elections by universal suffrage and neglected to specify the applicability of the penal code.[95] The ministry and the central consistory negotiated these two points for several months.[96] The consistory refused to accept universal suffrage, which, it pointed out, entailed drawbacks that the last elections had made clear in many localities.[97] By February 1856, the ministry had yielded on the suffrage issue, but was persistent in its refusal to grant the Jewish consistories recourse to sanctions which the other non-Catholic religions did not have, and which were reserved for the area of public administration.

Adolphe Franck then began a personal campaign to obtain this prerogative for the consistory. On February 14, 1856, he warned the Minister of Cults that dangerous ideas could be taught in the name of religion, and it was therefore imperative that the consistories be able to prevent unauthorized private prayer meetings. The *mohelim* must also be under supervision, he added, because circumcision puts health, and even life, at stake.[98] Without the provision of penalties for infractions, the consistories would be totally unable to control these institutions.

Persisting in his refusal to satisfy the request, the minister replied that in order for the proposed bill modifying consistory organization to be enforced as a *règlement d'administration publique,* and thereby to qualify for the requested penal code sanctions, it would have to be submitted to the *conseil d'état.* The *conseil d'état* would be certain to reject the provision of limited suffrage, the point on which the ministry had yielded to the consistory's wishes. Nevertheless, the central consistory decided that Franck would reply to the minister that it was essential to submit the bill to the *conseil d'état,* and Cerfberr, Anspach, Franck, and L. Halphen undertook to seek support among members of the *conseil d'état*.[99] Franck apparently made several trips to the ministry in pursuit of this aim, but always without success.[100]

A new obstacle to the negotiations was introduced by the government sometime before September 1856, when the ministry attempted to reserve to itself the right to confirm the election of the central consistory president. Despite the quasi-governmental nature of the consistory institution from the beginning, and the close control it permitted the authorities to maintain, this was the first time that such a proposal had been introduced. It is not known when or how it originated, but an internal note dated September 5, 1856, makes reference to it, and another, undated, asks the Minister if he wishes to reserve to the government the right to name the central consistory president:

Question: Son excellence entend-elle que le consistoire central continue à élire son Président (qui est toujours un laïque de même que les présidents des consistoires départementaux)? Ou veut-elle réserver au gouvernement la nomination de ce personnage qui joue un rôle assez important dans l'administration du culte israélite?[101]

Although the final bill did allocate this right to the government, no law was ever adopted which abrogated consistory independence in this way.

Adoption of the bill continued to be delayed while the parties argued over whether to incorporate penalties for its infraction. On March 17, 1857, a departmental memo informed the minister that work on the project had come to a halt. The note referred to the consistory's insistence on sanctions and described the loss of consistory authority that had been caused by the 1851 court decision.

The minister penned his final refusal in red on the bottom of the memo: "M. le ministre ne voit aucun moyen de satisfaire aux voeux du consistoire central."[102] The battle seems to have been lost at that point.

The following month, April 1857, the government printed a new draft of the project for distribution to the departmental consistories. This version appears to have been the result of three years of discussions between the government and the central consistory, since the November 1854 central consistory draft. Opinions on this bill were then directed to the ministry by departmental consistories and by individuals. The Jewish periodicals stated their views on the issue, with the two major journals taking their customarily opposing stands.

What were the issues raised by the draft? Rabbinical hierarchy, as we have already seen, was firmly established by the fifties, and did not appear again as a live question. The consistories now voiced negative reaction to central consistory encroachment on local prerogatives, increased lay domination of the rabbinate, abrogation of universal suffrage, and lack of enforceability of consistory control. In addition, Metz wanted the departmental consistories empowered to tax the Jews of their districts in order to balance their budgets; Strasbourg repeated its old request for periodic rabbinic synods; the Colmar consistory (which was having difficulty gaining control of a dissident rabbinical school opened by orthodox Grand Rabbi Klein) proposed an additional article putting all Jewish institutions in each district under departmental consistory control.

By a vote of five to two, the Nancy consistory adopted a motion which sought to mitigate lay domination of the central consistory by having two rabbis in that body. Five consistories (all except Nancy and Colmar) protested the provision whereby the central consistory could censure or transfer grand rabbis, or even request the ministry to dismiss them. Paris and Metz would have at least limited such action to cases in which the departmental consistory first registered a complaint with the central consistory. The remaining consistories, Strasbourg, Bordeaux, St. Esprit, and Marseille went further and argued that assignment of such powers to the central consistory contradicted the concept of tenure (*inamovibilité*), also accorded by the bill, and prevented the grand rabbi from exercising independence. A petition from some individuals of the Haut-Rhin (Colmar) district and a letter from Grand Rabbi Klein of Colmar echoed consistory protest against granting the central consistory the right to censure grand rabbis.

The only consistory to refrain from complaining about the growing power of the central consistory was Colmar, which was currently receiving the aid of the central consistory in a local struggle against the orthodox. Bordeaux had attempted to unite all the local consistories in a protest against the central consistory's proposed domination of the departments. Bordeaux was especially alarmed at the bill's provision for the central consistory to name all rabbis and grand rabbis. The Bordeaux consistory minutes of April 16, 1857, record the decision to solicit concerted action by all the departmental consistories:

Le Consistoire se pénétrant de la haute importance de ce remaniement de nos Règlements organiques, procède à l'examen du projet soumis au ministre, et la première impression qu'il éprouve, c'est de voir dans cette oeuvre projetée la tendance d'étendre outre mesure l'action du consistoire central sur tout ce qui concerne le culte et la direction religieuse dans les communautés de France. . . . Il est décidé que M. le Président communiquera aux Présidents des autres circonscriptions l'impression du consistoire afin d'arriver à ce que les observations qui seront transmises au Ministre aient autant que possible un caractère uniforme.

With the single exception of Colmar, all the consistories

agreed with Bordeaux and insisted on maintaining the election of the grand rabbis and the communal rabbis at the district level. An anonymous ministry official accurately reported consistory reaction when he noted that rabbis cannot be imposed from above, but must answer the needs and desires of the local communities:

Le premier pasteur de la communauté ne saurait lui être imposé; il est urgent qu'il soit sympathique à son troupeau; qu'il n'arrive qu'autant qu'il est appelé; que le consistoire central ne peut pas connaître assez les rabbins pour savoir s'ils conviennent à telle ou telle communauté, telles sont les principales raisons émises par les consistoires.

In a further effort to limit central consistory encroachment, Nancy asked that the phrase "for serious cause" (*pour causes graves*) be added to the article that allowed the central consistory to censure lay members of the departmental consistories. None of the other consistories thought to protest this point. Administrative hierarchy in the consistorial system, like the rabbinical hierarchy, was becoming an accepted institution. But the local consistories had drawn the line at complete eradication of their authority. The consistory of St. Esprit, protesting to the ministry that the 1857 project would destroy the authority of the local consistories and the rabbis, expressed a typical concern:

En terminant ces observations et ces voeux, nous ne pouvons nous empêcher de protester contre la tendance générale du projet de décret, qui involontairement sans doute, ne conduit à rien moins qu'à annihiler l'autorité des consistoires départementaux et les droits des populations, et à placer nos chefs spirituels dans un état de dépendance et de compression incompatible avec le caractère dont ils sont revêtus. Nous sommes profondément convaincus que telle n'a pas été la pensée des auteurs du projet, mais les conséquences se déduisent fatalement des principes et nous manquerions à un devoir de conscience si nous ne signalions pas celles qui résulteront de l'oeuvre qui nous est soumise, et que la sagesse du Gouvernement, nous n'en doutons pas, saura prévenir.

The government had yielded on the issue of direct universal suffrage, and the 1857 bill had proposed indirect, or two-degree, elections of consistory lay members. Metz and Colmar accepted this provision, but the other departmental consistories preferred direct elections. Paris and Strasbourg, though requesting direct elections, did not desire universal suffrage. They would have liked to see the elections limited to those who contributed financially or "morally" to consistorial institutions.

Surprisingly, none of the consistories complained about the provisions in Articles 9 and 14 of the project that would have transferred to the government the right of approving the elections of presidents and vice-presidents of the central and departmental consistories.

Finally, the lack of penal sanctions in the 1857 bill was deplored by four of the consistories. Paris sought to remedy this situation by having the *mohel* and *shochet* named directly by the Minister of Cults, and by asking for the addition of an article to cover the case of private prayer meetings. Nancy suggested the addition of an article that would specify that infractions of the law be punished by the penalties provided by Article 471, paragraph 15 of the penal code. Marseille simply asked for a means of coercion (*des moyens coërcitifs*), and Metz requested penal sanctions, also without specifying the kind.[103]

It was not only the consistories that voiced opinions of the new bill. The press presented its views, as did various individuals. The most prolific writer of letters and *memoires* directed to the central consistory and to the ministry was Benjamin Gradis of Bordeaux. In 1856, while the members of the central consistory were negotiating the terms of the 1857 project, Gradis sent them a letter pleading for maintenance of the status quo. He was loath to see further power gains made by the central consistory or by the laity over the rabbinate, and especially opposed the central consistory's desire to obtain for itself the appointment of all the rabbis. After having argued, in 1850, against universal suffrage, he now made a plea in its favor:

Depuis les temps les plus reculés, les Israélites ont toujours joui de la faculté de nommer leurs Rabbins. La leur retirerez-vous sous le régime du suffrage universel qui est de droit public en France? On ne pourrait pas citer un seul mauvais choix qui ait été fait, depuis la promulgation des lois du grand Sanhedrin. Il n'y a donc pas lieu à changement. L'Eglise primitive nommait ses évêques. La synagogue aurait-elle moins de libertés?[104]

Gradis had obviously modified his stand in order to support local community rights and combat the centralizing aims of the central consistory. The curious argument that he used to support his position was that the central consistory was obligated to honor the Sanhedrin decisions, and that the old form of consistory organization was among their decisions. (He glossed over the problem of how to handle the existence of the 1844 and 1853 laws, of which he approved, despite the fact that they had already considerably modified the original organization.)[105]

The Jewish press took up the argument soon after. Editor Simon Bloch of the "conservative" journal *Univers Israélite,* who had recently been fired from his post as secretary to the central consistory because of his dissident views, informed his readers in February 1857 that the central consistory was asking for new legislation to counteract universal suffrage and put the entire rabbinate into its own hands. He recommended that his readers address letters of protest to the ministry in order to prevent the implementation of what he termed the central consistory's "ukase." He suggested a sample letter:

le consistoire central a soumis au gouvernement un projet de règlement organique qui enlève aux israélites de France la liberté religieuse garantie par la constitution de notre pays; qui les dépouille surtout d'un droit séculaire et imprescriptible dont ils ont joui à toutes les époques de l'histoire et dont leurs coreligionnaires jouissent encore aujourd'hui dans tous les pays du monde: celui de choisir leurs chefs spirituels. Or, nous priver de ce droit, c'est blesser notre conscience, c'est frapper notre religion, c'est nous retirer notre emancipation, c'est mettre la Synagogue française hors la loi commune. . . . On veut aussi abolir le suffrage universel dans les élections consistoriales, système qui a eu de si heureux résultats dans la constitution politique de l'empire et qui n'a montré aucun inconvénient dans l'organisation de notre culte.

To resist the serious threat posed by the central consistory, Bloch urged the founding of a permanent committee of resistance to combat all the usurpations and abuses of power in religious matters.[106]

Samuel Cahen, editor of the "reform" journal *Archives Israélites*, took up the argument in September and October, after the April 1857 draft had been criticized by the departmental consistories. Although he opposed the central consistory's plan for the election of lay members of the consistories, he deemed the popular outcry against the project a "tempête dans un verre d'eau." In regard to the central consistory proposal for the naming of the rabbis, he expressed his approval in these terms:

Avant de déclarer contre l'absolutisme consistorial, il faudrait donc, selon nous, qui certes prisons très fort l'indépendance, démontrer si, pour bien des choses, il ne vaut pas mieux s'en rapporter à l'intelligence de quelques-uns qu'à l'aveugle entraînement de la multitude.

In defense of his position, Cahen pointed out that universal suffrage had *not* been the traditional usage unswervingly followed in the choice of local rabbis. He cited the case of Metz just prior to the institution of the consistories, where a council of six and a council of three made the most important religious decisions. Cahen's point is notable in that he is the only one to use a historical argument *against* universal suffrage. History was generally invoked to *prove* that in traditional Jewish communities the Jews elected their rabbis democratically.

Surprisingly, the reform journal argued for an increase in the amount of rabbinic participation on the central consistory. Cahen claimed that such a move would help the cause of progress, because people were prone to assume that all reform measures had been decided under severe lay pressure placed on one grand rabbi. If there were at least two rabbis, Cahen estimated, the central consistory's reform measures would be regarded less suspiciously.[107]

Four years of work and polemics had ended, but no new law had emerged.

3. 1857–1862

The new law did not come into existence until 1862. The five years that preceded it were more years of negotiating and redrafting. In November 1857 a joint central consistory–ministry commission on the reorganization project was named, which consisted of the following government representatives: R.-E.-N. Cuvier, *conseiller d'état,* president; A.-A.-A. de Contencin, *conseiller d'état, directeur général de l'administration des cultes;* Prosper Duvergier, *conseiller d'état;* Pierre-André Sayous, *sous directeur à l'administration des cultes;* A.-F.-L. Tardif, *chef de bureau au cabinet du ministre;* and A.-J.-E.-B. de Salverte, *auditeur au conseil d'état,* secretary.[108] The central consistory representatives on the commission were Philippe Anspach, *conseiller à la cour impériale;* Adolphe Franck, *vice-président du consistoire central;* Salomon Ulmann, *Grand Rabbin du consistoire central.*[109]

From June 1858 to May 1861, this commission met nine times and produced at least three drafts for a new law. Their work terminated, the commission forwarded its report to the minister in July 1861. After certain changes introduced by the *conseil d'état,* the new decree was promulgated on August 29, 1862.

The commission's work radically changed the type of new legislation to be introduced. Whereas previously it had been planned to introduce an all-embracing reorganization of the cult, the new drafts were now for a supplementary decree that would make some modifications but leave intact the remainder of the 1844 *ordonnance.* This revision of the basic concept is evident in the April 1861 draft, which was already very much the final project submitted in July of that year to the *conseil d'état.* Whereas the 1857 project had contained fifty-seven articles, this one, and the decree of 1862, consisted of thirteen. All of them increased consistorial authority, and especially that of the central consistory, and restricted the voice of the people in the choice both of rabbis and of lay consistory members. The central consistory won its long struggle for the right to appoint departmental grand rabbis, although it failed to gain control over naming *all* the rabbis throughout the country: the 1853 provision for the choice of the communal rabbis by the departmental consistories was retained.

A new post of *sous-rabbin* was established. These assistant rabbis were to replace the *ministres-officiants* in some of the small communities, thus placing in these remote areas a larger number of personnel trained at the rabbinical school.[110] The central consistory won also the right to grant all rabbinic diplomas, both of the first degree—required of communal rabbis and formerly conferred by the departmental consistories—and of the second degree—required for posts as grand rabbi. The central consistory also obtained supervisory rights over the Algerian consistories.

The long debate on universal suffrage and direct or indirect elections was finally resolved by establishing a list of categories to which one must belong in order to qualify to vote in direct elections for the lay members of the consistories.[111]

The effect of the categories was to eliminate from the electorate the people who did not participate in the consistory institutions and expenses. This included the indigent and the people (mostly poor) whose major Jewish affiliation was with a mutual aid society. The fact that people of this class were among the purchasers of kosher meat, which was taxed in most places for the communal treasury, does not seem to have been taken into account.

Once again, none of the voices raised in favor of the rabbinate were heeded. The lay-rabbinic relationship remained essentially that which had been wrought by the 1844 *ordonnance* and by a half-century of consistory experience.

The thorny problem of legal sanctions was not handled to consistory satisfaction. The compromise measure that emerged required the *mohel* to have a certificate from a doctor designated by the prefect of the department, attesting to his capacity. The *shochet* was to obtain the mayor's countersignature on the authorization given to him by the consistory. Private prayer meetings escaped all penal sanctions.

Despite its partial losses, the consistory emerged a victor in 1862. A ministry memo underscored its bolstered position:

il [le décret] aura seulement pour effet principal d'augmenter l'action et le pouvoir du consistoire central qui a rendu de si utiles services . . . le décret confie au consistoire central la nomination des Grands Rabbins départementaux . . . [l'ancien mode de nomination] avait été souvent contraire aux intérêts du culte lui-même en créant des partis.[112]

D. 1862–1905: The Period of Consolidation

The consistories remained officially constituted by the two laws of 1844 and 1862 until the 1905 law of separation of church and state dissolved them. They then reconstituted as private associations under the liberalized law of associations of

1901 and adopted names such as *Association cultuelle israélite* or (in the case of Paris) *Association consistoriale.*

Central consistory strength and control remained at the level and limits reached in 1862, except that Algeria came more closely under its supervision. By law of September 16, 1867, all three Algerian consistories were authorized to name representatives to the central consistory. This scheme eliminated the intermediary function of the Algiers consistory between the central consistory and the consistories in Oran and Constantine. (That step may properly be viewed as preparatory for the "Crémieux decree" of October 24, 1870, which granted the Algerian Jews French citizenship.)

On November 11, 1870, the Provisional Government of National Defense reintroduced universal suffrage into consistory affairs. Local communities were empowered to elect communal rabbis by direct elections. In the various consistory districts the Jews were to elect the grand rabbi in indirect (or two-degree) balloting. Only one grand rabbi, however, was actually elected under the provisions of that law. The departmental and central consistories protested, and a law of 1872 rescinded the 1870 measure. After 1872 the only remnant of democracy that remained was the addition of some local delegates to join with the departmental consistory lay members to elect the communal rabbis and to draw up the list of three nominations to the post of grand rabbi, from which the central consistory would make the final choice.[113]

Many communities never reconciled themselves to the 1862 provisions for the election of rabbis. The right of the departmental consistories to name communal rabbis and the central consistory's right to name departmental grand rabbis were contested until the end of the nineteenth century. During the periods both before and after the brief reintroduction of local autonomy, frequent, unheeded complaints were addressed to the ministry.[114]

The limited suffrage defined in 1862 and again in 1872 was also hotly contested, though with no greater success. Bordeaux, a community that had consistently championed local rights and fought the central consistory's growing power, arose again in the seventies, trying to wrench itself free. In 1873 a *Comité libéral israélite de Bordeaux* was constituted. Its avowed aim was "de réclamer toutes les réformes libérales que pourrait nécessiter la gestion des intérêts de la circonscription consistoriale de la Gironde." The committee's petition to the government in January 1879, resulted in a proposal for changing the system of electing consistory members. The committee had argued that suffrage should not be limited to those who worked for or supported consistory institutions, but should include those whose Jewishness was expressed in institutions that were not controlled by the consistory. Although the ministry elaborated more than one draft of such a measure and solicited the advice of the departmental and central consistories, no law to this effect was ever promulgated, apparently because of negative consistory reaction.[115]

Consistory structure retained essentially its 1862 form until the separation of church and state. Both the strengths and the limitations of the consistories had been defined. In the absence of penal sanctions, there were repeated infractions of the rules concerning ritual slaughterers and private prayer meetings. The number of rival, nonconsistory institutions increased. The *minyanim,* especially, multiplied with the influx of Polish and Russian Jews at the end of the century.

A. Structure

The seven departmental consistories were the administrative units charged with running the Jewish communities. They were composed, at first, of one rabbi and three lay members. Although the initial legislation had ordered the election of a second rabbi, if possible, no second rabbi was in fact elected in any of the districts. Some consistories had named an additional lay member; others had not. In 1823 a new law required all districts to elect a fifth member, preferably a rabbi. Only the Strasbourg *notables* chose a rabbi as the fifth consistory member; elsewhere the consistories continued to be composed of one rabbi and four lay members until an 1850 decision raised the number of lay members to six.

The average number of meetings for routine work was one or two a month, but varied from as many as eight per month to as few as one every two months. The central consistory met less often than did the departmental consistories.

The Paris consistory decided, on March 18, 1838, that their meetings would be held twice a month, on Monday evenings at 7:30.[1] This decision merely formalized the practice that had already emerged. The frequency of Paris consistory meetings during the previous eight years had been slightly higher than two per month, additional meetings being called whenever problems arose. The available minutes books show that the fewest meetings per year, 10, occurred in 1827. The most meetings per year, 37, occurred in 1839 and again in 1851. We can summarize the frequency of meetings as follows: an average of 13 per year from 1826 to 1830; an average of 26 per year from 1831 to 1839; an average of 20 per year from 1840 to 1846. There were 37 meetings in 1851, 36 in 1852, and 21 in 1853.

We can see from this that after 1830 there was a marked increase in the number of meetings, which corresponds to the beginning of a significant development of consistory control of Parisian Judaism.

The Strasbourg consistory's meetings followed a similar pattern. From 1839 to 1845 they averaged 17 per year. After 1845 the average increased considerably. In 1848 the consistory met 47 times. By 1853 the practice had become established to meet twice a month (on the second and fourth Thursdays) and more frequently when necessary. The necessity did, in fact, arise frequently, and the Strasbourg consistory met more frequently than any of the other departmental consistories studied. From

1859 to 1862 meetings averaged 36 per year, with a range of 32 to 47.[2]

In each consistory the situation varied somewhat. In Bordeaux the frequency of meetings was slightly lower than in Strasbourg and Paris. Between 1848 and 1857 this consistory met an average of 21 times per year, but the yearly rate fluctuated considerably according to annual needs. The most meetings per year, 35, occurred in 1850; the fewest, 14, in 1847. The Metz consistory convened still less frequently. From 1845 to 1861 they met a total of 238 times, for an annual average of 14 meetings per year.

The central consistory met considerably less frequently than any of the departmental consistories we have studied. Their meetings, throughout the entire period under consideration, rarely attained the order of one per month. Table V-1 is a record of meetings in sample years.

TABLE V-1
*Frequency of Central Consistory
Meetings*

Year	*Number of Meetings*
1839	10
1840	9
1842	9
1848	10
1849	13
1857	8
1858	16
1860	6
1861	6

At first no by-laws were adopted to regulate procedures during consistory meetings. Experience eventually led to certain ways of handling the work, which in turn were formalized in some places by the adoption of by-laws (*règlements intérieurs*).

The first mention of such a *règlement* is to be found in the minutes of the Paris consistory, October 20, 1835. On this day it was decided to draw up a *règlement intérieur* "to govern our meetings and work." The *règlement* was considered and approved on January 12 and February 23, 1836.[3] It specified that meetings were to be held once or twice a month. Decisions were to be taken by majority vote, by standing, unless a secret ballot was requested. The consistory's treasurer would not be a member. (This was not a fixed practice of the consistories; the Bordeaux treasurer *was* a member of the consistory.) The treasurer was to render his accounts quarterly for inspection by the comptroller, who was chosen by the members from among themselves. The secretary was a salaried employee of the consistory and was responsible for minutes, correspondence, archives, and financial records. (The secretary of the Paris consistory in 1844 was Raphael Jeramec, who was hired for a salary of 1800 francs per year.) There was also a salaried office boy.

The *règlement* ordered that the names of people who made propositions, or who argued for one or another viewpoint during the consistory's deliberations, would not be recorded in the minutes, unless the member asked for his name to be inserted. Although it was not always followed, this regulation has resulted in disappointment to the researcher who cannot always identify the members whose views are recorded in the minutes. An analogous decision was reached on November 17, 1853, by the Strasbourg consistory, although here, too, the rule was not always followed. In Bordeaux the minutes often omit even the discussions, and record only decisions reached.

An 1860 *règlement* records the procedures of the Strasbourg consistory. There were meetings on a twice-monthly basis, plus extra sessions as needed. The secretary read the minutes of the previous meeting, and their adoption was voted. The consistory next took up the business indicated on the agenda. If a member wished to request priority for another affair, the consistory was asked whether to grant his request. Letters to be discussed were circulated first among the membership. The president was expected to see to the implementation of the consistory's decisions. Decisions were made by a simple majority of those present. The necessary quorum for voting was a majority of the membership. All decisions reached by the majority obligated the minority, who, nevertheless, could register their protests in the minutes. Balloting was secret any time that two members requested it. If the issue at hand referred to specific people, the secret ballot would automatically be used.[4]

Although the consistories functioned in slightly differing ways, depending largely upon their needs and the size of their populations, certain generalizations about their work can be made. All the consistories delegated work through networks of committees and representatives for the supervision of charity, cemeteries, schools, and temples. The number of subcommittees varied, as did the number of synagogues and therefore of *commissaires surveillants* (local delegates in the individual synagogual districts). The consistories of the east had the largest number of committees and representatives because they had the highest number of communities and the largest population to administer. (Even when the Paris Jewish population had overtaken that of the Haut-Rhin and Bas-Rhin, it was mostly concentrated in Paris alone, and there were fewer temples to supervise.)

The subcommittees, such as those for schools, held their own meetings, kept their own records, and corresponded in writing with the consistories. Although their letters have been partially preserved, they are often disappointing. Most of the detailed documentation, the minutes and other records that these committees kept, have been lost. An analysis of consistory activity must take into account the work of all the subcommittees. Even though these bodies were not comprised of consistory members, they received their authority from the consistories and should be viewed as arms of the consistories themselves.

The laws governing the consistories specified that the synagogues were under their control. All of the consistories established temple administrations, which were theoretically responsible for carrying out the orders of the consistories. Often, however, the temple administrations were fairly autonomous, and even became indignant if the consistory suddenly decided to make changes, especially if the changes were of the nature of "reform."

In Paris this kind of jealousy developed between the consistory and its commissions. For example, a considerable degree of antagonism developed between the charity committee (*comité de bienfaisance*) and the consistory. The latter complained often that the committee did not properly respect the hierarchy.

The minutes of the Paris consistory reveal some details concerning the apportioning of the consistory's work. On October 24, 1850, after some power struggles with its various subcommittees, the consistory decided to appoint from within its own membership three subcommissions to handle liaisons with the *comité de bienfaisance,* the temple, and the butchers.[5]

Another decision more than three years later indicates that this system was not altogether satisfactory. On February 8, 1854, the consistory decided that the charity board, which already was in charge of fund raising, the manufacturing of matzoth, burials, and some other jobs, would assume supervision also of the kosher meat trade.[6]

The control of *kashrut* was handled by the consistories, generally through the grand rabbi. In addition to supervising the practice of ritual slaughter, most consistories received tax money from the sale of kosher meat, and they depended upon this income.

In Strasbourg the minutes from the 1840's reveal that an *administration locale* handled the synagogue, charity, and cemeteries of the community of Strasbourg. A separate school committee was responsible for the Jewish schools. The consistory delegated authority to that administration to run local institutions in the same way that it delegated authority to administrative committees in the more than one hundred communities of the Bas-Rhin district. (This was a sharp contrast to the practice in places like Paris and Bordeaux, where almost all the Jews of the district lived in one city and the consistories dealt directly with local problems.) In 1854 the structure of the local administration of Strasbourg was slightly changed, to meet the needs of the growing population. Indicating that their purpose was to achieve a smoother running of Jewish affairs and a tighter control of expenses, the consistory divided the *administration locale* into two separate committees: a three-member commission to handle the temple, and a five-member committee to run the charity and burial services. New rules were adopted for the rendering of accounts by each of the groups.[7] An additional change in this organization intervened in 1857, when it was decided to have one nine-member *comité consistoriale* with three sections: charity, temple, and cemetery. The president and secretary of this committee would be named by the consistory.[8] Less than a year later the arrangement was again slightly altered. This body was re-named *commission administrative de la communauté de Strasbourg* and was divided into two sections: the first was in charge of the temple and the cemetery; the second handled charity. The two offices of *commissaire administrateur* and *commissaire adjoint* were rotated among the members.

Thus the method used in administering the Jewish communities was based on the needs that arose, and varied with both time and place. Yet all the consistories created essentially the same kinds of institutions and governed them in basically similar ways.

B. Membership

Who were the members of the consistories? The 1806 *règlement* specified only that they must be thirty years old, not known to have been usurers, and not have been bankrupt unless "honorably rehabilitated." It did not require that they be chosen from among the twenty-five *notables,* who were to be named from among the richest men and highest taxpayers of the district. However, in early years, the members of the consistories were, in fact, the wealthy, and were often members of the *collège de notables*. A decision of June 8, 1829, made membership in the consistory incompatible with notability, but in 1837 (law of October 12) it again became permissible to hold both posts simultaneously.

Because the consistory members were rich, there were critics, such as Olry Terquem, who complained that members were far removed from the reality of Jewish problems and were not sufficiently active in seeking solutions. The wealthy members, Terquem said, turned the consistory into a mere commercial enterprise:

Notre communion n'étant plus qu'une vaste confédération commerciale, à propos d'une religion toute hiérarchie y doit être

*basée sur la richesse. Ayez de l'argent, vous devenez notable; de
l'or, vous arrivez aux consistoires; des diamants, vous atteignez
le central. Cette administration est donc et doit être une
argyrocratie pure, tempérée par des moeurs turcarétiques.*[9]

Terquem protested the religious indifference that he de-
tected among the rich consistory members. He claimed that
religious reforms were necessary, and that they could be introduced only by men who still retained an interest in religion.
Terquem's desire for religious reform was part of his analysis of
the need for social and economic improvement of the poor
Jewish population. These people had been emancipated but
not integrated. Transfer of the Sabbath services to Sunday and
the abrogation of some of the holidays would help to integrate
them into the national work force.

Terquem spoke sarcastically of the consistories, saying that
they were not attempting to help the people get rid of traditional practices that interfere with successful integration.
Religion, he observed, is for the poor, to protect the property
of the rich. Claiming that the consistories took no interest in
religion, he contended that they concerned themselves only with
administration and formalities: "Elles font, au nom d'Israél, des
compliments de félicitation ou de condoléance, rient ou
pleurent officiellement suivant la circonstance."[10]

At the time Terquem wrote, it was true that only the wealthy
were consistory members, and because the wealthy were in the
"economic" professions—commerce, banking, and manufacturing—these were the professions represented on the consistories.
In Paris from 1809 to 1840, seventeen people were members of
the consistory and thirteen of them pursued "economic" professions: four bankers, one capitalist, one manufacturer of por-
celain, three *négociants* (two in jewelry), one gold dealer, one
wholesaler of oil, one manufacturer of buttons, and one
propriétaire and army purveyor. Of the others, two were rabbis,
one a doctor, and one a lawyer. The doctor had been the first
member of the liberal professions to be elected to the consistory (in 1828). Some time later he wrote that he had accepted
the post even though the work was in direct opposition to the
nature of his occupations and his personal tastes.[11]

Not only were consistory members generally from the
"economic" professions, but the occupations of the *notabilité*
(the twenty-five electors in each consistory district) were no
more diversified. Terquem complained about this, pointing out
that eminently qualified lawyers, doctors, military men, writers,
were to be found among the Jewish population, but that they
were not chosen as *notables*. Writer Michel Berr had had great
difficulty in getting himself named, and Charles Narcisse Oulif
(a lawyer who founded the first Jewish primary school in Metz
and who pleaded a *More Judaïco* case) had been rejected twice:
"Nous avons parmi nous des juriconsultes, des médecins, des
militaires décorés, des hommes de lettres, etc.; pourquoi n'en

rencontre-t-on que quelques noms comme égarés sur la liste de notabilité?"[12]

When the 1844 *ordonnance* widened the ranks of the electorate, the conservative journal *Univers Israélite* called upon the voters to use their franchise to alter the character of the consistories: "Le temps est venu où la synagogue française peut et doit sortir de cet état de négligence et d'abandon où une législation vicieuse et la domination exclusive de l'argent l'ont laisée végéter." The article asked that the newly enfranchised *notables* make themselves the true representatives of the people and elect men who had not simply big fortunes and good reputations, but also religious qualifications. It argued that France was a country of intelligence and civilization, where moral and intellectual qualifications should have weight in political life:

Nous sommes, Dieu merci! loin des tristes époques, de ces tristes pays, où il a fallu, où il faut encore placer à la tête des communautés des hommes riches, ayant de vastes relations commerciales et industrielles, pour satisfaire la cupidité intolérante de nos oppresseurs, et imposer à la foule ignorante et fanatique par la puissance de l'or et l'éclat des titres.

Editor Bloch went on to insist that those who are named consistory members should be people who will frequent the temples and take an active interest in the needs of the religion.[13]

The polemics were in vain. In 1852 the Paris consistory's lay membership was composed of two bankers, two *négociants,* and the same one physician. Two new members just elected were Gustave de Rothschild (banker) and Adolphe Israél (*négociant*).

Michel Berr was another early critic of the consistories. His bitterness stemmed largely from the fact that he had not succeeded in becoming a member himself. The son of Alsatian Jewish leader Berr Isaac Berr, he ostensibly remained conservative in his religious views until the death of his orthodox father but then came out openly in favor of religious reforms. As early as 1819, in his Bible extracts and religious textbook, he had borrowed from the writings of the German reformers, especially those of Hamburg. In 1828 he attacked the consistory members for their lack of interest in religion: "le consistoire dont on a écarté les hommes honorables uniquement parce qu'ils sont religieux et où on a appelé des hommes sans honneur et sans éducation uniquement parce qu'ils ne le sont pas."[14]

Although the Parisian and central consistory members were characterized correctly as being indifferent to religion, the same was not always true in the provinces. Both eastern and southern consistory members were, for a long time, traditional in their outlook. Whereas there is ample testimony that consistory members in Paris rarely went to the synagogues,[15] we have many indications from the minutes books of the Strasbourg consistory that these members were familiar with, and involved in, synagogue ceremonies. For example, in 1856 an assistant rabbi was hired in Strasbourg. The minutes record a consistory member's request that the new rabbi's name be included in the blessings: "Un membre demande que le nom de M. le Rabbin adjoint ne soit pas omis dans la bénédiction récitée à l'occasion des offrandes faites au temple par les personnes appelées à la lecture de la loi."[16] Reading this, we see that those consistory members were sensitive to the details of the ritual and to the dignity of the rabbi. It is difficult to believe that a similar statement would have been made in analogous circumstances in Paris.

Of the various provincial consistories, that of Metz probably most resembled Paris. Metz had had its *haskalah* and was a center of reform agitation, with close links to Germany. When the old Metz synagogue was about to be destroyed to make way for the construction of a new one, the consistory decided that all the members would attend services on Friday evening and Saturday morning in honor of the closing of the temple: "tous ses membres assisteront à l'office de ce soir et à celui de samedi matin dans l'ancien temple, comme une marque de convenance parce que ce sera pour la dernière fois que le service du culte se fera dans ce temple."[17] Evidently, the Metz consistory members were less than assiduous in attending synagogue services.

Although the members of the consistories were often not observant, that does not imply a high level of assimilation. We have noted, for example, that on several occasions consistories held meetings on Christmas Day. Such observations give us the right to assume that this Christian holiday was not a vital part of the cultural associations of consistory members.[18]

The lack of religious observance among consistory members was important to the orthodox and their spokesman, Abraham Ben Baruch Créhange. In 1844 Créhange protested the timidity of the new law of that year, which enlarged the electorate but did not enfranchise all the Jews. He observed that the continually growing power of the rich laity prejudiced the interests of the orthodox Jews and the traditional rabbinate. Moreover, he found absurd the idea of a consistory composed of men who were not concerned with religion:

Un consistoire qui a la police des temples et qui ne fréquente pas les temples; qui accorde des diplômes [aux rabbins] et qui veut faire la loi aux rabbins; qui nomme le mohel, et qui ne fait pas circoncire ses enfants; qui nomme le sohet, et qui ne mange pas de la viande kasser, qui règle les cérémonies relatives à l'exercice du culte, et qui ne pratique pas le culte; un consistoire enfin qui veille à l'éducation religieuse, je le dis à regret, tant cette vérité me paraît triviale, mais un tel consistoire nous rendrait la risée de tous les peuples civilisés.[19]

There was very little turnover in the membership of the consistories. During the first thirty years of the Paris consistory's existence, members were usually elected when they were about fifty years old, and they remained in office for about ten years. After the 1844 *ordonnance* widened the electorate, and especially after the 1850 law increased the lay membership to six, younger men began to enter. In 1853 twenty-three-year-old Gustave Rothschild and thirty-eight-year-old Adolphe Israél were elected.

In some cases, members remained for much longer, and dynasties even emerged, with sons and nephews almost automatically named to succeed retired or deceased members. This was most noticeable in the cases of the Ratisbonne and Rothschild families. Alphonse de Rothschild entered the central consistory in 1852; in 1902 he was awarded a medal to celebrate fifty years of membership in that body. As we have seen, his brother Gustave was elected to the Paris consistory in 1853. Until this day there has almost always been a Rothschild in the Paris or the central consistory.

At least one other case is known of a consistory member remaining in office for fifty years. Elie Lantz, textile manufacturer in Colmar, was elected to the Haut-Rhin consistory around 1860 and remained in office under the German occupation until at least 1910.

The Ratisbonne family of Strasbourg and their relatives, the Cerfberr family of Paris, were both active in the consistories. In 1837 Max Cerfberr replaced Alphonse Cerfberr in the central consistory, and in 1854 he became its president. The Ratisbonne family was represented on the Strasbourg consistory, first by Auguste Ratisbonne, then by Louis Ratisbonne. When the latter, who had been president of the consistory, died in 1855, his nephew Achille Ratisbonne was named his successor, and was immediately elected president. In his acceptance speech, Ratisbonne thanked his colleagues for their confidence, emphasizing, however, that he knew that his election was principally an act of respect to his late uncle: "tout en ne voyant dans cet honneur qu'un hommage rendu à la mémoire de son digne et regrettable oncle, [son] prédecesseur." The reply to Ratisbonne's speech indicated that this factor had indeed been an important consideration:

Bien qu'une légitime part doive être faite au nom si vénéré que porte Mr Président, il est néanmoins juste de reconnaître que les services rendus personellement par Mr Achille Ratisbonne à la cause israélite . . . ont vivement contribué au témoignage d'estime et de déférence qui vient de lui être décerné.[20]

Toward the middle of the nineteenth century, members of the liberal professions and academicians began to be elected to the consistory. Often membership was accepted half-heartedly by these representatives of "the people." (We have already quoted Dr. Cahen on the subject of his reluctance to accept membership.) In some cases this lack of initiative in seeking the post did not entail a lack of initiative in fulfilling its tasks, but often it did. François Halévy, the celebrated musician, was elected a member of the central consistory even though, as a *notable* from Paris, he had never attended a single meeting. When he became a central consistory member, his zeal for Jewish administration did not improve much, and he was frequently absent from meetings.[21] Lateness and absences had always plagued the consistories. In 1820, David Singer, in his pamphlet attacking the consistories, had complained that consistory members were so casual about appearing at meetings that some of them arrived when others were leaving.[22] In 1846 the Paris consistory instituted a ten-franc fine for unexcused absences and a five-franc fine for late arrival.[23]

In summary, the consistory members were generally advanced in age, wealthy, frequently nonobservant, although not assimilated. They were politically conservative, and we should add that they believed in working through constituted authority rather than in resorting to publicity. This led them into differences with the younger liberals and with the emerging Jewish press, and was a crucial factor in the subsequent foundation of the *Alliance Israélite.*

C. Electorate

The electorate (or *notabilité,* or *Collège des notables*) was limited by the original *règlement* to twenty-five of the richest and most respected Jews named by the government in each consistory district. Although they were originally charged with drawing up the Jewish tax roles for their districts, the 1831 law that put Jewish religious expenses on the state budget eliminated this function. The *notables* subsequently had as their sole task the election of consistory members.

Olry Terquem, whose criticisms of the consistory have already been cited, in his rejection of the 1839 project, demanded that the tasks of the *notables* be expanded to include periodic review of consistory actions and convocations of synods.[24] Nevertheless the *notabilité* remained uniquely an electoral body, losing to the departmental consistory even some of its electoral functions in 1853 (when the naming of departmental grand rabbis was entrusted to the consistories).

Originally the prefect chose the twenty-five *notables* from among the most highly taxed and most respected Jews of the district. No procedure was specified for replacing the *notables* in the event they died, resigned, or failed to participate.

The 1823 *ordonnance* ordered the total renewal of the several *collèges de notables,* and specified a procedure for their renewal by fifths every two years. The central consistory was to submit a list of twice as many names as there were positions to fill, and the government was to select the *notables* from this list. Because the consistory often asked the advice of the departmental consistories, it became the general rule that the departmental consistories made the nominations. Although they were expected to submit two names for each post, the consistories were allowed to indicate their first and second choices, and their first choices were usually honored by the ministry.

It was so well known that the departmental consistories were, in reality, the ones to make the nominations that the government frequently forgot that the prerogative was that of the central consistory. On September 26, 1831, for example, the Paris consistory read a letter from the Prefect of the Seine, who requested a list of ten names, from which the government would choose five notables. In reply, the Paris consistory pointed out that it was the job of the central consistory to draw up such lists, and that the Paris consistory only advised.[25] In Marseille several years later a similar error occurred, this time on the part of the local consistory. The Marseille consistory, forgetting the proper procedure, sent a list of candidates for the *notabilité* directly to the Ministry of Cults. The ministry forwarded the list to the central consistory to be properly channeled.[26]

Occasionally the central consistory exercised selective choice in the monitoring of nominations. Thus in April 1844 it received a list of ten candidates for the five places open in the Colmar *Collège,* and it decided to try to obtain information on the merits of each candidate.[27] This move was related to the central consistory's involvement in the local dispute between the "enlightened" and "retrograde" factions of the Colmar community. The central consistory did not only reserve to itself the right to disapprove departmental consistory choices; it also, occasionally, exercised its prerogative of drawing up the list of candidates without consulting the local consistory.[28]

The 1823 *ordonnance* had specified the procedure for the periodic renewal of the *collège de notables* by fifths: five of the twenty-five members were to be replaced every year. In 1840 the minister complained to the central consistory that since the election of a totally new group of *notables* in 1823, the prescribed renewal by fifths had not taken place with any regularity. He outlined a procedure to rectify this situation.[29] In Paris some *notables* whose terms had theoretically expired in 1836, 1838, and 1840 were still in office on January 28, 1841, when the Paris consistory received a letter from the central consistory repeating the minister's complaint of laxity in renewing the *collège de notables.* The confusion caused by failure to renew the *notabilité* dated back to 1834; the 1834 replacement of *notables* had not taken place until 1837. As a result, three-fifths of each *collège* had to withdraw at once, and the newly elected members were to be grouped into fifths, to retire in 1846, 1848, or 1850.[30]

All this complicated arranging was made obsolete a scant three years later when the 1844 *ordonnance* redefined *notabilité* to include all those who qualified under certain categories:

1. Les fonctionnaires publics de l'ordre administratif.
2. Les fonctionnaires de l'ordre judiciaire.
3. Les membres des conseils généraux, des conseils d'arrondissement et des conseils municipaux.
4. Les citoyens inscrits sur la liste électorale et du jury.
5. Les officiers de terre et de mer, en activité et en retraite.
6. Les membres des chambres de commerce et ceux qui font partie de la liste des notables commerçants.
7. Les grand rabbins et les rabbins communaux.
8. Les professeurs dans les facultés et dans les collèges royaux et communaux.
9. Le directeur et les professeurs de l'école centrale rabbinique.

The *ordonnance* provided for the optional addition of adjunct *notables* up to a number equal to one sixth of the regular list. This provision was designed to enable the consistories to reward Jewish leaders and prominent citizens who were not otherwise qualified to be *notables*. The *notables* to be named as a result of the 1844 *ordonnance* were to elect completely new consistories throughout France. For this reason Dr. Cahen, president of the Paris consistory, urged that his consistory not take advantage of its faculty of naming adjunct *notables*. He expressed a fear that *notables* so named might feel themselves bound to vote for the re-election of the current consistory members in order to show their appreciation. In the discussion that ensued, Halphen disagreed, pointing out that there were many worthy and knowledgeable people who had rendered services but who were not in any category. He added that since many of the new regular *notables* did not have much knowledge of Judaism, worthier people should be added as adjuncts.[31]

It is interesting to examine the practical results on the consistories of the enlarged electorate of 1844. In Paris the 1845 election returned three of the four lay members to the consistory. Only one new member was elected in that year—Olry Dupont, a wealthy jeweler. In all seven districts there were a total of twenty-eight lay members, sixteen of whom were retained by the 1845 election. Of the twelve new members who entered, we have an indication of the liberal modern attitudes of only one of them: Léon Werthe, elected to the Colmar consistory. He had been instrumental in the founding of a Jewish trade school in Mulhouse, and his son had celebrated the first confirmation (*initiation religieuse*) ever held in Alsace. Table V-2 shows the re-elections and the changes resulting from the 1845 elections.

During the period of restricted *notabilité* (through 1844), *notables* whose terms expired were generally re-elected. Sons, brothers, or fathers frequently replaced members who retired or died. The consistories were usually able to control the appointments by indicating to the government those candidates whom they preferred. (They used the simple device, understood by the government, of putting their first choices at the top of their lists.) Consistory policy was to seek re-election of outgoing members and to keep certain prominent families represented in the *notabilité*.

The number of electors until 1844 was uniformly twenty-five

TABLE V-2
Results of the 1844–1845 Consistory Elections,
Showing the Effects of the 1844 Ordonnance *on the*
Composition of the Consistories

Consistory	Consistory Members	Re-elected	Replaced by
Bordeaux	Léon, Jacob Alfred	*	
	Lopes-Dubec, Félix	*	
	Rodrigues, Abraham		Perpignan, Josué
	Alexandre, David		Pereyra, Joseph
Colmar	Mannheimer, Meyer Baer	*	
	Schoengrun, Nathan Lévy	*	
	Lehmann, Raphael		Werthe, Léon
	Meyer, Aron		Bicard, Isaac
Marseille	Cahen, Jonas Joseph	*	
	Altaras, Jacques Isaac	*	
	Crémieu, Jacob Haim	*	
	Foa, Octave		Rodrigues, Fils aîné
Metz	Cahen, Louis-Aron	*	
	Schwabe, Isaïe	*	
	Dupont, Auguste	*	
	Worms, Adolphe		Lippman, David
Nancy	Picard, Goudchaux	*	
	Levylier, Joseph	*	
	Cain, dit Lajeunesse		Levylier, Abraham
	Lippman, père		Spire, Sigisbert
Paris	Cahen, Moise	*	
	Allegri, Benedict	*	
	Halphen, Edmond	*	
	Lévy, Michel		Dupont, Olry
Strasbourg	Ratisbonne, Louis	*	
	Half, B.		Bloch, C.
	Samuel, B.		Hirtz, I.
	Sarrazin, L.		Picard, Z.
Central Consistory	Worms de Romilly		Franck, Adolphe
	Crémieux, Adolphe	*[a]	Anspach, Philippe
	Maas, Myrtil		Halévy, Fromenthal
	Simon, Philippe		Hemerdinger, Michel
	Halphen, Anselme	*	
	Raphael, aîné	*	
	Cerfberr, Max	*	
Number of Members	35	19	16

[a]Crémieux declined his re-election.

per district, although not all of them actually participated. In 1844 all Jews who qualified as electors under the new categories were invited to make known their eligibility. Then the consistories named adjuncts, as allowed by Article 27 of the 1844 *ordonnance*. After prefectoral approval, the first electoral list compiled under the new law totaled 910 (Tables V-3, 4). Of these, 714 were on the jury lists or were electors in the general elections (a position determined by the level of wealth). The others were members of municipal councils, public functionaries, soldiers, members of the chamber of commerce, rabbis, and teachers in the public high schools (*collèges royaux*). These were the categories that conferred the right of *notabilité*.

TABLE V-3
Electors, 1845, by Consistory District

District	Number of Electors
Bordeaux	136
Colmar	110
Marseille	137
Metz	65
Nancy	112
Paris	206
Strasbourg	144
Total	910

TABLE V-4
Electors, 1845, by Basis of Qualification[a]

Qualification	Number of Electors
On election or jury lists	714
Members of municipal councils	70
Rabbis	56
Soldiers	33[b]
"Notables commerçants" [c]	2
Public-administrative functionaries	13
Public-judicial functionaries	7
Member of general council (local government)	1
Professors in *Collèges Royaux*	4
Unknown	10
Total	910

[a] Many of the electors qualified in more than one way, but if they were eligible on the basis of the first category (on the election and jury lists), they were placed there.
[b] Only a fraction of the eligible soldiers registered to vote.
[c] The term cannot be translated. It is an honorary title assigned to prominent businessmen.

The electorate was considerably enlarged again in 1849, when universal suffrage was introduced. All electors on general election lists (now constructed on the basis of universal suffrage) and over twenty-five years of age were eligible to vote in the consistory election.

From 1850 to 1854 the size of the registration for consistory elections depended upon the local level of interest in the work of the consistory. Thus twice as many voters were registered in Strasbourg as in Paris, even though the Jewish population of the Paris consistory was almost equal to that of Strasbourg. The data available are incomplete, and it is to be hoped that the voter registration information for the other three consistories will eventually be recovered. Table V-5 shows the level of registration in five districts. In these five districts, 12,176, or 16½ percent of the total Jewish population of these districts, were registered to vote.[32]

TABLE V-5

*Number of Electors Registered for Consistory
Elections in Five Districts, 1850–1854*

District	Date	Number of Registered Electors[a]
Bordeaux	1850	408
Paris	1852	2295
Nancy	1853	1683
Colmar	1853	3323
Strasbourg	1854	4467

[a]The sources of these figures are as follows: Bordeaux, Arch. B.C., 2 A 6, January 6, 1850; Paris, Arch. P.C., AA 4, December 26, 1852; Nancy, Arch. P.C., I[CC] 31, Nancy consistory to central consistory, February 8, 1853; Colmar, A.D. Haut-Rhin, 1 V 91, *procès verbal* of the consistory elections, January 30, 1853; Strasbourg, Arch. S.C., minutes, uncatalogued, August 17, 1854.

Studying the evolution of voter registration in Strasbourg, we discover a progressive decrease from 4467 in 1854, to 4264 in 1855, to 3887 in 1859, to 3781 in 1863.[33] During the same period the Jewish population of the district did decline somewhat, but not enough to explain this drop of 700 voters (16 percent). Lack of interest was apparently a major factor in the decreased voter participation.

Not all of those registered actually voted. From the time the consistories were established, lack of interest in consistory elections plagued the system. *Notables*—the only electors until 1848—were picked for their prominence and wealth rather than for a knowledge of Judaism or an interest in Jewish affairs. These men frequently failed to attend meetings and participate in elections. In some cases they would have had to travel some distance to the seat of the consistory, at their own expense.

Even when they lived in the city, however, their interest was not assured. Meetings often lacked quorums; *notables* stayed away without explaining their absences. In 1834 the central consistory received numerous complaints by the various consistories about the difficulties caused by repeated absences of *notables* from meetings and elections. In that year, at the request of the central consistory, the Ministry of Cults ruled that any *notable* who missed three consecutive meetings would forfeit his post unless a valid excuse was offered. Still, on October 4, 1841, only eight of the twenty-five *notables* were present at a meeting of the Paris *Collège de notables*.[34] At that meeting Allegri was re-elected, and Jules Lan, the youngest *notable* present, protested against the illegality of the past three elections. He pointed out that there had not been a quorum for any of them: of the twenty-five *notables* there had been only ten, twelve, and eight present at these elections. His objections were overruled, but his protest was included in the record of the election which was sent to the central consistory. Benoît Cohen, of the Paris charity board, supported Lan and requested that the Paris consistory enforce the rule that banned *notables* from their functions if they missed three successive meetings. Cohen named several *notables* who had never attended a meeting. Perhaps all of the publicity and agitation concerning the crisis of the *collège de notables* had a beneficial effect. In 1842 an unusually large number—twenty of the twenty-five—were present to elect Michel Lévy *notable*.[35]

When the newly expanded electorate gathered for the complete renewal of the consistories in September 1845, interest still did not run high. In Paris 233 electors had been registered but only eighty-three appeared for the election, which had to be postponed for lack of a quorum.[36] At a second gathering, two weeks later, a quorum still was not attained, although this time it was not required.[37] Only 107 of the 233 *notables* voted in this election, despite the fact that it was the first opportunity for most of them to participate directly in Jewish communal government.[38]

The indifference of the successful Parisian Jews to the organized Jewish community was repeatedly evident. Even the rather low participation of 107 out of 233 *notables* in the September 1845 election of a Paris representative to the central consistory was unusually high. When Crémieux, elected in that ballot, declined to serve, and another meeting of the *notables* had to be called to name his successor, fewer than half as many as had voted in the previous election appeared. Again, the meeting had to be adjourned for lack of a quorum.[39] On December 28, sixty-nine of the 233 *notables* elected Philippe Anspach (also a lawyer) to replace Crémieux.[40]

Interest in the 1845 elections varied considerably from one district to another. We have some statistics (Table V-6) concerning the number of *notables* who took part in the 1845 elections in each district. The percentage of registered voters who turned out to vote ranged from 13 percent in Marseille to 95 percent in Colmar.

In Paris interest ran higher two years later when elections were called to name a grand rabbi. The Paris consistory had publicly endorsed Mayer Charleville, the most liberal candidate. Crémieux led an angry section of *notables* who objected to the method used by the consistory to influence the election. Crémieux's choice was Lazard Isidor, the rabbi of Phalsbourg, who had become famous for his refusal to administer an oath *More Judaïco*. As a result of Cremieux's campaign, the issue was discussed in the Jewish press and additional polemics were published. Sixty-seven percent, 150 of the 225 *notables,* turned out to vote, and Isidor was elected.[41]

In Bordeaux in the same year, slightly more than half, forty-six of the eighty-nine registered voters appeared and re-elected the consistory members whose terms had expired.[42] It is obvious that the involvement of the Jewish community in its administrative affairs had not significantly increased as a result of the 1844 *ordonnance.*

TABLE V-6

Percentage of Registered Electors who Voted in 1845 [a]

District	Number Registered	Number Voting	Percentage
Bordeaux	136	67	49
Colmar	128	121	95
Marseille	143	29	13
Metz	65	51	78
Nancy	114	65	57
Paris	233	107	46
Strasbourg	144	122	85

[a] Calculated on the basis of data published in *A.I.,* 6 (1845), p. 835.

The next major change in the *notabilité* was the introduction of universal suffrage. It was first in effect during the 1850 consistory election. Interest varied but was low enough to elicit a ministry ruling of April 24, 1850, that a quorum of one third of the registered voters would suffice for validating an election.[43]

The rate of voter turnout in the consistory districts between 1850 and 1853 is shown in Table V-7. The percentage of registered voters who voted in those years ranged from 35 percent in Paris to 59 percent in Bordeaux. Ten years later (after the introduction of categories for qualification as an elector) we note a 71 percent voter turnout in Strasbourg.[44]

In all these cases we must bear in mind that the percentage of eligible men who voted was even lower than the figures cited, as even registration to vote was dependent on initiative and interest. Many simply did not register.

What were the professions of the *notables* or electors? We

have pointed out that initially they were twenty-five of the highest taxpayers in each district, ordinarily men involved in commerce and banking. However, when the 1844 *ordonnance* broadened the electorate to all those qualified by virtue of being included in any of several categories, the percentage of voters in economic professions decreased significantly.

TABLE V-7
Percentage of Registered Electors who Voted, 1850–1853[a]

District	Date	Number Registered	Number Voting	Percentage
All France	1850	15,000	6,381	42.5
Bordeaux	1850	408	238	59
Paris	1852	2,295	797	35
Colmar	1853	3,323	1,794	54
Nancy	1853	1,683	860	51

[a] Calculations are based on figures from the following sources: France (1850), Zosa Szajkowski, "Electoral Battles," p. 140; Bordeaux, Arch. B.C., 2 A 6, January 6, 1850; Paris, Arch. P.C., AA 4, December 26, 1852; Colmar, A.D. Haut-Rhin, 1 V 91, *procès verbal* of Colmar consistory, January 30, 1853; Nancy, Arch. P.C., ICC 31, Nancy consistory to central consistory, February 8, 1853.

Of the thirty people whose names had been proposed in February 1841 by the Marseille consistory for fifteen vacant posts on the *collège de notables,* all but four were involved in business or other capitalist enterprises. (The other four were at the bottom of the list and therefore not included in the preferred choice of the consistory.) Most of the rest were *négociants;* two were *rentiers;* two were employed by large commercial or banking firms; two were brokers in business transactions. Of the four who were not in the business world, two were public functionaries and two were lawyers.[45]

Again in October of the same year, the Marseille consistory was called upon to elect six *notables.* All those presented as the first choices were *négociants* or other businessmen.[46] The situation was similar everywhere. We have a list (Table A-16 in Appendix A, below) of the twenty-five *notables* of Colmar in 1841. Twenty-one of them were involved in business, but only eight of these earned their living by commercial transactions. The other thirteen lived on income from property. Three manufacturers and one physician completed the list.

In Bordeaux in the same year twenty candidates were proposed for ten vacant posts of *notables* (Table A-17). The professions of eighteen of the candidates were given: all were in banking and business (including nine *propriétaires*), except for the physician, Isaac Pereire.

An incident that occurred in the Haut-Rhin in 1842 underscores the fact that posts as *notables* were limited to the rich. Claiming that they had been usurers, the government rejected the re-election of two incumbents (the candidates favored by the consistory). If we study the list (Table V-8), we see that the two wealthiest alternates were chosen instead of the poorer incumbents. The table shows the five preferred candidates plus the five alternates and indicates the government's choice. Seven were *propriétaires* and one was a *négociant*. A very wealthy manufacturer (the highest taxpayer of all of the candidates) and a physician were the only two noncommercial candidates.[47]

TABLE V-8
Wealth of Candidates to the Notabilité, *Colmar District, October 10, 1841*[a]

Candidates	Occupations	Tax Assessment (in francs)
Incumbents, recommended by consistory:		
SÉE, ISRAEL GABRIEL	*Propriétaire*	371.84
DREYFUSS, LÉOPOLD	*Propriétaire*	519.93
LÉVY, MICHEL	*Médecin*	112.62
Lévy, Samuel	*Propriétaire*	73.56
Wahl, Josué	*Propriétaire*	137.24
Alternate candidates:		
BLUM, SAMUEL	*Négociant*	145.59
PARAFF, BENJAMIN	*Fabricant*	939.65
Schwab, Isaac	*Propriétaire*	92.74
Hirtz, Marx Aron	*Propriétaire*	64.98
Wahl, Samuel	*Propriétaire*	64.53

[a] Names in capital letters indicate successful candidates. Source: A.D. Haut-Rhin, 1 V 81.

After the 1844 *ordonnance* had permitted new categories of men to become *notables,* the occupational distribution of the *notables* did, in fact, broaden. Public functionaries, members of local government, soldiers, rabbis, and teachers (from the universities to the public secondary schools) were included. Members of the liberal professions, writers, and researchers, were still not included, unless they happened also to qualify in one of the named categories, but they could be named adjunct *notables*.

In the Seine 175 *notables* were on the regular list in 1844. All but four of them qualified because they were on the election and jury lists. Three more were soldiers and one was a professor (at the *Collège de Nancy*).[48]

The Jewish press attempted to analyze the professions of the 963 electors in the 1845 elections. Both the *Archives Israélites* and the *Univers Israélite* ran articles on this, but neither had been able to obtain complete data. Neither analyzed the occupations of the adjunct *notables* of Paris and Colmar. In an

attempt to show that the distinguished *notables* among the Jews
had moved significantly away from commerce and into "les
carrières les plus honorables," editor S. Bloch of *Univers
Israélite* analyzed the lists from Colmar and Strasbourg. These
consistories were located in Alsace, in the areas most likely to
be highly populated by businessmen. He showed that of the 110
notables in Colmar and of the 144 *notables* in Strasbourg, only
thirty-two and sixty-nine respectively (or 29 and 48 percent)
were *négociants*. Thus, of the 254 *notables* in both Alsatian
departments, 101, or 40 percent, were actively involved in commerce. The rest were *propriétaires* (seventy-nine), manufacturers, physicians, rabbis, soldiers, and public functionaries.[49]
Bloch's analysis may have satisfied his apologetic aims, but it
cannot withstand close examination. He failed to specify that
many of the seventy-nine *propriétaires,* who lived on the income from their investments, had made their fortunes in commerce. If we add these people to the group of businessmen
whom Bloch reported at the time, we find that 71 percent, not
40 percent, of the Alsatian *notables* had commercial occupations.

Had Bloch calculated the occupational distribution of the
notables for the entire country, according to the categories we
propose (Table V-9), he would have found that the percentage
of regular *notables* whose living was earned in various ways from
business (including "capitalists," industrialists, merchants) was
highest in Paris and Marseille, where it reached 80 and 82 percent respectively. Lower figures in the eastern provinces are
explained by the larger number of rabbis and members of
local government who qualified as electors under the 1844
ordonnance.

The liberal professions were represented in the new electorate of 1844. Of all the *notables* whose professions are known,
8 percent belonged to this group. They qualified, however, not
because of their occupations but because of their elevated
economic status, which entitled them to figure on the general
election lists. They represent, therefore, the wealthiest among
those in the liberal professions. The percentage of *notables* in
the liberal professions ranged from a low of 2 percent in Colmar
to a high of 12 percent in Metz.

The naming of additional (adjunct) *notables* hardly affected
the occupational or class distinction of the electorate. Occasionally an aged cantor or charity board member who had rendered
great service to the community was named *notable* as a mark
of honor, but this did not affect the course of the elections.

In fact, the effect of the 1844 law never could have been
great. Although a larger number of people were enfranchised,
they were men whose range of opinion was the same as that of
the older, more restricted *notabilité:* they were progressive and
moderately liberal in religious outlook, integrationist socially
and economically.

It appears that very few men were named adjunct *notables*.

There were twenty-two in Paris, eighteen in Colmar, and two in Nancy. There were no additional adjunct appointments two years later, when another election was held. In fact, the Paris consistory complained in that year that the government had frozen the number of adjunct *notables* allowed.[50]

TABLE V-9

Occupation Distribution, by Consistory District, of Electors, 1845[a]

	Bor-deaux[f]	Colmar	Mar-seille	Metz	Nancy	Paris	Stras-bourg	Total Electors per Oc-cupation
Commercial occupations	(5)	77	117	39	72	182	85	577
Liberal professions[b]	(1)	7	13	8	4	22	11	66
Rabbis	(2)	20	1	2	5	2	17	49
Soldiers[c]			2	4	12	13	10	41
Public functionaries[d]	(1)		3	1	1	3	1	10
Members of government[e]	(9)	20	7	11	18	6	19	90
Other		4			2	5	1	12
Total electors per consistory	136	128	143	65	114	233	144	963[g]

[a] Sources: *A.I.,* 6 (1845), 831–835; Arch. P.C., B 25, central consistory to Paris consistory, July 1, 1845; A.D. Haut-Rhin, 1 V 91.
[b] Liberal professions include physicians, notaries, lawyers, judges, professors, intellectuals, pharmacists, engineers, etc.
[c] Active and retired.
[d] Includes police commissioners, tax collectors, postmasters, etc.
[e] Includes mayors, deputies, diplomats, members of municipal councils.
[f] We know the occupations of only 18 of the 136 Bordeaux electors.
[g] This total includes all 136 Bordeaux electors.

But the events of 1848 changed the system again, bringing in universal suffrage and with it a significant change in the opinion of the electorate. The masses of the Ashkenazi Jews were orthodox and traditional in outlook. All Jews over twenty-five years of age and eligible to vote in political elections were now *notables,* or electors. A significant increase in orthodox opinion was felt in the 1850 election. As a result, the 1853 law was promulgated, taking the choice of rabbis out of the hands of the people and giving it to the consistories. Universal suffrage continued to elect lay members to the consistory for another ten years.

In 1862, after a twelve-year struggle which we have described in chapter four, the electorate was narrowed and restricted to people who qualified in certain categories:

1⁰ Ceux qui exercent des fonctions relatives au culte ou qui sont attachés, soit à titre d'administrateurs, soit à titre de souscripteurs annuels, aux établissements placés sous l'autorité des Consistoires;

2^O Les fonctionnaires de l'ordre administratif, ceux de l'ordre judiciaire, les professeurs ou instituteurs dans les établissements et écoles fondés par l'Etat, par les communes ou par les Consistoires, et tout israélite pourvu d'un diplôme obtenu dans les formes établies par les lois et Règlements;

3° Les membres des Conseils Généraux, les Conseils d'arrondissement et les Conseils municipaux;

4° Les officiers de terre et de la mer en activité ou en retraite;

5° Les sous-officiers, les soldats et les marins de la Légion d'honneur ou décorés de la médaille militaire;

6° Les membres des Chambres de Commerce et ceux qui font partie de la liste des notables commerçants;

7° Les titulaires d'offices ministériels;

8° Les étrangers résidants dans la circonscription depuis trois ans et compris dans l'une des catégories ci-dessus, sans que, toutefois, la qualité d'électeur leur confère l'éligibilité.[51]

The effect of the 1862 decree was to disenfranchise those who did not contribute financially to consistory-recognized institutions. This tactic was successful in protecting the financial interests of the consistory and in preventing the orthodox poor from influencing the elections significantly.

In order to bring some of the financial resources of the mutual aid societies into the consistory treasury, the consistories (first in Paris, then elsewhere) demanded financial contributions in return for consistory "recognition" of these societies.

The second aim of the 1862 change, that of minimizing the influence of the orthodox, was based on a realistic appraisal of the situation. It aimed at preventing a repetition of the Colmar events of the 1850's, when universal suffrage had elected a traditionalist consistory, causing a split between the consistory and the liberal Philanthropic Society.

The 1862 restriction of the electorate achieved its purpose. The consistories remained unrepresentative of the people, and for that reason they remained vulnerable to the competition of separatist traditional institutions.

D. Elections, Installations, and Oaths

1. Elections

All consistory elections, of both laymen and clergy, were subject to the approval of the government. Oaths were administered, and official acts were issued by the ministry to name the successful candidates to their posts. Thus the consistory had quasi-official status, and all its authority and power derived from the government.

Elections were rather quiet and simple before 1848, when the electorate was restricted. But when the 1850 elections were about to take place and universal suffrage was being used for the first time, there was much publicity. The consistories sought a means of channeling public opinion. This they accomplished through ad hoc committees to "prepare" the election, and through circular letters recommending certain candidates. By obtaining impressive signatures on these letters, they were able to influence the vote for the candidates they endorsed. In Paris another means was used to ensure the compliance of the people: the consistory co-opted, to serve on the nominating committee, the presidents of twenty officially recognized mutual aid societies. A single slate was then presented in Paris, and was endorsed by elected leaders of these grass roots organizations as well as by consistory members and committee appointees. The total nominating committee, however, had been weighted in favor of the consistory. It comprised twenty presidents of mutual aid societies and forty-six members of consistory commissions and committees.[52] A similar procedure was followed elsewhere. In Nancy a committee slate was endorsed by 150 people and published on May 14, 1850.[53] In Strasbourg, also, a committee was formed to influence the election outcome ("dans le but de dessigner aux suffrages des électeurs les candidats qui offrent des garanties . . . ."). This committee seems to have been independent of the consistory, at least officially, but was of the same tendencies.[54]

Universal suffrage brought confusion to the method of election of communal rabbis. Previously, communal rabbis had been elected in varying ways, but most frequently by ad hoc commissions formed for this purpose by the *commissaires surveillants,* the consistories' delegates in the communities. In the wake of the revolution and the institution of universal suffrage, some republican enthusiasts among the Jews felt compelled to democratize Jewish affairs, even if democracy produced results contrary to their own personal religious views. This was the case in Metz, where the consistory was both enthusiastic about the republic and sympathetic to moderate religious reform. By allowing universal suffrage in the 1851 election of the communal rabbi of Sarreguemines, the Metz consistory caused an orthodox victory. Several Jews of Sarreguemines complained of this election by universal suffrage, and the Minister of Cults asked the central consistory's opinion. The central consistory replied that it favored the retention of the 1844 provision for nomination of rabbis by local commissions.[55]

After the 1853 law had eliminated universal suffrage in the election of rabbis, the consistories continued their attempts to influence the popular election of the consistory members. In Strasbourg in 1856 the consistory members disputed among themselves the appropriateness of such action. President Ratisbonne had taken it upon himself to circulate a statement of support for a liberal candidate who was running against an orthodox incumbent, and this circular enabled his preferred candidate to win. But the rest of the consistory was very angry because Ratisbonne had signed his name to the circular and indicated his capacity as *Président du consistoire.* They felt that Ratisbonne had given the impression that he was speaking for the entire consistory. One member claimed that the circular broke the tradition whereby the consistory maintained silence on the issue of elections. Ratisbonne angrily replied that he had acted within his rights, as an individual, in no way implicating the other members. He added that he fully intended to act in the same way during the next elections. Another member asked what would happen to the dignity of the consistory if each member had his personal list of favored candidates. The discussion turned into a tumultuous argument, and Ratisbonne adjourned the meeting. For at least two months the argument raged between the president and the rest of the consistory. Both sides threatened to resort to publicity, but they appear not to have done so. Ratisbonne complained to the central consistory of his consistory's attitude. Some individuals complained to the ministry, and the prefect was called upon to intervene.[56]

In his letter to the central consistory Ratisbonne aired his feelings about the bad effects of universal suffrage. He claimed that it had given expression to an unintelligent and backward majority. He insisted that universal suffrage had produced bad choices in Alsace: "a produit de facheux effets en Alsace . . . il est sorti une majorité inintelligente, arriérée, absurde." His own action, he continued, speaking of his circular, had brought into the consistory an enlightened and educated lawyer, and caused the defeat of an ignorant member:

membre . . . nul, profondément ignorant et imbu, au plus haut degré, d'idées rétrogrades, chef et instrument d'un parti aussi audacieux que stupide, a dû céder la place à un homme instruit et éclairé, à un membre du barrau, à l'honorable président de notre école de travail.[57]

This method of preparing slates of candidates that were officially endorsed continued to be practiced and was effective in influencing the vote.

2. Installations and Oaths

From the beginning of the consistory system, the lay members, rabbis and cantors were sworn in by local prefects or mayors, who administered an oath. This was prescribed by Article 2 of the decree of October 19, 1808. The form of the oath was based on that prescribed by Article 6 of the law of 18 germinal, An X, for installation of public functionaries. Whereas the oath for public functionaries was sworn on the Gospels, the version for the Jews was sworn on a printed Bible:

Je jure et promets à Dieu, sur la sainte Bible, de garder obéissance aux constitutions de l'empire, et fidélité à l'empereur. Je promets aussi de faire connaître tout ce que j'apprendrai de contraire aux intérêts du souverain ou de l'Etat.[58]

By law of August 31, 1830, a new oath for public functionaries was substituted, by which the person only promised allegiance to the king, the constitution, and the laws. The religious references and the promise to report to the authorities all things contrary to the public interest were dropped. However, the Jews were sometimes given a special form of oath, on the Bible. The record of Philippe Anspach's 1842 installation by the Prefect of the Seine to his Paris consistory post shows that Anspach took the oath on a Hebrew Bible. The prefect wrote that Anspach appeared before him

à l'effet de prêter entre nos mains et sur la bible le serment prescrit par l'article 2 du décrêt du 19 octobre 1808 et dont nous lui avons donné lecture conformément à la nouvelle formule.

Cette lecture achevée M. Anspach (Philippe) a prêté à haute voix entre nos mains sur une bible hébraïque ouverte à cet effet sur notre Bureau, le serment dont la teneur suit:

"Je jure sur la Sainte Bible, fidélité au Roi des Français, obéissance à la charte constitutionnelle, et aux lois du Royaume."[59]

Although the oath before the prefect generally constituted the installation of consistory members, rabbis' oaths were frequently followed by a separate installation. Communal rabbis were installed by consistory delegates in the synagogues of the various communities. Grand rabbis were installed by the consistory members themselves in the consistorial synagogue. Practices varied, and there are records also of lay members being officially installed by the consistory after having taken the oath. In Strasbourg this occurred in the consistory meeting room.[60] In Bordeaux it was done in the synagogue on Friday evening before the services.[61]

The 1844 *ordonnance* changed the installation practice. Article 36 specified that lay members of the central consistory and departmental consistories were to be installed by the prefect, who would administer the oath prescribed by the law of August 31, 1830, and that the person taking the oath would raise his hand, without any other formality. Thus the special Jewish version of the oath was eliminated. According to Article 58 of the 1844 *ordonnance,* the grand rabbis and rabbis were to take the oath prior to their installation.

The 1848 revolution abolished political oaths, and the Ministry of Cults ruled that Article 36 of the 1844 *ordonnance* no longer applied. Thus in Strasbourg an 1850 installation of consistory members was as follows: the members appeared before the prefect's delegate, who read the decree issued by the President of the Republic approving the election. The prefect's delegate then declared them installed. This procedure continued to be followed for some time in the Bas-Rhin and was used in 1863 when the entire consistory was renewed as a result of the 1862 changes in the electoral laws.

Sometime between 1863 and 1867 the oath was reintroduced in the Bas-Rhin. The minutes of the installation of Strasbourg consistory members in 1867 mention an oath for the first time since 1848: "Je jure obéissance à la constitution et fidélité à l'Empereur."[62] In the Haut-Rhin such an oath had been administered as early as 1861.[63]

For purposes of our analysis, the various tasks assigned by the
legislation to the consistories may be classified into three categories which we call "administrative," "regenerative," and
"police." The administrative functions of the consistories involved organizing and supervising the communities and their
institutions. "Regeneration"—a popular term of the nineteenth
century—meant socioeconomic and moral improvement. The
police functions, perhaps the least exercised, were nevertheless
the *raison d'être* of the consistories, which had been established
to exercise surveillance over the Jews, and especially over the
rabbis.

The consistories, however, did not consider themselves bound
to limit their activities to the prescribed tasks in these three
areas; once established, they developed a certain degree of
autonomy and were in a position to take some initiative in deciding on their future course. However, the degree of initiative
varied with the period and the place, and many critics of the
consistory system blamed them precisely for a lack of vigorous
initiative. Often the consistories claimed that the tasks being
attributed to them by such critics were beyond the scope of the
definition of their powers. Yet, as we shall show, the consistories did, in fact, step beyond their assigned tasks, and it is
interesting to speculate just how far they could have gone in
initiating action, had their members wanted to do so.

A. Administration

The administrative functions of the consistories occupied most
of their attention. Article 12 of the 1806 *règlement* had prescribed three administrative tasks. The consistories were to
maintain "order in the synagogues," supervise the administration of private synagogues, and receive and handle the tax
money destined for religious expenses.

We note that the minutes of the Metz consistory meetings of
November 1855 to November 1856 contained reports exclusively of an administrative-financial nature, including the rental of
seats in the temple, the sale of honors, raising and distributing
charity money, elections, building, renovating, paying, administering the rabbinical school, hiring staff and admitting
students.[1]

Elsewhere, also, consistory meetings were often devoted entirely to administrative and financial considerations; others were largely concerned with them. The consistories received money, at first from special Jewish taxes and later from the state, private donors, the sale and lease of temple seats, fund-raising campaigns (often lotteries) and taxes on kosher meat. Administrative tasks of the consistories included organizing and running elections; building, running, repairing, and enlarging the temples; supervising charities and *kashrut;* hiring, firing, and paying personnel (in Metz this included the rabbinical school); regulating circumcision; and controlling burial procedures and cemeteries (purchase of land, repair of walls, etc.). They drew up regulations for the functioning of their own administration and for the committees under them. The consistories supervised the schools that belonged to the community until, as we shall note, many of them were turned into public schools. The consistories served as intermediaries between the government and local Jewish communities and institutions. When, for example, synagogues sought government funds for repairs, when clergy needed emergency funds to supplement meager salaries, or when Jewish schools sought to be taken over by the city (*communalisation*), the consistories served as the transmitter of messages.

The consistories administered the many communities of their districts by appointing delegates (*commissaires surveillants*) in the various towns, but the consistories alone had the right to approve the naming of cantors, teachers, and rabbis. They listened to the communities' many complaints concerning taxes, teachers, *commissaires surveillants,* cantors, rabbis. The consistories intervened in all manner of conflicts that arose in the communities. In some districts (e.g., Strasbourg) the consistories also reviewed and approved local community budgets.

The consistories transmitted government requests for the special services or prayers to celebrate events of national importance, such as births of princes, escapes from assassination, battles, and royal birthdays. They cooperated, more or less willingly, with administrative procedures for the repayment of the various Jewish communal debts remaining from the pre-Revolutionary period.

The various consistories apportioned their time differently, according to the needs of their districts. Because the Jewish population in the eastern districts was diffusely located in several hundred small communities, administrative tasks in those consistories were more numerous than in places like Paris and Bordeaux, where the population was concentrated mainly in one city. Analyzing the work of the Bordeaux consistory in 1853 and that of the Paris consistory in 1840 and 1853, we find that two thirds of the discussion items during these consistories' sessions were related exclusively to affairs of the local community. The other one third concerned either other communities of the district or the entire district. This second category includes the running of the consistory itself.

In the eastern regions, on the other hand, the consistory was a coordinator of the work of the administrations of many local communities, including that of the local administration. It did not, itself, act directly to control the affairs of the Strasbourg community. It was the highest regional authority, from which power was delegated. Reports were made to the consistory; the consistory's approval was sought. The administrative role of the consistory was paramount. We have noted that during the years 1853 to 1856 the Strasbourg consistory dealt at each of its sessions, on behalf of the more than one hundred communities of its district, with three to eight problems regarding hiring and replacements of various personnel (teachers, rabbis, cantors, *commissaires surveillants,* etc.). At each meeting the consistory handled one to five requests of government aid for schools, temples, cantors, widows, etc. These they forwarded to the government, and when the responses were received, they made them known to the individuals or communities concerned. At each session there were also one to five cases of conflict that were discussed and handled. These included complaints against teachers, consistory delegates, cantors, rabbis, and also against taxes or membership dues in local communities. Examining the analysis that we have made of the distribution of their efforts (Table VI-1), we find that the overwhelming majority (between two thirds and three quarters) of their discussions concerned the various areas of business that we have called administrative and which dealt with the smooth functioning of the communities' Jewish institutions. Next in frequency among the items of consistory attention were various efforts to supply protection, either to individuals or to communities. This includes defense against anti-Jewish writings or actions, obtaining favorable publicity, and administrating charity to the Jewish poor. Twelve percent of the 385 discussions analyzed were in regard to such topics. Another 10 percent of the consistories' time was spent on affairs that tended to develop the consistories' monopoly on control of Jewish institutions, generally in order to (mildly) reform them. Also included in this category, however, are *all* issues of religious ceremonies, whatever the aim or intentions, including the transmission of government orders for national events to be celebrated in the district's temples.

B. Regeneration

"Regeneration" was clearly one of the basic functions of the consistories from their inception. Article 12 of the 1806 *règlement* specified that it would be the job of the consistories to encourage the Jews to exercise "useful" professions. In a circular of May 8, 1809, the central consistory emphasized this task even before the departmental consistories were established. The circular stated that the departmental consistories would be "la base fondamentale de notre régénération religieuse et poli-

TABLE VI-1

Items of Deliberation, Paris and Bordeaux Consistories, 1853

Item	Paris		Bordeaux	
	Number of Items Concerning Chef Lieu	Number of Items Concerning Remainder of district	Number of Items Concerning Chef Lieu	Number of Items Concerning Remainder of district
Administration				
Financial aid	10	15	1	7
Schools	1	0	0	3
Conflicts	5	9	4	0
Personnel	24	14	10	4
Finance	50	8	16	5
Burials	15	2	2	0
Kashrut	4	0	0	0
Rabbinic School	0	7	0	0
Elections	1	4	0	5
Buildings	0	0	5	0
Total	110	59	38	24
Protection				
Non-financial Aid	2	2	0	0
Charity	20	0	5	0
Total	22	2	5	0
Monopoly				
Ceremonies	11	8	4	1
Control	0	0	1	2
Total	11	8	5	3
Total Items	143	69	48	27

tique."[2] It was well known that this meant, as Anchel put it, "moral and social assimilation."[3] An 1831 report by the Strasbourg consistory's commission on regeneration displayed the same concept:

En effet, messieurs, quel doit être le résultat de notre régénération, sinon de nous porter au niveau de la population des autres cultes au milieu de laquelle nous vivons en minorité, c'est à dire d'avoir les mêmes moeurs, les mêmes habitudes, les mêmes occupations qu'elle.[4]

Regeneration programs caused conflict and a certain amount of cleavage within the Jewish community. In order for the traditional-minded Jewish beggars and peddlers to be integrated into the economic pattern of the country, they would have to make some compromises with orthodox practices. Even if Jewish trade schools would hold classes on Sundays, instead of Saturdays, and close for Jewish holidays, the Jewish laborer could not expect to maintain a skilled job unless he agreed to be available on the usual working days.

Another Strasbourg commission on regeneration (this one established in 1853) realized this when it called for a program of religious reform without which, it said, integration of the Jews was materially impossible. Such reforms were the elimination of the second days of holidays (except *Rosh Ha Shanah*) and the extension of the dispensations which the "Sanhedrin" granted to Jews in military service to include those citizens and public functionaries whose jobs conflicted with traditional observance. The commission asked that the half holidays be declared working days. Furthermore, it requested the enforcement of the regulation which prohibited unauthorized people from giving religious instruction, and the institution of an examination on the central consistory's approved "catechism" prior to the celebration of Bar Mitzvah. This plan meant a radically reformed style of Jewish education, one that concentrated on morality and civic duty, Bible stories and history. Such a reform program could not avoid alienating the orthodox masses.

In Colmar a philanthropic committee was established in 1835, which opened a trade school in Mulhouse in 1842, and worked for the economic integration of the Jews. It kindled the hostility of the orthodox, including most of the Colmar consistory members. This issue resulted in a deep-rooted division of the Jewish population of the Haut-Rhin which continued for two decades. It led, eventually, to the intervention of both the central consistory and the government. The institution of universal suffrage had allowed the orthodox to get the upper hand in this largely traditional province. In 1858 an orthodox victory in the consistory elections was annulled by government action, and in 1861 a new (manipulated) election brought in the Mulhouse group.

All of the consistories attempted to regenerate their populations. In all of them there were committees, both consistorial and private. There were both inducements and threats to convince parents to enroll their children in the primary schools, rather than send them to peddle thread on the streets. Attempts were made to get parents to have their children trained for some kind of skilled work. Enthusiasm varied with the consistories, and in Paris individual initiative seems to have been more useful than that of the consistories. David Singer, for example, seems to have been the first to think of arranging to place young Jews in apprenticeships. In 1819 he offered to place two poor children in apprenticeship at his own expense, and he appealed for others to imitate his action:

Je prends l'engagement de mettre en apprentissage à mes frais, les deux écoliers pauvres pris parmi ceux qui auront eu la meilleur conduite, lorsque l'âge de l'instruction leur permettront de quitter l'école.

*Si je trouve des imitateurs comme je me plais à le croire les
pauvres seront arrachés à la misère et la France aura acquis de
bons citoyens.*[5]

The consistories of the east were more active in sponsoring
regeneration projects than was Paris. On several occasions, the
consistories of Strasbourg and Colmar, together and separately,
formed committees to eliminate begging. During the years 1853
to 1855 a committee in Strasbourg worked to aid Jews to emigrate to the United States. The Strasbourg consistory had decided that this was the best means of regenerating the Alsatian
Jews.

But private philanthropy was perhaps more important than
consistory activity in many parts of the country. In Paris David
Singer *did* find imitators among other private individuals, including the Rothschilds, who played a large part in this kind of
work. Some of the charitable foundations that emerged from
individual endeavor in Paris were *la société des amis du travail*
(1823), *la société pour l'établissement des jeunes filles israélites*
(1844), and *la société de patronage des apprentis et ouvriers
israélites de Paris* (established in 1846 under a different name;
reorganized under this name in 1853).

Not only did private initiative often exceed that of the consistories, but even the government sometimes seemed more concerned than the consistories. In fact, governmental ideas frequently underlay the regeneration projects. In 1820 the Rector
of the Academy of Moselle asked a series of questions of the
Jewish school committee for that *canton*. He wanted to know
the size of the five-to-fifteen-year-old male population and the
state of education and training among the Jews.[6]

The Haut-Rhin philanthropic committee and its *école de
travail* in Mulhouse had, as we have said, alienated the Colmar
consistory. Yet in 1850 even the conservative members of the
Colmar consistory called for the elimination of begging and the
opening of trade schools (*écoles d'arts et métiers*) in each of
the communities. They announced the institution of a program
in modern religious education, including an examination on the
official catechism, as a requirement for the Bar Mitzvah celebration. They even drew up a program for the celebration of
confirmation (*initiation religieuse*), which they appended to
their announcement of their altered stance.[7]

When attempts at regeneration were resisted by the population, the consistory tried to find methods to enforce its
decisions. In 1829 the Paris consistory decided to withhold
charity from poor parents who neither sent their children to the
consistory's primary school, nor had them learn a trade.[8] It is
not known whether this threat was actually implemented, but
it was repeated in 1832, 1834, and 1841.[9] The Strasbourg
consistory minutes of 1858 mention this Parisian practice in
connection with a similar provision in Strasbourg.[10]

The charity committee of Paris continued to warn against conduct it found improper. In 1845 it threatened to cut from the charity rolls parents who, despite warnings, allowed their daughters to pose for artists.[11]

The major methods of the consistories and individuals of promoting regeneration consisted of establishing primary and trade schools, forming societies and committees to eliminate begging, and encouraging apprenticeship and work. Finally, there were some programs to encourage agriculture. Some proponents of a return to the soil wanted to establish a farm school and model farm in France. Others advised emigration to Algeria. The agricultural debate continued throughout the first half of the century and found new inspiration when European Jews, in the 1840's, began raising money for an agricultural project in Palestine, and again in the 1860's when the *Alliance Israélite Universelle* began its work for an agricultural colony in Palestine. But despite publicity and pledges of funds for a French Jewish agricultural school, the project did not materialize.

1. Schools

Nineteenth-century French liberalism placed great stress on the school as a prime institution conducive to progress. For the Jews it was no different. "Regeneration" meant immersion in French language, culture, and mores. It meant acquiring skills that would be essential in the acquisition of useful jobs. The school was the institution that could satisfy these needs. Prior to the Revolution Jewish schools in France were traditional religious institutions that did not teach secular subjects. Wealthy commercial families, to be sure, acquired the French language and culture, and Sephardi families, because of their particular history and demographic balance, were less noticeably non-integrated, even at an early date. By the time the consistories were created there was a generation of enthusiastic liberals among the Ashkenazim. They blessed the French Revolution (if they did not worship it), and they dreamed of a network of Jewish schools which would mold a new brand of *Israélite français.*

Initiative in the actual creation of schools was divided between the consistory and "enlightened" individuals. During the Empire the central consistory requested permission to open schools, but it was not forthcoming. When the first schools were finally opened, they were the work of private individuals, although they were immediately put under the protection of the consistories. Consistorial schools were all organized along modern lines. The most prevalent pedagogical method was the "mutual" system, perfected at the turn of the nineteenth century by Lancaster and Bell in England.[12] Curricula included French reading and writing, mathematics, and sometimes rudimentary sciences, history, and geography. This reflected the contemporary curriculum in all French primary schools. By 1821 there were twelve modern primary schools for Jewish students in France. They were located in six of the seven consistory seats (only Colmar had none), and in six other towns: Thionville and Sarreguemines, in the Metz district; Haguenau, in the Strasbourg district; and three in the Haut-Rhin: Bergheim, Sierentz and Ribeauvillé.[13]

Centralized supervision of these schools did not yet exist. Through their school committees, the consistories succeeded in keeping an eye on the education of the poor in their own towns. Outside these cities curricula and standards were at the discretion of the individual communities.

In 1818 the central consistory had already seen the need for a uniform religion textbook, and had solicited manuscripts. In 1820 the central consistory adopted the *Précis Elémentaire* of Samuel Cahen. The *Précis* and its subsequent additions and imitations were frequently referred to as "catechisms," by analogy with the Catholic texts, whose question and answer format they adopted.

In analyzing the development of modern Jewish schooling, we must bear in mind the contemporary state of primary education among the general population. Although an 1816 law had required all communities to maintain schools, it had been materially impossible to enforce. The 1833 *Loi Guizot* restated this obligation, adding a coercive factor: the government was empowered to add educational expenses to municipal budgets. Where local resources proved insufficient, the government could grant subsidies. Even so, the movement was slow and varied from one part of the country to another. There was a much higher rate of illiteracy in rural than in urban areas. Conditions until well after the middle of the century were often very primitive: schools lacked decent quarters and were often short of paper, pens and ink. One of the biggest problems they faced was a lack of uniform textbooks. The schools were staffed by underpaid, often underqualified, and generally overworked teachers, who frequently combined teaching functions with all manner of church duties, from janitorial work, to singing, to grave digging. Although both supervision and inspection were required by several laws and court decisions of the 1830's, 40's and 50's, they were often perfunctory, or even fictitious. Against this background, the progress of the Jewish schools seems favorable. The growth of a Jewish primary school system was, nevertheless, slow and beset both by financial difficulties and resistance from the population. State and municipal aid to the schools was nowhere a requirement. The 1833 *Loi Guizot* only *allowed* municipal aid, thereby leaving total discretion to local authorities. Although the 1850 *Loi Falloux* required, where the population warranted it, separate public schools for the children of the various religions, municipalities (especially in Alsace) continued to refuse to allocate funds for Jewish schools, and the Ministry of Public Education could not, or would not, find a means of forcing them to do so.

Consistory control and supervision varied with time and place. That of the central consistory was minimal for many years. Although it had approved and recommended several texts for use in Jewish schools, conditions prevented the realization of the goal of uniformity in school curricula. After soliciting manuscripts for the religion textbook, the central consistory failed to take any further initiative with regard to the schools for almost thirty years. It is true that consistory members read many books submitted to them over the years, and decided whether to approve them for use in the schools, but they did not solicit such works or offer prizes for them. They did not issue instructions, gather information, or in any way stimulate the development of the schools.

Because the departmental consistories saw the school as an instrument of regeneration and integration, they were not generally concerned with its faithful maintenance of the traditional religious heritage. What they expected from religious education was instruction in religion as morality, which would be conducive to good citizenship and economic utility.

In 1831 the government assumed some of the cost of financing Jewish institutions. As part of this program it offered to assume the cost of printing a textbook for use in the public Jewish schools. The central consistory decided to issue a revised edition of Cahen's *Précis,* and it developed and extended the section which stressed religion as morality.[14]

Although the central consistory did not take any initiative in inspecting or supervising the schools, the departmental consistories did do so. In 1830, upon his accession to the throne, Louis-Philippe announced that he would organize methods of inspecting the primary schools of the various cults. By *arrêté* of April 17, 1832, it was decided to form in the *chefs-lieux* of the seven consistories committees of surveillance and encouragement for the Jewish schools. The committees were to be composed mainly of Jews. Similar committees would be established in *arrondissements* with sufficient Jewish population.

The April 17, 1832 *arrêté* specifying the inspection procedures for Jewish schools also listed certain kinds of data that should be obtained concerning the number of pupils who paid and the number who were instructed free of charge, the subjects taught, and the number of teachers. The consistories did not have this data, however, not even for their own departments, and the central consistory had none whatsoever. In 1833 the Metz consistory distributed a questionnaire to its various communities, in an effort to obtain the required data. Thus the initiative for much of this kind of useful supervision came from the government.[15]

In Paris the minutes prior to 1833 reveal no discussions about desirable improvements for the schools. On January 8, 1833, shortly after the institution of the new *comité cantonnal* prescribed by the 1832 decision, two of its members suggested to the Paris consistory some ways of improving the schools.[16] A certain tension then developed between the consistory and this *comité*, and Léon Kahn assumes that this was one of the factors that led the consistory to ask for the "communalization" of the schools.[17]

The consistories had financial reasons also for seeking to turn their Jewish schools into public schools. The 1831 law which accorded Judaism the benefit of state support had simultaneously deprived the consistories of the right to tax the Jews. The result was that institutions provided for by the 1831 law were protected, but all others were doomed to lack of funds. The schools were in the latter category.

It was not only economic considerations that made the consistory look favorably on the substitution of public for consistory schools. The consistories were anxious to rid themselves of the problem of supervising and administering the schools. Furthermore, they believed that public schools would be more effective in integrating Jewish pupils into French society.

The municipalities did not rush to build, equip, or staff Jewish schools, however, and did not even concern themselves with already existing schools that had been officially "communalized" (made into public schools). Thus in Paris the boys' school lacked decent quarters for several years after the consistory gave up its lease on the school rooms, in the expectation that the city would arrange suitable quarters. Because the city failed to construct a school building during the next ten years, the school was forced to move into an available small room in the temple building and to reduce its enrollment. Although the city was to blame for its lack of responsibility, the consistory, in its anxiety to rid itself of the school, had acted precipitously.

Even as the Paris municipality was beginning to assume responsibility for the Jewish schools, these schools were rapidly becoming insufficient for the needs of the poor Parisian Jewish population. Kahn has described in detail the work of the charity board in placing the overflow in private schools. The charity board paid tuition for these pupils, although part of the cost was eventually reimbursed by the city.[18] No advance planning for schools emerged. The consistory and the *comité* simply tried to plug the gaps as they occurred.

In Paris the charity board (*comité de bienfaisance*) was decidedly more active than the consistory, and frequently took independent decisions and actions. It was staffed by a group of men who were on a slightly lower rung in wealth and prominence than the consistory members. They were generally more devoted to Judaism, and this devotion, rather than any prestige they might acquire, was usually the motivation for their service. Inasmuch as French citizenship was a requirement for consistory membership, the *comité* frequently enjoyed the services of enthusiastic immigrant members who were not qualified for the higher offices. Benoît Cohen and Albert Cohn were two notable examples.

In 1846, while the city was completing two buildings to be used by the Jewish school, the *comité* took the initiative of hiring a teacher for fifty poor children. It made available its own meeting room for use as a classroom.[19]

In Strasbourg, as a result of the *Loi Guizot*, a *comité local de surveillance pour les écoles israélites de Strasbourg* was formed in 1834. Copies of this committee's correspondence through 1843 indicate that it handled mainly the administrative aspects of this school, although it *did* occasionally take action to improve the quality of its teaching. Thus, for example, it voted to dismiss a teacher because of the poor results he had achieved in the teaching of Hebrew.

It was only in 1842 that the Strasbourg consistory expressed any interest in opening a girls' school. In February 1843 the mayor of Strasbourg (probably in reply to the consistory's request for a girls' school) announced that in compliance with the law of June 23, 1833 (*Loi Guizot*), Adjunct Mayor Charles Boersch had been named to the school committee. Compliance had trailed enactment by ten years. This was typical of nineteenth-century compliance with laws on education.[20]

In some places, the 1831, 1832, and 1833 legislation prompted more regular inspections of the schools, and uniform instruction. But such an effect was very limited. In 1834 the Parisian Jewish school committee announced an examination of the students at the boys' school. At the same time a Mme. Bernheim was appointed to organize a group of women for a similar examination of the girls. This was done in compliance with the 1832 *arrêté*. Many schools, however, especially those far from consistory seats, were not supervised according to the requirements of the law.

The central consistory was still relatively unimportant as a motivator or coordinator of primary education. In 1834 it solicited information from the departmental consistories on the numbers of schools in the various districts and the type of instruction received by the children.[21] It is hardly likely that the central consistory acted spontaneously; evidently the government had requested the data, as it had in 1832.

In general, government inspections of the Jewish schools, both the public ones and those of the Jewish community, occurred with great irregularity. However, some inspections may have taken place without any contact being made with the consistory, and we may therefore lack records of them.

According to a historian of French education in the nineteenth century, the departments of Lorraine were among the most active in creating and inspecting their primary schools.[22] It is not surprising, therefore, that the first instance of a *comité local d'instruction primaire* inspecting a Jewish primary school in a small town occurred in this province, in the town of Hellimer. On August 1, 1838, the *comité local* in Hellimer informed the Metz consistory of its entire satisfaction with the quality of the schools in its district.[23]

The Strasbourg consistory was the first to take the initiative in introducing periodic inspections of the schools. Its minutes of June 15, 1842, report this decision:

M. Samuel signalant l'état déplorable où se trouve l'instruction primaire dans beaucoup de communes propose de désigner chaque année un membre du consistoire pour inspecter les écoles.[24]

In requesting government funds for this purpose, the consistory argued that the state inspectors do a good job of supervising the secular education of the Jewish schools, but they obviously cannot inspect the religious instruction:

Messieurs les Inspecteurs de l'université remplissent leur devoir avec conscience, mais l'enseignement religieux n'est pas dans leurs attributions.[25]

It is probable that the consistory's claim to be interested only in the religious part of the curriculum was tactical. The best case for government funding could be made by stressing religious supervision. Although the consistory does not appear to have received the requested funds, Grand Rabbi Aron did make several inspection trips, and it is clear from his 1843 report that he was not solely interested in religious education. Progress toward regeneration is what the consistory was looking for, and Rabbi Aron commended the work of the communal rabbis toward this goal. He spoke of the zeal that the local rabbis manifested in their educational work:

Tous rivalisent d'efforts pour perfectionner l'instruction de la jeunesse, pour diriger celle-ci vers les occupations utiles, tous désignent la religion comme base d'une bonne éducation, enfin tous sympathisent avec l'école de travail à Strasbourg.[26]

Although supervision of the schools remained inadequate, in 1847 there was a sudden increase in interest in school inspections. The Metz girls' school was inspected in 1847 by a *comité des dames surveillantes des écoles israélites des filles* which reported to the Metz consistory that the religious education needed reorganizing.[27] In the same year the rabbi of Soulzmatt informed the Colmar consistory of the pressing need to improve religious instruction in the Haut-Rhin. This departmental consistory could not decide what to do, and transmitted the rabbi's complaint to the central consistory. The central consistory notified Colmar that the problem should be handled locally.[28]

Two months later Grand Rabbi Ennery, recently elected to the central consistory as Grand Rabbi of France, advised the departmental consistories how to supervise teachers and choose school books.[29] This was the first time in thirty years of existence that the central consistory took the initiative in the practical aspects of running the primary schools. In November of the same year Eugène Halphen accepted the function of inspector of Jewish schools in Paris.[30]

What caused the flurry of activity in 1847? In 1845 the government, aware of the insufficiency of inspection procedures for public schools, had developed a plan for centralizing primary school inspections.[31] It appears likely that the inspection of Jewish schools in Metz and the Haut-Rhin and the central consistory initiative all reflect governmental requirements.

In the case of Ennery's initiative, however, there are other possible explanations. All newly inaugurated grand rabbis circulated pastoral letters, indicating the direction which they hoped to give to French Judaism. It is also possible that Ennery's 1847 letter was influenced by Adolphe Franck, who had been elected to the central consistory in 1844. Franck held strong views concerning the need for educational improvements and was active in campaigning for them.[32]

The inspection system for the public primary schools remained spotty and often fictitious throughout much of the century. But in 1854 the Strasbourg consistory organized a system of semi-weekly inspections and semi-annual reports to be carried out by the rabbis in the communities of their districts. Although concerned largely with the quality of religious education, they also reported on enrollment and on children who were receiving no education. The Strasbourg consistory corresponded with its delegates (the *commissaires surveillants*) in these towns and urged them to encourage parents to send their children to school. In 1858 the Strasbourg consistory asked that the communities deny charity to families that refused to send their children to school.[33] At a time when French children in rural areas were still often illiterate,[34] this kind of involvement by the consistories is an indication of a sustained effort to regenerate the Jewish population.

The educational situation was critical in the Haut-Rhin district of Alsace, where popular anti-Jewish feeling and low consistory enthusiasm combined to prevent the creation of a sufficient number of publicly supported Jewish schools. Jewish communities and individuals complained frequently of the lack of schools, and the ministry was often consulted. In 1861, in the wake of the manipulated elections which brought enthusiastic "reformers" into the Colmar consistory, the consistory became more active. It decided to improve education by granting aid to Jewish communities that could not afford to maintain a school, and it instituted annual inspections of the Jewish schools of the Haut-Rhin. In a letter to the central consistory it explained these new measures to help the poor of its district:

il est bien douloureux de voir de nos jours des enfants privés de toute instruction religieuse, parce que leurs parents sont trop

*pauvres pour entretenir un instituteur. Le consistoire a voulu
pourvoir, et, dans ce but, a formé dans son sein, un fonds
consistorial destiné, en partie, à venir au secours de ces pauvres
communautés. . .*

*Le consistoire a encore décidé, dans l'intérêt de l'instruction
primaire qu'il visitera tous les ans les écoles israélites de
Haut-Rhin.*[35]

In 1855 the Metz consistory decided to institute annual conferences of the teachers in the district's Jewish schools. The
rabbi of Sarreguemines was asked to hold local conferences in
his district. The instigator of this plan was Gerson Levy, book-
store owner, newspaper editor, activist in the development of
public schools, and Jewish school committee member for the
Metz area for many years.[36]

Fund-raising for the schools was an area where consistories
and charity boards could have taken greater initiative. The
schools were in constant financial peril; teachers were forced to
combine several jobs in order to be certain of an income. In
Strasbourg, when the school committee was established in 1834,
it paid one half of the back wages owed to the teachers, who
were required to waive their claims to the remainder!

Only the Strasbourg consistory was really active in fund-
raising for education. It raised money to support its vocational
school (which served the entire district) by insisting that local
communities write into their budgets an allowance for that
school. It used its prerogative of approving local budgets in
order to enforce this ruling. Unfortunately, the consistory did
not go further and use its right of supervision of local budgets
to allocate funds for community schools. As we have already
seen, however, the consistory did undertake regular inspections
of the schools, and it did encourage their improvement, inter-
ceding to urge municipalities to contribute toward their
maintenance.

Often it was individual initiative and unsolicited philanthropy,
rather than the Jewish institutions, which came to the rescue.
The Rothschilds and Furtados were among the benefactors of
Jewish schools. In 1840 Moyse Alcan published a book of
poetry (inspired by the Damascus Affair) for the benefit of the
free Girls' School of Metz. Mme. la Baronne de Rothschild
subscribed for 100 copies.[37]

After they learned reading, writing, and arithmetic in the free
primary schools, the children of the poor needed vocational
training. However, if it was difficult to enforce school attendance because of financial hardships caused by the loss of
the children's small peddling incomes, it was even more difficult
to convince families to allow older children to receive vocational training. Beginning in the 1820's there developed societies to encourage, place, and assist apprentices. Trade schools
were also established. They were instrumental in convincing
many parents to give their children vocational training, because

in them it was possible to observe Jewish religious practices, including abstention from work on holidays. Religious observance was often an impossibility in apprenticeship programs.

It was in Strasbourg that the first trade school (*Ecole de Travail*) was established, in 1825, four years before even the rabbinic school had opened. Some years later Noé Noé of Bordeaux wrote that this was the only school to have been established by consistory initiative; all the others, he claimed, were the result of private initiative.[38] From 1855, as we have seen, the Strasbourg consistory required all the communities of its district to budget a fixed annual sum for support of the school. Although there were at first objections, this measure eventually guaranteed the school the security of a regular income.[39]

A similar institution was founded in 1842 in Mulhouse (Haut-Rhin) by the initiative of individuals, independent of consistory effort. Despite the fact that in 1839 the consistory had nominated a commission to found a trade school (*une école d'arts et métiers*) and to eliminate begging, Leon Werthe, president of the Philanthropic Society of Haut-Rhin, complained in 1844 to the central consistory that the Colmar consistory members took no interest in the new trade school.[40] Funds for the Mulhouse school were raised in a variety of ways; in 1849 a local rabbi, S. Dreyfus, published and sold copies of a sermon.[41]

In 1844 Créhange tried in vain to have a similar school established in Paris.[42] The Paris consistory continued its policy of placing children in apprenticeship when they left the consistorial school, but the orthodox complained that these children were not permitted to fulfil religious obligations. The *Ecole de Travail* of Paris was not established until 1865.

In 1847 Jérome Aron, editor of the Strasbourg journal *L'Ami des Israélites,* campaigned unsuccessfully for additional trade schools. Arguing for the need to train workers, he stressed the idea that only work can ensure a livelihood and thereby guarantee morality. Despite excellent results and high tribute paid to them from all quarters, the Haut-Rhin and Bas-Rhin trade schools remained without imitators until 1865.

2. Societies, Commissions, and Training Programs to Combat Begging and Train Skilled Workers

Regeneration efforts were also aimed at eliminating two practices common among the Jews of the eastern provinces: begging and money-lending. Efforts to eradicate these practices were the repeated theme of several private and consistorial committees. In 1837, in an effort to put an end to such practices, the Colmar consistory requested permission to impose religious punishments on people who disregarded the consistory's prohibition. The central consistory ruled, however, that Colmar could not impose religious penalties.[43] In 1839 the Colmar consistory tried to reach the same goal in another way: it proposed the creation of a vocational training school. This school eventually came into being but was not in itself sufficient to solve the problem completely. The situation was similar in the Bas-Rhin, where the trade school had existed since 1825.

Several times committees were organized in the Bas-Rhin and the Haut-Rhin (sometimes jointly, sometimes separately) to handle the dual prohibitions against usury and begging.[44]

There were also continuous attempts to encourage job training and manual labor. Although much of this encouragement stemmed from the initiative of private individuals, these were not always wealthy philanthropists. Regeneration of the poor population was a liberal ideal, enthusiastically embraced by much of the educated and enlightened population. Such individuals often waged verbal battles against the consistories, who, they claimed, did nothing to discharge their obligations to the poor.

The critics were not wrong. Although the consistories were continually plagued with financial difficulties, there was much they could have done in providing leadership and recruiting private philanthropic aid. Instead, the role of leadership was exercised by others, such as Olry Terquem. In Paris, in 1823, Terquem founded a *Société des amis du travail,* apparently under the influence of David Singer. The *Société* undertook the placement of apprentices and the raising of funds through subscriptions. It had limited success, mainly because orthodox parents refused to put their children into apprenticeship programs that did not permit Jewish observance. At the time of its dissolution (in 1834) the society was supporting very few children, although it had the resources for placing more. Perhaps its most significant influence was on the outlook of the French Jewish population, especially on consistory members. When the society dissolved, its members were determined that this kind of work would continue. They met with the Paris consistory, members of the charity board, and some of the Parisian *notables,* and discussed other means of improving the education and the job training received by the poor: "l'on devait s'occuper de réaliser le voeu de tous les hommes qui veulent franchement la régénération des Israélites indigents."[45]

The consistory's charity board then took over the work of encouraging and placing apprentices, but with no better results. In 1839 the Paris consistory decided on a reorganization of the charity board, and a new membership was elected and installed. It was charged with the task of handling several kinds of charitable work: distributing aid to the poor, founding a Jewish hospital, and deciding on a means for reviving the *amis de travail* to encourage the learning of trades.[46] The charity board continued to handle the placement of apprentices for several years, and in 1846 a *société de patronage des apprentis et ouvriers israélites de Paris* was organized by some private individuals, notably Albert Cohen (who served as the agent for funneling Rothschild charity into the community). Central consistory member Hemerdinger urged the central consistory to take the new society under its protection, but the consistory declined, as an institution, to patronize it. As individuals, the members announced, they were all favorably disposed to the new society.[47]

The Paris consistory was not more encouraging. Although it admitted that the project had merit, the consistory stressed that its own charity board did much of the same type of work. The consistory "regretted" its lack of funds to aid the new society.[48]

Private attempts to organize charity for poor immigrants met with no greater encouragement from the consistory. Although mass immigration did not begin until the 1880's, there was a constant light stream of Central and Eastern European Jews into France. In 1846, when a "Society for the Aid of Poor Foreigners" was organized in Paris, the Paris consistory reacted by warning the Police Prefect that the society was not under its auspices. The consistory's position, as stated by Halphen during the May 8th meeting, was that under the appearance of morality this group could tend to attract poor Jews from other countries to the generosity of Paris. Some of the people attracted might not be worthy of this hospitality, the consistory claimed.[49] We may conclude that one of the official methods of regeneration was discouraging the arrival of untrained poor Jews from foreign countries.

A similar situation existed in other consistory districts. In 1825 a group of prominent Jews in Nancy organized a society to encourage skilled work among the Jews. They raised funds through subscriptions, and acquired the voluntary services of a physician, Dr. Turc.[50] Similarly, in the Haut-Rhin district, in 1835, a *société d'encouragement pour l'instruction, les arts et métiers* was organized by private individuals, including the lawyer Hemerdinger.[51] This society was obviously the impetus that caused the Colmar consistory to nominate an 1839 committee for a like purpose.[52]

In order to finance the work of its new committee, the Colmar consistory required the communities of the district to pledge sums for this purpose and divide the cost among the local population. The contribution was by no means voluntary. The consistory threatened to use government aid to collect the money if it was not forthcoming:

vous aurez à nommer une commission locale, composée de 5 membres, qui aura à faire la répartition de la cotisation à laquelle vous aurez été imposés par l'assemblée générale des délégués et des membres de notre commission.[53]

In Bordeaux, also, the initiative came from private sources. Mme. Robles (founder of the first free boys' school) undertook to place poor Jewish boys in apprenticeship and to aid them financially. Between 1826 and 1838 her committee received 600 francs per year from the department, but this subvention was stopped when the boys' school became a public school and the department could not find sufficient funds to aid both institutions. Grand Rabbi Marx appealed for a revival of the support, comparing the Gironde with the department of the Bas-Rhin, where, since 1832, 500 francs per year had been allocated to help finance Jewish apprentices. He told the prefect that the work of the society helped prevent vagabondage and peddling:

depuis l'année 1826 jusqu'en 1838, Mme. Robles recevait une somme annuelle de 600 fr. pour un comité dont elle fait partie et qui s'occupe du placement et de l'encouragement des apprentis indigents israélites. Ce comité a fait beaucoup de bien parmi la classe indigente de nos coreligionnaires. Bon nombre d'enfants pauvres qui, abandonnés à eux-mêmes et à la misère de leurs parents, se seraient livrés au vagabondage et au colportage, se trouvent aujourd'hui, grâce aux encouragements du comité, dans une position heureuse, pourvoyant honorablement par leur industrie aux besoins de leurs familles.[54]

Almost everywhere the pattern was repeated: first, energetic individuals, critical of the lack of initiative manifested by the consistories in more than fifteen years of existence, took the initiative to create societies to encourage work; the consistories later became involved as nominal or real administrators of the groups.

In Strasbourg, the situation appears, however, to have been different. Its Society for the Encouragement of Work (founder, in 1825, of the *école de travail*) seems to have been consistory-organized. Again, in 1853, the Strasbourg consistory took similar action. It decided to form a *société pour l'amélioration matérielle et intellectuelle des nos coreligionnaires.* Four local committees were established, one in each of the four *arrondissements* of the department.[55] Consistory members realized that regeneration had not yet occurred, almost fifty years after the foundation of the consistory system, and that vigorous action on their part was going to be required in order to achieve it. M. Hirtz, of the consistory, warned his colleagues that the Jews of the countryside were hardly likely to cooperate without being threatened: "il faut leur inspirer la crainte de poursuites directes." Grand Rabbi Aron cooperated by addressing a circular to the delegates in which he asked them to single out any Jews who refused to cooperate with this charitable work.[56]

Proceeding vigorously, the consistory collected reports on the economic state of Jews all over its district and supervised the collection of funds in the communities. The *commissaire surveillant* in Marmoutier was dismissed from his post for failing to contribute.[57] A *Comité Central* in Strasbourg (with Achille Ratisbonne at its head) coordinated the work on this project. Its preferred method of regeneration was emigration to the United States. During a four-year period the funds collected helped about forty Jews to emigrate. Around 1856 the committee ceased to exist.[58]

Poverty and begging continued to be a problem among the Jews of Alsace throughout the 1860's. In 1862 another joint commission for the elimination of begging was formed by the Strasbourg and Colmar consistories.[59] But the Alsatian poverty problem was "solved" only in 1870, when the department was lost to Germany.

3. Agriculture

The idea of the Jews taking up agriculture was an old one that had developed under the *ancien régime* and had become an important part of the ideology of the emancipation. Hertzberg traces the idea back to the Abbé Claude Fleury, whose book *Les moeurs des Israélites* was written at the end of the seventeenth century. Fleury believed that the way to regenerate the Jew was to encourage him to take up agriculture. The popularity of the book in the eighteenth century suggests to Hertzberg that it was a prime factor in the later development of the theme.[60]

Toward the end of the eighteenth century the theme was repeated by Christian Dohm, in a pamphlet written on behalf of the Alsatian Jews. Shortly after that, in 1784, the Jews of Alsace were permitted by royal decree to rent farms.[61] It seemed as if the Jew might, after all, return to the soil.

No large-scale agricultural movement developed, however, and the pastoral ideology continued to find proponents through the nineteenth century. In 1820 Grand Rabbi Wittersheim of Metz, in his inaugural address, urged the Jews to leave their accustomed profession of second-hand dealing and return to agriculture.[62]

From 1825 the *société d'encouragement au travail* in Strasbourg considered fostering agriculture, but its efforts were finally directed to running the trade school instead. In 1831 the Strasbourg consistory, dissatisfied with the progress of Jewish regeneration, appointed a committee to study the obstacles that still existed and to suggest the means of overcoming them. The committee's report urged three means of regeneration: education, job training, and agriculture. These ideas were not new. The committee, in fact, acknowledged that it was repeating ideas that Strasbourg consistory members had long been expounding. Its own innovation was the proposal that a model farm be created.[63]

In 1835 a philanthropic society (*société philanthropique*) was formed in the Haut-Rhin, and in 1842 this society founded a trade school (*école d'arts et métiers*). According to one of the founders, it had also attempted several times to found a Jewish agricultural colony, and had contacted the central consistory for support for the plan. The central consistory deliberated the request, and, together with S. Cahen, editor of the *Archives Israélites,* decided to encourage it. They urged the *Société philanthropique du Haut-Rhin* to seek the aid of the Rothschilds and other wealthy Jews in France and Germany.[64] After two years without any success, and lacking the support of their own consistory, this society contacted the Strasbourg consistory in an attempt to organize jointly a school of agriculture for the two departments.[65] The Alsatian agricultural school project remained a live issue for the next twenty-five years.

Algeria was considered by some a better location for agricultural projects. Several plans to establish Jews from France and Eastern Europe in Algeria were discussed during the forties and fifties. Seen as a solution to problems of poverty in Alsace and persecution in Russia and Poland, these plans envisaged settling the proposed immigrants on the land. In 1846 J. I. Altaras, a wealthy merchant and ship owner in Marseille who did business with Algeria, undertook personally to arrange for the settlement of Russian and Polish Jews in Algeria. His plan failed (partly because it was rejected by the French War Ministry, which governed Algeria), but the idea did not die quickly, and the *Archives Israélites* repeated it several years later.[66] In 1858 an Algerian journal took up the issue and urged implementation of the plan. This article recommended the resettlement project not only to rescue Jews from oppression but to regenerate them: "car c'est à nos yeux le moyen le plus puissant pour régénérer la race israélite."[67]

The 1853 Strasbourg commission for the regeneration of the Jews, which accomplished little other than the embarkation to America of a few dozen poor Alsatian Jews, had considered the encouragement of agriculture in Alsace as a means of improving the Jewish position. Although the commission and some prominent individuals were in favor of such a plan, the president of the consistory, Louis Ratisbonne, opposed it on grounds of impracticality. Several months later the consistory reconsidered the issue, but Ratisbonne insisted that with no Jewish farmers or landowners in Alsace, trained Jewish farm workers would find no market for their skills. The consistory took a formal decision to encourage industrial trades in preference, saying that "avec quelques outils un ouvrier trouve toujours de l'occupation."[68]

Ratisbonne's assumptions were not entirely correct. In 1860–61 a study was made by M. Masse of the Strasbourg consistory on the situation of agriculture among the Jewish population of the Bas-Rhin. Masse found that although there was only one Jew in the department who did farm labor (in Niederroedern), there were several Jews who owned land cultivated by Christian workers. (Another group of Jews, he said, possessed land for investment but did not exploit it agriculturally.) He recommended that the consistory try to interest wealthy Jews in buying land for agricultural exploitation.[69] There are records of two

Jewish landowners in other departments whose land was used for farming: Léopold Javal of the Yonne and M. Worms of the Vosges.[70]

In 1855 the Metz consistory received a large donation from Mme. la Duchesse de Plaisance. The income from this foundation was to be used to place poor children in apprenticeship, and the Metz consistory enrolled the first beneficiaries of the charity in a model farm that existed in Forbach. When this farm closed, however, the consistory was unable to convince any families to place their children in apprenticeships on private farms. Jewish parents feared Christian religious influence on the children who would be living with Christian farmers.[71]

In March 1862 the four eastern consistories (Nancy, Metz, Strasbourg, and Colmar) held a joint meeting to discuss the proposition of establishing an agricultural school. At the close of their meeting they issued a statement on the importance of encouraging agriculture: "Populariser l'agriculture parmi les Israélites, c'est enlever le germe du pauperisme, c'est donner une autre direction à cette population exubérante et nomade qui est l'aliment de la mendicité."[72] The central consistory approved the agricultural project, emphasizing the importance of such an institution:

un établissement consacré à faire prendre à nos jeunes co-religionnaires le goût de l'agriculture. Nous voudrions les pousser dans cette voie, qui aurait le double avantage de les faire sortir des habitudes d'un commerce qui n'est pas toujours en rapport avec les exigences de notre époque, et ensuite, de les initier à cette grande existence agricole dont l'Ecriture nous a laissé un si magnifique tableau, et qui conduirait les générations qui nous suivent, non seulement à la fortune, mais, ce qui vaut encore mieux, à la considération publique.[73]

The Metz consistory responded to this circular by expressing their enthusiastic hopes for the establishment of an agricultural school. It promised that if the school were created, the Metz consistory would provide some scholarships from the Duchesse de Plaisance charitable fund established for the placement of apprentices.[74]

In the meantime, the *Alliance Israélite Universelle* was founded in 1860, and by 1863 had begun to express interest in agricultural projects. In May of that year the *Alliance* named a commission to report on the possibility of founding an agricultural colony in Alsace.[75] Three years later, on December 3, 1866, the Central Committee of the *Alliance* recommended agriculture as a means of improving the situation of the Jews in Palestine. It took five years (1866–71) for this recommendation to lead to the opening of an agricultural colony (Mikveh Israel) near Jaffa. During those years the *Alliance* campaigned extensively for funds to cover the enormous costs involved in the clearing and planting of the land and for the necessary construction. French Jews contributed generously to the Palestinian agricultural project advocated by *Alliance* founder Charles Netter, a Parisian Jew. But in France no colony emerged. The *Alliance's* own 1863 hope for one seems to have been abandoned. The consistories and the various committees dropped the project.

In 1868, while the *Alliance* was developing the agricultural school of Jaffa, Léon Werthe (who had been instrumental in the founding of the *école d'arts et métiers* of Mulhouse almost thirty years earlier) undertook to found an agricultural colony for French Jews. He launched an appeal for subscriptions and announced that about twenty acres of land had already been donated.[76]

Although the *Archives Israélites* published his appeal and opened a subscription in its columns, this reform journal expressed disapproval of the plan. Werthe was very hurt and angry. Yet this time it appeared that a French Jewish agricultural colony might succeed. Land and money were donated. By May 1868 (less than a year after Werthe's appeal), 6270 francs had been contributed for the project. Werthe published the amounts he had collected, together with his correspondence with skeptics and supporters. Among his supporters was the director of a successful non-Jewish agricultural colony that had opened with resources of only 2950 francs and one teacher. The Alsatian Jewish agricultural colony seemed on the verge of materializing, but the following year, as a result of the Franco-Prussian War, France lost Alsace.

C. Police

The third task attributed to the consistories, that of police, was their primary role in the eyes of Napoleon. It was with the idea of ensuring proper control of the Jews (this "dangerous" element) that Napoleon had convened the Assembly of Notables. In November 1806 Napoleon's delegates (*commissaires*), who had been working together with nine representatives of the Assembly to plan the consistory system, stressed to Napoleon the advantage of imposing consistorial supervision over the Jews. The consistories would, in turn, be accountable to the government.[77] Napoleon himself emphasized in a note of June 1807 that the consistories "doivent exercer une police sévère sur les rabbins."[78]

Grand Rabbi David Sinzheim (member of the Assembly of Notables, president of the Sanhedrin, and later central consistory grand rabbi), writing to the Ministry of Cults, reflects on the purpose of the government in creating the consistories. Sinzheim places the police functions before the administrative ones: "Le gouvernement a voulu, dans la création des consistoires, conformité de doctrine, soumission aux lois, centralisation de rapports de travaux, de correspondance."[79] Despite Georges Wormser's claim that the Assembly had accepted these police functions against its will, only about four members had bothered to protest the provisions for registering Jews, supplying lists of army conscripts and denouncing indigent Jews. These four *notables* argued that the consistories' job should be to administer religious institutions and not to police fellow Jews. But their view did not prevail.[80]

Despite the liberal philosophy of the pre-revolutionary and revolutionary theoreticians, it was not really possible to maintain a conception of Judaism as limited exclusively to matters of faith and piety, or organization of ceremony and ritual. The consistories, like the Jewish syndics and community organizations of the eighteenth century, were delegates of the government, and their prime function was to police the Jewish community on behalf of the government.

A typical example of the police role of eighteenth-century Jewish leaders is the case of Prussia. The Prussian Jewish constitution of 1750 required that all Jews belong to the community and accept the authority of the rabbis and elders. The rabbi was required to report to the authorities anything which threatened the government: "The [rabbi] . . . upon noticing that something is happening in Jewry which concerns Our and Our country's highest interests, shall reveal the same instantly [to the authorities]."[81] Earlier in the eighteenth century, in Berlin, a court Jew, Marcus Magnus, had been directed by the authorities "to attend the meetings of the Jewish elders in the name of his Majesty, faithfully and diligently to safeguard his best interests."[82]

In the Ashkenazi communities of early modern Europe, it was common for the appointment of *kehilla* (Jewish community) officers to be ratified by the authorities, who required an oath of allegiance. Jewish leaders, Jacob Katz says, "were responsible to the authorities for the actions of individuals, and they were asked, on occasion, to punish individual violators of the law, or even to surrender them to the authorities for trial."[83]

Arthur Hertzberg reports a similar situation regarding the eighteenth-century Jewish communities in France. Speaking of Alsace, Hertzberg says, "The prime function of the parnass was to carry out the orders of the local nobleman."[84] Similar surveillance responsibilities assigned to the consistories in the Napoleonic legislation fall into six specific categories: (1) the consistories were to exercise surveillance over the rabbis, making certain that everything the rabbis taught conformed to Sanhedrin doctrine; (2) they were to prevent the holding of unauthorized prayer meetings; (3) they were to register all Jews who arrived in the district from elsewhere, and (4) report those who had no apparent source of income; (5) they were to deliver certificates of good behavior which were necessary in order to get the *patente* to carry on business; and lastly, (6) they were to publish annual lists of conscripts.[85]

These provisions merely continued a pre-revolutionary attitude. The syndic of the Parisian Jews, just prior to the Revolution, had been Jacob Hollander, who was immediately responsible to the police lieutenant. No Jew could stay in Paris without the syndic's authorization, and Hollander was responsible for the behavior of the Parisian Jews.

Far from being reluctant to comply with the requirement that it police the Jews, the Paris consistory complained in 1811 that its rights of control were not being sufficiently respected by the Parisian police. As a result, the consistory was assured (on February 19, 1811) that in the future no Jews would receive a *permis de séjour* (permission for temporary residence) or a renewal of such permission without first obtaining a certificate from the consistory.[86]

During the Empire, the consistories took their authoritarian role very seriously. They policed the Jews at least as rigorously as the state would have done. Discussing the granting of certificates to enable Jews to obtain *patentes* for commerce, Anchel indicates the severity of consistory control: "Ils se firent un point d'honneur de se montrer très rigoureux envers leurs administrés et même ceux de Strasbourg et Wintzenheim prétendirent refuser leurs certificats à tous ceux qui ne se pliaient pas doucement à leurs ordres."[87] The job of reporting conscripts was not continued beyond the period of the First Empire. In Paris the last such list was drafted in 1812.[88]

Anchel points out that during the Empire no one protested against the consistory's police powers.[89] This was generally true in subsequent years as well. Although the consistories' role did change somewhat, so that conscripts were not reported, nor were the penniless turned over to the police, it is incorrect to state that the consistory's police functions disappeared.[90] The consistory long remained a police instrument of the state, and expressly referred to itself as a *civil* authority exercising supervision over the Jewish population. This view is manifest in an 1822 letter to Grand Rabbi Wittersheim of Metz, by Schwab, a member of the Metz consistory. Schwab writes of the need to exercise surveillance over the behavior of the Jewish population. If bad behavior of a *civil* nature is observed, he said, it is up to the consistory to intervene; if such behavior is of a *religious* nature, it is up to the grand rabbi to show the person his error:

Si la conduite d'un individu devient repréhensible, si c'est en matière civile, c'est au consistoire à le faire appeller pour le faire entrer dans le devoir; les exemples à cet égard, ne sont pas rares, est-ce en matière religieuse, c'est à vous monsieur le grand Rabin [sic] de la ramener par des paroles de paix.[91]

Not only did the consistories continue, after the Empire, to think of themselves as exercising police authority, but the government also believed this to be the case. This is clear in an 1828 report by the Paris Police Department. The Prefect had complained that there was a large element of the Jewish population that seemed to be at odds with the consistory. The police investigated and reported that there were many poor and fanatic Jews who considered themselves in exile in France and who resented the consistory's efforts to regenerate them. The honest Jews, the ones sincerely attached to France, were in favor of the consistories and consistory measures. But the large group of very poor Jews opposed the consistories because of their police function: "parce que les consistoires ont été établis précisément pour les surveiller et les réformer s'il est possible."[92]

Another way in which the consistories were expected to police the Jews was in regard to marriages. It will be remembered that one of the questions asked the Assembly of Notables by Napoleon's government had to do with marriages. In Jewish law a marriage was valid without any special ceremony, or the intervention of a rabbi. Only the presence of two witnesses was necessary. Napoleon's preoccupation with centralized bureaucracy and control over his empire extended to the proper recording of marriages by the state. He therefore required obedience to the civil laws controlling marriage and divorce. It was decided by the Sanhedrin that no rabbi could celebrate a marriage without evidence that the civil marriage had first been performed. But this did not solve the problem, as many traditional Jews, especially immigrants from the east, did not feel the need for a rabbi's presence at a wedding. All during the period under consideration, traditional Jewish marriages continued to be celebrated in France, often in ignorance of the law. Other times they indicated conscious opposition to the consistories and to modern synagogue marriages, introduced by the consistories to bring money into the treasury and imitate the Christian ritual.

In 1821 the *Tribunal de première instance* of the Seine asked Grand Rabbi de Cologna to explain exactly what constituted a legal marriage. Must it be performed by a rabbi? May the rabbi delegate his authority to someone else? The court insisted on the seriousness and urgency of this issue, indicating that it was very common for the Jews to neglect to be married in a civil marriage, as required by law: "La justice a absolument besoin pour fixer son opinion sur un délit qui malheureusement est très commun parmi les personnes de votre religion et que vous devez avoir le plus grand intérêt à punir."[93] Despite efforts to eliminate them, clandestine marriages continued to be celebrated. In 1825, acting on a complaint of the charity board, the Paris consistory adopted a measure to achieve proper registration of all marriages.[94] This unspecified measure was apparently unsuccessful. The problem was not unique to Paris, and the central consistory was asked to act on it. In 1833 the central consistory, in a circular letter to the departmental consistories, asked that a commission of consistory members be named in each district to examine together with the grand rabbis the following two questions:

*Is a religious marriage valid when a man and woman declare
themselves married with the usual formula, and before two witnesses, without the permission of the father or widowed
mother, and without any civil marriage?*

*If so, what are the religious means of putting this doctrine in
harmony with the civil legislation, which our religious laws
say we must obey?*[95]

The Paris consistory established a commission and filed a
report the following March.[96] We have not been able to locate a
copy of this report, or of any others that may have been written
in other districts. Whatever new measures may have been proposed in Paris, they were not successful. In September 1834 the
consistory decided that the charity board would no longer
grant aid to poor Jews who had not been married in accordance
with civil law. All the poor currently receiving aid were invited
to re-enroll themselves on the lists and bring proof of their civil
marriage.

The problem persisted. In 1839 a Paris consistory member
reported that a clandestine marriage had been celebrated by a
certain Mayer Marx. The consistory decided to obtain information on this violation of the civil law and turn it over to the
authorities.[97] A letter sent by the Paris consistory to the police
prefect in 1841 shows that the consistory understood French
Judaism's laws to be those of the Sanhedrin. The letter informed the police of a clandestine marriage which was about to
take place and said that such an act was a breach of both civil
law and religious law, the latter requiring, in France, obedience
to the Sanhedrin decisions. The consistory asked the police
prefect to prevent the marriage from taking place,[98] and this
was done.[99]

An interesting variation of the marriage problem occurred in
1844, when Grand Rabbi Ennery refused to perform a marriage between a Sr. Landsberg and a Mlle. Goldner, because he
heard that an attempt was going to be made to annul the civil
marriage. As a foreigner from a "country where marriages are
in the hands of the rabbis," Landsberg believed that the civil
marriage had no validity without the religious ceremony, and
when the rabbi did not perform the ceremony, he abandoned
the girl and left Paris. The consistory sharply reprimanded
Ennery for having made his decision alone.[100]

A significant number of Parisian Jews continued to marry
according to Jewish tradition and without bothering about a
civil marriage. In 1850 the Police transmitted a file of documents concerning such a marriage between Henriette Demuth
and M. Léon, celebrated by Isaac Cahen, "prétendu prêtre de
cette religion."[101]

The problem continued to trouble the consistories elsewhere,
too. As late as 1862 the Strasbourg consistory reported to the
central consistory that many secret marriages occurred in its

district, usually by foreigners who wished to avoid the bother of the civil marriage. Such marriages, the Strasbourg consistory said, are performed by a "soi-disant rabbin, sans avoir préalablement satisfait à la loi concernant le mariage civil." The central consistory, by this time, had lost its zeal for "informing." It counseled the Strasbourg consistory to take no action, inasmuch as no illegal ,act had been committed by any (officially recognized) rabbi.

The original police powers of the consistory included that of surveillance of the rabbis to be sure that they preached nothing that disagreed with the Sanhedrin decisions. Although there were no real problems of infractions of these decisions, the nature of the consistory system favored a continued policing of all clergy, cantors as well as rabbis. Before anyone received official appointment to such posts, a police investigation was conducted. The consistories did not participate in the compilation of these reports; they were done by the local police, mayor, prefects, etc. The system continued so long as the consistories were official bodies constituted to administer the cult (i.e., until the separation of church and state in 1905).

The consistories had undertaken the job of eliminating money-lending as a Jewish occupation, because it led frequently to charges of "usury." The *Commission d'enquête pour l'extirpation de l'usure et pour la fondation d'une école d'arts et métiers, et l'extinction de la mendicité* was named by the Colmar consistory on May 2, 1839. It proposed to seek out all instances of usury in the district and to turn the guilty over to the authorities for judicial action. It promised "une surveillance sévère, une enquête consciencieuse, et des rapports réguliers établis avec les autorités judiciaires et administratives du département."[102]

The consistories were even called upon to police the political behavior of the Jews. For example, the Prefect of the Bas-Rhin requested the Strasbourg consistory to use its influence to persuade Jews to vote for the government's officially endorsed candidates in the June 21, 1857 legislative elections. This was the first legislative election since the declaration of the Second Empire, and Louis Napoleon mobilized the entire machinery of the state bureaucracy to see that the official candidates were elected. The consistory cooperated by forwarding the request to all its delegates in the communities of the Bas-Rhin.[103] Although the Strasbourg consistory minutes are the only ones to reflect consistory involvement, there is little doubt that similar requests were addressed to the other Jewish consistories as well.

The consistories policed their constituents through their delegates in the communities, the *commissaires surveillants*. In 1821 the Metz consistory appointed to such a post in Sedan Israel Créange, manufacturer. His job was to inform the consistory of the behavior, sources of income, and morality of the Jews of Sedan, and to promote among them good behavior and useful occupations. He was to report all improper conduct to the consistory in order that it be referred to the authorities:

1º il tiendra le consistoire informé de la conduite de la moralité, des moyens d'existence de chacun des pères de famille israélite habitant le sus dit département.

2º il usera de toute son influence pour maintenir les israélites de ce département dans les bons principes et moraux. Il les exhortera à embrasser des états honorables, à élever leurs enfants dans l'amour du travail manuel, et il leur rappellera souvent ce qu'ils doivent à Dieu, au Roi, et à leurs semblables.

3º Il désignera au consistoire sans ménagement tout israélite qui se rendrait repréhensible par sa conduite et sa moralité, afin que le consistoire puisse le cas échéant, en reférer à l'autorité compétente.[104]

The government continued to regard the consistories as an arm of the state. In 1859 the Strasbourg consistory was notified by the Inspector of the Strasbourg Academy (investigator of primary education) of the existence in the department of several private Jewish schools whose directors had not made the necessary declarations. The consistory was asked to exercise greater surveillance, and the inspector threatened to prosecute such schools. The consistory sent a circular to its communal rabbis asking them to verify the legality of all schools.[105] The obligations of the elementary schools had been defined by the *Loi Falloux,* which provided for separate free schools for the various cults, under certain circumstances. Private schools could exist, if their teachers met certain standards. Jewish communities that were unable to obtain free Jewish schools in their towns maintained teachers at their own expense in order to avoid sending their children to the Christian-oriented public elementary schools. Such teachers were often also the cantors and ritual slaughterers. Frequently they were not properly qualified to teach.

Although the consistories no longer reported the foreign poor during our period, and although the 1844 *ordonnance* had dropped such a requirement from the laws, the consistories often took the initiative in preventing the settlement of foreign poor among themselves. There were two reasons for this: the consistories' charity funds were already strained, and they naturally sought to minimize the burden of the poor on the rest of the community. Secondly, poor foreign Jews presented an undesirable image to the general public. They were, by French standards, strangely dressed and dirty. They were thought of as dangerous, suspicious, barbaric, lazy, cunning. This was especially true of the small number of Polish Jews who began to arrive in Paris in the 1840's. Although by the 1840's the reporting of foreign poor for expulsion was no longer practiced, the Paris consistory notified the police that they could not vouch for the activities of the "Society for the Aid of Poor Foreigners." This indication of the consistory's bias against the foreign poor was not very different from its 1812 act of handing to the prefect a list of penniless Jews slated for expulsion. The times had not really changed.[106]

CHAPTER VII THREE FUNCTIONS NOT

ASSIGNED BY THE LEGISLATION

The consistories did not limit themselves to the functions prescribed by the law, but took it upon themselves to react as they saw fit to the situations that arose. We have discerned three primary areas of consistory activity that had not been required by legislation: protection of Jews, modernization of the rabbinate, and creation of a consistory monopoly on Jewish institutions.

A. Protection of the Jews

The consistories were moderately active in combatting anti-Jewish manifestations, in protecting Jewish rights, and in improving the public image of the Jew. Because they were reluctant to make themselves conspicuous, their methods were very conservative and defense measures took the form generally of discrete intervention with the authorities. Only in order to keep before the public eye the dignity of the semi-official consistories and their members did the consistories resort to publicity. Thus every time a new member was named to the Paris or central consistory, his name was inserted in the official journals.[1]

Immediately after their inception, the consistories began to concern themselves with Jewish welfare. One of the earliest acts of the central consistory was to solicit demographic data on the Jews for the period since the emancipation. They wanted to show proof of progress, in order to convince the government to nullify the "infamous acts" of 1808, which limited Jewish settlement in certain areas and required Jews to obtain patents for the exercise of business.

Throughout the rest of their official existence, the consistories continued to exercise this role they had first assumed in 1809. There were, however, many critics who found them lax in offering protection to the Jews. Simon Bloch, of the *Univers Israélite,* was one such critic. In 1857 he wrote of the consistory:

Nous voyons aussi que jamais il n'intervient pour défendre l'honneur des israélites, souvent attaqué par des écrivassiers des rues qui déjeunent de calomnie et dînent de la boue qu'ils jettent à tout ce qui est vénéré et vénérable. Les feuilles judiciaires accolent le mot juif à celui de voleur et excitent ainsi le mépris contre une classe de citoyens et contre un culte reconnu par la loi. Quand donc le consistoire central,—s'il n'est pas orthodoxe en religion, l'est au moins en honneur civil et en morale sociale,—a-t-il demandé aux tribunaux justice contre les ignobles blasphémateurs d'Israël et de sa foi?[2]

Despite such accusations the central consistory did act on some occasions, exerting the utmost caution, and appealing to constituted authority. This mild approach of the older generation was one of the factors that led to the alienation of the young future organizers of the *Alliance Israélite Universelle*. The new organization was formed by men who believed in publicity and in the utility of public opinion.

In 1860, in a rare move, central consistory president Max Cerfberr sent a letter to the editor of the *Journal des Débats* to refute calumnious statements that had appeared in the French press alleging Jewish involvement in a recent attack on Christians in Damascus. Cerfberr had taken this step very hesitantly, and consequently felt compelled to justify it in some detail at the following central consistory meeting; his colleagues voted their approval.[3]

Although the principal gain of the emancipation had been an ideology of equality under the law, reality did not correspond to the theory. Two 1808 decrees (on patents and domicile) discriminated in law against the Jews, and Judaism did not receive state funding on a par with the other recognized religions until 1831. A special Jewish oath (*More Judaïco*) was abolished by the high court only in 1846, and at even later dates some courts tried to reinstitute the Jewish oath. The validity of the pre-revolutionary Jewish communal debts was reaffirmed throughout the century, and special taxation for the repayment of the Alsatian debt was approved as late as the end of the 1860's. Such a legal situation is inconsistent with a liberal philosophy, but the philosophy was not consistently maintained, either by the country as a whole or by the consistories. In the cases of both the oath *More Judaïco* and the communal debts the consistories looked for the quickest and most practical way to achieve the resolution of the problem. They did not concern themselves with maintaining a liberal stance. They were willing to cooperate with special taxation to put an end to the debt which was a gnawing wound, reminding everyone of the limitations of the emancipation. Similarly, they were willing to collaborate on a modern version of a special Jewish oath that would replace the one inherited from the middle ages.

In addition to legal inequities, Jews feared the practical effects of local attitudes. Municipalities often refused to allocate funds for public Jewish schools; pamphlets incited riots against Jews of the eastern provinces; courtroom speeches referred to the religion of Jewish defendants. All these acts of unorganized antisemitism had serious consequences for the Jewish community. Thus the Nancy consistory complained in 1838 that it had been refused a troop detachment for the Besançon synagogue's celebration of the king's *fête* (a ceremony ordered in all churches and synagogues by the government). Officials at the garrison had claimed that Catholics alone had this right. The mayor, also, refused to support the Jewish claim, and the Nancy consistory appealed to the central consistory to bring the issue to the attention of the government. By letter of May 28, 1838, the central consistory protested the discrimination.[4]

Individual Jews and departmental consistories considered the central consistory their intermediary to the government, to protest anti-Jewish actions or publications. Occasionally the central consistory initiated action by itself. Often it refused to act, claiming that this was beyond the scope of its duties.

At stake throughout the nineteenth century was the maintenance of the liberal gains of 1789–1791. With each successive change of regime, with every bill that was passed, with all the local variations in the implementation of national policy, the Jews were watching, often tensely, for any change that might affect the Jewish position. There was always an undercurrent of anti-Jewish feeling, nurtured by the Church, which found occasional expression in riots (as in Alsace in 1848 and again during the 1850's), in the press (especially Catholic), and occasionally in administrative decisions. There was reason to be tense and defensive. When a new law was being written (as in the case of the educational law, *Loi Falloux*) it was necessary to read it carefully to see which of its provisions might affect the Jews. Consistory members were generally politically alert and often politically active. They read the bills carefully and were often able to prevent "oversights" that would have had a negative effect on the Jewish population. Legal equality was the basis upon which they expected to improve their absorption into French society.

Thus in 1849 the government was preparing a new bill on education (subsequently the *Loi Falloux*), which would allow greater freedom for the establishment by religious groups of secondary schools, provide public elementary schools for all recognized faiths, and reorganize the system of administration and inspection of public schools. "Inadvertently," the bill provided for priests and ministers, but not rabbis, to be members of the educational boards (*conseils*) at both the departmental and national levels. Most of the consistories spotted this omission and complained to the central consistory. On July 4, 1849, the central consistory informed the legislative committee examining the bill that Judaism had the same legal status as Christianity in France. Pointing out that this equality had been protected in 1833 under the *Loi Guizot,* which regulated public education, the central consistory complained that the new bill failed to recognize the right of Judaism to be represented. The consistory proposed that one of its members be delegated a member of the *conseil supérieur,* on the national level, and that a delegate of the local consistory or its grand rabbi be a member of the *conseil académique,* at the departmental level.[5]

The central consistory reported to the departmental consistories that the Minister of Cults had given his assurance that the omission was an oversight and that it had not been intended to prejudice Jewish interests. The minister had promised to support the proposed changes.[6]

When passed, the new law provided for the establishment of separate public primary schools for each religious group. The 1833 law had also allowed this, and many Jewish schools had become communal schools in the late thirties and early forties. The new law theoretically guaranteed this privilege, but in fact its implementation was subject to the decision by the communities to appropriate funds for that purpose. Again a liberal principle was at stake, and again the consistories were not consistent in the solution to the problem. The Paris consistory, when asked in 1843 by the prefect to contribute toward the expense of building the public Jewish school, at first refused, saying that this was asking the consistory to accept a compromise on the equality of rights that Jews were assured by law. But the consistory ultimately agreed to the request, for practical reasons, in order to speed up construction of the long overdue building. (The building, on rue des Blancs Manteaux, was finally opened in 1847.)[7]

The central consistory did not take a vigorous stand on this issue of public education. Throughout the entire period under consideration it continued to receive complaints of the refusal of local administrations to convert Jewish schools into communal schools, but the consistory did not wish to make it a public issue, believing that a wise government must respect the prejudices of its constituents and that publicity would be an adverse factor. As late as 1861 and 1862, private individuals and the Colmar consistory complained that anti-Jewish feeling in Upper Alsace prevented the communalization of the Jewish schools. Whereas in the Bas-Rhin there were forty-two such schools, the Haut-Rhin had only eight:

Notre circonscription renferme plus de quarante communautés israélites. Presque toutes devraient avoir une école communale israélite si la loi était exécutée avec sincérité. La loi ne doit cependant pas rester une lettre morte pour nous seulement.

The Colmar consistory asked the central consistory to request that the ministry enforce the communalization of two schools, which ten years previously had already been declared communal by the "conseil académique du département." Despite earlier complaints, the central consistory had done nothing to help. Colmar believed that by making an example of these two communities and by forcing them to budget funds for the Jewish schools, the problem would be solved elsewhere too.[8]

In their attempt to obtain the benefits of state-supported

education, Jews encountered difficulty at the secondary-school level as well. Frequently Jews encountered difficulty in gaining admission to the various *Ecoles Normales,* which prepared secondary school teachers. These normal schools were established by many of the departments in their largest cities and often supplied lodging and board so that students from all parts of the department could attend. Boarding was sometimes compulsory, and Jews were refused permission to live out of the school and board with Jewish families. Moreover, the schools frequently had Jewish quotas. If admitted, Jews had difficulty obtaining the right to receive Jewish religious instruction in the school at state expense. The Strasbourg and Colmar consistories tried to obtain these advantages for the Jewish students, but the central consistory refused to second their efforts. The local consistories were forced to make compromises with their liberal principles in order to achieve increases in Jewish enrollment in these schools. In Strasbourg, for example, the Jewish students of the *Ecole Normale* were housed, fed, and given religious instruction at the *Ecole de Travail* for several years during the 1850's.[9]

In 1853 the community of Macon (Bas-Rhin) prohibited Jewish children from entering the *lycée.* When the government applied pressure, they were finally admitted but were forced to attend Catholic religious lessons with everyone else. This time the central consistory agreed to intervene, and did so successfully. The ministry issued orders for the children to be excused from religious instruction at the school.[10]

By choosing its causes carefully, the central consistory was assured of almost total success in achieving its demands. Although it insisted on having the Jewish children exempt from Catholic lessons, it did not insist upon Jewish instruction for these children at public expense, even though publicly supported religious instruction for the Jewish pupils of secondary schools was guaranteed by the *Loi Falloux.*

Everyone knew that true equality under the law meant equal funding by the state and that the Jewish taxes authorized until 1831 were an exceptional measure. But it was impolitic to admit this. If the Jews acknowledged that prior to 1831 they had been less than equal, they would have destroyed the myth of the revolution and the emancipation. In 1831 an argument developed between central consistory president Worms de Romilly and his colleague Benjamin Rodrigues over whether the central consistory should admit that prior to 1831 Jews had not enjoyed equal status. The consistory members had been invited to an audience with King Louis-Philippe on New Year's Day, and they composed a message to be presented on the occasion. The first draft of the greeting thanked the new monarch for his intention to eliminate the "line of demarcation" between the Jews and the rest of the population by funding Judaism. Rodrigues took exception to this statement and warned that the Jews must never admit to any distinction between themselves and the rest of the population. In a note to Worms de Romilly he advised:

Observez que vous représentez tous les Israélites de France et qu'il ne faut pas qu'ils puissent vous reprocher d'avoir manqué de dignité et de les avoir déconsidérés aux yeux du Roi en parlant d'une ligne de démarcation que nous ne devons jamais avouer avoir existé . . . car ne pas salarier notre culte n'était pas une ligne de démarcation civile.[11]

The revised speech omitted the reference to the "ligne de démarcation," and the members simply thanked the king for putting Judaism on the national budget.[12]

Even after the 1831 law there continued to be financial discrimination against the Jews. We have seen this in the case of the schools, but there were other ways in which it was manifest. In order to reinforce the principle of equality, consistories and individuals often requested equal shares of municipal funding for charity. Thus when the Parisian government distributed contributions to many charities in the city, a Paris consistory member brought this to the attention of his colleagues, and suggested that the consistory claim its share. He emphasized that he was concerned with the principle, and not with the funds. Similarly, the Strasbourg consistory requested government aid to pay for inspections in the Jewish schools. Because such funds were available to the Protestants, the consistory argued that it was important to assure the Jews of equal treatment: "il s'agit de défendre des droits acquis par la loi du 8 février 1831, de combattre des mesures exceptionelles qui dégradent notre sainte religion."[13]

As late as 1857 it was not impossible for a local community to impose a special tax on the Jews. The Jewish population of Itterviller (Bas-Rhin) complained to the Strasbourg consistory of a special Jewish tax "qui n'aurait d'autre cause que la malveillance de l'autorité locale." The consistory asked for a complaint to be registered through normal channels, and undertook to make an unofficial inquiry at the prefecture.[14]

According to law there were no posts for which Jews were disqualified because of their religion, but here again there was a discrepancy between theory and practice. In 1856 a lawyer of Alsace applied to the court of Colmar for a judgeship. He was refused on the grounds that the population of Alsace held strong anti-Jewish feelings and it was unlikely that the situation would change rapidly. The central consistory refused to intervene.[15]

Similarly, Jews were sometimes discriminated against in teaching posts, on the grounds that they might have too great an influence on the young. In 1849 Isidore Cahen was named professor of philosophy in Luçon (Vendée), but when he arrived the local archbishop refused to allow him to assume his post. Despite the central consistory's intervention, no satisfaction was given. This consistory, already feeling that it was not getting the necessary support from the government in other issues, offered its resignation.[16] Such extreme action was not normal for the central consistory, nor did it achieve much. Cahen was never restored to his post, and the experience was traumatic for him. His activities as a journalist for the Jewish press and as co-founder of the *Alliance Israélite Universelle* can be understood only in relationship to his discovery early in life that the emancipation had not been completed.

Extending equality to Jews incarcerated in French prisons was an issue discussed by the consistories many times during this period, although it did not involve many individuals. At stake was the right to celebrate Jewish holidays, receive ritual objects and food, and be given religious instruction (generally considered the way to reform prison inmates). The consistories supported prisoners' religious rights, although they were very careful to keep their demands highly reasonable and practicable. They even considered the possibility of establishing their own penal institutions for the Jews, in order to solve the problems posed by the government's lack of cooperation in making special arrangements for the small number of Jewish prisoners. Frequently it was the prisoners themselves who contacted the consistories to ask for aid, books, or religious instruction. For example, inmates at the *Maison Centrale* of Gaillon had been accorded a place for prayer, and they asked the Paris consistory to supply books and religious instruction.[17]

In 1843 the Strasbourg consistory complained that of the three recognized religions, only Judaism was not represented on the departmental prison committee. It asked the central consistory to bring this to the attention of the Minister of the Interior and to request that Grand Rabbi Aron be named to the commission:

Nous avons à Strasbourg une commission des prisons composée de plusieurs membres laïques, d'un curé, et d'un pasteur protestant, les Israélites seuls n'y sont pas représentés. . . . Cette exception a cela de fâcheux qu'elle autorise par continuation l'habitant de l'Alsace à croire que les Israélites se trouvent toujours placés en dehors du régime commun.[18]

The central consistory declined to intervene, saying that the Strasbourg consistory could bring the matter directly to the attention of the local prefect.[19]

The Paris consistory frequently received appeals for aid from Jewish prisoners in Melun, the Colmar consistory from prisoners in Ensisheim, the Marseille consistory from prisoners in Nîmes and Toulon. In all cases the local consistories attempted to improve conditions and help the Jews obtain the right to practice their religion and receive instruction. Occasionally the central consistory spoke in support of Jewish prisoners' rights, in response to the Paris consistory's prodding. A plan that was repeatedly proposed but never implemented was to group the prisoners together, so that they would be numerous enough to justify special treatment.

Several times permission to observe Jewish holidays in the prisons was given and retracted. In 1846 such permission was withdrawn and the central consistory requested its restoration. By letter of September 9, 1846, the Ministry of Cults informed the central consistory that its request had been granted:

Vos coreligionnaires pourront donc pratiquer toutes les cérémonies de leur culte durant les jours que vous indiquez dans votre lettre du 6 septembre, autant du moins que les localités et les exigences de l'ordre et de la discipline le permettront.[20]

In the 1850's and 1860's both the Strasbourg and Paris consistories were disturbed by the lack of a good solution to the problem of young offenders held in *correction paternelle*. Children were detained with no notification having been made to the consistories; they were sent to the provinces, far from Jewish communities, and were sometimes transferred to convents and baptised. As late as 1870 the problem was not solved, partly because there were so few children concerned, and a proposal for an agricultural colony for young Jewish prisoners was rejected on those grounds.[21]

We have already shown that the consistories did not always defend the liberal principle that no official distinction should be made between French Jews and French Christians. Several prominent Jews, however, felt very strongly that the consistories should insist upon this point. Benjamin Rodrigues, whose 1831 argument with Worms de Romilly over just such an issue was quoted above, had previously made a similar argument in 1827. In Upper Alsace in that year, the local government was considering passing a law against vagabondage among Jews. When the central consistory was asked to offer an opinion, it suggested that the issue be discussed and decided between the Colmar consistory and the local prefect. Rodrigues, a member of the central consistory, knew that an exceptional measure could serve as a precedent for additional discriminatory laws, and he argued that it was crucial to prevent passage of this bill. In an eloquent and impassioned letter to his colleagues, Rodrigues wrote that he had been unable to sleep the previous night because the implications of the "Colmar Affair" had tormented him all night:

L'affaire de Colmar est d'une haute conséquence; cela m'a tourmenté toute la nuit et je n'en ai pas dormi. J'ose même avancer que cela attaque les droits civils de tous les israélites de France puisque cette mesure fait exception sur ceux qui professent les autres cultes.

Rodrigues advised a firm stand against exceptional legislation. He asked the consistory to argue that inasmuch as ordinary laws against vagabondage apply to Jews as well as to everyone else, there is no justification for a special measure concerning only the Jews.[22]

The Metz consistory often championed liberal principles. For a long time it refused to cooperate with the commission that had been established to repay the Metz debt, but was eventually forced to yield. In 1846 the Metz consistory refused to compile statistics concerning the Jews, arguing that such research might imply a distinction between Jews and other Frenchmen.[23]

The consistories protected the Jewish population in a variety of ways. In an unusual case, in 1840, the Colmar consistory tried to influence the government to choose a particular priest for the post of Bishop of Strasbourg! In explaining its request, the consistory cited the priest's tolerance and his ability to establish good relationships among the various religious groups.[24]

Negative attitudes toward Jews were not rare throughout the century, but physical violence appears to have occurred only in Alsace. In 1848 the Strasbourg and Colmar consistories, Rabbi Nordmann of Hegenheim, and a French school teacher working in Switzerland all forwarded to the central consistory first-hand reports of such violence. Even the distant but concerned community of Bordeaux asked the central consistory to take some action. Although the central consistory intervened promptly and energetically, the local authorities were sympathetic to the anti-Jewish feeling and refused to protect the Jews. Hemerdinger—a native of Haut-Rhin, a member of the central consistory, and "commissaire général pour les départements de Haut-et Bas-Rhin"—was sent by the provisional government to quell the riots. Rabbi Nordmann, describing acts of violence against Jewish men, women, and children, asked that the perpetrators be tried outside the department, as this would be the only way to obtain a trial not prejudiced against the Jews. Carnot, the Minister of Cults, asked that the Justice Department prosecute the offenders and that the Minister of the Interior take steps to prevent such events from recurring. Nevertheless, from February to May the riots continued. At the end of June, twenty-three people were tried in Marmoutier (Bas-Rhin), the scene of some of the worst riots. Nordmann's skepticism was justified. To the astonishment of everyone—including the defendants themselves —they were acquitted on all counts by a sympathetic jury.[25]

Despite popular misconceptions, the 1848 troubles in Alsace did not end quickly or without repercussions.[26] In July 1851 the Colmar consistory reported serious riots in Bollwiller (Haut-Rhin):

depuis une quinzaine de jours des attroupements considérables d'ouvriers s'étaient formés dans la commune de Bollwiller, et ont traversé le village en proférant des cris de menace contre les Israélites et en se portant même à des voies de fait.[27]

The Jews of Bollwiller had expected the troubles to end spontaneously and had been prepared to wait quietly for events to run their course; when the rioting became serious, however, they asked the Colmar consistory to register a complaint with the authorities, who had thus far taken no action. It was only after receiving the official consistory complaint that the prefect finally intervened.

The Bas-Rhin had further anti-Jewish outbursts. In 1857 the Jews of Scharrachbergheim and Westhausen complained of violence directed against them by the people of Dachstein. Local authorities allowed the acts to pass unpunished. When the Strasbourg consistory intervened, it received promises from the *Procureur impérial* of Strasbourg that the guilty would be prosecuted.

The consistories were called upon to defend the Jews against the press. Throughout the entire period the press persisted in publishing the religion of Jewish defendants in criminal cases. The term used was *Juif,* intended as a means of derision and an insult to the religion. (*Israélite* was the acceptable term of the day.) Several departmental consistories complained of this practice to the central consistory, which registered at least one complaint with the ministry. As late as 1862 the official French government newspaper, *Moniteur,* ended an article on some business frauds with the words "ce sont des juifs."[28]

The press was no kinder during the Damascus Affair of 1840 and the Syrian massacres of 1860. When the news of the Damascus Affair first reached France, French newspapers printed the accusations against the Jews as though they were established fact and without comment or rebuttal. Again, in 1860, when Christians were massacred in Syria and Jews were accused of being participants, the French newspapers carried the news without comment.

Throughout the period there were pamphlets and books hostile to the Jews.[29] In 1853 an inflammatory anti-Jewish brochure was advertised in the newspaper of Guebwiller (Haut-Rhin), and was distributed in Alsace. The Colmar consistory complained to the prefect, but without success, and then turned to the central consistory.[30]

The following year the grand rabbi of Strasbourg complained to the central consistory of an anonymous pamphlet that was being sold in Strasbourg entitled "Conseils aux paysans contre l'usure." This brochure accused the Jews of being usurers. The Strasbourg consistory alerted the prefect, and the central consistory complained to the prefect, but did not expect to achieve success.[31]

Again in 1861 the Strasbourg consistory brought to the attention of the central consistory two anti-Jewish pamphlets, one entitled *L'Eglise et la Synagogue,* by Rüpert, and another in the

Alsatian dialect. The Alsatian pamphlet attained a very large circulation and the Strasbourg consistory was unsuccessful in convincing the courts to withdraw it from sale. This consistory then appealed to the central consistory to intervene directly with the government in Paris, pointing out that the local courts, because of their anti-Jewish attitude, would obey only an order from Paris.[32]

From 1856 to 1858 Eugène de Mirecourt published several attacks upon the Jews and created a disturbance among the Parisian Jewish population. He published a series of biographies called *Les Contemporains,* in which he included unsympathetic works on Crémieux and Rothschild. He also wrote a work on Heine, and although Heine fared better than either Crémieux or Rothschild, Mirecourt took the opportunity to speak disparagingly of the poet's racial origins: "la race absurde et brutale des adorateurs du veau d'or, qui se perpétue depuis Moïse jusqu'à nos boursicotiers actuels."[33]

Although the *Procureur général* warned Mirecourt to cease making provocative statements, he repeated his attacks on March 3, 1857, in his paper, *Les Contemporains.*

In 1857 a group of alarmed Parisian Jews requested that the central consistory take some action to counter Mirecourt's attacks. The consistory not only refused to follow such advice but recommended to the government, to which appeals had been sent by the same group of concerned Jews, that no action be taken. Samuel Cahen, editor of the *Archives Israélites* and one of the men who sought to silence Mirecourt's attacks, learned of the central consistory's communication to the government and wrote an indignant letter to that administration. Cahen accused the consistory of having insulted the religious feelings of the Jews and thereby having forfeited its "moral authority" among the Jewish population:

On peut demander comment l'administration qui représente les israélites de France a pu tenir si peu de compte de leur susceptibilité religieuse, non seulement en ne faisant pas la moindre démarche pour y répondre, mais même en entravant celle faite par d'autres. . . . La plus grande force d'une administration, vous le savez, Messieurs, est dans son autorité morale, et dans cette occasion cette autorité a reçu une atteinte dans l'esprit d'un grand nombre d'assistants.[34]

Mirecourt's writings were often muck-raking and sometimes scandalous. He attacked dozens of prominent people and several of his writings were seized. A newspaper he owned was closed down, and he spent some time in prison. From there, in 1858, he issued a book called *La Bourse, ses abus et ses mystères,* in which he attacked the capitalism of the stock exchange, the immorality of its transactions, the rapidly made fortunes, and the frauds. He claimed that the stock exchange in modern nations was invented by the Jews, "a decadent people with a great love for wealth." He wrote mockingly of the British Jews and their important political positions, obtained because of their wealth, and included several facetious anecdotes about a Jew named "Issachar."[35]

Another anti-Jewish writer was Louis Veuillot, editor of the Catholic paper *L'Univers.* On November 19, 1858, Veuillot printed a blood ritual accusation against the Jews. This was a great shock to many people who firmly believed in a liberal France of the Enlightenment, Revolution, and Jewish Emancipation and to whom the blood ritual smacked of the middle ages. The Colmar consistory members wrote that Veuillot's article reminded them of the worst days the Jews have ever known, and that it was especially dangerous for the Jews of Haut-Rhin, where their position was most precarious. The consistories in Strasbourg, Nancy, and Paris also asked that Veuillot be prosecuted. The situation became more tense when the respectable and usually fair *Journal des Débats* reprinted part of the calumnious article.[36]

This time, however, the central consistory did not wait for the departmental consistories to prod it to action. It met the day after the appearance of the article and accepted a motion by Anspach that the Minister of Cults be requested to prosecute Veuillot for inciting hatred ("délit d'excitation à la haine"). One cautious member suggested that they only request that a warning be given to Veuillot, but this motion was overruled. The central consistory decided that if the government prosecuted, the consistory would enter the case as a civil plaintiff (*partie civile*).[37]

A central consistory circular notified all the departmental consistories of the decision, and all wrote to express approval.[38] Upon receipt of the central consistory complaint, the Ministry of Cults requested that the Ministry of Justice handle the prosecution. The government agreed that the article was "unjust" and "dangerous," and the central consistory was informed of the procedure to follow if it wished to press charges against Veuillot. However, the government itself refused to prosecute in its own name, desiring to take no stand on religious issues.[39]

The government, in refusing to take a stand, had, of course, taken a stand. It had refused its protection to the Jewish population, which was now more vulnerable than ever to violent press attacks. The central consistory was left to its own devices, and the only remaining option appeared to be the institution of a lawsuit against Veuillot. Opinion was divided; one member warned that a trial would call attention to the Jews, and that the central consistory should remain aloof to the attacks of a journalist. Requests for action, which had been received from the departmental consistories, could be rejected, inasmuch as these consistories were not always in a position to judge the long-term effect of the measures they solicited. Other consistory members opposed this view, pointing out that *L'Univers* was the major journal of the clergy, and had an enormous influence. The clerical party, the argument continued, is unenlightened and believes that it is permissible to direct such attacks against the Jews. It is necessary to teach them that they cannot succeed in such actions, or persecution of the Jews is likely to result. All Jewish eyes are on the central consistory, and if it fails to act, there will be reproach from all sides.[40]

Permission to prosecute was requested,[41] and the central consistory consulted lawyers Crémieux and Eugène Bethmont. To their surprise, Crémieux advised against prosecution. He pointed out that the chances of failure because of legal technicalities were great. The central consistory did not have a clear case; no specific legal prohibition applied to Veuillot's long invective against Jews and Judaism. To lose a just case, Crémieux said, would be much worse than to abstain from prosecuting it: "Succomber dans une lutte où nous aurions porté tant de vérités, tant de lumières, quel échec; quelle consternation pour la bonne cause! Quel triomphe, quelle victoire pour les ennemis du progrès!"[42]

At least one central consistory member insisted on the utility of the prosecution in order to have the opportunity to refute Veuillot's calumnies. His colleagues pointed out, however, that this would not be the case, inasmuch as publication of court debates was not permitted. The central consistory vacillated. At first it decided to withdraw the lawsuit but send a bold letter of complaint to the government denouncing the lack of legal protection.[43] At its next meeting it reconsidered this last decision and adopted a policy of "protecting the freedom of the press." Once again the consistory had decided not to take a principled public stand. It withdrew the case, stating that its lawyers had judged that the Veuillot article contained no passage which explicitly violated the law.[44] The unidentified member who had been holding out for prosecution now suggested that the central consistory publish a refutation of Veuillot's article. This was quickly vetoed.[45]

It seems likely that the member eager for prosecution—or at least publicity—was Adolphe Franck. The controversy over the use of publicity and recourse to public opinion had divided Jewish leadership increasingly since the 1840 establishment of Samuel Cahen's journal, *Archives Israélites*. In 1858 the conflict was on the verge of giving birth to the *Alliance Israélite Universelle*. Franck was the only member of the consistory who was also a founding member of this society.[46] When the central consistory decided against publishing a refutation of Veuillot's article, Rabbi E. Aristide Astruc, also a founding member of the *Alliance*, did publish such a refutation. In it he wrote that it is natural for people who are attacked to defend themselves:

Il était naturel que ceux qu'on attaquait élevassent la voix pour se défendre. Les Juifs pouvaient bien, quand on violait, pour les opprimer, la loi la plus naturelle de toutes, celle qui lie l'enfant au père, les Juifs pouvaient bien en appeler à l'opinion publique, aux pouvoirs de la terre, à tous enfin.[47]

Astruc's publication was obviously a response and a challenge to the central consistory position.

The central consistory knew that the confidence in public opinion exhibited by many of the younger men could find no reconciliation with the older generation's "prudence"; it also feared disapproval of the departmental consistories, which had been demanding action against Veuillot. In announcing to the departmental consistories the decision to drop the case, the central consistory deliberately abstained from forwarding copies of Crémieux's consultation, for fear that the departmental consistories might contest his conclusions. Rather, the central consistory stressed that it would be imprudent to risk failure.[48]

The departmental consistories replied that the central consistory's decision would leave the way open to further attacks, and they were correct. One month after the central consistory withdrew its request to sue Veuillot, the same journalist published another attack[49] in which he reiterated the "blood libel." Strasbourg immediately demanded that the central consistory request the government to warn Veuillot against his continual attacks and his tendency to arouse hatred ("sa tendance à exciter sans cesse et méchamment à la haine et au mépris d'une classe de citoyens").[50] The central consistory again debated whether to ask the government to repress the calumnies. Some members continued to insist upon freedom of the press, but it was ultimately decided to request that the government issue a warning to Veuillot.[51] In the weeks that followed, the consistories of Nancy and Paris complained that lack of success in dealing with Veuillot had led to an outbreak of anti-Jewish publications in the press.[52]

The government finally acted, apparently issuing a warning to Veuillot. The departmental consistories received the news with satisfaction. Strasbourg commented: "avec quel sentiment de satisfaction nous avons appris que des ordres, émanés de haut lieu, sont venus mettre un frein salutaire à la verve calomnieuse de cette fanatique feuille."[53] But the press attacks did not end. On October 19, 1861, *Le Monde,* successor to *L'Univers,* attacked Jews in a story entitled "La Banque Noire." The Colmar consistory immediately complained to the central consistory.[54] Strasbourg undertook this time to register its complaint directly with the Ministry of Cults.[55] By the end of November the central consistory had taken no action. (It had not even met during that month.) Colmar wrote again to ask for action, adding that a simple warning would not be sufficient.[56]

The central consistory deliberated the issue on December 3, and decided that it was analogous to the previous affair. It forwarded to the two provincial consistories the consultations of Crémieux and Bethmont that had been made in regard to the first Veuillot case three years previously, together with the ministry's instructions on how to proceed with such a prosecution. It pointed out, moreover, that if the courts agreed to prosecute, the departmental consistories need not be party to the case.[57]

The Strasbourg consistory brought suit against the newspaper, but the Colmar consistory urged that the case be transferred to Paris because the chances of success were far greater there. Success in Paris would also be more useful. Colmar brought pressure to bear, suggesting that the central consistory, as protector of Jewish interests, would certainly want to take this affair into its own hands:

nous pensons que le consistoire central, protecteur des intérêts moraux et religieux des Israélites français, voudra, sans doute, prendre cette affaire entre ses mains, en déposant une plainte au parquet de Paris; la satisfaction à obtenir dans la Capitale serait plus sûre et plus éclatante qu'à Colmar ou à Strasbourg; elle sera aussi plus efficace, pour tous les Israélites français, si sa représentation légale près du gouvernement voulait user de son droit et de son influence pour protéger la population israélite contre les attaques des calomniateurs et des persécuteurs sous quelque forme qu'ils se montrent.[58]

The central consistory refused to bring charges, claiming that the case, like that of Veuillot, was not governed by the law. The Colmar consistory disagreed, saying that whereas Veuillot had been careful to protect himself, the present article was an open and simple "excitation directe à la haine." Colmar repeated that the Strasbourg case should be transferred to Paris.[59]

In dramatic opposition to the central consistory's conservative view, the government itself decided to prosecute. The three ministries (Cults, Justice, and Interior) examined the issue, and the Minister of the Interior found the terms of the article under question far too serious for a simple warning to suffice. He therefore requested that the Ministry of Justice prosecute:

Les termes de cet article m'ont paru empreints d'un tel caractère de malveillance, que je n'ai pu considérer un avertissement comme une répression suffisante.

En conséquence, j'ai transmis le dossier à M. le Ministre de la Justice pour que S. Exc. livrât aux tribunaux le rédacteur du feuilleton, d'autant plus coupable qu'il est revêtu du caractère ecclésiastique.[60]

It was not only the press that persisted in its habit of defaming the Jews. Even worse, in the eyes of the Jews, was the usage of the pejorative term, *Juif*, in the courtroom by judges and lawyers. Individuals and consistories complained repeatedly about such practices, especially because the courtroom was an official forum of the state, and the nineteenth-century French

Jew liked to believe himself equal in the eyes of the law, if not in the hearts of his countrymen. More than that, he liked to believe in a secular state in which a person's religion was a private affair. We have found traces of several campaigns to eliminate such courtroom abuses during the nineteenth century. In 1847 the central consistory complained to the ministry that such practices tended to make the religion somehow an accomplice to the crime ("à rendre en quelque sorte la religion solidaire du crime").[61]

The consistories argued that the repetition of the term *Juif* in the courts and thereby the press constituted an attack on one of the three religions protected by the state. In 1847 the central consistory thought that a warning by the Ministry of Justice would suffice to put an end to such courtroom practices:

C'est à vous, M. le Ministre, au chef de la justice, que nous devons signaler un abus offensant pour notre culte. . . . Nous sommes sûrs . . . qu'un avertissement émané d'une sphère aussi élevée ne tardera pas à faire disparaître un reste de préjugés aussi peu en harmonie avec les lumières de notre siècle qu'avec l'esprit de nos institutions.[62]

Although the minister requested the *Procureur général* to take some action in this regard,[63] the practice continued as before.

Not only did the judiciary permit such excesses in the courtrooms, but it even became involved in the circulation of anti-Jewish publications. In 1853 the *Procureur impérial* of Colmar published a circular asking for a solution to the problem of Jewish usury, which, he said, was ruining farmers and artisans. The Strasbourg and Colmar consistories made this pamphlet known to the central consistory and offered to collect documentary evidence disproving the claim of widespread Jewish usury. Cerfberr, president of the central consistory, who was at that time in Strasbourg, informed his consistory that he, too, was gathering evidence to show the exaggerations resorted to by the enemies of the Jews. The central consistory decided to assemble all the evidence and bring it before the government.[64] We have not seen the results of such research, nor do we know the outcome of the central consistory's complaint to the government. The only reaction from the government that has been preserved is the claim that none of the high officials in the Ministries of State or Justice had known about the Colmar circular in advance.[65]

Another courtroom incident occurred in Paris, in 1855, when a M. Nathan Lévy, together with several other witnesses against a man charged with fraud, was called *Juif* during the trial. The defendant's lawyer, Arond, attempted to dismiss the significance of the charges against his client by pointing out that each witness was a "Jew and usurer" (*juif, juif-usurier*). Although the judge reminded Arond that the law recognized no religious distinctions, Lévy was shocked by his experience and wrote a letter to the central consistory describing his reaction: "profondément attristé de toutes ces injures, de toutes ces atroces calomnies dans lesquelles je venais d'être englobé." Lévy announced that he had decided to bring charges against the lawyer, and he asked the central consistory to take appropriate steps to assist him. He urged that they put an end to such problems before they became bigger ones. To sue a calumnious lawyer today would be to prevent a judge from discriminating tomorrow. Lévy, a seventy-year-old leather-worker, emphasized that he was bringing charges not merely in his own name ("il me reste peu de temps à vivre") but in the name of the Jewish community.[66]

The central consistory refused to help, or even to send any written advice to Lévy, on the grounds that what he had asked was not within the scope of consistory authority. The members felt that if they involved themselves by sending a written reply, their responsibility would be engaged. They charged their secretary with reporting orally to Lévy that the law forbade bringing any charges against lawyers for anything relative to their functions.[67]

Three years later, in July of 1858, a similar case occurred in the *Cour d'Assise* of Caen (Calvados). This time the initiative was taken by a group of Parisian Jews who were shocked by the language of Me Berthauld, the attorney for the *partie civile* at the trial of a certain Péchard. In a petition to the central consistory, the group stressed the importance of punishing Berthauld as an example to other lawyers, in order to prevent any recurrence of such comportment: "tellement étrange, tellement innouï, qu'on serait tenté de se demander s'il est bien possible . . . au dix-neuvième siècle, au centre de la civilisation."[68]

On July 13, when the central consistory and the Paris consistory met in an emergency session to discuss the Caen affair, opinion was divided.[69] There were those who wanted to use the utmost reserve and tact and avoid a public debate, and those who believed in the efficacy of vigorous self-defense. The second group stressed the need to show that Jews had dignity and honor and would not allow themselves to be attacked. Adolphe Franck announced that he had called the meeting in order to decide on a measure that would not only avenge Berthauld's insult, but prevent the recurrence of this kind of problem: "non seulement d'obtenir une réparation éclatante des insultes prodiguées à notre Culte, mais aussi de prendre des mesures efficaces pour prévenir des faits semblables."

The conservative opinion was voiced first by Anspach, who offered to write to the judge in the Caen case. Alkan and Munk defended the vigorous approach, arguing that a simple letter was insufficient and would probably remain unanswered, as had happened in 1847. They favored wide publicity. Alkan suggested publishing an article in the Jewish press and distributing a large number of reprints. Munk felt that even this was not strong enough. He recommended that the central consistory request an audience with the minister. He proposed, secondly, that the central consistory bring defamation charges against Berthauld, and pursue the case all the way to the supreme court if necessary and possible. The Jews, he declared, had nothing to fear from an open debate with widespread publicity, and he cited the courage of the British Jews in bringing up the issue of their rights in Parliament every year. He pointed out that although many derogatory statements were made about them during the yearly debates, the British Jews had ultimately obtained a triumphal success.

Arguing against Munk, Rothschild warned against any large-scale publicity: "il pense qu'il serait imprudent d'ouvrir une polémique qui peut-être ne tournerait pas à l'avantage des Israélites." Another member (not named, but probably Anspach) agreed that caution should be used: "ce n'est pas par le bruit et par la polémique qu'on peut vaincre les préjugés." He hoped that a letter to the court would have the effect of producing a retraction by Berthauld. If not, the consistory should publish an article in the judicial press.

The decision was, typically, conservative: both Anspach's letter to the Caen court and a central consistory audience with the ministry would be tried. Neither Alkan's proposal of a publication nor Munk's more extreme proposal that they sue Berthauld for defamation was accepted.[70]

Berthauld retracted his statements in a publication inserted in *La Presse,* July 13, the very day of the central consistory–Paris consistory joint meeting. It is not clear what actually provoked this retraction, but it does not appear possible that it was the consistory action. In view of the retraction, the central consistory decided there was nothing more to do. However, the Strasbourg, Bordeaux, and Lyon consistories disagreed and continued to press for more satisfaction, such as a statement from the Ministry of Justice.[71] The Paris consistory was angry and dismayed to find that the decisions reached at its joint meeting with the central consistory were not to be put into effect.

The departmental consistories were not wrong to attack the conservative nature of the central consistory, and the lack of a general solution to the problem. By September a similar incident had occurred. Again the judge in the case had let it pass. The Paris consistory noted: "Ce n'était donc pas seulement contre l'avocat Berthauld qu'il fallait agir, mais il était urgent de faire connaître par des actes virils que les Israélites n'acceptent pas les outrages." In its strongest statement thus far on fighting for Jewish honor, the Paris consistory said that it hoped its initiative would help the honor and dignity of the Jews: "contribuer à l'honneur et à la dignité d'Israél, titres précieux pour lesquels il faut combattre . . . et non courber la tête avec résignation."[72]

Even in the face of the new attack, the central consistory took no decisive action. It had resolved to address a complaint to the government, but the Veuillot affair broke out on November 19 and distracted its attention.

The government, however, took action. Upon a complaint from the Ministry of Cults, the Ministry of Justice promised equal protection for all religions before the law and gave instructions to the courts to prevent similar occurrences in the future. It promised the central consistory that if similar happenings occurred, prompt measures would be taken to repress them.[73] The central consistory was satisfied and reported its "success" in a circular to the departmental consistories.

Not everyone was equally certain that the ministry's statement represented a success. The Strasbourg consistory expressed concern that this policy of the Justice Ministry would not receive sufficiently wide application. It stressed that in Alsatian courts the same abuses occur daily: "En Alsace, par exemple, ces mêmes expressions offensantes abondent journellement devant toutes les juridictions."[74]

Perhaps the governmental action produced the desired results. According to the documents at our disposal, there were no further complaints against lawyers and judges for several years following the 1858 proclamation of the policy.

B. Redefinition of the Rabbinate

The second major activity that was assumed by the consistories, although not required by the legislation, was the redefinition of the rabbinate. Although one of the main reasons for the creation of the consistory system had been to achieve close supervision of the rabbis, neither the Jewish *notables* nor the legislation they helped draft fully anticipated the type of modern rabbi that was to emerge in the nineteenth century.

The principal instrument for the creation of modern rabbis was the *école rabbinique* (rabbinic school) opened in 1829. In addition to the fact that the school was consistory controlled, the consistories alone were empowered to ordain the rabbis, upon the recommendation of the school's examiners. At first the departmental consistories granted the lower diplomas (those needed for communal rabbi posts) and the central consistory awarded the higher degree of grand rabbi. By 1862 ordination was entirely in the hands of the central consistory.

In 1829 the *école rabbinique* opened in the rue de l'Arsenal, the main street of the old Metz ghetto. Although it was designed from the beginning as a modern seminary with secular, as well as religious studies, many of the hopes vested in the institution did not materialize. Despite the rule that French was to be spoken in the school, the language of instruction was, in fact, German. (Most of the students came from the east and had not learned French.) Not all of the subjects listed on the original curriculum were actually taught. At an early date the Parisian

Jewish leaders were dissatisfied with the location of the school. It seemed to them symbolically medieval to allow the "modern seminary" to remain in the ghetto. In 1844 the central consistory began to campaign for the transfer of the school to Paris, where the students could benefit from the academic advantages of the capital and also be under the watchful eye of the central consistory.

The official status of the Metz school meant that its graduates were to be preferred above all other candidates for posts. An early example of this policy occurred in 1833, when the Marseille consistory needed a new grand rabbi to succeed one who had died in 1831. There had been two candidates for the post: Rabbi A. Muscat of Avignon, former member of the Sanhedrin, and Rabbi Michel-David Cohen, graduate of the *école rabbinique*. Rabbi Muscat's letter of candidacy stressed his qualifications: "d'ancien Grand-Rabbin et comme membre du Sanhedrin . . . appuyé . . . sur l'article 27 du règlement." It is true that the *règlement* had provided that preference be given, in the selection of grand rabbis, to those who had been members of the Sanhedrin. By 1833, however, the consistories were not interested in aged rabbis of pre-*école rabbinique* days, notwithstanding their Sanhedrin qualifications. Rabbi Michel David Cahen was chosen.[75]

Adolphe Franck was the most ardent proponent of the plan to move the rabbinic school to Paris. From 1844 to 1859 the project was debated and finally implemented. Michel Lévy, member of the Paris consistory, published an article in favor of the project in which he pointed out that the young rabbis were not breaking away from the prejudices of their masters, who belonged to another generation. He cited the case of Lazare Wogue, a brilliant young graduate of the rabbinic school and protégé of the Paris consistory. Wogue had refused to participate in a Paris consistory commission on revising the ritual because Grand Rabbi Ennery had refused. Lévy pointed out that a generation of real "Jewish pastors" could be formed only by teaching rational and scientific theology in Paris. Such "pastors" could then be sent throughout the country to preach the message of "life and regeneration":

Nos jeunes grands rabbins ne résisteront pas aux arguments et aux réprimandes de leurs doyens, n'avons-nous pas vu un jeune disciple [Wogue] refuser de siéger dans la commission pour la révision des prières . . . translation de l'Ecole de la rue de l'Arsenal de Metz à Paris . . . vienne une génération de rabbins, une seule génération de vrais pasteurs israélites, formés sous les yeux du consistoire central, nourris d'une théologie scientifique et rationelle . . . vous enverrez ces hommes au loin, parmi vos communautés des villes et des campagnes; vous leur direz à votre tour: Allez et enseignez la vraie parole du Dieu d'Israél, la parole de vie et de régénération, non la lettre morte et inerte.[76]

The school was transferred to Paris in 1859. In 1862 a decree provided that assistant rabbis (*sous-rabbins*) could be substituted for cantors. This was another important step in the control of the clergy because there was no standardized training program for cantors.

A crucial factor in the training of the new kind of rabbi was the secular education he was to receive in public secondary schools, prior to entering the rabbinical school. This kind of preparation for rabbinical studies was a radical departure from traditional patterns, which stressed thorough Talmudic preparation. In 1853 orthodox Jews of the Haut-Rhin district of Alsace, with Rabbi Salomon Klein as their leader, opened a traditional patterns, which stressed thorough Talmudic preparation. In 1853 orthodox Jews of the Haut-Rhin district of contrary to the specific decision of the central and Colmar consistories that students be prepared in secular secondary schools. It led to a schism within the Colmar community.

The 1831 legislation, which put rabbis on the state payroll, had been an important aid to the consistories in controlling the accession of rabbis to posts. State law now determined the official qualifications to be required of rabbis. Furthermore, by limiting the amount of money available for rabbis' salaries, the law also had the effect of limiting the total number of rabbis in France. (No local Jewish taxes were authorized to supplement this funding.) The central consistory attempted to put the law immediately to its advantage by excluding thirty rabbis from the newly created state-salaried posts. Grand Rabbi of France Emmanuel Deutz protested vehemently, saying that all the rabbis should benefit equally from the new measure:

Tous les rabbins doivent jouir du bénéfice de cette loi et le consistoire n'a nullement le droit de supprimer tels rabbins et de conserver tels autres; qu'il serait plus convenable que le consistoire central fixe une somme quelconque qui sera répartie entre tous les rabbins communaux.[77]

The consistory image of the modern rabbi was clearly influenced by that of the Catholic clergy: the role was viewed as priestly or sacred and was therefore said to be incompatible with commercial activities. (Although the European rabbinate had gradually been evolving in that direction since the beginning of modern times, rarely had rabbis actually been prohibited from engaging in business.) Even an intermittent period of commercial activity was considered disqualifying for future appointment to a rabbinic post in the location where the rabbi had practiced his commerce. A case in point was the 1851 election of Michel Wimphen as rabbi of Sarreguemines, and the central consistory's ruling that Wimphen was disqualified for the post. After obtaining his rabbinic degree at the *école rabbinique,* Wimphen had for several years aided his wife in her furniture business while, he later claimed, he continued his rabbinic studies.[78] The Jewish communities of the Sarreguemines district were adamant that Wimphen be installed; they re-elected him in several subsequent ballotings and petitioned the central consistory on his behalf. The consistory eventually compromised and offered Wimphen a post elsewhere.

This tendency to Christianize the rabbinate led Grand Rabbi Arnaud Aron of Strasbourg to explain to his lay colleagues on the consistory the difference between Judaism and Christianity with regard to the ecclesiastical role. In 1853 the consistory's commission on "amelioration" had recommended some reforms of the rabbinic role, which, Aron claimed, were based on a misunderstanding of the rabbinate. The reformers wanted the rabbis to visit the sick and the bereaved, accompany the dead to the cemeteries, and say the prayers for all critical life-cycle events. Aron pointed out that all these activities could be done by laymen. He said that Judaism recognized every Jew's prayers as equally valid, those of the rabbi having no special significance.

Christian influence is shown also in the 1862 decision to substitute *sous-rabbins* for cantors. Traditionally, if a community could afford to hire only one religious leader, it hired a cantor in preference to a rabbi. The cantor's role as reader of the service was that of layman. (No ecclesiastical role existed.) Because the rabbi's role was scholarly and judicial, he was not an everyday necessity, and a poor community that could not pay his salary could obtain rabbinic decisions by correspondence. A rabbi's presence was in no way necessary to the daily religious practice of the community. Only under the influence of Christianity could the rabbinic role have so evolved that it was deemed desirable to replace cantors by rabbis in 1862.

Another method used by the consistories to control and shape the rabbinate was to influence the choice of rabbis and thereby to obtain the appointment of men who agreed with their own views on the evolution of Judaism. Adolphe Franck seems to have been the one to develop the method of questioning candidates to rabbinic posts on their views on the future of Judaism. In 1846, when the central consistory was about to elect a grand rabbi, Franck composed a questionnaire for the candidates to the post. The rabbis were asked to express their views on nine points of reform that the central consistory suggested. This questionnaire and the use made of it for the purpose of improving lay control of the rabbinate are discussed in Chapter 10.

C. Creation of a Consistorial Monopoly

The third major consistory activity not expressly envisaged by the legislation, was the attempted creation of a consistorial monopoly on Jewish expression and institutions. The consistories sought the monopoly largely for financial reasons, although also in order to change French Judaism through certain (moderate) reforms. We discuss the attempt at development of this monopoly, and the extent to which it was achieved, in the next chapter.

Because its organization was hierarchical, the consistory expected to control all Jewish communities and all Jewish institutions. Yet there were some communities that resisted consistory authority, and even within consistory-controlled communities there were Jews who created independent societies for mutual aid, study, or prayer. Throughout the nineteenth century the departmental consistories attempted to bring within their control all recalcitrant groups, and the central consistory, in turn, sought the subordination of the departmental consistories. Such centralization, both at the departmental and central consistory levels, reached its pinnacle by 1862. By the same year, however, the consistories were forced to recognize that they would not succeed in achieving a total monopoly on all forms of French Jewish expression.

A. Consistory Control of the Various Communities within Each District

1. Legal Status of the Consistories and of the Communities

The organizational structure of nineteenth-century French Judaism offers a marked contrast to that of the traditional Jewish communities. Robert Anchel has correctly described the consistories as totally new institutions with no roots in Jewish traditions ("institution nouvelle et sans racine dans la tradition").[1] It is true that there were preconsistory *superkehillot*,[2] but it should be remembered that the authority of those institutions rested on the voluntary consent of the constituent communities. Perhaps a closer ancestor of the consistories was the Alsatian Provincial-Wide Organization, which was invested with power by the French government.[3]

In an 1810 letter to the ministry, the central consistory itself analyzed the structure of the Jewish communities prior to the consistory system: the Jewish communities designated their own leaders, the *parnassim* or "syndics" and the *gabbai* (the treasurer who received taxes and administered the funds). Principal sources of income were the rental of temple seats, sale of honors, and voluntary contributions. (Although not mentioned by the central consistory, we know that the tax on kosher meat was also a principal source of income in many places.) The officers were elected yearly and were expected to

give an accounting of their use of the funds.[4] With the creation
of the consistories, the several hundred individual Jewish communities lost their legal autonomy, and even their officially
recognized existence. The consistories were the only Jewish
organizations with recognized legal status; they acted on behalf
of the communities of their districts. The consistories negotiated
contracts, purchased land and buildings for synagogues and
cemeteries, and, when necessary, went to court as official
representatives of the Jewish communities.

The acknowledgment of the consistories as the official
representatives of the communities evolved during the nineteenth century. While that was occurring, centralization of
power continued to deprive the private sector of control over
the institutions it had created in pre-emancipation days. Even
after the establishment of the consistories, it often happened
that several individuals of a community joined together privately to finance the acquisition of a synagogue or cemetery, which
either remained private or became community property. The
status of such community and privately owned land and buildings was subsequently questioned. If a synagogue had been built
by the contributions of one or several Jews, could it continue
to be considered private property? Did it make a difference
whether the rabbi or cantor was paid by the government or by
the community? Must the consistory, as the only legal body,
act to make relevant contracts in the name of the private
individuals or the communities, and represent them in court?
Was it the local community or the consistory that bore legal
responsibility? After some administrative hesitations and rever-
sals of opinion, it was ultimately decided that the regional consistory must act for the community in all such instances, and
that even if the local rabbi or cantor did not receive a government salary, buildings used for religious purposes were still to
be considered public buildings. In this way synagogues that had
been built privately became public if they were used by the
Jewish community.

Thus in 1855 the *Cour de Cassation*, ruling on a claim for
damages to the synagogue of Altkirch in the 1848 riots, decided
that despite the fact that the synagogue had been built by
private funds, the building could no longer be considered
private property, and only the consistory could represent it in
legal action for the recovery of damages.[5]

The following year another court decision established that
only the consistory could be sued for debts resulting from construction work on a synagogue. The case concerned the synagogue of Brumath (Bas-Rhin):

*Au cas de travaux exécutés pour une synagogue, l'action en
paiement de ces travaux ne peut être exercée que contre le
consistoire départemental représentant cette synagogue, et non
contre la commission administrative à laquelle le consistoire
aurait délégué le droit de faire exécuter les travaux.*[6]

Even the right to create local synagogues was not uncontested. The 1806 *règlement* had specified that only one "consistorial" synagogue could be built, but that private synagogues could be created upon the recommendation of the consistorial synagogue. This created some doubts about the conditions under which additional (private) synagogues could be built.

It became the practice that the departmental consistory would routinely approve all first requests for synagogues from each community. The power to rule on such requests, however, was used to prevent the formation of second congregations within the same communities. The guiding principle of the consistory was to preserve unity.

The principle of honoring all first requests for local synagogues was established early. In 1812 the Jews of Sélestat (Bas-Rhin) had been prohibited by the mayor from continuing to meet for prayers in the private home of a certain Dreyfus. The mayor claimed that since there were only seven Jewish families in that town, there was not a large enough Jewish population to warrant a synagogue, and that these seven families did not have the required permission for holding private prayer meetings. Moreover, the mayor protested, Dreyfus was suspected of having sheltered a band of thieves during the winter of 1808–09.

The departmental prefect realized that at stake was the general principle of whether the practice of Judaism was going to be tolerated. He asked the Ministry of Cults for a general ruling. The minister replied that inasmuch as Judaism was an officially authorized religion in France, the Jews had the undeniable right to solicit permission from the consistory to gather for prayers:

*Comme les juifs de cette commune n'ont ni synagogue ni
maison de prière pour y remplir leus devoirs religieux et que
leur culte est autorisé dans l'empire, ils ont incontestablement
le droit de solliciter du consistoire de Strasbourg et des
autorités civils dont ils dépendent, la permission de s'assembler
pour faire leurs prières en commun sous la surveillance,
néanmoins, de la police.*[7]

Following this 1812 ministerial ruling, it became automatic for Jewish communities to receive permission to open a first synagogue. Thus, for example, when the developing community of Chalon-sur-Saône requested permission of the Paris consistory to open a temple in 1833, they were informed that they had this right automatically, provided that they would divulge their intentions to the consistory and obey the local police regulations in effect.[8]

This reply to Chalon-sur-Saône was possible only because there was no other synagogue in the town. Almost all separatist prayer meetings were ferreted out by the consistories and were relentlessly prosecuted. In 1857 the Strasbourg consistory successfully brought charges against Benjamin Dreyfus of Wissembourg, who was condemned "pour l'exécution du culte sans la permission de l'autorité municipale" and ordered to pay fifty francs plus court costs.[9]

Once the permission of the departmental consistory was obtained, there remained the question of acquisition of a building. In 1847 the Jewish community of Libourne (Gironde) requested the permission of the local prefect to purchase a building which already served as a synagogue. The prefect passed the request on to the Minister of Cults, who was himself not certain whether the purchase of a synagogue building by a Jewish community that had no government-supported rabbi or cantor had to be handled by the consistory. (It was clear to everyone that this would have been the case had there been a state-salaried "clergyman.") The Minister of Cults refused to approve the acquisition, claiming that such approval would be tantamount to granting the community official status. Because it had no state-salaried clergy, the Libourne Jewish community was not entitled to official status. After the Bordeaux consistory interceded, the ministry approved the acquisition *by the Bordeaux consistory* of a building for use as a synagogue by the Jewish community of Libourne.[10]

2. Consistory Control of the Jewish Community in the Chef-Lieu

Consistory control of Jewish institutions within the city in which the consistory was located (the *chef-lieu*) was more direct and more complete than its control of the other communities within the consistory's district. Some consistories spent entire sessions discussing problems of administering the local synagogue, setting the rental rates of seats, balancing the budget, and repairing the building. In the other communities such problems were handled by local commissions; the consistories became involved only when conflicts arose.

Around 1839 the Paris consistory began to assume control of the various Jewish institutions of the capital. Within a short period several changes were made: the charity board was reorganized under tighter consistory control; the presidents of about twenty mutual aid societies (which the consistory wanted to crush) were co-opted to serve on the charity board; the government, yielding to consistory pressure, banned prayer meetings in the mutual aid societies; the kosher meat trade was reorganized so as to obtain greater financial benefit for the consistory (entailing a ban on nonrecognized *shochetim* from the slaughter houses); the *notables* began meeting less frequently, and consequently the consistory began to assume more responsibility. In 1843 the consistory decided that henceforth all its dealings with "lower" administrations would be in writing. Oral reports were no longer to be allowed, since they were not considered befitting the dignity of a hierarchical administration.[11]

The characteristics of the Jewish communities in the *chefs-lieux* varied, as did the methods of administration. The local community of Strasbourg was a rare example of a *chef-lieu* community that managed to retain much of the flavor of a traditional Jewish community. It was run by a local administration which exercised a remarkable degree of local autonomy in administering the three primary institutions of Jewish life: synagogue, charity, and cemetery. Even the word *communauté*, frequently used in reference to the Jewish population of Strasbourg, is a clue to the actual existence of such a "community."

Joining the Strasbourg *communauté* was not simply a matter of living in Strasbourg and being Jewish, as it was in Paris or Bordeaux. In Strasbourg one made a formal request for admission to the community, and was assessed a fee, according to ability to pay, for cemetery rights, contributions to "cultic" expenses, and charity. That the fees were set at meetings of the administrative commission, to which the candidates were invited, probably helped assure the remarkable harmony that prevailed in Strasbourg.[12]

Similar administrations were established in other *chefs-lieux*. In 1829 the Metz consistory established a "commission administrative des synagogues de Metz" for the two temples.[13] In Bordeaux there was also a "commission administrative," which administered the temple and choir through various internal regulations which it drew up and submitted for consistory approval.[14] In 1851 the Bordeaux commission was reorganized by the consistory, and its new by-laws provided for a commission of five to nine members, to be named by the consistory. Each year one third of the members' terms would expire, but outgoing members could be reappointed. The commission was to supervise the maintenance of order in the synagogue and propose the nomination of all synagogue personnel to the consistory. It was in charge of collecting the temple income, making announcements in the temple, maintaining the building, and buying all ritual materials needed in the synagogue.[15]

A temple administration existed in Paris, but conflict arose between that organization and the consistory. In 1828 the consistory decided to put the temple under its direct supervision, and to delegate one of its members as administrator of the temple. Two of the officers of the former administrative commission were retained: T. Simon, comptroller, and Michel Goudchaux, treasurer.[16] Apparently the new system did not work out well, and the consistory relinquished direct administration of the synagogue some time before 1833. In that year it was decided to replace Alkan, the current administrator of the temple, by holding an election. This was to be the first of regular biennial elections. Only men over twenty years of age who owned or rented seats in the synagogue were eligible, and each man was entitled to only one vote even if he held several seats. Balloting was to be secret, and the winner would be determined by the absolute majority of those present. The consistory would approve of the choice before the administrator could enter into his functions.[17]

Yet before two years had elapsed, there was again discord between the consistory and the temple administrator. In 1835 the consistory repeated an order to Alkan (still administrator) that no announcements were to be made in the temple without consistory approval.[18] The following month Alkan resigned, and the consistory asked Grand Rabbi Ennery to assume the job of *commissaire surveillant* of the temple, thus establishing direct consistory control.[19]

The consistory continued sporadically throughout the period to assert its direct authority over the temple; it was loath to delegate responsibility. Isaac David, cantor and choir leader, was severely reprimanded in 1839 for admitting children to the choir without consistory approval.[20] By 1844 the system had changed again, and a *commission administrative* had been established. Its members were anxious to modernize the synagogue atmosphere through moderate reforms, but the consistory persisted in its refusal to delegate real authority to these administrators, and the commission felt itself powerless. In 1844 it complained about this, pointing out to the consistory that it was unable to take effective steps to remedy daily abuses because it lacked statutes describing its authority. The temple employees, in particular, refused to acknowledge the authority of the commission.[21]

Yet the Paris consistory refused to change its attitude and to relinquish any of its authority. Seven years later, in 1851, the same battle was being fought. In that year the temple administration hired two employees and asked the Paris consistory to ratify their choice. The consistory, jealous of its rights and powers and fearful of usurpation of them by the commission, refused. It was only when the temple administration resigned in protest that the consistory reconsidered its policy and ratified the nominations.[22]

In 1853 the consistory published a *règlement* governing the temple administration. This document established a commission of seven members, appointed by the consistory and replaced, several at a time, on a rotating basis, with each person's term being three years. The administration was to be responsible for the *police générale* of the temple, but the consistory alone would rule on the ceremonies. The grand rabbi would decide on the hour and length of services. The administration would be responsible for the finances of the temple—setting rates and collecting fees. Its members would, on a rotating basis, be present at all ceremonies in the synagogue and make sure that order was maintained ("veillera à ce que pendant la durée des offices les fidèles observent le plus profond silence"). In case of disturbance they would intervene to restore order. (The commission had previously been rebuffed in this attempt by some of the congregants who charged that it had no authority; this *règlement* attempted to reinforce its authority.) The commission also was given limited authority to discipline temple employees, including the right to fine them and suspend them temporarily. The consistory, however, was to exercise all final authority, such as continued suspension or dismissal. By the terms of the *règlement* the commission could make no announcements or post any notices in the temple without approval of the consistory president. No one could preach a sermon or officiate in the temple without consistory authorization.[23]

The newly appointed temple administration immediately resigned to protest the *règlement,* which left it little latitude. Firm in the desire for ultimate control, the consistory accepted the resignations.[24]

The Paris consistory struggled not only to control the main (Ashkenazi) temple, often called the "consistorial temple," but also to bring under its supervision and authority the Portuguese temple, which never completely submitted to consistory control. The 1806 *règlement* provided that there could be only one consistorial temple per district; the Portuguese temple was therefore a "private synagogue" that was "administered" by the consistory. What this meant before 1831 was that the Sephardi population paid twice: they were taxed (as were all the Jews) for the expenses of the Jewish cult and they were responsible for the private financing of the Sephardi synagogue. Control of their synagogue, nevertheless, rested, by terms of the *règlement,* with the consistory. The Paris consistory examined and approved the accounts of the Portuguese synagogue but did not finance it. The hostility of the Sephardi "aristocrats" can be imagined.

When the consistorial temple was built in 1822, a room in an adjoining building was made available to the Sephardim for their synagogue. In 1831, although Judaism was put on the public payroll, the official Jewish cult in Paris was Ashkenazi, and the Sephardi cantor did not receive a state salary until 1834.[25]

For a long time Allegri, *commissaire surveillant* of the Portuguese synagogue, was a member of the Paris consistory, which facilitated the administration of his temple, whose status was ambiguous. The consistory continued to be consulted in many matters of administration, but the financing remained the Portuguese temple's own responsibility. Thus in 1837 when Allegri sought and obtained permission for some structural improvements in the synagogue, the Paris consistory stressed that the improvements were to be made at the temple's own expense.[26] The Portuguese community outgrew its tiny quarters in the temple annex, and in 1846, when the boys' school left this building to move to the newly erected communal school, the Portuguese asked permission to expand into that space.[27]

Until the 1870's, when three new consistorial temples were built and one was designed for the Sephardi rite, the status of the Portuguese synagogue remained unclear. In an 1845 letter to the Paris consistory approving the election of Aaron Lopes Silva, cantor of the Portuguese temple, the central consistory referred to the temple as though it were, in fact, a consistorial institution: "votre temple consistorial du rite portugais."[28]

The Portuguese population was split between two factions. There were those who favored an attempt to merge with the Ashkenazi population into a single *rite français*. Members of this group were willing to put themselves totally under the control of the Paris consistory and simultaneously to benefit from the broader income base of this large Ashkenazi population. The other group of Sephardic leaders waged a constant struggle to maintain their independence from the consistory.

Without consulting the consistory, the Portuguese synagogue administration, in 1854, re-located its temple at 29 rue Lamartine, which was at that time in the second *arrondissement*. This administration developed its own funeral regulations and fees and denied that it was accountable to the consistory. It claimed that the Portuguese temple was a private chapel allowable under the terms of the 1844 *ordonnance,* with consistorial approval. The dissident Sephardi Jews petitioned the consistory to intervene, facilitate fusion with the Ashkenazim, and exert financial control in order to lower the expenses of the congregation attending the Portuguese temple.[29]

The building in which the Portuguese temple was located was, indeed, a privately acquired building. It belonged to Allegri, president of the administration of that temple. It was taxed by the city as a private building, although Allegri asked the consistory to intervene to get the city to accept its classification as a tax-exempt place of public worship.[30]

The Portuguese remained in their semi-autonomous position, while a commission tried to work out a "fusion" of the two rites. Although some of the Sephardi chants and customs eventually entered the French consistorial ceremony, complete "fusion" never took place, and the Paris Sephardim have maintained their independent existence, under the supervision of the consistory, to this day.[31]

The refusal of the Paris consistory to delegate authority was reflected not only in its relations with the two Paris synagogue authorities, but also in its power struggle with the charity board (*comité de bienfaisance*). This board was composed of zealous and charitable Jews, of a somewhat lower social group than the men of the consistory. They were frequently pious and often foreign-born, so not eligible for membership on the consistory. Benoît Cohen, for one, served for many years as president of the *comité,* and he felt very much antagonized by the consistory's condescending attitude. In 1843 Cohen appended a note to his long statistical analysis of the committee's work of the past year, in which he asked that the consistory try to realize that even though the charity board was administered by the consistory, it need not be constantly made to feel inferior:

> *L'Administration du Comité est, il est vrai, inférieure dans la hiérarchie administrative à celle du Consistoire, mais il serait de bon goût, que celle-ci ne cherchât pas à le faire sentir au Comité dont les membres sont toujours prêts comme les siens, à sacrifier leurs occupations et leurs plaisirs au bien de leur coreligionnaires.* [32]

3. Control of the Other Communities of the District

Consistory control of Jewish institutions scattered throughout the consistory district differed markedly from the situation within the *chef-lieu*. It was never possible for the consistory to keep as close an eye on the affairs of the other communities as on those of its own city. Actual levels of control varied with the consistory, the community, and the year.

As we have shown, the community itself had no legal status. No specific mention had been made in the original *règlement* of the mechanism for governing the communities, but it was generally considered that they were to be governed by the regulations concerning private synagogues. Such synagogues were, according to the *règlement*, to be administered by two *notables* and a rabbi, appointed by the departmental consistory and approved by the central consistory. Although the consistories considered that their authority over the communities stemmed from this provision, they never followed the procedure that had been prescribed. They began, instead, to appoint delegates, called *commissaires surveillants*, in the various communities, and because these officers had no legal status, the government refused to participate in their installations.[33] Even after the *ordonnance* of August 20, 1823 prescribed the appointment of *commissaires surveillants*, the government maintained its refusal to recognize the legal status of these delegates.[34] For this reason, the consistories were refused the right of postage-free communication with them, although they did have this privilege for their correspondence with the communal rabbis.[35]

The communities were generally insistent upon adherence to hierarchical forms, both within the *chef-lieu* and in the communities. For example, when a cantor of Rouen wrote to the Paris consistory in 1831 to inquire whether he could receive a salary from the state according to the new law, he was told to correspond in the future through the intermediary of the *commissaire surveillant*.[36]

Although the system of appointing *commissaires surveillants* was eventually instituted everywhere, the change took place at varying rates. In Bayonne, in 1819, for example, the *Hebera* still existed.[37]

Although the 1823 *ordonnance* gave the consistories the right to appoint the *commissaires surveillants*, the consistories frequently allowed the communities to elect them. Such elections represented a vestige of communal democracy in the communities, even when there was none in the *chefs-lieux*. It was not love of democracy, however, but practicality, that induced the consistories to permit elections in the communities. The consistory members did not know the inhabitants of the various communities, and were in no position to choose leaders. Furthermore, the authority of the consistory in outlying areas was difficult enough to assert without risking also the imposition of unpopular leaders.

Because of the frequent conflicts that arose within the communities, it was often difficult to find someone to accept the job of *commissaire surveillant*. In 1839 M. B. Lecerq, cantor in Brest, informed the Paris consistory that he had not been able to find anyone in that city who was willing to take the job.[38]

The details of the administration of the consistories varied from one consistory to another. Some communities forwarded their budgets for approval; others did not. Thus the Paris consistory's communications with its communities were less detailed than those of the Strasbourg consistory. Yet the job of *commissaire surveillant* of the Lille community (Paris district) was described in 1846 as one of reporting yearly to the consistory on the local budget, religious instruction, and charitable institutions.[39]

In 1846 the Metz consistory took stock of its relationship with the various communities of its district. Conflicts in the communities had been a frequent source of difficulty for the consistory, and it was decided that a uniform procedure would be established for the nomination, installation, and functioning of local administrative commissions. It was resolved that new commissions of three to seven members would be established in each community, the size depending upon the local population. The mayors of the communities with Jewish populations were asked to conduct the elections, at which the Jews would designate a double list of candidates. The consistory would then choose the members of the commission from this list.[40]

In submitting this new *règlement* to the central consistory for its approval, the Metz consistory explained that by allowing the communities to participate in the selection of their leaders, frequent conflicts might be eliminated.[41]

The difficulties encountered in administering the communities were of several kinds. Sometimes the *commissaire surveillant* refused to obey consistory orders and had to be reprimanded or dismissed.[42] Often the local population refused to honor the authority of the *commissaire surveillant*. This problem was not as easily solved. If the community rejected consistorial authority it rejected any *commissaire surveillant* imposed by the consistory. It was, therefore, of no use for the consistory to install a new one. In 1860, when the rabbi of Lauterbourg informed the Strasbourg consistory that the *commissaire surveillant* of Wisserbourg was without real influence on the community, the consistory kept the man in office but reprimanded him for his ineffectiveness.

On the other hand, it was not rare for *commissaires surveillants* to resign from their uncomfortable posts. Frequent resignations were a tremendous hardship to the consistories, which often refused to accept them and tried instead to pressure the men into retaining their posts.

Although Anchel thought that during the Empire the *commissaires surveillants* were the influential representatives of the consistories in the communities, it appears that such an estimation of consistory influence at this early period is an exaggeration. Anchel says: "dans l'ensemble, les commissaires surveillants furent les informateurs actifs et les auxiliaires précieux des consistoires, tant pour l'administration culturelle que comme agents de propagande dans l'oeuvre régénératrice."[43] It was, in fact, after the Empire that the consistories became active in seeking, with more or less prudence, to impose their aims upon the communities. But despite apparent increases in their powers, because of additional laws, the consistories continued to encounter legal difficulties in imposing their authority. The more prudent among them adopted conciliation as the wisest political tactic, attempting to avoid protests against their authority. Others attempted to impose consistorial views and ways on the communities, a policy that led to confrontations between the consistories (or their *commissaires surveillants*) and the local population.

The range of consistory control in the various communities can be illustrated by the two cases of Rouen in 1836 and Lyon two years later. In 1838 S. Levy protested that the Marseille consistory had imposed two delegates on the Lyon community, in an effort to mold that community to its own way of thinking. Both delegates, Levy complained, were foreigners, not naturalized, unknown to the Jewish community, who lived entirely apart from the community.[44]

At the other extreme, Paris consistory control of Rouen was very lax and offers an interesting contrast to the situation in Lyon. At its meeting of February 26, 1836, the Paris consistory discussed a request by the cantor of Rouen for the appointment of a *commissaire surveillant* in that city. Confused and surprised, the consistory noted that its records showed that a Sr Molina had been *commissaire surveillant* for a long time. The following month the consistory was informed by Rouen that Sr Molina had been dead for several years.[45]

A perusal of the minutes books of the Strasbourg consistory shows the same variations in consistory–community contacts. For the two-year period, June 24, 1858, to June 21, 1860, this consistory discussed the affairs of ninety-one communities within its district. During these same years Jews were actually located in more than 130 communities, but some of these congregations were very small. The Jewish communities whose affairs were not discussed by the consistory during the two-year period we analyzed were mainly, but not exclusively, the very small ones. Thus of the forty Jewish communities not mentioned in these minutes, twenty-six had (according to the 1861 census) two to forty-one Jews each, another ten were more substantial communities of fifty-one to seventy-eight Jews, and four more held over one hundred each: Benfield, 127; Bischwiller, 216; Wingersheim, 101; and Wittersheim, 124. In 1861 the total Jewish population of these forty communities was 1620 (out of 20,951 for the entire department). At most, then, 7.7 percent of the Bas-Rhin Jewish population escaped consistory control. It is possible, however, that the percentage was lower and that some of the smaller communities worshiped together and shared the facilities of larger neighboring communities.

Strasbourg consistory involvement with the communities varied from one place to another. Several of the larger communities whose affairs were discussed during the two-year period are mentioned only once or twice during the minutes of those years. Other communities, especially those with recalcitrant members, are mentioned frequently in the minutes books. The community most mentioned in the minutes is that of Strasbourg, indicating the tendency we have already noted of the *chef-lieu* to dominate consistory considerations and to be directly under consistory supervision, while other communities maintained greater autonomy.

Significant consistorial influence on the communities developed slowly during the early years of the consistorial system. The influence increased more rapidly from 1839 to 1862.

Sometimes an entire community would refuse to subordinate itself to the consistory but still manage to benefit from the special aid that was, in theory, available to Jewish communities only through the consistory. In 1854, for example, the Nancy consistory complained that the cantor of Bar-le-Duc, M. Chetels, had received financial aid from the government, without the intermediary of the consistory. The Nancy consistory explained that the Jewish community of Bar-le-Duc had consistently refused to submit to consistory authority. In reply the central consistory regretted the breach of hierarchy and informed Nancy that the central consistory itself had not been consulted in the matter. M. Chetels had received the aid because of the intervention of an influential friend.[46]

Normally the situation was quite the reverse, and it was not possible for a Jewish community to establish its right of existence and to be assured of its security without formal constitution through the consistory. For this reason the developing Jewish community of Chalon-sur-Saône took the initiative, in 1835, to be officially constituted as a community under the authority of the Colmar consistory. When this consistory ignored several of their letters (for reasons we cannot determine) the Jews of Chalon-sur-Saône complained to the central consistory that they were unable to negotiate with the local consistory. Without official status they feared they would not be able to acquire a cemetery and their temple might be closed down. For the communities, then, the consistory meant the lifeline to the privileges and aid that could come from the state. This, if no other reason, inclined them toward cooperation with the consistory.

The effectiveness of the consistory influence in the communities continued to vary and to be far from total throughout the entire period. As late as 1856 the Strasbourg consistory complained to the central consistory that it had not been able to bring the rather large Jewish community of Bischwiller under its control. The consistory wished to integrate Bischwiller into one of its rabbinic districts, but had been unable to get the community to cooperate.[47]

In 1856 Rabbi B. Mossé of Avignon complained about the jealously guarded autonomy of several communities, which prevented them from adopting the decisions of the 1856 rabbinic conference.[48]

Similarly, there were communities in the Haut-Rhin district as late as 1862 which appear to have avoided contact with the Colmar consistory. When the 1862 decree limited suffrage to men who participated financially in consistory-approved Jewish institutions, the Colmar consistory inquired about the electoral rights of the Jews in communities that did not submit to consistory authority:

Quelques rares communautés ne soumettent jamais leur
budget à l'approbation du Consistoire; elles n'ont aucune
fondation pieuse ou religieuse autorisée ou administrée par
le consistoire; ces communautés en masse sont-elle privées par
cela même du droit de voter?[49]

The relationship between the communities and the consistories was based on necessity and characterized by hostility. The establishment by law of the consistorial system and the subsequent decision to grant state-funding to Judaism had destroyed not only the legal autonomy of the communities, but also their initiative. Communities quickly learned to expect aid from above in solving all difficulties. In 1836, for example, the Nantes community requested financial aid in order to hire a ritual slaughterer. The consistory emphasized that such expenses must be borne by those who benefit locally from the service and that the consistory had no funds for such purposes.[50] Similarly, the Fontainebleau community complained that it had buried a pauper at communal expense and wished to be reimbursed for the twenty francs of their costs. The consistory again had to make it clear that the individual communities must support their own charges and their own public charity.[51] In 1843 it was the turn of the Nantes community to ask the consistory to help recover the burial costs of two poor Jews, at a total cost of eighty francs.[52]

The consistories administered the communities from the exterior. They named, confirmed, and dismissed *commissaires surveillants,* cantors, teachers. They corresponded with the communities (primarily about financial matters). The consistories transmitted requests for aid from the communities to the ministry, and received the replies and the funds, which it forwarded to the communities. When conflicts arose, the consistory intervened to reestablish peace.

Conflicts generally revolved around financial and ceremonial issues. The people of the communities often felt that the consistory-appointed leaders were imposing foreign (consistorial) ways upon the community. Resentment arose about the sums of money asked as "contributions." When appealed to, the consistories generally endorsed the penalties imposed by *commissaires surveillants* on people who refused to comply with their orders. Hundreds of letters and petitions of protest against *commissaires surveillants* were submitted to departmental consistories and the central consistory, and some were even published in the press.

The consistories generally took it upon themselves to restore harmony. Often consistory members or rabbis visited the community involved and attempted to correct the problem. We have already mentioned the conflict between the Jews of Lyon and their *commissaire surveillant,* Heyman de Ricqlès. This Dutch Jew with "reform" notions was disliked both for his religious views and his fiscal policies. In 1840 during a visit to the girls' school, he made a point of informing the girls that intermarriage was permitted by the Sanhedrin decisions. This led to a scandal. De Ricqlès was charged also with attacking traditional beliefs in public speeches. His fiscal policies were denounced. He had raised the funeral tax from a twenty-franc to a seventy-five-franc minimum and was charged by S. Lévy with extracting as much as he could get from the rich by the severe pressure tactics of his agents. Lévy said that de Ricqlès forced the poor to sign an agreement to pay before he would allow a funeral to be held.

The Jews of Lyon were unable to get the Marseille consistory to acknowledge their complaints. In desperation they communicated with the grand rabbi through the intermediary of the departmental prefect. After more than two years of hostilities, the Marseille consistory was forced to hold an election to replace de Ricqlès, but even then it was charged with unfairly influencing the elections.[53]

Although the consistory sometimes supervised local institutions, it was the community that created them. The consistories took almost no initiative in anticipating local needs. When a community's population grew to a sufficient size to deserve a rabbi, the community requested that a rabbinic post be established, and it supported the request with census lists or population levels. Routinely, the consistory would endorse the request and transmit it to the central consistory, which alone could ask the government to fund the post.

Because the original *règlement* had given the consistories the job of administering the private synagogues and supervising the collection of taxes, the consistories developed a practice of supervising local budgets. In some cases communities forwarded budgets and accounts for consistorial approval and auditing even after 1831, when the tax system was discontinued. Whereas complaints against the taxes had been frequent before 1831, a new sort of dissension arose in the 1830's. Strapped for funds and unable to finance local needs other than by voluntary contributions, the communities' administrators resorted to an unofficial, "voluntary" taxation—or *cotisation*. This was equivalent to the imposition of membership dues on those who wished to participate in the organized Jewish community life. Failure to comply was punished with what amounted in fact, if not in name, to excommunication. Such people were not allowed to receive honors, and in some cases they were even excluded from praying in the synagogues. Sometimes the butchers were told not to sell to them, and the *mohelim* were instructed not to circumcise their children.

Freedom to make budgetary and fund-raising decisions by the communities varied tremendously from place to place. In their typically pragmatic way the consistories based their judgment of the permissible upon immediate political considerations, rather than upon a definite ideology. Sometimes the communities were refused even the most elementary fund-raising rights. In 1853 the Versailles community was refused permission to solicit funds for the construction of a new temple. Versailles then turned to the Paris consistory for aid and received 200 francs, the same amount of aid previously accorded in that year to both the Rheims and Orléans communities for similar purposes.[54]

Arguments over local administration of funds were sometimes referred directly to the government by angry Jews who could obtain no satisfaction from the consistory. The issue of "dues" or "taxes" thus became public, and the central consistory and the government examined together the question of the rights and limitations of the Jewish administrations.

In 1853 and 1854 the communities of Ribeauvillé and Colmar and several others in the Haut-Rhin were split over the payment of dues and the religious sanctions that were being used to enforce them. Dissenters of Ribeauvillé and Colmar complained to the Ministry of Cults, and the central consistory's opinion was then solicited by the government. In response to the ministry's request, the central consistory sent a detailed account of the financial problems faced by the Jewish communities. The central consistory began by explaining that since 1830 there were still many religious expenses that remained at the charge of the communities and that even salaries for the clergy were often paid by the small communities where there were no state-salaried posts. Income in these small communities, however, was almost nonexistent. Synagogue seats were generally owned by those who cooperatively built the edifice, and therefore there was no rental income. The sale of honors generated very little income. The general method adopted for financing the communities had been one of *répartition*—the division of the costs among members of the communities. Ordinarily this procedure was amicably arranged and agreeable to all parties and was handled *en famille* with no recalcitrants. In fact, the central consistory pointed out, the two petitioners from Alsace, M. Dreyfus of Colmar and his brother-in-law, M. Sée of Ribeauvillé, had themselves been *commissaires surveillants* and in that capacity had used the same method of financing the communities they were now protesting. They changed their opinions, the central consistory charged, only because they were removed from office by the Colmar consistory when they refused to render their accounts to that consistory. Although they were professing to believe that the "tax" was illegal, the consistory insisted, they were in reality attempting to camouflage bad faith behind references to liberal principles and charges of illegal taxation. Moreover, the central consistory claimed, the only supporters of Dreyfus and Sée were men who found it profitable to benefit from community institutions without supporting them.

Defending the sanctions imposed by the Colmar consistory as very moderate, the central consistory pointed out that the recalcitrants had been refused admission, not to the synagogue, but only to the honors. In regard to *kashrut,* they were told that either they must contribute toward the salary of the *shochet* or they would be denied his services. The central consistory declared that it gave its entire approval to the Colmar consistory's administrative procedure for financing the communities. This procedure consisted of four provisions: the communities were permitted to impose dues on their members; they were to draw up annual budgets based on their expenses of the preceding three years; the administrative committee of each synagogue was to handle the finances; it was to submit an annual report to the consistory.[55]

The Haut-Rhin communities continued to use this method of raising funds, and the consistory appears to have organized its supervision of the system in an increasingly efficient manner. In 1861 the consistory published a notification that all *rôles de répartitions* had to be addressed by the communities to the consistory during the months of November and December.[56]

A similar system appears to have been in effect during the 1850's in the Bas-Rhin, although it was not uniformly enforced and only some of the communities actually forwarded annual financial reports.[57] In 1858 the Strasbourg consistory drew up a new *règlement,* which prescribed the establishment by all the communities of an annual list of dues (*rôle annuel des cotisa-tions*), calculated on the basis of each person's capacity to pay. This list was to be submitted for consistory approval, together with the accounts for the preceding year. It was specified that those who refused to pay their share would be excluded from the rights and honors of the synagogues.[58]

Another source of conflict over community financing was the question whether the consistory had the right to insist that local communities appropriate funds for consistory-run institutions which benefited the entire district. A case in point is the *Ecole de Travail* (trade school) for Alsatian Jewish youth, established in Strasbourg in 1825. Financing this institution was always a problem, and both the school and the consistory were constantly soliciting funds to maintain it. In the 1850's the Strasbourg consistory ruled that every community in the district must allocate a set annual sum for this purpose. When some communities refused to comply, the consistory, confident of its authority, added this item to their budgets.[59]

Ten years earlier a similar issue had caused bitter conflict within the Haut-Rhin district. The zealous "regenerators" of the Philanthropic Society had been authorized by the Colmar consistory to solicit contributions for a proposed *Ecole des Arts et Métiers,* but issued instead a threatening letter *demanding* contributions from the budget of each community. The letter warned the *commissaires surveillants* of the various communities that if they did not comply, they would be dismissed, or the funds would be written into their budgets by the Society. The Colmar consistory protested that the Society had gone too far, but the central consistory chose to back the high-handed tactics of the Philanthropic Society against what it judged to be a retrograde consistory.[60]

Regulations (*règlements*) for the governing of the communities were either made locally and approved by the consistory or imposed upon the communities by the consistory. As early as 1809 the Strasbourg consistory published a set of regulations according to which the communities of its district would be governed uniformly.[61] In 1858 the same consistory published a revised *règlement* for the communities of its district. This document specified that administrative committees of varying sizes (depending upon the local population) would be created in each community. The duties of the committees included the policing of the local synagogues and maintaining the monolithic structure of Judaism by preventing prayers and weddings outside the temple. They were to handle the finances, cemeteries, division of honors, and charitable institutions. The hierarchical system was emphasized, and financial penalties were prescribed for synagogue employees who refused to recognize the authority of the *commissaire surveillant*. In addition, certain ceremonial practices were ordered. During weddings and confirmations (*initiations religieuses*) women were to be allowed in the men's section; at other ceremonies men and women were to remain separated. The consistory also ordered an end to the practice of auctioning honors in the synagogues. In place of this system of raising funds, the Jews of the communities were to share the costs of the religious institutions by paying dues (*cotisations*).[62]

The 1844 *ordonnance* had given the consistories the right to approve the *règlements* by which the communities were to be governed, and in that year the Colmar consistory published a similar document governing its district.

Although these documents were duly approved by the consistories and then by the central consistory, the government refused to make them official by reading and approving them. In 1861 the Strasbourg consistory attempted to enforce its authority on the basis of its 1858 *règlement* through court action. The court advised that the consistory's rights would be clearer if the prefecture would give official approval to the *règlement*. When the prefect requested a ruling on this from the ministry, he was informed that no such approval was required by the terms of the 1844 *ordonnance*.[63] This ministerial policy drastically limited the effect of consistorial authority. It was but another in the series of events which revealed the 1844 *ordonnance* to be unenforceable.

By imposing regulations on the communities, some of the consistories, like that of Strasbourg, sought to assure a certain level of modern religious instruction. They did so by requiring an examination and a confirmation ceremony (*initiation religieuse*) as prerequisites to the acquisition of honors in the synagogue. The examination was based upon the official "catechism," the *Précis* by Samuel Cahen. This requirement had the effect of refusing the celebration of the *Bar Mitzvah* to children who had not received modern religious education. Not unexpectedly, this decision was protested by the traditional Jews. In 1858 a Sr. Loeb of Strasbourg protested that his son was refused the right to read the Torah in the synagogue because he had not participated in the ceremony of *initiation religieuse*. The consistory agreed to reverse the decision on the condition that M. Loeb promise to send his son to religious instruction.[64] Several of the communities reported difficulty in implementing this regulation, but the consistory insisted that it was its intention to refuse the celebration of Bar Mitzvah to boys who had not participated in the confirmation ceremony. The consistory called for increased surveillance of the religious instruction given in the Jewish schools. If at all possible it was to be given by the rabbis themselves. When they could not do so, the regular teacher was to give it, but the rabbis were to make frequent visits and inspections.[65]

The same *règlement* required the abolition of the sale of honors by auction in the synagogue. For a long time this practice had been under attack as one that turned the synagogue into a financial exchange. It had the merit, however, of assuring an income to the communities, and many of them were afraid to give it up. Recalcitrance was treated harshly by the consistory, which was successful in getting the courts to agree to prosecute. Apparently this was all that was needed; actual prosecution seems not to have occurred. The remaining communities (Zellwiller, Brumath, Lauterbourg, Mutterholtz, Schirrhoffen) complied.[66]

In order to create uniform ceremonial practices, the consistories began to be concerned that only "authorized" people conduct the services. Since 1823 they had the right to name the cantors in the various communities, but this applied only to those who held official posts as cantors. Judaism, however, permitted any male over thirteen to lead the services, and there were many traditionally religious individuals for whom this was a coveted honor. By 1846 the Metz consistory was able to insist that the town of Thionville add a clause to its proposed *règlement* which limited the right to officiate to the cantor except for certain named persons who might participate during the week prior to *Rosh Ha Shanah* and during the High Holy Days.[67]

A handful of reforming spirits since the beginning of the century had wanted to see the consistories make rapid and significant changes in the ritual and practices of the communities. They believed that a hierarchical administration was the ideal mechanism for the imposition of uniform and progressive changes in the direction of "reform." It was only after 1840, however, that the consistories began insisting on the abolition of the sale of honors, on the establishment of the confirmation ceremony, and on the imposition of order during synagogue ceremonies. It was much later (around 1870) that it imposed a uniform prayer in French for the government. Consistory concern with ritual was for a long time limited to the transmission of government requests for prayers in celebration of national events. Some consistories prescribed programs to be followed on such occasions. The communities' expectations of directions from the consistories increased gradually, and they became dependent upon the consistories. In 1832 during the great cholera epidemic the Versailles community asked the Paris consistory what prayers should be said for the cessation of the epidemic.[68]

This kind of expectation continued. In 1845 the *commissaire surveillant* of Rouen asked the Paris consistory to indicate the prayers and hymns to be used for the inauguration of the temple, and the consistory requested Grand Rabbi Ennery to instruct the *commissaire surveillant* of the procedure to follow.[69]

Similarly, the *commissaire surveillant* of Dijon (Mannheimer) turned to the Paris consistory for advice on imposing order and dignity during funerals. The consistory suggested that Mannheimer was in a better position to handle the problem and suggested that he draft a *règlement* which the consistory would approve.[70]

Although the consistories monitored the sermons that were

delivered in the consistorial synagogues[71] it does not appear that they gave prior approval to the sermons of the other communities in their districts. In 1843 the Marseille consistory decided, as a result of de Ricqlès' controversial sermon attacking Christianity, that all sermons in the Lyon synagogue had to be submitted for consistory approval. This control was extended only to Lyon and was not the general rule for all of the communities in the district.[72]

B. Competition Between the Central and Departmental Consistories

The competition for power that existed between the communities and the departmental consistories was mirrored on the next level by a similar struggle between the departmental consistories and the central consistory. In Chapter 4 we have shown that the legislative changes proposed throughout the century by the central consistory aimed at increasing its own centralized authority, and that the departmental consistories generally reacted with hostility to such attempts. The departments were sometimes extremely sensitive about issues concerning their prerogatives. Thus in 1828 the Paris consistory members complained to the ministry that they had not been consulted when the central consistory drew up a list of candidates for the Parisian *notabilité,* and they threatened to resign if their right to make recommendations was not honored.[73]

The central consistory, on the other hand, was jealous of its position at the top of the hierarchical consistory structure and did not easily forgive transgressions of the rules of proper channels. In 1858 the central consistory distributed a circular complaining that the departmental consistories had not respected the hierarchy but had sent directly to the Emperor letters of congratulation at his having escaped an assassination attempt. Indignant at being among the recipients of this circular, the Paris consistory wrote to say that it, for one, had forwarded its letter through the intermediary of the central consistory.[74]

Similarly, when the eastern consistories held a collective meeting in Strasbourg in 1846 to discuss some of the problems French Judaism was facing and some of the reforms that it might be necessary to institute, the central consistory was quick to state its disapproval. It even claimed that such a meeting was illegal according to the terms of Article 54 of the 1844 *ordonnance.* The Metz consistory disagreed, claiming that the article in question referred exclusively to meetings of the rabbis. The Metz consistory insisted on the departmental consistories' right to meet for discussion and to seek solutions to contemporary problems. It protested that in no way did this usurp the authority of the central consistory, especially since that organization had received a copy of the minutes of the Strasbourg discussions. Moreover, Metz continued, rather than simply "annul" the decisions of the eastern consistories, the central consistory should have given them serious consideration and made useful recommendations.[75]

It was not paranoia that caused the central consistory to be suspicious of departmental consistory encroachments on their own prerogatives. There were indeed such encroachments, sometimes in ignorance or haste; sometimes for opportunistic reasons. In 1838, despite its full knowledge of the central consistory's ruling that no religious sanctions could be used to force payment of dues, the Paris consistory recommended such sanctions to the Reims community as the best method for collecting debts.[76]

In another example of disregard for central consistory authority, the Colmar consistory, in 1844, published a *règlement* that ordered the dismissal of cantors who failed to meet newly established criteria for the post. Dismissal of the cantors, however, was a prerogative of the central consistory, and the *règlement* therefore represented a usurpation of central consistory powers, as the press was quick to point out.[77]

Despite their differences, the consistories worked together harmoniously most of the time. The departmental consistories were generally deferential to the higher authority of the central consistory. In the absence of any legal requirement for them to do so, for example the departmental consistories frequently submitted their *règlements* for central consistory approval.[78]

The long-range program of the central consistory to gain control over all aspects of French Judaism threatened the authority of the local consistories. In 1854, immediately after the passage of the law transferring from the electorate to the departmental consistories the right to name grand rabbis, the central consistory went on record as opposing this system, and it indicated that it wished to acquire this right for itself.[79] By 1862 its ambition was realized.

By 1862, also, the central consistory had succeeded in acquiring, at the expense of the local consistories, the right to award the lower rabbinic degree. (Since the inception of the consistorial system it had had the right to award the higher degree.) The departmental consistories had unsuccessfully fought this further encroachment on their powers by arguing that as local authorities they were in a better position to judge the morality and merit of the candidates.[80]

The departmental consistories of the south united in a protest against the central consistory's plan of training assistant rabbis to take over the posts held by cantors. The southern communities protested that the Metz school did not and could not teach the Portuguese ritual, and that the needs of the southern communities could be served only by people trained in the south at the special cantorial school maintained in Bordeaux.[81] The struggle was waged for ten years, until the 1862 decree did indeed create the post of *sous-rabbin* (assistant rabbi). The post of cantor (*ministre officiant*), however, continued to exist, and in the south was filled by men trained in the Portuguese *minhag*.

The bitterest conflict that occurred between the central consistory and a departmental consistory was with the Colmar consistory—a struggle that lasted almost twenty years during the 1840's and 1850's. In an attempt to bring Upper Alsace firmly under the influence of modernized French Judaism as it was being developed in Paris, the central consistory ignored the proper channels of the hierarchy and entered into direct communications with some of the more liberal rabbis, the philanthropic society, and the trade school (1844). It requested (unsuccessfully) the dissolution of the Colmar consistory (1849), annulled a consistory election (1858), and involved the government in a project to control elections in favor of "desirable" candidates (1861).

The central consistory's reason for this extreme action was its certainty that Alsatian Jews needed thorough and drastic reforming. It was commonly believed that they were the black sheep of French Judaism, being less educated and less enlightened than those in the rest of the country. That anti-Jewish outbreaks occurred almost exclusively in Alsace was attributed partly to this defect in the Alsatian Jewish community. The central consistory set itself the task of bringing about sufficient changes in the Alsatian Jewish population so that further attacks would not be provoked. Jewish leadership of the nineteenth century had clearly adopted the prevailing image of the Jews, and its method of handling all problems was therefore one of attempting to correct Jewish defects. This meant agreeing that Alsatian Jews who were itinerant peddlers were untrustworthy, that usury, a serious problem, was practiced by large numbers of Jews. It meant believing that only by training Jews to be skilled industrial workers would they be useful members of society and achieve integration.

Opposition to such a program, the central consistory felt, must be crushed as rapidly and effectively as possible, and therefore methods of coercion must replace methods of persuasion. This policy led to the twenty-year schism between the central consistory and the Alsatian reformers or proponents of regeneration on the one hand, and much of the local population on the other. A large part of the Alsatian wealthy and influential leadership also objected to coercive measures (such as the consistory's revising local budgets to assure appropriation of funds for the trade school). They opposed the use of threats against the poor who refused to cooperate with their own regeneration.

An ideological dispute arose, too, between the Colmar consistory and the more zealous Philanthropic Society (backed by the central consistory) over how much of the population needed reforming. The consistory was concerned mainly with the itinerant peddlers and beggars, the ones who gave Alsatian Jewry its bad image. The Philanthropic Society, on the other hand, was anxious to industrialize the entire poor population of Upper Alsace through its own training program and school. It wanted to raise more funds by force than were forthcoming by voluntary contributions. The consistory wished to limit action to what it viewed as legal means. The central consistory found itself more in sympathy with the vigorous approach of the Philanthropic Society, thus helping to create a split in the community.[82]

C. Growth of the Consistorial Monopoly

In addition to centralized power in a hierarchical organization, the consistory system tended toward a monopoly on Jewish institutions in the country. By 1862 this monopoly was far from complete, but it had developed to the limit of its potential. By this year also, the identity and security of several nonconsistorial institutions had been fairly well established. Those institutions outside the scope of the consistory included the Jewish press, the *Alliance Israélite Universelle,* mutual aid societies, and *minyanim* (prayer meetings), many of which were maintained by mutual aid societies.

Among the institutions of a Jewish community there are always cemeteries, synagogues, pious societies, small prayer gatherings, kosher meat shops, and charity boards, and it was not a new thing in nineteenth-century France that the officially recognized Jewish leaders sought to control or tax them, or—in the case of the charity board—to prescribe the conditions under which aid might be given. In Paris an attempt had been made in 1809 to disband independent charitable societies to strengthen the newly created consistorial charity board. Despite their interdiction, however, mutual aid societies continued to exist, and to provide major competition for the consistories. In these small societies poor men could be presidents and treasurers; they found companionship and warmth—a reminiscence of traditional life.

In order to crush the independence of some of its subcommittees, the Paris consistory resolved, in 1829, that all organizations that were financially supported by the consistory would be headed by a consistory member. This practice did not last long, but it marked the beginning of rigorous efforts by the consistory to assert its preeminence over these groups, including the temple administration, the school committee, the women's committee for the girls' school, and the charity board.

The major group of rival institutions, the mutual aid societies, continued to exist. In 1839 the consistory was unable to obtain a ministerial ruling forcing these societies to disband or to reorganize as exclusively charitable organizations, not permitted to hold prayer meetings. It proved difficult and often impossible to enforce this measure. The 1844 *ordonnance* was

designed to give consistorial pretentions to monopolistic control
a legally secure basis. The consistories were soon to find, however, that the law could not be enforced and that the authorities were not anxious to remedy the situation.

The Revolution of 1848 gave the consistories a setback. The
orthodox Jewish masses began to talk about freedom of trade
and the unfair consistory monopoly on the kosher meat trade.
Several independent kosher butcher shops appeared in Paris.
The people entered seriously into the struggle against the
sole authority of the consistory. The Jewish press helped to
mold public opinion. Simon Bloch of *L'Univers Israélite* was
particularly outspoken about the consistories' misuse of power.
In 1857 he attacked the *"absolutisme consistorial."*[83] He
told the story from the point of view of a man who understood the intentions and the mentality of the central consistory; he had been secretary to this organization and was
fired after many years of publicly disagreeing with his em-
ployers.

Bloch was not overstating his case when he denounced
consistorial absolutism. This was precisely the goal of the
consistories, one they believed had been implicit in their very
conception. Total control was sought more for financial reasons
than for philosophical ones. At no time were the consistories
assured of the funds they required; before 1831 taxes were insufficient, and after 1831 government funds and voluntary
contributions were insufficient.

1. Prayer Meetings

The major sources of income in Jewish communities usually
included the sale and rental of synagogue seats, the sale of
ritual honors, and voluntary offerings made by individuals at
significant times in their lives. Because the *minyanim* (private
prayer meetings) competed with the consistories' temple for this
revenue, they were a prime target for consistorial attacks. Moreover, the consistory was not satisfied with the traditional style
of service generally celebrated by these private prayer meetings,
nor with the freedom from supervision that they enjoyed.

The most common reasons for the existence of private Jewish
prayer meetings in nineteenth-century France were financial
and social. The lack of space in the consistorial synagogue and
the distance of that synagogue from areas of Jewish residence
provided additional motivations for the holding of private
minyanim. Traditionalist attitudes toward the ritual also played
a part, because the consistorial temples began to modernize
their practices, making some liturgical changes and installing
organs.

Only rarely was the creation of a private chapel attributed
to the reforming aims of the dissidents. In Reims, in 1838, and
in Nice, in 1867, unauthorized synagogues were established by

groups which claimed they desired liturgical reforms.[84] In both cases the consistories denied the claims of the "reformers" to have introduced innovations.

In Paris there was talk of reform services at least as early as 1836. Shortly after his arrival in Paris, Albert Cohn, together with Samuel Cahen and Solomon Munk[85] petitioned the Paris consistory for the right to hold private High Holy Day services for those Jews of the capital who were "both religion and enlightened."[86] The three men criticized the disorder that characterized the services at the consistorial temple and stated their belief that the liturgy was in need of modification. In requesting the use of the small synagogue adjoining the main temple, they threatened to seek quarters elsewhere if they did not receive a positive reply. The Paris consistory refused the requested permission, but unfortunately the records do not tell us whether the dissident group managed to implement its plans.

Competition between the official synagogue and private prayer meetings was not a development of the nineteenth century.[87] A similar situation existed in eighteenth-century Metz, due obviously to financial considerations.[88]

The attempts of the official community to prevent competition from independent groups continued throughout the entire nineteenth century in France, but whereas traditional communities were frank about their financial motives, the consistories often claimed that their interests were of a "moral" nature.[89] They frequently warned the government of supposed moral and political dangers in allowing Jews freedom of assembly for religious worship. Consistory minutes show unquestionably, however, that the major concern of the consistories in regard to these meetings was financial.

From their inception, the consistories found that their financial obligations were difficult to meet unless all of the funds from charity, the sale of religious honors, marriages, rental of synagogue seats, supervision of *kashrut,* etc., were received exclusively by them. All the consistories attempted, with partial and variable success, to close down prayer meetings and to eliminate both private weddings and independent slaughterings of *kasher* meat.

Mayors, prefects, and police, to whom complaints of such independent initiative were addressed, gave various interpretations to the relevant laws. When they failed to satisfy the consistories' demands, the consistories often sought satisfaction either by appealing to other branches of the government, or by waiting a short time and repeating their claims.

The consistories rejected the government's claim that prohibiting the meetings would be in opposition to the 1830 *Charte,* the constitution, or the principle of freedom of religion. The legal basis for the consistories' claims to a monopoly on synagogues and all associated revenue was their interpretation of several articles of the 1806 *règlement:* Articles 3 and 4 provided for only one consistorial synagogue per department, and Article 12 attributed to the consistories the job of preventing unauthorized prayer meetings.[90]

From the time the consistories were established, they disputed among themselves and with the government the correct interpretation of these articles. The Paris consistory, interpreting the *règlement* as meaning that only one consistorial synagogue (i.e., "temple") could be maintained, immediately proceeded to close down several Parisian synagogues. The central consistory disagreed with this interpretation, arguing that the word "synagogue," as used in the *règlement,* meant the administrative body (i.e. the consistory) and argued that it was absurd to think that the law intended there to be only one temple per district. Freedom to open houses of worship belonged to the people, as a right which derived from the recognition of Judaism as a state religion. The meaning of the term "private synagogues," the central consistory argued, was not chapels or temples but subordinate administrations. In certain cases such subordinate administrative bodies would be established and would have to be authorized and controlled by the departmental consistories. Interpreting the *règlement*'s use of the word "synagogue" as "temple," the central consistory claimed, would have the effect of "disorganizing instead of organizing" and of preventing most of the French Jews from exercising their right of freedom of religion.[91]

The interests of local consistories diverged from those of the central consistory. The Bordeaux consistory agreed with Paris that "synagogue" meant "temple." Arguing against the central consistory's interpretation of the word as meaning "administration," the Bordeaux consistory cogently argued that if this had, in fact, been the intention of the legislation, we should expect to find the word "synagogue" used in the articles of the *règlement* which speak of the central consistory. However, this is not the case; the word "synagogue" is used exclusively in speaking of the departmental consistories.

Bordeaux also said that the central consistory was wrong in claiming that if "synagogue" meant "temple," most of the French Jews would be deprived of the right to public worship. The *règlement* provided for the establishment of private "synagogues" ("temples"), which would be available for public worship by Jews who do not attend the consistorial synagogue because they live outside the consistory seat. Such private temples were to be opened in cities and towns where the Jewish population could support the expense of a building and a rabbi. Even in the city with the consistorial temple, private synagogues might be opened if the size of the population warranted it. In Jewish communities that were too small to support a temple, prayer meetings might be established with the approval of the consistory.[92]

In further support of its argument that "synagogues" meant "administrations," the central consistory pointed out that the decree of April 13, 1809, had named the "membres des treize synagogues." Since this was the act naming consistory members, "synagogue," in this case, had been used to mean "consistory."

The central consistory conceded that the usage was ambiguous and that in some cases the word did mean "temple." It agreed that this was the case in Article 12, which charged the consistories with maintaining order in the synagogues, and again in Article 21, which provided that the rabbis would preach in the synagogues. The word "synagogue," in fact, had three meanings, the central consistory pointed out. Sometimes it referred to Judaism and the Jews, sometimes to the administrative bodies (consistories), and sometimes to the temple. In the case of Article 3 ("il ne pourra y avoir plus d'une synagogue consistoriale par département") the central consistory continued to insist that "synagogue" meant "consistory." This article was therefore interpreted to mean that there could be only one consistory (and not only one temple) per department.[93]

The central consistory continued to argue against the notion that there must be only one consistorial temple. Its members insisted that this was not what the Assembly of Notables or the Committee of Nine had discussed or intended in formulating the concept of the consistory system. These men were in a position to know. They had all been members of the Assembly of Notables, and three of them (Rabbi Sègre, Rabbi Abraham de Cologna, and one lay member, Jacob Lazard) had been on the Committee of Nine. But we cannot be certain of the accuracy of their contention. The major reason for their argument appears to have been their wish to prevent the construction of a single, large, pompous, expensive synagogue in each district. At this early stage the central consistory was predominantly traditional-minded; it was only later, as it became increasingly a lay organization, that it began to adopt the aims of consolidation and hierarchy and encouraged the construction of large synagogue edifices, imitative of churches. In 1809 the central consistory, opposing plans to erect large consistorial synagogues, argued that if such temples were built, only the Jews of the large cities would benefit, but the entire population of the district would pay for them. In only three consistorial districts (Paris, Metz, and Bordeaux), the central consistory noted, did more than one eighth of the Jewish population live in the *chef-lieu*, where these new temples would be built.

From June to September the consistories awaited the minister's ruling on the interpretation of the *règlement* before acting on the issue of private synagogues and prayer meetings. But the minister was not as anxious as the consistories to interpret the law. In September the central consistory again requested that the ministry rule on the question.[94]

Despite the existing ambiguities, a careful study of the use of "synagogue" in the various passages of the *règlement* confirms the view held by the Paris and Bordeaux consistories that "synagogue" meant a building for the public celebration of the cult. The word appears in the following places: Article 3—there

can be only one consistorial synagogue per department; Article
5—there will be one grand rabbi per consistorial synagogue;
Article 6—the consistories will supervise the administration of
private synagogues; Article 12—the consistories must maintain
order inside the synagogues; Article 21—the rabbis will preach
and recite prayers for the Emperor and his family in the synagogue. Although the word, as used in Articles 3, 5, 6, and 12,
could also be interpreted as referring to the consistory administration, in Article 21 it clearly means only "temple."

In arguing in favor of their differing interpretations, both
the Paris consistory and the central consistory had both compared the 1806 *règlement* with a similar document governing the
Protestants. They were correct to do so, because the Jewish
consistorial organizations were clearly modeled after those of
the Protestants. To support its contention that "synagogue"
meant "administration," the central consistory's statement
cited Article 16 of the reformed church's *règlement:* "Il y aura
une église par 6000 âmes de la même communion." In that
context "église" clearly meant administrative body. However,
the Paris consistory's argument was based on Title 2, Article 18,
Section 2 of the same *règlement:* "Le consistoire de chaque
église sera composé du Pasteur ou des Pasteurs desservant cette
église." In this context, it said, it was evident that the word
"église" meant "temple." The Paris consistory then went on to
show the correspondence between this passage and Article 6 of
the 1806 *règlement:* "Les consistoires seront composés d'un
grand rabbin." There is only one difference between the wording of the relevant articles of the two documents; and the Paris
consistory argued that this resulted from an error. The text,
the consistory claimed, should have read "du grand rabbin"
(of the synagogue), rather than "d'un grand rabbin." As the
Protestant pastor of the consistory was pastor of the church,
so the grand rabbi, who was to be a member of the consistory,
was the one who was rabbi of the "synagogue consistoriale."
As "église" meant "temple" in the Protestant *règlement,*
"synagogue" meant "temple" in the Jewish one.

Hoping that the government would accept this argument and
authorize the closing of five of the six synagogues that existed
in Paris, the Paris consistory enthusiastically painted a picture
of the future benefits it anticipated from such action: All the
Parisian Jews, closely supervised by the consistory, would
gather together in great solemnity in a single dignified temple,
and be aroused to patriotism by the fiery speeches of the rabbis,
whose eloquent preaching would rival that of the great Christian
orators.[95]

Nevertheless, the government accepted the central consistory's contention that Jews had to be free to open temples, at
least in areas outside the consistory seat. We have already seen
that in 1812 the Minister of Cults was consulted about a case
involving a tiny Jewish community of seven families in the Bas-
Rhin town of Sélestat. He ruled that followers of Judaism, a

state-recognized religion, were free to practice their religion. All Jewish communities, therefore, had the right to request authorization to open synagogues. The authorization was to be automatically granted by the responsible consistory and then by the local municipality. The government distributed a circular to all the mayors, outlining the procedures to be followed in such cases, and guaranteeing to the consistory the right to authorize and control the private temples.

Although the government had adopted the central consistory's interpretation, the departmental consistories were not deterred from their plan to close many synagogues. As Robert Anchel has noted, there were many instances during the Empire when the consistories invoked police assistance to eliminate private prayer meetings in the consistorial districts of Paris, Colmar, Bordeaux, and Strasbourg. The authorities, Anchel added, responded positively to consistorial appeals to prohibit these reunions; they were always ready to imagine dangerous conspiracies (*noirs complots*) in any Jewish gatherings.[96] Thus the government's acceptance of the freedom to open synagogues was, in practice, limited to areas that were not within the consistory seat.

As an example of the procedure followed in closing down private prayer meetings, we may cite an 1812 letter of the Strasbourg consistory to the mayor of Strasbourg. The consistory complained that although the 1806–08 legislation gave it the job of seeing that no prayer meetings took place without consistory permission, and although the mayor had already issued an 1811 order supportive of the consistory's authority and ordering all private synagogues to close, several *minyanim* continued to function:

tous les matins à 7 H où 7 heures et ½ il se tient des assemblées de prières chez Jacob Abraham place Victoire No. 3, chez Samuel Goldschmitt rue Jeu des enfants No. 13, et chez Samuel Weyl [illegible] No. 66, en conséquence nous prenons la liberté de vous en prévenir, dans l'espoir que vous voudrez bien prendre les mesures convenables pour se faire cesser [ces] assemblées.[97]

With the change of regime after the Empire, the basic principles of consistory authority were thrown into doubt. Individuals challenged the Paris consistory's right to authorize or prevent prayer meetings. In 1816 this consistory reported two prayer meetings that functioned without its permission. When the organizers were called before the police prefecture, one of them agreed to stop holding meetings unless he secured permission. The other, however, showed written permission from the mayor, in accordance with the requirements of Article 291 of the Penal Code. The Paris consistory claimed that such permission should not have been given without their consent, and the minister was asked to rule.[98]

The minister consulted the central consistory as to whether the departmental consistory should be the administrative authority empowered to grant permission for prayer meetings. The central consistory replied that the provisions of the Penal Code were construed for public security and that it was therefore up to the general authorities and not the consistory to grant permission for prayer meetings. However, the central consistory added, the provision of the 1806 *règlement* that gave the departmental consistories the right to control prayer meetings was based on serious financial needs of the consistories. Therefore, the government should be the power that authorizes the meetings, but it should do so only on the recommendation of the departmental consistory. The ministry accepted this argument and ruled in accordance.[99]

This decision added nothing new to public policy. It prescribed the same procedure for authorizing private synagogues that had been adopted as early as 1812. What was interesting, however, is the central consistory's argument. Although historically inaccurate, the central consistory's statement clearly demonstrates its ideology in 1816. The power to control prayer meetings had been given to the consistories—not for financial reasons, as the central consistory now claimed, but because the government wished to limit private gatherings. Napoleon had feared that in the guise of assembling for religious worship, people might gather to foment conspiracies. In 1816 the central consistory had good reason for denying that this was the reason for the law. It was anxious that the new political regime repudiate the Napoleonic policy that had made of the consistories a police power. Only if the consistories were viewed as purely religious bodies, not exercising any kind of civil authority, could the consistory insist that a French Jew was in every respect a Frenchman like all others and that only his faith was different. For this reason, then, it was necessary not only to deny the history of the consistories' police functions, but to urge that such functions be performed solely by the government. The central consistory could not suggest that the departmental consistories should have the right to authorize prayer meetings.

We have found only one case in which the authorities refused permission for public Jewish worship. In 1835 the prefect of the Haute-Marne (in the Nancy consistory district) refused permission for a synagogue to a group of Jews who had consistory support. When the case was investigated, it was discovered that the prefect had feared that his administration would have to pay the costs of such a chapel.[100] The rest of the opposition to private prayer meetings came from the consistories themselves.

The 1816 ministry decision was cited by several consistories as providing a precedent and a method for closing down unauthorized prayer meetings. For example, when the consistory of the Haut-Rhin (then located in Wintzenheim) requested central consistory advice on how to close down prayer meetings, the central consistory forwarded a copy of this decision.[101] When the Bordeaux consistory found the local authorities unwilling to enforce the ban on unauthorized private chapels, it asked that the ministry send copies of the 1816 decision directly to the prefects of the five departments comprising the Bordeaux district.[102]

The consistory struggle to dominate the prayer meetings was never won. For the next forty-five years each new law appeared for a time to sanction consistory power, but the consistories continued to have only partial success in closing down private chapels or prayer meetings. The consistories waged a continual war on these *minyanim,* but were always dependent upon the willingness of local authorities to support their claims. Their legal position was so weak that many of their successes were due to ignorance of the law on the part of the Jews who complied. In many instances, Jews who continued to refuse to comply found that the courts ruled that no penalties were prescribed for refusal to acknowledge the consistories' authority.

Of all the consistories, the Paris consistory made the greatest attempt to obtain a monopoly on public prayer. Although it repeatedly authorized the *minyan* organized by Sr. Sauphar, it did so only because of the regular attendance of the grand rabbis de Cologna and Deutz. Sauphar lost the consistory's protection after de Cologna left France and after Deutz became unpopular because of the 1825 conversion of his son-in-law, Rabbi Drach, the teacher at the consistorial school. On June 15, 1826, the Paris consistory unanimously rejected Sauphar's request for permission to hold prayer meetings.[103]

The budget of the consistorial temple in Paris continued to experience deficits attributed to the existence of prayer meetings. In 1828 Baruch Weill, administrator of the temple, complained about the loss of revenue in this way.[104] Another strong campaign against the prayer meetings was then mounted, and the aid of the police was enlisted. The police again agreed to seek out and report all infractions of Article 294 of the Penal Code, which forbids the use of private homes for prayer meetings without municipal permission.

The pressure brought by the consistories increased, and the issue became the object of a police investigation. In a report prepared by Police Commissioner Masson, the history of the Parisian Jews' resistance to consistory authority was reviewed. Masson attributed this resistance to a "horror of civilization." His version of Jewish history was that the Jews had made no progress in "civilization" during the seventeenth and eighteenth centuries, despite the great gains made in the country during that period. He assured the prefect that Voltaire's opinion of the Jews was correct, despite the fact that his views might appear to be extreme.

The consistories were established, Masson continued, in order

to police the Jews and to reform them in accordance with the
Sanhedrin decisions. For this reason the poor, traditional-
minded masses hated and resisted the consistories:

*Mais cette grande masse de Juifs misérables, croupis dans la
fénéantise, entichés de ce fanatisme qui les porte à se regarder
comme jettés dans une terre étrangère qu'ils peuvent exploiter
à leur gré jusqu'à ce que la crainte les arrête, n'aime point les
consistoires, parce que les consistoires ont été établis précisément pour les surveiller et les réformer.*

Masson continued his account by observing that after the
Revolution most Jews continued to live in the old way and to
embrace their religion fanatically. Their religion, he said, included the Biblical concept that they would rule the world one
day. These Jews also continued to adhere to the letter of
Talmudic law. The Sanhedrin's concessions, Masson charged,
were made under governmental pressure, and he appears to
doubt their sincerity when he refers to them as "concessions
au moins verbales."

The Jews were continuing to practice usury, Masson claimed.
The Sanhedrin had deliberately mistranslated the Hebrew in
order to prove that Jews were not allowed to charge usurious
rates when lending money to non-Jews. The Sanhedrin had
claimed that the charging of *any* interest was prohibited among
Jews, but permitted between Jew and non-Jew. Basing his
argument on the Latin translation of the Bible by St. Jerome,
Masson contended that the section referred to usurious rates of
interest. He claimed that the Jews understood the law in this
traditional sense. The reason for the Jew's lack of progress, he
asserted—in the tradition of the enlightenment—was the poor
treatment he had received: "Si Voltaire avait voulu bien re-
chercher les causes de l'avilissement moral des juifs, il les aurait
trouvées principalement dans la conduite des gouvernements à
leur égard."

Returning to the specific cases at hand, Masson explained
that the Paris consistory was in need of the funds that it
derived from the rental of seats in its synagogue, and that five
private prayer meetings were threatening the stability of the
consistory budget. The five men responsible were Sauphar,
Théodore, Lazare, Moïse Ephraïm and Grodwol. The last four,
Masson thought, would close their chapels with just a bit of
police pressure, but Sauphar, who had lost most of his pupils
when the consistory opened its free school, was bitter and
determined. He ran his prayer meetings for his livelihood, and
those who attended did so primarily because the cost was lower
than the price of the seats in the temple: "for Jews, money is
everything," Masson asserted. Sauphar attempted to escape the
Penal Code prohibition of the use of private dwellings for prayer
meetings by breaking his congregation into several groups of

fewer than twenty each. Masson took this as an indication that Sauphar did not accept the Sanhedrin ruling that in civil and political matters French law was supreme.[105]

Despite the financial prejudice to the consistory budget caused by the prayer meetings, the situation was tolerable as long as the consistories continued to receive tax money. Thus the 1828 reports both by Baruch Weill of the synagogue and Masson of the police department pointed out that the situation was not yet critical but threatened to become so if the opposition to the consistory remained unchecked. Masson wrote: "Cette scission ne produit pas encore un grand préjudice aux revenus du consistoire; mais elle peut s'étendre et devenir dangereuse."[106]

Although both the government and the consistories often claimed that private chapels were an ever-present security risk, Masson admitted that the prayer meetings did not threaten the government. He claimed, however, that they were bad for the "morality" of the Jews. The consistory, composed of enlightened and honest men, had already made progress in improving the morality of the Jews, through education and apprenticeship programs, a modern temple, and sermons. He thought that for this reason the state should protect the consistory's interests.

In order to close down Sauphar's *minyan,* Masson offered some tactical advice on when to catch him with more than twenty people:

Quant à Sauphar, d'ici au prochain phase (Pâques) je crois qu'on l'attaquerait en vain, mais le vendredi soir et le samedi de la semaine des Azymes (vers le 20 Mars) il aura certainement plus de vingt personnes réunies chez lui et il pourra être attaqué, car c'est à lui principalement qu'il importe de s'attacher.[107]

It is evident that the consistory had chosen Sauphar as the principal target.

The sources do not indicate whether Sauphar's Passover prayers were in fact disturbed. Several months after Passover, however, the Paris consistory was still engaged in correspondence with the police over the continued existence of prayer meetings. The police prefect offered to cooperate with the consistory in checking the meetings, but needed their addresses. The Paris consistory replied that it needed the help of the police to locate the secret meetings, but forwarded the names and addresses of those it did know at that time.[108]

When the period of the High Holy Days approached, the Paris consistory gave its permission for some *minyanim* to form, and it notified the police of the names, addresses, and sizes of the authorized meetings.[109] This step was significant in two ways. First, the Paris consistory had acted as though it had the right not merely to recommend prayer meetings for government authorization, but to authorize them itself. Secondly, the step was an admission by the consistory that its official temple—only seven years old—was insufficient for the needs of the Parisian Jewish population. For almost fifty years there existed only one consistorial temple in Paris, and during this time the Parisian Jewish population multiplied to five times its 1829 size. The need to accept the existence of *minyanim,* at least for holiday periods, was met with resignation throughout the fifty years, although the consistory tried, nevertheless, to minimize the effect that this would have on its pretentions to monopoly.

All the consistories reacted to the private *minyanim* in a similar way. They prohibited and attacked prayer meetings, whether held for reasons of financial speculation or economy, infirmity, distance from the temple, piety, or dissident religious views. The Metz consistory repeated its prohibition of prayer meetings several times during the 1820's.[110] In 1829 the Nancy consistory firmly requested a certain widow Goudchaux to cease holding prayer meetings in her house. The consistory threatened to prosecute her under the provisions of the Penal Code.[111]

In more than one way the liberalism of the July monarchy was to prove a handicap to organized Judaism. First, although it provided state funding, it abrogated the consistories' right to tax the Jews. Then, when the consistories complained that private prayer meetings were cutting into their limited income, the ministry ruled (in July 1833) that the prayer meetings were protected by the provision for freedom of religion contained in the 1830 *Charte.* The financial distress suffered by the consistories became extreme for the first time. The Paris consistory claimed that it lost more than two thirds of its anticipated income to the prayer meetings. In 1833 the Paris consistory was able to name and place only six *minyanim,* although it knew that others existed.[112]

Sauphar operated the largest unauthorized chapel and posed the greatest threat to the consistory. Despite almost ten years of protests against his chapel, the Paris consistory had been unable to eliminate it. In 1833 the consistory indicated to the police prefect that it suspected that Sauphar had the protection of someone highly placed.[113] As we have noted in Chapter 4, the Paris consistory, when asked by the police in 1834 about Sauphar's "guarantees of morality," gave evasive answers. Sauphar was refused permission to operate his chapel,[114] but he managed, nevertheless, to keep it open. In September 1834 the consistory reported him to the police.[115] When Sauphar appealed directly to the consistory to support him, it refused to do so.[116] Sauphar bitterly asked why the Jews should have less protection in the exercise of their freedom of religion than other Frenchmen:

Pourquoi les juifs seraient-ils soumis à plus de restrictions dans l'exercice de leur culte, après qu'ils ont été appelés à jouir des mêmes avantages que les catholiques et les protestants?[117]

By 1835 a *modus vivendi* began to emerge between the Paris consistory and some of the mutual aid societies that wished to hold prayer meetings. The societies sent financial contributions and copies of their constitutions to the consistory. In return, the consistory issued its authorization of the constitutions, and accorded limited privileges to meet for prayer (generally for the High Holy Days, when the consistorial temple could not accommodate everyone who desired to attend). The first record we have of such an arrangement concerns an unnamed society headed by Jaffa and Dreyfuss, who received the privilege in June 1835, and in November donated 100 francs to the consistorial charity board.[118]

It appeared for a while that this *modus vivendi* would enable the consistory to salvage its dignity and authority, meet its financial obligations, and hide its inability to provide sufficient synagogue space. In December 1835 Messieurs Hoffman and Simon, on behalf of their mutual aid society, *Société des amis de l'ordre,* requested permission to hold prayer meetings. The prefect had agreed to authorize the *minyan* if the Paris consistory approved, but the society failed to make a financial contribution, and the consistory did not grant the request.[119] It is clear that by 1836 the consistory was tolerating prayer meetings in several mutual aid societies which were contributing to the consistory treasury.[120]

The police prefect vacillated continuously between requiring and not requiring consistory permission before authorizing prayer meetings. In 1833 it had been ruled unnecessary by the ministry's interpretation of the *Charte*. In 1834 and 1835 it was again being required. By 1837 the police had once again stopped consulting the consistory, which renewed its complaint against unauthorized prayer meetings. The consistory claimed these meetings were in violation of the 1806 decree:

nombreuses assemblées de prières qui existent à Paris sous le titre de sociétés de bienfaisance et qui autorisées par la préfecture de police ne l'ont pas été par le consistoire, bien que cette formalité soit imposée par le décret organique de 1806 qui a force de loi.[121]

The consistory was still trying to pursue its policy of exchanging permission for financial contributions, and therefore it requested that the police send a list of all municipally authorized prayer meetings so that the consistory might "regularize" their situation.[122]

At this point the financial situation of the Paris consistory was in the midst of a serious crisis, and it should have been apparent that the prayer meetings alone could neither be blamed for the problem, nor solve it. Yet they provided the consistory with an issue on which it could focus. The consistory was at that time trying to obtain government permission to reinstitute a special Jewish tax in order to cover consistory expenses (especially the debt outstanding on the temple). The consistory knew, however, that it was going to be refused the right to tax the Jewish population, and it was therefore preparing to pounce on the prayer meetings when the refusal came.

In response to the consistory's request of 1837, the police forwarded a list of twelve societies, and the consistory pressured them to contribute to its budget. Calling the presidents of the societies to appear in two groups of six at two successive meetings, the consistory bartered its tolerance against financial contributions. Whether the police actually had agreed in that year to respect consistory opinion before according authorization is unclear, although the consistory gave this impression to the mutual aid societies in its attempt to coerce them into contributing. The consistory itself characterized its plan as making its tolerance work to the profit of the charity fund: "Faire tourner la tolérance du consistoire à cet égard au profit de la Caisse du Comité de Secours."[123] The societies filed formal requests for consistory approval, together with copies of their statutes. After studying their statutes and pronouncing on the orthodoxy of their religious views (!), the consistories duly approved.[124]

The following year a ministerial decision outlawed "mixed societies"—that is, societies with both a philanthropic and a religious character. The prefect of police was asked by the ministry to see that all authorization given by the Paris consistory to societies be withdrawn immediately. The police notified the consistory to this effect, enclosing a list of twenty societies registered and authorized by the police to meet for prayer. Although the terms of the notification do not specify that the ruling was specific to Jewish societies, or the Parisian ones, we have not found any references to this ruling in regard to non-Jewish groups or to non-Parisian groups. The ruling was obviously the result of several years of Paris consistory pressure on the authorities. The wording of the decision seems to indicate that the consistory had suggested that it hurt the dignity of Judaism to allow the services to be held outside the temple:

aucune association de Secours Mutuels ne pourrait avoir de caractère mixte, comportant tout-à-la-fois des intérêts pécuniaires et des exercises de religion, attendu que le bon ordre et le principe religieux lui-même sont intéressés à ce qu'un culte ne soit célébré que dans les Eglises, temples ou autres édifices exclusivement consacrés aux exercices de piété et reconnus comme tels par l'autorité publique.[125]

The consistory lost no time in communicating this message to the twenty societies indicated by the police. Representatives of the societies were invited to a consistory meeting to discuss what should be done. It would be difficult to overlook the manner in which the consistory staged this event. Its members assumed an innocent and protective air, appearing to convey the bad news with reluctance and concern and inviting the societies to help find a solution to the problem that had been posed by this ministerial ruling.

On June 24, 1839, the consistory met with delegates of eighteen societies to decide what steps to take. Three of the representatives who appeared announced that their societies did not recite prayers, and they left the meeting.[126] The presidents of the remaining fifteen societies were all heard. All agreed with the proposal, made by one of their number, that the consistory find a way of opening a second temple for those who did not live close enough to the consistorial temple on the rue Notre Dame de Nazareth. Until a second temple was made available, the consistory should request government authorization for them to continue their prayer meetings.[127]

All the representatives were in agreement that a second temple would provide a solution, which seems to indicate that they did not consider themselves seriously opposed to the consistorial version of Judaism. If a consistorial temple near their homes were opened, at prices they could afford and providing sufficient room, they would attend.

Abraham Ben Baruch Créhange, an orthodox merchant of the capital, was spokesman for the societies at the meeting on June 24. He was obviously far more radical than the men he spoke for. His speech was sharp and bitter. Behind a formal politeness, there was barely disguised contempt for the men of the consistory and for their institutions, which he did not accept as his: "Votre temple, rue Nazareth, est trop petit, trop cher et hors de la circonscription territoriale de la majorité des israélites de Paris."

Arguing further for the continuation of the *minyanim* within the societies, Créhange pointed out the historic relationship in Judaism between ritual and charity. Most of the income received by the societies, he said, came from offerings made in connection with the religious services. Most of the members joined because of the opportunity to say *kaddish,* which they would otherwise not have. If the societies lost their right to pray together, the charitable aspect of the societies would also be destroyed. Moreover, this charitable work was very important to the people; none of it was duplicated by the consistory's charity board. Only the *hebroth* (mutual aid societies) cared for the sick in the spirit and dignity of Judaism; only they prevented poor Jewish heroes from going to paupers' graves (a reference to a recent celebrated case of a Jewish soldier, Jonas) and the sick from dying under a crucifix. He berated the consistory for not acting more vigorously to promote the interests of Judaism, although they posed as its defenders:

Vous defendrez donc nos intérêts et la religion. Ces principes

posés, messieurs, il nous sera facile de nous entendre sur la
question importante qui nous amène aujourd'hui dans cette
enceinte.

Créhange went further. He complained that it was shocking that the Paris consistory had rushed to execute the ministerial decision (even he did not guess that they had *caused* it!), rather than ask for a postponement. The Paris consistory president, Dr. Cahen, replied indignantly that he did not have to defend his behavior to anyone but the *notables* who elected him and the government which placed its confidence in him.[128]

Although Créhange had been asked by the societies to prepare this plea on their behalf, there is a significant difference between their willingness to accept a second temple as a solution to the problem and Créhange's insistence on the need to retain prayer meetings within the societies. As a result of the joint meeting, it was decided that a commission of five of the presidents would prepare a written proposal to present to the Paris consistory. Créhange was delegated by the commission to write the petition. On July 3 he appeared before the Paris consistory, read his petition, and left. The consistory found that Créhange's view that prayer meetings must continue as in the past was not acceptable. The June 24th agreement had been that the societies would request the establishment of a second temple and the temporary authorization to hold prayer meetings until this could be accomplished. The petition was returned to Créhange with an invitation to re-word it in accord with the agreement of June 24.[129]

A second petition was prepared and submitted to the consistory. It is not clear whether Créhange was responsible for the second draft. (A document refers to the fact that the Paris consistory secretary, Polack, had offered his services to the societies in the drawing up of their petition, yet the wording of this second draft is characteristic of Créhange.) The petition complains once again of the consistory's zealous execution of the ministry's order to suppress mixed societies ("un zèle peu charitable"), but it also requests the right to meet temporarily for prayers until such time as a second temple of sufficient size and proximity to the homes of the majority of Jews could be opened.[130]

Upon receipt of the new petition in mid-July, the consistory appointed a three-man commission to search for a site for a second temple. The consistory thought it would be able to complete satisfactory arrangements for the installation of a synagogue in the Marais (the present fourth *arrondissement,* old sixth and seventh, center of the nineteenth-century Jewish population of Paris) before the High Holy Days in September. It therefore omitted to ask the police for a stay on the order to close down the *minyanim.*[131]

Sauphar, the long-standing arch competitor of the Paris consistory temple, had not been included in the joint meetings. His was a separate case. His prayer meetings were held in a private chapel, not a mutual aid society. The police asked him again to close his chapel. Sauphar objected, saying that the Paris consistory should have supported his request for authorization. The consistory decided to reply that it was its duty to enforce the law:

On fera observer au Sr. Sauphar que le consistoire a le devoir, d'après le règlement de 1806, de veiller à ce que sous aucun prétexte, il ne se forme d'assemblée de prières sans autorisation que par conséquent il a dû appuyer la mesure qui a été arrêtée par M. le Préfet.[132]

After two weeks of intensive searching for a place to open a second synagogue in the heart of the Jewish quarter, the commission was able to find only one suitable space, and its price was far too high. (It would have cost 6,000 francs rent per year plus renovation and construction costs.) The commission decided to abandon the project because of the nearness of the holidays and the obvious impossibility of finding a suitable solution before them. Only then did the consistory ask the police to permit the *minyanim* during the holiday season.[133]

On the recommendation of the ministry, the police accorded authorization for prayer meetings between September 8 and October 1, 1839, with the condition that they cease after that period. The consistory was to furnish the police with a list of all the locations where the prayer meetings were to be held, so that proper supervision and maintenance of public order could be assured.[134]

The "victory" for the prayer meetings was communicated to the societies. Contrary to Paris consistory aims and expectations, they were not at all grateful. Créhange, replying on their behalf, once more claimed the right of the *minyanim* to worship throughout the year, and not merely for the holidays. He insisted that the location of the consistorial temple, far from the homes of the Jews of the Marais, was a continual impediment to the fulfillment of religious obligations. This was especially true during periods of illness and mourning, but was also a problem for weekly sabbath observance. Créhange argued that it made no sense to forbid prayer meetings on a regular basis but allow them during the High Holy Days. Indeed, at this point the consistory was caught in its own contradiction. It had urged the ministry to forbid mixed societies on the grounds that worship must be held in a special edifice to assure both the dignity of the religion and the security of the state. It was a definite contradiction, then, to allow worship in these societies precisely on the days when the services are the most solemn and the congregations the largest, and therefore potentially the most dangerous:

Car il est évident que s'il y avait eu raison d'Etat pour interdire les réunions religieuses aux sociétés qui sont en possession de ce privilège depuis longtemps cette Raison subsisterait pour 25 jours comme pour 50, comme pour 100; pour des jours de fêtes, jours de réunions nombreuses bien plus que pour des jours non-fériés où les réunions ne dépassent jamais 20 hommes.[135]

After the holidays the societies were afraid to resume their prayer meetings without authorization. It appeared that the police were determined to act. Several of the societies proposed to Benoît Cohen, president of the consistorial charity board, that he be their spokesman before the Paris consistory. They offered to make annual contributions to the charity board if their requests were satisfied. Cohen was sympathetic and wrote to the Paris consistory that the promised funds would greatly benefit the poor and recommended that the consistory accord the requested permission.[136]

By now the consistory was playing harder to get than ever before. Whereas for years its *modus vivendi* with the societies was based on financial contributions to the consistorial treasury, the consistory now replied that despite the attractive nature of the offer, it would be injurious to the dignity of the religion for them to accept:

Le consistoire après avoir entendu la plupart des membres décide qu'il répondra au comité que quelque puissante que soit la considération sur laquelle la demande est appuyée la dignité de la religion s'oppose à ce qu'elle puisse être accueillie.[137]

A study of the consistory minutes reveals that, despite public statements about dignity, the only serious fear the consistory ever had in regard to the societies was a financial one. For tactical reasons the consistory members emphasized different concerns to their various correspondents. To the authorities they stressed the need for public order and moral progress, which, they implied, could be guaranteed only by consistory control. This was the surest argument against the *minyanim,* as the government was primarily concerned with security. The consistories also told the government of their financial problems and their attempts to improve religious dignity, emphasizing the latter. To the public they spoke mainly of their obligation to obey the law and to enforce the ministry's ruling.

Continually denying any part in the ministerial decision outlawing the mixed societies, the Paris consistory insisted that the whole issue was in the hands of the authorities. Thus, for example, the consistory replied to Isaac David, who requested permission for his private society to continue meeting on Saturdays at noon for religious lessons and *mincha* service, that only the authorities could rule on his request: "cette autorisation est de la compétence de l'autorité supérieure dont la décision a été signifiée aux diverses sociétés de secours mutuels."[138]

It is clear from the minutes book of one of the mutual aid societies that the societies were not fooled by the consistory's pretention of helplessness, and that they understood that freedom to meet in prayer depended entirely on the will of the consistory. On November 3, 1839, one month after the High Holy Day permission for the *minyanim* had expired, the *Société de l'union de secours mutuels,* noting that many other societies had been continuing to meet, voted to continue its own prayer meetings. The members agreed that to cancel their *minyan* would be "immoral and irreligious." The president of the society had been to the police prefecture and had been informed that if the consistory did not oppose the prayer meetings, the authorities would permit them to continue.[139]

The consistorial temple on the rue Notre Dame de Nazareth continued to be the only authorized Parisian synagogue except for the Portuguese temple. Although the Paris Jewish population reached 8000 in 1840, this synagogue could accommodate only 500 persons.[140] Despite a severe lack of facilities, the consistory continued to pursue rival chapels. To the observant Jews of the capital it was evident that the consistory was anti-religious. Abraham Ben Baruch Créhange, still their spokesman, began to publish a journal called *La Sentinelle Juive,*[141] in which he argued against consistorial monopoly on public prayer and attacked the reform propaganda being agitated by people like Olry Terquem. To Créhange's chagrin, his arch-enemy Terquem joined him in the plea for the freedom to form *minyanim.* Terquem (now signing his articles in the newly created *Archives Israélites* with the Hebrew letter צ) argued that freedom to form *minyanim* was a traditional Jewish liberty.[142] Créhange angrily retorted that he had no need for support from such quarters.

The struggle against the prayer meetings continued in all the consistory districts. Each consistory seems to have decided the merits of prayer meeting requests on an individual basis. Thus in November 1839 the Strasbourg consistory fined a certain Sr. Ulmann, who had admitted to his chapel people who had not received consistory authorization to attend.[143] Apparently the Strasbourg consistory authorized some *minyanim* and specified who could attend.

In the meantime, the central consistory had begun work on its project of revising the laws that governed the consistories. In the 1839 draft of what became the 1844 *ordonnance* there was a clause that gave the consistories the right to authorize private prayer meetings. This was supposed to look like a liberal stance, and it fooled some people. Terquem, usually an astute critic of the consistories, wrote that it was a wise provision, which would restore to the Jews a traditional liberty.[144] The truth was exactly the opposite. The consistory aimed only at assuring to itself the right, continually disputed with the authorities, to authorize—and therefore *not* to authorize—the prayer meetings.

After the 1839 ministerial ban on "mixed" societies, the

police cooperated with the Paris consistory. They were in frequent contact concerning illegal and unauthorized prayer meetings. The mutual aid societies were warned by the police that they were not to hold prayer meetings, even for the High Holy Days, unless they received consistory authorization. Such authorization had to be shown to the police commissioner. The Paris consistory reinstituted the procedure of "selling" authorization in exchange for charitable contributions. It also suggested to the societies that authorization would be forthcoming if their members rented seats in the temple.[145]

The pattern of paying for toleration of their religious activities was accepted only partially by the societies. Some of them stopped their payments or paid only when absolutely necessary. In January of 1844 the charity board denounced several societies to the consistory as not having contributed in 1843. At least one such society held prayer meetings throughout the year.[146]

The struggle between the official temple and private prayer meetings took place not only in the consistorial seats—the major centers of Jewish population—but also in the smaller cities and towns. Frequently, a dissident group would rebel against the local Jewish administration (the consistory's authorized representative) and establish a separate chapel or *minyan*. The local *commissaires surveillants,* in such instances, would enlist the aid of the consistory and the government to suppress the unauthorized establishments.

It was generally assumed that the prohibition of unauthorized prayer meetings was sanctioned by several provisions of the Penal Code. Article 291 of the code prohibited associations larger than twenty persons from meeting without government authorization. Article 294 penalized anyone who allowed his house to be used for religious services without having obtained municipal permission. In 1844 the Nancy consistory attempted to defend the interests of the official Jewish community of Mittelbronn against a rival *minyan* of twelve men who met at the house of Sr. Raphael Séligmann. In reply to the consistory's claims, the local authorities pointed out that the small size of the group gave it complete freedom. The Nancy consistory argued that regardless of the size of the group, Article 294 applied in this case. However, it was commonly accepted that groups of fewer than twenty members were exempt from this restriction also. The consistory pointed out that it was charged with "maintaining order and peace in the community" and with "seeking moral progress." In order to do so, it needed the prefect's support in enforcing the 1806 ban on private prayer meetings. If the Penal Code was not applicable, the consistory argued, the decree should be enforced in some other way. Because the argument for law, order, and morality impressed the local authorities, they agreed to prosecute offenders, but the court denied permission to prosecute, ruling that groups of fewer than twenty men had full freedom of assembly. A series of additional court cases further revealed the impotence of the consistory's claims.[147]

In 1846 similar conflicts arose in Rouen and in Reims, both of which were in the Paris consistory district. In these two cities the consistory supported the authorized community against rival groups, but the government cautioned local authorities to show great leniency in matters of religious dissent and conscience.[148]

Contrary to expectations, the restatement in the 1844 *ordonnance* of the consistories' right to authorize private prayer meetings did not improve their ability to control the *minyanim*. The struggle continued in precisely the same way. Although local authorities often supported the consistories' position and some local courts decided in their favor, all appeals to higher courts revealed a lack of enforceability of consistory authority. However, the consistories maintained control unless the dissidents were persistent enough to push their claims as far as the higher courts.

In Paris the system of payment in return for consistory authorization became a permanent arrangement. The charity committee and the consistory worked together on this, and the former unabashedly sent letters of reminder to the societies, prodding them about their unpaid "contributions" and reminding them that the High Holy Days were approaching.[149] The authorities sometimes assisted by issuing warnings or by closing the recalcitrant prayer assemblies. Those that cooperated were not troubled.

It was the policy of Louis-Philippe to be as liberal about religious tolerance as was compatible with public order. For this reason, several *minyanim* which failed to contribute were nonetheless unmolested. An interesting example is the case of Samuel Lévy, furrier, who lived at 95 rue St. Martin. The consistory had denounced him, informing the police that on October 11 (Yom Kippur) he would have public prayers at his house. The police arrived late—at five o'clock in the afternoon—and found twenty-six people present, some of whom were members of Lévy's own family. The police noted that Lévy wore a "particular costume" and "seemed to be engaged in some kind of religious exercises." Lévy admitted this, specifying that the prayers had begun at ten that morning and that with nightfall approaching they would soon end. He claimed to be ignorant of the requirement to obtain permission for such ceremonies, and promised to request such permission in the future. Respectfully, the police withdrew, permitting the services to conclude.[150]

In 1846 the idea of constructing a second Parisian temple was again discussed a short time before the holiday season. The Jewish population of the capital now exceeded 10,000. Furthermore, not only the poor Jews of the Marais lived at a great distance from the temple; the wealthy Jews had moved out to fashionable areas on the outskirts of the expanding city and could no longer walk to the synagogue. An argument arose over whether the new temple should be built in the Marais or in the fashionable neighborhood around the rue de la Victoire. To make matters worse the old temple was found to be in need of significant repairs, and it had to be temporarily closed. The outstanding debt on the existing structure was still large, and the government was giving substantial aid to the consistory in order to help pay back the loans it had received when it constructed the temple. Some people argued that the building should be turned over to the municipality, which would then be responsible for all repairs. Although this possibility was considered, it was never accepted by the consistory, which insisted that it was obligated to protect the property rights of the seat-owners. For many months while the temple was being repaired, services were held in the schoolrooms.

A second temple was not built for another thirty years. The Paris consistory was able to provide extra synagogue space during the High Holy Days only by using the schoolrooms for auxiliary services. Apart from these seasonal chapels and the small Portuguese synagogue (whose maintenance was due entirely to the initiative of its own congregation) the only official synagogue services in Paris until after 1870 (when the Parisian Jewish population reached about 25,000) were those of the one consistorial temple.

It is hardly surprising, then, that private *minyanim* flourished throughout the nineteenth century. It is highly probable, in fact, that there were more than the twenty groups whose names appear in the consistory archives. It is likely that there were not only the holiday *minyanim* for which permission was asked and obtained, but also unrecorded and unauthorized Sabbath or even daily *minyanim*. Unaware of this factor, historians looking at the considerable size of the Parisian Jewish population and at the small number of synagogue seats sometimes erroneously concluded that Parisian Jews had largely abandoned Jewish practices.

The 1848 revolution threw the legitimacy of the 1844 *ordonnance* into question. Once again, as in 1833, it appeared as though any attempt to limit freedom of religious expression would be found to conflict with the state's basic principles. An increased number of prayer meetings developed (or surfaced) in the wake of the events. The Paris consistory sounded out the police on the enforceability of their old arrangement. The situation had indeed changed. The police answered that they would restrict prayer meetings only for reasons of public order or morality.[151] Articles 14 and 19 of the law of July 28, 1848, had guaranteed freedom to nonpolitical meetings. The law of June 19, 1849, later added that religious assemblies could be prevented only if they posed a threat to public security or peace.

The situation was in a constant state of flux. For a while the Paris consistory lost control and temple receipts fell drastically. Revenues from seats, honors, and marriages, which had totaled

19,600 francs in 1847, reached only 12,940 francs in 1848.[152]

Although the Metz consistory was able to obtain a lower court conviction in 1851 against a private prayer meeting held without consistory authorization,[153] it lost the case on appeal. While the appeal was pending, the supreme court, ruling on a similar case from Colmar, decided that Article 471, Paragraph 15 of the Penal Code did not apply to violations of the consistory's control of prayer meetings.[154] The Metz consistory realized that it, too, would lose its case.

Metz had recently built a large temple, and the problem of adequate space for worship did not exist there.[155] The consistory was anxious to suppress all who competed with its new temple, and appealed to the prefect for administrative support. Just before the High Holy Days of 1851 the prefect forwarded to the mayor of Metz the consistory's request that private prayer meetings be prohibited by an administrative measure.[156] By the following spring, however, the Metz consistory had lost its court case against the *minyanim*. It then turned its attention to the central consistory's project of redrafting the consistory legislation and tried to include provisions for punishment of transgressions.[157] Such penalties, as we have seen in Chapter 4, never materialized.

In Paris shortly before the holidays of 1851, a private chapel called *Cercle Israélite* was opened at 44 rue de la Victoire, in the heart of the residential district of the wealthier Parisian Jews. When the Paris consistory objected, the police prefect (despite his previous pledge of support for the consistory) requested directions from the Ministry of Cults.[158]

The minister replied that the constitution and the laws of July 29, 1848, and June 19, 1849, allowed freedom of association to religious groups provided they did not threaten public order; therefore it had to be ascertained in this case whether the meeting involved was purely religious, and whether it endangered public order. Of the men who had opened the chapel, the minister continued, Oppenheim and Hermann offered very few moral guarantees, while the other two, Duval and Vienot, were Catholics. The minister thought that the police should investigate, but he reminded them that the consistory was a valuable collaborator in guaranteeing public order and that it would be regrettable to rule against it, and thereby diminish its authority. Nevertheless, the minister suggested, it appeared that the provisions of the 1844 *ordonnance* were at variance with the more recent laws and constitution.[159]

The prefect carried out the requested investigation and consulted legal experts. It was decided that the new chapel was, in fact, protected by the constitution, and therefore the police granted it authorization. Furious, the consistory members considered resigning to protest their lack of power, but decided against such a move. They contented themselves with inserting notices in four newspapers, declaring that the prayer meeting in question was established merely for financial gain.[160]

By the following June (1852), the political situation in Paris had changed drastically. A *coup d'état* had promoted Louis Napoleon from president to prince. A new constitution had been written, and De Maupas had taken over as prefect of police. The Paris consistory decided to see what change in policy might come from the new regime. It asked De Maupas to reaffirm consistory rights ("de consacrer de nouveau le droit du consistoire") based on the 1844 *ordonnance*,[161] and the police prefect promised his support.

The consistory had tested its strength prematurely. It was not ready to act, as a second temple was not yet available. Auxiliary services for the High Holy Days, held as usual in the school building, were again insufficient. The *minyanim* still had to be tolerated. Each year from 1852 to 1855 the consistory looked around for a while in July and August for a possible site for a second temple. It never found anything other than the school buildings. In 1856, when the Parisian Jewish population had reached 20,000, several branches were opened, which accommodated a total of 800 men in addition to the 1200 worshipers at the main temple. No women or children were able to attend the auxiliary services.

The consistory continued to rely on sporadic local administrative support, and tried to convince the authorities that one or another of the laws of provisions of the Penal Code supported their claim. For example, despite the legal changes of 1848–49, the Strasbourg consistory was able to persuade some officials that private prayer meetings violated Article 291 of the Penal Code and the Law of April 10, 1834.[162] Of course, the consistory also emphasized the economic prejudice to the temple treasury caused by the prayer meetings and on the tendency of such meetings to cause internal division within Judaism and to hurt the dignity of the cult. Unlike the Paris consistory, however, the Strasbourg consistory refrained from accusing the dissidents of immorality and untrustworthiness. The language of its appeal for government support reveals its awareness that its own authority depended entirely on municipal backing:

La mission du consistoire consiste à veiller sur l'exercice régulier du culte, à entretenir la concorde parmi les fidèles et à les maintenir dans la ligne du devoir religieux. Le bienveillant appui de l'autorité lui est nécessaire pour l'accomplissement de cette tâche; nous osons le solliciter dans la présente circonstance.[163]

Despite the previous administrative and legal decisions to the contrary, the prefect of the Bas-Rhin accepted the consistory's argument that Articles 291, 292, and 294 of the Penal Code applied to transgressions of the 1844 *ordonnance* governing the consistories. However, because membership in the *minyan* was kept to nineteen people, the consistory failed to eliminate it.[164]

The number of dissident groups seeking to escape consistory

authority continued to increase throughout the century as it became increasingly apparent that the consistories could do little to combat them. In Bliesbruken (district of the Metz consistory) a dissident *minyan* in 1856 even included two members of the local administrative commission! When asked for its advice by the official community of Bliesbruken, the only recommendation the Metz consistory could make was that the community should remove these men from official office.[165] In Strasbourg during the High Holy Days of 1858, the temple was not large enough to accommodate Strasbourg's Jewish population of 2300. The consistory wanted to forbid *minyanim,* and attempted to open an official annex. However, the only potential site that was located was too expensive, and no subscribers could be found. The attempt was abandoned and the private *minyanim* flourished.[166]

In Paris the consistory continued to grant authorization to nineteen or twenty *minyanim,* and additional ones probably existed as well. In 1858 the consistory regretfully informed the central consistory that it could not do otherwise, in view of the size of the Jewish population—24,000 or 25,000, according to the consistory's estimate. (The Paris consistorial temple could accommodate only 1200.)

In 1856 a private chapel was approved for Polish Jews of the capital, who formed a society called *Israélites polonais de la loi rabbinique.* In 1866 an additional Polish chapel was approved for the *Enfants de Daniel Polonais.* Although the size of the Polish immigration did not yet necessitate two chapels, the consistory could not reconcile the conflict between the two groups and therefore allowed them their separate organizations.[167] In 1858 a chapel was approved in Montrouge, a suburb far from the consistorial temple, in which a Jewish community had developed. For similar reasons a chapel was authorized in 1860 at 10 rue du Moulin de Beurre, in the fourteenth *arrondissement.*[168]

In 1859 a serious attempt was made to open a second temple in a building on the rue de Jouy, which the consistory wished to acquire. The location would have been convenient for the large Jewish population of the Marais—the neighborhoods along both sides of the Seine and the adjacent neighborhood of the left bank. The synagogue would have cost one million francs, and would have accommodated 3000 people. The projected cost was too high, however, and the consistory proposal to fund it through the sale of seats, selling of shares, and city aid did not materialize. The temple was never built. In 1862 an attempt was made to establish two temples, one in the Marais and one in the ninth *arrondissement* (at that time the first and second *arrondissements*), the area to which the wealthier Jews had been moving for many years. The first of these projects materialized in 1870, when a temple in the Marais was finally established on rue des Tournelles (Place des Vosges). Four years later the new temple of the ninth *arrondissement* was opened at 44 rue de la Victoire.

This address is the same as that of the chapel opened in 1852 by Hermann and Oppenheimer, and it would therefore appear likely that the private chapel had endured for twenty years until the new synagogue was constructed upon the site. This temple was succeeded by yet another, in 1877, in the same *arrondissement*, rue Buffault, for the Portuguese rite. Eight hundred seats were available for congregants in this new building, which replaced the smaller synagogue of the adjoining rue Lamartine. Within a seven-year period three new synagogues had been constructed. Together with the synagogue of rue Notre Dame de Nazareth, there was seating capacity for about 5000. But the building spurt, so long delayed, could not keep pace with the growth of the Parisian Jewish population, or its geographical dispersion. The population had already reached 30,000, and the eastern immigration had not yet begun. After 1880 Jews from Eastern Europe began streaming into the capital, and they sought to re-create their traditional communities through a proliferation of new institutions—especially the *schul* (small synagogue) and the *landsmannschaft* (society of immigrants from a single area). The consistory was forced to acknowledge definitively that it was not the sole arbiter of what constituted Jewish expression.

2. Marriages

Although the consistories were interested in modernizing the form of synagogue ceremonies, the financial factor was clearly the more crucial one in the consistory's search for monopoly. Fees from synagogue weddings, sale and rental of seats, honors, etc., were the backbone of the treasury, without which the consistories would have had no income other than voluntary contributions.

Synagogue weddings had both financial and ceremonial implications for the consistory, but they were insisted upon for several additional reasons. The consistories were charged with seeing that religious weddings were performed only after a civil ceremony, and the ("clandestine") traditional weddings generally omitted this step. Secondly, it appeared to the consistory that social integration would be fostered by the development of a set of synagogue ceremonies that paralleled standard Christian practice. Thus the "dignity" of the religion required that marriages take place in the synagogue. Curiously, however, "dignity" was automatically acquired in weddings held at home, provided the financial contributions to the synagogue and to the charity board were substantial.

Marriage fees were set in various ways in the different districts. In Metz in 1829 they were set by the consistory according to the amount of taxes a person paid.[169] Bordeaux classified its population into categories according to estimates of wealth, and used the person's class to determine the rate at which he would pay for burials, marriages, etc. In Paris there were six classes of weddings, at widely varying prices, from which one could choose. They ranged in luxury from a ceremony with the barest essentials in an almost dark synagogue, through various sizes of choirs and numbers of lit chandeliers. The cost of a synagogue wedding was not limited to the set fees, but included in addition almost mandatory charitable contributions. During the wedding ceremony, members of the charity board were authorized to pass around collection plates. For this reason the board was loath to see permission granted for weddings to be held outside the synagogue, and it frequently brought pressure to bear on the consistory to refuse such permission. Eventually it was decided that permission would be granted only in exceptional cases and only if equivalent contributions were promised by the family. For example, in 1839 a certain Sr. Heller, ill and unable to leave his house, asked for permission to celebrate his son's marriage at home. The consistory accorded permission, with the provision that the offering for the temple be no less than it would have been if the marriage had been celebrated there.[170] In Strasbourg, in the same year, the indigent Samuel Schwartz paid three francs to the temple administration for the privilege of celebrating his marriage outside the temple.[171]

The Paris consistory vacillated over its policy. Perhaps the fees for weddings outside the synagogue were difficult to collect. In December 1839, the consistory granted permission for another home wedding in order that a ninety-nine year old grandfather could be present, but it decided to allow no more weddings outside the synagogue.[172] Yet three years later, Paris consistory president Cahen took it upon himself to approve a home wedding between the prominent Pisarro and de Castro families, requested because of the illness of one of the grandmothers. The letter of request had specified that the temple treasury would not suffer: "Sans cependant nuire ni préjudicier aux intérêts du temple."[173]

In 1843 the Paris consistory ruled that poverty was not a sufficient excuse for celebrating weddings at home. A certain "femme Byr" had argued that she and her future husband were not in a position to purchase suitable clothing for a synagogue wedding. The consistory refused to grant an exemption to the rule and replied that the couple would not be expected to make a charitable contribution.[174] The consistory did, however, continue giving permission for weddings to be held out of the temple. In 1854 the temple administration complained of the small contributions received on such occasions, and it was decided to obligate the wedding couple to pay for one of the established classes, as determined by the temple administration jointly with the grand rabbi.[175]

Ritual food had always been a traditional source of income in Jewish communities. When the fees charged by the religious authorities for inspection and approval were greater than the actual costs of supervision, the surplus constituted a tax which entered the community's treasury. Meat was, of course, the most important commodity of the income-producing ritual foods. (In nineteenth-century France it was calculated that despite their poverty, Jews ate more meat per capita than did the general French population.) This meat had to be, at least for those who were observant of the ritual law, unquestionably kosher. The consistories, through their grand rabbis, were held to be the arbiters of the fitness of the meat; they examined and licensed the slaughterers and provided the inspectors. In some places the cost of the meat reflected only the actual cost of supervision. Elsewhere, notably in Paris, it included a generous amount of tax money for the consistory treasury.

The meat tax in Paris affected mainly the poor and the lower middle classes, the principal purchasers of kosher food. The wealthier Jews had moved out of the Jewish quarter of the Marais, and away from the Jewish butcher shops. In their new neighborhoods of the first and second *arrondissements* (today, the ninth), no kosher meat was sold. Those who remained observant had their meat delivered to them from the old neighborhood; the majority, however, abandoned this observance.

The poor and the lower middle classes began to object that although they did not attend the consistorial temple because they lived too far away or could not afford to rent seats, the meat tax which they paid was used to support the temple. By the 1840's slaughterers and butchers not authorized by the consistory had attracted the patronage of Jews who sought to escape the meat tax. The consistories attempted to suppress these shops in order to guarantee a market to the butchers it licensed and taxed.

The 1848 revolution led the now politically conscious, poor, orthodox Parisian Jews to declare that the consistory monopoly on kosher meat was an illegal restraint of trade. There developed a new, more vigorous attempt to escape consistorial control. This competition, like that of the prayer meetings, has never ended; it is still common for advertisements inserted in *Le Monde* to declare that meat sold by butchers who do not display the consistory certificate is not ritually fit.[176]

The origin of the kosher meat tax is much older than the consistory system. There are records of a community monopoly of the meat trade, established for financial reasons, in the sixteenth-century Jewish community of Salonica. Salo Baron points out that the trend in this direction began as early as the fourteenth century, and he judges it "inescapable."[177] In pre-consistory France the meat tax was an essential item in the community budgets of the eastern provinces.[178]

Legally the consistories had no support for their claims to control the meat market before 1823. The *ordonnance* of that year attributed to the consistories the right to name slaughterers for the first time, and this right was confirmed by the 1844 *ordonnance.* However, the consistories found it difficult to enforce these laws. Almost immediately after the passage of the 1823 *ordonnance,* recalcitrants began challenging consistory authority. In 1825, for example, the Strasbourg consistory complained to the prefect that a dissident group in Ittersviller was competing with the consistory-approved *shochet* (slaughterer). When the prefect referred the case to the courts, the *procureur-général* and the *procureur* of Séléstat ruled that no law had been broken.[179] It was apparent that consistory authority was going to be unenforceable.

In 1829 the Metz consistory reorganized the meat trade so as to ensure that only consistory-authorized *shochetim* could enter the slaughterhouse. The financial benefit to the consistory was 300 francs per year per *shochet.* Fees for slaughtering were to be paid directly by the butcher to the *shochetim.*[180]

In Paris the system underwent several changes during the course of the century. Initially, the butchers paid the slaughterers directly and made a "contribution" of twenty-five francs per week to the charity fund. There were three butchers, and the meat trade provided a total of 3600 francs per year for the consistory charities. Until 1821 the system remained essentially the same, with the number of butchers varying between three and four. In 1821 it was decided that income from the meat trade would no longer be used for charity, but would be allocated to the repayment of the debt on the temple. At the same time the system for payment was changed, and the butchers began to pay the consistory instead of the slaughterers. The rate depended on the number of cattle slaughtered. Slaughterers became consistory employees, and the consistory also hired several full-time inspectors, whom they stationed at each of the four butcher shops. Slaughterers earned 1200 francs and inspectors 1000 francs in 1832.[181]

There was constant friction between the butchers and the slaughterers. In 1833, because of charges by the butchers against the slaughterers, the consistory requested the slaughterers to be more exact in the execution of their duties.[182] The butchers' livelihoods were not secure, and they rebelled if one of them received more advantageous terms and was able to compete more favorably than his colleagues. Thus in 1836 a butcher named Hedlin was paying only ten francs per head of beef, while his competitor, Talot, paid seventeen and one-half francs. Both paid an additional five francs for the inspector's fees.[183] The consistory changed its policy several times in attempts to keep the system viable.

The consistory's income from the meat trade was threatened, not only by competing butchers and slaughterers, but also by its own approved agents. In 1839 there were five approved butchers in Paris. They were paying fees to the consistory based on the number of cattle slaughtered. Paris consistory member Halphen calculated, however, that the consistory was not earning as much money as it should from the volume of the meat trade. It appears (although the sources are not explicit) that Halphen was charging the butchers and *shochetim* with conspiring to underestimate the number of animals slaughtered. A new arrangement was reached, whereby each butcher agreed to pay a flat weekly fee to the consistory, in exchange for the right to be the exclusive dealers in kosher meat. The weekly payments were set between forty-five francs and seventy-five francs (based on the volume of business done by each butcher). Total weekly receipts to the consistory amounted to 325 francs. This made a yearly income of 16,900 francs, which represented a significant increase. The butchers were now free to purchase as many animals as they could sell. In exchange for the butchers' acceptance of these new terms the consistory agreed not to license three additional butchers who were seeking the right to sell kosher meat in Paris.[184]

The official slaughterers, Elie Kulmann and Moïse Mayers, were sworn in by an oath administered by Grand Rabbi Ennery, and they were instructed to slaughter only for authorized butchers. Five full-time inspectors were named, one for each shop. Each received a salary of 800 francs per year. Governmental aid was enlisted in enforcing consistory control of the meat trade, and the Inspector General of the Markets agreed to admit to the *abbatoirs* only the slaughterers appointed by the consistory.[185]

Outside Paris the handling of income from the meat trade varied. The Metz consistory, which in 1829 was receiving 300 francs per *shochet* per year, subsequently renounced all revenues from this source.[186] In Strasbourg in 1832 the *shochetim* began paying a weekly contribution of five or eight francs to the charity board.[187]

The Nancy consistory found it difficult to maintain control over the butchers of that city. In 1840 M. Horviller was refused the services of the *shochet* because he refused to obey the consistory ruling that butchers who wished to sell kosher meat must not carry non-kosher meat as well. Horviller went to Metz, where he obtained a certificate as a slaughterer from Grand Rabbi Lambert by pretending to live in a community of the Metz district. He returned to Nancy and did his own slaughtering, continuing his business despite the prohibition of the grand rabbi of Nancy.[188]

In Paris the government condoned and even encouraged the use of the meat tax for the payment of the temple debt. When the consistory, in 1841, requested city aid to help repay the loan, it expected to be able once again to assign the meat tax to charity. However, the minister ordered that these funds be reapplied to the debt.[189]

What the Paris consistory insisted upon for itself, it did not always permit others. In 1843 the Jewish community of Lille (Paris consistory district) decided to open a school. It requested permission to tax kosher meat to finance the school. The *commissaire surveillant* of Lille, M. Sriber, proposed a tax of ten centimes per one-half kilogram of meat. The consistory refused permission, claiming that such a tax was "impossible."[190]

The control of the meat trade was not exercised exclusively for financial reasons, but the documents testifying to the religious aspects of the issue are rare. One of the few examples of the religious issue was the 1844 rejection by inspector M. Lévy of meat prepared during several days by the *shochet* Kulmann. This was reported to Grand Rabbi Ennery, who issued a warning to Kulmann.[191]

The 1844 *ordonnance,* designed to strengthen consistory authority, repeated the provision that only the consistory could name slaughterers, but it was no more effective than the old law had been. Several months after the passage of the new *ordonnance* the Nancy consistory complained to the prefect that a *shochet* was slaughtering meat in Mittelbronn, despite the fact that the consistory had withdrawn his permit. The consistory charged that the man, a certain David Ettinger, had violated Article 258 of the Penal Code, which prohibited the usurpation of public functions.[192] When the case was brought to court, however, the *procureur du roi* in Sarrebourg ruled that Article 258 applied only to the usurpation of civil and military functions, and not to religious functions.[193] The court decision led to additional cases of recalcitrance in the communities, and the rural communities were now convinced of the impotence of the consistory.[194] The Nancy consistory turned to the central consistory for help in enforcing its authority, but the central consistory could offer no solution to the lack of legal sanctions to enforce consistory authority. It suggested that the only recourse available to the consistories was to declare the meat from unauthorized slaughterers non-kosher.[195] Nancy refused to accept this affront to its dignity. The following year it prosecuted another case, in Saint Michiel, against a certain Bolack. This time it based its charges on Article 471, Paragraph 15, of the Penal Code (the section that punishes infraction of *règlements* concerning public administration). The *tribunal de simple police* of Saint-Michiel ruled on June 20, 1845, that Bolack had not exercised the functions of *shochet* but had merely slaughtered animals for his own butcher shop; this, the court found, did not constitute an infraction.[196]

In the wake of these cases an unauthorized butcher shop was opened in Paris by M. Rottembourg of Metz, and in due course Grand Rabbi Ennery declared his meat *tréfa* (non-kosher). The consistory appealed to the Inspector of Markets to refuse Rottembourg access to the slaughterhouse, and the government supported the consistory by convicting Rottembourg of not slaughtering in the manner prescribed by the official regulations. (Only official *shochetim* were exempt from the regulations.)[197] While Rottembourg's case was pending, the consistory, not at all certain of an ultimate victory, tried to convince the authorized butchers to lower their prices in order to compete with Rottembourg. However, the authorized butchers were able to prove to the satisfaction of the consistory that they could not afford to lower prices.[198] Rottembourg was able to charge less only because he paid no fees to the consistory.

The consumers were torn between financial advantage and respect for consistory authority. They sought to reconcile the two, and protested the monopoly of the four authorized butchers, the high prices, poor quality, and the great distance of the shops from many Jewish homes.[199] The central consistory investigated the case, and Paris consistory member Halphen defended the consistory's position in a long *mémoire* recounting the history of the kosher meat trade in Paris. Halphen argued that the consistory's experience had shown that increasing the number of butchers never improved quality or lowered prices. Rather, it increased the costs of religious supervision.[200] The central consistory, under the influence of Adolphe Franck, then ruled that the Paris consistory had been correct in limiting the number of butcher shops.[201]

For a short while, despite the lack of serious legal controls, the butchers of Paris accepted consistory discipline. Then the February 1848 revolution gave new impetus to their anarchical tendencies. Several butcher shops opened without bothering to request consistory authorization; other, more disciplined, people petitioned for permission to open shops. The consistory met with the charity board and some *notables* to decide how to handle this new threat to its authority.[202] Forced to acknowledge that the situation was temporarily beyond its control, the consistory tried to salvage the financial benefits from the meat trade by declaring ritually unfit all meat not slaughtered and inspected by consistory-authorized officials. These services were available to new butchers at a reduced rate of forty francs per week for three weeks, and fifty francs thereafter. The strategem quickly proved a failure, however, and observant Jews, with complete disregard for consistory declarations of kosher or non-kosher, bought meat where the prices were lowest. The consistory resorted to enlisting the government's aid in repressing the unauthorized slaughterers.[203] Popular pressure was brought to bear by the orthodox poor under the leadership of Abraham Ben Baruch Créhange. His journal, *La Vérité,* was the organ of the Jewish revolutionary *Club démocratique des fidèles.* His paper protested consistory monopoly and the tax of ten centimes per pound on meat. It announced a boycott of the authorized butchers in favor of the new independent ones and called on Grand Rabbi Isidor, newly installed, to support the people's cause: "M. le grand rabbin Isidor ne voudra pas débuter à Paris en se prêtant complaisamment aux volontés et aux mesures arbitraires *du consistoire des privilégiés* [Créhange's italics]."[204]

Isidor was suitably impressed. The following month he urged the consistory to abolish the meat tax and to reduce all contributions from the butchers to the actual cost of supervision. He proposed that the loss incurred be replaced by fundraising. The consistory insisted upon maintaining its former system, and Isidor was embarked upon his new career as religious figurehead and messenger boy. He was sent to the police to complain about unauthorized slaughterers and to the *abattoir* to bring the news that the police prefect had agreed to enforce the prohibition of entry to nonauthorized *shochetim*. The consistory decided that a weekly contribution of 380 francs to the consistory would be divided among all the butchers using the services of the consistory's *shochetim* and inspectors. Thus freedom of trade and competition was tacitly acknowledged, while a means was sought to retain the financial benefits of the meat trade. The government, in response to a protest by a Parisian butcher, investigated and authorized the consistory's practice of taxing meat.[205]

The effect of the revolution had been to increase rapidly the number of kosher butcher shops from four to eleven and to reduce the tax profits from 7000 to 4000 francs. Isidor quickly adopted the consistory way of thinking, and only a year after urging that the consistory not seek to gain any profit from the meat trade, he presented the Paris consistory with his own proposal for increasing the profits from 4000 to 10,000 francs per year! The eleven butchers were each paying thirty francs per week, for a total of more than 17,000 francs per year. After the expenses of supervision, the consistory retained only 4000 francs. Isidor suggested reducing the number of licensed butchers to eight and increasing their weekly contribution to fifty francs, demonstrating that this would increase the profit to 10,000 francs. The consistory applauded Isidor's initiative and urged him to implement his plan.[206] He evidently failed in the attempt, for three years later there were thirteen authorized butchers in Paris, four of whom filed a joint complaint that none was able to earn a living because the community was not large enough to support them all.[207]

In the meantime consistories elsewhere were also having difficulty controlling the meat trade. The government of the Second Republic was sympathetic to free trade. On February 20, 1851, a supreme court decision ruled that unauthorized *shochetim* could not be convicted and fined on the basis of Article 471, Paragraph 15, of the Penal Code, a provision punishing disobedience to local or municipal administrative regulations.[208] The Marseille consistory immediately complained that it could not control the meat trade in Lyon and in Avignon. It suggested that the new law (then under preparation) restore consistory authority, or that the government be

prevailed upon to grant state salaries to "ministers" in communities as small as 100 Jews, so that the communities would not have to depend upon the meat tax.[209]

In Paris the struggling butchers found that the only way to earn a living was to lower their prices, and this could only be done by cutting their expenses. The method was familiar: do away with consistory control. An unauthorized *shochet*, M. Lévy, began supplying Paris with ritually slaughtered meat. Consistory response was also familiar: it asked the police to ban Lévy's entrance to the slaughterhouse. This time, however, the government refused to cooperate. The Ministry of Agriculture and Commerce ruled that it was not the business of the administration to enforce the 1844 *ordonnance;* inasmuch as Lévy fulfilled all requirements for entry into the slaughterhouse, he could not be restrained.[210]

The Second Empire was not more favorable to consistory authority than the Republic had been. As we have shown in Chapter 4, it was during this regime that the consistory failed in attempts to assure passage of a new law that would apply penal sanctions to infractions of consistory authority. The consistories were reduced to the application of religious penalties. In 1857 the Colmar consistory noted that Ebstein Goetsch of Colmar slaughtered meat without authorization. The consistory threatened with fines and withholding of religious honors any butcher who bought meat from him.[211]

The question of freedom of trade in regard to the kosher meat trade continued throughout the century and into our own times. In 1877 a candidate for election to the Lyon consistory based his campaign on a platform that included "Liberté complète de la Boucherie."[212] In France today the consistory continues to warn the Jews of the capital that some butchers who claim to sell kosher meat are not under consistory supervision. Notices to this effect are even published in the daily press.

Another item of ritual food supervised by the consistories was the *matzoth* (unleavened bread for Passover). The financial advantage to the control of this product was not in the form of cash, but in the special lower prices at which the approved bakers were expected to supply the charity board for distribution to the poor. The acquisition of *matzoth* for the Passover ritual was a very serious problem for the poor, as its cost was always much higher than that of bread. The distribution of *matzoth* has therefore always been a principal activity of Jewish charities, and often consumed a very high proportion of their total annual expenditures (a fact frequently criticized by early nineteenth-century reformers).

In December 1838, Benoît Cohen, president of the Paris charity board, began to prepare for the following Passover. Attempting to reduce the cost of the *matzoth,* he asked for bids for the exclusive right to manufacture consistory-approved *matzoth.* Only one baker entered the bidding, and Cohen knew that the other bakers were not concerned with obtaining consistory approval, but would bake and sell their *matzoth* independently, as they had always done. In order to prevent this, he asked the consistory to announce that only consistory-approved *matzoth* was ritually acceptable. The consistory refused, knowing from its experience with the meat trade that lack of approval would not prevent the cheaper *matzoth* from being sold. The consistory decided instead to negotiate with the bakers, and an agreement was made whereby all authorized *matzoth* bakers paid a tax to the consistory. However, this tax turned out to be no easier to collect than were the meat taxes. In 1845 a Parisian baker refused to pay the tax and sold his *matzoth* cheaper than did the other bakers. Upon the Paris consistory's complaint, the central consistory replied that there was nothing to do but have the grand rabbi make the announcement that this *matzoth* had not been prepared under rabbinical supervision.[213]

In Bordeaux the consistory also followed the practice of naming an official *matzoth* baker each year. There was no competition for the post, however; one Solomon Dias was the only baker who owned the equipment necessary for its manufacture, and his monopoly was not challenged. In December 1847, he agreed to furnish *matzoth* to the poor at twenty-five centimes per pound, instead of the usual price of thirty-five centimes.[214]

After the 1848 revolution the Paris consistory dared not attempt to control the *matzoth* production. In 1849 it decided to finance the distribution of free *matzoth* for the poor through a special fundraising campaign.[215]

4. Control for Non-financial Reasons

In addition to the financial reasons for which the consistories sought control of Jewish institutions, there were also strong social reasons. To further the effect of the emancipation through greater integration of Jews into French society, the consistories felt it necessary to render their institutions relatively inconspicuous to the general public by Christianizing Jewish practices. We have pointed out this phenomenon in the cases of synagogue weddings and the development of a modern rabbinate; it occurred also in the reform of synagogue ceremonies so that they would not shock honored guests who occasionally attended services in an ecumenical gesture.

Ceremonial control of Judaism was minimal in the first decade of consistory existence. The consistories' early orders regarding ceremonial issues seem to have consisted solely of transmitting government requests for prayers to be said on various state occasions. Ceremonial changes began around 1820 with a movement toward order and decorum. Sermons in French were encouraged, limited—at least in Paris—to rabbis, and scrutinized by the consistory prior to being authorized. A choir was added and music was written, often in imitation of German and Austrian compositions. Priest-like costumes were designed for the rabbis and cantors. Choir uniforms were inspired by those of church choirs. The congregation was instructed to pray together—often silently and never loudly enough to drown out the cantor. Rabbinic sermons in the vernacular were instituted. Paris and Metz took the lead in such changes. Bordeaux claimed that it had been running its services this way for a long time. This was true; the Sephardic practice seems to have been the model for the French reformers.

Substantive changes, such as the introduction of new ceremonies (for example, confirmation) and revision of old ceremonies (for example, circumcision) did not take place until after 1840. Because they were initially established as an administrative and police force, only gradually did the consistories see themselves as religious authorities with the power to introduce reforms. Moreover, large consistorial synagogues were a necessary precondition for effective ceremonial control.

Men outside the consistory system were the first to realize the potential of the consistory as an instrument of religious reform. By 1820 they began asking why the consistories had accomplished so little. Olry Terquem began attacking the consistories in a series of pamphlets and journal articles which he signed "Tsarphati" (Hebrew for "French"). Because of the inflammatory tone of his writings, initially he won few converts; gradually, however, many of his suggestions were incorporated into Jewish institutional life (between 1840 and the end of the century). In 1840 the journal *Archives Israélites* was founded in order to further the cause of the reformers. That Terquem's earlier publications had been an important influence in the foundation of this periodical is obvious from the fact that he was a collaborator on the new journal from the first issue. The role of *Archives Israélites* in awakening and stimulating public opinion on ceremonial reforms was, in turn, a further factor in the preparation of such reforms.

For many years the central consistory took no initiative in regard to religious reform. At first it was principally a rabbinic body, composed of old traditional rabbis. When consulted by the Copenhagen community in 1819 on the permissibility of the reforms introduced in Hamburg, central consistory rabbis de Cologna and Deutz ruled negatively on all points. As the situation evolved over the next twenty years, however, the central consistory became progressively lay-dominated and influenced by the writings of Terquem, which pointed the way toward strong consistory leadership and modernized Jewish institutions.

By 1839 the central consistory was ready to seek control of the synagogue ceremonials for the departmental consistories and itself. This right was granted by the 1844 *ordonnance*. The first actual central consistory initiative in regard to ceremonies seems to have been the establishment of a committee (named in 1845 and reactivated in 1847) to consider the revision of burial ceremonies. In 1846 the central consistory approved the Paris consistory's reform of the circumcision procedure, and the following year, because of Paris consistory pressure, it formed a commission to examine the circumcision ritual.[216]

Traditional practice of circumcision came under attack as early as 1822 by Terquem. As practiced at that time, this ritual occasionally caused infections and even death. Terquem urged changes in the circumcision method to modernize the procedure in accordance with contemporary medical knowledge.[217] His brother, Metz Jewish community leader, and physician, Elie Terquem, had invented a surgical instrument for this purpose. In the late 1830's the Paris consistory had already attempted to introduce reforms into the practice of circumcision, but the 1844 *ordonnance* was the first law that authorized the consistories to exercise control over the *mohelim* (operators of circumcision). Although the law proved to be unenforceable, the Paris consistory at first thought that it could implement reforms in the ceremony by selectively authorizing the *mohelim*. On August 22, 1844, the Paris consistory assembled the *mohelim* and requested that they take an oath to obey consistory rules regarding the methods of circumcision and promise never to perform the part of the ceremony known as *mezizah* (sucking the blood). Seven *mohelim* were present, and four took the oath. These four men were appointed as authorized *mohelim*. One asked for two weeks to think it over. Two others decided not to practice, but the following week one of them changed his mind and took the oath.[218] Several weeks later it was discovered that Louis Lévy, one of the men who had taken the oath, was continuing to practice the *mezizah*. Called before the consistory, he declared his intention to continue obeying this Talmudic injunction and made it known that he had consulted lawyers and theologians and was confident that he could not be prohibited from continuing to practice traditional circumcision. The consistory resolved to ask the police prefect to prevent Lévy from operating.[219] We have no indication of the response of the police, but it is difficult to believe that they could have given the consistory satisfaction, for circumcision was not controlled by state law.

The consistory, which wanted to improve the public image of the Jew in order to aid his absorption into French society, wanted to eliminate the chances of newspaper reports of syphilitic infections and deaths due to ritual circumcision. The orthodox rejected the need for such protection. Conservative leader S. Bloch, of the *Univers Israélite,* wrote that the consistory had no competence, either as a religious or an administrative authority, to change the mode of circumcision. He said that only the government was qualified to act in the interests of public health. As a religious authority, the consistory would have to defend religious law and could no more prohibit *mezizah* than it could prohibit the fast of *Yom Kippur* or the Sabbath rest.[220]

The quarrel expanded. Orthodox Parisian groups petitioned the Paris consistory to choose carefully the *mohelim* it authorized, but not to change the traditional method. Suitable control of operators, they pointed out, was sufficient precaution to prevent infections. The grand rabbis of the eastern departments agreed, and publicly protested the Parisian measure. They accused the consistory of coercing Grand Rabbi Ennery into approving the reform measures by threatening that the government would take even more dramatic measures if he did not approve.[221]

The central consistory approved of the Paris consistory's circumcision reforms, and directed other consistories to imitate them. Several consistories instituted changes in the circumcision procedure, and in 1846 the Metz consistory threatened to prosecute an unauthorized *mohel.*[222]

The Jewish community, sensitive to the severity of public criticism, was its own worst critic, and attempted to handle all issues *en famille.* By the 1850's, regulations and controls regarding circumcision were established everywhere. In Alsace in 1859 a baby died of a hemorrhage after a circumcision. The *mohel* was found guilty of disobeying the *règlement,* which required him to call a doctor if a hemorrhage began, and he was dismissed from his functions.[223] The following year the consistory revised its circumcision regulations.[224]

Another target of attack of the reformers was the practice of selling synagogue honors (*mitzvot*) by auction in the synagogue. In the 1840's the consistories began to eliminate this practice. They had been slow to act because they were concerned that abolishing the auctions might jeopardize their source of income. Once convinced of the merit and feasibility of this change, the consistories became the ardent proponents of the new system and ordered the elimination of auctions in all officially recognized temples of their districts. In the Bas-Rhin consistory district the communities were given a final deadline of April 1, 1859, by which to abolish the auctions or risk prosecution. In September of that year the *Procureur impérial* of Strasbourg promised to prosecute the recalcitrant communities. Armed with this promise, the Strasbourg consistory extended the deadline to the first of November and issued another warning to the communities. Letters of compliance began arriving, and prosecution was unnecessary. The closest the consistory came to prosecution was the summoning of the *commissaire surveillant* of Zellviller before the justice of the peace in Obernai. This menace sufficed, and the *commissaire surveillant* promised to eliminate the auctions.[225]

The public image of the Jews was affected by other ceremonies of the Jewish tradition. Because burial ceremonies were of a public nature, they were frequently criticized. Straggling processions of ill-dressed mourners, dirty funeral attendants, the cacophony of prayers without an ecclesiastical leader—all were judged unsuitable. In 1845 the central consistory agreed to consider the creation of a standard burial procedure and appointed a commission. Reactivated two years later, this commission appears not to have accomplished anything. In 1853 the Paris consistory submitted for approval to the central consistory a set of regulations regarding burial ceremonies. By now the central consistory had begun to interest itself in ceremonial policy. On the recommendation of Anspach, it approved the *règlement*.[226] In 1860 the Strasbourg consistory adopted a new regulation regarding burials.[227] These regulations provided for orderly processions and rabbis' prayers. Horse-drawn hearses, being adopted everywhere for Christian burials, replaced the old practice of carrying the coffin by hand. Funeral attendants were to wear specified clothing.

Control of burial procedures was facilitated by the consistories' exclusive role as representative of the Jewish communities in negotiating for burial space. Napoleonic law had placed ownership of the cemeteries in the hands of the municipalities, and the consistories were responsible for making suitable arrangements with local authorities. Burial procedures varied with the varied attitudes of the consistories regarding traditional Jewish practices. At times it was difficult to obtain separate space where Jewish law could be observed, and in some cases Jews were forced to conform to the regulations regarding Christian burials.

Several different classes of funerals could be purchased, according to the economic status of the family. The city of Paris made extensive use of cheap, temporary burial plots and common graves for the poor. Because of their poverty, only about 20 percent of the Parisian Jewish population was able to purchase permanent burial plots in the middle of the nineteenth century. Since exhumation and multiple burials in a plot were stringently regulated by Jewish law, the need to conform to local regulations worked a religious hardship on the orthodox.

Although dissident groups could meet in prayer, bake their own *matzoth* and slaughter their own meat, they could not bury their own dead. There was no way to obtain land for a cemetery without entering into negotiations with the government, and only the consistories and their official representatives could do that. The consistory generally complied with local customs and procedures, rather than insist that Jewish law govern procedures at Jewish cemeteries (or sections of cemeteries). Thus in Paris in 1841 a group of orthodox Jews under the leadership of Abraham Ben Baruch Créhange and a certain Bollwiller complained to the Paris consistory about a municipal decision to demolish the temporary graves. The orthodox wanted the consistory to insist that the graves be saved and that the Jewish part of the cemetery be governed by Jewish law, which knows no temporary graves. Religious arguments failed to persuade the consistory to defend Jewish religious interests. Although Adolphe Crémieux, president of the

central consistory, supported the religious rights of the orthodox, the Paris consistory disregarded his recommendation and
announced that it was important to conform to Parisian ways
as much as possible.[228]

The position of the Nancy consistory offers a contrast. In
that city the authorities decided to close the Jewish cemetery
in 1842, and they ordered that people of all religions be buried
together in the same cemetery, with one set of regulations. The
Nancy consistory president resigned in protest, and the city
yielded on the issue.[229]

The question arose in several places at various times as to
who owned the Jewish cemetery and who had the right to rule
on procedure within it. Most of the cemeteries used by the Jews
had been the property of the communities before the revolution. The revolution decided not to nationalize Jewish property
(and therefore Jewish debts), but the law attributed to the
municipalities control of the cemeteries. Jewish rights were challenged in some places, but elsewhere were acknowledged, despite
the fact that a strict interpretation of the legislation would
have determined that only the consistories had the legal right
to own property. In several cases consistories challenged local
ownership, but the issue was never formally resolved. Throughout the period of several years when the consistories were
drafting what became the 1844 *ordonnance,* none of the consistories thought to include a provision granting the consistories
control of all Jewish cemeteries. In January 1844, when the
new law was on the verge of being adopted, the Strasbourg
consistory requested the help of the central consistory in acquiring the Schlestadt cemetery. The central consistory admitted
that it was incompetent to instruct the Strasbourg consistory on
this matter, because of a gap in the legislation. Although the
central consistory attempted to have control of the cemeteries
added to the list of consistory attributions in the bill, this was
never done.[230]

In Bordeaux the cemeteries and burial services were handled
exclusively by a pious society called *Guémilout Hassadim.*
This society had been founded in 1730 as a mutual aid and
burial society. Under the consistory regime it became quasi-
official. The consistory exercised supervision over its treasury,
regulations and procedures, and, until 1860, granted it full
authorization to function both as a mutual aid society and as
the official Jewish burial society in Bordeaux. The society
charged for nonmembers' burials according to its estimate of
the family's wealth, but the consistory reserved the right to
require modifications of the fees charged if families complained.
In 1860 *Guémilout Hassadim* lost its right to handle the
burials.[231]

The earliest form of control sought by the consistories for
ideological–political reasons was control of schools and education. The reasons are evident: the consistory had been formed
to police and mold ("regenerate") the backward masses of poor

Jews. The instrument of regeneration *par excellence* was the consistory-controlled school. Although French Judaism did not await the coming of the consistories to develop schools which taught secular subjects,[232] it was only with consistorial pressure that the traditional schools which taught only religion were closed. The central consistory had adopted a uniform religious textbook ("catechism") as early as 1820, but it was only the 1823 *ordonnance* (Article 18) that guaranteed to the central consistory the exclusive right to approve books for use in the Jewish elementary schools. The book that was approved in 1820, the *Précis élémentaire d'instruction religieuse et morale pour les jeunes Français israélites* by Samuel Cahen, and all subsequent books adopted by the central consistory stressed the consistory's interpretation of Judaism as primarily a universal moral ethic. Hard work and good citizenship made a good Jew.

Unauthorized books were barred from use in the schools, but the history of effective control in this domain followed roughly the development of consistory control in other areas. Control of textbooks and the standardization of interpretation were officially in the hands of the consistories for the private Jewish schools as well as for the consistorial schools. Moreover, in order to standardize religious instruction along lines approved by the consistory, the public examinations gradually introduced everywhere as a prerequisite to the celebration of the *Bar Mitzvah* were based on the *Précis*. This examination eventually developed into a confirmation (*initiation religieuse*) ceremony for both boys and girls. Its purpose was to ascertain that the child had received a proper and thorough religious education, as defined by modern consistory standards. This meant that the pupil had learned the catechism by heart and understood his duty to the state.

The consistory program for a modern education stressed general training in French language and civilization, arithmetic, and practical skills (needlework, mechanical drawing, etc.). Religion was defined in the modern way we have indicated and was limited to an aspect of the curriculum. It did not include Talmudic studies. The modernizing trend was accentuated by the communalization of many of the Jewish schools.

The orthodox resisted the influence of the modern school, and the competition of their own traditional schools hurt the recognized schools financially. As the French public school system grew during the nineteenth century, the government became increasingly vigorous in its inspection and authorization of schools. It sought to suppress the unauthorized traditional religious schools. For example, the Metz consistory enlisted the aid of the Sarreguemines rabbi in closing down an unauthorized school in Forbach which competed with the public Jewish school there.[233]

Charitable institutions were another area where consistories sought a monopoly. This was especially true in Paris. Only by controlling the dispensation of aid could the consistories use charity as a weapon to pressure people to conform to certain prescribed standards of behavior. Beggars, parents who refused to send their children to school, and people whose morality was questionable were all threatened with loss of financial aid.

Although multiple charities are a normal feature of the traditional Jewish society, in 1809 all existing Parisian mutual aid societies were officially merged into a single consistorial charity board, *Le comité de bienfaisance*. Despite their official dissolution, however, many of the societies continued to exist (as we have seen in our discussion of the prayer meetings they often held). The consistory made no attempt to prevent either the mutual aid practiced by these societies or the charity they extended to nonmembers, disaster victims, or pious scholars in Jerusalem. Moreover, the consistory had developed a system whereby it received charitable contributions from these societies in exchange for the favor of approving prayer meetings. Parisian Jewish poor were then supported by these funds, and it is permissible to believe that without the concurrence of the private societies, sufficient funds could not have been raised. Yet the manner of distribution—centralized through the consistory—was such as to mask the real source of much of the money and to credit the consistory with providing for all the charitable needs of the Jews of the capital.

This monopoly of the *comité* in the realm of charity was attacked in 1847 by Goudchaux Baruch Weill, who contended that of the eighty Parisian charitable associations, only one was Jewish. That one, the *comité*, had an income of 36,000 francs, which was used to assist an estimated 3000 people. Weill compared this with the situation prevailing in other large European Jewish centers. In Hamburg there were fifty-nine Jewish charitable associations. In London 750,000 francs per year were spent. In Amsterdam 15,000 poor were supported by the community. As though the independent societies did not exist, Weill argued for a decentralization of institutionalized Jewish charity. He was not altogether incorrect, for the primary purpose of the Parisian societies was mutual aid and not general philanthropy.

Weill's recommendations included the establishment of charity groups to help the poor receive job training, to supply layettes, and to pay rent on behalf of poor laborers and the aged. He urged that all such charitable activities be under the patronage of influential and wealthy people. He went so far as to propose the Rothschild women as the natural presidents of some of the societies he envisaged. (In 1845 they had given financial aid to 950 pregnant women.) He insisted that the multiplicity of institutions would increase the total amount of money available.[234]

Weill's letter appears to have stimulated the Rothschilds to action. Before many years had passed they had, in fact, established or helped to finance every kind of charitable institution called for by Weill.

The severe financial hardship wrought on the consistory the following year by the 1848 revolution—discussed above with regard to the loss of synagogue income in that year—caused the consistory to reorganize the *comité* along broader lines. The consistory co-opted leaders of the societies, making them representatives to the *comité*. (It was clear that these small groups were far better equipped than the consistory to command voluntary adherence.) Twelve societies sent representatives to the *comité* as a result of the 1848 reorganization.

The societies and the consistory continued to struggle for authority throughout the period under consideration. In 1853 the mutual aid society *Japhet* announced a dance to raise funds for the poor. Incensed at such independence, the consistory contemplated forbidding the dance, but wisely refrained from doing so. Tickets had already been sold and expenses contracted by the society. The consistory contented itself with sending a circular to the various societies announcing that in the future such activities would require consistory permission and strict police surveillance during the affair. The terms in which the president addressed the consistory about this event reveal the assumptions of the consistory. Consistory authority and hierarchy were at stake. The consistory also manifested its tendency to impute ulterior motives or dangerous inclinations to all spontaneous actions:

M. le président fait observer . . . que le consistoire ne peut tolérer que des particuliers ou des associations prennent la place de l'administration dans quelque circonstance que ce soit et quelque soit le but honorable que l'on aurait pour objet d'atteindre. Sous le manteau de la charité, il se commet des abus de tous genres; les actions échappent au contrôle de l'autorité, et le principe de bienfaisance qui guide ces sortes d'entreprises toujours pompeusement annoncées, est presque toujours négatif. Il y aurait donc lieu de prévenir désormais toute démarche de l'espèce, de ne pas laisser usurper l'autorité de l'administration à qui appartient l'initiative de tous les actes pouvant intéresser ses administrés, et de tenir ses coreligionnaires en garde contre des sollicitations qui ne peuvent que préjudicier aux intérêts généraux.[235]

The Metz consistory also tried to limit competition from private individuals in the creation of charitable societies. The *société de la jeunesse israélite* of that city, which celebrated its one hundredth anniversary in 1947, was at first refused authorization by the Metz consistory because of its potential threat to the consistorial charity board.[236]

In 1847 the Metz consistory had reason to be suspicious of private charities. It was engaged in a struggle with a burial society (*Hevra Kaddisha*) of women, whose pious members refused their services to women whose lives had not been sufficiently orthodox. After attempts at conciliation, the consistory dissolved the group in October 1848, when the society refused religious honors to a *"dame honorable"* of Metz.[237]

Hierarchical control of charities was not limited to Paris and Metz. In 1856 the Bordeaux consistory decided that the treasury of the mutual aid and burial society, *Guémilout Hassadim,* which had been periodically audited, should now be controlled by the consistory. The consistory felt that it was obligated to protect the society's funds, which were deposited mainly by humble workers. It therefore limited the amount of money that could be kept in the treasury, and required the rest to be deposited with the consistory.[238]

In Strasbourg, also, attempts were made to put all charitable societies under the financial control of the consistory. In 1861 a member made such a proposal to the consistory, but some doubts were raised as to the legality of the measure. It was decided to investigate the merits of the proposal, and its sponsor was asked to make a general report on all charitable societies. We do not have any indication of the outcome of this proposal.[239]

CHAPTER IX   THE RABBINATE

The French rabbinate, rather than being a truly independent institution, functioned more as the religious conscience of the consistory. Because the rabbis were organized within the hierarchical and lay-dominated consistory, no rabbinic societies were formed and no instrumentality developed whereby rabbis could cooperatively exert pressure on lay leaders. The only rabbinic conference that was held, at least until 1870, was called by Grand Rabbi Ulmann in 1856 to prepare the ground for some ritual reforms the central consistory wished to implement from above. The rabbis maintained no communication through any professional journal or bulletin. Even direct interpersonal communication among the rabbis was impossible, since the hierarchical structure required that all communications between rabbis pass through the intermediary of the consistory administration. If we may judge from the available documentation, the great majority of communications among rabbis were the published and unpublished letters and circulars sent by the grand rabbis to the local rabbis and by the central consistory grand rabbi to the rest of the French rabbinate.

A. Rabbinic Districts

The French rabbinate consisted of grand rabbis who were members of consistories and communal rabbis who were assigned to one or several Jewish communities. Thus, the district of a communal rabbi was often comprised of several small Jewish communities, and the total Jewish population varied greatly from one district to another. In 1841 the central consistory attempted to reorganize the rabbinic districts along a more rational basis. Central consistory member Myrtil Maas and secretary Polack prepared a plan in which each canton or set of contiguous cantons with a total population of 300 Jews would form a rabbinic district,[1] but the government rejected these revisions.

For several reasons the existence of the consistory system tended to limit the size of the rabbinate. The minimum rabbinic salary of 1000 francs specified in the original legislation, although not high, was expensive for the impoverished Jewish communities, whose funds were being siphoned off into the large cities in the form of taxes for the grand rabbis' salaries and for modern schools and synagogue buildings. Communities were therefore frequently not in a position to create rabbinic posts, and were only able to employ one man as cantor-slaughterer-teacher.

Nor did the financial situation improve and favor the growth of the rabbinate after the government's 1831 assumption of the cost of the rabbis' salaries. Rather, the Ministry of Cults was careful to maintain the size of the rabbinate at a steady level, even refusing at times to create new posts when the Jewish population level justified requests for new posts. The consistory itself even suggested decreasing the number of rabbis, thereby enlarging the size of the individual districts and improving the salary level and the amount of incidental fees for each rabbi. However, a central consistory plan to this effect in 1849 and another in 1860, both of which were proposed for Alsace, were not implemented by the government.[2]

The cities in which the consistories were located, regardless of their size, were originally entitled only to one rabbi (the grand rabbi) at state expense. As the Jewish population grew, the consistorial synagogues in some places needed additional rabbis. In Paris an assistant rabbi was authorized by the government around 1855. As early as 1851, however, the Paris consistory had hired Rabbi Trenel for this post, while waiting for government approval. By 1861 there were two salaried posts for assistant rabbis in Paris. The three rabbis served a Jewish population in that city of about 25,000. Although there was a Portuguese synagogue, it did not have its own rabbi, nor did any of the authorized chapels or prayer meetings.

Before the post of assistant rabbi was created in Paris, there were always some semi-official assistants to the Paris grand rabbi. Two traditional rabbis, Marcus Prague and a certain Mosbach, who had none of the modern credentials, lived in the capital and were occasionally called upon to render their services. They were even referred to as *sous-rabbins* although they never collected regular salaries, but only *secours* (occasional financial aid from the government). In 1837 Prague requested that the Paris consistory solicit a regular salary for him, but the consistory decided that Grand Rabbi Ennery was able to handle the spiritual needs of the Parisian Jewish population by himself. The consistory, while conceding that Prague had occasionally replaced Ennery when he was away, pointed out that Mosbach could have done the job as well.[3] The Paris consistory solicited annual aid from the government on behalf of both Mosbach and Prague, in order to keep them available to substitute for Ennery when needed.[4]

The situation was similar in Strasbourg. The consistory hired an assistant rabbi for the consistorial synagogue in 1855 and paid him at communal expense for several years before the government agreed to authorize a state-salaried post. (The Jewish population of Strasbourg at that time was about 2300.)

The number of state-salaried rabbinic posts in France in 1861 was sixty-one, including ten grand rabbis—nine in the departmental consistories and one in the central consistory. The other fifty-one were communal rabbis, including the two assistants in Paris. There were therefore forty-nine communal rabbis who held posts outside the *chefs-lieux* (seats) of the consistories. Of these, thirty-nine were in Alsace (twenty-one in the Haut-Rhin, eighteen in the Bas-Rhin). Another five were in Lorraine (four in Meurthe, one in Moselle). The remaining five were divided among the districts of Paris, Bayonne, Marseille and Lyon. The Bordeaux consistory alone counted no communal rabbis in its district. In addition to the sixty-one official rabbinic positions, there were sixty-four cantorial posts, which were also state-salaried. The cantors' role will be discussed below.[5]

B. Rabbinic Training and Scholarship

Although only forty-eight rabbis were trained in the Metz rabbinic school from its founding in 1829 to 1860, a total of ninety-eight rabbis held state-salaried posts during the same thirty-year period. Thus more than half of the first generation of nineteenth-century French rabbis had received traditional training.[6] In order to make sure that they would be the kind of rabbis that Napoleon and the Jewish *notables* had agreed upon, the legislation specified that preference would be given to rabbis who had been members of the Sanhedrin. The rabbis were also required to take an oath that their teachings would conform to Sanhedrin principles.

It was 1816 before the central consistory first discussed the idea of creating a school of theology that would respond to the desire of educated Jews that rabbinic studies be modernized.[7] The Metz consistory took the first steps to put such a plan into action. Early in 1820 Metz established a *Comité de l'enseignement religieux,* including Grand Rabbi Wittersheim, Mayer Anspach, Samuel Cahen, and Olry Terquem among its members, to prepare a new program of studies for the education of rabbis. On June 8, 1820, the committee recommended a school with three classes; the elementary class would accept graduates of the consistory's primary school who seemed fit for the rabbinate. Each of three levels would require more than one year to complete, and pupils would be promoted from one class to another according to their progress.[8]

Although it was the Metz community that was planning this school, the suggestion seems to have been made that the school be established in Paris. In November at a meeting of the Metz *notables,* a member pointed out the advantages of Metz with regard to space, lower costs, families who would freely board poor students, and the city's location in the midst of the eastern concentration of French Jews.[9] The project was adopted and a curriculum was planned, consisting of Hebrew grammar, Pentateuch, Prophets, Talmud, and commentaries. It was anticipated that the students would also learn French and arithmetic in the local primary school while studying at the rabbinic school.[10]

In 1823 the *notables* of Metz expressed pride in their two-year old modern Talmudic school and said that they expected the school to supply "virtuous, educated and enlightened rabbis."[11] According to Olry Terquem, however, the Metz school did not live up to its promises. In 1824 Terquem wrote that the language of instruction in the rabbinic school was Yiddish, the students knew little French, and they attended primarily for the free food available to students: "Il serait plus exact de dire qu'ils viennent manger le Talmud que l'apprendre."[12] Terquem charged that the future rabbis studied no secular or religious literature, no philosophy, and no sciences: "aucune des connaissances portant nom chez les hommes."[13] We do not know the level of competence actually achieved in Hebrew, Talmud, and Bible, the subjects which formed the major part of the program.

Terquem published his critique of the school in order to protest an 1824 proposal of the central consistory that each consistory organize a Talmudic school modeled on the one founded in Metz in 1821. We can therefore assume that as late as 1824 the central consistory thought that religious studies in Yiddish and minimal secular education constituted a sufficiently modern training program for rabbis.

Terquem ridiculed not only the model chosen by the central consistory for its proposed additional schools, but also the idea of creating as many as seven such schools for the small French Jewish population (which he overestimated at about 70,000). He pointed out that three theological schools sufficed for three million Protestants and warned that the rabbinic schools would prove expensive and increase the already high Jewish taxes. He suggested that the money would be better spent on elementary schools. Terquem proposed that all the traditional Talmudic schools in the provinces be closed and that all efforts be concentrated on the development of a single modern rabbinic school in Paris. Only in the capital would it be possible to organize a rabbinic school correctly without increasing communal expenses, and to achieve the necessary "regeneration" of the rabbinate.

Terquem went on to make very specific proposals for the organization of a program of rabbinic studies. Despite widespread antipathy to him and to his manner of writing, his suggestions were influential in determining the eventual direction of French Judaism. Terquem's immediate influence on consistory policy was the abandonment of the plan for seven rabbinic schools and the decision to create one central rabbinic school. His proposal that the school be located in Paris, which would afford the rabbinic students the opportunity of studying simultaneously at the university, was not accepted by the central consistory. Yet in 1859 the school was moved from Metz to Paris in the anticipation that students would benefit from the proximity of the university. Terquem seems also to have influenced rabbinic training with his proposal for a three-stage educational program. He suggested that they begin with elementary school studies of French, Hebrew, arithmetic, and mechanical drawing. Their secondary education would be in public institutions, and therefore secular. It would be supplemented by instruction in Biblical exegesis, Jewish literature, and history given by the grand rabbi. Twenty-three years later, in 1847, the central consistory, influenced by Adolphe Franck and Solomon Munk, recommended precisely the same plan to some district consistories which had wanted to establish Talmudic secondary schools to prepare students for the rabbinic school. The third stage of Terquem's plan was for the rabbinic training itself. While studying at the rabbinic school the students would augment their studies by courses at the various institutions of higher learning in Paris. They would study rhetoric and history at the *facultés,* Arabic at the *Collège de France,* agriculture at the *Jardin du roi,* elementary astronomy at the *Observatoire,* and hygiene at the medical school. Terquem was thirty-five years before his time. After the *Ecole rabbinique* had moved to Paris, this kind of cross-fertilization was finally achieved.

After the abandonment of the central consistory's 1824 proposal to establish seven rabbinic schools, no further action in this regard was taken for several years. In 1827 the Paris consistory raised the question again of what was to be done to ensure the training of French rabbis. It requested that the central consistory take serious steps toward the founding of a theological school. The central consistory then decided to open a central rabbinic school in Metz, citing as reasons for choosing that city rather than Paris, that costs would be lower in Metz, that the Metz Talmudic school had offered to close and make its building available, and that the talents of the local rabbis and the professors of the *lycée* in that city would assure an adequate local teaching staff.[14]

The program of studies planned by the central consistory in 1827 included much of what Terquem had found wanting in the Metz Talmudic school: French, German, Latin, logic, rhetoric and elocution, Jewish history, French history, geography. It is notable, however, that it was the government, and not the central consistory, which insisted upon secular education for all rabbinic students. The central consistory's proposal had been for two distinct courses of study, one leading to the diploma of communal rabbi and requiring only religious studies, the other sanctioned by the diploma of grand rabbi and requiring secular learning as well as religious studies. The ministry protested that this system would prevent the communal rabbis from rising eventually to higher posts. Insisting that its own views prevail on this issue, the government took yet another step in the control of its Jewish population through the rabbis, pursuing the course of action that had begun with the Sanhedrin.

Religious studies were to include Hebrew, Bible and Talmud, the *Shulkhan Aruch* and works by Alfasi and Maimonides. It was specified that the professor of Talmud was also to teach the Sanhedrin decisions, demonstrate the harmony between state law and religious law, and encourage patriotism.[15]

Despite the impressive program announced in 1827, the school failed during its Metz period (1829–59) to actually teach all of these subjects at all times. It failed to live up to expectations in other ways also. It accepted students who were not prepared for advanced work. Although the government had urged that candidates for admission be required to first spend two years in public secondary schools, this requirement was officially waived for the first class and was subsequently not enforced.

The 1829 *règlement* governing the functioning of the school required the following for admission: a knowledge of French (minimal, described as "les principes de la langue française"), skill in arithmetic, some background ("des notions") in history and geography. Prerequisite religious study included the principles of Hebrew and ability to interpret portions of the Bible, Mishna, and Talmud.

When the school opened in 1829, it was placed under the immediate supervision of the Metz consistory, although its direction was theoretically lodged in Paris with the central consistory. Only around 1839 did the central consistory begin to raise questions about the school's functioning and to take steps to improve it.

In 1841 Adolphe Franck published a severe critique of the rabbinic training being received in Metz. The *Archives Israélites,* which printed his letter in its February issue, joined its voice to his, and made the suggestion that the school be moved to Paris, where general educational opportunities were better. This seems to have been the first time that anyone suggested moving the school, although, as we have already seen, some people had favored establishing it in Paris originally. The consistory of Metz, backed by the local prefect, opposed moving the school, and the move was not accomplished until 1859.

In response to the *Archives Israélites* article, the ministry investigated the quality of the rabbinic training, and agreed that improvement of the school was necessary. A memo for the Minister of Cults, prepared by an aide on the basis of a report by the school's governing board, took note of the poor preparation of the students who entered the school, some of them barely knowing how to read and write. It charged that the rabbinic school resembled more a primary school than an institution of higher learning. The writer estimated that the quality of the teaching was poor and the program had no fixed aim. He proposed that future rabbis receive a solid and varied education, including instruction in morality, to ensure that they would be a good influence on the Jews. Furthermore, the writer of the note suggested that the grand rabbis be required to obtain the *bachelier* (secondary school) diploma, or at least spend some years studying the humanities in a public secondary school.[16]

The question whether the rabbinic school should affiliate in some way with the university was frequently raised in nineteenth-century Europe. In Germany, for many years, Rabbis Abraham Geiger and Ludwig Philippson campaigned unsuccessfully for a Faculty of Jewish Theology, to be established at one of the German universities. The creation of a faculty would have entailed official recognition of Judaism.

The history of the issue in France is less well known. In 1831 the Metz consistory requested that the central consistory try to obtain the title of *Faculté de théologie israélite* for the school, but inasmuch as there was no branch of the university in Metz, it is not clear if the consistory expected the change of title to be accompanied by affiliation with the university. The central consistory at that time rejected the proposed new title as inaccurate, claiming that there is no theology in Judaism.[17]

In 1841 an aide to the minister of cults proposed replacing the rabbinic school with a university chair of Jewish dogma and ethics ("une chaire de dogme et de morale hébraïque"), to be established either in Metz or, preferably, in a city with a university. His proposal reflected a low opinion of the rabbinic school and a feeling that by supporting an entire school, which taught secular as well as religious subjects, the government was doing more for the Jews than for others.[18]

In 1846, the Metz consistory requested again that the *école rabbinique* be placed under the Ministry of Public Education, as a Faculty of Jewish Theology. This time it was explicitly requested that the school obtain university status, and the central consistory supported the proposal.[19] The government rejected the request.

In 1841 the central consistory sent out a circular asking the departmental consistories to test the candidates for the *école rabbinique* to be sure they met the minimum requirements. Previously the admissions committee of the Metz school, not wishing to embarrass either the boys or the recommending consistories, had accepted many unqualified students. The central consistory announced that in the future only candidates who met the requirements would be accepted.[20]

Despite this attempt to improve the level of instruction, Adolphe Franck, shortly after his 1844 election to the central consistory, renewed his complaint about the poor results obtained by the rabbinic school. On his suggestion, it was decided that a delegation be sent to visit the establishment and report to the consistory.[21]

It was two years before the delegation was sent; in May 1846 an impending visit by Franck and Munk was announced to the Metz consistory,[22] which appears to have been inspired or frightened by the improvements suggested. It decided to ask the ministry to place the school under its authority and turn it into a *Faculté de théologie* on the same plane as the Protestant and Catholic *facultés*.[23] The project was supported by part of the central consistory and then was either temporarily abandoned or went slowly through administration channels, to emerge again in 1848. After the 1846 visit of Franck and Munk to the school, the central consistory began making improvements in the curriculum; new courses in Bible exegesis and religious history were added.[24] Although these courses had already been listed on the 1827 program for the rabbinic school, the program had not been implemented. Adolphe Franck was very anxious to improve the school. He made suggestions for improvements in the admissions policy, the teaching program, and the physical plant of the school.[25] As a result of his urging, the central consistory, in consultation with the government, ruled that entry into the rabbinic school should be dependent upon the candidate's having achieved a level of knowledge equal to that of a student finishing the class of *quatrième* (eighth grade) at a *Collège Royal* (public secondary school).[26]

Franck and Munk also reported that the school's library was shockingly undersupplied. None of the basic classical works that were standard possessions of libraries in the *lycées* and *collèges* were to be found there. Even the theology books published in France and Germany in the previous thirty years were lacking. As long as the school remained in Metz, this situation did not improve, and in 1852 the prefect reported that the entire library was worth only 700 francs![27]

Further recommendations by Munk and Franck in 1846 included examinations of the students before they could go on to the second division, introduction of the Sephardi pronunciation of Hebrew, a thesis to be required of candidates for the higher degree of grand rabbi, establishment of a series of regular inspections, and introduction of a course in "eloquence" and one in theology. Finally, they recommended that the best of the school's graduates be sent to Paris for a few years of further study of literature and theology.[28]

The two questions, of moving the rabbinic school to Paris and turning it into a *faculté de théologie,* had not been resolved. French Jewry was divided on both issues. Some felt that an advantage in status, facilities, and quality of teaching would result from the establishment of a theology faculty under government supervision. Others insisted on retaining Jewish control of the rabbinic school for religious and (unstated) ethnic reasons. Metz, itself, was divided, and especially ambivalent on the issue of the move to Paris. In 1848 the central consistory, under the leadership of vice-president Adolphe Franck, negotiated with the government to move the school to Paris as a *faculté de théologie.* The proposal was submitted to the National Assembly, which rejected it in 1849.[29]

The idea of turning the school into a theology faculty was definitively abandoned at this point, but the plan to move it to Paris was pursued. It was discussed in 1850, and then (because of disagreement among central consistory members) lay dormant for a while,[30] was raised again in 1854, and was finally implemented in 1859.

The school's faculty included five men in 1850: Grand Rabbi Mayer Lazard, director and professor of Talmud; L. Morhange, professor of Hebrew and Biblical exegesis; M. Solomon, professor of Latin and Greek literature; M. Bourgeois, professor of philosophy and oratory; and M. Helmann, professor of religious music.[31] The following year Franck succeeded in having a chair of theology and religious history established, and in naming Lazare Wogue to the post.[32] Franck was also responsible for the introduction of a German course, on the dual grounds that it was a practical necessity for rabbis in Alsace and that many theology books were written in German.[33] Again, it should be noted that these so-called new courses were really part of the original program that had remained a dead letter since the establishment of the school.

In 1850 the building that housed the rabbinic school was in severe disrepair. For the twenty-one years of the school's existence no repairs had been made and none of the equipment had been replaced. In 1850 the central consistory temporarily abandoned the plan to move the school to Paris, and the government authorized reconstruction of the Metz building. The state even offered to pay demolition costs. The Metz consistory bought three buildings adjacent to the school in order to expand the school's facilities. Clearly everyone concerned assumed at that point that the school would remain in Metz. The money ran out before the job had been completed, and the Metz consistory turned to the other departmental consistories for help in financing the rest of the work.[34]

When help was not forthcoming, the project to move the school to Paris was once more considered; the Metz consistory president went for discussions to Paris, but on his return reported that the projected move had been "definitely" abandoned.[35] The financial problem was not solved, it was only temporarily shelved. Restoration had ceased and money was sought.

In 1855 central consistory Grand Rabbi Ulmann visited the school and examined the students. He reported to the central consistory that he was satisfied with their progress. He praised especially the new course in Biblical exegesis, taught by Morhange, and the course in theology by Wogue. Ulmann described Wogue's theology course as an explanation of several works of religious philosophy. By 1856 an additional professor had been added: M. Krüger, who taught homiletics.[36] But the courses were held, and the students were housed, in the midst of suspended renovations.

In March 1856 it was finally realized that the rabbinic school was not going to receive the funds it needed in order to finish the necessary rebuilding. The government had contributed 60,000 francs and the Metz consistory had contracted an additional 60,000 francs worth of debts.[37] Once again the central consistory proposed moving the school to Paris. Central consistory member Javal argued that if it were transferred, it would be easier to get financial support.[38] Two months later the assembly of rabbis meeting in Paris to discuss the possibility of making some reforms voted to move the rabbinic school to Paris. That vote put an end to the vacillation.

It would appear that the Rothschilds were partisans of the move to Paris, because although they did not come to the rescue of the school while it was in Metz, their representative, Albert Cohn, announced that he would not have any trouble raising the 60,000 francs necessary to establish the school in Paris.[39] No one had any solution for the problem of the other 60,000 francs needed to cover the Metz consistory's contracted debts.

A commission of Adolphe Franck, Albert Cohn and Grand Rabbi Salomon Ulmann was appointed to arrange for the transfer of the school to Paris.[40] The opinions of the various consistories were solicited; five of the eight consistories supported the move. Opposed were Metz and Bordeaux, which insisted on maintaining the school in Metz, and Nancy, which proposed moving it to Nancy, where it could share the facilities of the new university. This proposal was supported by Hervé Faye, the rector of the Nancy Academy, who suggested the addition of chairs of Hebrew and classical Arabic at the Nancy University. He argued that there was more of a Jewish community in the east; in Paris, he said, the Jews were submerged in the large population of that city, and they lost their corporate identity. One could train scholars and Hebraists there, but not rabbis.[41]

Before granting permission for the transfer of the school to Paris, the ministry requested information about how the central consistory planned to indemnify the Metz consistory.[42] A commission was appointed to investigate and answer the ministry. The commission members were Grand Rabbi Ulmann, Max Cerfberr, and L. Halphen of the central consistory; Grand Rabbi Isidor, Gustave de Rothschild, and Emile Oulmann of the Paris consistory; and Albert Cohn of the *Comité*.[43] Although Metz sought total indemnity of its expenses, Adolphe Franck pointed out that this was an exaggerated claim. The rabbinic school's building remained the property of the Metz consistory, which had already installed its elementary schools in it. The upper floors, he added, could easily serve to house temple employees. He recommended that Metz be indemnified for one half the amount claimed—that is, 30,000 francs. This was agreed upon, and the minister was informed that enough money had been raised by the consistories to indemnify Metz and to begin the transfer of the school. Government approval was requested.[44] The ministry was favorable, having decided that the enlightened views of Paris were more patriotic than the "old Judaism" of the east: "le vieux judaïsme qui a son quartier général dans l'Est est quelque peu ennemi des idées sociales que nous cherchons à propager. Quant à celui de Paris, plus éclairé, mieux dévoué...."[45]

With the transfer of the school to Paris an entirely new period began. Instead of *école rabbinique,* the school now had the title *séminaire israélite*. Only two members of the faculty survived the move—Trenel and Wogue, the only two who had, themselves, been educated at the school. In Paris new courses were added. Albert Cohn taught Jewish history. Isidore Cahen (*agrégé* of the university, who had been refused a teaching post in a *lycée* several years earlier, because of his religion) taught French literature and modern history. Paul Janet, the well-known philosopher at the university, taught the philosophy courses. Eugène Manuel taught ancient history and literature. Wogue seems to have dropped his German courses and taken over the course in Bible exegesis that Morhange had taught in Metz. Grand Rabbi Trenel taught Talmud.[46]

The rabbis who finished their studies at the rabbinic school did not emerge great scholars. They were neither traditional Talmudists nor modern theologians. They produced only some Bible translations, prayer translations and compendia of prayers, and outlines of Judaism and Jewish history for adults and children. The original research, the publication and study of rabbinic sources, was done by Christians first and later also by Jewish scholars of the university, the *Collège de France* and the *Ecole Pratique des Hautes Etudes.* Solomon Munk was such a person. He was curator of the oriental manuscripts collection of the *Bibliothèque Nationale* and professor of Hebrew, Chaldaic, and Syriac at the *Collège de France.* Munk published scholarly studies of medieval Hebrew grammarians; on Saadia Gaon; on the geography, history, and archeology of Palestine; on Phoenician inscriptions; and on Hebrew manuscripts in private and other collections. He also published the Arabic text, plus a French translation and commentary, of Maimonides' *The Guide for the Perplexed.* Together with Joseph Derenbourg, Adolphe Franck, and Herman Zotenberg, he published a catalogue of the oriental manuscripts at the *Bibliothèque Nationale.*

Derenbourg and Munk had come to Paris from Germany in order to enjoy the greater opportunities open to Jews in France. They had left behind a great friend and kindred soul—Abraham Geiger. It is not too much an exercise of the imagination to assume that the same people who in France looked forward to academic and public careers, membership in the Institute, etc., would have envisaged rabbinic posts in Germany.

Only toward the end of the nineteenth century did the rabbis of the seminary begin to do work that we would call modern scientific Jewish scholarship. In 1840 Samuel Cahen, in the first issue of his *Archives Israélites,* expressed his regret that there were no works of scholarship by French grand rabbis. The rabbis were the very people, he argued, whose mission should be to work on oriental, and especially Hebraic, sources. The gap, he said, had been filled by Christian scholars like de Sacy, Pichard, Abbé Glaire, Lécluse, Abbé Latouche, Préaux. Cahen concluded with a scathing attack on the French rabbinate: "Le rabbinat est, en France, nous ne dirons pas un soporifique fauteuil académique, là on n'y arrive du moins que par le travail; il ne faut pas tant pour devenir grand-rabbin."[47] In 1865

Hippolyte Rodrigues unsuccessfully attempted to establish a Jewish Scientific and Literary Society, but it was not until 1880 that the *Société des Etudes Juives* was founded.

The lack of scholarship among the rabbis is, of course, a consequence of the low academic achievements of the rabbinic school, at least until the 1860's, and the lack of university training of the rabbis for even longer than that. A comparison with the situation in Germany is instructive; in the period that concerns us, some German rabbis held university degrees. The reason is that an educated German Jewish laity, contemptuous of the traditional rabbinate, wanted rabbis whose own learning matched theirs and who could therefore be respected. Because German Jews were not emancipated and because they lived in a religious country, they did not turn from religion to seek absorption in a secular society, as did French Jews. In several parts of Germany, therefore, university training was made a formal requirement for the rabbinate. In 1838 the Breslau congregation, seeking a university-trained rabbi to work together with traditional Rabbi Titkin, chose Abraham Geiger. The following year the Frankfurt community voted that in order to qualify as a rabbi in that city, the candidate must hold a diploma from a German gymnasium and have studied oriental languages, history, and philosophy at a university. This contrasts sharply with the requirements for the French rabbinate, where candidates were not required to have even the secondary school diploma. Whereas educated German Jewry actively sought enlightened and vigorous religious leadership, French Jewish leaders seem to have consciously preferred more malleable men of lesser learning.

It was not until 1839, and especially after 1845, that improvements in the Metz school were sought for the purpose of introducing the rabbis to the scientific study of Judaism that had begun in Germany with the founding in 1819 by Leopold Zunz of the *Verein für Cultur und Wissenschaft der Juden.* The addition of Morhange's Biblical exegesis course (1846) and of Lazare Wogue's theology classes (1851) marked the beginning of modern Jewish science in the school. Its library, which in 1847 did not own any of the recent theological or scientific books published in France or Germany, acquired, shortly after that date, Jost's history (four copies) and Zunz's *Zur Geschichte und Literatur* (published in 1845).[48]

Although one of the reasons the rabbinic school moved to Paris in 1859 was to enable the students to take advantage of the university, this did not happen quickly. The seminary was run in a strict way. Students' time was carefully accounted for, and permission to leave the building was severely limited. In 1878 a committee recommended improvements in the general education of the rabbis by revising admissions requirements and programs of study. It urged that entering students have the *bachelier* diploma, and that daily instruction be limited to four or five hours per day. The committee further suggested that upper division students should attend courses at the *Faculté des Lettres* and *Collège de France,* and that the seminary should reinstitute a Jewish history course. The results were meager. The students were granted the right to leave the seminary on Thursdays from four to six in the afternoon to attend Joseph Derenbourg's rabbinic Hebrew course at the *Ecole Pratique des Hautes Etudes.*[49]

Even before the rabbis began to study at the universities, the universities began to come to them. Hartwig Derenbourg taught Arabic; Paul Janet and Elie Rabier taught philosophy; Eugène Manuel taught ancient literature; Arsène Darmsteter taught linguistics and French literature. By the end of the century the rabbis were actively participating in research on the medieval documents and inscriptions of French Jewry. Grand Rabbi of the central consistory, Israel Lévy, the second seminary student who had been born in Paris, became professor at both the seminary and the *Ecole Pratique des Hautes Etudes* (of the university). (Before him, Arsène Darmsteter, another former rabbinic school student, had achieved a university post. However, Darmsteter had never finished his rabbinic studies, having left after only two years at the school.) Grand Rabbi Lévy, who graduated from the seminary in 1879, was a contributor to *The Jewish Encyclopedia* and wrote many scholarly articles for the *Revue des Etudes Juives.* His topics included early modern rabbinic responsa and exegesis, Hebrew inscriptions of medieval France, the effects on the Jews of both the Inquisition in southern France and of Napoleon. He wrote a history of the Jews of France to the tenth century.

Although the 1806 *règlement* required that after 1820 rabbis must know French, the extent of the knowledge actually required was rudimentary. As we have shown, the language of instruction in the Metz Yeshiva (1821–29) was Yiddish. Until 1833 all the rabbis assuming French posts had been trained in such traditional Talmudic schools. Many had studied in Germany. They were subject to no systematic examination, but needed only a certificate of competence from three grand rabbis of their own choosing. Their lack of proficiency in French delayed the use of that language for synagogue sermons, much to the chagrin of Jewish lay leadership.

The effect of the rabbinic school on the character of the French rabbinate could not be felt immediately. An 1832 law specified that rabbis must be examined by the new school, but did not require that they study there. The law provided for two degrees: *Morénou, docteur de la loi,* communal rabbi, and *morénou harab (rabbin-maître),* grand rabbi. It listed the topics on which candidates for each post would be examined. For both degrees these included Hebrew, Bible, Talmud, French, Latin, Jewish history, the works of Maimonides, Alfasi and Karo, and the doctrinal decisions of the Sanhedrin. The grand rabbis would also be examined on Greek and more advanced Latin, rhetoric, philosophy, and ancient and modern history. The 1832 requirements were not to be in effect until 1836, and even after that date all rabbis who already held posts were permitted to continue in office and even to change locations when other posts became available. From 1836 until about 1865, then, the French rabbinate was still composed of men who had the various types of training mentioned above, but by the middle of the century more than half of the rabbinate was composed of men trained in Metz. Thus in 1860, of the sixty-four rabbis who occupied posts in France and Algeria, thirty-nine (61 percent) had been trained at the Metz school.[50] The effect of the school's 1859 move to Paris was not felt until after 1865 and then, of course, only slowly, as the new graduates began to obtain rabbinic posts. Only toward the end of the century was the French rabbinate composed mostly of Parisian-trained rabbis.

The first central consistory grand rabbi to have been trained at Metz was Salomon Ulmann, a member of the first class at the rabbinic school. He was elected to the central consistory in 1853 to replace German-trained Marchand Ennery. In the departments the first Metz-trained rabbis were Ulmann and three of his classmates from the first class of the school: M. D. Cahen was named grand rabbi in Marseille in 1833; D. Marx became Bordeaux grand rabbi in 1837; S. Ulmann was elected grand rabbi of Nancy in 1843; and L. Isidor became grand rabbi in Paris in 1847. When the Lyon consistory was created in 1857, its grand rabbi was also a rabbinic school graduate. The other four consistories were not served by rabbinic school grand rabbis until some time after 1862[51]

The hierarchical system worked to keep the younger and more recently trained of the rabbis in posts of lesser influence, under the tutelage of their superiors. By the time they achieved positions where they could influence policy, they were mature men with histories of traditionalism, and therefore not likely to seek change.

With the opening of the *école rabbinique* in Metz, it was expected that all traditional Talmudic schools would close. The Metz school was to forge a modern French rabbinate, competent in secular studies, knowing French well, talented in rhetoric, and capable of delivering eloquent sermons and inspiring morality among the Jews. In order to achieve these goals it was decided that the future rabbis should have a modern secular education, such as the kind that was being acquired by the pupils in the (free) consistorial elementary schools in many districts. The effect of this change was to bring into the rabbinic school students with a rudimentary French education, some Hebrew and Bible, a moralistic, charity-giving interpretation of Judaism, and little Talmudic training. The difference between the religious training of the old and the new generations was clear. Thus in 1856 the Nancy consistory, in drawing up a list of its district rabbis and their educational levels, noted that three of them had gone to the Metz school and had a satisfactory level of secular education. The fourth, Durckheim, fifty-one years old, who had received traditional training, had religious knowledge that far surpassed that of his younger colleagues: "La faiblesse de l'instruction laïque de M. Durckheim est compensée, par une instruction religieuse bien supérieure à celle de ses collègues."[52]

Much of the Alsatian French Jewish community was dissatisfied with the lower level of Talmudic studies achieved by the new rabbis. Several of these communities decided to create alternative institutions which would provide serious Talmudic training. The central consistory, which at first did not categorically oppose such plans, ultimately ruled that pre-rabbinic training was to be in secular secondary schools. In 1849, when the Colmar consistory requested permission to open a Talmudic school in Upper Alsace that would prepare students for entry into the rabbinical school, the central consistory said that it did not disapprove in principle, although the time was not opportune for requesting government permission.[53]

In 1847 the consistories of Strasbourg and Colmar both proposed to create Talmudic schools to prepare students for the Metz rabbinic school. The central consistory refused to authorize such schools, noting that the financial resources of the departmental consistories would be better spent in aiding prospective rabbinic students to finance their studies in the *collèges royaux* (public secondary schools), where they would acquire a broad secular education. The central consistory directed that the rabbis should instruct these candidates privately and guide them in their religious education and help them prepare to enter the *école rabbinique*.[54] In the same year, and as though to reinforce their position on the preparatory training of the rabbis, the central consistory raised the standards of secular education to be required of the candidates to the rabbinic school.

The Strasbourg consistory accepted the central consistory's ruling and dropped the project of a Talmudic school, but the Colmar consistory did not. In 1850, taking advantage of Louis Napoleon's liberalized regulations concerning independent (religious) secondary schools, Colmar began to plan for a preparatory school. In 1853 the school opened.[55] The Colmar consistory had difficulty in obtaining government approval, because the director of the school had not attained the requisite age of twenty-five years. The consistory considered having the school recognized as a *petit séminaire* which, because of the new regulations, would be under the sole supervision of the consistory. For several years this school was run by the Colmar consistory and its Grand Rabbi Klein, with no difficulties. But in 1856 a fierce conflict erupted between Klein and the consistory as a result of Klein's public denunciation of the decisions of the 1856 rabbis' conference. Without consulting the Colmar consistory, Klein decided to turn his Talmudic school into a rival rabbinic seminary to train orthodox leaders.[56] The threat to French Jewish unity was intolerable to the central consistory. Franck urged his colleagues to have the school closed down. He described it as retrograde and as an institution by which Klein sought to cause disharmony, impede progress, and damage more useful and more liberal institutions.[57]

Throughout the period there were unofficial rabbis, who merited and used this title in the traditional sense, but were not recognized as rabbis by the consistories or the state because they did not have the new diplomas prescribed by the 1832 law. Such men were frequently accepted as rabbis by traditional Jews or entire communities, and sometimes they performed so-called clandestine weddings. They were referred to contemptuously by the consistories as "soi-disant rabbins." In 1860 one of these "rabbis" in Alsace solicited the aid of the Strasbourg consistory in solving some problems in his community. The consistory refused even to debate the issues he raised and did not answer his letter. The minutes record this:

Lettre de Sr. Jacques Lévy, se disant rabbin à Hochfelden et soumettant ses vues sur des questions intéressant ladite communauté et pour la solution desquelles il prie le consistoire d'aviser. Le signataire étant sans qualité pour traiter ces questions, le consistoire passe à l'ordre du jour.[58]

C. Socio-Economic Status of Rabbis

In order to understand the character of the French rabbinate, we must consider the socioeconomic background of its recruits and the level of prestige that the post afforded. In most cases accession to the post of rabbi represented a rise in social status for the candidate. He invariably came from a humble background and aspired to the post because his traditional family saw it as prestigious despite its low income potential. Rabbinic posts—especially for communal rabbis—paid such low salaries that sons of middle-class families were not tempted by such prospects. Furthermore, the wide availability of careers to Jews during much of the nineteenth century (notable exceptions occurred between 1830 and 1860 when Jews found certain university and judicial posts barred to them) served to attract the best minds toward a university education. Those, like Hartwig and Joseph Derenbourg, Adolphe Franck,[59] James Darmsteter, Solomon Munk, and Joseph Salvador—who were interested in traditional texts, theoretical issues of religious philosophy, and history—were even prevented from pursuing a rabbinic career by the kind of training required. In Germany, on the other hand, a man like Abraham Geiger could receive his university degree and add to that the rabbinic title bestowed by a rabbi who recognized his scholarly capabilities. A six-year course of study in a designated institution was not required.

The salaries paid to the rabbis were low, and the effect of the 1831 law, which made rabbis' salaries payable by the government, was to lower them further. According to the 1806 law, communal rabbis were paid by the community, and the minimum legal salary was 1000 francs. The law of August 1831 sharply diminished the minimum to 300 francs and established a maximum of 700 francs (depending on the size of the local Jewish population and the size of the town).[60] By 1860 rabbis' salaries had been raised to a range of 600–1200 francs. Salaries could be supplemented only by incidental fees, such as those from marriages. No commercial enterprises were permitted the rabbis, on the grounds that such activities would taint their sacred character. In 1843, of eighteen communal rabbis in the Bas-Rhin, six received 600 francs, nine received 400 francs, and three received 300 francs salary.[61] In 1846, seventeen French rabbis received 400 francs and twelve were paid only 300 francs.[62] In 1849 the central consistory attempted to revise the rabbinic districts of the Alsatian consistories in order to reduce the number of rabbis and enlarge each one's district.[63] This would have increased the population served by many rabbis, thereby qualifying them for higher state salaries and more frequent extra fees from marriages and other special occasions.

It is clear that these salaries were grossly inadequate. A study of the nineteenth-century French working class has shown that in 1853 an average salary for laborers was 500 francs per year. In 1864 a shoemaker in Paris could earn 950 francs. The cost of bread alone for an average family was 305 francs. The minimum salary needed to support a family of four in the 1850's was about 1000 francs (but varied according to the geographic area).[64] Frequently (but not uniformly) local communities voted a supplement for the rabbi and/or succeeded in having the municipality allocate free lodging for him. Although rabbis salaried by the state were entitled by law to free lodging from the municipality, this provision was not always honored. Some municipal councils refused, as in the case of the schools, to vote funds for this purpose. (Lodging for a family of workers during the Second Empire cost between 100 and 400 francs per year and consumed, on the average, 30 percent of the salary.)[65]

Salaries paid to grand rabbis were considerably better. In the departmental consistories they received 3000 francs; after 1850 this was raised to 3500 francs, and to 5000 for the Parisian grand rabbi. The grand rabbi of the central consistory received 6000 francs. Yet even these higher salaries did not make rich men of the rabbis; we have numerous examples of their being in financial straits. In 1828, when Grand Rabbi Deutz was arranging the marriage of his daughter, he requested an advance of 1500 francs on his salary, plus 1300 francs, the portion of his salary owing, in order to pay the dowry and the expenses of the wedding.[66] In 1837 Grand Rabbi Ennery of the Parisian consistory requested and received a supplement of 300 francs to his 1836 salary.

The grand rabbis were expected to have a certain prestige in the community because of the fact that they represented Judaism (alongside the Catholic and Protestant clergy) on public occasions. In Paris, especially, the consistory was very sensitive to the image that its spiritual representative had in the community at large. The consistory believed that if it was a good one—if the rabbi's manners and speech were dignified, his clothing proper, etc.—then Jews as a whole would reap the benefits of general esteem. The Christian population would understand the Jew and his religion by being able to equate the rabbi with the priest. Similar costumes helped. It was decided in 1853 that Grand Rabbi Isidor of Paris must travel in a carriage worthy of his position, for all official visits. The consistory authorized him to order such a carriage each time he needed it, and decided that the consistory would pay the costs.

Although the consistories tried consciously to assure a respectable image of the grand rabbis in the general community, it was very difficult to raise the low prestige of the rabbinate in the Jewish community. For several years after the death of central consistory Grand Rabbi Deutz, the central consistory periodically solicited funds throughout the country to help support his widow. The public reaction was of almost total disinterest in 1842. The Strasbourg, Metz, and Bordeaux consistories sent nothing. A collection in Marseille raised 313.50 francs. By 1844 the Paris consistory protested to the central consistory that Deutz's widow was living in misery, forgotten by everyone. It asked for an annual pension for her, to be contributed jointly by all the consistories. Paris offered 200 francs as its share of the cost:

Il est pénible de voir la femme du premier ministre de la religion israélite en France trainer une existence qui nuit à la dignité de notre culte et qui peut attirer à nos coreligionnaires le reproche de manque de tout sentiment de charité.[67]

It is evident that the concern of the consistories was not for the person of the rabbi (as represented by his widow) but for the role the rabbi had and the public image the role generated. In response to subsequent central consistory appeals, Metz and Marseille each promised fifty francs; Bordeaux offered 140 francs. Nancy refused help, and Strasbourg and Colmar did not answer the appeal.[68] It was this kind of problem which led the 1856 rabbinic conference to vote for a *Caisse de Secours* that would provide emergency financial assistance and pensions for rabbis and their widows.[69] The spontaneous concern of the population would have obviated this need had the rabbinate enjoyed higher prestige.

We have already said that for the men who entered the rabbinate the post represented an improvement in social status.

They generally came from humble backgrounds and were of limited education. They almost never had received a classical secondary education, partly because secondary education was not free during most of the nineteenth century. For the sons of the Jewish families scattered throughout the countryside of Alsace-Lorraine, secondary education would have been possible only by boarding at a school in one of the larger cities, and such an arrangement would have required the student to abandon traditional Jewish practices.

When the rabbinic school was being organized in 1828, the government wished to see Latin included as one of the prerequisites for admission, but the central consistory objected, noting that the parents of the future rabbinic students would almost all be too poor to give their sons instruction in Latin.[70] From this it is clear that even before the school had opened, Jewish leaders expected that the rabbinate would be drawn from the poor. Moreover, it seems that such a selection was purposeful. The consistories, in arranging details of the training and paying of the rabbis, seemed to be working toward a rabbinate of humble background. It had been decided that a large part of the student population at the rabbinic school would receive total scholarships. This factor, plus the school's location in Metz, would appeal mainly to the sons of poor Jews of Alsace-Lorraine, and that is precisely what happened. From 1829 to 1859, of the 109 students who entered the rabbinic school, 106 were from the eastern provinces. Two were from the south (Gard and Gironde) and one was from Fontainebleau.[71] Even after the center of Jewish population began to shift toward Paris, and during the first twelve years after the rabbinic school itself had moved to Paris, the future rabbis continued to be drawn almost exclusively from the eastern provinces. Although the Parisian Jewish population increased mainly as a result of migration from the east toward Paris, the same families, once transplanted to Paris, underwent significant socioeconomic change, and the rabbinic career no longer appealed to them. It was 1871 before the seminary received its first Paris-born student, David Haguenau, born in 1854. From 1871 to 1890 seven students from Paris entered the seminary. At about this time the eastern European immigrants began to seek rabbinic careers, and they replaced the students who stopped coming from Alsace-Lorraine when the Germans sealed the border. A small number of Parisian-born students (an average of one every three years) continued to enter the seminary from 1870 to 1929. Gradually, first-generation Parisian-born sons of families from Alsace-Lorraine began to be replaced by first generation Parisian-born sons of east European immigrants.

The extent of the Metz community's contribution to the French rabbinate was in disproportion to its small size. From 1829 to 1879 the Metz consistory sent thirteen students to the rabbinic school, despite the fact that the Jewish community of that city never exceeded 2900. Moreover, by 1857 this community had contributed the first three directors of the rabbinic school (Lambert, Lazard, and Trenel), a professor of exegesis and Hebrew (Morhange), two grand rabbis, and six other practicing rabbis.[72] Although the Alsatian community was more populous, Metz contributed more to French Jewish leadership, both lay and rabbinic.

D. The Type of Modern Rabbi

The consistory's aim in controlling the training of the rabbis was to produce a new kind of rabbi, essentially different from the traditional one. In general, the model was the Christian minister, and the Paris consistory even attempted, in 1844, to have the government change the title of grand rabbi of the central consistory to *Pasteur Supérieur,* that of the other grand rabbis to *Pasteur Consistorial,* and that of the communal rabbis to *Pasteur Communal.*[73]

During the nineteenth century the entire concept of the rabbinate underwent transformation. Traditionally the rabbi had three main functions: he was chief teacher of the academy, he was head of the court, and he preached in the synagogue. (This last was especially true of Sephardi rabbis; in the Ashkenazi communities it was more common for itinerant lay preachers to give the sermons.)[74] In the late eighteenth century and during the nineteenth century the rabbi lost his juridical function when the Jewish judicial system was abolished, and he lost his position as head of the academy as most traditional Talmudic schools disappeared. The Assembly of Notables, convened by Napoleon in 1806, described the rabbis' activities since the revolution as preaching morality in the synagogues, blessing marriages, and pronouncing divorces. We may assume that this is a fairly accurate reflection of the situation, although undoubtedly the Assembly neglected to mention that the rabbis advised people on matters of religious law and observance, and some of them taught in *yeshivot* (traditional Talmudic schools).

The tendency of the consistories to develop a modern rabbinate based on the model of the Christian clergy began early. As early as 1809, in one of its first communications, the central consistory described the rabbis as the Jewish equivalents of ministers and priests: "Toutes les religions ont leur culte, et chaque culte a ses ministres, connus sous des dénominations différentes, telle qu'évêques, curés, pasteurs, rabbins, etc., etc."[75]

The kinds of jobs assigned to rabbis during the nineteenth century, and seen as a Christian influence by some, included officiating at marriages, visiting prisoners, preaching, accompanying funeral processions into the cemetery, reciting prayers over the graves, and reciting prayers at the bedside of the dying and in the houses of those in mourning. When the Strasbourg consistory, in 1853, insisted that Grand Rabbi Aron assume these functions, Aron unsuccessfully attempted to demonstrate their Christian origin and their lack of necessity in Judaism.[76] Other rabbis refrained from disagreeing, and followed the consistories' recommendations more or less exactly. Because the consistories were emphasizing the moral-charitable aspect of Judaism, they were insistent that the rabbis be models of charitable behavior. Thus the Metz consistory in 1853 reminded Grand Rabbi Lambert to pay occasional visits to the prisons, the military hospital, and other institutions of public charity.[77]

Samuel Dreyfus, the communal rabbi in Mulhouse and journalist-critic of French Judaism, complained that the public view of the rabbi had changed much in recent times. Instead of a serious scholar, commanding respect, the people wanted a man who gave pleasant little talks at weddings and funerals and who visited prisons and hospitals. Above all, the modern rabbi had to be "affable." Dreyfus was not wrong. This image of the modern rabbinate, although originally conceived by the laity, had already been accepted by Grand Rabbi Ulmann. In 1853 Ulmann, recently elected central consistory grand rabbi, sent a circular letter to the French rabbinate in which he said: "Le premier devoir du pasteur est . . . celui de se recommander, par sa conduite et par son caractère personnel, à la confiance, au respect et à l'affection des fidèles."[78] The nineteenth-century definition had restricted Judaism to its ethical and charitable aspects, and the rabbi had been transformed accordingly.

In a letter of praise of its grand rabbi, Samuel Marx, the Bayonne consistory said that its free schools and public charitable societies had all benefited from Grand Rabbi Marx's "inspiration."[79] Whether the rabbi really took the initiative in regard to these institutions, and whether he succeeded in being the new type of modern rabbi, is difficult to know. Since the letter in question was praising Marx in order to solicit for him the *légion d'honneur* award, it is not possible to accept the statement at face value.

It was after the midpoint of the nineteenth century that the modern type of rabbi began to emerge. The last member of the Sanhedrin to attain the post of central consistory grand rabbi was Emanuel Deutz, who died in 1842. His replacement was Marchand Ennery, Grand Rabbi of Paris, German-trained and traditional. The reformers had suggested other candidates. Olry Terquem's choice was Solomon Yehuda Löb Rapoport, Polish rabbi and scholar, and friend of Zunz.[80] Terquem argued that no French rabbi was qualified for the post. Michel Lévy, physician and Paris consistory member, suggested Solomon Munk because he was a great scholar and had been recognized as such by his university and library posts. Munk would have been the type of modern rabbi whom the "enlightened" young French Jews sought. However, he was not qualified according to French law, as he did not have the official rabbinic diploma prescribed by the 1832 law, nor had he acquired French citizenship.

Dr. Michel Lévy agreed with Terquem that none of the French rabbis could provide proper leadership. Ignoring Munk's ineligibility, Lévy urged that unless Munk accepted the post, the election should be postponed. The money allocated to the grand rabbi's salary could be used instead for transferring the rabbinic school to Paris and placing it under the watchful eye of the central consistory. Within six or seven years a new generation of rabbis could be trained in "rational and scientific theology." Lévy wanted reforms in the ritual and expected that in Paris the rabbinic school would stop teaching the inviolability of Talmudic law. He suggested that men like Munk, Franck, and Léon Halévy could be the new teachers of the rabbis. Dr. Lévy proposed himself as teacher of hygiene, which the rabbis could compare with the hygiene taught by the Talmud![81]

Although the central consistory did postpone the election of a successor to Deutz while it completed its work toward the passage of the 1844 *ordonnance,* it held the election in 1846. The successful candidate, Grand Rabbi Ennery of Paris, opposed the introduction of reforms by the consistory or its grand rabbi. He believed that ritual changes should be introduced only after a decision of all French rabbis, meeting in a synod. Previously, while Ennery was a member of the Paris consistory, he had refused, on these grounds, to join a committee named by the consistory to consider reforms. When the commission's work was completed, Ennery refused to approve it. Yet he was considered moderate in his views. He had accepted the introduction of a confirmation ceremony for boys and girls, and he had been the first Parisian rabbi to preach frequently in French (although it was generally felt that his sermons were uninspired).

After Ennery's death the election of his successor provided the occasion for Jewish leaders to describe the kind of rabbinate they desired for France. Simon Bloch, editor of the *Univers Israélite,* was the spokesman for the traditional Jews. He argued that the choice of a grand rabbi was going to be a choice for or against Jewish law, for or against tradition. A "conservative," Bloch wanted to see renewed scholarly achievement within the rabbinate. Judaism, he said, had sunk to an inferior and ignorant condition. Sharply criticizing the new methods and new education, he argued that the old way had produced brilliant scholars. If modern secular education can do the same, Bloch cried, let us see the proof. He called for the leadership of a rabbi who was a scholar, rather than a "rabbi of style and elegant manners." "Nous ne voulons pas avoir un grand rabbin du budget, un grand rabbin de l'émargement, un grand rabbin des modes et des manières élégantes, mais un docteur de la loi qui sache faire rayonner sur Israél une vive et sainte lumière." Bloch deplored the electoral arguments between reformers and traditionalists, and pointed out that in traditional communities the only important issue in the choice of rabbi was how to get the best scholar available.[82]

Throughout the campaign Bloch continued to publish his

views on the rabbinate. On the eve of the elections he called for the election of a rabbi who possessed three qualities: "la science, l'autorité, la piété." He opposed the tendency to substitute communal and administrative functions for the "real mission" of rabbis, which was to teach, preserve, and propagate religious studies ("la science sacrée"). He argued that religious authority is traditionally founded only on excellence of scholarship. He ridiculed the modern idea that a diploma determines who is a rabbi: "On n'est rabbin que par le savoir qu'on a acquis, que par les élèves qu'on forme, que par les lumières qu'on répand et les noeuds qu'on ajoute à l'antique arbre de vie de notre céleste Thôra." In addition to demonstrating traditional qualities of piety, scholarship, and authority, the rabbis should exercise the modern function of defenders of Jewish rights. They should obtain from the authorities a guarantee of respect for Jewish religious law in public institutions such as schools, hospitals, prisons, and cemeteries.[83] Bloch's insistence on the Jew's right to be different and to have his differences accepted by the state was a logical interpretation of the emancipation and of official recognition of Judaism. In fact, the structure of French law in regard to the status of Judaism *did* imply that Jewish practices should be respected by the state. The consistories, however, did not always defend this right.

Other critics joined Bloch in condemning the popular image of the rabbi as a Jewish priest. We have alluded above to a conflict in this regard between Grand Rabbi Aron and the Strasbourg consistory. In 1853 a *comité d'amélioration,* inspired by the pastoral role of Catholic priests, had tried to impose new tasks on the rabbi. A member of the consistory, Hirtz, spoke for many of his contemporaries when he denounced a Judaism that did not provide the same comforts in times of crisis that were provided by Christianity:

dans les plus graves situations de la vie, la religion [juive] nous fait complètement défaut, dans les écoles comme au chevet du lit des malades, comme pour accompagner les morts à leur dernière demeure, comme pour présider aux inhumations, comme pour prier sur la tombe des fidèles à la grand différence des autres cultes où curé et pasteur prodiguent, en toute circonstance les consolations de leur ministère.

In reply, Grand Rabbi Aron tried vainly to explain that Judaism was different from Christianity:

notre religion est la religion israélite, on ne peut pas la christianiser, elle a ses coutumes, ses lois. Pour les prières des agonisants, il existe de saintes confréries d'hommes et de femmes qui récitent ces prières et ainsi dites elles ont la même valeur religieuse que faites par les rabbins eux-mêmes, et si ceux-ci dont le devoir est d'assister aux convois, ne vont pas jusqu'aux cimetières, c'est qu'ils n'y sont appelés par aucun acte particulier de leur ministère, et que le premier israélite venu y peut prier.

In complete ignorance of the fundamental tenets of Judaism, Hirtz replied that laymen cannot pray as well as rabbis. He asked what would be the function of the rabbinate if just any Jew, and not only rabbis, said the prayers on important occasions.[84]

This episode clearly demonstrates the crisis of the French rabbinate in the nineteenth century. The definition of the rabbinic role was in a state of flux, and the Jewish community was far from unanimous on the shape it should take. Many, both conservatives and reformers, agreed that France needed an educated rabbinate, well-versed in the "science of Judaism." But the understanding of this term varied. The reformers were interested in a critical and historical attitude toward Jewish tradition, because they believed that this would lead to an understanding of the evolutionary nature of Judaism, and therefore to an acceptance of reforms. Terquem and Lévy were prominent examples of people who thought this way. Conservatives, like Bloch, believed that "Jewish science" meant a scholarly familiarity with traditional Jewish literature and the continuation of this tradition of religious scholarship. He believed that rabbinic authority stemmed from familiarity with Jewish sources and he expected that improvement of training in such sources would serve to reinforce respect for the tradition.

Both groups were united toward the middle of the century in agreeing that the educational level of the rabbis left much to be desired. For the first thirty years of the consistory system (and in accordance with Napoleon's aims) the consistories had allowed and encouraged the progressive weakening and deterioration of the rabbinate. As we have seen, during the 1840's and 1850's under the guidance of men like Crémieux, Munk, and Franck, the central consistory began to realize the need for more serious training of the French rabbis.

In the middle of the century the rabbis disagreed on the direction French Judaism should take. Some had been influenced by thirty years of French reformist polemics and by developments in Germany, but lacked both the academic training and the freedom for individual initiative to implement reforms. According to the 1844 *ordonnance,* the central consistory grand rabbi had sole authority to approve ritual. It was generally considered essential that a single usage prevail throughout the country, and therefore local attempts at reform could not be condoned.

A myth of unity within French Judaism prevailed. The motivation for maintaining the myth lay in the wishes and needs of French Jewish leaders. Upon his election to the central consistory in 1853, Grand Rabbi Salomon Ulmann wrote that the French synagogue was "calm and united." He may have been blissfully ignorant of reality, but more probably he was trying to use his writings as a means of attaining such unity.[85] After the 1856 rabbinic conference, however, the French synagogue was even further from unity. The rabbis had voted to allow a measure of independence to the departmental consistories. With the agreement of their grand rabbis, they could implement certain ceremonial reforms in the synagogues of their districts. This decision formally acknowledged the existence of diverse opinions within French Judaism, while seeking to preserve at least the external unity of the synagogue within the consistory system. Those who aimed at developing a unified "French rite" were dissatisfied, as were the staunch conservatives. One of the immediate results of the conference was an anticonsistorial movement led by Grand Rabbi Solomon Klein of Colmar. He and several other rabbis published a condemnation of the reformist views endorsed by the majority of the rabbis who attended the conference. For the first time a denominational split in French Judaism threatened to materialize. Although the consistory, backed by governmental authority, succeeded in suppressing Klein's movement and in censuring other outspoken rabbis, internal dissension continued within the rabbinate, and for a long time serious disagreement lay buried beneath a façade of harmony. This external appearance of harmony and unity was what French Judaism required in order to convince itself that its situation was considerably more stable than that of chaotic German Jewry.

Grand Rabbi Salomon Ulmann was the most modern and the most inclined toward reform of the grand rabbis to have entered the central consistory. He was the one who convened the rabbinic conference in Paris in 1856. A majority of the rabbis attending the conference declared the permissibility—although not the necessity—of certain ritual changes and reforms, including the reduction of the *piyyutim,* the introduction of the organ, and the addition of a synagogue ceremony to mark the birth of a girl. Although inclined toward reforming Jewish ceremonies and modeling the rabbinic role after that of Christian priests, Ulmann is nonetheless a good example of the Metz-trained rabbis who believed that the liberal ideals of post-revolutionary France implied that Judaism had the right to insist upon its own individual identity, and to grow and develop from its own roots. Ulmann was a spokesman for those who realized by the middle of the nineteenth century that Jewish enthusiasm for integration into French society had caused a neglect of Jewish studies and that an appreciation for traditional learning had been lost. He called for a return to the sources, to the "science of Judaism," to the development of an evolutionary Judaism based on its own, rather than foreign, traditions. He agreed with Simon Bloch, of the *Univers Israélite,* that sermons based on classical secular sources did not add any luster to Judaism. Ulmann directed the French rabbis to make exclusive use of traditional Jewish literature as material for rabbinic sermons:

Que dans vos prédications surtout respire l'esprit du judaïsme; qu'elles soient marquées du caractère israélite, puisées dans les sources israélites, et pures de toutes citations empruntées à des ouvrages traitant de matières étrangères à notre culte, et déplacées dans un enseignement donné du haut de la chaire israélite.[86]

This was the kind of vision, then, which the grand rabbis—trained by the new methods, brought up in post-Emancipation France, and interested in progressive developments in Judaism—indicated as the path for the French rabbinate to take. It was a combination of a new emphasis on the ethical teachings of Judaism and a rediscovery of the ancient traditional roots of Judaism: "rendre aux formes de notre culte leur puissance moralisatrice, tout en leur conservant leur caractère antique et traditionnel, tel est le problème que nous sommes appelés à résoudre."[87]

In 1865 Rabbi Ulmann's death and the election of his successor created a new opportunity for French Jews to analyze the functions of the rabbinate and to decide what kind of rabbi would best fulfill the role of central consistory grand rabbi. Benoît Lévy hoped that Ulmann's successor would be a man capable both of preventing disharmony within the synagogue, and creating a unified "rite israélite français" which had been proposed for many years. The new grand rabbi should reunite French Judaism by annulling the 1856 decision that allowed district grand rabbis to institute changes in their own areas. Moreover, Lévy said, the new grand rabbi must be well-educated, respectable, and capable of defending Judaism against unjust attacks.[88]

Although there were repeated calls for a grand rabbi of superior learning, there were not many such people available in France. Moreover, the official requirements for the state-salaried post prevented the recruiting of non-nationals or of university-trained scholars who lacked the diploma of the single recognized rabbinic seminary. The successful candidate was Grand Rabbi Isidor of Paris, who had been trained in Metz. No serious changes in the nature of French Judaism or its rabbinate occurred immediately. The gradual movement toward synagogue reform progressed slowly, and in 1870 Isidor announced the suppression of some *piyyutim*.

E. Functions of the Rabbis

The rabbis' duties as defined by law and custom underwent certain changes during the consistory period. The 1806 *règlement* prescribed the following duties for the rabbis: (1) teaching religion and Sanhedrin doctrine; (2) teaching obedience to

French law; (3) encouraging military service and teaching that Jewish law permits breach of observance during such service; (4) preaching; (5) reciting the prayer for the Emperor; (6) performing marriages and divorces after the civil act had been recorded.

In 1824 Olry Terquem complained that the rabbis' functions were ill-defined and not performed. He said that their first duty prescribed by the 1806 *règlement,* that of teaching, was not executed; in Paris, the three grand rabbis did no teaching, not even in the new consistorial elementary school.[89]

Although the rabbis did, occasionally, in the early years, encourage military service and emphasize Sanhedrin doctrine and obedience to state law, these functions fell quickly into disuse. With the rapidly awakening Jewish consciousness during the nineteenth century, Jews considered such reminders a slight against Jewish morality and evidence of a suspicion that Jews were less patriotic than other Frenchmen. Preaching was irregular for many years, despite the injunction of the *règlement* and despite an 1810 decision of the central consistory that every Saturday and holiday the rabbis should preach on morality, duty, love of the sovereign, and obedience to French laws.[90]

Terquem was not wrong in complaining of the lack of initiative taken by the three Paris-based grand rabbis in regard to religious education. When Grand Rabbi Ennery assumed the office of central consistory grand rabbi in 1847, he sent a circular letter to the departmental rabbis on the need for improving religious education in the country. This was the first example of such initiative.

The officially prescribed rabbinic tasks were modified by subsequent legislation, especially in regard to the developing hierarchy. Thus the 1844 *ordonnance* provided for the surveillance of lower ranking rabbis by the grand rabbis. It also repeated an earlier provision giving the grand rabbi the right of veto in central consistory decisions regarding "les objets religieux ou de culte." We have already seen elsewhere that this was often ignored.

The entire description of the communal rabbi's job in 1844 is included in Article 46 of the law: "the rabbis officiate and preach in the temples of their districts." The insufficiency of this provision caused confusion as to the precise limits and definitions of the powers and duties of the rabbis. In 1847 Max Cerfberr, president of the central consistory, recommended to his colleagues a *règlement* that would define the rabbis' duties. The proposal was adopted, and, for models, the consistory resolved to check the regulations governing rabbis in Germany.[91] It does not appear that this was ever done.

A debate developed over whether the rabbi was to have legislative power. The consistory legislation had specified that the rabbi's voice was preponderant in cases where the consistory wished to make religious decisions. The orthodox, who wished no changes introduced into the cult, objected that the rabbis had no right to make any changes; it was their job simply to preserve and protect Judaism. Thus Benjamin Gradis, warning against the projected rabbinic conference of 1856, argued that the rabbis no longer had legislative functions and could not change ritual or ceremonial: "[Les rabbins] ne possèdent pas plus le pouvoir législatif ou constituant . . . Il n'entre dans leurs attributions de changer ni les usages, ni les rites, ni les cérémonies."[92]

One of the trends in the nineteenth-century French rabbinate was the development of a notion of the sacred character of the rabbinic role. It became a generally held view that the rabbinate was incompatible with secular affairs, especially business. This was made formal by a provision in the 1844 *ordonnance* (Article 57): "Les fonctions de rabbin sont incompatibles avec toute profession industrielle ou commerciale." The consistories went further and decided that commercial activities for a period of seven years disqualified a rabbi from ever assuming a post in the same town where he had been engaged in commerce. Accordingly, in 1851, when several communities of the Moselle elected Michel Wimphen (a graduate of the *école rabbinique* who had been in business for a number of years) as their district rabbi, the central consistory annulled the election. The communities' choice was fixed, however, and they elected Wimphen in several successive ballots, despite the fact that the central consistory repeatedly annulled the election results. The central consistory had been too insistent in its modern views; the communities would not yield. In order to put an end to an embarrassing situation, the central consistory decided to find Wimphen a rabbinic post elsewhere and to secure passage of a new regulation that would take the choice of communal rabbis out of the hands of the people.

By 1877 the proponents of what we might call the "sacred role theory" were trying to push it further. In that year B. Lévy, in a circular written in regard to the Lyon consistory elections, asked for candidates to run on a platform including a prohibition against a grand rabbi's becoming vice-president of the consistory. He cited the "caractère sacré et tout religieux" of the grand rabbi and the fact that the consistory's vice-president had to handle money.

In fact, grand rabbis often did handle money, and not only as vice-presidents of consistories. In both Paris and Metz the grand rabbis were in charge of the synagogue accounts for many years. In Paris, Ennery was appointed administrator of the temple when difficulties erupted between the consistory and the temple administration. For many years Ennery paid the small bills of the temple, received the donations, arranged for the lighting fixtures to be cleaned, and turned over the temple accounts to the consistory. Grand Rabbi L. M. Lambert performed the same functions in Metz.[93]

Several contemporary documents describe the rabbinic role

as it developed during the period under consideration. In 1842 in a letter requesting a salary increase for Benjamin Roos, rabbi of seven communities of the Bas-Rhin, including Saverne, seat of his rabbinate, the Strasbourg consistory cited the fact that he traveled among the various communities of his district, where, among other things, he resolved religious questions for his congregants.[94] Three years later, in 1845, Benjamin Wahl and others, in a brochure critical of Rabbi Samuel Dreyfus of Mulhouse, wrote that the only functions of a rabbi were to resolve religious questions, recite the prayer for the king, and deliver two sermons a year.[95] It is important to note that both documents mention that rabbis were still called upon to answer religious questions, although Wahl implied that this did not happen frequently.

Most of the *yeshivot* had closed and Talmudic studies were on the decline. Rabbis now taught religion in elementary schools and *lycées*. When the Strasbourg consistory, in 1855, sought an assistant rabbi, the job description specified two hours per day of religious instruction.[96] In many towns the rabbis were the only religious teachers available, and they gave lessons in the public schools, after the hours of instruction in secular subjects or while the Christian children were receiving religious instruction.

Sometimes the public schools attended by the Jewish children were exclusively Jewish schools, where teachers taught both secular and religious subjects. In these cases the rabbis were expected to visit the schools for the purpose of inspection and examination of the pupils. In the 1850's the Strasbourg consistory began to request and to receive periodic reports by the Bas-Rhin rabbis concerning the quality of the schools in their districts.[97] In the Metz district the grand rabbi was expected to visit the schools. This became too much for the aging Rabbi L. M. Lambert, and the consistory in 1858 requested permission to hire an assistant for him.[98]

The rabbis also sat on boards of education at several governmental levels, where their function was to protect the interests of Judaism in the public schools.

Preaching was expected with increasing frequency, and the rabbis were supposed to deliver their sermons in good French and according to contemporary standards of eloquence. Frequent sermonizing, however, developed slowly. Even after the middle of the century many rabbis spoke French poorly. When they did speak, their sermons were more often traditional expositions of the weekly Torah portion than the edifying moral discourses that reformers demanded. French Jews who sought an improvement in the rabbinic sermons impatiently asked when France would have her Mannheimers.[99] The traditional two sermons per year remained the norm through the middle of the century, even in the case of Rabbi Samuel Dreyfus of Mulhouse, the first French rabbi to have received the *bachelier* degree.[100] In the cities where consistories sat, the grand rabbis began to preach more often. Ennery of Paris was the first to deliver fairly frequent French sermons, but the press found his oratorical talents wanting. Grand Rabbi Lambert, who occupied the post of Metz grand rabbi until shortly before the German occupation, never developed a facility in French.[101]

Rabbis performed weddings, although there continued to be a significant number of traditional (clandestine) weddings which did not use the services of a rabbi. Although synagogue weddings with a rabbi officiating were another modern innovation in imitation of Christian practice, rabbis did not protest this as they protested other modern demands, such as their participation in funerals and visits to prisoners. The wedding was a borrowing that had occurred earlier, and it had therefore gained acceptance. Moreover, weddings were one of the few sources of additional income which the rabbis had at their disposal.[102]

No divorce records exist in any of the extant consistory archives, nor do we know whether any ever existed. We have located no references to religious divorces in any of the documents consulted. It is therefore not possible to say whether the rabbis' functions included the issuing of divorces.

Although prayers for the government had been instituted at an early date, it was only with the establishment of the consistories (1806 *règlement*) that the rabbi began to recite them. It remained the practice that the prayer for the government was recited by the rabbi, and throughout much of the nineteenth century this was the only part of the service that was his responsibility. (The cantor led the prayers, and a sermon was not always pronounced.)

The nineteenth-century's delineation of the rabbinic role included, as we have already shown, visits to hospitals and prisons and attendance at funerals. Expected to be models of charitable activity, rabbis also attended meetings of charitable and mutual aid societies. Gradually the rabbis came to accept the new demands made on them, and the modern definition of the rabbinic role solidified. All of these modern rabbinic tasks were included in the job descriptions written by the Paris, Strasbourg, and Metz consistories during the 1850's, when they hired assistant rabbis to share the work of the grand rabbis.[103]

Another new dimension of the rabbinic role in the nineteenth century resulted from the creation of districts in which rabbis had the exclusive right to practice. In the manner of the church's ecclesiastical division, all of France was divided into consistorial districts, which were in turn subdivided into rabbinic districts. In this way even small Jewish communities had the services of a district rabbi. It then became his job to visit schools in his district and to report to the consistory on the institutions, people, and problems of the communities under his jurisdiction.

In a striking transformation, some grand rabbis became experts on the French laws pertaining to the consistories, as their predecessors had been experts on Jewish law. French law had replaced Jewish law in all aspects of the governing of the Jewish communities that were not considered "religious" in the modern, narrow sense of that term. Although Jewish law was still the theoretical foundation upon which purely religious decisions were made, French law began to absorb more of the time and attention of Jewish community leaders. The consistories were generally careful to base their actions on their best understanding of pertinent laws. Thus the Strasbourg consistory, each time it needed an interpretation of the laws regulating the consistories or when the draft of a new law was being studied, called upon its Grand Rabbi, Arnaud Aron, to give an explanation in the light of an historical résumé of relevant French laws. Aron was respected as the authority on consistorial law for the entire tenure of his office. One cannot but conclude that French law filled the vacuum left when Jewish law ceased to be the basis upon which the Jewish community was organized.

During the 1850's rabbis began to suggest the organization of periodic rabbinic conferences. When the Alsatian communal rabbis took such initiatives, they met with hostility from the laymen of the central consistory. In January 1854 the communal rabbis of the Haut-Rhin gathered in Colmar to formulate plans for semi-annual conferences.[104] In the Bas-Rhin it was not until 1859 that such an idea was broached, and then it came from a lay member of the local consistory who suggested "l'utilité qu'il y aurait d'organiser des conférences périodiques entre les rabbins de notre circonscription." Grand Rabbi Aron endorsed the plan, and the consistory requested the appropriate permission of the central consistory.[105] No union of French rabbis came about during the period under consideration, and since the majority of the communal rabbinic posts were located in the territory lost to Germany, the period after 1870 constitutes an entirely new chapter in the development of the French rabbinate.

F. Hierarchy in the Rabbinate

We have discussed in Chapter IV the development of hierarchy within the rabbinate from the point of view of the legislation. The original *règlement* of 1806 did not spell out a rabbinic hierarchy. The grand rabbis of the central consistory, as members of the central consistory, were entitled, however, to exercise supervision over the rest of the French rabbis, and therefore a hierarchy slowly developed.

The rabbis' views on the desirability and the significance of the hierarchy were not uniform. Rabbis seem to have been aware from an early date that a hierarchy was developing. As early as 1822 Grand Rabbi Wittersheim of the Metz consistory refused to make an independent decision on a religious question submitted to him. When he was asked whether Jewish apprentices could work on the half-holidays, he insisted, despite pressure from the lay members of his consistory, that the question be submitted to the grand rabbis of the central consistory. He said that the central consistory should rule on the question for the entire country because it would not look good if contradictory decisions were rendered by various rabbis.[106]

After 1823 the hierarchy began to be defined. The grand rabbis of the central consistory had the right to rule on textbooks to be used in all Jewish schools in the country; they had the (theoretical) right of veto in all religious decisions made by the central consistory for the entire country. In 1844 the new *ordonnance* created an explicit hierarchy, with supervision and censure to be exercised by the higher placed rabbis over the lower. This was an entirely new phenomenon—even the Sanhedrin (in the response to the question on how rabbis are named) had emphasized that there was no ecclesiastical hierarchy in Judaism. The basis for the hierarchy, however, is clearly in the 1806 *règlement,* which gives the central consistory the job of surveillance over the rabbis.

Both because of the administrative hierarchy and because of the salary differences, there was a great gap between the grand rabbis and communal rabbis. In 1855 communal rabbi Mayer Charleville of Dijon accused the consistory of fostering this separation, declaring that there had developed a "high and low clergy."[107] The notion of a high and low clergy was not a private hallucination of Charleville's. It will be remembered that in 1828 the central consistory had attempted to institute separate courses of study for communal and grand rabbis. This had not been implemented because of the government's refusal to allow an unbridgeable gap between the two posts.

Some communal rabbis bemoaned a loss of prestige and autonomy which resulted from the hierarchy. Others, such as Samuel Dreyfus of Mulhouse, ambivalently stated both a dissatisfaction with the status of the communal rabbis and an enthusiastic support of the hierarchy. But Dreyfus saw, as the major impediment to improved status, not the hierarchy within the rabbinate but the effect of the lay administration on the consistories.[108]

The majority of the communal rabbis were not satisfied to see themselves under the supervision of the grand rabbis. Many of them protested that such hierarchy was foreign to Judaism and therefore had no validity. A critical moment occurred in 1856 after the rabbinic conference, at which only the grand rabbis were present. Protests against the decisions of the conference were circulated, and signed by several communal rabbis. Furious at the challenge to its authority, the central consistory requested the departmental consistories to take appropriate action against the insubordination. In Strasbourg the rabbi of Bischeim was summoned to a consistory meeting to explain his behavior in this regard. Arguing that hierarchy did not exist, this rabbi declared that he had committed no fault; he had merely replied, according to the dictates of his conscience, to some religious questions about which he had been consulted professionally. He argued that, far from being in the wrong, he had been obliged to reply. Furthermore, he argued, had the majority of the Alsatian communal rabbis (who had met to discuss the propositions before Grand Rabbi Aron went to the Paris conference) voted in favor of the reforms, he would have kept silent. But only ten of the forty rabbis had approved them. Asked directly if he accepted the grand rabbi as his superior, he said he did not. The Strasbourg consistory voted to censure the rabbi:

L'autorité hiérarchique n'existant pas, il [le rabbin] ne croit pas être en faute et qu'il a été de son devoir de répondre avec bonne foi aux questions qui lui ont été posées sous forme de consultation ... interpellé ensuite s'il ne reconnaît pas les grands rabbins pour ses supérieurs et pour les chefs religieux des circonscriptions, il répond qu'il ne reconnaît cette supériorité que sous le rapport administratif, leur déniant le droit de rien entreprendre de leur seule et unique autorité en matière de religion et de culte. Il n'y a chez nous, dit-il, ni pape, ni évêque et le pape lui-même ne peut rien faire sans un concile. Donc, il ne saurait, lui, approuver les changements faits, par les grands-rabbins ... le rabbin de Bischeim se borne à dire qu'il n'a pas agi par esprit d'opposition, mais avec bonne foi et pour l'acquit de sa conscience. Le consistoire ... considérant que le comparant n'a nullement cherché à témoigner le moindre regret de sa conduite et que loin de là, il a persisté à s'insurger contre l'autorité de ses chefs et les décisions prises dans la conférence des grands rabbins ... décide à la majorité de quatre voix contre deux de demander l'application du droit de censure au rabbin de Bischeim et que la délibération à intervenir soit insérée textuellement dans les journaux religieux.[109]

S. Bloch, editor of the *Univers Israélite* and defender of the traditional role of the rabbi, was outraged by the attitude of the central consistory in censuring the rabbis who disagreed with the conference decisions. He wrote that the grand rabbis and communal rabbis who expressed views contrary to the decisions of the conference had done so in response to questions put to them by some Parisian Jews whose consciences were disturbed by the conference. Bloch added that the rabbis would have violated their most sacred duty if they had refrained from answering. In a furious outburst against the central consistory and against its hierarchy, Bloch pointed out that Rabbi Lambert, the oldest member of the French rabbinate and the former teacher of Rabbi S. Ulmann, was among those Ulmann censured. Bloch charged Ulmann with conspiring against religion and the rabbis: "Vous conspirez contre l'autorité de nos chefs spirituels et contre la religion!"[110]

It is difficult to estimate the potential strength of the post of grand rabbi of the central consistory. Although in theory he alone had the right to approve ceremonial and ritual decisions for the entire country, a certain amount of decentralization was a necessity in order to prevent overt rebellion and the disintegration of the consistory system. At least one rabbi in the middle of the nineteenth century estimated that he could exert greater influence by remaining in his post as departmental consistory grand rabbi than by seeking the position of central consistory grand rabbi. In 1853 Rabbi David Marx turned down the nomination offered him to be a candidate to replace Grand Rabbi Ennery:

après avoir puisé dans le passé du Grand Rabbinat de France l'indication et la mesure de l'action que peut exercer le fonctionnaire religieux appelé à ce poste, il n'a pas acquis la conviction que le poste auquel on désire le porter lui facilite les moyens de travailler avec efficacité, comme il le désirait, au progrès religieux de ses coreligionnaires de France; il espère au contraire, en conservant sa position et sa sphère d'action dans la Gironde, pouvoir comme il en a le désir et la ferme volonté, y servir mieux, par ses efforts et sa persévérance la sainte cause Israélite à laquelle il a consacré sa vie.[111]

The hierarchy was dealt a blow by the 1856 rabbinical conference, which declared that initiative in instituting changes would be left to local rabbis with the approval of their grand rabbis. Such a decision was declared illegal by many, who cited the fact that the rabbinic conference had no decision-making power, having failed to obtain government approval for its convocation. For many years the ritual continued to develop minor variations in the several areas of France, and those who deplored this development called repeatedly for the reimposition of a strict hierarchy and uniformity. But there had never been uniformity of rite in the French synagogues, and all nineteenth-century attempts to create a *rite français* from a blend of Ashkenazi and Sephardi traditions failed.

G. Elections and Installations of Rabbis

The election system was another factor that contributed toward the impression that there existed a high and a low clergy. The choice of grand rabbis was vested in a limited number of people, which varied only slightly throughout the period. The communal rabbis, however, were elected by a broader base, although there was a tendency to concentrate their election in fewer and fewer hands. Because the rabbis themselves never elected their own leaders, the pattern was one of lay-imposed higher clergy, which exercised supervision over the communal (lower) rabbis. In 1853, however, in the midst of a controversy over whether the grand rabbi of the central consistory should be elected by universal suffrage, the central consistory had submitted a plan to the government according to which the departmental grand rabbis would elect the central consistory grand rabbi. Benjamin Gradis of Bordeaux urged the passage of this measure as a means of offsetting the lay domination of the French rabbinate.[112]

In 1853 Rabbi Samuel Dreyfus of Mulhouse appealed to his colleagues in the rabbinate to exercise their influence locally on the choice of the sixteen electors who were to vote with the central consistory for the new central consistory grand rabbi:

Seize délégués nommés par l'influence du corps rabbinique auraient pu éclairer la religion du consistoire central pour n'élever sur le premier siège rabbinique de France que celui que le même corps rabbinique aurait désiré le plus.

But the notion that French rabbis could gain control of the choice of their superior was unrealistic. Neither Gradis' nor Dreyfus' suggestion was implemented, and the elections continued to rest firmly in the hands of the laity.

In 1853 the central consistory succeeded in depriving the communities of their traditional right of selecting their own rabbis, vesting this power in the departmental consistories. (It reverted to local choice for only two years, from 1870 to 1872.) By 1862 a similar kind of hierarchy had intervened in the system of naming the departmental grand rabbis. These were no longer chosen in their own districts, but three nominees were submitted by the consistory to the central consistory. The grand rabbi was then chosen by the central consistory. (In practice departmental consistory members were generally able to obtain their first choice of consistorial grand rabbi.) All rabbinic nominations were thus in the hands of the laymen of the consistories and the central consistory.

At the inception of the consistory system the three grand rabbis of the central consistory were chosen by the government. The 1823 *ordonnance* provided that this system would continue, but no grand rabbi was ever chosen under the provisions of that *ordonnance*. By 1846, when France was about to have its first new central consistory grand rabbi since 1810, new election provisions had been instituted by the 1844 *ordonnance*. Grand Rabbi Ennery was elected by the members of the central consistory plus two representatives of each consistory. Central consistory members, although they represented the various districts, were residents of Paris. The two delegates per district were also frequently chosen from among the residents of Paris, because of the difficulty of traveling from the provinces to Paris to participate in the election. Thus the grand rabbis of France, from 1846 on, were named by laymen, mainly

Parisians. In this way Parisian views dominated French Judaism.

In order to inform electoral opinion, the consistories adopted the practice of making known which candidate they preferred. The announcement took the form of a published report or an oral announcement to a meeting of *notables*. An example is the report (*"détaillé et impartial"*) prepared by Baruch Weill in 1829 for the Parisian *notables* who were about to elect a successor to Grand Rabbi Michel Seligmann.[113] In 1846, however, when the same procedure was attempted for the replacement of deceased Grand Rabbi Ennery, the *notables,* under the leadership of Adolphe Crémieux, rebelled, and refused even to listen to the report, charging the consistory with trying to influence the elections.

The procedure of selecting grand rabbis included asking the candidate to deliver a sermon in the consistorial synagogue. In 1846 the central consistory went further, and asked a series of questions designed to indicate the willingness of the candidates to accept reforms. The following year the Paris consistory imitated this procedure, in "preparing" the election of its grand rabbi. Crémieux, sponsor of the candidacy of Lazare Isidor, was irritated by the fact that the Paris consistory had asked its preferred candidate, Rabbi Charleville, to hold the post temporarily (as a means of improving his chances for being elected). Arguing that the consistory had no right to question the rabbis on their willingness to conform to central consistory views on religious questions, nor to attempt to manipulate the elections by instructing the *notables* on how to vote, he led a rebellion and secured the election of Lazare Isidor.[114]

In Nancy, in 1854, the consistory failed in an attempt to impose a written work as a part of the competition, when the six candidates for the post of grand rabbi refused to submit compositions. The consistory at first refused to alter this procedure, but was eventually forced to yield in view of the insistence of the candidates, who were supported by Grand Rabbi Ulmann of the central consistory. Ulmann had often opposed the method of choosing rabbis by competition (*concours*) as contrary to the dignity of the rabbinate.[115]

Throughout the nineteenth century the consistories attempted to obtain the election of rabbis whose views were sympathetic to their own. But their methods were haphazard, and it is far from certain that the results would have been significantly different had the consistory not attempted to manipulate the outcome of the elections.

The chief effect of the consistory system in regard to the election of rabbis was to put an end to the democratic system that had been in effect since the Revolution. Although some people held the romantic notion that traditional European Jewish communities had functioned in a democratic way, a number of scholars have shown that this was by no means the uniform practice of such communities. Yet elections by universal suffrage do appear to have been the case in France in the eighteen years from the Revolution to the institution of the consistories.[116]

With the institution of the consistories, selection of local rabbis was entrusted to a consistory-appointed ad hoc committee in the town. Chief rabbis were named by the *notables* alone. All election results were forwarded through the consistory hierarchy, requiring approval at each level, and the government officially named the rabbis to their posts upon the recommendation of the central consistory.

When, in the wake of the revolutionary events of 1848, universal suffrage in consistory elections was instituted, the question arose whether the communal rabbis were also to be chosen by universal suffrage. From 1850 to 1853 this question caused agitation. The Metz consistory attempted to institute general elections for the choice of rabbi of the Sarreguemines district, but complaints were filed and the government issued an administrative decision against such elections.[117]

The popular movement then turned its attention toward the highest rabbinic office in the land. In 1853 several petitions were circulated, at least in the Colmar and Paris districts, demanding the election of the central consistory grand rabbi by universal suffrage.[118] Benjamin Gradis suggested, rather, that universal suffrage be employed to name the two delegates per district who would select the grand rabbi of the central consistory.[119] He later supported a suggestion that the central consistory grand rabbi be elected by the departmental grand rabbis.[120]

None of these proposals succeeded in gaining acceptance. Moreover, the central consistory was able to convince the government to pass the election law of 1853, which put the choice of communal rabbis and departmental grand rabbis in the hands of the consistories at the departmental level. Thus all the effects of universal suffrage were neutralized. The only long-term effect that the popular movement had was to slightly increase the amount of provincial involvement in the election of the central consistory grand rabbi. Whereas in 1846 Ennery had been elected by the central consistory plus a body of fourteen representatives, nine of whom lived in Paris and five in the departments, in 1853 Ulmann was elected by the central consistory members plus a body of sixteen delegates, seven from Paris and nine from the provinces.[121]

The rabbi was officially named by the Ministry of Cults, upon the recommendation of the central consistory, after an administrative investigation of his moral and political attitudes. In most cases these security checks were perfunctory, and certificates of good conduct were easily obtained from police and mayors of the local communities.

The procedure for the installation of the rabbis was also prescribed by law, thus confirming the public nature of the post.

Oaths of allegiance to the state were required from 1808 to 1848, and were reinstituted toward the end of the Second Empire. The original form of the oath included the promise that the rabbi would report anything that he discovered that was contrary to the interest of the government. With the succession of political regimes, the oath underwent changes. In all cases it was similar to the oath prescribed by law for public functionaries. Grand rabbis were sworn in by the departmental prefects or their delegates, and the consistories installed them with a synagogue ceremony. The installation ceremony was improvised by the consistory according to its ideas of dignity and pomp and with an eye toward impressing the local dignitaries who were invited. The grand rabbi of the central consistory was installed in a similar way after the central consistory had failed in an attempt to have him installed by the Minister of Cults.

At the level of the communal rabbi, it is not clear from the extant documentation whether both installations and swearing-in ceremonies by Jewish leaders were practiced. In at least some cases, oaths were administered by mayors or by *sous-préfets.* For those rabbis whose installation records have survived, however, we have no record of an oath, and in the cases where an oath is reported, the records do not indicate an installation. It would seem likely that both ceremonies (the swearing-in and the installation) took place in at least some of the cases. Installation proceedings consisted of a ceremony in the synagogue, conducted by an appointed representative of the district consistory (often the local *commissaire surveillant,* more rarely a member of the consistory itself). The ceremony generally consisted of reading a letter of appointment and declaring the rabbi installed. The letter was sometimes the official letter sent by the Ministry of Cults to the central consistory, sometimes the central consistory letter announcing this appointment to the departmental consistory, and sometimes the departmental consistory letter announcing the appointment to the local community.

H. *Ministres Officiants*

1. Description

Traditionally Jewish communities that could not afford to hire both a rabbi and a cantor were advised to choose a cantor. His services in leading the daily prayers were considered more critical than those of a rabbi, whose rulings were not a daily need; when the need did arise, it was always possible to obtain a consultation elsewhere. In nineteenth-century France the cantor took the name *ministre officiant* (officiating minister), which seems to describe the post well. Small poor communities had as their sole religious official the *ministre officiant.*

Napoleon, hence the Assembly of Notables, had been exclusively concerned with the rabbis. No one had worried about policing the *ministres officiants,* or regulating their handling of synagogue ceremonies; concern had been limited exclusively to doctrine and teaching. Napoleon wanted only to be sure that the rabbis, the arbiters of Jewish law and morality, guided their followers according to socially accepted standards and that they encouraged obedience to French law; he was not in the least concerned with synagogue order, harmonies, length or language of prayers.

The tradition that small poor communities hired only cantors remained operative under the consistory system. The 1806 *règlement* had set a minimum rabbinic salary at 1000 francs, but *ministres officiants* were paid less and could also double as *shochetim* and assume teaching duties as well. Although the post of *ministre officiant* (especially when combined with those of *shochet* and teacher) was the ritualistic core of institutional Judaism, it was at first totally unofficial. It was not mentioned in any of the laws before 1823. In that year a new *ordonnance* attributed to the consistory the right to name the *ministres officiants* for the city where the consistory was located. The *ministres officiants* in the local communities were to be elected by an ad hoc committee in the town concerned. The 1844 legislation repeated these provisions.

2. Status, Training and Requirements

The post of *ministre officiant* paid very little. Often, without the secondary functions he exercised, he could not have earned a living. The post carried very little prestige and attracted uneducated men from the lowest socioeconomic class. Except in Bordeaux, where a school trained *ministres officiants* for the Sephardi rite, the cantors received no professional education. Their pronunciation of Hebrew was considered defective, and they were blamed for their tendency to improvise the melodies. When the hierarchical system for the "Jewish clergy" was established, the *ministres officiants* were at the lowest level. They could be censured or suspended by the local consistories without the intervention of the central consistory, and the central consistory could dismiss them from office without government approval.

The first law to take note of the *ministres officiants,* the 1823 *ordonnance,* discussed only methods of election and did not specify any requirements for the office. In 1832 when the state assumed the payment of rabbis' salaries, the *ministres officiants* of communities of more than 200 Jews were included on the payroll, but the law still specified no particular qualifications for the post. In line with French policy that only nationals might receive government appointments and salaries, however, the state began to insist that only Frenchmen be named to these posts. The consistories were asked on several occasions to withhold approval of elections if the nominee was not qualified. In 1837 the community of Forbach (Metz consistory district), as a result of a dispute with its *ministre officiant,* M. Samuel, elected a foreigner, N. Strauss, to the position. When Samuel complained to the prefect that the new appointee was not a French citizen, the ministry ruled for the first time that all *ministres officiants* supported by the state were to be French.[122] A similar incident occurred again in 1841, this time in the Nancy district. M. Courwicki, born in Posen and not naturalized, was elected *ministre officiant* of the synagogue of Pont à Mousson. The ministry ruled that the 1831 legislation (by which the state agreed to pay salaries of rabbis and *ministres officiants*) implied that the recipients must offer the same "guarantees" as other *fonctionnaires:*

La législation qui régit le culte israélite en France, n'a pas jusqu'à présent déterminé les conditions à exiger des ministres officiants. Mais la loi du 8 février 1831, en assurant aux ministres de notre culte les mêmes avantages qu'aux ministres des autres cultes reconnus, leur a implicitement imposé l'obligation de donner au gouvernement les mêmes garanties. Il est donc parfaitement juste et légal que les fonctions salariées par l'Etat ne soient données qu'à des nationaux français ou à des étrangers naturalisés.[123]

The following year a certain Cahen was named *ministre officiant* of Grosbliederstroff (Metz district), but the ministry ruled that he lacked the necessary qualifications and refused to approve his nomination. It charged that the Metz consistory had failed to screen the election results properly. Metz argued the extent of consistory responsibility to verify the qualifications of the men elected, saying it was its job to certify only to the legality of the election procedure and not to the aptitude of the nominee.[124]

The controversy with the Metz consistory led the government to request new legislation specifying the qualifications to be required of a *ministre officiant*. In a letter of April 4, 1842, to the central consistory, the Minister of Cults declared inadmissible the contention of the Metz consistory that the departmental consistories were not responsible for screening the elections.[125] The following year the central consistory directed the departmental consistories to verify that all *ministres officiants* were twenty-five years old, of French nationality, and fluent in both French and Hebrew.[126] The May 25, 1844 *ordonnance* required simply that the *ministre officiant* be twenty-five years old and have a certificate from the district grand rabbi that he had the required religious knowledge. The central consistory was to determine the form of these certificates, and, therefore, the precise prerequisites for the post. Despite the flurry of activity, the simple requirements of French and Hebrew continued to be all that was officially expected of the cantors.

Jewish leaders seeking to improve the social and intellectual status of their coreligionists began, around 1847, to consider the influence exerted upon the people by the example of the *ministre officiant.* In the rural areas, where traditionalism and low levels of education prevailed, the *ministres officiants* were the only permanent religious officials. Parisian Jewish leaders realized that the cantors did not provide the kind of model they wanted to introduce into these communities. Moreover, the cantors were unwilling or unable to cooperate with consistory aims of improving decorum or instituting ceremonial changes. As early as 1847 it was suggested (by Adolphe Crémieux) that the solution to this problem was to replace the *ministres officiants* by *sous-rabbins* (assistant rabbis) to be trained in the rabbinic school. But it was 1862 before the post of *sous-rabbin* was created, and the *ministres officiants* continued to exist even after that date.

As a part of the deliberations of the rabbinic conference in 1856, the grand rabbis of France decided on the following educational requirements for the cantorial post: a knowledge of the Torah and first prophets, the entire ritual, and elementary Hebrew grammar, especially the rules for correct reading.[127] This decision of the rabbinic conference created no law and was never put into practice.

Although it was around 1900 before the central consistory's official rabbinic training school (*séminaire israélite*) included in its curriculum courses for the training of cantors,[128] the Bordeaux cantorial school was operating as early as 1852, for the training of men in the special requirements of the Portuguese ritual.[129] The course of study offered by the Bordeaux school included instruction in the skills later requested by the rabbinic conference and ultimately taught at the Paris seminary. It appears likely that this school served as a model for the proposals of the conference and for the training program of the seminary.

The Bordeaux school had a faculty of four in 1853. The grand rabbi was in charge of the school. Abraham Castro, *ministre officiant* at the Bordeaux temple, gave one lesson per week on the "recitation of the services" and one on the translation of prayers and Hebrew grammar. Juda Fereyra, cantor,[130] taught three lessons a week on reading the Torah and translating the Bible and on the sections of the law concerning cantors. Elie Paz, director of the Bordeaux temple choir, taught vocal music and liturgical chants. Part of the training consisted of practice officiating at the temple. Upon the completion of the training, the student received a certificate of capability for the cantorial functions from the grand rabbi.[131]

The consistories of Bayonne and Marseille, the Portuguese temple, rue Lamartine in Paris, and the temples of Libourne and Clermont-Ferrand were invited to send students to the school. No tuition was charged, but the sponsors of students from outside Bordeaux were asked to pay the expenses of room and board.[132] This school continued in existence until at least 1870, at which date it was receiving 800 francs per year subvention from the department of the Gironde.[133] Unfortunately, no records of the enrollment have survived to clarify the extent to which other consistories and temples made use of this training program to satisfy their own needs.

No program was available to train cantors for the Ashkenazi communities. For a while Jewish leadership hoped that the decisions of the rabbinic conference concerning the qualifications to require of cantors would upgrade their qualifications. But no action was taken to implement those decisions. In 1861 Dr. Wormser, editor of *Le Lien d'Israél,* called for the establishment of a school to teach *ministres officiants*—to give them good religious training and prepare them to teach children.[134] His advice was not followed and, as we have already seen, it was not until around 1900 that such a training program was implemented.

3. Elections

The *ministres officiants* were elected locally. Prior to 1823 no legislation governed the method of election. It is unlikely that a uniform system existed. The *ordonnance* of 1823 called for an ad hoc commission, named in the community by the consistory, for the purpose of electing the *ministre officiant.* The consistory members themselves were to select the *ministre officiant* for the consistorial synagogue.

After 1831 the practice began of forwarding election announcements through channels to the ministry. Thus developed a system of consistorial "approval" which, as we have seen, regarded solely the form of the election. The 1844 *ordonnance* did not change the election procedure; it merely specified that the ad hoc commission was to be comprised of at least five (preferably local) *notables,* and the central consistory was to confirm the election. We know from government documents[135] that before the government gave its approval to elections, police checks were made on the candidates. Ministry approval of the *ministres officiants* always preceded their installation. Such approval should not be confused with nomination; it was only for consistory members and rabbis that the ministry issued an act of nomination after approving an election.

The installation of the *ministre officiant* was generally performed by the *commissaire surveillant,* as representative of the consistory. It often consisted of reading the consistory's letter of approval of the election. In some cases the minutes of the installation specified the salary and other benefits (for example, lodging) accorded to the *ministre officiant.*[136]

The 1862 decree did not make any change in the election procedure or prerequisites for the *ministre officiant* post. But it did provide that *sous-rabbins* might replace the *ministres officiants* anywhere that a state salaried post existed.

4. Numbers

The law provided state salaries for *ministres officiants* in Jewish communities whose population exceeded 200, but for budgetary reasons the government did not always approve the creation of posts when requested. (There was a yearly fixed limit to the total funds allocated to the Jewish cult.) In addition to the state-salaried *ministres officiants*, there were numerous communities that hired cantors at their own expense.

Some of the large communities employed more than one *ministre officiant*. In 1832 Paris was accorded two cantorial posts by law (at 2000 and 1000 francs salary). The Portuguese temple of that city had its own cantor also. In the early 1840's the Paris synagogue employed three cantors, Mayer, Isaac David, and Samuel Naumbourg.

In most regions there were more cantors than rabbis. The major exception to this pattern was in Alsace, the area of densest Jewish concentration and from which most of the rabbis came. Thus in 1861 there were nineteen rabbis and sixteen *ministres officiants* in the Strasbourg district. In Colmar in the same year there were twenty-two rabbis and approximately ten cantors.[137] In the rest of the country the proportion of cantors was higher. The Nancy district in 1856 was served by eight cantors and four rabbis. In all of France in 1841 there were 123 state-salaried "Jewish clergy." Of this number, sixty-seven were *ministres officiants* and fifty-six were rabbis (forty-eight communal rabbis plus eight grand rabbis).[138] A slight movement toward the equalization of the size of the two groups took place over the next twenty years. By 1861 the number of rabbis had climbed to sixty, and the number of *ministres officiants* had probably decreased somewhat.[139]

A. Historical Background

In view of the fact that no clear distinction between the jurisdiction of the laity and that of the rabbinate had emerged prior to the Emancipation, it is not surprising that the nineteenth-century French Jewish community encountered difficulty in determining the division of authority between these two groups. The reason for the lack of clear delineation between their respective powers must be sought in the character of the Jewish community in the diaspora and the historical development of the rabbinate.[1] Throughout the middle ages no clearly defined rabbinical class existed on the basis either of ordination or of professional appointment. There was no post of rabbi to which a man was elected and for which he was paid a salary. The professional rabbinate began to develop only in the fifteenth century, and only then did a modern system of ordination come into use. Posts were developed in increasing numbers, and the men named to them were given contracts and fixed salaries for the first time. Previously, rabbinic competence had been informally acknowledged on the basis of scholarly reputations.

Throughout the middle ages judicial authority had been shared by the scholars and nonscholars, a situation that was fostered by the fact that there were no official criteria for identifying the scholar class. Men of learning, however, had always disputed the wisdom of the practice of including the uneducated on the tribunals, citing the fact that the Talmud enjoins the community to choose the best possible judges, in order that the rulings be in harmony with rabbinic precepts. Nevertheless, judicial authority continued to be shared by the learned and the unlearned (the equivalent of the "rabbinic" and the "lay" groups of the modern period). With the emergence of a clearly defined class of "rabbis" in the fifteenth and succeeding centuries, an objective distinction could be drawn between rabbis and laymen for the first time, and their competition for authority could be defined by these terms.

As the professional rabbinate developed, it began to assume most of the judicial authority. There were some areas, especially in Italy, where this was not the case, and where the laity continued to dominate the scholars, but the general trend was toward a strong rabbinate. In fifteenth-century Spain, for example, appeals from lay tribunals could be made to the rabbis, but from the rabbis litigants could appeal only to the king. Thus the period from the fifteenth to the seventeenth centuries in western Europe (to the nineteenth century in eastern Europe) has been called the "heyday of the rabbinate."[2]

The development of a strong rabbinic faction did not prevent continual competition from lay leaders. The latter sought to preserve power and authority within the community by exercising judicial prerogatives, especially in the area of civil cases (business, testaments, etc.), which involved considerable economic patronage.[3] In the area of ritual decisions, on the other hand, the rabbis remained the undisputed authorities and began to be challenged in this only after the French Revolution.[4]

Before laymen could dispute rabbinic jurisdiction in ritual matters, a very important change had to take place: the authority both of the rabbinate and of the *halakhic* tradition it represented had to be questioned. As long as the communities operated on the assumption that answers to religious questions could be found by reference to traditional texts, rabbinic authority remained unquestioned. The rabbis were the acknowledged experts in the interpretation of the texts.

It is well-known that by the eighteenth century rabbinic prestige in the Ashkenazi communities had begun to decline and the authority of the rabbinic literature was no longer unquestioned. Many factors had entered into this development, and without attempting to elaborate the role of each, we can briefly remember that mysticism, the Sabbatian heresy, Hasidism, the Polish political and social upheavals and consequent migrations, the purchase of rabbinic posts, combined with the developments in secular society—enlightenment, rationalism, modern economic developments, the emergence of the secular modern state, and deism—all contributed to this change.

In the eighteenth-century Sephardi community, on the other hand, there was a diminution not of prestige but of scope of function. The rabbis of southern France were more limited in their jurisdiction than most rabbis in the Ashkenazi communities of the northeast. Thus the Bayonne constitution of 1760 specifies that the rabbi will take no part in the "affairs" of the *Nation,* but will concern himself only with his "ministry."[5] This was no rebuff to the rabbinate, which had been voluntarily reconstituted by the ex-Marranos less than a century before. Rather, this provision of the Bayonne constitution reveals a modern conception of the rabbinate, which the Sephardim had evolved according to the Christian pattern of the minister and the scope of his "religious" role.[6]

Not only would it be incorrect to say that the Sephardim had a negative attitude toward their rabbis, but it must be stressed that it was from among the Sephardim that the rabbis found their staunchest support. It was Benjamin Rodrigues, representative from Bordeaux to the Assembly of Notables (and later a member of the central consistory), who obtained for the rabbis, in his dealings with Napoleon's representatives, a guaranteed minimum income. In an 1825 letter to the central consistory, Rodrigues reminds them of this:

Messiers [sic!] les rabbins . . . savent bien que c'est moi qui ai été leur défenseur dans l'assemblée pour obtenir le salaire dont ils jouissent qu'on ne voulait porter qu'à moitié.[7]

Although a narrowed definition of religion had evolved among the Sephardim, they did not draw a distinction equivalent to the nineteenth-century's sharp delineation of civil authority from religious authority. Scholars who deny that the eighteenth-century Sephardi community lacked all civil jurisdiction do not take into account all of the evidence.[8] Cirot's researches show that community authority was considerably broader than a narrow definition of religion would allow.[9] He speaks, for example, of a *Beth Din* (rabbinic court) which tried a case of seduction and imposed certain financial penalties and support costs in favor of the unborn child. Moreover, the community was responsible for keeping records of birth, marriage, and death. In the absence of any governmental records and civil status, it was the *Nation* which kept the records. Certainly this constitutes civil jurisdiction. Mandatory arbitration of business cases, by the lay leaders of the community, not necessarily resolved according to Jewish law, is another example of civil jurisdiction exercised by the *Nation.*

The consistory system emerged from a combination of factors: the trend toward a modern definition of the rabbinic role in the south, skepticism about the rabbinic tradition in Paris and in the east, and the dawn of the modern secular state, which recognized the possibility of multiple religious traditions —all under the control of a strong centralized state. The price of the Emancipation fifteen years earlier had been the acceptance of a narrowly defined concept of religion and comparably narrowed fields of activity for the rabbinate. Fearing that the rabbis might not accept their redefined role, the laity took it upon themselves to supervise them. Once the government and Jewish lay leaders had defined the rabbinic role as subservient to laity, it was a simple step for the skeptical among the lay leaders to claim the right to disagree with the rabbis' religious decisions.

When nineteenth-century scholars began to use modern scientific research for critical study of Jewish institutions and history, initial interest was directed toward antiquity and the medieval (rabbinic) period. When the medieval period was explored, researchers were attracted to the Spanish experience, and the Ashkenazi medieval tradition was downgraded. The recent past was very little understood, especially in regard to the relative roles of rabbis and laymen. It was often claimed that traditional communities always elected their rabbis democratically. The orthodox used this contention in their fight for local choice of rabbis by universal suffrage. Samuel Cahen, editor of the *Archives Israélites,* was the only polemicist to argue that the choice of rabbi had been far from democratic. He cited eighteenth-century Metz, where six *parnassim* made most of the choices on behalf of the community.

Adolphe Franck used his knowledge of ancient Israel to argue that there was no lay-rabbinic distinction in Judaism, and thereby to justify lay predominance in official nineteenth-century Judaism. But such a contention ignored 1800 years of history and especially the distinction that had developed during the early modern period.

Neither the rabbis nor the laymen, who were disputing religious authority, seem to have been aware that they were participating in the final act of a drama that had begun in the fifteenth century. Neither seemed to realize that in the preceding four centuries of professionalization of the rabbinate, lay leaders and rabbis had been engaged in "quarrels over authority, the division of functions and prestige," nor that "the balance of forces varied with each community."[10]

The tension between the rabbinic and lay elements in the consistory began with the creation of the consistory system, and the addition of two laymen to the rabbinic council that Napoleon had ordered established in Paris. This addition of laymen, made at the request of Napoleon's representatives, probably at the instigation of the Jewish *notables,* made the central consistory a mixed lay-rabbinic body, rather than the purely rabbinic council originally envisaged by Napoleon.[11]

The central consistory began as a five-member body, with three rabbis and two laymen, but the ratio of rabbinic to lay members immediately began to decline. There were only about three years during which three rabbis actually participated on the central consistory. On November 9, 1812, central consistory Grand Rabbi David Sinzheim died, and he was never replaced. The 1823 *ordonnance* legalized this by officially reducing the number of grand rabbis to two, while simultaneously increasing the lay membership to seven. Thus, for the first time, laymen formed a large majority of the membership of the central consistory. But the maintenance of two grand rabbis on the central consistory did not last for very long either. In 1826 Grand Rabbi Abraham de Cologna returned to his native Italy and he, too, was not replaced. Once again the legislation caught up with reality, and in 1844 the number of central consistory grand rabbis was reduced to one. (Already an 1831 law which granted state salaries to the rabbis took into consideration only one post of central consistory grand rabbi.)

The tendency toward a lay consistory did not end with the reduction of the number of rabbis to one. From 1833 to 1835, as a result of disagreements between Grand Rabbi Deutz and the lay members of the central consistory, Deutz was not invited to consistory meetings. Again, from 1842 to 1846, between the death of Deutz and his replacement by Grand Rabbi

Marchand Ennery, the central consistory was composed entirely of laymen. When Ennery died the central consistory allowed eighteen months to elapse before the election of Grand Rabbi Ulmann. During all of these periods the central consistory continued its work without the collaboration of a grand rabbi.

The lay membership of the consistories increased several times. In 1823 the central consistory jumped from two to seven, and it increased by one every time a provincial consistory was added. In 1850 the departmental consistory lay membership was increased from four to six, to further reduce rabbinic influence on these administrations and to attempt to neutralize the orthodox influence feared as a result of universal suffrage.

Although the 1823 *ordonnance* gave the rabbis veto rights in religious decision-making, the lay members often took matters into their own hands, voted by simple majority, and even, as we have seen, had recourse to the exclusion of the rabbis from consistory meetings.

Several attempts were made by conservatives to require the concurrence of a majority of the grand rabbis before any reform could be undertaken, but the legislation that emerged never required more than the permission of the grand rabbi of the central consistory. Neither the 1823 nor the 1844 *ordonnance* required the departmental consistories to have the permission of their grand rabbis before making "religious decisions."

The choice of rabbis was, at all levels, in the hands of the laity. We have already described a futile attempt to establish a rabbinic assembly which would have had the power to name the grand rabbis. The education of the rabbis was under consistory control from 1829, when the official rabbinic school opened. The legislation governing the consistories provided for censure, suspension, and dismissal of rabbis by, or upon the complaint of, the laymen of the consistories. This lay power first emerged in the 1839 project, and it remained in effect until the separation of church and state in 1905.

Throughout the nineteenth century there were recurrent complaints against the "secularization" of French Judaism. In 1857, when an early draft of the 1862 decree was being debated, S. Bloch, editor of the *Univers Israélite,* charged the laity with usurpation of powers and with raising themselves to the position of "infallible popes":

Déjà, après la promulgation de l'ordonnance organique du 25 mai 1844, un célèbre évêque catholique reprocha au gouvernement la sécularisation d'une religion révélée par Dieu, et aux israélites d'avoir consenti à cette sécularisation qui profanait, selon lui, leurs sanctuaires. Que dirait-on de ce progrès dans la profanation de cette religion qui aurait pour papes infaillibles quelques laïques chargés de conférer les ordres sacrés, de nommer les chefs religieux, de fixer les matières de l'enseignement théologique, de diriger le séminaire et d'en choisir les maîtres, d'agir, de réformer, de bouleverser dans la Communauté du Seigneur tout ce qui bon leur semble, et de considérer le sanctuaire du Très-Haut comme une ville conquise, où l'on arrache le drapeau du souverain légitime pour arborer les couleurs de l'usurpateur![12]

The level of lay control over the rabbinate that was achieved through the legislation did not remain theoretical. It is the purpose of this chapter to illustrate the lay domination as it, in fact, occurred.

B. Civil Jurisdiction and Religious Jurisdiction

The area of jurisdiction that was disputed between rabbis and laymen in nineteenth-century France was purely religious. Although the rabbis had a share in the civil administration of Jewish institutions[13] when the consistories were first organized, and although their participation in it diminished progressively throughout the century, the rabbis did not protest their loss of influence in this domain; it was purely their religious authority that the rabbis attempted to preserve.

Only when the laity attempted to dispute rabbinic religious authority did conflicts develop between the two groups. Part of the problem was in defining those areas that were religious. Since the purpose of the consistory in contesting the religious authority of the rabbinate was to introduce reforms into the ceremonies and rituals, the consistory attempted to draft the regulations in such a way as to deny that ceremonial form was a religious issue. Thus in the final stages of the drafting of the 1844 *ordonnance,* the Paris consistory unsuccessfully tried to introduce some changes in Article 38, which provided that the grand rabbi's consent be obtained before the central consistory could make decisions concerning *questions religieuses.* Since this phrase could lend itself to broad interpretations and to claims by the rabbinate over ceremonial matters, the Paris consistory recommended that the wording describing the rabbis' area of authority be changed to *ressortissant au dogme* or *touchant aux principes fondamentaux de la croyance.* The final wording did not, however, deprive the grand rabbi of his authority, as it spoke more generally of *objets religieux ou du culte.*

When the 1844 *ordonnance* was being considered for revision in 1849, S. Bloch urged that the consistories be composed primarily of rabbis. He argued that consistory responsibility, which in 1806 had been primarily administrative, was now mainly religious:

aujourd'hui, les consistoires ne ressemblent presque en rien à leurs devanciers de 1806. Aujourd'hui ce sont de véritables assemblées ecclésiastiques chargées de donner l'ordination aux jeunes rabbins, de choisir les livres d'instruction religieuse et morale, de faire les règlements pour les cérémonies du culte, de représenter la synagogue, de nommer les agents de la loi mosaïque, tels que le mohel et le schohet, de veiller sur les établissements de charité et de bienfaisance: toutes ces fonctions, nous le demandons à la bonne foi de chacun, ne sont-elles pas de l'essence même du ministère sacré, de la direction spirituelle, et peuvent-elles être convenablement remplies par des hommes du monde, par des banquiers, des négociants, des officiers ou des industriels?[14]

Even in Strasbourg, where the lay leaders showed great respect for the grand rabbi, and Grand Rabbi Aron shared many of their inclinations toward mild ceremonial reform, the question of jurisdiction was a touchy one. In 1857 Aron introduced some changes into the services of the High Holy Days, modifying some prayers and eliminating others. (Unfortunately, the sources are not more specific.) As a result the consistory voted their thanks and expressed the hope that Aron would continue to make changes of this type. Aron accepted the thanks but refused the advice; he would not be told by the lay members what religious decisions he should make. He reminded his lay colleagues on the consistory that all initiative in religious matters was up to him and should stem from his own free will:

Tout en appréciant le motif qui a dicté ce sentiment, M. le grand-rabbin dit qu'il ne saurait agréer la partie secondaire de la proposition, vu que toute initiative en pareille matière doit émaner de son seul et libre arbitre.[15]

The fact that modern rabbis did not seek administrative responsibilities was cited by men who sought to strengthen the position of the rabbinate and to clarify the division of power between laymen and rabbis. Créhange was one of those who argued this way. In his series of pamphlets called *La Sentinelle Juive,* which he wrote in protest against the central consistory's 1839 project to revise the laws governing Judaism, Créhange deplored the central consistory's aim of making the "spiritual authority" dependent upon the "temporal authority":

[le projet] n'avait pour le moment d'autre but que de placer l'autorité spirituelle sous la dépendance du pouvoir temporel; ce qui serait d'autant plus injuste chez nous, que les Rabbins n'ont jamais fait invasion dans le domaine de l'administration.[16]

In the Strasbourg district the communal rabbis were expected to help the consistory in the governing of the district. Whenever a dispute arose, or when a *commissaire surveillant* had to be named, the consistory requested, and generally followed, the advice of the communal rabbi of the district, but such activity on the part of the rabbis seems to have been the exception.[17]

C. Defining the Respective Powers

Several attempts were made to define and understand the respective roles of the rabbis and the laymen. During the 1833–35 controversy between Deutz and the central consistory, the government was almost drawn into the discussion, but the Minister of Cults discreetly remained silent. Deutz had sent him several letters of complaint about having been excluded from central consistory decisions on religious questions. His letters had stimulated some interest within the ministry, and an investigation was made into the religious functions the central consistory was exercising without consulting Deutz. Although the government found that Deutz' complaint was justified and that the central consistory was violating the 1823 *ordonnance,* it was decided that nothing would be said. The central consistory and its rabbi were left to reach an accord themselves.[18]

During the same period, a disagreement between Grand Rabbi Ennery and the Paris consistory led the consistory to seek a definition of the scope of rabbinic authority. The choir leader employed by the Paris consistory was Jacques Offenbach, later to be known for his theatrical music. In 1834 Offenbach was already employed in a theater orchestra, where he played every evening, including Friday, and Grand Rabbi Ennery insisted that he either stop working on Friday evenings or give up his post with the choir. The consistory argued that Offenbach's choir job was not a religious post and that, furthermore, it was not the grand rabbi's job to supervise the religious behavior of the temple employees. The regulations, they claimed, gave the right to hire such personnel to the consistory alone.

The incident led to a central consistory decision on the limits of rabbinic powers, which was all the more remarkable in that it was made during the quarrel with Deutz and therefore reflected the views of the lay members only. The central consistory ruled that rabbis have no particular rights in regard to the supervision of the behavior of temple employees, except during the time that they are exercising religious functions in the temple. Furthermore, the consistory agreed that the post of choir director was not a religious position.[19]

Ennery and the consistory clashed again in 1844 when the grand rabbi refused to allow the use of an organ and a girls' choir in the confirmation ceremony. The consistory felt that the grounds for the rabbi's decision were not religious, because his opposition was based on the principle *Hukkot ha-Goyim,* by which the rabbinic tradition disapproved of imitating the practices of non-Jews, rather than on a specific text which forbade the innovations. The Paris consistory turned to the central consistory (which was once again without a rabbi) for a clarification of the rights and powers of lay members and rabbis.[20] Since the law required that the rabbis be followed in questions of religion, and since the Paris consistory was anxious to make these ceremonial changes, it argued that the innovations it sought were not matters that "essentially concern the religion." The consistory insisted upon the difference between dogma and the form of the ceremonies. After several months had passed without a reply, the Paris consistory requested and obtained a joint meeting with the central consistory for the purpose of defining "les limites des attributions respectives du rabbin et des laïques."

Adolphe Franck of the central consistory also felt the need for such a definition, but he warned his colleagues not to respond hastily. He reminded them that such a distinction does not really exist for the Jews, or at least it had not existed for the ancient Jews:

M. Franck désire qu'on puisse fixer les limites des pouvoirs respectifs des rabbins et des laïques; mais cette question importante appelle toutes les méditations et ne saurait être décidée à la hâte. Quant à lui, il pense que, parmi les juifs, il n'y a pas de laïques; du moins les distinctions de pouvoir clérical et de pouvoir laïc n'existaient pas chez les anciens juifs.[21]

No decision of principle was even attempted at that time, and the issue was resolved by postponing the confirmation ceremony, in order to give Ennery the opportunity to confer with his colleagues, the other rabbis of France. (Ennery's opposition to ceremonial reform was consistently based upon a belief that reforms should not be authorized by individual rabbis, but only by the rabbis together, deliberating in a synod.)

Three years later, in the midst of another conflict with Ennery, the Paris consistory again asked for a definition of rabbinic powers. This occurred during the election, discussed above, of a successor to Ennery on the Paris consistory. Ennery had been elected to the position of grand rabbi of the central consistory, but attempted to maintain his former post until a new Paris consistory grand rabbi was chosen. When the Paris consistory instead appointed Rabbi Charleville of Dijon as interim rabbi, a large part of the Parisian Jewish population protested, and cited Article 38 of the 1844 *ordonnance,* which defined the powers of the grand rabbi of the central consistory. The central consistory interpreted the article in question in favor of Ennery's claim, and the Paris consistory resigned in protest.[22] The affair did not come to an end until Charleville had been defeated in the election. The definition of lay and rabbinic powers was never made.

Rabbi Samuel Dreyfus of Mulhouse (the first rabbi trained at the Metz school; an "enlightened" leader of modernists and promoter of "useful" trades among the Alsatian Jewish population) repeatedly insisted on the need for a clear distinction between rabbinic and lay functions. He claimed that the blurring of this distinction had contributed to the diminution of rabbinic prestige. In 1855 he reminded the readers of his journal,

Le Lien d'Israél, that the rabbis have purely religious functions and the consistories have purely administrative functions.[23]

Similarly, the need to maintain the distinction between the laity and the rabbinate was repeatedly emphasized by Benjamin Gradis of Bordeaux. When a religious publication society was founded by laymen in 1854, Gradis opposed it on the grounds that even though the grand rabbi of the central consistory was theoretically at the head of the society, he might lack time for proper supervision. The tendency of the society's publications, Gradis feared, might be toward innovation:

Il n'y a rien de si contraire à la religion que d'organiser une publication régulière et incessante de livres pieux dont on confie la composition et la rédaction à des laïques. . . . Les laïques ont la passion depuis quelque temps de s'immiscer dans tout ce qui a trait à la religion et au culte, au lieu de s'en rapporter entièrement sur ces matières à leurs chefs spirituels. . . . Il est à craindre que dans la société dont il s'agit, les laïques ne finissent par dominer et compromettre l'élément religieux.[24]

D. Lay Control of the Rabbinate

The rabbis were correct in judging that the laity was deliberately attempting to minimize their voice. One of the areas in which this was done was public education. An 1850 reform of the educational system (*la Loi Falloux*) brought into existence boards of public education at both the departmental and national level. Jews were to be represented on these boards by delegates of the consistories. Whereas the Catholics and Protestants were represented by priests and ministers, the consistories in some cases elected to send laymen to represent Judaism. Thus, although the representatives from Strasbourg and Paris were Grand Rabbis Aron and Isidor, the Metz delegate was lay member Schwab.[25] At the national level the central consistory delegated Adolphe Franck to the *conseil supérieur de l'instruction publique.* Grand Rabbi Ennery, prior to Franck's election, realized that the central consistory was considering naming a layman to represent the religious interests of the Jews, and he refused to take part in the election.[26]

If Simon Bloch is to be believed,[27] it was by secret petition to the government that the central consistory had obtained the wording of the 1850 law which allowed the central consistory the option of appointing a lay member to the *conseil supérieur.* Bloch said it had been the intention of the government that the Jews be represented by the grand rabbis, just as Catholics were represented by bishops and Protestants by pastors:

La Chambre des députés allait voter la loi organique du Conseil supérieur de l'instruction publique. Dans le projet élaboré par le gouvernement, le culte catholique devait être représenté par des évêques, le culte protestant par des pasteurs et le culte israélite par le grand rabbin du Consistoire central. Mais, pour éloigner le vénérable pontif de la Synagogue française du poste qui lui était dû, on fit des démarches secrètes auprès de la commission de la Chambre pour obtenir que les mots "grand rabbin du Consistoire central," écrits dans la loi, fussent remplacés par ceux de membre du Consistoire central. *Cette substitution clandestine une fois obtenue, on proposa au gouvernement de nommer un laïque représentant du judaïsme dans le sein du Conseil supérieur de l'instruction publique. Le judaïsme et ses docteurs ont été ainsi mis hors la loi commune, un saint ministre de Dieu outragé dans son honneur et dans sa religion; et encore aujourd'hui, le grand rabbin du Consistoire central est soumis à l'humiliation inouïe de céder la place à un professeur déiste ou panthéiste!*[28]

Similarly the consistory managed to minimize the effect of the rabbi's presence at official presentations. It was the custom of the government to receive a delegation from the consistory on New Year's Day and on certain other occasions. Bloch denounced the consistory's action in keeping the rabbi from speaking on such occasions:

Nous ajouterons que, dans les présentations officielles aux Tuileries, où les évêques et les pasteurs parlent au nom de leurs cultes respectifs, on n'a jamais permis à notre grand rabbin d'ouvrir la bouche. C'est tantôt un ancien fournisseur de l'armée, tantôt un avocat qui laisse baptiser ses enfants, tantôt un théologien à grosses épaulettes, qui représentent la foi d'Israël devant le chef de l'Etat! . . . Voilà comment le Consistoire central respecte l'autorité et la considération de nos guides spirituels![29]

In still another example, taken this time from its own minutes, the central consistory showed itself in active competition with its own grand rabbi for the role of official representative of Jewry. In 1852 Napoleon III gave a public celebration for the re-establishment of the Empire. He invited the grand rabbi of Paris to represent the Jews, because central consistory Grand Rabbi Ennery had just died. The central consistory was angry that the government had chosen the rabbi, rather than a layman, to represent Judaism at this public celebration. It delegated one of its members, Auguste Furtado, to complain to the *ministre d'état* and to ask that in the future the central consistory president, as well as the grand rabbi, be invited to represent Jewry at public events.[30]

Despite the judgment of Georges Wormser that "the reduction of the rabbinic representation was possible because of a disposition adopted by the consistory almost from its inception which gave the grand rabbis the right of veto in purely religious matters,"[31] and despite Article 12 of the 1823 *ordonnance,* which required that all central consistory decisions concerning religion be made only with the consent of the two grand rabbis, and despite Article 38 of the 1844 *ordonnance,* which gave the one remaining rabbi the same right of veto, it is clear that many religious decisions in the central consistory, as well as in the departmental consistories, were made without the consent of a rabbi.

Grand Rabbi Deutz, for instance, during his conflict with the central consistory (1833-35), complained to the ministry that the central consistory failed to inform him of meetings and then made religious decisions in his absence.[32] During his absence, on May 2, 1833, the central consistory discussed a project of reorganization of the cult and proposed it to the government. The following day, May 3, the consistory approved a book for use in the Jewish schools. On June 17 it expelled a student from the rabbinic school.[33] Between June 25, 1833, and May 31, 1835, still in the absence of Deutz, the central consistory ordained four rabbis and awarded them the second (higher) rabbinic degree. It also appointed eleven rabbis to posts.[34]

At its meeting of July 3, 1834, also in the absence of Deutz, the central consistory had received a complaint from Ennery, grand rabbi of Paris, against the central consistory practice of excluding Deutz from their meetings. The central consistory's reply, that its decisions were made by simple majority vote, totally ignored the rabbinic veto provision of the 1823 *ordonnance.*

Within the Paris consistory the situation was analogous. On December 26, 1842, a religious question was being debated: a niece of the brothers Max and Alphonse Cerfberr had died and the family wanted her buried in the Jewish cemetery. Ennery was opposed, on the grounds that the girl's mother was Christian, and that the girl had not during her lifetime observed the ritual requirements. The Cerfberr brothers insisted that their niece had considered herself Jewish, and despite the opinion of Ennery, the consistory ordered her buried in the Jewish cemetery.[35]

It is not difficult to find further examples of lay decisions on religious questions. During the 1820's the Paris consistory forbade preaching in German, despite the contrary opinion of Grand Rabbi Seligmann.[36] On October 15, 1829, after the death of Seligmann and before the election of his successor, the Paris consistory decided that boys would not be allowed to celebrate their *Bar Mitzvah* by reading the *Torah* unless they had passed an examination on the official catechism, *Précis élémentaire d'instruction religieuse.*[37]

Nevertheless, lay leaders voluntarily imposed certain limits on their claim to religious authority. In 1843 the central consistory had not yet replaced Grand Rabbi Deutz, when the Paris consistory requested approval of its new regulations concerning circumcision. The central consistory was afraid to make this decision by itself, and decided to request the opinions of all the grand rabbis.[38] In another case, after the death of Paris Grand Rabbi Seligmann, the consistory wanted his body brought to the temple for an elaborate funeral with a eulogy. Deutz informed them that Seligmann had specifically requested that his body not be brought to the temple, and that, furthermore, Judaism forbade long eulogies at that time of year. Although the consistory members disputed Deutz's views, they ultimately yielded to his veto.[39]

Again, in 1850, the Metz consistory backed Grand Rabbi L. M. Lambert in his attack on reforms introduced (without rabbinic approval) by the *commissaire surveillant* of Sarreguemines. This administrator had decided that the *Cohanim* and *Leviyim* would no longer be called first to the Torah. A letter of protest from the traditional members of the community reached the Metz consistory, and Grand Rabbi Lambert declared the new procedure contrary to religious law. The Metz consistory reprimanded the *commissaire surveillant* for instituting the change without first consulting Grand Rabbi Lambert, "who alone has the right to make any changes in the public services."[40]

The respect and deference shown to Lambert in this case is hardly typical of consistorial attitudes toward the grand rabbis. More representative is the case of Grand Rabbi Solomon Klein of Colmar, whose orthodoxy brought him into sharp conflict with the Colmar consistory, the central consistory, and the government. The "Klein Affair" started in 1856 when Klein repudiated the decisions of the rabbinic conference. At their conference in Paris that year the majority of grand rabbis had agreed that some reforms of the ceremonies were permissible (but not mandatory). Klein joined with some other conservatives in written objection to the decisions, and was censured by the central consistory for his "insubordination." He next expanded his local Talmudic school[41] into a rabbinic school to compete with the official, central consistory-controlled rabbinic school, which the conference had voted to move from Metz to Paris. Klein's school was designed to train orthodox rabbis and to attract students of the eastern provinces who did not wish to go to Paris.

When the Colmar consistory refused him permission to publicize the school in the Colmar temple, Klein had the temple's sexton post the notices anyway. The sexton was fired by the consistory. Klein rehired him and also gave his father the job of slaughterer in competition with the consistorial slaughterer. Klein also refused to cooperate with the consistory's attempts to open a trade school in Colmar, and the consistory accused him of diverting funds raised for that purpose to his Talmudic school. Colmar requested the intervention of the central consistory, which in turn appealed to the government. Stopping short of requesting Klein's dismissal, the central consistory asked that the ministry use its authority to request that Klein respect the rules and regulations governing the consistory. The central consistory implied that the government should threaten Klein, holding over his head the possibility of eventual dismissal. This tactic seemed to work, and in the face of the threat Klein agreed to come to terms with the consistory. The controversy was long (1856 to 1858) and bitter, and brought the government into internal Jewish affairs. Most notably, it led to a government-manipulated consistory election in Alsace, in which mayors, prefects, and police departments all cooperated to see that the "right" (reform-oriented) candidates won.[42]

In other instances the consistories did not limit themselves to intimidation but exercised to the full their right of censure. Suspension and dismissal, however, were rarely practiced. In 1856 the Marseille consistory requested the dismissal of Nîmes communal rabbi Alexandre Seligmann, because of a *déplorable scandale* which had occurred as a result of a disagreement between the rabbi and the *commissaire surveillant* during a religious service. The central consistory suspended him.[43]

Rabbis' sermons and letters were always subject to lay criticism. In 1822 Grand Rabbi Wittersheim of Metz announced that if children decided to work on the half-holidays of *Pesach,* it would be by their own decision, and not because he gave them permission. The consistory, whose job it was to encourage useful trades among poor children, had asked for a statement by Wittersheim that would make work on these days permissible. They were outraged by the rabbi's sermon, and Schwab, of the consistory, criticized him for it. Wittersheim replied sharply that as grand rabbi of Metz he could not be prevented from expressing his views in his sermons. He objected to the consistory's attitude in criticizing him and in telling him what to say.[44]

Eighteen years later the Metz consistory was again at odds with its grand rabbi; this time it was L. M. Lambert who held the post. Lambert had participated in the circulation of a written protest against the central consistory's 1839 program for revamping the consistorial system, a program that was designed to increase lay control of the rabbinate. The Metz consistory felt that Lambert's public rejection of the project and his disagreement with the consistory had injured its prestige. The members resolved to have nothing further to do with him until they obtained the cooperation of the government in revising the laws so as to give them control over the rabbi. When the new law was not ready quickly enough, they resigned in protest.[45]

Again, in 1846, Lambert was under criticism for his writings. Together with Grand Rabbi Goudchaux of Colmar, he had issued a pastoral letter disapproving of the introduction of ceremonial reforms on the German pattern. Lambert specifically attacked the young rabbis of Germany who sought "disastrous" reforms, and warned their would-be imitators in France that if they persisted, they would be faced with severe opposition. His letter, he later said, was designed to alert the public to the dangers of the proposed reforms and to prevent people from being fooled by the "utopias" described by reformers. Both the central consistory and the Metz consistory reprimanded Lambert for his letter and accused him of exceeding the limits of his authority.

In reply Lambert courageously defended his rights of freedom of speech, religion, and the press, declaring that the rights granted by the *Charte* existed for rabbis as they did for everyone else:

comme si les Rabbins étaient exceptés dans la loi sur la liberté de la presse! On pourrait donc librement attaquer la religion et les Rabbins, et ceux-ci ne pourraient pas répondre! . . . je ne reconnais qu'aux tribunaux le droit de me demander compte de mes publications; la Charte existe pour les Rabbins comme pour les autres citoyens.[46]

The attitude of Jewish leaders toward the rabbinate was one of employer to employee. At every opportunity the consistories attempted to influence the choice of rabbis and to define for the rabbis the work that they were expected to do. Opposition to this attitude was repeatedly expressed, but, with rare exceptions, it had no effect. We have already discussed the fact that the election of rabbis was in the hands of the laity. The consistories attempted, moreover, to enlist the government's aid in screening candidates for these posts. Thus it is obvious that the 1831 *ordonnance,* which put the rabbis' salaries on the state payroll, was sought by the consistories, not only for financial benefits, nor merely to consecrate liberal principles of equality, but to create a situation in which the government would closely control appointments to rabbinic posts. In fact, the following year another measure was enacted which regulated the awarding of rabbinic degrees and which detailed the studies required of rabbis.[47]

In 1830 and 1846, during his installations, first in the Paris consistory and then in the central consistory, Grand Rabbi Ennery was addressed by lay leaders, who spoke of the duties awaiting him in his new post. Although we have no record of how the 1830 speech was received by the public, S. Bloch has recorded *his* reaction to the one of 1846. Bloch deplored the fact that central consistory president Cerfberr had criticized traditional Jewish practices and had publicly urged Ennery to understand his "duty":

Le président de cette administration monta devant l'arche sacrée et prononça un discours; mais, au lieu de se borner à proclamer la nomination du nouveau grand rabbin et à lui adresser quelques mots d'hommage et de respectueuse sympathie, l'orateur, entièrement étranger aux études et aux pratiques religieuses israélites, catéchisa le patriarche du judaïsme français, étalant devant Israél et devant le monde un système religieux rationaliste qui n'a presque rien de commun *avec la religion positive révélée à nos pères au pied du Sinaï, avec la religion historique qui s'est transmise de génération en génération jusqu'à nos jours, s'est gravée dans notre âme, s'est établie dans nos maisons, s'est élevée des autels dans nos sanctuaires. Le prédicateur-soldat fit plus: s'érigeant en juge et en critique de nos usages sacrés traditionnels, il appela nos prières et nos jeûnes "des prières et des jeûnes d'esclaves qui ne conviennent pas à l'homme libre," et nos invocations pour Sion et Jérusalem "des espérances de proscrit qui n'ont aucun sens dans notre bouche! . . ." Voilà la leçon que le président du Consistoire central osa faire publiquement au chef de la Synagogue de France en l'apostrophant par ces paroles blessantes: "Ne vous trompez pas, monsieur le grand rabbin,* nous sommes les interprètes d'une génération plus religieuse qu'on ne pense . . . *Nous croyons avoir rempli notre devoir;* vous comprendrez aussi le vôtre!" Voilà la flétrissure que le président du Consistoire central, en présence de représentants du gouvernement et de cultes étrangers, osa imprimer sur le front du judaïsme.*[48]

But the consistory went even further. It undertook to control the elections of rabbis, and to elicit statements from the candidates on their attitudes toward the reform measure the consistory wished to introduce. Notably, this occurred in 1846 and 1847 when grand rabbis were being elected to the central and Paris consistories. It occurred again in 1853 when another central consistory grand rabbi had to be chosen.

In March 1846 the central consistory sent a circular to all the departmental consistories.[49] It solicited nominations for the post of grand rabbi and invited all candidates to submit a written statement on their views of the ritual needs of Judaism and on their conception of the grand rabbi's obligations. The candidates were to indicate whether they would be willing to cooperate with the central consistory in bringing about nine reforms which the central consistory enumerated. The rabbis were asked whether they believed that such changes were in harmony with the essential and eternal principles of Judaism (which the central consistory insisted it wished respected). The nine reforms the consistory listed were:

(1) The fusion of the Ashkenazi and Sephardi rites in a *synagogue française* by adopting uniform melodies and the Sephardi pronunciation of the Hebrew.
(2) Greater pomp and "dignity" in synagogue ceremonies, including weddings, funerals, and confirmations (*initiations religieuses*).
(3) The suppression of the *piyyutim* and of any prayers that might be considered incompatible with the Jews' civil and political position in France ("our only homeland").
(4) The introduction of the organ for all religious and national celebrations in the synagogues of France.

(5) The improvement of the role of women in the synagogue by adopting a synagogue ceremony to celebrate the birth of a girl, by including the girls in the ceremonies of *initiation religieuse,* and by allowing women to participate in public prayer in the synagogue.

(6) The reform of the circumcision operation in the light of modern scientific knowledge.

(7) The adoption of the following definition of a Jew: any individual born of a Jewish father or mother, and claiming to be a Jew himself.

(8) Several changes in the program of the rabbinic school: the addition of courses in theology, Biblical exegesis, religious controversy, civil and political law; the substitution of French for German as the language of instruction in the courses where German is still used; the substitution of the Sephardi for the Ashkenazi pronunciation of the Hebrew.

(9) The redefinition of the rabbi's duties to include charity as well as instruction. Charitable duties would include visits to the sick, to the bereaved, and to prisoners, and encouraging Jews to a love of study and of work.[50]

The central consistory received a number of replies to the circular, but unfortunately we have not been able to locate all of them. Although Rabbis Nordmann of Hegenheim and Dreyfus of Mulhouse, as well as Grand Rabbi Ennery of Paris, all stated their views on the central consistory program, their answers are missing from the archives. The Archives of the Jewish Theological Seminary in New York have acquired three documents that are replies to the nine points of reform. One is a statement of his views on the reforms by Rabbi Mayer Charleville of Dijon. The second is a petition against the reform program by members of the Strasbourg Jewish community. The third is a statement of his views on the nine questions by Bordeaux consistory lay member Benjamin Gradis.[51]

What interests us in the context of this chapter is not the issue of reform and the many opinions that were expressed on the nine points, but the concept of the publication of such a program and the attempt to give preference to a candidate who was amenable to its implementation. For this the consistory was sharply criticized by those who defended the rabbinate against lay domination. Gradis sent a circular of his own to all of the delegates who were to elect the grand rabbi. In it he emphasized that he would not recommend that any of the rabbis reply to the central consistory circular. He urged that they maintain the official silence that their position permitted. Gradis chided the central consistory for deliberating on religious questions and arriving at a reform program in violation of Article 38 of the 1844 *ordonnance,* which required the consent of the grand rabbi in religious decisions. He claimed that the central consistory should have discussed these matters *after* the election and not before.[52]

In January 1847 the central consistory and the Paris consistory met in joint session to decide how to arrange the election of Ennery's successor to the post of Paris grand rabbi. A suggestion was made that they prepare a report on the candidates and present it to the *notables* who would participate in the elections, but the proposal was rejected at that time, on the grounds that it was too official and might excite opposition. Instead, the individual consistory members were to speak out at a "preparatory" meeting of the *notables* prior to the election.[53] By March the consistories had discarded their cautious stance and decided to appoint a commission to prepare a program to submit to the candidates. (This was analogous to the procedure used the preceding year to select the central consistory grand rabbi.) However, the consistory members were not all in accord with this procedure; two of them, Halphen and Allegri, refused to participate, and a third, Olry Dupont, participated only with reluctance.[54]

The choice of grand rabbi remained suspended for several months while the procedural and ideological disputes raged. In June a commission to prepare the elections was appointed from the membership of the central and Paris consistories and the Paris college of *notables*. The commission met seven times, from June 24 to October 12.[55] The commission members debated whether their function was to influence the vote and whether the members should try to discourage certain candidates from running (those who "seem to have little chance of winning"). The commission resolved to use its influence to urge the election of the candidate that it preferred. Any member who might dissent from the majority opinion would be expected to keep this information to himself. Three screening devices were adopted: (1) a sermon in the synagogue, (2) written replies to some questions on the candidates' opinions of Judaism's current needs, and (3) oral replies to similar questions.[56]

Adolphe Franck, vice-president of the central consistory, was responsible for drawing up the questions to be submitted to the candidates for written replies. The questions were as follows:

(1) How can we reconcile love of country with messianic hopes, and our duty to the state with our religion?
(2) What is the position of the Jewish woman according to the Bible and the Tradition?
(3) What is the function ("mission") of the rabbi?[57]

Further questions were posed orally to the four candidates, who were invited to a meeting, two at a time. On September 13 Rabbis Dreyfus and Charleville were asked to reply orally to the following questions:

(1) Under the present circumstance of religious indifference that exists among the Jews, what would be the most effective way of bringing the youth back to the temples?

(2) What would be the best method of increasing Jewish fulfillment of religious duties?

(3) How much power would a synod have? Could it do more than an individual rabbi could do, working in his own community?

(4) What are the advantages of retaining Hebrew in the public prayers and religious instruction?[58]

Several weeks later the commission questioned Rabbis Isidor and Klein on the following points:

(1) What should we do about the increasing number of Jews who do not attend the temple? Should we abandon them to their lives of irreligion and lack of moral culture?

(2) What is the reason for the increasing abandonment of religious practice? Is it due to new ideas, real disbelief, or changes in conditions? What can be done to remedy the situation?

(3) Are all the customs (*minhagim*) equally obligatory? If not, how do we distinguish among them?[59]

Adolphe Franck analyzed the written replies and reported that Charleville's replies were the best, both in content and in style. Franck admitted Rabbi Klein's erudition but found that his orthodoxy was too extreme to permit Jews to be integrated into general French society ("la grande famille française"). Rabbi Dreyfus, Franck reported, had liberal ideas, but they were too general and weak and his style was not well developed. Rabbi Isidor was orthodox in his views on the validity of the Talmud, but he allowed great individual latitude to the rabbis, a factor, Franck said, that tempered Isidor's own severity.[60]

The candidates' replies to the oral questions did not change anyone's opinion. On October 12 the commission voted to support Charleville for the post by a vote of seven to five. Of the five dissenters, two (G. Weil and S. Munk) favored Dreyfus because he was more liberal and three (Ennery, Sciama, and Allegri) favored Isidor because he was more conservative.[61]

The *notables,* under the leadership of Crémieux, refused to accept the commission's findings, or even to listen to its report. In a turbulent protest move, it disrupted and walked out of the preparatory meeting called at the beginning of November to announce the commission's preference for Rabbi Charleville. It is not clear whether the *notables'* protest and subsequent election of Isidor should be ascribed to conservative religious leanings and support of the rabbinate against the consistory's attempt to dictate religious views, or to resentment of the commission's attempts to direct the *notables* how to vote, or, again, to respect for Crémieux's leadership or liberal views.

The election of Isidor was a significant failure for the consistory, which had put much time into preparing the way for a liberalization of Judaism. It was now clear that French Judaism was not going to move quickly in the direction of reform and that the consistory could not be certain of its ability to manipulate the rabbinate. Yet it did not stop trying, and met with some success.

Several years later, in 1853, when Grand Rabbi Ennery died, the central consistory was determined to replace him with someone who would agree to implement reforms. Despite its failure with this method in 1847, the central consistory met to evaluate and rank the candidates, hoping thereby to influence the election.[62] We have no records of the proceedings of this preparatory meeting, but it resulted in the election of the relatively liberal Rabbi Salomon Ulmann of Nancy, in preference to the orthodox candidate, Solomon Klein. Ulmann went on to call the first French rabbinical conference, which ultimately paved the way for ceremonial reforms, such as the elimination of some *piyyutim* (liturgical poetry) and the installation of organs in some synagogues.

It is almost certain that the election of Rabbi Klein would have put a very different stamp on the face of French Judaism. Fierce conflict would undoubtedly have arisen between this very orthodox Rabbi and the reform-minded central consistory. During the decade that followed Klein's unsuccessful bid for the grand rabbinate, he became embroiled in bitter controversy with his departmental consistory in Colmar because of his insistence that orthodoxy had the right to develop freely and maintain its own independent institutions. Had Klein been in Paris rather than Colmar to fight this battle, the history of French Judaism might have been very different.

SUMMARY AND CONCLUSIONS

We have studied several aspects of the modernization of French Jewry, including demographic patterns, Jewish status under French law, and social, religious and institutional evolution. We have investigated these changes from the perspective of the consistory, whose own archives and whose correspondence preserved in government archives have been the major sources of documentation for the study. An emphasis on the consistory is natural. It was the single most comprehensive French Jewish institution of the nineteenth century, it interacted with most of the other Jewish institutions, and it was involved directly or indirectly in almost all the historical developments affecting French Jewry. Although the communities retained some traditional institutions, the development of the consistory was accompanied by a major break with tradition. Judaism in France today reflects the impact of this clash between traditional European Judaism and the novel reformist and integrationist attitude of the consistory.

Because the Jewish consistory of France has never before been the subject of a thorough systematic study, we have described and analyzed consistory structure and action, in order to present the documentation necessary to an evaluation of its effects, merits, and weaknesses. After summarizing our findings we will draw some conclusions about the nature of the consistory and its significance as a new institution in Judaism.

A. Demographical Aspects

After the Revolution the Jews did not spread throughout the country and achieve geographic integration. They remained primarily in the departments where they had been living, although many moved into the larger towns and cities. Several attempts to encourage a movement of Jews toward agriculture were unsuccessful. The Jewish rate of urbanization was much higher than general rates because the Jews led an urban existence even prior to the Revolution. Not residents of the largest cities and towns, they nevertheless held urban-type jobs, mainly in commerce. When the emancipation granted them freedom of movement, they gravitated toward larger centers, where business opportunities were better. In addition to a movement into the cities of Alsace-Lorraine (Colmar, Stras-bourg, Metz etc.), there was a distinct shift of Jewish popula-tion toward Paris. In 1808 79 percent of the Jewish population lived in Alsace-Lorraine and 6 percent in Paris; by 1861 only 57 percent lived in Alsace-Lorraine, while 26 percent lived in Paris (only 5 percent of the general French population lived in Paris in 1861).

Rates of Jewish density varied considerably from one area to another. We have shown that density was highest in the eastern provinces. With the exception of Bordeaux, the only towns with a density of Jewish population greater than 2 per-cent (and up to 8 percent) were located in Alsace-Lorraine. Perhaps the persistent conservatism of the Jewish population of Bordeaux and Alsace-Lorraine is linked in part to this factor of higher ratios of Jews to general population.[1]

Changes in the occupational distribution of the Jewish popu-lation came slowly. Some Jews entered the liberal professions and others became craftsmen, but the majority retained com-mercial occupations. Within commerce there was gradual im-provement in the level of business carried on and in the income earned. We have estimated on the basis of several different sources that in the middle of the century, varying with the location, 42 to 55 percent of the Jews were engaged in trade and 10 to 30 percent in manufacture of goods, 10 to 17 percent were *capitalistes,* 7 to 10 percent were professionals, and 0 to 3.5 percent chose military service. Some Jews achieved public office as mayors, municipal councillors, or members of cham-bers of commerce.

Poverty remained a persistent problem in the Jewish com-munities. Until at least 1870 more than 50 percent of the Parisian Jewish burials were at public expense; a Jewish leader noted in 1868 that only one half of the Alsatian Jewish popula-tion of 35,000 to 40,000 had a secure livelihood. The social distinctions between the large mass of the poor and the elite of the consistory leadership, aggravated by the steep prices of temple seats, weddings, *kashrut* control, etc., created ill will to-ward the consistory institutions and the development of a set of parallel, non-consistory institutions.

Analysis of the demographical pattern thus demonstrates that the emancipation did not bring about the expected and hoped-for rapid socioeconomic improvement and acculturation of the Jewish population, and with these, an absorption into the gen-eral French society. One of the goals in establishing the consis-tory had been to promote that process.

B. The Functioning of the Consistory

The consistory was a mixed lay-rabbinic body, exercising both civil and religious authority, vested by state law with the competence to govern all French Jewish communities and institutions through a system of hierarchical administration. Although their control over the various communities of their districts was at first weak, by 1840 the consistories began to develop efficient patterns of operating through administrative networks and systems of inspection and control. The drafting of more precise legislation (leading to the *ordonnance* of 1844) helped all the consistories to clarify their view of themselves as administrative supervisors over the entire range of French Jewish institutions. Despite aggressive consistory behavior, however, there were some groups and even entire communities that succeeded in escaping consistory control.

Through a series of laws which the consistories, especially the central consistory, urged upon the government, the consistory structure underwent several changes and became increasingly hierarchical, centralized, and lay-dominated. The major laws of 1844 and 1862 defined the consistory until, and even largely beyond, the 1905 law of separation of church and state. There were disputes over each bill, and the major issues that caused contention were the introduction of hierarchy into the rabbinate, the centralization of power in the hands of the central consistory, limitation of suffrage to the wealthy or to those who contributed to consistory institutions, and the problem of the enforceability of the laws guaranteeing certain prerogatives to the consistories.

In describing the consistory's structure and methods of functioning, we have emphasized the lack of representation of the masses in the electorate (except for a brief period during the 1850's). Prior to 1844 almost all the electors (*notables*) were wealthy businessmen, and only an occasional lawyer, government functionary, or physician made his way onto the list. Even after the 1844 *ordonnance* had enlarged the electorate, members of the liberal professions were not given suffrage unless their wealth was sufficient to place them on the general election lists. About 70 to 80 percent of the *notabilité* continued to be chosen from among the businessmen. Since the composition of the *notabilité* had not significantly changed, its outlook remained stable, and the views it expressed were mildly liberal in regard to religion and integrationist socially and economically. Only when universal suffrage was introduced in 1849 did the views of the electorate change, and orthodoxy and traditionalism were reflected in the 1850 elections. The consistory responded by devising new laws which rescinded the communities' right to choose their own rabbis. (The elections of consistory members, which remained in the hands of the people until 1862, were manipulated by the consistories, especially through consistory-endorsed slates and through pamphlets distributed by the consistories.) Many members of the *notabilité* were re-elected repeatedly, and members of the same families were often chosen in hereditary fashion.

The consistory members, also, were mainly businessmen.

They were generally non-observant, although not assimilated. Like the *notables,* they, too, were re-elected repeatedly, and passed their offices on to other members of their families. They were politically conservative, and believed in achieving their goals through constituted authority rather than in resorting to publicity. A few members of the liberal professions and some academicians began to be elected to the consistory by the middle of the century.

The consistories, as was shown, functioned in six main areas, three of which were specifically prescribed by the initial legislation, and three of which were the result of consistory initiative after its original conception. In the first category we have discerned the administrative, "regenerative," and police duties of the consistories. The first task, administration, occupied most (often about two thirds) of the consistories' time. The second, regeneration, encouraged secular education, trained Jews for "useful" occupations, and urged "moral" and social improvement through the prohibition of begging and the elimination of poverty. In order to achieve this second goal, the consistories discouraged foreign poor from entering France, and the Strasbourg consistory exported some of its poor to America.[2]

The third prescribed function was policing the Jews. Although the most objectionable of the police tasks were dropped after the Empire, the consistory continued to be used by the government for occasional police purposes and as an instrument to effect the government's political aims.

The second category—the three functions adopted voluntarily by the consistories—included protection of Jewish interests, development of a monopoly on French Judaism, and modernization of the rabbinate. Not a required function of the consistory, protection of Jews and of Jewish interests was naturally expected of the consistory by the Jewish population. Although consistory leaders sometimes embraced the causes referred to them, they did not do so automatically, nor with much enthusiasm. The cases they chose either were certain to win government support or threatened Jewish security so seriously that they could not be ignored. The central consistory generally had to be prodded by the departmental consistories or by individuals before it acted, and when it did, it eschewed publicity in favor of behind-the-scenes political maneuvering. Even in the campaign to eliminate the special Jewish oath (*More Judaïco*) the central consistory did not take the initiative. Although it was informed by the Nancy consistory about the case of Rabbi Lazard Isidor of Phalsbourg, who was being prosecuted for refusal to administer the oath, the central consistory refused its support, preferring to await the outcome of the case.

The second task assumed voluntarily by the consistories—the creation of a monopoly on French Jewish institutions—was undertaken primarily for financial reasons. It tried to bring into consistory treasuries the funds that would otherwise have entered the coffers of *minyanim* and mutual aid societies.

The third attribution voluntarily assumed was the development of a modernized rabbinate. The consistories tried to ensure that the rabbis had a tolerable level of French culture, could preach sermons in French, and would perform pastoral duties similar to those of the Christian clergy. They wanted rabbis to visit hospitals and prisons, give talks at weddings and funerals, and represent Judaism at public ceremonies or on committees, alongside the Christian clergy. Although the model for this new kind of rabbi was mainly the priest or minister, the Sephardi rabbinate served as an additional model because its authority had been narrowed to a modern religious scope during the previous century. In addition to redefinition of functions, the nineteenth-century rabbis underwent a diminution of prestige. That loss appears to be the result of two factors: skepticism regarding the rabbinic tradition had already developed in the Ashkenazi communities during the second half of the eighteenth century, and secular professional opportunities had opened up to Jews after the Revolution.

The new rabbis were not men of advanced education; it was rare for them to acquire a thorough secondary school education, and university studies were not available to them until about 1880. Rabbinic posts did not pay well, and it is clear from the structure of the *école rabbinique* that the profession was designed to attract men of comparatively low socioeconomic background, for whom the career of rabbi represented an improvement in status.

If the rabbis did not have a good secular education, they were equally deficient in their knowledge of traditional Jewish sources. Because the consistory and the government insisted upon some years of public secondary education prior to enrollment in the rabbinic school, the rabbinic students could not study at Jewish preparatory schools, and they consequently entered the *école rabbinique* unprepared for advanced work. For these reasons they failed to develop into serious scholars, either as Talmudists, or as modern theologians. They produced very little scholarship—only some Bible translations, prayer translations and compendia of prayers, and outlines of Judaism and of Jewish history for adults and children. The original research, the publication, and the study of medieval rabbinic sources were done by Christian and Jewish scholars at the universities.

Within the rabbinate a strict hierarchy was instituted, which gave the chief rabbis the right of guiding and admonishing the communal rabbis and of ordering which ceremonial procedures were to be followed. As we have seen, the hierarchy was implicit in the consistory system from the beginning, for it had been one of Napoleon's chief purposes to establish a system of supervision and control of the rabbis. In 1844 the hierarchy was fully defined by law, and by about 1850 it was generally, though not unanimously, accepted by the rabbis.

The supervisory power of the laity over the rabbinate was also anticipated when the consistory system was instituted. Thus lay preponderance was prescribed in all but the central consistory. After a brief initial period the central consistory, too, became a predominantly lay board, although this transformation was resisted by almost all the consistories, with the single exception of Paris. The dominance of the laity in the consistories became such an established fact that it was common usage to contrast the consistory with the rabbinate, in which phrase "consistory" referred only to the lay members. The mixed nature of the consistory as initially conceived had been entirely forgotten, and it was now argued whether the duties of the consistory were essentially religious or essentially administrative.[3]

C. The Nature of the Consistory

Although liberal ideology would have required that the consistories be essentially religious bodies—religion in the modern Western narrow sense of the term being the only permissible differentiation between Jews and other Frenchmen—the consistories were, in fact, both religious and civil administrations. The consistory had been established largely for policing purposes, and even after the Empire, when consistories no longer registered Jews, provided lists of conscripts, or denounced those without a livelihood, the consistories tended to retain a civil character. They were involved, for example, with the drafting and interpretation of state laws governing Jewish organization; they worked through the police and courts to collect taxes and, later, dues (*cotisation*); and they imposed financial penalties on offenders. Moreover, the government occasionally made use of the consistories to police the schools and control political elections. We have already seen that some rabbis separated their religious functions from the consistories' administrative functions.

It is clear, both from the legislation[4] and from actual practice, that the consistory had religious functions and authority. During the first few years of consistory existence it was debated whether the consistories could apply religious penalties in order to enforce their authority. The formula that generally prevailed was that they could not invoke bans or excommunications but could withhold synagogue honors. In fact, however, the consistories exceeded this restriction. There were cases in which Jews were denied access to a synagogue or to the services of a burial society—almost tantamount to a ban.

On the other hand, even the withholding of religious honors

was not unambiguously condoned by the central consistory. Although in 1832 the central consistory had approved of such penalties, and in June 1837 it had confirmed the Colmar consistory's right to apply "des peines spirituelles,"[5] two months later it ruled that Colmar could not use religious penalties to enforce a plan for the elimination of poverty.[6]

For various reasons of expediency some people denied that the consistory was a religious body. Thus in 1843 Benjamin Gradis of Bordeaux protested that the central consistory's attempt to reform the circumcision ritual tended to *transform* the consistory into a religious authority. In 1861, in response to complaints from orthodox Jews that the government had interfered in the consistory elections ("a purely religious matter"), a regional governor insisted that the consistory was not a religious authority: "L'élection des membres du consistoire n'a pas un caractère religieux mais plutôt civil, car le consistoire ne peut toucher aux matières rituelles, mais qu'il s'occupe surtout des règlements des [illegible] temporels des communautés israélites."[7] After the polemics have been discounted, it is clear that the consistory combined both religious and civil aspects.

In some ways the consistories resembled their predecessors, the government of the traditional "autonomous" communities. All of their authority stemmed from the government, for ultimate control had always rested with the general authorities. Traditionally, communal constitutions were subject to the approval of the government, which specified the extent and limit of Jewish jurisdiction and its relationship to the general juridical system. Tax collection was also enforced by the authorities, who protected the official community by prohibiting rival organizations. Reciprocally, the primary task of Jewish leaders was to carry out the orders of the local noblemen. In a similar way, in the nineteenth century all consistory elections were subject to the approval of the government. Successful candidates took oaths of fidelity and were named to their posts by official acts of the ministry.

In several additional ways the consistories were similar to traditional Jewish community administrations. Even the existence of a hierarchy, which is often cited as a new phenomenon in Jewish communal structure, had some precedent in the *superkehillot*. Although these were usually voluntary associations, the eighteenth-century provincial-wide organization of Alsace[8] was already a compulsory institution. Its authority was enforced by the government, and it had the right to confirm all local choices of Jewish leaders. By the end of the century there were several rabbis in Alsace who had authority even over the rabbis of their districts. The *superkehillot* were frequently asked (as were the consistories later) to intervene to protect individuals or local communities threatened or falsely accused. "For obvious reasons the words of *medina* [*superkehilla*] representatives carried greater weight than those of local functionaries."[9]

The leadership of the Jewish communities had been oligarchical even in preconsistory times. Nowhere in the sixteenth to eighteenth centuries had direct elections by universal suffrage been the practice. In France an oligarchy had been formally instituted in Bayonne and Bordeaux and written into their constitutions. In Metz it was common for a *parnass* to hold office for life and for children of the *parnassim* to inherit the office. The same trends have been seen in the nineteenth-century consistory.

Despite these similarities, however, the status of the French Jewish communities in the nineteenth century was diminished in comparison with that of the traditional communities. As a result of the Emancipation and the loss of autonomy, some aspects of communal organization, which had previously been of solely Jewish concern, became public matters. Thus, the cemeteries, whose ownership by the Jewish community was a traditional right, now passed into public control. This fact made it difficult to enforce Jewish burial law. Also as a result of the Emancipation, the authorities began regulating what rabbis may teach. This was achieved by indoctrination, oaths, laws and a prohibition against convening synods or promulgating new religious decisions without the government's authorization.

With the loss of communal autonomy, Jewish leaders lost the tight control they had once exercised on all aspects of the behavior of the community's members. Sumptuary laws regarding behavior and dress were no longer written, and lay religious leaders found it difficult to enforce standards of behavior even among community employees. Thus Grand Rabbi Ennery was unable to stop the choir leader, Jacques Offenbach, from playing in theaters on Friday evenings,[10] and the central consistory could not convince Grand Rabbi Deutz to renounce his son after the latter had betrayed the Duchess de Berry to Louis-Philippe's forces. The controls still available to community leaders when they were dissatisfied with members' behavior usually involved firing or ignoring the individuals. Thus the Strasbourg consistory fired its secretary when he failed to circumcise his son; the central consistory fired its secretary, Simon Bloch, who publicly disagreed with the consistory's reformist attitude; Grand Rabbi Deutz was not invited to attend central consistory meetings for two years following the Duchess de Berry affair. The difference between the old and the new forms of control was that the new tended toward dissolution of the community, while the old helped to maintain its cohesiveness.

The most serious problem the communities faced after the abrogation of communal autonomy was the loss of the power to tax. This power was temporarily prolonged by the Napoleonic regime, which did not wish to accord public support to Judaism. However, even during the period when the communities could levy taxes (1809–31), Jewish institutions suffered financial difficulties. Only certain expenses (temple, rabbi, schools) could be charged to the taxes; the central consistory had ruled in 1810 that the communities could not collect a tax for charity. After

1831 the state assumed (some) Jewish cultic expenses and the consistories were denied all rights of taxation, which resulted in increased difficulty for the Jewish institutions not funded by the government. The consistories had no way to enforce contributions in order to finance Jewish schools which had previously been supported by taxation, to repay the debts incurred in the construction of large new temple buildings, or to supplement the rabbis' small state salaries. Apart from meager voluntary contributions, the schools had no steady funding until they were "communalized," which occurred very late in some areas (especially in Haut-Rhin). The ability to maintain quality institutions had depended upon a solid tax structure.[11]

The establishment of the consistory system was the Jewish response to the Napoleonic centralization of civil bureaucracy and church administration. A hierarchical system with pretensions to total monopoly on Judaism could not have occurred prior to the Napoleonic conception of the state, and its history naturally paralleled general developments in French society. Progressive centralization in Paris, anticlericalism, lay domination, arguments over universal suffrage, manipulations of elections—all took place in the general, as well as the Jewish, arena. There is a parallel between the factions in the general Church–State debates and those within the Jewish community. The "Gallicans," the French Catholic higher ecclesiastical officers established by Napoleon's Concordat with the Pope, were appointed by the state and swore allegiance to the government, and it was in their interest to foster cooperation between church and state. In Judaism their parallel was the consistory. The "Ultramontanes" (under the inspiration of royalist-papist leaders Louis de Bonald and Joseph de Maistre) demanded separation of church and state. Their attempts to free themselves of state control resemble the efforts of the orthodox Jews to be rid of consistory restrictions. Both groups were the traditionalists of their cults, although the orthodox Jews had no loyalty to a foreign hierarchical figure like the Pope. Yet in its repeated attempts to convince the government to suppress the *minyanim,* the consistory played on the same fears that the state harbored concerning papists, and claimed that private prayer meetings could be politically dangerous. Lastly, the ideology of the "liberal Catholics," who represented the interests of the lower clergy against all hierarchical direction, paralleled that of the communal rabbis as expressed in *Le Lien d'Israél,* the journal begun in 1855 by Rabbi Samuel Dreyfus of Mulhouse, and in several conferences of communal rabbis in the eastern provinces.

D. Consistory Aims and Achievements

The consistory had two fundamental purposes, both of which were implicit in its conception and which were, to an extent, contradictory: to preserve Judaism and to integrate the Jews into French society. It appears to the modern researcher that those contemporary critics were correct who accused the consistory of valuing integration more than the maintenance of the traditional values of Judaism.

The consistory members disagreed among themselves on the extent to which integration was compatible with the maintenance of Jewish differences, separate institutions, and preservation of specific ethnic historical consciousness. The majority of the leaders opposed, or were at best indifferent to, the establishment of particularist institutions, such as the Jewish press, Jewish schools, a Jewish publication society, and a network of Jewish libraries. They rejected the use of international Jewish political pressure, and even refused to help gather Jewish statistics for government use, an exercise that they feared might imply a distinction between Jews and other Frenchmen. In order to minimize the barriers to acceptance and shield Jews and Judaism from the public eye, most consistory members were ready to accept compromises not only with Judaism, but even with the liberal principle that others saw as the ultimate basis of Jewish security: the right to be different.

This position was criticized by staunch liberals, such as Adolphe Crémieux, who insisted that the political principles of the *nouveau régime* guaranteed the Jews' right to be different. On the other hand, they fought to secularize all areas of public life and to banish all religious references from courtrooms, oaths, etc., and they denied that the government had the right to distinguish among its citizens on the basis of religion. They claimed that practices such as a Jewish oath, even an "inoffensive" one, or taxing Jews for the payment of pre-revolutionary communal debts, violated the notion of equality before the law.

The majority of the consistory leadership feared that protests would antagonize public opinion, and preferred to cooperate prudently with the government. For this reason the consistory refrained from any political stance, but pledged its loyalty to each successive regime. Duly constituted government was its guarantee of stability.

While fostering integration, the consistories had yet to maintain Judaism, whether in its old form or some new form. A major impetus for the establishment of the consistory had been the deterioration of Jewish institutions following the Revolution. The Jewish leaders who requested state aid in reorganizing the communities had anticipated that the consistory would provide stability and security for the rebuilding and maintenance of Jewish institutions.

Did the consistory succeed in either of its missions—acculturating the Jews or preserving Judaism? In regard to the first, we must ask ourselves whether there would have been any appreciable difference in the rate of integration and absorption of the French Jews if community structures had been allowed to re-emerge individually and locally without the help of the government and the wealthy and ambitious Parisian Jews. We are forced to conclude that the existence of the consistory was not decisive in the work of acculturation and economic integration, because much of the impetus and groundwork for instituting schools and apprenticeship programs came from private individuals whose initiative might have been even greater in the absence of a central authority to which they could look expectantly for leadership and aid. Repressive measures—such as the consistory's threat to withhold financial assistance from poor families whose children did not attend schools or vocational training programs—do not appear to have made any difference in the rate of acculturation. What had a greater effect than either private or consistory efforts to encourage education was the improved and enlarged system of public primary schools instituted after 1833 by the government.

As for the second mission—preserving Judaism—the consistories re-established order in the Jewish communities, and offered confidence and optimism to the demoralized communities. The quasi-official status of the consistory system made state funding possible, although French Judaism would have survived without state funds. The communities, thrown back on their own resources, would probably have found the necessary funds to meet their needs, as traditional communities—no matter how extreme their poverty—had always done. Without the consistory, institutions would have developed differently. Smaller, old-fashioned chapels would have predominated, rather than the imposing modern edifices constructed in nineteenth-century France. The continued survival of the independent *minyanim* and mutual aid societies, despite consistory pressure against them, is evidence that the people had the will and the ability to maintain Judaism and its traditional institutions. Charity certainly would have been organized differently, on a more personal and traditional basis, rather than through the doles of the modern Jewish charity boards, which offered prestigious office to socially mobile Jews hoping for eventual election to consistory posts. Inasmuch as poor Jewish communities always maintained a multiplicity of charitable institutions, and Jews in Alsace had to be pressured by the consistory before they abandoned some of their traditional charitable practices, it is likely that in this area also traditional Jewish initiative would not have failed to manifest itself.

As a unifying force the consistory only partially succeeded. Although the country's many Jewish communities were brought together in a single administrative unit, the various regions retained a strong sense of individuality. Several abortive attempts were made by the central and Paris consistories to achieve a *rite français*, through the fusion of Sephardi and Ashkenazi rites. Yet a certain amount of homogeneity in ceremonial practices eventually evolved, because the consistories gradually began to prescribe the chants and ceremonies to be used in all the synagogues of their districts. The practices of the larger synagogues provided models for imitation, such as the confirmation ceremony and the use of the organ.

Was the hierarchical and centralized control of Judaism by the consistory a factor which prevented Reform Judaism from taking root in France? It is true that consistory regulations prevented local initiative and experimentation. The law required ceremonial changes to be approved by the grand rabbi, prohibited rabbis from preaching new doctrines without the permission of the grand rabbi and the government, and prevented the free establishment of religious institutions. Theoretically, denominationalism within Judaism (as it occurred in America) could not take place within consistory-controlled Judaism. However, dissidents (generally orthodox) who chose to establish independent Jewish institutions often succeeded in escaping consistory control. The courts repeatedly refused to grant the consistories the benefit of penal sanctions to enforce the powers granted to them by the laws. We must therefore remember that in France there were other factors besides the hierarchy which prevented reform from developing.[12]

Perhaps the most important accomplishment of the consistory, especially in the early years, was to prevent the leadership class from assimilating; many educated and enlightened Jews retained their identity with Judaism because they were provided with community offices. Although Jews of the highest socioeconomic class moved out of Jewish neighborhoods, stopped going to the synagogue, and began to socialize with Gentiles, they remained Jewish through their mission of "civilizing" their poor coreligionists and reassuring the government that Jews made good citizens. As the official spokesman for the Jews on the one hand and the representative of the government to the Jewish people on the other, the consistory served two essential purposes: it guaranteed to the state that the Jews were trustworthy and patriotic citizens, and it afforded the Jewish population a sense of security as a recognized religious group.

APPENDIX A

DEMOGRAPHICAL DATA:
POPULATION TABLES AND LISTS
OF OCCUPATIONS

TABLE A-1

French-Jewish Population, 1808–1861

Date	Jewish Population	Comments on Source
1808	46,280	Decree of December 11, establishing the consistories.
1815	46,863	Author, based on Posener, "Les juifs sous le premier empire, les statistiques generales," *REJ*, 93 (1932), 197. (Posener neglected to subtract the 303 Jews of Alpes Maritimes—lost to France in 1815.)
1831	60,000	A.N. F^{19} 11016 and 11024 (source unknown).
1831	73,000	Central consistory estimate (Anchel, *Frais*, p. 43).
1831	c. 70,000	Author.
1841	70,324	Consistory figures, A.N. F^{19} 11024 (low).
1845	85,910	Consistory figures, A.N. F^{19} 11016, and *U.I.*, 5 (1849), 40.
1851	73,975	General census, *Statistique de la France*, 2ème series, tome 2, p. xxv (low).
1853	61,239	A.N. F^{19} 11024, marked "census of 1853" (we have not been able to determine the source of this figure; low).
1853	88,331	Consistory figures, A.N. F^{19} 11024. (Because of an error of tabulation, their total is 88,376.)
1853	89,220	Author, using the consistory figures as a basis, and filling the gaps by using the 1851 general census (for the small Jewish population in 34 departments).
1861	79,964	General census, *Statistique de la France*, 2ème series, tome 13 (low).
1861	92,381	Consistory figures, A.N. F^{19*} 1821.
1861	95,881	Author, based on the above two sets of figures.

TABLE A-2
Jewish Population by Department, 1808–1861

Department	1808, Decree of Dec. 11, 1808	1808, Posener[a]	1841, Consistory Figures[b]	1851, General Census[c]	1853, Consistory Figures[d]	1853, Author[e]	1861, Consistory Figures[f]	1861, General Census[g]	1861, Author[h]
Ain			0	18		18		3	3
Aisne	5	5	0	67	37	67		52	52
Allier			0	12		12		4	4
Alpes (Basses)			0	6		6		1	1
Alpes (Hautes)				6		6		8	8
Alpes-Maritimes							i	321	321
Ardèche				4		4		10	10
Ardennes	11	115	96	73	81	81	j	119	119
Ariège				2		2	k	0	0
Aube			0	21		21		31	31
Aude	4	4	0	18		18	k	16	16

a Posener, "Les juifs sous le premier empire, les statistiques generales," REJ, 93 (1932), 197.
b Response to government circular of October 3, 1840, which ordered a census. In A.N., F19 11024.
c J. Ch. M. Boudin, Traité de Geographie et de Statistique Medicale, Vol. 2 (Paris, 1857), pp. 133–134.
d A.N., F19 11024. This document lists the Jewish populations by commune and some rural and floating populations are sometimes added into the totals after the list by commune.
e Based on 1851 general census and 1853 consistory figures.
f A.N., F19* 1821.
g Statistique de la France, Series 2, Vol. 13.
h Based on consistory and census figures of the same year.
i Not yet counted into population figures.
j Included in Moselle figure.
k See footnote b on page 323.

TABLE A-2 (Continued)

Department	1808, Decree of Dec. 11, 1808	1808, Poséner	1841, Consistory Figures	1851, General Census	1853, Consistory Figures	1853, Author	1861, Consistory Figures	1861, General Census	1861, Author
Aveyron			0	1		1		0	0
Bouches-du-Rhône	942	942	1462	1371	1944	1944	a	2532	2532
Calvados			0	44		44		26	26
Cantal			0	2		2		5	5
Charente	8	8	0	18	20	20		19	19
Charente-Inférieure	70	70	39	80	130	130		51	51
Cher			19	15		15		13	13
Corrèze			0	4		4		5	5
Corse			0	4		4		9	9
Côte-d'Or	251	251	312	364	558	558	393	407	407
Côtes-du-Nord			0	1		1		2	2
Creuse				5		5		9	9
Dordogne	1	1	0	8		8		8	8
Doubs	86	86	619	745	698	745	756	842	842
Drôme			0	63	14	63		34	34
Eure			0	6		6		5	5
Eure-et-Loir			2	8		8		21	21
Finistère	11	11	0	80	42	80	26	38	38
Gard	425	425	477	494	499	499	375 b	375	375
Garonne (Haute)	107	107	404	104	215	215		394	394
Gers			0	7		7		4	4
Gironde	2131	2131	3169	2454	3687	3687	3000 c	2253	3000
Hérault	141	141	112	158	128	158	d	171	171
Ille-et-Vilaine	11	11	0	9	3	9	7	19	19
Indre			0	6		6		4	4
Indre-et-Loir			0	35	31	35	48	52	52
Isère	4	4	0	20		20		24	24

a The document gives only a total Jewish population for Bouches-du-Rhône, Var, and Hérault of 2200.
b See footnote b on page 323.
c Estimate, but probably not high. Cf. Szajkowski, Jews and the French Revolutions, p. 87, who points out that in 1861 there were 2771 Jews in chefs-lieux of Gironde.
d See Bouches-du-Rhône.

TABLE A-2 (Continued)

Department	1808, Decree of Dec. 11, 1808	1808, Posener	1841, Consistory Figures	1851, General Census	1853, Consistory Figures	1853, Author	1861, Consistory Figures	1861, General Census	1861, Author
Jura			0	59		59		50	50
Landes	1198	1198	1239	836	1171	1171	a	96[b]	96
Loir-et-Cher	10	10	0	9	5	9		1	1
Loire			40	29	119	119	300[c]	167	300
Loire (Haute)			0	2		2		0	0
Loire-Inférieure	11	11	154	45	148	148	159	133	159
Loiret	7	7	57	62	64	64	56	81	81
Lot			0	0		0		0	0
Lot-et-Garonne			0	22	20	22		16	16
Lozère			0	1		1		0	0
Maine-et-Loire			0	23	20	23	14	20	20
Manche			0	9		9		60	60
Marne	2	2	335	415	397	415	401	446	446
Marne (Haute)	41	41	284	309	332	332	127	301	301
Mayenne			0	0	0	0		7	7
Meurthe	3289	3544	5332	5675	6029	6029	5934	5116	5934
Meuse	405	405	662	699	666[d]	699	993	769	993
Morbihan			0	20	13	20	10	15	15

aSee footnote b on page 323.
bSt. Esprit was annexed to Bayonne in 1857, and its Jewish population therefore "moved" from Landes to Basses-Pyrénées.
cAll 300 reported were in St. Etienne (Metz consistory district), which had a salaried rabbi from 1860 on.
dPlus Bar-le-duc (figure left out of source).

TABLE A-2 (*Continued*)

Department	1808, Decree of Dec. 11, 1808	1808, Posener	1841, Consistory Figures	1851, General Census	1853, Consistory Figures	1853, Author	1861, Consistory Figures	1861, General Census	1861, Author
Moselle	6506	6506	8081	7768	7994	7994	7853ᵃ	7250	7734ᵇ
Nièvre			0	10		10		26	26
Nord	166	166	226	271	315	315	437	584	584
Oise			0	44		44		49	49
Orne			0	6		6		12	12
Pas-de-Calais	63	63	76	157	92	157	90	140	140
Puy-de-Dôme	38	38	80	85	120	120	350ᶜ	82	350
Pyrénées (Basses)	127	127	341	394	452	452	d	1197ᵉ	1197
Pyrénées (Hautes)			32	16	36	36	d	22	22
Pyrénées-Orientales			0	21		21	d	28	28
Rhin (Bas)	16,155	16,155	20,749	20,935	22,806	22,806	20,682	20,936	20,936
Rhin (Haut)	9915	9915	14,316	14,882	16,547	16,547	16,719	14,062	16,719
Rhône	67	195	762	458	1107	1107	1100ᶠ	967	1100
Saône (Haute)	5	5	409ᵍ	536	492	536		616	616

aIncludes (119?) Jews of Ardennes.
bThis figure is the 1861 consistory figure minus the 119 Jews of Ardennes.
cAn estimate by Bordeaux consistory for Clermont Ferrand and environs.
dSee footnote b on page 323.
eThe great increase is due to the annexation of St. Esprit by Bayonne.
fEstimate by Lyon consistory; reasonable.
gIn 1838 there were 167. Préfet, Haute-Saône, to Préfet, Haut-Rhin, April 20 and May 23, 1838, in A.D. Haut-Rhin, 1 V 89.

TABLE A-2 (*Continued*)

Department	1808, Decree of Dec. 11, 1808	1808, Posener	1841, Consistory Figures	1851, General Census	1853, Consistory Figures	1853, Author	1861, Consistory Figures	1861, General Census	1861, Author
Saône-et-Loire			[a]	167	145	167	89[b]	96	96
Sarthe			0	12		12		4	4
Savoie	[c]	[c]	[c]	[c]	[c]	[c]		42	42
Savoie (Haute)	[c]	[c]	[c]	[c]	[c]	[c]		0	0
Seine	2733	2733	8000	10,978	18,000[d]	18,000	25,000[e]	15,196	25,000
Seine-Inférieure	47	47	331	222	370	370	464	396	464
Seine-et-Marne	132	132	91	165	154	165	181	228	228
Seine-et-Oise	95	95	114	216	227	227	230	415	415
Sèvres (Deux)			0	7	25	25		2	2
Somme	14	14	17	36	30	36		81	81
Tarn			0	3	3	3		1	1
Tarn-et-Garonne			0	7	7	7		9	9
Var	14	14	0	79	35	79	[f]	67	67
Vaucluse	631	631	776	673	766	766	650	638	650
Vendée			0	1	1	1		11	11
Vienne			0	24	47	47		12	12

[a] No data; in 1838 there were 116. Préfet, Saône-et-Loire to Préfet, Haut-Rhin, April 26, 1838, in A.D. Haut-Rhin, 1 V 89.

[b] These 89 Jews were residents of Châlons (mistakenly reported in Haute-Saône).

[c] Not yet French.

[d] Paris consistory estimate; cf. Boudin, who claimed there were 16,512 Jews in 1848.

[e] Paris consistory estimate. Cf. Isidor Loeb, *Biographie d'Albert Cohn* (Paris, 1878), p. 28, who says there were 26,298 Parisian Jews in that year.

[f] See Bouches-du-Rhône.

TABLE A-2 *(Continued)*

Department	1808, Decree of Dec. 11, 1808	1808, Posener	1841, Consistory Figures	1851, General Census	1853, Consistory Figures	1853, Author	1861, Consistory Figures	1861, General Census	1861, Author
Vienne (Haute)	29	29	0	27	15	27		161	161
Vosges	345	441	1090	1194	1273	1273	1524	1428	1524
Yonne	27	27	19	33	12	33	13	41	41
Scattered throughout the St. Esprit-Bayonne District Bayonne[b]					200	200	2200[b]		447[a]
Total for France	46,280	46,863[c]	70,324	73,975	88,331[d]	89,220	92,381	79,964[e]	95,881

[a]The consistory figures of 1861 did not give a breakdown of the Bayonne consistory by department. Using 1861 general census figures for those departments, we get a total of only 1753. The figure of 447 is the difference between the Bayonne consistory estimate and the census figure.

[b]The consistory figure of 1861 for the Bayonne consistory is not broken down by the seven departments, but represents the total of these departments. The seven departments are Landes, Basses-Pyrénées, Hautes-Pyrénées, Pyrénées-Orientales, Aude, Ariège, Haute-Garonne.

[c]Posener gives a total of 47,166 because he includes 303 Jews of Alpes-Maritimes (*not* in post-1815 boundaries).

[d]The consistory tables add up to 88,376, because of two errors: (1) they give a total for the Haut-Rhin of 17,183 instead of 17,184, and (2) they total Marseille consistory as 4658 instead of 4612.

[e]Low.

TABLE A-3
Relative Distribution of Jewish Population in the 33 Departments of Major Concentration, 1808–1861

Department	1808, Posener Total French Jewish Population: 46,863		1841, Consistory Figures Total French Jewish Population: 70,324		1851, General Census Total French Jewish Population: 73,975		1853, Author Total French Jewish Population: 88,331		1861, Consistory Figures Total French Jewish Population: 79,964		1861, Author Total French Jewish Population: 95,434[a]	
	Departmental Jewish Population	% of Total Jewish Population	Departmental Jewish Population	% of Total Jewish Population	Departmental Jewish Population	% of Total Jewish Population	Departmental Jewish Population	% of Total Jewish Population	Departmental Jewish Population	% of Total Jewish Population	Departmental Jewish Population	% of Total Jewish Population
Bas-Rhin	16,155	34.47	20,749	29.50	20,935	28.30	22,806	25.82	20,936	26.18	20,936	21.94
Haut-Rhin	9915	21.16	14,316	20.30	14,882	20.12	16,547	18.63	14,062	17.59	16,719	17.52
Meurthe	3544	7.56	5332	7.58	5675	7.65	6029	6.83	5116	6.40	5934	6.22
Meuse	405	.86	662	.94	699	.94	666	.75	769	.96	993	1.04
Moselle	6506	13.88	8081	11.49	7768	10.50	7994	9.05	7250	9.07	7734	8.10
Vosges	441	.94	1090	1.55	1194	1.61	1273	1.44	1428	1.79	1524	1.60
Seine	2733	5.83	8000	11.38	10,978	14.84	18,000	20.38	15,196	19.00	25,000	26.20
Bouche-du-Rhône	942	2.01	1462	2.08	1371	1.85	1944	2.20	2532	3.17	2532	2.65
Gironde	2131	4.55	3169	4.51	2454	3.32	3687	4.17	2253	2.82	3000	3.14
Landes	1198	2.56	1239	1.76	836	1.13	1171	1.33	96	.12	96	.10
Basses-Pyrénées	127	.27	341	.48	394	.53	452	.51	1197	1.50	1197	1.25
Ardennes	115	.25	96	.14	73	.10	81	.09	119	.15	119	.12
Cote d'Or	251	.54	312	.44	364	.49	558	.63	407	.51	407	.43
Gard	425	.91	477	.68	494	.67	499	.56	375	.47	375	.39
Haute-Garonne	107	.23	404	.57	104	.14	215	.24	394	.49	394	.41
Hérault	141	.30	112	.16	158	.21	128	.14	171	.21	171	.18
Nord	166	.35	226	.32	271	.37	315	.36	584	.73	584	.61
Rhône	195	.42	762	1.08	458	.62	1107	1.25	967	1.21	1100	1.15

aOmitting 447 individuals of unknown location in the Bayonne consistory.

TABLE A-3 (*Continued*)

Department	1808, Posener Total French Jewish Population: 46,863		1841, Consistory Figures Total French Jewish Population: 70,324		1851, General Census Total French Jewish Population: 73,975		1853, Author Total French Jewish Population: 88,331		1861, Consistory Figures Total French Jewish Population: 79,964		1861, Author Total French Jewish Population: 95,434	
	Departmental Jewish Population	% of Total Jewish Population	Departmental Jewish Population	% of Total Jewish Population	Departmental Jewish Population	% of Total Jewish Population	Departmental Jewish Population	% of Total Jewish Population	Departmental Jewish Population	% of Total Jewish Population	Departmental Jewish Population	% of Total Jewish Population
Seine-et-Oise	95	.20	114	.16	216	.29	227	.26	415	.52	415	.43
Seine-et-Marne	132	.28	91	.13	165	.22	154	.17	228	.29	228	.24
Vaucluse	631	1.35	776	1.10	673	.91	766	.87	638	.80	650	.68
Doubs	86	.18	619	.88	745	1.01	698	.79	842	1.05	842	.88
Loire-Inférieure	11	.02	154	.22	45	.06	148	.17	133	.17	159	.17
Marne	2	.004	335	.48	415	.56	397	.45	446	.56	446	.47
Haute-Marne	41	.04	284	.40	309	.42	332	.38	301	.38	301	.32
Seine-Inférieure	47	.10	331	.47	222	.30	370	.42	396	.50	464	.49
Haute-Saône	5	.01	409	.58	536	.72	492	.56	616	.77	616	.65
Loire			40	.06	29	.04	119	.13	167	.21	300	.31
Puy-de-Dome	38	.08	80	.11	85	.11	120	.14	82	.10	350	.37
Saône-et-Loire					167	.23	145	.16	96	.12	96	.10
Alpes-Maritimes	–		–		–		–		321	.40	321	.34
Pas-de-Calais	63	.13	76	.108	157	.21	92	.10	140	.18	140	.15
Haute-Vienne	29	.06	0	.00	27	.04	15	.02	161	.20	161	.17

TABLE A-4

Jewish Population Increase/Decrease in the
21 Departments of Original Concentration, 1808–1861

Department	Increase/Decrease
Ardennes	3.5
Bouches-du-Rhône	168.8
Côte d'Or	62.2
Gard	–11.8
Haute-Garonne	268.2
Gironde	40.8 (estimate)
Hérault	21.3
Landes et Basses- Pyrénées[a]	–2.4
Meurthe	67.4
Meuse	145.2
Moselle	18.9
Nord	251.8
Bas-Rhin	29.6
Haut-Rhin	68.6
Rhône	464.0 (estimate)
Seine	815.0 (estimate)
Seine-et-Marne	72.7
Seine-et-Oise	336.8
Vaucluse	3.0 (estimate)
Vosges	245.6

[a]Based on the combined population of these two departments because St.
  Esprit (suburb where the Jews of Bayonne lived) was in Landes in 1808
  but in Basses-Pyrénées when St. Esprit was joined to Bayonne in 1857.

TABLE A-5
Jewish Population by Department in the Bordeaux Consistory District, 1808–1861

Department	1808, Decree of Dec. 11, 1808	1808, Posener	1841, Consistory Figures	1851, General Census	1853, Consistory Figures	1853, Author	1861, Consistory Figures	1861, General Census	1861, Author
Arriège[a]			0						
Aude[a]	4	4	0						
Aveyron			0	1		1		0	0
Cantal			0	2		2		5	5
Charente	8	8	0	18	20	20		19	19
Charente-Inférieure	70	70	39	80	130	130		51	51
Corrèze			0	4		4		5	5
Creuse			0	5		5		9	9
Dordogne	1	1	0	8		8		8	8
Garonne (Haute)[a]	107	107	404						
Gers			0	7		7		4	4
Gironde	2131	2131	3169	2454	3687	3687	3000[b]	2253	3000
Landes[a]	1198	1198	1239						
Lot			0	0		0		0	0
Lot-et-Garonne			0	22	20	22		16	16
Puy-de-Dôme	38	38	80	85	120	120	350	82	350
Pyrénées (Basses)[a]	127	127	341						
Pyrénées (Hautes)[a]			32						
Pyrénées-Orientales[a]			0						
Sèvres (Deux)			0	7	25	25		2	2
Tarn			0	3		3		1	1
Tarn-et-Garonne			0	7		7		9	9
Vendée			0	1		1		11	11
Vienne			0	24	25	25		12	12
Vienne (Haute)	29	29	0	27	15	27		161	161
Total	3713	3713	5304	2755	4042	4094	3350	2648	3663

[a]Became part of the St. Esprit-Bayonne consistory in 1846.
[b]Estimate, but probably reliable.

TABLE A-6
Jewish Population by Department in the Colmar Consistory District, 1808–1861

Department	1808, Decree of Dec. 11, 1808	1808, Posener	1841, Consistory Figures	1851, General Census	1853, Consistory Figures	1853, Author	1861, Consistory Figures	1861, General Census	1861, Author
Ain[a]				18		18			
Jura[a]				59		59			
Rhin (Haut)	9915	9915	14,316[b]	14,882	16,547	16,547	16,719 [c]	14,062	16,719
Saône (Haute)	5	5	409 [d]	536	492	536		616	616
Saône-et-Loire[a]				167	145	167			
Total	9920	9920	14,725	15,662	17,184[e]	17,327	16,719[f]	14,678	17,335

[a] Became part of Lyon consistory in 1857.

[b] In 1841 the general census reported 13,845.

[c] Figure for Haute-Saône is missing from the 1861 consistory tables.

[d] A.D. Haut-Rhin, 1 V 89, Préfet, Saône-et-Loire to Préfet, Haut-Rhin, April 26, 1838, gives population as 116 (in Châlon); but the 1841 consistory census did not report any Jews.

[e] They reported (error in addition) 17,183.

[f] Figure is low (see footnote c, above).

TABLE A-7
Jewish Population by Department in the Marseille Consistory District, 1808–1861

Department	1808, Decree of Dec. 11, 1808	1808, Posener	1841, Consistory Figures	1851, General Census	1853, Consistory Figures	1853, Author	1861, Consistory Figures	1861, General Census	1861, Author
Alpes (Basses)			0	6		6		1	1
Alpes (Hautes)			0	6		6		8	8
Ardèche			0	4		4		10	10
Bouches-du-Rhône	942	942	1462	1371	1944	1944	[a]	2532	2532
Corse			0	4		4		9	9
Drôme			0	63	14	63		34	34
Gard	425	425	477	494	499	499	375	375	375
Hérault[c]	141	141	112	158	128	158	[b]	171	171
Isère[c]	4	4	0	20		20			
Loire[c]			40	29	119	119			
Loire (Haute)			0	2		2		0	0
Lozère			0	1		1		0	0
Rhône[c]	67	195	762	458	1107	1107		42	42
Savoie[d]	[e]	[e]	[e]	[e]	[e]	[e]		67	67
Var	14	14	0	79	35	79	[b]		
Vaucluse	631	631	776	673	766	766	650[f]	638	650
Alpes-Maritimes	[e]	[e]	[e]	[e]	[e]	[e]		321	321
Total	2224	2352	3629	3368	4612[g]	4778	3225	4208	4220

aThe only available figure here is 2200, which includes the departments of Var and Hérault.
bSee Bouches-du-Rhône.
cBecame part of the Lyon consistory in 1857.
dEntered France in 1860.
eNot in France.
fNot yet counted in the population totals.
gBy an error, the consistory counted a total of 4658.

TABLE A-8
Jewish Population by Department in the Metz Consistory District, 1808–1861

Department	1808, Decree of Dec. 11, 1808	1808, Posener	1841, Consistory Figures	1851, General Census	1853, Consistory Figures	1853, Author	1861, Consistory Figures	1861, General Census	1861, Author
Ardennes	11	115	96	73	81	81	a	119	119
Moselle	6506	6506	8081	7768	7994	7994	7853[b]	7250	7734[c]
Total	6517	6621	8177	7841	8075	8075	7853	7369	7853

[a] Total for Ardennes included in the figure for Moselle.
[b] Includes (119?) Jews of Ardennes.
[c] Consistory figure, minus 119 (approximate figure for Ardennes).

TABLE A-9
Jewish Population by Department in the Nancy Consistory District, 1808–1861

Department	1808, Decree of Dec. 11, 1808	1808, Posener	1841, Consistory Figures	1851, General Census	1853, Consistory Figures	1853, Author	1861, Consistory Figures	1861, General Census	1861, Author
Doubs[a]	86	86	619	745	698	745		301	301
Marne (Haute)	41	41	284	309	332	332	127		
Meurthe	3289	3544	5332	5675	6029	6029	5934	5116	5934
Meuse	405	405	662	699	666	699	993	769	993
Vosges	345	441	1090	1194	1273	1273	1524	1428	1524
Total	4166	4517	7987	8622	8998	9078	8578	7614	8752

aBecame part of the Lyon consistory in 1857.

TABLE A-10
Jewish Population by Department in the Paris Consistory District, 1808–1861

Department	1808, Decree of Dec. 11, 1808	1808, Posener	1841, Consistory Figures	1851, General Census	1853, Consistory Figures	1853, Author	1861, Consistory Figures	1861, General Census	1861, Author
Aisne			0	67	37	67		52	52
Allier	5	5	0	12		12		4	4
Aube			0	21		21		31	31
Calvados			0	44		44		26	26
Cher			19	15		15		13	13
Côte d'Or	251	251	312	364	558	558	393	407	407
Côtes-du-Nord			0	1		1		2	2
Eure			0	6		6		5	5
Eure-et-Loir			2	8		8		21	21
Finistère	11	11	0	80	42	80	26	38	38
Ille-et-Vilaine	11	11	0	9	3	9	7	19	19
Indre			0	6		6		4	4
Indre-et-Loire	10	10	0	35	31	35	48	52	52
Loir-et-Cher	11	11	0	9	5	9	1	1	1
Loire-Inférieure	7	7	154	45	148	148	159	133	159
Loiret			57	62	64	64	56	81	81
Maine-et-Loir				23	20	23	14	20	20
Manche			0	9		9		60	60
Marne	2	2	335	415	397	415	401	446	446
Mayenne			0	0		0		7	7
Morbihan			0	20	13	20	10	15	15
Nièvre			0	10		10		26	26
Nord	166	166	226	271	315	315	437	584	584
Oise			0	44		44		49	49
Orne			0	6		6		12	12
Pas-de-Calais	63	63	76	157	92	157	90	140	140
Sarthe			0	12		12		4	4
Seine	2733	2733	8000	10,978	18,000	18,000	25,000	15,196	25,000
Seine-Inférieure	47	47	331	222	370	370	464	396	464
Seine-et-Marne	132	132	91	165	154	165	181	228	228
Seine-et-Oise	95	95	114	216	227	227	230	415	415

TABLE A-10 (Continued)

Department	1808, Decree of Dec. 11, 1808	1808, Posener	1841, Consistory Figures	1851, General Census	1853, Consistory Figures	1853, Author	1861, Consistory Figures	1861, General Census	1861, Author
Somme	14	14	17	36[a]	30	36		81[b]	81
Vienne	27	27	19		22	22	13	41	41
Yonne				33	12	33			
Total	3585	3585	9753	13,401	20,540	20,947	27,529	18,609	28,507

a Twenty-four in Vienne were reported in the Bordeaux consistory.
b There were twelve Jews in Vienne, according to the 1861 general census. It is unclear whether they were in the Paris consistory or Bordeaux consistory districts, so I have arbitrarily included them in the Bordeaux consistory figures.

TABLE A-11
Jewish Population by Department in the Strasbourg Consistory District, 1808–1861

Department	1808, Decree of Dec. 11, 1808	1808, Posener	1841, Consistory Figures	1851, General Census	1853, Consistory Figures	1853, Author	1861, Consistory Figures	1861, General Census	1861, Author
Rhin (Bas)	16,155	16,155	20,749	20,935	22,806	22,806	20,682	20,936	20,936
Total	16,155	16,155	20,749	20,935	22,806	22,806	20,682	20,936	20,936

TABLE A-12
Jewish Population by Department in the St. Esprit-Bayonne Consistory District,[a] *1808–1861*

Department	1808, Decree of Dec. 11, 1808	1808, Posener	1841, Consistory Figures	1851, General Census	1853, Consistory Figures	1853, Author	1861, Consistory Figures	1861, General Census	1861, Author
Ariège				2		2		0	0
Aude				18		18		16	16
Garonne (Haute)				104	215	215		394	394
Landes				836	1171	1171		96	96
Pyrénées (Basses)				394	452	452		1197	1197
Pyrénées (Hautes)				16	36	36		22	22
Pyrénées-Orientales				21		21		28	28
Scattered in St. Esprit consistory district					200	200			
Corrective addition to district[b]									447
Total				1391	2074	2115	2200[c]	1753	2200

[a]Consistory established in 1846.
[b]See footnote [a] on last page of Table A-2.
[c]The only figure available is an estimate of 2200 for the entire Bayonne consistory district.

TABLE A-13
Jewish Population by Department in the Lyon Consistory District,[a] 1808–1861

Department	1808, Decree of Dec. 11, 1808	1808, Posener	1841, Consistory Figures	1851, General Census	1853, Consistory Figures	1853, Author	1861, Consistory Figures	1861, General Census	1861, Author
Ain[b]								3	3
Jura[b]								50	50
Saône-et-Loire[b]							89	96	96
Doubs[c]							756	842	842
Isère[d]							[e]	24	24
Loire[d]							300	167	300
Rhône[d]							1100	967	1100
Total							2245	2149	2415

[a] Consistory established in 1857.
[b] From Haut-Rhin.
[c] From Nancy consistory.
[d] From Marseille consistory.
[e] No data.

TABLE A-14
Jewish Population by Consistory District, 1808–1861

Consistory	1808, Decree of Dec. 11, 1808	1808, Posener	1841, Consistory Figures	1845, Consistory Figures[a]	1851, General Census	1853, Consistory Figures	1853, Author	1858–60, Szajkowski[b]	1861, Consistory Figures	1861, General Census[c]	1861, Author[c]
Bordeaux	3713	3713	5304	3500	2755	4042	4094	3053	3350	2648	3663
Colmar	9920[d]	9920	14,725	16,871	15,662	17,184	17,327	??	16,719	14,678	17,335
Lyon[e]	—	—	—	—	—	—	—	2189	2245	2149	2415
Marseille	2224[f]	2352	3629	3958	3368	4612	4778	3550	3225	4208	4220
Metz	6517	6621	8177	8071	7841	8075	8075	7253	7853	7369	7853
Nancy	4166	4517	7987	10,479	8622	8998	9078	6792	8578	7614	8752
Paris	3585	3585	9753	17,000	13,401	20,540	20,947	25,410	27,529	18,609	28,507
St. Esprit-Bayonne[g]	—	—	—	2500	1391	2074	2115	1204	2200	1753	2200
Strasbourg	16,155	16,155	20,749	23,531	20,935	22,806	22,806	16,455	20,682	20,936	20,936
Total	46,280	46,863	70,324	85,910	73,975	88,331	89,220	Incomplete	92,381	79,964	95,881

a *U.I.*, 5 (1849), p. 40.
b Szajkowski, *Jews and the French Revolution*, p. 147.
c These figures include, in some cases, populations that escaped consistory control (were unknown to the consistory), as is evidenced by the difference between the consistory and general census figures by department.
d Decree gives 10,000, including 80 in Léman, separated from France after 1815.
e Consistory established in 1857.
f Decree gives 2527, including 303 in Alpes-Maritimes, separated from France after 1815.
g Consistory established in 1846.

TABLE A-15

*Percentage of Jews in General
Population of Each Department, 1861*

Department	1861 Population (General Census)	1861 Jewish Population Numbers[a]	Percent
Ain	369,767	3	0.0008
Aisne	564,597	52	0.0092
Allier	356,432	4	0.0011
Basses-Alpes	146,368	1	0.0007
Hautes-Alpes	125,100	8	0.0064
Alpes-Maritimes	194,578	321	0.1650
Ardèche	388,529	10	0.0026
Ardennes	329,111	119	0.0362
Ariège	251,850	0	0.0000
Aube	262,785	31	0.0118
Aude	283,606	16	0.0056
Aveyron	396,025	0	0.0000
Bouches-du-Rhône	507,112	2532	0.4993
Calvados	480,992	26	0.0054
Cantal	240,523	5	0.0021
Charente	379,081	19	0.0050
Charente-Inférieur	481,060	51	0.0106
Cher	323,393	13	0.0040
Corrèze	310,118	5	0.0016
Corse	252,889	9	0.0036
Côte d'Or	384,140	407	0.1060
Côtes-du-Nord	628,676	2	0.0003
Creuse	270,055	9	0.0033
Dordogne	501,687	8	0.0016
Doubs	296,280	842	0.2842
Drôme	326,684	34	0.0104
Eure	398,661	5	0.0013
Eure-et-Loir	290,455	21	0.0072
Finistère	627,304	38	0.0061
Gard	422,107	375	0.0888
Haute-Garonne	484,081	394	0.0814
Gers	298,931	4	0.0013
Gironde	667,193	3000	0.4496
Hérault	409,391	171	0.0418
Ille-et-Vilaine	584,930	19	0.0032
Indre	270,054	4	0.0015
Indre-et-Loire	323,572	52	0.0161
Isère	577,748	24	0.0042
Jura	298,053	50	0.0168
Landes	300,839	96	0.0319
Loir-et-Cher	269,029	1	0.0004
Loire	517,603	300	0.0580
Haute-Loire	305,521	0	0.0000
Loire-Inférieur	580,207	159	0.0274
Loiret	352,757	81	0.0230
Lot	295,542	0	0.0000

[a]Author's figures; see Table A-2.

TABLE A-15 (*Continued*)

Department	1861 Population (General Census)	1861 Jewish Population	
		Numbers	Percent
Lot-et-Garonne	332,065	16	0.0048
Lozère	137,367	0	0.0000
Maine-et-Loire	526,012	20	0.0038
Manche	591,421	60	0.0101
Marne	385,498	446	0.1157
Haut-Marne	258,501	301	0.1164
Mayenne	375,163	7	0.0019
Meurthe	428,643	5934	1.3844
Meuse	305,540	993	0.3250
Morbihan	486,504	15	0.0031
Moselle	446,457	7734	1.7323
Nièvre	332,814	26	0.0078
Nord	1,303,380	584	0.0448
Oise	401,417	49	0.0122
Orne	423,350	12	0.0028
Pas-de-Calais	724,338	140	0.0193
Puy-de-Dôme	576,409	350	0.0607
Basses-Pyrénées	436,628	1197	0.2741
Hautes-Pyrénées	240,179	22	0.0092
Pyrénées-Orientales	181,763	28	0.0154
Bas-Rhin	577,574	20,936	3.6248
Haut-Rhin	515,802	16,719	3.2414
Rhône	662,493	1100	0.1660
Haute-Saône	317,183	616	0.1942
Saône-et-Loire	582,137	96	0.0165
Sarthe	466,155	4	0.0009
Savoie	275,039	42	0.0153
Haute-Savoie	267,496	0	0.0000
Seine	1,953,660	25,000	1.2796
Seine-Inférieure	789,988	464	0.0587
Seine-et-Marne	352,312	228	0.0647
Seine-et-Oise	513,073	415	0.0809
Deux-Sèvres	328,817	2	0.0006
Somme	572,646	81	0.0141
Tarn	353,633	1	0.0003
Tarn-et-Garonne	232,551	9	0.0039
Var	315,526	67	0.0212
Vaucluse	268,255	650	0.2423
Vendée	395,695	11	0.0028
Vienne	322,028	12	0.0037
Haute-Vienne	319,595	161	0.0504
Vosges	415,485	1524	0.3668
Yonne	370,305	41	0.0111
(Scattered through departments of Bayonne District)		447	
Total	37,386,313	95,434[a]	0.2553

[a]Does not include last entry, "Scattered through . . . Bayonne."

TABLE A-16

Occupations of the
25 Notables of the Colmar District, 1841[a]

Name	*Professions*
Manheimer, Meyer Baer	Banquier
Schoengrün, Nathan-Lévy	Propriétaire, rentier
Dreyfuss, Léopold	Idem
Lévy, Samuel	Marchand de cuir
Bicard, Léopold	Propriétaire
Hirtz, Isaac	Idem
Pareff, Arnold	Courtier de marchandises
Katz, Mathis	Fabricant d'indiennes
Piquart, Constant	Fabricant de rubans
Lantz, Elie	Fabricant d'indiennes
Wohl, Josué	Propriétaire
Raphaël, Lehmann	Idem
Lang, Isaac	Marchand de fer
Sée, Israël-Gabriel	Propriétaire
Lévy, Benjamin	Idem
Boumsel, Léon	Négociant
Netter, Louis	Propriétaire
Gros, David	Idem
Duckos, Benjamin	Marchand de boeufs
Weil, Joseph	Propriétaire
Duckos, Bloch-Goudschoux	Négociant
Mayer, Aron	Propriétaire et maire
Lévy, Michel	Médecin
Sée, Jacques	Propriét. et marchand de farine
Greilsamer, Mayer	Propriétaire

[a]Data from *Réfutation de plusieurs articles calomnieux publiés contre le consistoire israélite de Colmar (par un Israélite du Haut-Rhin)* (Strasbourg, 1841).

TABLE A-17

Age and Occupation of 20 Candidates for
Election to the Notabilité *of the Bordeaux District, 1841*

Candidate	Age	Occupation
Raba, Hypolite	50	Négociant
Raba, Elisé	52	Propriétaire
Mendès, J^or Abraham	55	Banquier
Solar, Ainé	51	Propriétaire
Gonzales, Ainé	65	Propriétaire
Lopes, Dias	34	Banquier
Fonseque, Aaron	—	Propriétaire
Patto, David	—	Propriétaire
Pereire, Isaac	42	Dr. Médecin
Léon, Hayman	35	Négociant
Peixotto, Isaac	76	Propriétaire
Rodrigues, Joseph	57	Banquier
Léon, Benjamin	55	Propriétaire
Léon, Isaac	60	Négociant
Furtado (fils)	—	—
Nonnés, Jacob Louis	—	—
Rodrigues, Gustave	39	Propriétaire
Lopes Dias, Jacob Thomas	36	Agent de Change
Norzy, David	46	Propriétaire
Valéry, David	49	Négociant

APPENDIX B

**TEXTS OF THE MAJOR LEGISLATION
REGULATING THE CONSISTORIES**[1]

RÈGLEMENT, 1806

Les députés composant l'assemblée des israélites, convoqués par décret impérial du 30 mai 1806, après avoir entendu le rapport de la commission des neuf, nommée pour préparer les travaux de l'assemblée, délibérant sur l'organisation qu'il conviendrait de donner à leurs coreligionnaires de l'empire français et du royaume d'Italie, relativement à l'exercice de leur culte et à sa police intérieure, ont adopté unanimement le projet suivant:

Art. 1er. Il sera établi une synagogue et un consistoire israélite dans chaque département renfermant deux mille individus professant la religion de Moïse.

2. Dans le cas où il ne se trouvera pas deux mille israélites dans un seul département, la circonscription de la synagogue consistoriale embrassera autant de départements, de proche en proche, qu'il en faudra pour les réunir. La siège de la synagogue sera toujours dans la ville dont la population israélite sera la plus nombreuse.

3. Dans aucun cas, il ne pourra y avoir plus d'une synagogue consistoriale par département.

4. Aucune synagogue particulière ne sera établie, si la proposition n'en est faite par la synagogue consistoriale à l'autorité compétente. Chaque synagogue particulière sera administrée par deux notables et un rabbin, lesquels seront désignés par l'autorité compétente.

5. Il y aura un grand rabbin par synagogue consistoriale.

6. Les consistoires seront composés d'un grand rabbin, d'un autre rabbin, autant que faire se pourra, et de trois autres israélites, dont deux seront choisis parmi les habitants de la ville où siégera le consistoire.

7. Le consistoire sera présidé par le plus âgé de ses membres, qui prendra le nom d'*ancien* du consistoire.

8. Il sera désigné par l'autorité compétente, dans chaque circonscription consistoriale, des notables, au nombre de vingt-cinq, choisis parmi les plus imposés et les plus recommandables des israélites.

9. Ces notables procéderont à l'élection des membres du consistoire, qui devront être agréés par l'autorité compétente.

10. Nul ne pourra être membre du consistoire, 1° s'il n'a trente ans; 2° s'il a fait faillite, à moins qu'il ne soit honorablement réhabilité; 3° s'il est connu pour avoir fait l'usure.

11. Tout israélite qui voudra s'établir en France ou dans le royaume d'Italie, devra en donner connaissance, dans le délai de trois mois, au consistoire le plus voisin du lieu où il fixera son domicile.

12. Les fonctions du consistoire seront,

1° De veiller à ce que les rabbins ne puissent donner, soit en public, soit en particulier, aucune instruction ou explication de la loi qui ne soit conforme aux réponses de l'assemblée, converties en décisions doctrinales par le grand sanhédrin;

2° De maintenir l'ordre dans l'intérieur des synagogues, surveiller l'administration des synagogues particulières, régler la perception et l'emploi des sommes destinées aux frais du culte mosaïque, et veiller à ce que, pour cause ou sous prétexte de religion, il ne se forme, sans une autorisation expresse, aucune assemblée de prières:

3° D'encourager, par tous les moyens possibles, les israélites de la circonscription consistoriale à l'exercice des professions utiles, et de faire connaître à l'autorité ceux qui n'ont pas des moyens d'existence avoués;

4° De donner, chaque année, à l'autorité connaissance du nombre de conscrits israélites de la circonscription.

13. Il y aura, à Paris, un consistoire central, composé de trois rabbins et de deux autres israélites.

14. Les rabbins du consistoire central seront pris parmi les grands rabbins, et les autres membres seront assujettis aux conditions de l'éligibilité portées en l'art. 10.

15. Chaque année il sortira un membre du consistoire central, lequel sera toujours rééligible.

16. Il sera pourvu à son remplacement par les membres restants. Le nouvel élu ne sera installé qu'après avoir obtenu l'agrément de l'autorité compétente.

17. Les fonctions du consistoire central seront, 1° de correspondre avec les consistoires; 2° de veiller dans toutes ses parties à l'exécution du présent règlement; 3° de déférer à l'autorité compétente toutes les atteintes portées à l'exécution dudit règlement, soit par infraction, soit par inobservation; 4° de confirmer la nomination des rabbins, et de proposer, quand il y aura lieu, à l'autorité compétente, la destitution des rabbins et des membres des consistoires.

18. L'élection du grand rabbin se fera par les vingt-cinq notables désignés en l'art. 8.

19. Le nouvel élu ne pourra entrer en fonctions qu'après avoir été confirmé par le consistoire central.

20. Aucun rabbin ne pourra être élu, 1° s'il n'est natif ou naturalisé Français ou Italien du royaume d'Italie; 2° s'il ne rapporte une attestation de capacité, souscrite par trois grands rabbins italiens, s'il est Italien, et français, s'il est Français, et, à dater de 1820, s'il ne sait la langue française en France, et l'italienne dans le royaume d'Italie: celui qui joindra à la connaissance de la langue hébraïque quelque connaissance des langues grecque et latine sera préféré, toutes choses égales d'ailleurs.

21. Les fonctions des rabbins sont, 1° d'enseigner la religion; 2° la doctrine renfermée dans les décisions du grand sanhédrin;

3° de rappeler en toute circonstance l'obéissance aux lois, notamment et en particulier à celles relatives à la défense de la patrie, mais d'y exhorter plus spécialement encore tous les ans, à l'époque de la conscription, depuis le premier appel de l'autorité jusqu'à complète exécution de la loi; 4° de faire considérer aux israélites le service militaire comme un devoir sacré, et de leur déclarer que, pendant le temps où ils se consacreront à ce service, la loi les dispense des observances qui ne pourraient point se concilier avec lui; 5° de prêcher dans les synagogues, et réciter les prières qui s'y font en commun pour l'empereur et la famille impériale; 6° de célébrer les mariages et de déclarer les divorces, sans qu'ils puissent, dans aucun cas, y procéder que les parties requérantes ne leur aient bien et dûment justifié de l'acte civil de mariage ou de divorce.

22. Le traitement des rabbins membres du consistoire central est fixé à six mille francs. celui des grands rabbins des synagogues consistoriales, à trois mille francs; celui des rabbins des synagogues particulières sera fixé par la réunion des israélites qui auront demandé l'établissement de la synagogue; il ne pourra être moindre de mille francs. Les israélites des circonscriptions respectives pourront voter l'augmentation de ce traitement.

23. Chaque consistoire proposera à l'autorité compétente un projet de répartition entre les israélites de la circonscription, pour l'acquittement du salaire des rabbins: les autres frais du culte seront déterminés et répartis sur la demande des consistoires par l'autorité compétente. Le payement des rabbins membres du consistoire central sera prélevé proportionnellement sur les sommes perçues dans les différentes circonscriptions.

24. Chaque consistoire désignera hors de son sein un israélite non rabbin, pour recevoir les sommes qui devront être perçues dans la circonscription.

25. Ce receveur payera par quartier les rabbins, ainsi que les autres frais du culte, sur une ordonnance signée au moins par trois membres du consistoire. Il rendra ses comptes chaque année, à jour fixe, au consistoire assemblé.

26. Tout rabbin qui, après la mise en activité du présent règlement, ne se trouvera pas employé, et qui voudra cependant conserver son domicile en France ou dans le royaume d'Italie, sera tenu d'adhérer, par une déclaration formelle et qu'il signera aux décisions du grand sanhédrin. Copie de cette déclaration sera envoyée, par le consistoire qui l'aura reçue, au consistoire central.

27. Les rabbins membres du grand sanhédrin seront préférés, autant que faire se pourra, à tous autres pour les places de grands rabbins.

Certifié conforme:

Le ministre secrétaire d'Etat, signé: Hugues B.

Maret

DÉCRET, 1808

Au Palais des Tuileries,
le 17 mars 1808

Napoléon, empereur des Français, roi d'Italie et protecteur de la confédération du Rhin;

Sur le rapport de notre ministre de l'intérieur;

Notre conseil d'État entendu,

Nous avons décrété et décrétons, ce qui suit:

Art. 1er. Pour l'exécution de l'art. 1er du règlement délibéré par l'assemblée générale des juifs exécution qui a été ordonnée par notre décret de ce jour, notre ministre des cultes nous présentera le tableau des synagogues consistoriales à établir, leur circonscription et le lieu de leur établissement.

Il prendra préalablement l'avis du consistoire central.

Les départements de l'empire qui n'ont pas actuellement de population israélite, seront classés par un tableau supplémentaire, dans les arrondissements des synagogues consistoriales, pour le cas où des israélites venant à s'y établir, ils auraient besoin de recourir à un consistoire.

2. Il ne pourra être établi de synagogue particulière, suivant l'art. 4 dudit règlement, que sur l'autorisation donnée par nous en conseil d'État sur le rapport de notre ministre des cultes, et sur le vu, 1° de l'avis de la synagogue consistoriale; 2° de l'avis du consistoire central; 3° de l'avis du préfet du département; 4° de l'état de la population israélite qui comprendra la synagogue nouvelle.

La nomination des administrateurs des synagogues particulières sera faite par le consistoire départemental, et approuvée par le consistoire central.

Le décret d'établissement de chaque synagogue particulière en fixera la circonscription.

3. La nomination des notables dont il est parlé en l'art. 8 dudit règlement sera faite par notre ministre de l'intérieur, sur la présentation du consistoire central et l'avis des préfets.

4. La nomination des membres des consistoires départementaux sera présentée à notre approbation par notre ministre des cultes, sur l'avis des préfets des départements compris dans l'arrondissement de la synagogue.

5. Les membres du consistoire central dont il est parlé à l'article 13 dudit règlement, seront nommés pour la première fois par nous, sur la présentation de notre ministre des cultes, et parmi les membres de l'assemblée générale des juifs ou du grand sanhédrin.

6. Le même ministre présentera à notre approbation le choix du nouveau membre du consistoire central, qui sera désigné chaque année selon les art. 15, 16 dudit règlement.

7. Le rôle de répartition dont il est parlé à l'art. 25 dudit règlement, sera dressé par chaque consistoire départemental, divisé en autant de parties qu'il y aura de départements dans l'arrondissement de la synagogue, soumis à l'examen du consistoire central, et rendu exécutoire par les préfets de chaque département.

8. Nos ministres de l'intérieur et des cultes sont chargés de l'exécution de présent décret.

Signé: Napoléon
Par l'empereur:
Le ministre secrétaire d'Etat, signé: Hugues B.
Maret

ORDONNANCE, 1823

Au château des Tuileries, le
20 août 1823

Louis, par la grâce de Dieu, roi de France et de Navarre, à tous ceux qui ces présentes verront, salut.

Sur le rapport de notre ministre et secrétaire d'État au département de l'intérieur;

Vu les propositions des synagogues consistoriales et celles du consistoire central des israélites, à l'effet d'ajouter à leur règlement du 10 décembre 1806 de nouvelles modifications, en outre de celles qui y ont été faites par notre ordonnance du 29 juin 1819;

Notre conseil d'État entendu,

Nous avons ordonné et ordonnons ce qui suit:

Art. 1ᵉʳ. Dans le cours de l'année 1825, les notables israélites des divers arrondissements consistoriaux seront intégralement renouvelés.

2. Tous les deux ans, il sortira cinq membres du college des notables. Cette sortie se fera par la voie du sort, à la fin de la séance annuelle qui a lieu conformément à l'ordonnance du 29 juin 1819.

La majorité des notables devra avoir sa résidence dans la commune où est établie la synagogue consistoriale.

3. Les conditions d'éligibilité requises par l'art. 10 du règlement concernant les membres du consistoire s'appliquent également aux notables.

4. Dans le cours de l'année 1825, et un mois après le renouvellement des notables, ceux-ci s'assembleront pour procéder au renouvellement intégral des membres laïques des consistoires départementaux.

5. Tous les deux ans, il sortira un des membres laïques des consistoires départementaux. Cette sortie aura lieu par la voie du sort, et successivement entre les quatre, les trois et les deux, plus anciens membres, et ensuite par ancienneté de nomination.

Les membres laïques des consistoires et les notables peuvent être réélus indéfiniment.

6. Dans le chef-lieu de la circonscription où siége le consistoire, la nomination des ministres officiants de temple (chantres) et celle des autres desservants et agents, notament le sacrificateur, appartiennent immédiatement au consistoire.

Il nommera aussi, près les temples de sa circonscription, un ou plusieurs commissaires surveillants, qui exerceront, sous sa dépendance, les fonctions qu'il leur aura déléguées.

7. Les rabbins près les temples des communes autres que le siége du consistoire, les ministres officiants (chantres) et les autres desservants près ces temples, seront élus par une commission locale, nommée par le consistoire et présidée par le commissaire surveillant.

L'élection des rabbins est soumise à la confirmation du consistoire central, sur l'avis des consistoires; les autres ministres et desservants seront confirmés par le consistoire dont ils dépendent et sous la direction et surveillance duquel ils exercent leurs fonctions.

8. Le traitement des rabbins, ministres officiants, desservants ou agents dont il est parlé dans les art. 6 et 7, fait partie des frais locaux du culte.

9. Chaque consistoire, dans l'assemblée qui se tient annuellement pour la fixation et la répartition des frais généraux de la circonscription, s'occupera en même temps, avec le concours des notables qui résident dans le chef-lieu, de la formation du budget et du rôle de répartition des frais locaux du culte de la commune où siége le consistoire.

Quant aux frais locaux des communes hors le siége consistorial, le consistoire adjoindra, chaque année, autant de notables israélites qu'il jugera nécessaire, au commissaire surveillant et sous sa présidence, afin de procéder à la formation du budget des frais locaux du culte et du rôle y relatif, lesquels budget et rôle seront soumis à l'examen et à l'approbation des consistoires respectifs.

10. Les commissaires surveillants sont tenus de présenter annuellement à la commission chargée de dresser avec eux les budgets et les rôles locaux, le compte rendu de l'exercice précédent, lequel compte sera ensuite soumis à l'examen des consistoires respectifs.

Ces comptes, le budget et les rôles de répartition seront adressés par le consistoire au préfet du département, qui les transmettra à notre ministre de l'intérieur. Le consistoire central y apposera son avis. Les rôles, définitivement approuvés par notre ministre, seront renvoyés aux préfets pour être rendus exécutoires.

11. Dans le cours de l'année 1825, le nombre des membres composant le consistoire central sera porté à neuf, savoir: les deux grands rabbins et sept membres laïques. A cet effet, le collége des notables de chaque circonscription désignera deux candidats laïques qui devront être domiciliés à Paris, et dont l'un sera nommé par nous, sur le rapport de notre ministre de l'intérieur.

12. Tous les deux ans, il sortira un des membres laïques du consistoire central. Cette sortie aura lieu par la voie du sort, et successivement entre les sept, les six, les cinq, les quatre, les trois et les deux plus anciens membres, et ensuite par ancienneté de nomination. Le membre sortant est toujours rééligible d'après le mode prescrit par l'art. 11.

Le consistoire central ne peut jamais délibérer en moindre nombre que cinq.

En cas d'égalité de suffrages, la voix du président est prépondérante.

Cependant aucune délibération ne peut être prise, concernant les objets religieux ou du culte, sans le consentement des deux grands rabbins. Toutefois, si ces derniers diffèrent d'avis, le plus ancien de nomination des grands rabbins des consistoires départementaux sera appelé à les départager.

13. Les mandats de payement qui seront délivrés par le consistoire central sur son receveur, devront être signés par cinq membres au moins.

14. En cas de décès ou de démission de l'un des deux grands rabbins du consistoire central, chaque consistoire proposera un candidat, pris parmi les grands rabbins des consistoires départementaux; sur ces candidats, trois seront désignés par le consistoire central pour l'un d'eux être nommé par nous, sur le rapport de notre ministre de l'intérieur.

15. Ne pourront être ensemble membres d'un consistoire départemental, ni du consistoire central, le père, le fils, le gendre, les frères et beaux-frères.

16. Le consistoire central déterminera, par un règlement spécial, qui sera soumis à l'approbation de notre ministre de l'intérieur, les formalités à remplir par les aspirants au titre de rabbin, qui, s'il y a lieu, seront ensuite confirmés en cette qualité par le même consistoire.

17. Chaque consistoire nommera, tous les ans, son président et son vice-président; ils peuvent toujours être réélus. En cas de partage de voix entre les membres des consistoires de département, le plus ancien d'âge ou de nomination parmi les notables du siége consistorial sera appelé pour former la majorité.

18. Il ne pourra être employé dans les écoles primaires aucun livre qui ne soit approuvé par le consistoire central, du consentement des grands rabbins.

19. Le décret du 17 mars 1808, qui prescrit des mesures pour l'exécution du règlement israélite, et l'ordonnance du 29 juin 1819, continueront d'être exécutés dans toutes les dispositions qui ne sont pas modifiées par la présente.

20. Notre ministre et secrétaire d'État au département de l'intérieur est chargé de l'exécution de la présente ordonnance, qui sera insérée au Bulletin des lois.

Donné en notre château des Tuileries, le 20 août de l'an de grâce 1823, et de notre règne le vingt-neuvième.

Signé: Louis
Par le roi:
Le ministre et secrétaire d'État au département
de l'intérieur,
signé: Corbière

Nous ministre secrétaire d'État de la justice, chargé de l'administration des cultes,

Vu les art. 20 et 21 du règlement pour l'école centrale rabbinique de Metz, annexé à l'arrêté de notre prédécesseur, en date du 21 août 1829, ainsi conçus:

"A la suite de l'examen général prescrit par l'art. 18, il sera délivré aux élèves des certificats d'aptitude de degré différent, savoir: 1° au titre de rabbin (ou docteur de la loi); 2° au titre de grand rabbin (ou degré supérieur).

"Les conditions et le mode de délivrance des diplômes pour ces deux degrés, sont déterminés par un règlement particulier qui sera proposé à l'approbation de son Excellence le ministre de l'intérieur par le consistoire central."

Vu le projet de règlement présenté par le consistoire central pour l'admission des aspirants aux titres rabbiniques;

Vu l'avis du Comité de l'intérieur du conseil d'État du 23 juillet 1828;

Vu les lettres du consistoire central sur les modifications proposées à son projet,

Arrêtons:

Les dispositions du règlement présenté par le consistoire central pour l'admission aux titres rabbiniques, tel qu'il a été rectifié et annexé au présent arrêté, sont approuvées.

Il ne pourra être fait de modifications audit règlement sans notre approbation.

Paris, le 15 octobre 1832.

Signé: Barthe

REGLEMENT d'admission aux titres rabbiniques

Titre 1er
Des degrés rabbiniques

Il y a deux degrés rabbiniques, savoir:

1° Morénou, docteur de la loi, donnant l'aptitude aux fonctions de rabbin communal.

2° Degré supérieur: Morénou harab (rabbin-maitre), donnant l'aptitude aux fonctions de grand rabbin de circonscription ou du consistoire central.

Toutefois les rabbins-maitres pourront concourir pour les places de rabbins communaux.

Titre II
Des conditions requises des aspirants au premier degré rabbinique

1° La langue hébraïque par principes.

2° La bible.

3° Les principes du Talmud qui sont d'une application journalière.

4° Le résumé de l'Alphasi.

5° Le résumé de Maïmonides (Yad Hachsaka).

6° Le Thour et le Schoulchan Arouch (Karo).

7° La langue française par principes.

8° Les éléments du latin.

9° L'histoire des juifs tant anciens que modernes.

10° Les décisions doctrinales du grand sanhédrin de France.

Titre III
Des conditions requises des aspirants au deuxième degré rabbinique

1° Les connaissances exigées de l'aspirant au premier degré.

2° Outre les connaissances acquises au titre II, art. 8, 9 et 10, les langues grecque et latine.

3° La rhétorique.

4° La philosophie.

5° L'histoire ancienne et moderne.

Titre IV
De l'examen et de l'admission des aspirants

Les aspirants aux titres rabbiniques seront examinés à l'école centrale de Metz.

Tout aspirant, soit du premier, soit du second degré, devra être âgé de vingt-cinq ans, au moins.

Ceux qui auront fait leurs études en dehors de l'école centrale, devront produire en outre: 1° un certificat de bonnes vie et moeurs délivré par le maire du lieu de leur domicile et visé par le consistoire départemental de leur ressort; 2° des certificats attestant le temps d'études tant sacrées que profanes qu'ils auront faites, soit dans les institutions de l'université, soit chez des professeurs particuliers.

Les professeurs de l'école centrale de Metz, après s'être assurés que les aspirants possèdent les connaissances et remplissent les conditions exigées par le présent règlement, leur délivreront des certificats d'aptitude soit au titre de rabbin, soit à celui de grand rabbin.

Sur le vu des certificats d'aptitude et autres pièces à l'appui, le consistoire départemental délivrera s'il y a lieu, aux aspirants de son ressort, le diplôme du premier degré rabbinique.

La délivrance des diplômes du second degré ou de grand rabbin appartiendra au consistoire central, également sur le vu des certificats d'aptitude et autres pièces à l'appui.

Dispositions transitoires

Le présent règlement ne sera mis à exécution qu'à dater de l'année 1836 pour les aspirants qui auraient fait leurs études ailleurs qu'à l'école centrale rabbinique.

Néanmoins il sera transmis immédiatement aux consistoires central et départementaux et au grand rabbin du consistoire de Metz, président de la commission administrative de l'École, afin qu'il soit donné connaissance aux aspirants des conditions de leur admission future aux titres rabbiniques.

Provisoirement, les élèves du culte seront admis aux titres rabbiniques dans les formes et aux conditions usitées jusqu'à ce jour, sans toutefois qu'il puisse être dérogé à l'âge exigé par le présent règlement.

Vu pour être annexé à notre arrêté du 15 octobre 1832.

Le ministre secrétaire d'État de la justice, chargé de l'administration des cultes.

Signé: Barthe

Section Première
Organisation Administrative

§ *Premier*
Des Consistoires, de leur Nombre et de leur
Circonscription

Article Premier. Le culte israélite est administré par des Consistoires départementaux et un Consistoire central.

Art. 2. Il sera établi un Consistoire israélite dans chaque département renfermant deux mille individus professant la religion de Moïse.

Art. 3. Dans le cas où il ne se trouvera pas deux mille israélites dans un seul département, la circonscription du Consistoire embrassera autant de départements de proche en proche qu'il en faudra pour atteindre ce nombre. L'ordonnance royale qui autorisera la création d'un Consistoire, désignera la ville où il aura son siége. Dans aucun cas, il ne pourra y avoir plus d'un Consistoire par département.

Art. 4. Les Consistoires actuellement existans sont maintenus; leur circonscription déterminée par le décret du 11 décembre 1808, est conservée. En conséquence, le Consistoire de la circonscription de Paris aura dans son ressort les départements de l'Aisne, de l'Allier, de l'Aube, du Calvados, du Cher, de la Côte-d'Or, de l'Eure, d'Eure-et-Loir, du Finistère, d'Ile-et-Vilaine, de l'Indre, d'Indre-et-Loire, de Loir-et-Cher, de la Loire-Inférieure, du Loiret, de Maine-et-Loire, de la Manche, de la Marne, de la Mayenne, du Morbihan, de la Nièvre, du Nord, de l'Oise, de l'Orne, du Pas-de-Calais, de la Sarthe, de la Seine, de Seine-et-Oise, de Seine-et-Marne, de la Seine-Inférieure, de la Somme et de l'Yonne.

Le consistoire de la circonscription de Bordeaux comprendra les départements suivants: l'Arriège, l'Aude, l'Aveyron, le Cantal, la Charente, la Charente-Inférieure, la Corrèze, la Creuse, la Dordogne, la Haute-Garonne, le Gers, la Gironde, les Landes, le Lot, le Lot-et-Garonne, le Puy-de-Dôme, les Basses-Pyrénées, les Hautes-Pyrénées, les Pyrénées-Orientales, les Deux-Sèvres, le Tarn, le Tarn-et-Garonne, la Vendée, la Vienne, la Haute-Vienne.

Le consistoire de la circonscription de Marseille embrassera les départements des Basses-Alpes, des Hautes-Alpes, de l'Ardèche, des Bouches-du-Rhône, de la Corse, de la Drôme, du

Gard, de l'Hérault, de l'Isère, de la Loire, de la Haute-Loire, de la Lozère, du Rhône, du Var et du Vaucluse.

Le Consistoire de la circonscription de Metz, les départements suivants: les Ardennes et la Moselle.

Le Consistoire de la circonscription de Nancy, comprendra les départements: le Doubs, la Meurthe, la Haute-Marne, la Meuse et les Vosges.

Le Consistoire de Strasbourg, le département du Bas-Rhin.

Le Consistoire de la circonscription de Colmar embrassera dans son ressort les départements de l'Ain, du Jura, du Haut-Rhin, de la Haute-Saône, de Saône-et-Loire.

Art. 5. Le Consistoire central embrasse toutes les circonscriptions, et son action s'étend sur tout le culte israélite. Le siége de son administration est à Paris.

II
Formation des Consistoires

Art. 6. Le consistoire central est composé d'un ministre du culte, sous le titre de *Grand-Rabbin,* et de sept membres laïques.

Art. 7. Les Consistoires départementaux sont composés d'un ministre du culte, sous le titre de *Rabbin Consistorial* et de quatre membres laïques.

Art. 8. Les membres laïques du Consistoire central et ceux des Consistoires départementaux sont nommés par les notables dont il sera parlé ultérieurement. Le Grand-Rabbin, membre du Consistoire central, et les Rabbins consistoriaux, membres des Consistoires départementaux, sont nommés d'après le mode établi par les articles 60 et 61 de la présente ordonnance.

Art. 9. Dans le cours de l'année 1839, et un mois après la clôture de la liste générale des notables dans les sept circonscriptions consistoriales, les membres laïques des Consistoires départementaux et ceux du Consistoire central seront intégralement renouvelés. A cet effet, ·les notables des sept circonscriptions seront, sur l'autorisation des préfets respectifs, convoqués par les consistoires et par lettres spéciales, au chef-lieu de la circonscription, et procèderont d'abord à l'élection de quatre membres laïques du Consistoire départemental, et ensuite à celle d'un membre du Consistoire central.

Art. 10. L'élection des membres laïques des Consistoires a lieu à la majorité absolue des notables présents; elle est valable quel que soit le nombre des votans. Le bureau se compose d'un président, de trois scrutateurs et d'un secrétaire. La présidence appartient au plus âgé des membres présens; le plus jeune est secrétaire. Les trois scrutateurs sont nommés par l'assemblée à un scrutin de liste, à la majorité.

Art. 11. Toute difficulté élevée dans le cours de l'élection, est jugée par le bureau, à la majorité, sauf recours au Ministre des cultes qui prononcera sur l'avis du Consistoire central, mais sans que l'élection puisse être suspendue. Si le Ministre annule une élection pour un ou plusieurs membres, il est procédé à une nomination nouvelle dans les trois mois.

Art. 12. Un procès-verbal, signé des membres du bureau, fait mention de tout ce qui se passe dans l'assemblée électorale. Il est transmis au Préfet dans les cinq jours de l'élection.

Dans les dix jours de la réception, le Préfet adresse, avec son avis, le procès-verbal au Ministre des cultes qui consulte le Consistoire central.

Le Ministre transmet sa décision au Préfet qui convoque une nouvelle assemblée de notables dans les trois mois, en cas d'annulation; si l'élection est reconnue régulière, elle est soumise à la sanction du Roi, et une expédition de l'ordonnance est transmise au Préfet et une autre au Consistoire central. L'installation des membres des Consistoires est faite par le Préfet ou par un conseiller de préfecture, spécialement délégué, qui se rend à cet effet dans le temple consistorial, et y reçoit, de la part de chaque membre, le serment de fidélité au Roi des Français, d'obéissance à la Charte constitutionnelle et aux lois du royaume.

III
Des Consistoires départementaux, de leurs Attributions

Art. 13. Les notables seuls peuvent être élus membres de Consistoire.

Art. 14. La durée des fonctions des membres des Consistoires départementaux est de quatre ans. Les membres sortans sont indéfiniment rééligibles; ils continuent leurs fonctions jusqu'au jour de l'installation des nouveaux élus.

Art. 15. Les membres du Consistoire nomment leur président et leur vice-président pour deux ans; ils sont rééligibles.

Art. 16. Le Consistoire a la police des temples de sa circonscription; il nomme près les temples, autres que ceux du chef-lieu consistorial, des commissaires-surveillants qui exercent, sous sa dépendance, les fonctions qu'il leur délègue. Il a le droit de les révoquer. Il nomme les ministres-officiants, les desservans et agens dans le chef-lieu consistorial. Les sacrificateurs ne peuvent exercer sans son autorisation. Il confirme les ministres-officiants des temples communaux, et donne au Consistoire central son avis sur l'élection des rabbins et des sous-rabbins. Il a droit de suspension et de destitution à l'égard des ministres-officiants, après avoir, toutefois, pris au préalable l'avis du commissaire surveillant. Il propose au Consistoire central la suspension ou la destitution des rabbins et des sous-rabbins, et il adresse au Consistoire central les plaintes qu'il aurait à faire sur le rabbin consistorial.

Le Consistoire départemental délivre aux aspirants au titre de rabbin, domiciliés dans son ressort, et sur le vu du certificat d'aptitude accordé par l'autorité compétente, le diplôme du premier degré exigé par le règlement du 15 octobre 1832, pour l'exercice des fonctions de rabbin.

Art. 17. Les membres des Consistoires sont admis, quand ils le désirent, dans les établissements d'instruction publique qui reçoivent des élèves israélites. Les rabbins sont admis dans les hôpitaux civils et militaires, quand les malades les réclament, sauf la soumission aux mesures d'ordre intérieur. Ils concertent avec les autorités locales les mesures les plus favorables au développement et au progrès des lumières parmi leurs co-religionnaires. Tous les établissements de charité ou de religion destinés aux Israélites, sont sous leur protection et leur surveillance. Ils en nomment et révoquent les agens et les employés, forment des commissions qui leur présentent, le plus souvent possible, les rapports sur la situation morale et matérielle de ces établissements. Ils ont seuls, ou par leurs commissaires qui présentent annuellement leurs comptes, la distribution et l'emploi des sommes qui proviennent des dons, oblations ou tout autre produit, à moins que celui qui donne ne fixe lui-même une destination spéciale. Ils entretiennent, dans tout leur ressort, une correspondance active qui leur fait connaître les besoins intellectuels et moraux des Israélites. Ils ont avec le Consistoire central des rapports continuels, dans lesquels ils lui font connaître toutes les mesures qui peuvent être utiles au bien-être de leurs coreligionnaires. Dans les fêtes nationales, célébrées dans les temples de leur circonscription, ils ont une place marquée; dans les présentations ou cérémonies publiques, ils paraissent dans l'ordre établi par le décret du 24 messidor an XII.

Art. 18. Les Consistoires ne peuvent correspondre avec le ministre que par l'entremise du Consistoire central; toute pétition ou réclamation d'un agent, d'un employé, d'un ministre du culte israélite, adressée au Ministre des cultes, doit être d'abord transmise au Consistoire départemental qui l'adresse, avec son avis, au Préfet du département; ce magistrat la fait parvenir; le Consistoire central est consulté sur le mérite de la réclamation. La plainte contre un Consistoire départemental ou contre l'un de ses membres, est adressée directement au Consistoire central qui, s'il le juge utile, la renvoie au Ministre des cultes.

IV
Du Consistoire central, ses Attributions

Art. 19. Le Consistoire central est délégué par la population israélite de France, comme représentant des besoins et des voeux de chaque circonscription consistoriale. Les notables de chaque circonscription nommeront un des membres laïques du Consistoire central. La réunion des sept israélites ainsi choisis par les collèges des notables, forme, avec le Grand-Rabbin, le

Consistoire central, dont tous les membres doivent avoir leur résidence à Paris, et l'y conserver pendant toute la durée de leurs fonctions.

Art. 20. Le procès-verbal de nomination des membres laïques du Consistoire central est remis, par le bureau de l'assemblée des notables de chaque circonscription, au Préfet du département, siége de l'assemblée; le Préfet le transmet au Ministre des cultes. Une ordonnance royale confirme la nomination. Les membres du Consistoire central prêtent serment entre les mains du Préfet de la Seine.

Art. 21. Le Consistoire central est nommé pour huit années; ses membres sont indéfiniment rééligibles.

Art. 22. Le Consistoire central nomme son Président et son Vice-Président pour deux ans. Ils sont indéfiniment rééligibles. Le procès-verbal de ces nominations, signé par le Président et le Secrétaire, est transmis au Ministre des cultes, et une expédition également signée par le Président et le Secrétaire, est adressée aux sept Consistoires départementaux.

Art. 23. Le Consistoire central a un Secrétaire archiviste et d'autres employés salariés qu'il nomme et révoque. Le Secrétaire prête serment entre les mains du Consistoire. Le Trésorier du Consistoire central est pris hors de son sein, et ses fonctions sont gratuites.

Art. 24. Le Consistoire central est l'intermédiaire entre le Ministre des cultes et les Consistoires départementaux; la haute administration du culte lui appartient. Il fait, après avoir pris l'avis des Consistoires départementaux, les règlements qu'il juge utile pour la police générale du culte dans les temples, pour la durée des prières publiques, pour les changements que peut nécessiter le rituel. Il surveille les écoles israélites, ses membres sont admis dans tous les établissements d'instruction publique qui reçoivent des élèves israélites.

Aucun ouvrage d'instruction religieuse ou morale ne peut être employé dans les écoles, aucun livre de prières n'est admis à l'usage des temples israélites de France, s'il n'a été approuvé par le Consistoire central.

Art. 25. Le Consistoire central a le droit de surveillance et de censure à l'égard des membres des Consistoires départementaux. Il peut provoquer, pour des causes graves, auprès du Ministre des cultes, la révocation de ces membres, la dissolution par ordonnance royale d'un Consistoire départemental, qui doit alors être recomposé dans trois mois de sa dissolution. Au Consistoire central appartient la délivrance des diplômes du deuxième degré pour l'exercice des fonctions de Grand-Rabbin ou de Rabbin consistorial. Il confirme la nomination des Rabbins et des Sous-Rabbins. Conformément à l'art. 16, il a sur les Rabbins et les Sous-Rabbins droit de censure, de suspension et de révocation. Il présente le Grand-Rabbin et les Rabbins consistoriaux à la nomination royale, après qu'ils ont subi l'examen dont il est parlé aux articles 56 et 57. Il a sur ces derniers droit de censure et de suspension, et peut provoquer du Ministre leur révocation ou leur mise à la retraite.

Art. 26. La dissolution du Consistoire central peut être prononcée par ordonnance royale. Dans ce cas, il doit être recomposé dans les trois mois de la dissolution.

V
Des Notables

Art. 27. Il y a une liste de notables par chaque circonscription consistoriale.

Art. 28. Sont notables, et doivent à ce titre, être portés sur la liste, tous les Israélites qui se trouvent dans l'une des classes dont la nomenclature suit:

1° Les fonctionnaires publics de l'ordre administratif ou judiciaire;

2° Les membres de la liste des électeurs et des jurés, publiée en vertu de la loi de 1828;

3° Les ministres du culte, le directeur et les professeurs de l'école centrale religieuse et des colléges royaux, les anciens membres des Consistoires;

4° Les officiers de la garde nationale;

5° Les membres des chambres de commerce et ceux qui font partie de la liste des notables commerçants;

6° Les membres des conseils-généraux et des conseils d'arrondissement; ceux qui depuis cinq ans sont membres des administrations dans les bureaux de bienfaisance, des hospices et dans les sociétés de bienfaisance pour les Israélites, créés par les Consistoires.

Art. 29. Nul ne peut être notable, membre de Consistoire ou ministre du culte, s'il n'est Français par la naissance ou la naturalisation; s'il n'est âgé de 25 ans révolus; s'il ne sait lire et écrire; s'il a subi, sans réhabilitation, une condamnation criminelle ou correctionnelle, portée aux art. 401, 405 et 408 du Code pénal, ou faits analogues; s'il est failli non réhabilité. Ses droits sont suspendus pendant la durée de tout emprisonnement subi pour le nonacquittement d'une dette ou d'un dommage emportant contrainte par corps; le tout sans préjudice des conditions spéciales exigées pour les rabbins et autres ministres du culte.

Art. 30. Pour voter comme notable dans un collége, il faut avoir son domicile depuis un an révolu dans la circonscription de ce collége.

Art. 31. D'ici au prochain, il sera dressé, par les soins de chaque Consistoire départemental actuellement existant, une liste des notables de chaque circonscription. Ces listes seront transmises aux préfets et sous-préfets. Du 1ᵉʳ au 29 mars, elles seront exposées pendant un mois dans les temples ou synagogues; pendant ce délai, tout Israélite omis pourra réclamer son inscription. Tout notable inscrit pourra réclamer contre l'inscription d'un notable, mais seulement pour violation de l'art. 29. Les préfets statueront dans le mois sur les réclamations, et transmettront aux Consistoires les divers arrêtés de rectification avant le 1er mai.

Art. 32. Du 1er au 10 mai, chaque Consistoire dressera la liste définitive de sa circonscription, fixée par les arrêtés du préfet. Il en transmettra un double au Consistoire central, qui fera dresser une liste générale des notables par ordre alphabétique, dont expédition sera transmise au Ministre des cultes.

Art. 33. Du   au   1839*, sur la convocation des préfets, une réunion des notables de chaque circonscription aura lieu dans la ville où siége le Consistoire, il sera procédé à la nomination des membres laïques des Consistoires départementaux et du Consistoire central.

Art. 34. Les listes dressées conformément aux articles ci-dessus seront permanentes pendant quatre années. En cas de réélection pendant la durée des quatre années, il ne pourra y être fait aucun changement à moins d'incapacité survenue dans l'intervalle et constatée par jugement. Ce changement pourra être provoqué par tout notable inscrit, et sera prononcé par le préfet sur la production du jugement et non autrement.

Art. 35. En cas de décès ou de démission d'un membre du Consistoire départemental, le Consistoire auquel appartiendra le membre décédé ou démissionnaire préviendra le Consistoire central, qui en donnera de suite avis au Ministre des cultes. Le ministre fera connaître au préfet du département où siége le Consistoire le décès ou la démission, et dans les trois mois au plus tard, à dater de cet avis, le remplacement devra avoir lieu.

Art. 36. En cas de décès ou de démission d'un membre laïque du Consistoire central, ce consistoire en informera immédiatement le Ministre des cultes qui autorisera, par l'intermédiaire du préfet, la réunion des notables de la circonscription, dont le membre à remplacer était le représentant spécial, à l'effet de choisir un autre membre. Cette nomination devra être faite dans les deux mois, à dater du jour de l'autorisation ministérielle.

Section II
Organisation religieuse

Ier
Des Ministres du Culte Israélite

Art. 37. La hiérarchie des ministres du culte est ainsi déterminée:

1° Grand-rabbin, membre du Consistoire central;

2° Sept rabbins consistoriaux, membres des Consistoires départementaux;

*The dates were never added to the draft.

3° Rabbins;

4° Sous-rabbins;

5° Ministres-officiants.

Art. 38. Les communes ou réunions de communes, dont la population israélite est de 1,000 âmes et au dessus, et la population générale du siége de 5,000 âmes et plus, ont des *rabbins.*

Les communes ou réunions de communes dont la population israélite est de 601 individus et au dessus, et la population générale du siége de 3,000 âmes et plus, ont des *sous-rabbins.*

Les communes dont la population israélite est de 201 individus et plus, ont des *ministres officiants,* quelle que soit la population générale du siége.

Art. 39. Le traitement du grand-rabbin est de 6,000 fr. Le traitement du rabbin consistorial de Paris est de 4,500 fr. Celui des autres rabbins consistoriaux est de 3,000 fr. Le traitement des rabbins est de 800 fr.; ce traitement augmente de 100 fr. par 5,000 âmes de population générale, jusqu'à 25,000 seulement.

Le traitement des sous-rabbins est de 600 fr.; il augmente de 100 fr. par 2,000 âmes de population générale, jusqu'à 10,000 seulement. Le traitement des ministres officiants est fixé à 400 fr.; il augmente de 100 fr. par 100 individus israélites dans le siége de la synagogue.

Art. 40. Il y a un ministre officiant près le temple consistorial du chef-lieu de la circonscription, dont le traitement est évalué d'après les bases déterminées par l'article précédent pour les rabbins, sous-rabbins et ministres officiants. Toutefois, le temple consistorial de Paris aura deux ministres officiants. Le traitement du premier est fixé à 2,000 fr., celui du second à 1,000 fr.

II
Du Grand-Rabbin, des Rabbins consistoriaux

Art. 41. Le grand-rabbin a droit de surveillance et de censure sur tous les ministres; mais il ne peut censurer les rabbins consistoriaux qu'après avoir obtenu l'adhésion du Consistoire central.

Art. 42. Dans les cérémonies religieuses célébrées pour un événement national, le grand-rabbin a le droit d'officier dans les grands temples consistoriaux. A toute autre cérémonie, le rabbin consistorial officie. Néanmoins, il délègue aux ministres-officiants les prières qu'il ne fait pas lui-même.

Art. 43. Le rabbin consistorial et les autres ministres du culte bénissent les mariages, assistent aux inhumations. Les mariages religieux ne peuvent être célébrés par le rabbin consistorial ou par le ministre du culte qu'il délègue, que dans la ville, siége du Consistoire, ou dans les communes de la circonscription qui n'ont pas de rabbin, de sous-rabbin ou de ministre-officiant. Le rabbin, le sous-rabbin ou le ministre-officiant ne peut bénir le mariage que dans l'étendue de son ressort et dans les édifices consacrés à l'exercice du culte. Il ne peut être dérogé à cette disposition que par une décision spéciale du Consistoire départemental.

Art. 44. Les rabbins consistoriaux ont droit de surveillance et de censure sur les rabbins, sous-rabbins et ministres-officiants de leur circonscription. Ils ne peuvent néanmoins censurer les rabbins et les sous-rabbins qu'avec l'adhésion du Consistoire départemental.

Art. 45. Le grand-rabbin et les rabbins consistoriaux ne peuvent être suspendus que pour des causes graves soumises à l'appréciation du Consistoire central. La suspension ne peut durer plus de six mois. Ils ne peuvent être révoqués que sur la plainte du Consistoire central, adressée au Ministre des cultes et pour les seules causes suivantes: Condamnation à une peine afflictive ou infâmante, à une peine correctionnelle pour les délits qui entachent l'honneur, pour scandale public ou inconduite notoire. Ils sont, de droit, en état d'interdiction pendant la durée d'une procédure criminelle, et leurs fonctions sont suspendues, même pendant les délais de l'appel, après un jugement correctionnel qui les condamnerait à l'emprisonnement pour les délits cidessus énoncés. La révocation des rabbins et des sous-rabbins par le Consistoire central ne peut avoir lieu que pour les mêmes causes.

Art. 46. Le grand-rabbin et les rabbins consistoriaux sont nommés à vie. La présente disposition est applicable à ceux qui sont actuellement en exercice. Le grand-rabbin et les rabbins consistoriaux sont nommés par ordonnance royale, sur la présentation du Consistoire central et après avoir satisfait aux obligations prescrites par les art. 56 et 57.

Art. 47. Les rabbins, les sous-rabbins et les ministres officiants sont élus par une commission nommée *ad hoc,* par les Consistoires départementaux, et dont les membres sont choisis de préférence parmi les notables domiciliés dans la commune, chef-lieu du ressort. Cette commission est présidée de droit par le commissaire surveillant. Le nombre des membres de ces commissions est laissé à l'appréciation des Consistoires départementaux, qui prennent en considération l'importance du ressort à desservir. Néanmoins, le nombre des commissaires ne saurait être au-dessus de onze. L'élection des rabbins et sous-rabbins est soumise à la confirmation du Consistoire central; celle des ministres-officiants appartient au Consistoire départemental.

Art. 48. Pendant la suspension, le traitement est réduit de moitié; il reprend dans son entier après l'acquittement, sauf au Consistoire central à prononcer la suspension, à provoquer ou à prononcer la révocation s'il y a lieu.

Art. 49. Nul ne peut être grand rabbin s'il n'a au moins quarante ans, s'il n'est Français et s'il ne possède, outre les connaissances requises des aspirants au titre de morénou harab (docteur-maître), la connaissance par principes de la langue allemande. Entre des candidats égaux en mérite, celui qui connaîtra une ou plusieurs langues de plus que les autres concurrents, sera préféré.

Art. 50. Nul ne peut être rabbin consistorial s'il n'est âgé de trente ans au moins, s'il n'est Français et s'il ne réunit les conditions que le règlement du 15 octobre 1832 exige des aspirants, au titre de *morénou harab* (docteur-maître). Pour être rabbin consistorial dans les Consistoires de Metz, Nancy, Strasbourg et Colmar, la connaissance par principes de la langue allemande est rigoureusement exigée.

Art. 51. Pour l'exécution des art. 49 et 50, le Ministre des cultes pourra accorder, sur la proposition du Consistoire central, des dispenses d'âge.

Art. 52. Nul ne peut être rabbin ou sous-rabbin s'il n'est âgé de vingt-cinq ans, s'il n'est Français et s'il ne réunit les conditions exigées, par le règlement du 15 octobre 1832, des aspirants au titre *morénou* (docteur de la loi).

Art. 53. Les rabbins et les sous-rabbins, dans les circonscriptions consistoriales de Metz, Nancy, Strasbourg et Colmar, doivent, indépendamment des connaissances exigées pour l'exercice de leurs fonctions, savoir la langue allemande par principes.

Les ministres-officiants sont examinés par le rabbin consistorial de la circonscription dans le ressort de laquelle ils veulent exercer. Outre les connaissances religieuses, ils doivent savoir le français; et, pour les départements de la Moselle, de la Meurthe, du Bas-Rhin et du Haut-Rhin, ils doivent aussi connaître l'allemand.

Art. 54. Les ministres du culte ne peuvent donner, soit en public, soit en particulier, aucune instruction ou explication de la loi qui soit contraire aux décisions du grand sanhédrin.

Art. 55. Avant leur installation, le grand-rabbin, les rabbins consistoriaux, les rabbins et sous-rabbins jurent d'être fidèles au Roi des Français, d'obéir à la Charte constitutionnelle et aux lois du royaume, d'employer tous leurs efforts, toute leur influence, toute leur autorité à favoriser le progrès des lumières parmi les Israélites, à leur inspirer les principes de morale et l'amour de la patrie. Les rabbins consistoriaux prêtent serment entre les mains du préfet, le grand-rabbin entre les mains du Ministre des cultes, les rabbins et les sous-rabbins dans le sein du Consistoire départemental de leur circonscription; enfin les ministres-officiants entre les mains du rabbin dont ils relèvent. Il est dressé procès-verbal de chacun de ces serments. Ceux qui constatent le serment du grand-rabbin, des rabbins consistoriaux, des rabbins et sous-rabbins, sont transmis en expédition au Consistoire central.

Art. 56. En cas de vacance de la place de grand rabbin, par suite de décès, démission, mise à la retraite ou révocation, le titre et les fonctions seront mis au concours entre les sept rabbins consistoriaux et ceux des rabbins qui se feront inscrire au Consistoire central dans le délai de deux mois. Le programme du concours sera dressé par le Consistoire central, approuvé par le Ministre des cultes. Une commission de neuf membres, présidée par le président du Consistoire central, et dont les huit autres membres seront désignés par le Ministre, sera juge du concours. Les candidats devront présenter le diplôme du deuxième degré rabbinique.

Art. 57. En cas de vacance d'une place de rabbin consistorial, par suite de décès, démission, mise à la retraite ou révocation, le titre et les fonctions seront mis au concours entre les autres rabbins consistoriaux, les rabbins, les sous-rabbins et les élèves actuels ou anciens de l'école centrale rabbinique qui se feront inscrire dans le délai de deux mois. Le programme du concours sera dressé par le Consistoire central, approuvé par le Ministre des cultes. Une commission de sept membres, présidée par le Président du Consistoire départemental, et dont les six autres membres seront désignés par le Ministre parmi les notables de la circonscription, sera juge du concours. Les candidats devront présenter le diplôme exigé par l'art. 50.

Art. 58. Les places de rabbins et de sous-rabbins appartiennent de droit aux élèves de l'école centrale religieuse de Metz, qui remplissent les conditions prescrites par l'art. 52 de la présente ordonnance et qui ont reçu le diplôme de bachelier-ès-lettres. Si l'école ne fournit pas un nombre de sujets suffisants, tout Israélite qui remplit les conditions voulues est admis.

Section III
De l'Exercice du Culte

Art. 59. A chaque chef-lieu consistorial, il y a un temple, appelé *Temple consistorial.* A Paris et à Bordeaux il y a deux temples consistoriaux, l'un pour les Israélites du rit allemand, l'autre pour ceux du rit portugais. Dans les autres villes, siéges des Consistoires, il peut y avoir un second temple consistorial si les besoins du culte l'exigent, sur la demande du Consistoire départemental, l'avis du préfet et du Consistoire central. Il y a besoin du culte, lorsque les Israélites qui suivent le rit portugais forment une réunion de trois cents individus au milieu de la population israélite, composée en majorité d'Israélites suivant le rit allemand, ou *vice versa.*

Art. 60. Dans l'une ou l'autre circonstance, les temples consistoriaux sont desservis par le rabbin consistorial, et par des ministres-officiants nommés par le Consistoire départemental, lesquels remplacent le rabbin consistorial dans les offices divins, en cas d'absence ou de maladie, et lui servent d'aides dans les cérémonies religieuses.

Art. 61. Dans toutes les autres villes, les temples actuellement existants sont maintenus.

Art. 62. L'ouverture d'un temple nouveau pourra être autorisée dans toute ville ou dans toute commune qui réunira les conditions de population déterminée par l'art. 38 de la présente ordonnance. L'avis favorable du préfet, du Consistoire départemental et l'approbation du Consistoire central seront préalablement nécessaires.

Art. 63. La réunion de dix Israélites mâles qui ont atteint

l'âge requis, suffisant à la loi religieuse pour former une association de prières, il pourra être accordé à tout chef de famille, sur sa demande, et sur l'avis favorable du Consistoire départemental, l'autorisation d'établir chez lui, soit à la campagne, et sous les conditions que le gouvernement jugera nécessaires, un oratoire destiné à la prière, mais à ses frais et à la charge de se soumettre au règlement qui sera fait par le Consistoire départemental.

Section IV
De l'Ecole centrale religieuse des Israélites

Art. 64. L'école centrale rabbinique de Metz prendra le titre de: Ecole centrale religieuse des Israélites. Le gouvernement sollicitera des chambres les ressources indispensables pour lui donner les développements nécessaires.

Art. 65. Le nombre des élèves gratuits est fixé à neuf. Deux places seront affectées à chacun des Consistoires de Strasbourg et de Colmar; une place appartient à chacun des autres Consistoires.

Art. 66. Aux études profanes prescrites par l'art. 15 du règlement du 21 août 1829, devront se joindre l'étude de la langue allemande, les éléments de chimie et de physique, d'arithmétique, les éléments de l'algèbre et l'étude du chant.

Art. 67. Le directeur et les professeurs de l'école centrale religieuse seront nommés par le Consistoire central et devront être agréés par le Ministre des cultes. Leur traitement sera fixé par le Consistoire central sauf l'approbation des chambres.

Le directeur de l'établissement devra, une fois chaque année, adresser au Consistoire central et au Consistoire de Metz, un rapport détaillé sur les progrès et la conduite des élèves et sur la situation de l'établissement. La commission administrative adressa également chaque année au Consistoire central et au Consistoire de Metz, un rapport circonstancié qui embrassera toutes les parties de l'école; elle fera connaître les vues d'amélioration, s'il y a lieu, tant sous le rapport matériel que sous le rapport moral, et sur l'impulsion donnée à l'école par le directeur et les professeurs. Le Consistoire de Metz donnera son avis au Consistoire central sur ces deux rapports.

Art. 68. Il sera porté au budget du culte israélite une somme annuelle de cinq mille francs destinée au traitement de prédicateurs. Ces prédicateurs, désignés par le Consistoire central, porteront la parole sacrée et les instructions morales et religieuses dans la population israélite. Ils correspondront avec le Consistoire central. Chaque année, le Consistoire central adressera au Ministre des cultes un rapport détaillé sur les résultats de ces prédications.

Art. 69. Les décrets du 17 mars 1808, les ordonnances royales des 29 juin 1819, du 20 août 1823 et 6 août 1831 sont abrogés. Le règlement du 15 octobre 1832 est maintenu dans les dispositions qui ne sont pas contraires à la présente ordonnance.

**Ordonnance du roi portant règlement pour
l'organisation du culte israélite, du 25 mai 1844**

Louis-Philippe, roi de Français,

A tous présents et à venir, salut.

Sur le rapport de notre garde des sceaux, ministre secrétaire d'Etat au département de la justice et des cultes;

Vu les décrets des 17 mars et 11 décembre 1808, et le règlement du 10 décembre 1806, y annexé;

Vu les ordonnances royales des 29 juin 1819, 20 août 1823, 6 août 1831, 19 juillet et 31 décembre 1841;

Vu le règlement du 15 octobre 1832;

Vu la loi du 8 février 1831;

Vu la lettre du consistoire central des israélites à notre garde des sceaux, ministre de la justice et des cultes, en date du 10 mars 1842, et le projet du nouveau règlement y annexé;

Vu la lettre du 27 mars 1844, par laquelle notre garde des sceaux, ministre de la justice et des cultes, a communiqué, tant au consistoire central qu'aux consistoires départementaux, une nouvelle rédaction dudit projet de règlement;

Vu les observations présentées sur ce dernier projet par le consistoire central et par les consistoires départementaux de Paris, Metz, Nancy, Colmar, Marseille, Bordeaux et Strasbourg;

Notre conseil d'Etat entendu,

Nous avons ordonné et ordonnons ce qui suit:

Organisation générale du culte israélite

Art. 1er. Le culte israélite a un consistoire central, des consistoires départementaux, des grands rabbins, des rabbins communaux, et des ministres officiants.

Titre 1er
Des Consistoires

2. Le consistoire central siége à Paris.

3. Il est établi un consistoire dans chaque département renfermant 2,000 âmes de population israélite.

S'il ne se trouve pas 2,000 israélites dans le même département, la circonscription du consistoire s'étend de proche en proche sur autant de départements qu'il en faut pour que ce nombre soit atteint.

Dans aucun cas, il ne peut y avoir plus d'un consistoire par département.

4. Les consistoires actuellement existants, leur siège et leur circonscription, tels qu'ils sont fixés par le décret du 11 décembre 1808, sont maintenus.

Dans le cas où il y aura lieu de former un ou plusieurs consistoires nouveaux, l'ordonnance royale qui en prononcera la création désignera en même temps la ville où ils seront établis.

Ier. Du consistoire central

5. Le consistoire central se compose d'un grand rabbin et d'autant de membres laïques qu'il y a de consistoires départementaux.

6. Les membres laïques du consistoire central sont élus par les notables des circonscriptions consistoriales.

Ils sont choisis parmi les notables résidant à Paris.

7. Le grand rabbin du consistoire central est nommé suivant les formes prescrites par les art. 40 et suivants.

Sa nomination est soumise à notre approbation.

8. La durée des fonctions des membres laïques est de huit ans. Ils sont divisés en deux séries se renouvelant alternativement de quatre en quatre années. Les membres sortants sont rééligibles.

9. Le consistoire central nomme son président et son vice-président pour quatre ans.

10. Le consistoire central est l'intermédiaire entre le ministre des cultes et les consistoires départementaux. Il est chargé de la haute surveillance des intérêts du culte israélite.

Il approuve les règlements relatifs à l'exercice du culte dans les temples.

Aucun ouvrage d'instruction religieuse ne peut être employé dans les écoles israélites, s'il n'a été approuvé par le consistoire central, sur l'avis conforme de son grand rabbin.

11. Le consistoire central a le droit de censure à l'égard des membres laïques des consistoires départementaux.

Il peut provoquer, pour des causes graves, auprès de notre ministre des cultes, la révocation de ces membres, et même la dissolution d'un consistoire départemental.

12. Le consistoire central délivre seul les diplômes de second degré pour l'exercice des fonctions rabbiniques, sur le vu des certificats d'aptitude obtenus conformément au règlement du 15 octobre 1832.

Il donne son avis sur la nomination des rabbins départementaux et communaux.

Il peut, sur la proposition du consistoire départemental, et avec l'approbation de notre ministre des cultes, ordonner le changement de résidence des rabbins communaux dans le ressort du consistoire.

Le consistoire central a le droit de censure à l'égard des grands rabbins consistoriaux, mais seulement sur la plainte de leurs consistoires respectifs. Il peut provoquer auprès de notre ministre des cultes leur suspension ou leur révocation, suivant le cas.

Il a directement, après avoir pris l'avis du consistoire et du grand rabbin, le droit de censure à l'égard des rabbins communaux.

Il peut prononcer leur suspension pour un an au plus.

Il prononce leur révocation, sauf la confirmation de notre ministre des cultes.

Il statue sur la révocation des ministres officiants, proposée par les consistoires départementaux.

13. Le consistoire central peut être dissous par ordonnance royale.

Dans ce cas, l'administration du culte israélite est déléguée jusqu'à l'installation d'un nouveau consistoire, à une commission composée du grand rabbin et de quatre notables désignés par notre ministre des cultes.

2. Des consistoires départementaux

14. Chaque consistoire départemental se compose du grand rabbin de la circonscription et de quatre membres laïques, dont deux au moins sont choisis parmi les habitants de la ville où siége le consistoire.

15. Le grand rabbin et les membres laïques sont élus par l'assemblée des notables de la circonscription.

16. Les membres laïques sont choisis parmi les notables de la circonscription.

17. La durée des fonctions des membres laïques est de quatre ans.

Leur renouvellement a lieu par moitié tous les deux ans.

Les membres sortants peuvent être réélus.

18. Le consistoire nomme son président et son vice-président pour deux années.

19. Le consistoire a l'administration et la police des temples de sa circonscription et des établissements et associations pieuses qui s'y rattachent.

Il délivre les diplômes de premier degré pour l'exercice des fonctions rabbiniques, sur le vu des certificats énoncés en l'article 12.

Il représente en justice les synagogues de son ressort, et exerce en leur nom les droits qui leur appartiennent, sous la réserve portée en l'art. 64.

Il nomme les commissions destinées à procéder à l'élection des rabbins communaux et des ministres officiants, ainsi qu'il est réglé par les art. 48 et 51.

Il donne au consistoire central son avis sur ces élections.

Il nomme le *mohel* et le *schohet* pour le chef-lieu consistorial, sur l'avis du grand rabbin, et, pour les autres communes, sur le certificat du rabbin du ressort, confirmé par le grand rabbin.

Ces nominations sont révocables par le consistoire, sur l'avis du grand rabbin.

20. Le consistoire a le droit de suspension à l'égard des ministres officiants, après avoir pris l'avis du commissaire administrateur ou de la commission administrative ci-après instituée.

Il propose, quand il y a lieu, leur révocation au consistoire central.

Il adresse au consistoire central les plaintes qu'il peut avoir à former, tant contre le grand rabbin que contre les rabbins de sa circonscription.

Il fait, sous l'approbation du consistoire central, les règlements concernant les cérémonies religieuses relatives aux inhumations et à l'exercice du culte dans tous les temples de son ressort.

Il est chargé de veiller, 1° à ce qu'il ne soit donné aucune instruction ou explication de la loi, qui ne soit conforme aux réponses de l'assemblée générale des israélites, converties en décisions doctrinales par le grand sanhédrin; 2° à ce qu'il ne se forme, sans autorisation, aucune assemblée de prières.

21. Le consistoire institue, par délégation, auprès de chaque temple, et selon les besoins, soit un commissaire administrateur, soit une commission administrative, agissant sous sa direction et sous son autorité.

Le commissaire ou la commission rend compte annuellement de la gestion au consistoire départemental.

22. Chaque année, le consistoire adresse au préfet un rapport sur la situation morale des établissements de charité, de bienfaisance ou de religion spécialement destinés aux israélites.

23. Les consistoires départementaux peuvent être dissous par arrêté de notre ministre des cultes.

Dans ce cas, l'administration des affaires de la circonscription est déléguée, jusqu'à l'installation d'un nouveau consistoire, à une commission composée du grand rabbin consistorial et de quatre notables désignés par le consistoire central.

3. Dispositions communes au consistoire central et aux consistoires départementaux

24. La nomination des membres laïques des consistoires est soumise à notre agrément.

L'époque de leur entrée en fonctions est fixée au 1er janvier.

Le père, le fils ou les petits-fils, le beau-père, les gendres et les frères ou beaux-frères, ne peuvent être ensemble membres d'un consistoire.

Pour le premier renouvellement, la série des membres sortants est désignée par la voie du sort.

Les présidents et vice-présidents sont rééligibles.

En cas de dissolution d'un consistoire, il est procédé à de nouvelles élections dans les trois mois.

4. Des notables

25. Il y a, pour chaque circonscription consistoriale, un corps de notables chargé d'élire, 1° le grand-rabbin consistorial; 2° les membres laïques du consistoire départemental; 3° un membre laïque du consistoire central; 4° deux délégués pour l'élection du grand rabbin du consistoire central, ainsi qu'il est dit en l'art. 42.

26. Font partie du corps des notables les israélites âgés de vingt-cinq ans accomplis, et qui appartiennent à l'une des catégories suivantes:

1° Les fonctionnaires publics de l'ordre administratif;

2° Les fonctionnaires de l'ordre judiciaire;

3° Les membres des conseils généraux, des conseils d'arrondissement et des conseils municipaux;

4° Les citoyens inscrits sur la liste électorale et du jury;

5° Les officiers de terre et de mer, en activité et en retraite;

6° Les membres des chambres de commerce et ceux qui font partie de la liste des notables commerçants;

7° Les grands rabbins et les rabbins communaux;

8° Les professeurs dans les facultés et dans les collèges royaux et communaux;

9° Le directeur et les professeurs de l'école centrale rabbinique.

27. A cette liste pourront être adjoints, par notre ministre des cultes, sur la proposition du consistoire central et les avis du consistoire départemental et du préfet, et ce, jusqu'à concurrence du sixième de la liste totale, les israélites qui ne seraient pas compris dans ces catégories, et qui, par leurs services, se seraient rendus dignes de cette distinction.

28. Nul ne fera partie de la liste des notables s'il n'a la qualité de Français, s'il a subi une condamnation criminelle ou une des condamnations correctionnelles portées aux art. 401, 405 et 408 du Code pénal, s'il est failli non réhabilité, et s'il n'est depuis deux ans au moins domicilié dans la circonscription consistoriale.

29. Les listes seront dressées par les consistoires, elles demeureront exposées, à partir du 1ᵉʳ mars de chaque année, et pendant deux mois, au parvis du temple du chef-lieu consistorial.

Pendant ce délai, toutes réclamations seront admises; il y sera statué par le préfet, sur l'avis du consistoire, sauf recours à notre ministre des cultes par la voie administrative. Le ministre prononcera définitivement, sur l'avis du consistoire central.

Les listes arrêtées par le préfet serviront pour un an.

30. Chaque année, les consistoires feront les additions et radiations nécessaires, conformément aux dispositions de l'article précédent, de façon que la liste définitive soit publiée dans le temple du chef-lieux consistorial au 1er juillet de chaque année.

5. *Des assemblées des notables et de l'élection des membres du consistoire*

31. L'assemblée des notables est convoquée par le consistoire départemental, sur l'autorisation du préfet du département, pour procéder aux élections mentionnées en l'art. 25.

32. Les élections ont lieu à la majorité absolue des membres présents.

Le nombre des membres présents au vote doit être de la moitié au moins de la liste totale.

Si ce nombre n'est pas atteint, une seconde réunion est convoquée, et l'élection est valable, quel que soit alors le nombre des votants.

33. Le bureau se compose des membres du consistoire départemental.

34. Le bureau prononce sur les difficultés qui s'élèvent touchant les opérations. En cas de partage, la voix du président est prépondérante.

Les réclamations contre la décision du bureau ne sont pas suspensives. Elles sont portées, par la voie administrative, devant notre ministre des cultes, qui prononce définitivement.

35. Le procès-verbal, signé des membres du bureau, fait mention de toutes les opérations et des incidents survenus. Il est dressé en double expédition, dont l'une est transmise au préfet, et l'autre au consistoire central.

36. L'installation des membres laïques du consistoire central et des consistoires départementaux est faite par le préfet, qui reçoit de la part de chaque membre, le serment prescrit par la loi du 31 août 1830.

Le serment est prononcé en levant la main, sans autre formalité.

37. Si le consistoire se refusait à l'accomplissement des obligations qui lui sont imposées par la présente section, il y serait pourvu par le préfet.

Titre II
Des Ministres du culte

1er. *Du grand rabbin du consistoire central*

38. Le grand rabbin a droit de surveillance et d'admonition à l'égard de tous les ministres du culte israélite.

Il a droit d'officier et de prêcher dans toutes les synagogues de France.

Aucune délibération ne peut être prise par le consistoire central concernant les objets religieux ou du culte, sans l'approbation du grand rabbin.

Néanmoins, en cas de dissentiment entre le consistoire central et son grand rabbin, le grand rabbin du consistoire de Paris est consulté.

Si les deux rabbins diffèrent d'avis, le plus ancien de nomination des grands rabbins consistoriaux est appelé à les départager.

39. Le grand rabbin est nommé à vie.

Nul ne peut être grand rabbin s'il n'est âgé de quarante ans accomplis, muni d'un diplôme de second degré rabbinique, délivré conformément au règlement du 15 octobre 1832, et s'il n'a rempli pendant dix ans au moins, les fonctions de rabbin communal, ou pendant cinq ans celles de grand rabbin consistorial ou de professeur à l'école centrale rabbinique. Néanmoins ces deux dernières conditions ne seront exigibles qu'à partir de 1850.

40. En cas de décès ou de démission du grand rabbin, les assemblées de notables de toutes les circonscriptions nomment à l'époque fixée par le consistoire central, chacune deux délégués pour procéder, conjointement avec les membres du consistoire central, à l'élection du grand rabbin.

41. Les délégués sont choisis parmi les notables de la circonscription ou parmi ceux du collége de Paris.

Si plusieurs colléges choisissent à Paris le même délégué, le consistoire central tire au sort la circonscription dont le membre élu sera le représentant. Les autres ont à nommer un nouveau délégué.

42. La présidence de l'assemblée des délégués et des membres du consistoire central, réunis pour procéder à l'élection, appartient au président du consistoire central.

Le plus jeune des membres remplit les fonctions de secrétaire.

L'élection a lieu à la majorité absolue des voix et au scrutin secret. Elle n'est valable qu'autant que quinze membres au moins y ont concouru.

Le procès-verbal de l'élection est transmis à notre ministre des cultes par le consistoire central.

2. Des grands rabbins des consistoires départementaux

43. Les grands rabbins des consistoires départementaux ont droit de surveillance sur les rabbins et sur les ministres officiants de leur circonscription.

Ils ont droit d'officier et de prêcher dans tous les temples de leur circonscription.

44. Nul ne peut être grand rabbin consistorial s'il n'est âgé

de trente ans, et s'il n'est porteur d'un diplôme de second degré rabbinique.

45. Les grands rabbins des consistoires départementaux sont élus, 1° parmi ceux des grands rabbins des autres circonscriptions qui se font inscrire au siége du consistoire; 2° parmi les rabbins en fonctions sortis de l'école centrale rabbinique; 3° parmi les rabbins ayant cinq ans d'exercice, quand ils ne sont pas élèves de cette école, et parmi les professeurs de la même école. Leur nomination est soumise à notre approbation.

3. Des rabbins communaux

46. Les rabbins officient et prêchent dans les temples de leur ressort.

47. Nul ne peut être rabbin s'il n'est âgé de vingt-cinq ans accomplis, et porteur d'un diplôme du premier degré rabbinique.

48. Les rabbins sont élus par une assemblée de notables désignés par le consistoire départemental et choisis de préférence parmi les notables du ressort.

Le commissaire administrateur ou le président de la commission administrative préside cette assemblée.

Le consistoire règle, suivant l'importance du ressort à desservir, le nombre des membres qui la composent, lequel, en aucun cas, ne peut être au-dessous de cinq.

Le consistoire départemental transmet le procès-verbal de l'élection, avec les pièces à l'appui, au consistoire central. La nomination est soumise à l'approbation de notre ministre des cultes.

49. Les rabbins sont choisis parmi les élèves de l'école centrale rabbinique pourvus du diplôme exigé.

Si l'école ne fournit pas un nombre de candidats suffisant, tout israélite remplissant les conditions prescrites par l'art. 47 ci-dessus peut être admis comme candidat.

4. Des ministres officiants

50. Nul ne peut être ministre officiant s'il n'est âgé de vingt-cinq ans, et s'il ne produit un certificat du grand rabbin de la circonscription, attestant qu'il possède les connaissances religieuses suffisantes.

Le consistoire central déterminera la forme de ces certificats.

51. Les ministres officiants sont élus dans la forme déterminée par l'art. 48.

Leur élection est confirmée par le consistoire central.

Le consistoire départemental nomme directement le ministre officiant du chef-lieu consistorial.

Le consistoire central envoie à notre ministre des cultes l'avis des nominations faites et approuvées; il indique les justifications produites par les nouveaux titulaires.

5. *Du mohel et du schohet*

52. Nul ne peut exercer les fonctions de mohel et de schohet s'il n'est pourvu d'une autorisation spéciale du consistoire de la circonscription.

Le mohel et le schohet sont soumis, dans l'exercice de leurs fonctions, aux règlements émanés du consistoire départemental et approuvés par le consistoire central.

6. *Dispositions communes aux divers ministres du culte israélite*

53. Le grand rabbin consistorial et les rabbins ne peuvent célébrer les mariages que dans l'étendue de leur ressort.

Ils ne peuvent donner la bénédiction nuptiale qu'à ceux qui justifient avoir contracté mariage devant l'officier de l'état civil.

La bénédiction nuptiale n'est donnée que dans l'intérieur du temple, sauf le cas d'autorisation spéciale accordée par le consistoire départemental.

Les ministres du culte assisteront aux inhumations, suivant ce qui aura été réglé par le consistoire départemental, en vertu du paragraphe 4 de l'art. 20 ci-dessus.

54. Aucune assemblée délibérante ne pourra être formée, aucune décision doctrinale ou dogmatique ne pourra être publiée ou devenir la matière de l'enseignement sans une autorisation expresse du gouvernement.

55. Toutes entreprises des ministres du culte israélite, toutes discussions qui pourront s'élever entre ces ministres, toute atteinte à l'exercice du culte et à la liberté garantie à ces ministres, nous seront déférées en notre conseil d'Etat, sur le rapport de notre ministre des cultes, pour être par nous statué ce qu'il appartiendra.

56. Nul ministre du culte israélite ne peut donner aucune instruction ou explication de la loi qui ne soit conforme aux décisions du grand sanhédrin ou aux décisions des assemblées synodales qui seraient par nous ultérieurement autorisées.

Les rabbins ont, sous l'autorité des consistoires, la surveillance et la direction de l'instruction religieuse dans les écoles israélites.

57. Nul ne peut être nommé grand rabbin, rabbin communal, ministre officiant, s'il n'est Français.

Des dispenses d'âge peuvent être accordées aux grands rabbins, aux rabbins communaux et aux ministres officiants, par notre ministre des cultes, sur la proposition du consistoire central.

Les fonctions de rabbin sont incompatibles avec toute profession industrielle ou commerciale.

58. Avant leur installation, les grands rabbins et les rabbins prêtent, entre les mains du préfet ou de son délégué, le serment prescrit par la loi du 31 août 1830. Le serment du grand rabbin

du consistoire central est prêté entre les mains de notre ministre des cultes.

59. Il est procédé, selon les instructions du consistoire de chaque circonscription, à l'installation des rabbins et des ministres officiants.

Procès-verbal de cette installation est transmis, en double expédition, par le consistoire départemental, au consistoire central et au préfet du département où réside le nouveau titulaire.

Titre III
Des circonscriptions rabbiniques et des temples

60. Il ne peut être établi aucune nouvelle circonscription rabbinique, ni être fait aucune modification aux circonscriptions rabbiniques actuellement existantes, qu'en vertu de notre autorisation, donnée sur le rapport de notre ministre des cultes, et sur l'avis du consistoire central, des communes intéressées et du préfet du département.

61. Dans la ville chef-lieu du consistoire départemental, il peut être adjoint au grand rabbin un ou plusieurs rabbins communaux, selon les besoins de la population.

Il est statué à cet égard par ordonnance royale.

62. Il ne peut être créé de titre de ministre officiant à la charge de l'Etat que par un arrêté de notre ministre des cultes, sur la demande du consistoire départemental et l'avis du consistoire central et du préfet.

63. Tout chef de famille peut, en rapportant l'avis favorable du consistoire départemental, obtenir l'autorisation d'ouvrir un oratoire chez lui et à ses frais.

Cette autorisation sera donnée par nous, sur le rapport de notre ministre des cultes.

Titre IV
Dispositions diverses

64. Les consistoires israélites ne peuvent, sans autorisation préalable, intenter une action en justice ou y défendre, accepter des donations et legs, en faire l'emploi, vendre ou acheter.

65. Aussitôt après la formation et la clôture de la liste générale des notables dans chaque circonscription consistoriale, il sera procédé au renouvellement intégral des membres laïques du consistoire central et des consistoires départementaux.

Les membres nouvellement élus entreront en fonctions immédiatement après que leur élection aura été confirmée par nous.

Néanmoins, pour le renouvellement périodique, leur entrée

en fonctions ne comptera que du 1er janvier qui suivra leur installation.

66. Continueront à être observés, dans toutes les dispositions qui ne sont pas contraires à la présente ordonnance, les décrets des 17 mars et 11 décembre 1808, les ordonnances royales des 29 juin 1819, 20 août 1823, 6 août 1831, 19 juillet et 31 décembre 1841.

67. Notre garde des sceaux, ministre de la justice et des cultes, est chargé de l'exécution de la présente ordonnance, qui sera insérée au Bulletin des lois.

Au palais de Neuilly, le 25 mai 1844.

Signé: Louis-Philippe
Par le roi:
Le garde des sceaux, ministre de la justice et
des cultes,
N. Martin (du Nord)

Napoléon, etc.

Sur le rapport de notre Ministre Secrétaire d'Etat au département de l'instruction publique et des cultes;

Vu l'Ordonnance du 25 mai 1844, portant règlement pour l'organisation du culte israélite;

Vu les instructions réglementaires des 15 décembre 1849 et 24 avril 1850;

Vu les propositions du Consistoire central;

Considérant qu'il y a lieu de mettre en harmonie certaines dispositions de l'Ordonnance précitée, et notamment celle concernant la nomination des Grands Rabbins des Consistoires départementaux, et de régler cette nomination suivant le système adopté pour l'élection du Grand Rabbin et du Consistoire central;

Avons décrété et décrétons ce qui suit:

Art. 1er.—Les Grands Rabbins des Consistoires départementaux seront nommés par les membres laïques de ces Consistoires, conjointement avec une Commission de vingt-cinq notables délégués à cet effet par les électeurs consistoriaux de la circonscription dans le ressort de laquelle la place de grand rabbin est devenue vacante.

Art. 2.—Les Rabbins communaux seront nommés par les Consistoires départementaux sur une liste de mérite des élèves sortant de l'Ecole rabbinique, ou choisis parmi les Rabbins communaux en exercice qui demanderaient à changer de résidence.

En cas de partage des voix, celle du Grand Rabbin sera prépondérante.

Art. 3.—Sont et demeurent maintenues les dispositions de l'Ordonnance du 25 mai 1844 et des Règlements postérieurs qui ne sont point contraires au présent Décret.

Art. 4.—Notre Ministre Secrétaire d'Etat au département de l'instruction publique et des cultes est chargé du présent Décret.

Fait au Palais de Saint-Cloud.

Paris, le 9 juillet 1853.

Signé Napoléon

Napoléon, etc.

Sur le rapport de notre Ministre Secrétaire d'Etat au département de l'instruction publique et des cultes;

Vu les Décrets des 17 mars et 11 décembre 1808, et le Règlement du 10 décembre 1806, y annexé;

Vu la loi du 8 février 1831;

Vu les Ordonnances royales du 25 mai 1844 et du 9 novembre 1845;

Vu les Décrets des 15 juin 1850 et 9 juillet 1853;

Vu les propositions du Consistoire central et les observations des Consistoires départementaux;

Notre Conseil d'Etat entendu,

Avons décrété et décrétons ce qui suit:

Art. 1er.—Dans les communautés israélites desservies par un ministre officiant rétribué sur les fonds de l'Etat, il peut être établi, par arrêté de notre Ministre, sur la proposition du Consistoire central, un Sous-Rabbin à la place du ministre officiant.

Art. 2.—Les Sous-Rabbins doivent être âgés de vingt-cinq ans au moins.

Ils sont nommés par les Consistoires départementaux.

Les conditions d'étude pour le titre de Sous-Rabbin, les fonctions et les attributions des Sous-Rabbins sont réglées par le Consistoire central, sous l'approbation de notre Ministre des cultes.

Les règles de discipline établies pour les ministres officiants sont applicables aux Sous-Rabbins.

Il peut leur être accordé des dispenses d'âge.

Art. 3.—Les diplômes du premier degré, pour l'exercice des fonctions rabbiniques, sont, comme les diplômes supérieurs ou du second degré, délivrés par le Consistoire central.

Art. 4.—La durée des fonctions des membres des Consistoires départementaux est de huit ans, comme celle des membres du Consistoire central.

Le renouvellement a lieu par moitié tous les quatre ans.

Les membres sortants peuvent être réélus.

Le Consistoire départemental nomme pour quatre ans son Président et son Vice-président.

Art. 5.—Dans chaque circonscription consistoriale, les membres laïques du Consistoire départemental, le membre laïque du Consistoire central et les deux délégués pour l'élection du Grand Rabbin du Consistoire central sont élus par tous les israélites âgés de vingt-cinq ans accomplis et qui appartiennent à l'une des catégories suivantes:

1° Ceux qui exercent des fonctions relatives au culte ou qui sont attachés, soit à titre d'administrateurs, soit à titre de souscripteurs annuels, aux établissements placés sous l'autorité des Consistoires;

2° Les fonctionnaires de l'ordre administratif, ceux de l'ordre judiciare, les professeurs, ou instituteurs dans les établissements et écoles fondés par l'Etat, par les communes ou par les Consistoires, et tout israélite pourvu d'un diplôme obtenu dans les formes établies par les lois et Règlements;

3° Les membres des Conseils généraux, des Conseils d'arrondissement et des Conseils municipaux;

4° Les officiers de terre et de mer en activité et en retraite;

5° Les sous-officiers, les soldats et les marins membres de la Légion d'honneur ou décorés de la médaille militaire;

6° Les membres des Chambres de commerce et ceux qui font partie de la liste des notables commerçants;

7° Les titulaires d'offices ministériels;

8° Les étrangers résidant dans la circonscription depuis trois ans et compris dans l'une des catégories ci-dessus, sans que, toutefois, la qualité d'électeur leur confère l'éligibilité.

Art. 6.—La liste des électeurs est dressée par le Consistoire départemental et arrêtée par le préfet.

Art. 7.—Dans chaque communauté, il est procédé, par les soins du Commissaire-Administrateur ou de la Commission administrative, à la formation de la liste partielle, comprenant tous les électeurs israélites de la circonscription.

Les électeurs israélites habitant dans des communes qui ne feraient point partie du ressort d'un Rabbin ou d'un ministre officiant se font inscrire sur la liste dressée dans la communauté la plus voisine de leur domicile.

Les listes partielles sont affichées pendant un mois au parvis du temple.

A l'expiration du délai porté au paragraphe précédent, les listes partielles et les réclamations auxquelles elles ont donné lieu sont adressées au Consistoire départemental.

Il sera procédé sur le tout selon ce qui est prescrit dans l'article 29 de l'Ordonnance du 25 mai 1844.

Art. 8.—La liste des électeurs est permanente.

Elle est révisée tous les quatre ans.

Néanmoins, lorsque, dans l'intervalle d'une révision à l'autre, il y a lieu de faire une nomination, le Consistoire ajoute à la liste les israélites qu'il reconnait avoir acquis les qualités requises, et il en retranche ceux qui les ont perdues.

Le tableau des additions et des retranchements est affiché au temple du chef-lieu consistorial, un mois avant la convocation de l'assemblée des électeurs; il est en même temps adressé au préfet.

Les demandes en inscription ou en radiation doivent être formulées dans les dix jours, à compter du jour de l'affiche.

Art. 9.—Les Grands Rabbins des Consistoires départementaux sont nommés par le Consistoire départemental.

La nomination est soumise à notre agrément.

Art. 10.—Nul ne peut exercer les fonctions de mohel et de schochet s'il n'a obtenu une autorisation spéciale du Consistoire de la circonscription, accordée sur l'avis conforme du Grand Rabbin. En outre, le mohel doit être pourvu d'un certificat délivré par un docteur en médecine ou en chirurgie désigné par le préfet, et constatant que l'impétrant offre, au point de vue de la santé publique, toutes les garanties nécessaires.

Le schochet doit, dans toute commune où il veut exercer ses fonctions, faire viser par le maire l'autorisation à lui donnée par le Consistoire départemental.

Les autorisations peuvent être révoquées.

Art. 11.—Les attributions du Consistoire central, telles qu'elles sont réglées par l'Ordonnance de 1844 et le présent Décret, comprennent la haute surveillance du culte israélite en Algérie.

Le Consistoire central devient l'intermédiaire entre le Ministre des cultes et le Consistoire algérien, qui sera représenté dans son sein par un membre laïque choisi parmi les électeurs résidant à Paris et agréé par nous.

Art. 12.—Continueront à être observés, dans toutes les dispositions qui ne sont pas contraires au présent Décret, les Ordonnances du 25 mai 1844 et du 9 novembre 1845, et nos Décrets des 15 juin 1850 et 9 juillet 1853.

Art. 13.—Notre Ministre Secrétaire d'Etat au département de l'instruction publique et des cultes est chargé de l'exécution du présent Décret, qui sera inséré au *Bulletin des Lois.*

Fait au Palais de Saint-Cloud, le 29 août 1862.

Signé Napoléon

APPENDIX C

**CIRCULAR OF THE CENTRAL CONSISTORY,
MARCH 12, 1846, CONTAINING NINE
QUESTIONS OF REFORMING JUDAISM**

Notre intention étant de convoquer pour les premiers jours du mois de mai prochain M.M. les Délégués chargés de concourir avec nous à la nomination d'un grand rabbin du Consistoire Central, nous vous prions d'en faire part à tous les rabbins, de votre circonscription, et de nous signaler ceux d'entre eux qui se portent candidats à la place éminente dont il va être disposé.

Vous voudrez leur faire connaître les conditions de cette candidature telles que les définit l'article 39 de l'ordonnance royale du 29 mai.

Vous voudrez en même temps les inviter à nous adresser par votre ministère, d'ici à la fin d'avril, un exposé précis de leurs vues sur les besoins actuels de notre culte et des obligations qu'ils croiraient avoir à remplir s'ils étaient appelés au rang de premier pasteur des Israélites de France.

Nous leur demandons particulièrement si d'après leur conscience et leurs convictions, d'après les principes essentiels et invariables de notre croyance, que nous désirons avant tout voir respectés, le futur grand rabbin du Consistoire Central devra prêter le concours de son autorité et de son influence pour amener, dans le plus court délai possible, les résultats suivants:

1° Pour réunir en un seul rit, en une seule synagogue, qui prendrait le nom de synagogue française, les deux rits particuliers qui existent actuellement sous les noms de synagogue allemande et de synagogue portugaise. Cette réunion pourrait avoir lieu sans obstacle, par la fusion des deux rituels, par l'introduction des mêmes mélodies religieuses, dans toutes les synagogues, et par la substitution dans la lecture de l'hébreu de la prononciation portugaise à la prononciation allemande, également répudiée par le goût, par la tradition et la science.

2° Pour donner plus d'éclat, plus de dignité et surtout plus d'ensemble à nos cérémonies religieuses, à celles du moins qui se pratiquent dans nos temples, qui constituent à proprement parler le culte public et au nombre desquelles il faut comprendre les mariages, les inhumations et les initiations religieuses.

3° Pour retrancher de nos prières, soit publiques, soit privées, toute parole susceptible d'être interprétée dans un sens contraire à notre position civile et politique au sein de la France, notre seule patrie, et pour amener la suppression de ces compositions appelées Pioutim qui prolongent démesurément le service divin sans rien dire ni à l'esprit ni au coeur.

4° Pour autoriser à la célébration de nos fêtes religieuses et nationales dans toutes les synagogues de France où cette innovation ne sera pas trop dispendieuse, l'usage de l'orgue déjà adopté depuis longtemps par plusieurs synagogues françaises et étrangères.

5° Pour assurer aux filles, jusqu'à présent exclues de la synagogue, une position plus nette et plus digne dans notre communion, en les consacrant à notre culte dès leur naissance, par un acte dont la forme serait déterminée plus tard; en rendant obligatoire pour elles la cérémonie de l'initiation religieuse et en les admettant à prendre part dans nos temples à la prière publique.

6° Pour introduire partout dans la pratique de la circoncision les améliorations réclamées par les progrès de la science.

7° Pour faire cesser à l'occasion des mariages et des inhumations toute recherche intolérante à l'égard des personnes, et cela par l'adoption du principe que tout individu né d'un père ou d'une mère israélite et se disant lui-même israélite doit être considéré comme un membre de notre communion.

8° Pour compléter et réformer s'il y a lieu l'enseignement de l'Ecole rabbinique de Metz en ajoutant à son programme d'études la théologie proprement dite, l'exégèse biblique, la controverse religieuse, des notions générales de notre droit civil et politique et en substituant immédiatement la langue française à la langue allemande dans les branches ou celle-ci est encore en usage et la prononciation portugaise à la prononciation allemande pour la lecture de l'hébreu.

9° Pour répandre de plus en plus chez tous les rabbins de France la conviction que leur ministère est un ministère de charité aussi bien que d'enseignement; que leur devoir n'est pas seulement de faire connaître du haut de la chaire la loi de Dieu et de résoudre les questions douteuses, mais de visiter les malades et les affligés, soit dans les hôpitaux, soit dans les maisons particulières, de porter la consolation et le bienfait de leur parole dans les prisons et les maisons de détention, de développer dans tous les coeurs l'amour de l'étude, de l'ordre et du travail.

Ceux des candidats qui voudront joindre à leurs communications écrites des explications verbales et se mettre personnellement en relation avec nous et M.M. les Délégues, nous feront un sensible plaisir. Nous appelons de tous les côtés les moyens de nous éclairer et de faire un choix digne de notre temps, digne du pays dans lequel nous avons le bonheur de vivre, digne des grands intérêts qui nous sont confiés.[1]

BIBLIOGRAPHY

I. ARCHIVAL SOURCES

A. French Public Archives

1. Archives Nationales

F^{19*} 1821   Etat des ministres du culte israélite et de leurs traitements (1861).

F^{19} 11014   Attributions des consistoires (1810). Réclamations et projets concernant l'organisation du culte (an XIII-1828). Préparation des ordonnances du 20 août 1823 et du 19 juillet 1841 sur le renouvellement des notables et des consistoires (1820-1823). Pièces relatives à un projet de loi sur les frais du culte (1830).

F^{19} 11015   Ordonnances des 22 mars, 6 août 1831 et 30 mars 1838. Projets de réforme et préparation de l'ordonnance organique du 25 mai 1844 (1837-1844). Introduction du suffrage universel dans les élections (1848-1850).

F^{19} 11016   Décrets et projets concernant l'organisation du culte: décret du 29 août 1862; enquêtes, rapports, travaux de la commission préparatoire (1854-1862). Décret du 5 février 1867.

F^{19} 11017   Décret du 12 septembre 1872 sur la nomination du grand rabbin et des rabbins; demandes et projets de réforme (1879-1880).

F^{19} 11019   Circonscriptions ecclésiastiques, tableau des circonscriptions. Modifications de circonscriptions et créations de places de rabbins et de ministres officiants dans le Haut-Rhin et le Bas-Thin. 1824-1870.

F^{19} 11020   Créations de rabbinats et de places de ministres officiants (par départements). 1814-1877.

F^{19} 11023   Statistique. Dénombrement de la population juive. Réponses et états fournis par les préfets en réponse à la circulaire de l'Intérieur du 29 mars 1808.

F^{19} 11024   Statistique. Réponses et états fournis après la circulaire du 3 octobre 1840. Renseigements et recensements en 1853, 1890, 1894, 1897.

F^{19} 11025   Ecole centrale rabbinique: organisation et réformes; rapports sur la situation morale de l'école . . . 1829-1859.

F^{19} 11028   Délibérations et correspondance du consistoire central au sujet de la création d'écoles primaires et autres (1809-1817). Secours aux écoles primaires israélites (1819-1851).

Cumul des fonctions d'instituteur et de ministre officiant (1851). Rapports du consistoire central sur des ouvrages d'instruction religieuse. Subventions à divers ouvrages ou publications. Offres de livres (1813-1887).

F^{19} 11029 Police du culte. Règlements intérieurs, troubles à l'exercice du culte (an XI-1861). Réunions de prières illicites, ouvertures et fermetures d'oratoires (an XI-1905).

F^{19} 11030 Coutumes et usages. Mariages et divorces (an XIII-1906). Costume des officiants (1810). Serment *more judaico* (1807-1812). Circoncision (1813-1845). Pains azymes, boucheries et nourritures spéciales (1811-1893). Culte dans les prisons (1840-1904).

F^{19} 11031 Prières publiques, actions de grâces, fêtes, réceptions officielles, préséances (1809-1890). Plaintes et réclamations contre faits d'intolérance (1820-1902).

F^{19} 11034 Organisation des consistoires (1808-1811). Correspondance relative aux notables et à l'organisation des consistoires, tableaux de circonscriptions, désignation des notables (1808-1809). Procès-verbaux des assemblées de notables du consistoire de Paris (1809). Installation des consistoires, délibérations et circulaires (1809-1810). Organisation du culte israélite dans les nouveaux départements de Hollande (1811). Réunions de rabbins (1856).

F^{19} 11036 Plaintes contre des consistoires, des commissaires surveillants, des administrations de temples, 1810-1895.

F^{19} 11037 Conflits entre le consistoire de Colmar et le consistoire central (1849-1857). Conflit entre consistoire et commission administrative de la synagogue à Besançon (1888-1889), à Nancy (1838). Conflit entre les consistoires de Colmar et de Mulhouse [sic!] (1849).

F^{19} 11039 Nomination de membres laïcs du consistoire central. 1808-1905.

F^{19} 11146 Algérie Projet de colonisation juive (1846). Règlementation des quêtes (1880-1893). Passages gratuits (1862-1895). Mariages (1876). Troubles et persécutions (1843-1898).

2. Archives Départementales du Bas-Rhin

V 511 Rapport au préfet du Bas-Rhin sur les israélites du département et les moyens de les régénérer (1832). Rapport du préfet Sers au ministre de l'Intérieur sur l'émancipation des juifs dans le Bas-Rhin (1843). Application par le consistoire du Bas-Rhin des dispositions de l'ordonnance 29 juin 1819 relative à l'organisation du culte (1819). Instructions diverses données par le consistoire aux fidèles (1812-1819). 1812-1843.

V 512 Décret concernant les sépultures (1806). Autorisation d'exercer le culte à Sélestat et Stotzheim (1811-1837). Scissions dans les communautés et manifestations d'indiscipline à l'égard du consistoire; Haguenau, Itterswiller,

Pfaffenhoffen, Riedseltz, Strasbourg, Wissembourg (1812–1866). 1806–1866.

V 520   Grands rabbins, membres du consistoire départemental et délégués au consistoire central: instructions et correspondance; procès-verbaux d'élections; nominations par le gouvernement; procès-verbaux d'installation et de prestation de serment; réclamations. 1832–1867.

V 522   Rabbins: élections; enquêtes administratives; nominations; procès-verbaux d'installation et de prestation de serment; révocations; démissions; congés; extraits d'état civil (dossiers individuels classés par ordre alphabétique des communes). 1831–1868.
       Bergheim: Bigard (1856)
       Bischeim: Beer (1837–1838)
       Bouxwiller: Wolff (1845)
       Brumath: Levy (1852)
       Dambach-la-Ville: Strauss, Blum, Weil (1835–1856)
       Fegersheim: Aron (1834)
       Hagenau: Libermann, Bloch (1846–1854)
       Lauterbourg: Haas, Lehmann, Grumbach, Weill (1833–1868)
       Marmoutier: Levy, Wimphen (1846–1853)
       Muttersholtz: Strauss (1831)
       Mutzig: Levy (1864)
       Niedernai: Levy (1835)
       Sarre-Union: Levy (1833)
       Saverne: Sopher, Dreyfus (1845–1856)
       Schirrhoffen: Lazarus A., Lazarus Z. (1854–1855)
       Surbourg: Lang, Bloch (1847–1852)
       Wintzenheim: Lehmann (1832)
       Wissembourg: Erlanger, Bloch (1856–1862).

V 523   Ministres officiants: élections; enquêtes administratives; nominations; procès-verbaux d'installation; révocations; démissions; plaintes formulées à leur endroit (dossiers individuels classés par ordre alphabétique des communes).
       Balbronn: Blum (1865)
       Hatten: Cahen (1848)
       Hochfelden: Goldsmitt, Beccard (1846–1861)
       Ingwiller: Mayer, Kalmann (1835–1858)
       Mertzwiller: Blum, Carron, Eisemann, Moch (1846–1866)
       Mommenheim: Bauer, Wollff (1848–1849)
       Niederbronn: Dennery, Schornstein, Weill (1833–1855)
       Niederroedern: Bloch, Mayer, Roos (1847–1858)
       Oberbronn: Weiner (1866)
       Obernai: Cahn (1861)
       Reichshoffen: Blum B., Blum J. (1855–1864)
       Romanswiller: Gradwohl, Geismar, Banberger, Joseph, Rosenberg (1834–1853)
       Rosheim: Banberger, Bloch, Weill (1834–1863)
       Soultz-sous-Forêts: Trautmann (1841)
       Strasbourg: Loeb, Loewe (1844–1855)
       Surbourg: Weill (1866)
       Westhouse: Gradwohl, Dreyfus (1834–1858)
       Zellwiller: Cahn, Levy, Fischer, Hirtz (1836–1866).

V 556   Règlement général pour l'administration et la police des synagogues promulgué par le Consistoire du Bas-Rhin (1861).

Commissions administratives: généralités; révocation de la commission d'Ingwiller; correspondance relative aux commissions de Haguenau et Rosheim. Révocation de commissaires surveillants et plaintes formulées à leur endroit: communautés de Bischeim, Sélestat, Stotzheim et Westhouse. 1812–1867.

V 560   Projet anonyme de statuts d'une "Société pour la régénération des juifs," précédé de considérations sur leur état moral et intellectuel. S.d.

V 562   Hospice Elisa: reconnaissance légale, statuts, legs de Louis Ratisbonne (1854–1862); achat de terrain à Strasbourg (1869–1870); comptes pour 1860 et 1866; pension accordée à Mme Lehmann, ancienne directrice de l'établissement (1861–1867). 1854–1870.

V 564   Ecole israélite d'arts et métiers: Nomination de membres de la commission administrative; rapports de la commission administrative; secours accordés par l'Etat ou le département; don de livrets de caisse d'épargne à des élèves de l'école; visites du ministre de l'Instruction publique et du préfet à l'établissement. 1849–1870.

V 571–573   Législation; mode de répartition de la contribution et détermination de la quote-part des départements du Bas-Rhin et du Haut-Rhin; formation des rôles et opérations de recouvrement; réductions et décharges; cotes irrécouvrables; réclamations et remboursement des créanciers (instructions, correspondance, rapports, états et comptes). 1823–1869.
         V 571 — 1823–1855
         V 572 — 1856–1860
         V 573 — 1861–1869.

VII M 211   (Jewish population, 1840, by community.)

VII M 212   (Jewish population, 1841.)

VII M 213   (Jewish population, 1846.)

3. Archives Départementales de la Gironde

6 M 1   (Population statistics, 1806, 1808, 1810, 1812.)

6 M 4   (1851 census.)

6 M 6   (1861 census.)

1 V culte israélite 1   Instructions, circulaires (1805–1844). Acquisitions et ventes d'immeubles (1846–1863). Ecoles (1840–1868). Cimetière (an XIII–1880). Divers (1807–1894).

1 V culte israélite 2   Personnel (1837–1900). Recensement de la population (1803–1843). Communautés juives étrangères à Bordeaux aux membres y résidant (1810–1868).

1 V culte israélite 3   Consistoire de la synagogue de Bordeaux, Collège des notables, présentations, nominations (1809–1853).

1 V culte israélite 5	Bâtiments, Synagogues de Bordeaux et de Libourne (1810–1884).
1 V culte israélite 7	Frais du culte, Budgets, dépenses générales d'administration, ordonnances de délégation, secours et indemnités, traitements (1826–1898).

4. Archives Départementales du Haut-Rhin

1 M 138/224	(Population statistics, 1807.)
1 M 138/1	(Population statistics, 1841, 1846.)
1 V 89	Circonscriptions rabbiniques, Création de rabbinats, Recensement de la population israélite (1825–1870).
1 V 91	Consistoires et notables, Personnel, Elections et varia (1841–1866).
1 V 92	Rabbins et ministres officiants, Nominations, Congés, Plaintes, etc. (An 10; 1816–1870).
1 V 97	Réunions de prières (An 12–1856), Sépultures des israélites (1827–1830), Varia (An 11–1868).

5. Archives Départementales de Meurthe-et-Moselle

V culte israélite 3	*Affaires générales (1820–1904).* Nomination par le Consistoire de Nancy du sieur Lambert comme receveur de la circonscription de Nancy (févr., 1821). Frais d'entretien du culte israélite (1827); frais d'administration du Consistoire israélite de Nancy (1838; 1869; 1873). Paiement des dettes viagères de l'ancienne communauté des Juifs de Metz (1820–1823). Idem pour l'ancienne communauté des Juifs d'Alsace (1868). Autorisation ou refus d'assemblées de prières juives (1829–1844). Etats numériques de la population israélite du département de la Meurthe (1840). Etats nominatifs des Israélites des communes de Rosières-aux-Salines, Vic et Chambrey (1844). Réponses des sous-préfets des arrondissements de la Meurthe à l'enquête du gouvernement sur la situation des Juifs (1843). Dissensions à Gosselming entre Israélites et catholiques (1849). Requête des Israélites de la communauté de Lisheim (1835) [objet indéterminé]. Rixe à l'intérieur de la synagogue de Mittelbronn (1865). Renseignements sur la situation et l'état de réparation ou d'entretien des synagogues de la circonscription israélite de Nancy (févr., 1838). Diverses synagogues; Baccarat-Verdun: construction, agrandissements, réparations (1841–1904). Ecoles israélites: ouverture, demandes de secours (1821–1840). Cimetières israélites: agrandissement; inhumations (1832; 1871). Décret de création du Consistoire israélite de Besançon (1881) [copie]. Autorisation d'achat de rente française par la communauté israélite de Lunéville (1901). Décret d'autorisation de l'exercice public du culte dans la synagogue de Bar-le-Duc (22 août 1903) [copie]. Demande d'autorisation d'ouverture d'une synagogue particulière à Troyes (1904).

V culte israélite 5 — *Personnel:* Nominations; indemnités; secours [classement par lieux de culte: Baccarat-Vic-sur-Seille] (1808–1897).

V culte israélite 7 — *Oeuvres israélites. Société israélite des amis du travail:* souscriptions et dons (1825–1826). *Oeuvre israélite de secours aux malades et d'une maison de refuge pour les vieillards et infirmes de Nancy:* reconnaissance légale (16 sept. 1889) [copie]; fonctionnement (31 déc. 1900); états de l'actif et du passif (1891–1911); comptes des recettes et dépenses (1897–1911); listes des membres souscripteurs (1905–1908); dons et legs en sa faveur (1891–1911; 1930–1939). *Oeuvre des Dames de charité israélites de Lunéville:* statuts (Lunéville, 15 févr. 1861) [copie]; reconnaissance légale (4 septembre 1863) [copie]; états de l'actif et du passif (1891; 1901); budget (1893–1895); legs en sa faveur (1891–1902; 1940). *Société de bienfaisance israélite de Toul:* refus d'existence légale (arrêté préfectoral du 5 déc. 1905).

6. Archives Départementales de la Seine

DV 59 — (Miscellaneous on Judaism 1842–1924.)

DV 64 — Ordonnances, décrets, instructions, 1844–1875.

DV 65 — (On the central consistory, Paris consistory, Paris notables, 1829–1908.)

B. Jewish Consistory Archives

1. Central Consistory Archives

1 B 4 — Procès verbaux des séances et des délibérations du consistoire central, 19 janvier 1832–23 janvier 1848.

1 B 5 — Procès-verbaux des séances et des délibérations du consistoire central, 9 janvier 1848–1 janvier 1871.

1 C 8 — (Minutes of letters sent, 1843–1850.)

1 C 9 — (Minutes of letters sent, 1850–1859.)

1 C 10 — (Minutes of letters sent, 1859–1866.)

3 E — Affaires politiques: More judaïco, 1809–1844; Univers catholique, 1858–1859.

4 E — (Schools, 1816–1869)

2 G 1 — Grand rabbin de France.

3 G 1 — Rabbinat, 1830–1935.

3 G 2 — Rabbinat—Dossiers personnels.

M   Affaires étrangères: Affaire de Damas, 1840; Affaire Mortara, 1858–1859; Les Juifs du Maroc réfugiés à Oran, 1860; La Suisse, 1826–1864.

2. Bordeaux Consistory Archives

2 A 4   Registre des Délibérations No. 4, 8 janvier 1826–22 janvier 1843.

2 A 5   Registre des Délibérations, 14 février 1843–21 octobre 1847.

2 A 6   Registre des Délibérations No. 6, 24 octobre 1847–21 avril 1858.

3 A 2   Répertoire du Registre des Délibérations, mars 1839–décembre 1859.

4 A 5   Copie de Lettres, No. 5, 5 avril 1835–10 juin 1842.

4 A 6   Copie de Lettres, No. 6, 10 juin 1842–12 mai 1850.

4 A 7   Copie de Lettres, No. 7, 12 mai 1850–31 décembre 1861.

7 A 3   Livre de Comptes, 1835–1857.

7 A 4   Livre de Comptes, 1857–1869.

2 B 4   Procès Verbaux de la Commission Administrative du Temple, 6 juillet 1843–31 décembre 1859.

4 B 4   Temple-Commission Administrative, Copie de Lettres, 2 août 1854–8 février 1881.

7 B 4   Temple — Comptes, 1851–1889.

7 C 2   Recettes et Dépenses de l'Ecole Primaire Israélite, 1 janvier 1825–31 décembre 1863.

2 D 2   Société de Bienfaisance de *Guemilout Hassadim* (pour l'inhumation), Administration Supérieure, Registre de Délibérations, 12 juillet 1847–10 février 1870.

3. Metz Consistory Archives (conserved in Archives Départementales de la Moselle)

17 J 39   Délibérations du Consistoire, 1819–1831.

17 J 40   Délibérations du Consistoire, 1845–1868.

17 J 42   Délibérations, expéditions, Minutes, brouillons, 1791–1850.

17 J 46   Affaires diverses, cabinet du Président: antisémitisme, 1822. Conversions d'enfants au catholicisme, 1858, 1919. Plaintes pour affaires d'usure, 1820–1821. Serment "more judaico," 1818–1843. Distinctions conférées au président, 1855. Relations avec les autres consistoires, recherches dans l'intérêt des familles, 1833–1839. Secours, comité de bienfaisance, 1833–1839, s. d. Alliance israélite universelle, 1866, etc. 1820–1919.

17 J 55   Comptabilité générale: Affaires diverses; souscriptions, legs Schwabe, etc., 1800–1848.

17 J 57   Impositions: Assiette et recouvrement: exécutoires par communautés, comptes, correspondance, plaintes et doléances. Extinction des dettes de l'ancienne communauté de Metz: rôle, etc., 1810–1885.

17 J 66   Fêtes et cérémonies officielles, Vente des honneurs, Police du culte, réformes (orgue, majorité religieuse), sermons, visites pastorales, circoncisions, 1811–1869.

17 J 71   Ecoles: Géneralités; comités cantonaux d'instruction primaire; société d'encouragement aux arts et métiers; enseignement primaire à Metz: salle d'asile, école d'enseignement mutuel, école de filles, 1817–1858.

17 J 72   Enseignement secondaire: école talmudique (1820–1830); instruction religieuse au lycée de Metz, divers, 1820–1852.

4. Paris Consistory Archives

AA 2   Procès-verbaux du 17 novembre 1825 au 13 mars 1839.

AA 3   Procès-verbaux du 18 mars 1839 au 8 juin 1847.

AA 4   Procès-verbaux du 26 juin 1847 au 9 août 1854.

AA 5   Procès-verbaux, 1854–1865 (held by Brandeis University).

Series B   Relations avec les autorités religieuses et civiles: correspondance générale: lettres reçues.
     B 21 — 1838–1839
     B 22 — 1840–1842
     B 23 — 1843
     B 24 — 1844
     B 25 — 1845
     B 31 — 1854
     B 32 — 1855–1856.

BB 3   Répertoire du courrier, 7 juin 1809 – 2 août 1847.

CC 8   Comptabilité, Mandats, 1841–1852.

CC 10   Comptabilité, Temple, Caisse, 1851–1855.

F 1   Ecoles, 1812–1873.

GG 1   "Mariages célébrés dans le Temple Israélite de la rue N. D. de Nazareth, Paris." Relevé des mariages comprenant les dates, noms, prénoms des époux, domiciles, classes. Récapitulation générale, 24 novembre 1822 – 31 décembre 1841.

GG 3   Attestations du Grand Rabbin du Consistoire Israélite de la circonscription de Paris que les époux ont été unis civilement avant la cérémonie religieuse. Noms, prénoms, domiciles des époux, dates des mariages religieux. 5 sept. 1852 – 9 déc. 1857.

GG 4   Mariages, 13 février 1858 – 6 avril 1862.

Series I^{CC} (Letters received by the central consistory.)

I^{CC} 11 — Consistoire de Colmar. 1835–1854.

I^{CC} 12 — Consistoire de Colmar. 1855–1870.

I^{CC} 15 — Consistoire de Strasbourg. 1833–1854.

I^{CC} 16 — Consistoire de Strasbourg. 1855–1870.

I^{CC} 18 — Consistoire de Metz. 1831–1870.

I^{CC} 19 — Consistoire de Saint-Esprit et lettres de Saint-Esprit. 1835–1857.

I^{CC} 22 — Consistoire de Bordeaux. 1830–1905.

I^{CC} 25 — Consistoire de Lyon. 1857–1905.

I^{CC} 28 — Consistoire de Marseille. 1831–1879.

I^{CC} 31 — Consistoire de Nancy. 1829–1869.

I^{CC} 34 — Consistoire de Paris. 1831–1869.

I^{CC} 52 — Temples. 1832–1864.

I^{CC} 53 — Elections consistoriales. 1834–1869.

I^{CC} 58 — Lettres au Consistoire Central ne provenant pas des Consistoires, classées sous les noms des expéditeurs, chemises numérotées de 1 à 80. 1817–1839.

I^{CC} 59 — Même contenu, chemises numérotées de 81 à 148. 1823–1836.

I^{CC} 60 — Lettres adressées au Consistoire Central ne provenant pas des Consistoires départementaux. 1809–1905

I^{CC} 61 — Etat des mutations. 1832–1853.

I^{CC} 62 — Etat des mutations. 1854–1869.

I^{CC} 69 — Lettres du Ministre de l'Intérieur et des Cultes. 1841–1848.

I^{CC} 70 — Lettres du Ministre de l'Intérieur et des Cultes. 1849–1855.

I^{CC} 78 — Lettres des Ministres de la Guerre et de la Marine: Organisation intérieure du Consistoire Central; Liste des rabbins de la Synagogue de Livourne; Protestation des Communautés du Haut-Rhin contre le programme élaboré par le Consistoire Central et imposé aux candidats au poste de Grand Rabbin du Consistoire Central (mentions grattées en partie sur le carton et restituées). 1809–1846.

I^{CC} 97 — Pièces relatives aux établissements de Bienfaisance avant 1844; Demande de M. Buding pour l'obtention d'un brevet d'imprimeur d'hébreu à Metz; Pièces relatives à l'enlèvement des filles Carcassone; Commission de la dette de Metz; Consistoire de Paris: dette du Temple. Dettes de l'ancienne communauté de Metz; Légion d'honneur, Statistique de la population israélite de France, 1860–1890; pétition des habitants de Sélestat, 1818–1890.

JJ 1   Société de l'Union de Secours mutuels d'Israélites de Paris. Comptes. Titre à l'intérieur: "Registre de la Société de secours Mutuels d'israélites de Paris, Commencé le 1er janvier 1834 sous la session de Messieurs les Présidents Lion et Julien." 1834–1858.

K 1   Documents imprimés, 1846–1847.

K 4   Documents imprimés, 1860–1862.

5. *Strasbourg Consistory Archives (Uncatalogued)*

Minutes of the Administrative Commission of Strasbourg, 1830–1849.

Minutes of Strasbourg consistory meetings, June 1, 1842 – April 27, 1847.

Minutes of letters sent, Administrative Commission of Strasbourg, 1847–1854, 1858–1860.

Minutes of Strasbourg consistory meetings, 1853–1858.

Minutes of Strasbourg consistory meetings, 1858–1863.

6. *Société pour l'histoire des Israélites d'Alsace-Lorraine (conserved in Archives départementales du Bas-Rhin)*

Boites No. 1, 2, 16   (Assorted 19th and 20th century manuscript and printed documents, including pastoral letters.)

7. *Central Archives for the History of the Jewish People (Jerusalem), Microfilm Collection*

HM 1067   Procès-verbaux des séances et des délibérations du consistoire central, 9 janvier 1848 – 1 janvier 1871.

HM 5503   Procès-verbaux du Consistoire du Bas-Rhin, 1842–1847.

HM 5517   Copies des lettres du comité local de surveillance des écoles (Strasbourg), 1841–1843.

HM 5533   Copies des lettres de la communauté de Strasbourg, 1847–1860.

8. *Jewish Theological Seminary of America (New York) (Uncatalogued French Jewish Documents)*

Boxes No. 2, 4, 5, 7   (Miscellaneous.)

Box marked "French documents, miscellaneous."

Boxes No. 18, 19, 20   Three boxes marked "Nineteenth and Twentieth Century Arguments between Reform and Orthodoxy."

II. PRINTED PRIMARY SOURCES

A. Journals

Alliance israélite universelle, bulletin semestriel. Paris, 1860–1913.
L'Ami des israélites. Strasbourg, 1847.
Archives israélites de France. Paris, 1840–1935.
La Famille de Jacob. Avignon, 1859–1891.
L'Israélite français. Paris, 1817–1818.
Le Lien d'Israél. Mulhouse, 1855–1861.
La Paix. Paris, 1846–1847.

La Pure Vérité. Strasbourg, 1846.
La Régénération-Wiedergeburt. Strasbourg, 1836–1837.
Revue orientale. Brussels, 1841–1844.
La Sentinelle juive. Paris, 1839–1840.
L'Union israélite. Paris, 1847–1848.
L'Univers israélite. Paris, 1844–1940.
La Vérité. Paris, 1848.
La Vérité israélite. Paris, 1860–1862.

B. Books and Pamphlets

Baquol, Jacques. *L'Alsace ancienne et moderne.* First and second editions. Strasbourg, 1849 and 1865.

Biding, Moïse. *La Vengeance d'Israël.* Metz, 1840.

Cahen, Samuel. *Précis élémentaire d'instruction réligieuse et morale pour les jeunes français israélites.* First and second editions. Paris, 1820 and 1831.

Créhange, Abraham. *Discours prononcé le 24 juin 1839 dans la séance du consistoire [de Paris] . . . en faveur des réunions réligieuses des sociétes de secours israélites de Paris.* Paris, 1839.

——. *Projet présenté au consistoire centrale et aux consistoires des départements pour l'établissement à Paris d'une école de commerce d'arts et métiers pour les jeunes Israélites.* Paris, 1844.

——. *Discours de M. Créhange prononcé dans la réunion préparatoire des Israélites de Paris, le 1er Décembre, 1844.* Paris, 1845.

——. *Almanach religieux et moral pour l'an du monde 5611 (1850–1851) à l'usage des Israélites.* Paris, 1850.

——. *Annuaire parisien du culte israélite pour 5617 (1856–1857).* Paris, 1856.

——. *Annuaire parisien du culte israélite pour 5626 (1865–1866).* Paris, 1865.

Dreyfus, Samuel. *Discours à Mulhouse.* Mulhouse, December 13, 1849.

Halphen, Achille. *Recueil des lois, décrets, ordonnances, avis du conseil d'état, arrêtés, et règlements concernant les Israélites depuis 1789.* Paris, 1851.

Jacobson, Israel. *Les premiers pas de la nation juive vers son bonheur sous les auspices du grand monarque Napoléon.* Paris, c. June, 1806.

Legoyt, A. "De certaines immunités biostatique de la race juive en Europe." *Journal de la société de statistique de Paris,* 10 (1869), 81–98, 109–124.

Lévy, Benoit. *Les droits et les devoirs du Grand Rabbin.* Paris, 1865.

Liquidation des dettes de l'Ancienne communauté juive de Metz. Mise en recouvrement du rôle de 1853. Imprimerie J. Mayer Samuel. Metz, 1853.

Mirecourt, Eugène de. *Heine.* Paris, 1856.

——. *La Bourse, ses abus et ses mystères.* Paris, 1858.

Recueil général des lois et arrêts. Paris, 1851 and 1855.

Refutation par un Israélite du Haut-Rhin de plusieurs articles calomnieux, publiés contre le consistoire israélite de Colmar. Strasbourg, 1841.

Singer, David. *Des consistoires israélites.* Paris, 1820.

Statistique de la France. Second series 2, 13. Paris, 1861.

Statistique de la France, Assistance Publique. Paris, 1866.

Tsarphati. [Olry Terquem.] *Projet de règlement conçernant la circoncision.* Paris, 1822.

——. *Cinquième lettre d'un israélite français à ses coreligionnaires.* Paris, 1824.

——. *Sixième lettre d'un israélite français à ses coreligionnaires.* Paris, 1824.

——. *Huitième lettre d'un israélite français à ses coreligionnaires.* Paris, 1836.

Uhry, Isaac, ed. *Recueil des lois, décrets, ordonnances, avis du conseil d'état, arrêtés, règlements et circulaires concernant les Israélites, depuis 1850.* Bordeaux, 1887.

Wahl, Benjamin. *Réponses à la deuxième lettre de M. Samuel Dreyfus, rabbin à Mulhouse.* Altkirch, 1845.

Weill, Goudchaux. *Deuxième lettre.* Paris, 1847.

Werthe, Léon. *Quelques réflexions sur la nécessité d'établir une colonie agricole pour la jeunesse israélite de l'Alsace.* Reprinted from *Archives israélites,* August, 1868. Colmar, 1868.

III. SECONDARY SOURCES

Albert, Phyllis. "The Archives of the Consistoire Israélite de Bordeaux, 1809–1905." *Revue des Etudes Juives,* 131 (1972).

——. "Le rôle des consistoires israélites vers le milieu du xixe siecle." *Revue des Etudes Juives,* 130 (1971).

Anchel, Robert. *Notes sur les frais du culte.* Paris, 1928.

——. *Napoléon et les Juifs.* Paris, 1928.

——. *Les Juifs de France.* Paris, 1946.

Baron, Salo. *The Jewish Community: Its History and Structure to the American Revolution.* Three volumes. Philadelphia, 1942.

Bauer, Jules. *L'Ecole rabbinique de France.* Paris, 1930.

Baugey, Georges. *De la condition légale du culte israélite en France et en Algérie.* Paris, 1899.

Beaufin, Penel. *Législation générale du culte israélite en France, en Algérie, et dans les colonies.* Paris, 1894.

Biraben, Jean-Noël. "Inventaire des listes nominatives de recensement en France." *Population,* 18 (1963).

Blumenkranz, Bernard. *Bibliographie des Juifs en France.* Paris, 1961.

Byrnes, Robert. *Antisemitism in Modern France.* New Brunswick, New Jersey, 1950.

Cahen, Abraham. "Une Notice historique sur les Israélites de l'Algerie." *Recueil des lois, décrets, ordonnances, avis du conseil d'état, arrêtés, règlements et circulaires concernant les Israélites, depuis 1850.* Edited by Isaac Uhry. Bordeaux, 1887.

Catane, Moshe. "Les Communautés du Bas-Rhin en 1809." *Revue des études juives,* 120 (1961).

——. "Les Juifs du Bas-Rhin sous Napoléon Premier: situation démographique et économique." Unpublished thesis, University of Strasbourg, 1967.

Chouraqui, André. *L'Alliance Israélite Universelle et la renaissance juive contemporaine.* Paris, 1965.

——. *Between East and West: A History of the Jews in North Africa.* Philadelphia, 1968.

Cirot, Georges. *Recherches sur les juifs espagnols et portugais à Bordeaux.* Bordeaux, 1908.

Daumard, Adeline. *La Bourgeoisie parisienne, 1815–1848.* Paris, 1963.

——. *Les Bourgois de Paris au dix-neuvième siècle.* Paris, 1970.

Debré, S. "The Jews of France." *Jewish Quarterly Review,* 3 (April 1891).

Delpech, François. "Documents relatifs aux Juifs dans la série V des archives départementales." *Archives Juives,* 3.

——. "La Seconde Communauté Juive de Lyon." *Cahiers d'Histoire,* 13 (1968).

Duveau, Georges. *La vie ouvrière en France sous le second empire.* Paris, 1946.

Finkelstein, Louis. *Jewish Self-Government in the Middle Ages.* New York, 1924.

Gille, Bertrand. *Les sources statistiques de l'histoire de France*. Paris, 1964.

Ginsburger, M. "Les troubles contre les Juifs d'Alsace en 1848." *Revue des études juives*, 64 (1912).

Hertzberg, Arthur. *The French Enlightenment and the Jews*. New York, 1968.

Hoffmann, Frances Malino. "Abraham Furtado and the Sephardi Jews of France." Unpublished thesis, Brandeis University, 1971.

Kahn, Léon. *Histoire des écoles communales et consistoriales israélites de Paris (1809-1844)*. Paris, 1884.

——. *Les professions manuelles et les institutions de patronage*. Paris, 1855.

——. *Le Comité de bienfaisance, l'hopital, l'orphelinat, les cimetières*. Paris, 1886.

——. *Les Sociétés de secours mutuels philanthropiques et de prévoyance*. Paris, 1887.

Kaspi, André. "La fondation de l'Alliance Israélite Universelle." Unpublished *mémoire*, Paris, 1959.

Katz, Jacob. *Tradition and Crisis*. Glencoe, Illinois, 1961.

Léon, Henry. *Histoire des Juifs de Bayonne*. Paris, 1893.

Leveillant, I. "La génèse de l'antisémitisme sous la troisième république." *Revue des études juives*, 53 (1907).

Leven, N. *Cinquante ans d'histoire (1860-1910). L'Alliance Israélite Universelle*. Two volumes. Paris, 1911.

Lévy, S. *Coup d'oeil sur l'administration de M. Heymann, commissaire surveillant de la communauté israélite de Lyon, délégué du Consistoire de Marseille*. Lyon, 1841.

Loeb, Isidore. *Biographie d'Albert Cohn*. Paris, 1878.

Lucien-Brun, Henry. *La condition des Juifs en France depuis 1789*. Paris, 1900.

Malvezin, T. *Histoire des Juifs à Bordeaux*. Bordeaux, 1875.

Marcus, Jacob. "Israel Jacobson." *Yearbook of the Central Conference of American Rabbis*, 38 (1928).

Mirot, Albert. *Manuel de géographie historique de la France*. Paris, 1950.

Netter, Nathan. *Vingt siècles d'histoire d'une communauté juive*. Paris, 1938.

Pinchamel, Ph. "Les listes nominatives de recensement de la population." *Revue du Nord*, 36 (1954).

Poliakov, Léon. *Histoire de l'antisémitisme de Voltaire à Wagner*. Paris, 1968.

Posener, S. "Les juifs sous le premier empire, les enquêtes administratives." *Revue des Etudes Juives*, 90 (1931).

——. "Les juifs sous le premier empire; les statistiques générales." *Revue des Etudes Juives*, 93 (1932) and 94 (1933).

——. *Adolphe Crémieux (1796-1880)*. Two volumes. Paris, 1933 and 1934.

——. "The Immediate Economic and Social Effects of the Emancipation of the Jews in France." *Jewish Social Studies*, 1 (1939).

Prost, Antoine. *L'Enseignement en France 1800-1967*. Paris. 1968.

Rabi (pseudonym). *L'anatomie de Judaïsme français*. Paris, 1962.

Roblin, Michel. *Les Juifs de Paris*. Paris, 1960.

Samson, Christine. "Les Juifs de Paris (1808-1840)." Unpublished thesis, University of Paris, 1971.

Szajkowski, Zosa. "New Materials on Altaras' Colonization Plan." *Yivo Bleter*, 21 (1943).

——. "Growth of the Jewish Population in France." *Jewish Social Studies*, 8 (1946).

——. "The Revolution of 1848 and the Internal Conflicts Among French Jewry." *YIVO Annual of Jewish Social Science*, II–III (1947–1948).

——. "Electoral Battles." *Yivo Bleter*, 35 (1951).

——. "Anti-Jewish Riots during the Revolutions of 1789, 1830, and 1848." *Zion*, 20 (1955).

———. "Simon Deutz: Traitor or French Patriot?" *Journal of Jewish Studies,* 1-2 (1965).

———. *Jews and the French Revolutions of 1789, 1830, and 1848.* New York, 1970.

Tcherikower, E., ed. *Yidn in Frankreich.* New York, 1942.

Uhry, Isaac. *Monographie du culte israélite à Bordeaux.* Bordeaux, 1892.

Wormser, Georges. *Français israélites, une doctrine, une tradition, une époque.* Paris, 1963.

NOTES

Abbreviations

PART ONE: DEMOGRAPHICAL BACKGROUND

Chapter I: Population Levels and Changes in Geographic Distribution

1. For additional population figures, as given by other sources, see Appendix A, Table A-1.

2. Not counting territory lost after the treaties of 1814–15.

3. In 1861 only one percent of the Jewish population in France was living in areas that had been devoid of Jews before the emancipation.

4. For the Jewish population figures by department from 1808 to 1861 see Appendix A, Table A-2. See Appendix A, Table A-3 for the changing percentage of the total Jewish population which resided in each of the thirty-three departments of major Jewish concentration from 1808 to 1861.

5. The departments with one to nineteen Jews were Ain, Basses-Alpes, Hautes-Alpes, Ardèche, Cantal, Cher, Corrèze, Corse, Cotes-du-Nord, Creuse, Eure, Gers, Indre, Lot-et-Garonne, Mayenne, Morbihan, Orne, Sarthe, Deux Sèvres, Tarn, Tarn-et-Garonne, Vendée and Vienne. Those with twenty to 300 Jews were Aisne (fifty-two), Aube (thirty-one), Calvados (twenty-six), Drome (thirty-four), Eure-et-Loire (twenty-one), Indre-et-Loire (fifty-two), Jura (fifty), Loire (300), Maine-et-Loire (twenty), Manche (sixty), Nièvre (twenty-six), Oise (forty-nine), Hautes-Pyrénées (twenty-two), Pyrénées-Orientales (twenty-eight), Saône-et-Loire (ninety-six).

6. An apparent decrease in Landes and a concurrent increase in Basses-Pyrénées was a result of an administrative change of St. Esprit, a large Jewish center, from Landes to Basses-Pyrénées, and did not reflect any population movement. The total population in the two departments was

actually fairly stable. There was an overall decrease of 2 percent; see Appendix A, Table A-4.

7.   The three departments were Allier, Charente-Inférieure, and Loire-et-Cher. The other seven were Aude, Charente, Dordogne, Finistère, Ille-et-Villaine, Isère, and Yonne.

8.   The author's calculations. Cf. S. Posener, "Immediate Economic and Social Effects of the Emancipation of the Jews in France," *JSS*, 1 (1939), 271 ff., who calculated 78 percent.

9.   Author's calculations. Cf. Zosa Szajkowski, *Jews and the French Revolutions of 1789, 1830, and 1848* (New York, 1970), p. 96, where he calculates the percentage at 69.1 for 1851, and p. 104, where he gives 68.2 percent for the same year.

10.   Szajkowski, *Jews and the French Revolutions,* p. 96. Szajkowski found that in 1866, 57 percent of the Jews lived in Alsace-Lorraine. After the war, 45 percent of the Jewish population within the former boundaries of France lived in Alsace-Lorraine. The precipitous decline during those six years reflects the emigration of those Jews who opted for French citizenship.

11.   Ibid., p. 98.

12.   Michel Roblin, *Les Juifs de Paris* (Paris, 1960), p. 52.

13.   Inasmuch as we are not comparing the population decrease for exactly the same years, it is not possible to comment on the significance of the higher rate of decrease in the Jewish population.

14.   Szajkowski, *Jews and the French Revolutions,* p. 105.

15.   For the population breakdown by consistory and by department within the consistory, see Appendix A, Tables A-5 to A-14.

16.   S. Posener, "Les Juifs sous le premier empire: les statistiques générales," *REJ,* 93 (1932), 206–207.

17.   Szajkowski, *Jews and the French Revolutions,* p. 57

18.   If we break down the Alsatian urbanization statistics by department, we discover that in the Haut-Rhin Jews were always more highly urbanized than gentiles, but that in the Bas-Rhin, until 1861, Jews were somewhat less urbanized than the general population.

19.   Szajkowski, *Jews and the French Revolutions,* p. 106, says that in 1886 only 36 percent of the French population was urban. Cf. *Statistique de la France,* 2ème séries, Vol. 13, p. xx, which indicates that from 1846 to 1861, the proportion was roughly 25 percent urban to 75 percent rural.

20.   Author's calculations based on data in *Statistique de la France,* 2:278. Because of the unreliability of the religious data of this census, we may assume that the figure for the Jews is a minimum. Cf. Szajkowski, *Jews and the French Revolutions,* pp. 102–103, who reported only 13 percent of the French population in the *villes chefs-lieux,* based on the same census.

21.   The 63.2 percent figure for the Jews comes from Szajkowski, *Jews and the French Revolutions,* pp. 102–103, but I cannot accept his figure of 18.2 percent for the general population, as my own calculations, based on the 1861 census, show that 19.64 percent of the total French population resided in *villes chef-lieux.* A decrease between 1861 and 1871 seems unlikely.

22.   Author's calculations. Cf. Szajkowski, *Jews and the French Revolutions,* pp. 105–106, who used the general census figures and calculated that 30.2 percent of the Jews lived in those nine cities in 1851. Given the inaccuracy of that census, his figure is undoubtedly low.

23.   Author's calculations, based on both the general census and the consistory figures for 1861. Cf. Szajkowski, *Jews and the French Revolutions,* pp. 105–106, who found that in 1872, 63.6 percent of the Jewish and 7.5 percent of the total French population lived in five cities (Paris, Bordeaux, Lyon, Marseille, Nancy).

24.   Today the ratio of Jews to total world population is probably around .40 percent. It is thought by some to have reached 8–10 percent in the Roman Empire. Dubnov has claimed that more than 10 percent of the seventeenth century Polish population was Jewish, while Jacob Katz cites

a more conservative figure of 6–7 percent. In fifteenth century Castille Jews composed one to 1.5 percent of the total population, and in Europe at the beginning of the nineteenth century they are thought to have been about 4.2 percent of the total.

25. Cf. Szajkowski, *Jews and the French Revolutions*, p. 91, who cites a range of 1.19 to 3.62 percent.

Chapter II: Socio-Economic Situation

1. Moshe Catane, *Les Juifs du Bas-Rhin sous Napoléon Premier: situation démographique et économique* (unpublished thesis, University of Strasbourg, 1967), p. 149. Cf. Szajkowski, *Jews and the French Revolutions*, p. 99.

2. Moïse Biding, *La Vengeance d'Israél* (Metz, 1840), p. 23.

3. These French terms do not correspond precisely to the English terms, nor are they rigorously definable even in French. They indicate three levels of trade, on an increasingly large scale.

4. Christine Samson, *Les Juifs de Paris (1808–1840)* (unpublished doctoral dissertation, University of Paris, 1971), pp. 199–200. Cf. Michel Roblin, *Les Juifs de Paris* (Paris, 1960), p. 60, who found that in 1840, 25 percent of the Parisian Jewish population were still peddlers and second-hand dealers.

5. A.D. Gironde, I V Culte Israélite, N°2; A.D. Bas-Rhin, Culte Israélite, V 511; A.D. Meurthe-et-Moselle, Culte Israélite, V 3.

6. François Delpech, "La Seconde Communauté Juive de Lyon (1775–1870)," *Cahiers d'Histoire*, 13 (1968).

7. Szajkowski, *Jews and the French Revolutions*, pp. 129–130.

8. This 1853 Metz debt liquidation list is a very useful document, and one to which we will refer several times. It is the tax list compiled in 1853 for the purpose of sharing the expense of liquidating the pre-revolutionary Metz Jewish community debt. The descendants of members of this community were located in the twenty-eight departments to which they had spread by 1853, and their share in the debt liquidation was based on their current estimated wealth. In the printed list of the 1684 people required to pay this expense, the occupations of 1181 are specified (probably as a means of identification). We have analyzed the job distribution of these 1181 people, but it should be pointed out that it is possible that the results are not representative of all groups for the following reasons: 1) Although it includes Jews of twenty-eight departments, it indicates only Jews who have come from Metz or are descended from or related by marriage to Metz families; 2) the jobs of about 1/3 are missing, and they may be jobs in a particular grouping, such as the lowest levels of trade; 3) some of the occupations indicated are vaguely stated. It is difficult, in some cases, to tell if a person manufactures or sells a certain article, and at what level of the commercial transaction he is placed. The document was published as *Liquidation des dettes de l'Ancienne communauté juive de Metz. Mise en recouvrement du rôle de 1853* (Metz, 1853).

9. Roblin, *Les Juifs de Paris*, p. 62.

10. A.D. Bas Rhin, Culte Israélite, V 511.

11. Szajkowski, *Jews and the French Revolutions*, pp. 129–130.

12. Samson, *Les Juifs de Paris*, p. 152.

13. A.D. Meurthe-et-Moselle, Culte Israélite, V 3.

14. A.D. Gironde, I V Culte Israélite, N°2; A.D. Bas Rhin, Culte Israélite, V 511; A.D. Meurthe-et-Moselle, Culte Israélite, V 3.

15. Samson, *Les Juifs de Paris*, pp. 199–200. Cf. Michel Roblin, *Les Juifs de Paris*, p. 61, who estimates that in Paris in 1840 60 percent of the Jewish population were skilled laborers (printers, tailors, shoemakers, cabinet makers, hatters); this seems exaggerated.

16. Arch. P.C., I[CC] 22.

17. Szajkowski, *Jews and the French Revolutions*, p. 129.

18. In an analysis of some incomplete occupation data for Marseille, Szajkowski noted the following changes between 1844 and 1866: increases

in traders (including horse dealers), office workers, members of the liberal professions, *rentiers*, religious functionaries, and domestic servants; decreases in the number of those engaged in industry and handicrafts at all levels, in the number of *propriétaires*, and in the number of the unemployed. Szajkowski, *Jews and the French Revolutions*, p. 129. He interpreted these statistics as representing a general decline in *productivité* and an increase in trade, but in the light of our own findings with regard to the major trends of the century, his assertions must be viewed with caution. The fact that his data for 1866 relates only to males over twenty-five who were on the consistory voting list may explain his findings, as the poor who could not or did not contribute to consistory institutions were disenfranchised and would not be represented on the voting rolls.

19. Samson, *Les Juifs de Paris;* Adeline Daumard, *La Bourgeoisie parisienne, 1815–1948* (Paris, 1963) and *Bourgeois de Paris au dixneuvième siècle* (Paris, 1970).

20. Samson, *Les Juifs de Paris*, p. 158; Daumard, *Les bourgeois*, p. 22.

21. Samson, *Les Juifs de Paris*, p. 203.

22. Ibid., pp. 220–221.

23. Ibid., pp. 212–220; *Liquidation des dettes.*

24. Samson, *Les Juifs de Paris*, p. 60.

25. Roblin, *Les Juifs de Paris*, p. 60.

26. Samson, *Les Juifs de Paris*, p. 158.

27. Ibid., p. 157.

28. Léon Werthe, *Quelque réflexions sur la nécessité d'établir une colonie agricole pour la jeunesse israélite d'Alsace* (Colmar, 1868), reprint from *A.I.*, August, 1868.

29. Samson, *Les Juifs de Paris*, pp. 206–207, citing A.D. Seine, VD 4 381.

30. *Statistique de la France, Assistance Publique*, 1866, p. lxviii.

31. Szajkowski, *Jews and the French Revolutions*, p. 196. Cf. Léon Kahn, *Le Comité de bienfaisance, l'hôpital, l'orphelinat, les cimetières* (Paris, 1886), p. 129.

32. The charity board records suffered a worse fate over the years than did the consistorial archives. Perhaps this is because the charity committees frequently had their offices elsewhere than the consistory, and their books were not subject to the control of the secretary-archivist generally employed by the consistories.

33. Salo Baron, *The Jewish Community* (Philadelphia, 1942); Arthur Hertzberg, *The French Enlightenment and the Jews* (New York, 1968).

34. Such attitudes were by no means new to the nineteenth century. Finkelstein's description of the *Herem Ha-Yishuv* makes it clear that the communities reserved to themselves very early the right to limit the settlement of foreign Jews. Louis Finkelstein, *Jewish Self-Government in the Middle Ages* (New York, 1924), pp. 10–15. Hertzberg found hostility to the foreign poor in eighteenth century Alsace, St. Esprit and Bordeaux. In Alsace in 1746 the syndics convinced the military governor to expel penniless foreign Jews. "Since vagabond German and Italian Jews kept arriving [in St. Esprit] their stay was limited to three days." This was sanctioned in 1753 by the intendant's approval of the community's constitution. Similarly, a 1760 Bordeaux *règlement*, approved by the government, provided for the expulsion of vagabonds after a three-fourths vote of the nation. Hertzberg, *The French Enlightenment*, pp. 224, 229, 231.

35. *U.I.*, 1 (1844), p. 16.

36. Samson, *Les Juifs de Paris*, pp. 181–183.

37. François Delpeche, "La Seconde Communauté Juive de Lyon," *Cahiers d'Histoire*, 13 (1968).

38. Samson, *Les Juifs de Paris*, p. 308.

39. Roblin, *Les Juifs de Paris*, p. 60.

40. *U.I.*, 9 (1854), p. 540, reprinted from the *Allgemeine Zeitung des Judentums.*

41. Samson, *Les Juifs de Paris*, p. 250.

42. The reports from Châteausalins and Lunéville.

43. Tsarphati [Olry Terquem], *Projet de règlement conçernant la circoncision* (Paris, 1822), p. 7.

44. A.D. Seine, D V 64, Léon Kahn to the Prefet. Kahn estimates about sixty-six intermarriages per year as compared with 250 Jewish marriages per year.

45. Delpech, "La seconde communauté," p. 62.

46. A.D. Meurthe-et-Moselle, Culte Israélite, V 3.

47. Tsarphati [Olry Terquem], *Huitième lettre d'un Israélite français à ses coreligionnaires* (Paris, 1836), p. 15.

48. *U.I.*, 8 (1852), pp. 9–10.

PART TWO: THE CONSISTORY AND THE COMMUNITY

Chapter III: The Consistory: A General Description

1. Abraham Cahen, "Une notice historique sur les Israélites de l'Algérie," in Isaac Uhry, *Recueil des lois, décrets, ordonnances, avis du conseil d'état, arrêtés, règlements et circulaires concernant les Israélites, depuis 1850* (Bordeaux, 1887), p. 167.

2. Catholicism had been named the official religion; Napoleon had the right of naming its bishops, and France agreed to assume its expenses. The two Protestant sects (Reformed and Lutheran) were accorded the status of recognized religions, and they received financial support from the government. Their administrations were re-fashioned into hierarchical, centralized "consistory" systems, responsible at the top to the government. Only the Jews remained outside this system of religious organization.

3. From 1817 to 1818 *L'Israélite français* was published in Paris, and from 1836 to 1837 a bilingual journal appeared in Strasbourg under the dual name, *La Régénération-Wiedergeburt*. In 1839 and 1840 Abraham Ben Baruch Créhange published a series of pamphlets collectively entitled *La Sentinelle juive;* it is debatable whether or not these constitute a journal.

4. Simon Bloch, "Aux notables," *Univers Israélite* 1 (1844), 309–310.

5. Arch. S.C., minutes, uncatalogued, July 6, 1853.

6. Arch. P.C., AA 4, December 14, 1853.

7. Arch. P.C., AA 4, passim.

8. Arch. B.C., 2 A 6, 1853, passim.

9. This theme is further developed in Chapter Nine.

10. These questions are discussed more fully in Chapter Ten, and the full text of the questions is to be found in Appendix C (p. 385).

Chapter IV: Legislation

1. Anchel, *Napoléon*, pp. 42–57.

2. Ibid., pp. 57–58, citing A.N., F^{19} 11014; the commission was composed of Olry Hayem Worms, Mayer Marx, J. Rodrigues fils, Th. Cerfberr, Manus Polak, Wittersheim le jeune, Nathan Aron Schmoll, Emanuel Dreyfous, Joseph Lehmann, Mardochée Elie, Jacob Mayer, Hayem Worms, Benjamin Rodrigues Henriquez, Saûl Crémieux, Jacob Lazard.

3. Ibid., pp. 57–59.

4. Ibid., p. 43.

5. The exact date of the letter is not known. The French translation appeared in an anonymous pamphlet, *Les Premiers pas de la nation juive vers son bonheur sous les auspices du grand monarque Napoléon*, pp. 11–

12, which was published either by Jacobson himself or by his friend and colleague, Schottlaender, around June 1806. Cf. Jacob Marcus, "Israel Jacobson," *Yearbook of the Central Conference of American Rabbis*, 38 (1928), 386. Marcus suggests that the letter may have been read to the Assembly of Notables by Schottlaender, who addressed the Assembly on the need for better education among the Jews, in July or August, as Jacobson's envoy. Marcus, writing before he could have seen Anchel's work on the formation of the consistories, suggested that Jacobson's scheme may have served as the model for the consistories. We now know that the consistories had begun to take shape before Jacobson wrote this letter.

6. The Assembly of Notables was a meeting of Jewish leaders from the various regions of the Empire called by Napoleon in order to elicit statements of patriotism and commitment by Jews and to elucidate for Napoleon the structure of Jewish institutions and some of the Jewish practices.

7. A.N. F[19] 11005, quoted in Anchel, *Napoléon*, pp. 228–229.

8. Anchel, *Napoléon*, p. 230. This reply included also the call for the Sanhedrin, which was not only to give religious sanctions to the Assembly, but also to decide on the establishment of a rabbinic council in Paris for the surveillance and control of the Jews. In fact, it did not happen that way at all; the Sanhedrin never got to decide on an organizational scheme because one was adopted by the Assembly in December, several months before the Sanhedrin convened; and the rabbinic council turned into a mixed lay-rabbinic central consistory.

9. Ibid., p. 240.

10. Halphen, *Recueil*, p. 274.

11. For the complete text of these and all major legislation concerning the consistory organization, see the Appendix, below.

12. For the necessary qualifications for *notable* and consistory members, see the text of the *règlement* in the Appendix. The 1808 decree supplies the details on how they are to be named.

13. For details on eligibility and elections see the text of the *règlement*.

14. It was the confusion surrounding this provision that allowed Grand Rabbi Sinzheim to serve simultaneously as grand rabbi of the central and Strasbourg consistories; because of the provisions for one member's annual retirement, he did not consider the Strasbourg post permanent.

15. Only in Strasbourg was a second rabbi ever elected to the consistory. In 1840 the second rabbi on the consistory was Louis Sarrazin. *A.I.*, 1 (1840), 70.

16. Robert Anchel, *Notes sur les frais du culte* (Paris, 1928).

17. Sinzheim had died in 1812 and was never replaced, although legally there were still to be three rabbis on the central consistory.

18. Halphen, *Recueil*, contains all of these.

19. Arch. P.C., AA 2, October 21, 1834.

20. *Recueil général des lois et arrêts* (B.N. 4°F 65), 1838, 1.314. Cf. additional volumes of this series for other court decisions on this issue: 1836, 1.615; 1837, 1.561; 1837, 2.139; 1843, 1.633; 1848, 1.16; 1854, 1.284.

21. Arch. P.C., AA 2, May 14, July 2 and 16, 1833.

22. Sauphar's services were ostensibly for his students, but the gatherings were, in fact, open to everyone, and attracted many, including Grand Rabbi Simon Deutz. Because of this, and until the falling out between Deutz and the Paris and central consistories, his services were not disturbed. In 1833 this was no longer an impediment. See Phyllis Albert, "Le rôle des consistoires israélites vers le milieu du xixe siècle," *REJ*, 130 (1971). Cf. Zosa Szajkowski, "Simon Deutz: Traitor or French Patriot?", *Journal of Jewish Studies*, 1–2 (1965), 53.

23. Arch. P.C., AA 2, June 10, 1834.

24. It is not clear whether the authorities accepted the financial motive of the consistory or whether they were unaware of it. When Sauphar complained to the consistory that it should have supported his request to the

authorities, the consistory decided: "On fera observer au Sr Sauphar que le consistoire a le *devoir*, d'après le règlement de 1806, de veiller à ce que sous aucun prétexte, il ne se forme d'assemblée de prières sans autorisation; que par conséquent il a du appuyer la mesure qui a été arrêtée par M. le Préfet." Arch. P.C., AA 2, July 22, 1834.

25. Ibid., Sept. 1, 1834. (The consistory may have been referring to other *minyanim* as well as to Sauphar's.)

26. Ibid., September 25, 1834.

27. A.N. F^{19} 11015.

28. Arch. CC, 1 B 4, December 24, 1837. Cf. Crémieux's report to the central consistory on April 28, 1840—published in *A.I.*, 1 (July 1840), 354 ff.—which erroneously dates the establishment of the commission as January 22, 1838.

29. Adolphe Crémieux's report to the central consistory—in *A.I.* 1 (1840), 355—speaks of this: "Plusieurs consistoires départementaux, notamment Metz, Strasbourg et Nancy, réclamaient, du consistoire central, l'initiative d'une proposition générale, qui vînt prouver aux juifs de France qu'on s'occupait de mettre en harmonie avec les idées du temps où nous vivons, les institutions administratives qui régissent notre culte."

30. "Mémoire à consulter sur la réforme de la constitution consistoriale de la communion israélite de France; adressé au consistoire central israélite, séant à Paris, par le professeur N. Noé, de Bordeaux, employé de la bibliothèque publique, janvier, 1838," in Arch. JTS.

31. Although the government appointed the *notables*, it followed almost invariably the suggestions of the central consistory, which followed the recommendations of the departmental consistories.

32. Noé, *Mémoire*, p. 7.

33. Arch. CC, 1 B 4, July 9, 1839.

34. This had been the case *de facto* since 1826, and the 1831 law which put rabbis' salaries at the expense of the government spoke only of one central consistory grand rabbi. The 1823 *ordonnance* had changed the central consistory composition from three rabbis and two lay members to two rabbis and seven lay members.

35. The dates of the six drafts are as follows: (1) July 1839: a central consistory project; (2) March 10, 1842: a revised central consistory draft (after the departmental consistory responses); (3) November 2, 1843: a ministry version (prepared by a commission including central consistory members); (4) January 1844: a central consistory project, which reacted to No. 3, above; (5) March 1844: the bill as prepared by the legislative committee; (6) May 1844: the final draft, after the government received replies from the departmental consistories about No. 5, above. The departmental consistories prepared written reactions to numbers 1, 2, and 5.

36. Arch. CC, 1 B 4, October 23, 1839.

37. Ibid., February 23, 1843.

38. *A.I.*, 1 (July 1840), p. 353.

39. Arch. JTS.

40. A.N. F^{19} 11015.

41. The date of the Bordeaux rabbi's complaint is unknown. B. Gradis, "Observations sur un nouveau projet . . . ," Arch. JTS.

42. A.N., F^{19} 11015.

43. Abraham Ben Baruch Créhange, *La Sentinelle Juive* (1839), p. 6.

44. The collection of French documents in the JTS archives includes the corrected copies of the project received by the central consistory from the departments, and permits comparison with the Crémieux report. Such comparison reveals total fidelity to the documents.

45. Grand Rabbi M. D. Cahen of Marseille and Grand Rabbi Arnaud Aron of Strasbourg.

46. Gradis, "Observations," Arch. JTS.

47. In 1840 the Jews of Damascus were falsely accused of murdering a Christian monk for ritual use of his blood for Passover.

48. Arch. CC, 1 B 4, August 2, 1841.

49. Ibid., November 4 and December 26, 1841.

50. Central consistory to the ministry, March 10, 1842, in A.N. F^{19} 11015.

51. Ibid.

52. Arch. P.C., I^{CC} 69.

53. A.N., F^{19} 11015.

54. Ibid.

55. Arch. P.C., I^{CC} 69.

56. A.N., F^{19} 11015.

57. Ibid.

58. Ibid.

59. Arch. CC, 1 B 4, November 5, 1843.

60. A.N. F^{19} 11015.

61. Arch. CC, 1 B 4, November 23, 1843.

62. Central consistory to the ministry, November 28, 1843, in A.N. F^{19} 11015; cf. Arch. CC, 1 B 4, November 23, 1843.

63. Vivien to the minister, March 7, 1844, in A.N., F^{19} 11015.

64. Metz consistory to the ministry, April 12, 1844; Colmar consistory to the ministry, April 15, 1844; Nancy consistory to the ministry, April 18, 1844; Strasbourg consistory to the ministry, May 13, 1844; Grand Rabbi Aron to the ministry, April 19, 1844. All the replies are filed in A.N. F^{19} 11015. The discussion that follows is based on the same documents.

65. Paris consistory to the ministry, April 22, 1844. The replies from Bordeaux and Marseille are dated April 9 and 19 respectively. All are in A.N., F^{19} 11015.

66. Baugey, *De la condition*, p. xix.

67. When the 1905 law of separation was enacted the provinces of Alsace and Lorraine, then German territory, were not affected by the change. Upon their re-entry into France, the three Jewish consistories in these areas (Haut-Rhin, Bas-Rhin, and Moselle) were maintained as "concordatory" consistories. Even today their rabbis and institutions are financially supported by the government and are regulated by the law of 1844. Cf. *Statuts du consistoire central*, 21 novembre 1965 (Paris, n.d.), Titre II, Article 9; Titre III, Articles 29 et 30; Titre VII, Article 45.

68. Instructions du ministre des cultes, Carnot, au consistoire central, sur le système électoral israélite, 7 juin 1848, in Arch. JTS.

69. Créhange, *La Vérité*, April 17, 1848; cf. Szajkowski, "The Revolution of 1848 and the Internal Conflicts among French Jewry," *YIVO Annual of Jewish Social Science*, 2-3 (1947–48).

70. Arch. P.C., AA 4, April 26, 1848.

71. Créhange's italics. Créhange, *La Vérité*, April 27, 1848, reporting a speech he made at the *Club* meeting of April 9.

72. Carnot to the central consistory, June 7, 1848, copy made by central consistory secretary Munck, in Arch. JTS.

73. Arch. M.C., in A.D. Moselle, 17 J 40, June 26, 1848; Nancy consistory to the central consistory, August 25, 1848, in Arch. JTS.

74. Colmar consistory to the central consistory, July 30, 1848, in Arch. P.C., I^{CC} 11.

75. Nancy consistory to central consistory, August 25, 1848; Strasbourg consistory to central consistory, January 19, 1849; Metz consistory to central consistory, n.d., in Arch. JTS; Colmar consistory to central consistory, July 30, 1848, in Arch. P.C., I^{CC} 11.

76. Circular by the Paris consistory, dated July 19, 1848, in Arch. JTS.

77. Arch. CC, 1 B 5, September 17, 1849.

78. Arch. P.C., AA 4, October 24, 1849; Arch. CC, 1 B 5, November 22, 1849; Arch. P.C., AA 4, December 15, 1849. The minutes of the joint meeting do not specify further the central consistory's argument.

79. A.D. Gironde, 1 V Culte Israélite, copy of the letter.

80. Arch. P.C., I^{CC} 22, petition by Bordeaux Jews to the ministry, March 27, 1850.

81. Ibid., Benjamin Gradis to the central consistory, March 27, 1850.

82. Arch. B.C., 2 A 6, September 10, 1850.

83. Gradis to central consistory, October 6, 1850, in Arch. P.C., I^{CC} 60.

84. Arch. CC, 1 B 5, November 10, 1850.

85. Arch. P.C., AA 4, November 20, December 22, 1850; Arch. M.C., in A.D. Moselle, 17 J 40, December 8 and 12, 1850.

86. Arch. P.C., AA 4, December 22, 1850.

87. Arch. CC, 1 B 5, May 11, June 11, 1851.

88. Bordeaux consistory to central consistory, October 15, 1851, in Arch. B.C. 4 A 7.

89. The analysis that follows is based on documentation concerning seven of the replies sent in response to the central consistory project. The sources do not reveal any information about the reply from Marseille. Documents used for this study are: Arch. P.C., AA 4, December 28, 1851; Strasbourg consistory to central consistory, January 4, 1852 (majority and minority opinions), in Arch. P.C., I^{CC} 15 and Arch. JTS; Bordeaux consistory to central consistory, October 15 and December 16, 1851, in Arch. B.C., 4 A 7; Colmar consistory to central consistory, November 25, 1851, in Arch. P.C. I^{CC} 11; Nancy consistory to central consistory, November 20, 1851, in Arch. P.C., I^{CC} 31; Arch. CC, 1 B 5, October 15, 1851; Arch. M.C., in A.D. Moselle, 17 J 40, November 18, 19, and 24 and December 28, 1851; St. Esprit consistory to central consistory, January 13, 1852, in Arch. P.C., I^{CC} 19.

90. Article 471, par. 15 was added to the penal code in 1832. It provided for fines of one to five francs for those who violated the regulations of any "administrative authority." The consistories unsuccessfully tried to get themselves recognized as an administrative authority for this purpose.

91. A.N. F^{19} 11016.

92. Arch. CC, 1 B 5, February 13, 1854.

93. A.N. F^{19} 11016, central consistory to the ministry, May 3, 1854.

94. Ibid., ministry to the central consistory, July 5, 1854.

95. Arch. CC, 1 B 5, September 29 and November 13, 1854.

96. Ibid., December 1, 1855; Ministry to central consistory, November 3, 1855, and central consistory to ministry, December 9, 1855, both in A.N. F^{19} 11016.

97. Arch. CC, 1 B 5, December 1, 1855. The reference was to the election of orthodox candidates in some localities.

98. Franck to the ministry, February 14, 1856, in A.N. F^{19} 11016.

99. Arch. CC, 1 B 5, February 23, 1856.

100. Adolphe Franck to the minister, February 25, 1856, in A.N. F^{19} 11016. Cf. Szajkowski, "Electoral Battles" (in Yiddish), *Yivo Bleter* (1951), pp. 148-149.

101. A.N. F^{19} 11016.

102. Ibid.

103. The 1857 project was published in *U.I.* (May 1857), pp. 391 ff. The sources for the departmental replies are as follows: Arch. B.C., 2 A 6, April 16 and May 4, 1857; replies to the ministry from St. Esprit, April 29, 1857; Nancy, July 7, 1857; Marseille, May 5, 1857; Strasbourg, July 6, 1857; Metz, April 30, 1857; Colmar, June 5, 1857; Paris, May 20, 1857; various communities of the Haut-Rhin district (variously dated), all in A.N., F^{19} 11016; copies of seven of the above replies to the ministry and a central consistory summary of them, in Arch. JTS.

104. Gradis to the central consistory, March 9, 1856, in Arch. P.C., I^{CC} 22.

105. Gradis to the central consistory, January 22, 1856, in Arch. JTS; Gradis to the central consistory, March 19, 1856, in Arch. P.C., I^{CC} 22.

106. *U.I.*, 12 (February 1857), pp. 249–250.

107. *A.I.*, 18 (1857), pp. 491–496, 555–558.

108. Szajkowski, "Electoral Battles," p. 153, adds de Lavergne of the War Ministry (added for his knowledge of Jewish affairs in Algeria), but we did not find his name indicated in the sources. Szajkowski incorrectly dates the formation of the commission as May 1858.

109. Originally the rabbinate was not to have been represented on the commission. Ulmann was a last-minute substitute for the central consistory president, Max Cerfberr, who declined to participate. A staff memo to the minister suggests Ulmann as a replacement in order to have the "religious element" present. The note adds, however, that it would be prudent to consult Adolph Franck first on the tendencies of this rabbi, with whom the cabinet had had no previous contact. Undated, unsigned note, in A.N., F[19] 11016.

110. The rabbinic school had just been moved from Metz to Paris, where it was to be more closely controlled by the central consistory.

111. In the commission's meetings the ministry representatives had continued to insist upon direct universal suffrage in order to maintain uniformity of practice within the country and in order to make Jewish electoral practices reflect the spirit of the country's political mood. Anspach and Franck held out for restricted elections, however, and the committee's project proposed a two-degree system. It was only in the work of the *conseil d'état* that the final form was reached.

112. Undated, unsigned memo, in A.N., F[19] 11016.

113. Uhry, *Recueil,* p. 70, the text of the 1872 measure.

114. A.N., F[19] 11017.

115. Ibid.

Chapter V: Organization of the Consistories

1. Arch. P.C., AA 2, March 18, 1838.

2. We cannot be sure, because of insufficient data, whether the Lyon consistory habitually met very frequently also. The only indication we have is for a nine-month period in 1861, when the consistory met 30 times. It is possible that this high frequency was due to the particular needs of that year. Lyon consistory to central consistory, October 9, 1861, in Arch. P.C., I[CC] 25.

3. Arch. P.C., AA 2.

4. Arch. S.C., minutes, uncatalogued, January 12, 1860.

5. The people named were, for the *comité:* Bloch and Israel; for the temple: Dupont and Sciama; for the *boucheries:* Cahen, Halphen, and Bloch. Arch. P.C., AA 4, October 24, 1850.

6. Ibid., February 8, 1854.

7. Arch. S.C., minutes, uncatalogued, September 28, 1854. The five members of the committee on charity and cemeteries were M. Arnaud Aron, Grand Rabbi and president of the Strasbourg consistory; Cerf Simon; Jacques Strauss, general treasurer; E. Aron; and Leopold Joseph Weill.

8. Ibid., June 4, 1857.

9. Tsarphati [Olry Terquem], *Huitième lettre,* p. 10.

10. Ibid., p. 9.

11. Samson, *Les Juifs,* p. 63.

12. Tsarphati [Olry Terquem], *Huitième lettre,* p. 12.

13. *U.I.*, 1 (1844), 175.

14. A.N., F[19] 11014, *Rapport sur le culte.*

15. E.g., Samuel Cahen's 1856 complaint that no reforms were introduced into the ritual because consistory members rarely attended services. *A.I.*, 17 (1856), 244.

16. Arch. S.C., minutes, uncatalogued, February 14, 1856.

17. Arch. M.C., in A.D. Moselle, 17 J 40, April 16, 1847.

18. See, for example, Arch. CC, 1 B 4, December 25, 1839.

19. Abraham Créhange, *Discours de M. Créhange prononcé dans la réunion préparatoire des Israélites de Paris, le 1er décembre, 1844* (Paris, 1845), p. 3.

20. Arch. S.C., minutes, uncatalogued, August 30, 1855. The reply was by Dr. Hirtz.

21. Arch. CC, 1 B 5, passim.

22. David Singer, *Des consistoires israélites* (Paris, 1820), p. 42.

23. Arch. P.C., AA 3, January 13, 1846.

24. *A.I.,* 1 (1840), 16.

25. Arch. P.C., AA 2, September 26, 1831.

26. Arch. CC, 1 B 4, June 13, 1839.

27. Ibid., April 6, 1844.

28. Ibid., December 18, 1843.

29. Ibid., December 25, 1840.

30. Arch. P.C., AA 3, January 28, 1841.

31. Ibid., August 29, 1844.

32. We have no statistics to tell us precisely what percentage of the population was male and over twenty-five years. It would seem unlikely that it was higher than 25 percent.

33. Arch. S.C., minutes, uncatalogued, August 17, 1854; August 9, 1855; September 15, 1859. A.D. Bas-Rhin, V 520.

34. Feuille de Présence à la séance du 4 octobre, 1841, in Arch. P.C., B 22. Those present were Anspach, J. Lang, Singer, Patto, Haas, Dupont, B. Cohen, and A. Halphen.

35. Arch. P.C., B 22, procès verbal, collège de notables, December 5, 1842.

36. Arch. P.C., B 25, procès verbal, collège de notables, September 1, 1845.

37. The law allowed elections to proceed without a quorum the second time they were called, thus tacitly acknowledging the low level of interest in the elections.

38. Arch. P.C., B 25, procès verbal, collège de notables, September 16, 1845.

39. Ibid., December 15, 1845.

40. Ibid., December 28, 1845.

41. A.D. Seine, DV 64, Dossier Isidor; cf. Créhange, *La Vérité,* April 17, 1848, who says that 111 of the 220 *notables* voted in this election.

42. Arch. B.C., 2 A 6, October 24, 1847.

43. Arch. P.C., AA 4, December 26, 1852.

44. Procès verbal of Strasbourg consistory elections, January 4, 1863, in A.D. Bas-Rhin, V 520.

45. Arch. P.C., I^{CC} 28, No. 35, Marseille consistory to central consistory, February 11, 1841.

46. Ibid., No. 37, Marseille consistory to central consistory, October 28, 1841.

47. A.D. Haut-Rhin, 1 V 81.

48. Prefect to the Paris consistory, December 21, 1844, in Arch. P.C., B 24. A total of 206 regular electors was named for the entire Paris consistory district. The other thirty-one lived in additional departments of the Paris consistory district. In addition, there were adjunct *notables.*

49. S. Bloch, *U.I.,* 1 (1844–45), 415.

50. Paris consistory to central consistory, February 3, 1847, in Arch. P.C., I^{CC} 34.

51. Décret du 29 août, 1862, in Uhry, *Recueil,* pp. 45–46, reprinted below in Appendix B, pp. 380–382.

52. Circular beginning "Election d'un membre du consistoire [de Paris]. . . ." (Paris, 1850).

53. Circular beginning "Nancy le 14 mai 1850 . . ." (Nancy, 1850).

54. "Election consistoriale du Bas-Rhin, Strasbourg le 14 août 1850," circular signed by the *Comité*.

55. Arch. CC, 1 B 5, January 27, 1851.

56. Arch. S.C., minutes, uncatalogued, December 18, 1856, January 8, 22, and 28, and February 25, 1857; Ratisbonne to the central consistory, December 25, 1856, in Arch. P.C. I^{CC} 16.

57. Ratisbonne to the central consistory, December 25, 1856, in Arch. P.C., I^{CC} 16.

58. Halphen, *Recueil*, p. 55.

59. Procès verbal, 1842, in Arch. P.C., I^{CC} 69.

60. A.D. Bas-Rhin, V 520.

61. Arch. B.C., 2 A 6, January 26, 1848.

62. A.D. Bas-Rhin, V 520.

63. *Procès verbal* of oath, administered by a delegate of the prefect, A.D. Haut-Rhin, 1 V 91.

Chapter VI: Three Functions Prescribed by Law

1. Arch. M.C. in A.D. Moselle, 17 J 40.

2. Quoted by Anchel, *Napoléon*, p. 483.

3. Ibid., p. 530.

4. Report of the commission on regeneration to the Strasbourg consistory, September 6, 1831, in Arch. JTS.

5. Singer to the *Comité de Surveillance et d'Administration des Ecoles Consistoriales Israélites de Paris*, December 5, 1819, in Arch. P.C., I^{CC} 58.

6. Grand Rabbi Wintzenheim to the Metz consistory, May 24, 1822, in Arch. M.C. in A.D. Moselle, 17 J 71.

7. *Lettre pastorale du consistoire israélite de la circonscription du Haut Rhin*, October 7, 1850, in A.N. F^{19} 11037.

8. Arch. P.C., AA 2, April 31, 1829.

9. Arch. P.C., AA 2, May 24, 1832, and March 26, 1834; AA 3, September 13, 1841.

10. Arch. S.C., minutes, uncatalogued, August 5, 1858.

11. Financial and statistical report of the *comité de bienfaisance*, February 13, 1845, in Arch. P.C., B 25.

12. In this system one teacher can instruct a class of more than one hundred children. The children are grouped by ability for each subject and monitors from among the more advanced pupils help teach. The system was very highly regarded at the time, because of the spectacular results it claimed to achieve at comparatively low cost.

13. Léon Kahn, *Histoire des écoles communales et consistoriales israélites de Paris*, 1809–1844 (Paris, 1884), p. 7.

14. Samuel Cahen, *Précis élémentaire d'instruction religieuse et morale pour les jeunes Français israélites*, 2nd ed. (Paris, 1831), foreword.

15. Arch. M.C. in A.D. Moselle, 17 J 71.

16. Arch. P.C., AA 2, January 8, 1833.

17. Kahn, *Histoire des Ecoles*, p. 51.

18. Ibid., pp. 62–63.

19. Arch. P.C., AA 3, January 13, 1846.

20. Strasbourg consistory to Charles Boersch, in CAHJP, Jerusalem, HM 5517.

21. Arch. P.C., AA 2, September 15, 1834.

22. Antoine Prost, *L'Enseignement en France, 1800–1967* (Paris, 1968).

23. Arch. M.C. in A.D. Moselle, 17 J 71.

24. Strasbourg consistory minutes, June 15, 1842, in CAHJP, Jerusalem, HM 5509.

25. Strasbourg consistory to the Ministry of Cults, July 20, 1842, in Arch. P.C., I^{CC} 15.

26. Arch. S.C., minutes, uncatalogued, February 6, 1853.

27. Arch. M.C. in A.D. Moselle, 17 J 40, March 17, 1847.

28. Arch. CC, 1 B 4, April 27, 1847.

29. Circular letter by Grand Rabbi Ennery, Arch. CC, 1 B 4, June 21, 1847.

30. Arch. P.C., AA 4, November 22, 1847.

31. Prost, *L'enseignement,* p. 93.

32. In 1850, when a new law (*Loi Falloux*) provided that special primary schools be established by the municipalities for each religious group, it was Franck who brought this provision to the attention of the central consistory. He alerted the consistory to the need for collecting exact data on the Jewish schools, and upon Franck's recommendation, the central consistory solicited the information from the departmental consistories.

33. Arch. S.C., minutes, uncatalogued, August 5, 1858.

34. Thirty-five percent of the French conscripts in 1860 were illiterate.

35. Colmar consistory to central consistory, September 17, 1861, in Arch. P.C., I^{CC} 12.

36. Arch. M.C., in A.D. Moselle, 17 J 40, July 5, 1855.

37. *L'indépendant de la Moselle,* May 15, 1840.

38. "Le système d'enseignement primaire israélite est-il en France ce qu'il pourrait être?" *A.I.,* 4 (1843), 212.

39. Arch. S.C., minutes, uncatalogued, June 9, 1855.

40. Arch. CC, 1 B 4, December 18, 1843, February 25, 1844.

41. Dreyfuss, *Discours à Mulhouse,* December 13, 1849.

42. *Projet présenté au consistoire centrale et aux consistoires des départements pour l'établissement à Paris d'une école de commerce d'arts et métiers·pour les jeunes Israélites* (Paris, 1844).

43. Arch. CC, 1 B 4, August 28, 1837.

44. Arch. M.C., in A.D. Moselle, 17 J 40, May 9, 1852. Arch. S.C. minutes, uncatalogued, December 21, 1837; November 8, 1839; May 31, 1858; July 21, 1859. Cf. *A.I.,* 1 (1840), 21.

45. Arch. P.C., AA 2, March 18, 1834.

46. Ibid., February 25, 1839.

47. Arch. CC, 1 B 4, July 14, 1846.

48. Arch. P.C., AA 3, October 15, 1846.

49. Ibid., May 8, 1846.

50. A.D. Meurthe et Moselle, V, Culte Israélite, No. 7.

51. Hemerdinger to the central consistory, November 12, 1835, in Arch. P.C., I^{CC} 59.

52. *A.I.,* 1 (1840), 21.

53. Ibid.

54. A.D. Gironde, 1 V, Culte Israélite, No. 1, Grand Rabbi Marx to Prefect, September 13, 1846.

55. Arch. S.C., minutes, uncatalogued, March 14, 1853.

56. Ibid., March 15, 1853.

57. Ibid., March 24, 1853.

58. Ibid., 1853 to 1857, passim. The record is incomplete, but it does not seem likely that the number of *émigrés* aided by this project approached 100.

59. Ibid., August 11, 1862.

60. Hertzberg, *The French Enlightenment,* pp. 41–42.

61. Ibid., p. 320.

62. Tsarphati [Olry Terquem], *Projet . . . circoncision,* p. 13.

63. Report to the Strasbourg consistory, September 6, 1831, in Arch. JTS.

64. Léon Werthe, *Quelques réflexions,* pp. 4–6, and Werthe, letter beginning "Monsieur le rédacteur des Archives," March 4, 1869, p. 3.

65. Arch. S.C., minutes, uncatalogued, April 25, 1844.

66. Z. Szajkowski, "New Materials on Altaras' Colonization Plan," *Yivo Bleter,* 21 (1943), 47, and *A.I.,* 16 (1858), 24.

67. *Colonisation,* February 1, 1858, quoted in *A.I.,* 16 (1858), 215.

68. Arch. S.C., minutes, uncatalogued, January 5, 1854.

69. Ibid., January 17, 1861.

70. *A.I.*, 16 (1858), 215.

71. Metz consistory to central consistory, November 20, 1862, in Arch. P.C., I^CC 18.

72. Werthe, *Quelques réflexions*, pp. 4-6.

73. Central consistory circular to the departmental consistories, October 27, 1862, in Uhry, *Recueil*, p. 54.

74. Metz consistory to the central consistory, November 20, 1862, in Arch. P.C., I^CC 18.

75. Werthe, *Quelques réflexions*, p. 6.

76. Ibid., pp. 6-7.

77. Anchel, *Napoléon*, pp. 234-235.

78. Ibid., p. 240.

79. Grand Rabbi Sinzheim to the Ministry of Cults, August 23 1808, in A.N., F^19 11014.

80. Georges Wormser, *Français israélites, une doctrine, une tradition, une époque* (Paris, 1963), p. 30. Diogènes Tama, *Transactions of the Parisian Sanhedrin* (Cincinnati, 1956), pp. 77, 79. Frances Malino Hoffman, in "Abraham Furtado and the Sephardi Jews of France" (unpublished doctoral thesis, Brandeis University, 1971), p. 269, identifies one of these *notables* as Marc Foy.

81. Baron, *Jewish Community*, Vol. 2, pp. 358-359.

82. Ibid.

83. Jacob Katz, *Tradition and Crisis* (New York, 1961), pp. 91-92.

84. Hertzberg, *The French Enlightenment*, p. 235.

85. These provisions are contained in Articles 11 and 12 of the 1806 *règlement* and Article 7 of the 1808 decree on Jewish businesses. Both documents are in Halphen, *Recueil*, and the *règlement* will be found in the Appendix, below.

86. Albert Cohn, "Lettres Juives," *A.I.*, 25 (December 15, 1864), 1063-1064.

87. Anchel, *Les Juifs*, p. 259.

88. Samson, *Les Juifs de Paris*, p. 53.

89. Anchel, *Les Juifs*, p. 256.

90. See especially Wormser, *Français israélites*, p. 30.

91. M. Schwab to the Grand Rabbi Wittersheim, April 5, 1822, in Arch. M.C. in A.D. Moselle, 17 J 71.

92. "Préfecture de Police, Rapport en réponse à la lettre de M. le Préfet du 6 août dernier," October 27, 1828, in A.N., F^19 11029.

93. Tribunal de Première Instance du département de la Seine to Grand Rabbi Cologna, April 5, 1821, in Arch. P.C., I^CC 58.

94. Arch. P.C., AA 2, November 17, 1825.

95. Ibid., December 17, 1833.

96. Ibid., March 11, 1834.

97. Arch. P.C., AA 3, October 24, 1839.

98. Paris consistory to the Prefect of Police, November 18, 1841, in A.N. F^19 11030.

99. Commissioner of Police, Arsenal Division, to Prefect of Police, November 22, 1841, in A.N. F^19 11030.

100. Arch. P.C., AA 3, July 18, 1844.

101. Préfecture de Police to Procureur de la Republique près le tribunal de 1ere Instance de la Seine, July 11, 1850, in A.N. F^19 11030.

102. *A.I.*, 1 (1840), 21.

103. Arch. S.C., minutes, uncatalogued, 1857.

104. Arch. M.C., in A.D. Moselle, 17 J 39, September 20, 1821.

105. Arch. S.C., minutes, uncatalogued, June 6, 1859.

106. Arch. P.C., AA 3, May 8, 1846.

Chapter VII: Three Functions not Assigned by the Legislation

1. An oversight of this protocol was brought to the attention of the government by the Paris consistory in 1853, and promptly remedied. Arch. P.C., AA 4, April 18, 1853.

2. *U.I.*, 12 (February, 1857), 248.

3. Arch. CC, 1 B 5, October 18, 1860.

4. Central consistory to the ministry, May 28, 1838, in A.N. F^{19} 11031.

5. Central consistory to legislative committee, Letter no. 6361, July 4, 1849, in Arch. CC, 1 C 8.

6. Central consistory to the Colmar, Bordeaux, Nancy, Strasbourg, and Metz consistories, Letter no. 6362, July 5, 1849, in Arch. CC, 1 C 8.

7. Arch. P.C., AA 3, July 13, 1843, and passim to 1847.

8. Colmar consistory to central consistory, June 26, 1861, in Arch. P.C., I^{CC} 12.

9. Arch. S.C., minutes, uncatalogued, passim; Colmar consistory to the central consistory, January 15, 1847, in Arch. P.C., I^{CC} 11.

10. Arch. CC, 1 B 4, October 5, November 10 and 19, 1853.

11. Deuxième lettre 1er janvier 1831, 10 heures, Rodrigues to Worms de Romilly, in Arch. P.C., I^{CC} 58.

12. Ibid.

13. Strasbourg consistory to the central consistory, May 31, 1843, in Arch. P.C., I^{CC} 15.

14. Arch. S.C., minutes, uncatalogued, December 10, 1857.

15. Ibid., December 18, 1856, and March 25, 1857.

16. Furtado to the ministry, January 22, 1850, in A.N., F^{19} 11037.

17. Arch. P.C., AA 3, September 24, 1840.

18. Strasbourg consistory to the central consistory, April 5, 1843, Arch. P.C., I^{CC} 15.

19. Arch. CC, 1 B 4, April 30, 1843.

20. Minister of Cults to the central consistory, September 9, 1846, in Arch. P.C., I^{CC} 69.

21. On the prisons, see: Arch. CC, 1 B 4, February 7, July 26, August 18, 1847; Arch. CC, 1 B 5, April 30, 1860; Arch. S.C., minutes, uncatalogued, July 14, 1859; Arch. P.C., AA 3, April 30, 1845; Grand Rabbi Isidor to Paris consistory, April 11, 1855, in Arch. P.C., B 32; Colmar consistory to central consistory, July 19, 1846, in Arch. P.C., I^{CC} 11; Paris consistory to central consistory, April 12 and 15, 1858, and May 14, 1858. These three letters are in Arch. P.C., I^{CC} 34. Central consistory to Paris consistory, May 3, 1855, in Arch. P.C., I^{CC} 34; Marseille consistory to central consistory, August 19, 1846, and several other letters from the 1850's and 1860's, in Arch. P.C., I^{CC} 28.

22. Benjamin Rodrigues to the central consistory, May 15, 1827, in Arch. P.C., I^{CC} 58.

23. Metz consistory to the central consistory, February 24, 1846, Arch. P.C., I^{CC} 18.

24. Colmar consistory to the central consistory, July 12, 1840, Arch. P.C., I^{CC} 11.

25. *La Vérité*, April 17, 1848; *Courrier du Bas-Rhin*, June 30, 1848; Arch. CC, 1 B 5, March 5 and May 21, 1848; Arch. B.C., 2 A 6, 1848 passim; J. J. Kertz to the ministry, March 3, 1848, in A.N. F^{19} 11031; Nordmann to the central consistory, May 7, 1848, in A.N. F^{19} 11031; central consistory to the Ministry of Cults, May 14, 1848, in A.N. F^{19} 11031; central consistory to Ministry of Justice, July 4, 1848, in A.N. F^{19} 11031; Ministry of Cults to Ministries of Justice and Interior, May 26, 1848, in A.N. F^{19} 11031. Cf. M. Ginsburger, "Les troubles contre

les Juifs d'Alsace en 1848," *REJ*, 64 (1912); Zosa Szajkowski, "Anti-Jewish Riots during the Revolutions of 1789, 1830, and 1848," *Zion* (1955), pp. 82–102.

26. I. Levaillant, a student of Third Republic anti-Semitism, believed that the 1848 Alsatian uprisings were not linked, through any intermediary events, to Third Republic sentiment. He is clearly incorrect. Levaillant, "La génèse de l'antisémitisme sous la troisième république," *REJ*, 53 (1907), lxxxi.

27. Colmar consistory to central consistory, July 3, 1851, in Arch. P.C., I^{CC} 11.

28. Bordeaux consistory to the central consistory, October 26, 1862, in Arch. P.C., I^{CC} 22 and AA 3, July 13, 1846.

29. See, in this connection, Robert Byrnes, *Antisemitism in Modern France* (New Brunswick, N.J., 1950).

30. Colmar consistory to the central consistory, January 10, 1853, in Arch. P.C., I^{CC} 11. Unfortunately, the sources do not give us the title of this brochure.

31. Arch. S.C., minutes, uncatalogued, July 20, August 17, September 7, 1854.

32. Strasbourg consistory to the central consistory, February 26, 1861, in Arch. P.C., I^{CC} 16.

33. Eugène de Mirecourt, *Heine* (Paris, 1856), p. 9.

34. Samuel Cahen to the central consistory, March 8, 1857, in Arch. P.C., I^{CC} 60.

35. Eugène de Mirecourt, *La Bourse, ses abus et ses mystères* (Paris, 1858), pp. 32, 90, 275 and passim.

36. Colmar consistory to the central consistory, November, 1858; Nancy consistory to central consistory, November 21, 1858; Strasbourg consistory to central consistory, November 25, 1858, all in Arch. CC, 3 E.

37. Arch. CC, 1 B 5, November 20, 1858.

38. Arch. CC, 3 E.

39. Minister of Justice to Minister of Cults, November 24, 1858, in A.N. F^{19} 11031.

40. Arch. CC, 1 B 5, November 24, 1858.

41. Central consistory to Minister of Cults, November 28, 1858, in A.N. F^{19} 11031.

42. Adolphe Crémieux to the central consistory, December 10, 1858, in Arch. CC, 1 B 5, December 16, 1858.

43. Arch. CC, 3 E and 1 B 5.

44. Central consistory to the minister, January 4, 1859, in A.N. F^{19} 11031.

45. Arch. CC, 1 B 5, December 30, 1858.

46. If we are correct in our supposition that it was Franck who was eager to prosecute, it is interesting to note that by 1890 he had changed his opinion regarding the correct tactic to adopt in such cases. As president of *Société des Etudes Juives,* he advised against publishing any refutation of anti-Semitic literature. (Michael Marrus, *The Politics of Assimilation,* Oxford, 1971, p. 143).

47. E. A. Astruc, *Les Juifs et Louis Veuillot* (Paris, 1859), p. 7.

48. Arch. CC, 1 B 5, December 30, 1858.

49. *L'Univers,* February 25, 1859.

50. Strasbourg consistory to central consistory, February 28, 1859, in Arch. CC, 3 E.

51. Arch. CC, 1 B 5, March 2, 1859.

52. Arch. CC, 3 E, Paris consistory to central consistory, March 13, 1859, and Nancy consistory to central consistory, March 15, 1859.

53. Ibid., Strasbourg consistory to central consistory, March 23, 1859; Metz consistory to central consistory, March 21, 1859; Bordeaux consistory to central consistory, March 23, 1859.

54. Colmar consistory to the central consistory, November 6, 1861, in Arch. P.C., I^{CC} 12.

55. Strasbourg consistory to the Ministry of Cults, November 6, 1861, in A.N. F[19] 11031.

56. Colmar consistory to central consistory, November 27, 1861, in Arch. P.C., I[CC] 12.

57. Arch. CC, 1 B 5, December, 1861.

58. Arch. P.C., I[CC] 12, Colmar consistory to central consistory, Dec. 4, 1861.

59. Ibid., central consistory to Colmar consistory, December 23, 1861.

60. Minister of the Interior to the Minister of Cults, December 4, 1861, in A.N. F[19] 11031.

61. Arch. CC, 1 B 4, November 14, 1847.

62. A.N. F[19] 11031, central consistory to Ministries of Justice and Cults, Nov. 23, 1847.

63. Ibid., Ministers of Cults and Justice to Procureur général, n.d. (1847).

64. Arch. CC, 1 B 5, March 2, 1853.

65. Ibid., March 8, 1853.

66. Nathan Lévy to central consistory, June 6, 1855, in Arch. P.C., I[CC] 34.

67. Arch. CC, 1 B 5, June 13, 1855.

68. Petition by several Parisian Jews to the central consistory, July 12, 1858, in Arch. P.C., I[CC] 34.

69. Those present were Adolphe Franck, vice-president, Grand Rabbi Salomon Ulmann, Philippe Anspach, François Halévy, and Salomon Munk of the central consistory, and Gustave de Rothschild and M. Alkan of the Paris consistory.

70. Arch. CC, 1 B 5, July 13, 1858.

71. Arch. S.C., minutes, uncatalogued, July 22 and August 5, 1858; Lyon consistory to central consistory, September 7, 1858, in Arch. P.C., I[CC] 25.

72. Paris consistory to central consistory, September 5, 1858, in Arch. P.C., I[CC] 34.

73. Minister of Justice to Minister of Cults, December 17, 1858, in A.N. F[19] 11031.

74. Strasbourg consistory to central consistory, January 17, 1859, in Arch. CC, 3 E.

75. Rabbi A. Muscat of Avignon to central consistory, Jan. 1, 1832, and Marseille consistory to central consistory, June 4, 1833, in Arch. P.C., I[CC] 28, no. 9.

76. Nathan Netter, *Vingt Siècles d'histoire d'une communauté juive* (Paris, 1938), p. 387.

77. E. Deutz to the president of the central consistory, June 14, 1831, in Arch. JTS.

78. Arch. P.C., I[CC] 18.

Chapter VIII: Power and Control

1. Anchel, *Napoléon*, p. 496.

2. Katz, *Tradition and Crisis*, chapter 13, "Super-Kehilla Organizations"; Baron, *Jewish Community*, Vol. 1, chapter 8, "Supercommunity."

3. Hertzberg, *French Enlightenment*, p. 320.

4. Central consistory to the ministry, February 7, 1810, in A.N. F[19] 11030, reported by Anchel, *Napoléon*, p. 496.

5. *Recueil général des lois et arrêts* (Paris, 1855), 2.385–2.390.

6. *Recueil général des lois et arrêts* (Paris, 1856), 2.181–2.183.

7. A.D. Bas-Rhin, V 512.

8. Arch. P.C., AA 2, July 16, 1833.

9. Arch. S.C., minutes, uncatalogued, November 19, 1857.

10. Ministry to prefect, August 18, 1846; prefect to ministry, October 26, 1846; and royal *ordonnance*, September 2, 1846; all in A.D. Gironde, 1 V, section 4, N° 6.

11. Arch. P.C., AA 3, June 26, 1843.

12. Arch. S.C., minutes of the *commission administrative,* uncatalogued, 1837–1840, passim.

13. Arch. M.C., in A.D. Moselle, 17 J 39, May 7, 1829.

14. Arch. B.C., 2 A 6, November 2, 1847.

15. Ibid., July 28, 1851.

16. Arch. P.C., AA 2, February 10, 1828.

17. Ibid., October 2 and 22, 1833.

18. Ibid., October 20, 1835.

19. Ibid., November 24, 1835.

20. Arch. P.C., AA 3, July 15, 1839.

21. Temple administration to Paris consistory, March 31, 1844, Arch. P.C., B 24.

22. Arch. P.C., AA 4, November 19, 1851.

23. *Règlement Constitutif de l'Administration du Temple Consistorial de Paris,* adopted by the Paris consistory on June 28, 1853, and approved by the central consistory on August 3, 1853, in *U.I.,* 9 (1853), 119–123.

24. At the time this book was researched, the Paris consistory minutes for 1854–1874 were missing, and we were unable to follow the development further. A portion of the missing minutes, for 1854–1865, have since been located in Paris by M. G. Nahon, Archivist of the Paris consistory. (Personal communication from M. Nahon, July 1975.) We have located the rest in the collection at Brandeis University.

25. Arch. P.C., AA 2, April 8, 1834.

26. Ibid., June 20, 1837.

27. Arch. P.C., AA 3, July 13, 1846.

28. Central consistory to Paris consistory, October 8, 1845, Arch. P.C., B 25.

29. Arch. P.C., B 31, Prosper Lunel to Paris consistory, June 29, 1854.

30. Ibid., Allegri to Paris consistory, October 6, 1854.

31. The smoldering power struggle and mutual hostility between the Ashkenazi-dominated consistory and the Sephardi population has flared into new significance in the last twenty years, with the arrival in France of large numbers of North African Jews of the Sephardi ritual.

32. Financial report of *comité* to Paris consistory, February 12, 1843, Arch. P.C., B 23.

33. The use of the term "commissaire surveillant" for the consistories' delegate in the community dates from as early as 1809 in the Bas-Rhin. A decision of the Strasbourg consistory of August 21, 1809, provided for the appointment of these delegates in the various communities of its district. Their job was to receive taxes and forward the sums to the consistory, administer the funds of the community, prevent unauthorized prayer meetings, and compile a list of the poor who wished to be admitted to the *hospice.* "Schluss des Consistoriums der Israëliten des Nieder-Rheins," Strasbourg, August 21, 1809, in Moshe Catane, "Les communautés du Bas-Rhin en 1809," *REJ,* 120 (1961), 321–343.

34. Arch. M.C. in A.D. Moselle, 17 J 40, February 9, 1847.

35. Arch. CC, 1 B 4, May 28, 1846.

36. Arch. P.C., AA 2, November 17, 1831.

37. When the Bayonne Jewish community complained to the central consistory about its differences with the Bordeaux consistory concerning taxes, the letter was signed by "Les administrateurs de Hebera." Letter of June 18, 1819, Arch. P.C., I^{CC} 58.

38. Arch. P.C., AA 3, August 14, 1839.

39. Ibid., May 7, 1846.

40. Arch. M.C., in A.D. Moselle, 17 J 40, January 11, 1846.

41. Metz consistory to central consistory, March 8, 1847, in Arch. P.C., I^{CC} 18.

42. The *commissaire surveillant* of Pfaffenhoffen was dismissed by the Strasbourg consistory in 1859 for allowing dissenters from the town of

Walch to pray in Pfaffenhoffen, despite a consistory order to the contrary. Arch. S.C., minutes, uncatalogued, August 4, 1859.

43. Anchel, *Napoléon*, p. 496.

44. S. Lévy, *Coup d'oeil sur l'administration de M. Heymann, commissaire surveillant de la communauté israélite de Lyon, délégué du Consistoire de Marseille* (Lyon, 1841), p. 3. Cf. Delpech, "La Seconde Communauté."

45. Arch. P.C., AA 2, February 26 and March 22, 1836.

46. Arch. CC, 1 B 5, May 31, 1854.

47. Strasbourg consistory to central consistory, February 14, 1856, in Arch. P.C., I^{CC} 16.

48. *La Famille de Jacob* (1859), pp. 135 ff.

49. Colmar consistory to central consistory, October 15, 1862, in Arch. P.C., I^{CC} 12.

50. Arch. P.C., AA 2, June 14, 1836.

51. Ibid.

52. *Commissaire surveillant* of Nantes to Paris consistory, May 24 and November 1, 1843, in Arch. P.C., B 23.

53. S. Lévy, *Second coup d'oeil*, passim.

54. Arch. P.C., AA 4, April 4 and 18, 1853.

55. Central consistory to ministry, December 8, 1854, in Arch. JTS.

56. Colmar consistory to central consistory, September 17, 1861, in Arch. P.C., I^{CC} 12.

57. Arch. S.C., minutes, uncatalogued, 1850's passim.

58. "Consistoire Israélite, Circonscription de Strasbourg, Règlement pour les synagogues, 7 janvier 1858," in A.D. Bas-Rhin, V 556.

59. Arch. S.C., minutes, uncatalogued, February 9, 1860.

60. Arch. CC, 1 B 4 and 1 B 5, passim; several letters from the central consistory to the ministry, in A.N. F^{19} 11037.

61. Catane, "Les communautés du Bas Rhin."

62. "Consistoire Israélite, circonscription de Strasbourg," in A.D. Bas-Rhin, V 556.

63. Strasbourg consistory to prefect, January 8, 1861; prefect to the Ministry of Cults, January 19, 1861; Strasbourg consistory to prefect, June 7, 1861; prefect to the Ministry of Cults, July 6, 1861; Ministry of Cults to prefect, July 23, 1861; prefect to Strasbourg consistory, July 29, 1861, in A.D. Bas-Rhin, V 556.

64. Arch. S.C., minutes, unclassified, May 13, 1858.

65. Ibid., July 8, 1858.

66. Ibid., September 15, October 6 and 27, 1859.

67. Arch. M.C., in A.D. Moselle, 17 J 40, September 4, 1846.

68. Arch. P.C., AA 2, May 8, 1832.

69. Arch. P.C., AA 3, April 4, 1845.

70. Ibid., April 12, 1836.

71. This decision was made around 1830 in Paris. In 1839 M. Zay's sermon was read by every member of the consistory before permission was granted. See Arch. P.C., AA 3, March 18, 1839.

72. "Consistoire israélite de Marseille, extrait des registres de délibération," January 25, 1843, in Arch. JTS.

73. Arch. P.C., AA 2, August 27, September 15, October 14, 1828.

74. Paris consistory to central consistory, March 12, 1858, Arch. P.C., I^{CC} 34.

75. Metz consistory to central consistory, February 25, 1846, Arch. P.C., I^{CC} 18.

76. The Paris consistory specifically recommended that men who refused to contribute be barred not only from synagogue honors, but from their synagogue seats. Arch. P.C., AA 2, August 13, 1838.

77. *U.I.*, 1 (1844), 247–249.

78. On April 26, 1846, the central consistory returned a Colmar *règlement* with the observation that such *règlements* need not be sub-

mitted for approval, provided only that they were compatible with existing laws. The following year, however, when Metz submitted a *règlement* for approval, the central consistory made a slight change in that document before approving it. Arch. CC, 1 B 4, April 26, 1846, and April 25, 1847.

79. Ibid., February 13, 1854.

80. An example of this argument is in Strasbourg consistory to central consistory, January 4, 1852, in Arch. P.C., I^{CC} 15.

81. St. Esprit consistory to central consistory, September 15, 1851, ibid., I^{CC} 19.

82. "Réfutation par un Israélite du Haut-Rhin de plusieurs articles calomnieux, publiés contre le consistoire israélite de Colmar" (Strasbourg, 1841), B.N., Ld^{185} 5; Arch. CC, 1 B 4 and 1 B 5, passim; several items of correspondence between the central consistory and the ministry and between Hemerdinger and the ministry in A.N. F^{19} 11037 and A.D. Haut-Rhin, 1 V 91.

83. *U.I.*, 12 (May 1857), 386.

84. Arch. P.C., AA 2, August 13, 1838.

85. Munk was orientalist at the university and at the Bibliothèque Nationale.

86. Arch. P.C., AA 2, August 25, 1836.

87. Baron, *Jewish Community*, Vol. 2, p. 21.

88. Hertzberg, *The French Enlightenment*, p. 202.

89. E.g., Arch. P.C., AA 4, October 9, 1848.

90. See the 1806 *règlement* below, Appendix B, p. 345.

91. Anchel, *Napoléon*, pp. 475–477, quoting A.N. F^{19} 11019.

92. A.N. F^{19} 11019, Bordeaux consistory (signed by David Gradis, Abraham Andrades, Lopes-Dubec, and Rodrigues Aîné) to the ministry, n.d.

93. Ibid., central consistory to Ministry of Cults, June 28, 1809.

94. Ibid., central consistory to Ministry of Cults, September 4, 1809.

95. Ibid., Paris consistory to the Ministry of Cults, June 12, 1809.

96. Anchel, *Napoléon*, p. 516.

97. Strasbourg consistory to the mayor of Strasbourg, January 22, 1812, in Arch. S.C., Register of Letters, uncatalogued.

98. A.N. F^{19} 11029, police commissioner of the Ste. Avoye quarter to police prefect, October 2, 1816, and central consistory to the Minister of the Interior, October 20, 1816.

99. Ibid., central consistory to the Minister of Cults, October 20, 1816, and minister to Prefect of the Seine, October 26, 1816.

100. Ibid.

101. A.D. Haut-Rhin, V 97, and A.N. F^{19} 11029.

102. Central consistory to Ministry of Interior, November 30, 1816, in A.N. F^{19} 11029.

103. Arch. P.C., AA 2, June 15, 1826.

104. Ibid., March 4, 1828.

105. Masson, commissaire de police, 3ème bureau, 1ère division, to Prefect of Police, October 27, 1828, in A.N. F^{19} 11029.

106. Ibid.

107. Ibid.

108. Arch. P.C., AA 2, June 10, 1829.

109. Ibid., September 23, 1829.

110. Arch. M.C., in A.D. Moselle, 17 J 39, August 25, 1822, and passim.

111. Nancy consistory to Mme. Veuve Goudchaux, January 31, 1829, in Arch. JTS.

112. The six men who held prayer meetings and whose names were turned over to the government were Sauphar, teacher, 19 rue Simon Lefranc; Lazare, peddler, 25 rue Maubrée; Isaac Nettre, pastrymaker, 20 rue Geoffrey l'Angevin; Arons Jacmin, 6 rue de Vieilles Etuves St. Martin; Mayer Dennery, merchant, 28 rue Geoffrey l'Angevin; Gerson Dennery, shoemaker, 20 rue des Menetriers. "Liste des principales réunions de

prières tenues illicitement par des Israélites de Paris," in A.N. F^{19} 11029.

113. Arch. P.C., AA 2, May 14, July 2 and 16, 1833; Paris consistory to police prefect, May 15, 1833; Minister of Cults to police prefect, July 9, 1833; "Note pour M. Cuvier" (an internal memo of the Ministry of Cults), September, 1846. The last three documents are in A.N. F^{19} 11029.

114. Arch. P.C., AA 2, June 10, 1834.

115. Ibid., September 1, 1834.

116. Ibid., September 25, 1834.

117. "Note pour M. Cuvier," September, 1846, in A.N. F^{19} 11029.

118. Arch. P.C., AA 2, June 16, 1835, and November 24, 1835.

119. Ibid., December 8, 1835.

120. On June 29, 1836, the Paris consistory decided to celebrate a special thanksgiving service in honor of Louis-Philippe's June 25th escape from an assassination attempt. It sent invitations to the central consistory, the charity board, and the directors of the various mutual aid societies. Thus, it is clear that the consistory had full knowledge of the existence of and location of these societies. Ibid., June 29, 1836.

121. Ibid., November 28, 1837.

122. Ibid.

123. Ibid., January 22, 1838.

124. Ibid., March 4, 1838.

125. Prefect of police to the Paris consistory, June 6, 1839, Arch. P.C., B 21.

126. They were David Reins, Gaffré, and Louis Lévy, of *L'Accord Israélite*, *L'Assistance Mutuelle des Israélites*, and *Enfants du Roi David*, respectively.

127. The fifteen societies whose presidents appeared and admitted to holding prayer meetings were *Les Amis de l'Union* (Alkan), *Bienfaisance Israélite dite de Moïse* (Goudchau), *Bienfaisance Israélite dite de Paris* (Jaffa), *Des Enfants de la loi des 12 tables* (Isaac Lion), *Réunion pour l'étude et l'exécution de la loi sacrée* (Isaac David, cantor at the consistorial temple), *Réunion de la Maison d'Aron* (Lazard), *Amis de l'humanité* (Chailly), *Les Israélites de Paris dite du Père Abraham* (Tedesco), *Les Enfants de Solomon* (Isaac Solomon), *Les Lois Rabbiniques* (Moyse Heymann), *Inséparables Israélites* (Blum and Lévy), *Patriarches Israélites* (Isaac Lévy and Bloch), *Amis des enfants d'Israel* (Nathan Joseph and Kaufman), *Enfants de Sion* (L. Edinger), and an unnamed society not authorized by the police (Neymark and Netter).

128. Abraham Ben Baruch Créhange, "Discours prononcé le 24 juin 1839 dans la séance du consistoire [de Paris] . . . en faveur des réunions religieuses des sociétés de secours israélites de Paris." BN: Ld^{185} 54 and Arch. P.C., AA 3, June 24, 1839.

129. Ibid., July 3, 1839.

130. Petition by the delegates of the mutual aid societies to the Paris consistory, July 10, 1839, Arch. P.C., B 21.

131. Arch. P.C., AA 3, July 15, 1839.

132. Ibid., July 22, 1839.

133. Ibid., July 31, 1839.

134. Arch. P.C., B 21, Préfet de Police to Paris consistory, August 16, 1830.

135. Ibid., Créhange and Sociétés de Secours to Paris consistory, August 28, 1839.

136. Ibid., Benoît Cohen to Paris consistory, December 27, 1839.

137. Arch. P.C., AA 3, January 6, 1840.

138. Ibid., February 3, 1840. The consistory also took the opportunity to remind David that as cantor of the consistorial temple, he should remember that he belonged in the temple during prayers.

139. Arch. P.C., JJ 1, November 3, 1839.

140. The 1852 renovations enlarged its capacity to 1200, but by the time the consistory built a second synagogue, the Parisian Jewish population had increased to about 25,000.

141. Only three issues of this journal appeared, in 1839–1840.

142. *A.I.*, 1 (1840), 21.

143. Arch. S.C., minutes of the commission administrative, uncatalogued, November 8, 1839.

144. *A.I.*, 1 (1840), 21.

145. Police prefect to Paris consistory, March 30, 1842; police prefect to Paris consistory, September 3, 1842; Montchaux (of a mutual aid society) to Paris consistory, September 4, 1842; all three documents in Arch. P.C., B 22. Arch. P.C., AA 3, April 11, 1842. Société de Patriarches to Paris consistory, September 10, 1843, and other letters in Arch. P.C., B 23. Comité de bienfaisance to Paris consistory, January 23, 1844, in Arch. P.C., B 24.

146. Comité de bienfaisance to Paris consistory, January 23, 1844, Arch. P.C., B 24. "Les amis des enfants d'Israél" was mentioned as having held prayer meetings throughout the year, although it did not contribute to the charity board.

147. Préfet du Meurthe to sous-préfet, April 1, 1844; sous-préfet to préfet, April 12, 1844; préfet to Nancy consistory, April 16, 1844; Nancy consistory to préfet, May 17, 1844; préfet to sous-préfet, June 5, 1844; préfet to sous-préfet, June 30, 1844. All these documents are in A.D. Meurthe-et-Moselle, V 3.

148. In regard to the Rouen affair, see Arch. P.C., AA 3, April 30, 1846; Paris consistory to central consistory, November, 1846, in Arch. P.C., I^{CC} 34. In regard to the Reims case, see sous-préfet à Reims to préfet, August 29, 1846; ministry notes; préfet to minister, September 4, 1846; minister to Paris consistory, September 12, 1846; central consistory to minister, January 21, 1847; minister to préfet de la Marne, April 24, 1847. These documents are in A.N. F^{19} 11029.

149. See, for example, circular to several societies, by the charity board, July 26, 1844, in Arch. P.C., B 24.

150. Préfet de police to Paris consistory, October 19, 1845, in A.N. F^{19} 11029.

151. Arch. P.C., AA 4, September 5 and October 9, 1848.

152. Report (printed) of the Paris consistory, February 25, 1862, Arch. P.C., K 4.

153. The decision to prosecute was made against the objection of Grand Rabbi Mayer Lambert, who argued the religious importance of the *minyanim*, generally held for *kaddish*. Arch. M.C., in A.D. Moselle, 17 J 40, May 29, 1851, and Metz consistory to central consistory, June 5, 1851, in Arch. P.C., I^{CC} 18.

154. Article 471, Paragraph 15 of the Penal Code punished infractions of the rules governing the general administration of France. The consistories considered themselves part of this general administration. Moreover, since their discovery that Articles 291 and 294 were not applicable, they counted on this provision. The court decision against the Colmar consistory is reported in *Recueil général des lois et arrêts* (Paris, 1851), 1.70–1.71, which erroneously dates it as August 23, 1851. It must have occurred in May. Cf. Metz consistory to central consistory, June 5, 1851, in Arch. P.C., I^{CC} 18.

155. There were 18,000 Jews in Paris, but only 2300 in Metz.

156. Arch. M.C., in A.D. Moselle, 17 J 40, September 18, 1851.

157. Metz consistory to central consistory, May 5, 1852, in Arch. P.C., I^{CC} 18.

158. Police prefect to Ministry of Cults, September 5, 1851, in A.N., F^{19} 11029.

159. Minister to the prefect of police, September 13, 1851, in A.N., F^{19} 11029.

160. Arch. P.C., AA 4, September 23, 1851.

161. Ibid., June 16, 1852.

162. A.D. Bas-Rhin, V 512, Strasbourg consistory to prefect, September 26, 1852, and prefect to mayor of Haguenau, September 30, 1852.

163. Ibid., Strasbourg consistory to prefect (about an unauthorized *minyan* in Haguenau), October 22, 1852.

164. Ibid., Haguenau police commissioner to mayor, October 2, 1852, and prefect to Strasbourg consistory, n.d.

165. Arch. M.C., in A.D. Moselle, 17 J 40, January 16, 1856.

166. Arch. S.C., minutes, uncatalogued, July 29, August 7 and 12, 1858.

167. The disharmony was apparently between the Jews of the first and second waves of Polish immigration.

168. Paris consistory to central consistory, March 12, 1858, in Arch. P.C., I^CC 34; central consistory to ministry, August 27, 1860, letter no. 8627, in Arch. CC, 1 C 10.

169. Arch. M.C., in A.D. Moselle, 17 J 39, December 21, 1829.

170. Arch. P.C., AA 3, November 18, 1839.

171. Arch. S.C., minutes of the administrative commission, uncatalogued, November 16, 1839.

172. Arch. P.C., AA 3, December 2, 1839.

173. Pisarro and de Castro to Paris consistory, September 28, 1842.

174. Arch. P.C., AA 3, August 24, 1843.

175. Arch. P.C., AA 4, February 8 and March 1, 1854.

176. *Le Monde*, September 7, 1972, p. 14. Notices of this kind appear frequently in the Jewish and general French press and are an attempt to combat the competition of North African butchers, who do not recognize the consistory as the ultimate religious authority.

177. Baron, *Jewish Community*, Vol. 2, p. 108.

178. Hertzberg, *The French Enlightenment*, p. 199.

179. Strasbourg consistory to prefect, July 21, 1825, and prefect to Strasbourg consistory, September, 1825, in A.D. Bas-Rhin, V 512.

180. Arch. M.C., in A.D. Moselle, 17 J 39, March 7, November 23, December 22, 1829.

181. Arch. P.C., AA 2, April 24, 1832.

182. Ibid., March 7, 1833.

183. Ibid., August 25 and October 11, 1836.

184. Ibid., June 18, 1838; AA 3, October 24 and November 11, 1839.

185. Ibid., AA 3, November 25 and December 2, 1839.

186. The date of the change is unknown. In 1846 a proposal was rejected by the Metz consistory to institute a meat tax to finance the new temple. Arch. M.C., in A.D. Moselle, 17 J 40, January 29, 1846.

187. The amount is not clear. Arch. S.C., minutes, uncatalogued, September 1, 1839.

188. Arch. CC, 1 B 4, February 23, 1840.

189. Arch. P.C., AA 3, April 15, 1841.

190. Ibid., May 4, 1843.

191. Lévy to Paris·consistory, March 13, 1844, Arch. P.C., B 24.

192. Nancy consistory to prefect, December 14, 1844, in A.D. Meurthe-et-Moselle, Culte Israélite, 1 V No. 5.

193. Procureur du roi de la cour royale de Nancy to the prefect of Meurthe, December 24, 1844, in A.D. Meurthe-et-Moselle, Culte Israélite, 1 V No. 5.

194. Nancy consistory to central consistory, January 10, 1845, in P.C., I^CC 31.

195. Arch. CC, 1 B 4, February 2, 1845.

196. *A.I.*, 6 (September, 1845), pp. 714–716.

197. Arch. P.C., AA 3, October 30, 1845.

198. Ibid., November 19 and December 8, 1845.

199. Petition to the central consistory, January 7, 1846, Arch. P.C., I^CC 34.

200. Arch. P.C., AA 4, January 25, 1846.

201. Arch. CC, 1 B 4, January 25, 1846.

202. Arch. P.C., AA 4, April 4, 1848.

203. Ibid., April 10 and 26, 1848.

204. *La Vérité*, April 17, 1848.

205. Arch. P.C., AA 4, June 1, 1848.

206. Ibid., October 24, 1849.

207. Ibid., March 14, 1852.

208. *Recueil général des lois et arrêts* (Paris, 1851), 1.716-1.717.

209. Marseille consistory to central consistory, May 12, 1852, in Arch. P.C., I^{CC} 28 No. 132.

210. Arch. P.C., AA 4, July 12, 1854, and prefect of police to Paris consistory, August 18, 1854, in Arch. P.C., I^{CC} 34.

211. Extrait des registres des arrêtés du consistoire. Séance du 15 septembre 1857, in Arch. JTS.

212. Circular by Bernard Lévy to the voters in the Lyon consistory election, January 15, 1877, in Arch. JTS.

213. Arch. P.C., AA 2, December 2, 1838, and Arch. CC, 1 B 4, March 2, 1845.

214. Arch. B.C., 2 A 6, December 30, 1847.

215. Arch. P.C., AA 4, March 20, 1849.

216. Arch. CC, 1 B 4, November 14, 1847.

217. Terquem, *Projet . . . circoncision.*

218. Arch. P.C., AA 3, August 19 and 22, 1844.

219. Ibid., September 17, 1844.

220. S. Bloch in *U.I.*, 1 (1844), 277 ff.

221. Petition to the central consistory, September 18, 1844, ibid., pp. 281-282.

222. Arch. M.C., in A.D. Moselle, 17 J 40, May 3, 1846.

223. Arch. S.C., minutes, uncatalogued, November 3, 1859.

224. Ibid., April 5, 1860.

225. This was reported to the Strasbourg consistory by the *procureur impérial* of Séléstat, Arch. S.C., minutes, uncatalogued, January 20, September 15, October 6 and 27, 1859.

226. Arch. CC, 1 B 5, January 3, 1853.

227. Arch. S.C., minutes, uncatalogued, April 5, 1860.

228. Arch. CC, 1 B 4, July 7 and 14, 1841.

229. Ibid., December 22, 1842.

230. Central consistory to Strasbourg consistory, January 23, 1844, Arch. CC, 1 C 8.

231. Arch. B.C., 4 A 7, December 4, 1860.

232. Sauphar's school in Paris was one of the first modern Jewish schools.

233. Arch. M.C., in A.D. Moselle, 17 J 40, November 30, 1854.

234. Goudchaux Weill, *Deuxième lettre* (Paris, 1847).

235. Arch. P.C., AA 4, October 19, 1853.

236. Arch. M.C., in A.D. Moselle, 17 J 40, April 4, 1847.

237. Ibid., October 22 and 25, 1848.

238. Arch. B.C., 2 A 6, 1856 passim.

239. Arch. S.C., minutes, uncatalogued, May 23, 1861.

Chapter IX: The Rabbinate

1. Arch. CC, 1 B 4, November 25, 1841.

2. Arch. CC, 1 B 5, March 4, 1849 and Arch. S.C., minutes, unclassified, March 22, 1860.

3. Arch. P.C., AA 2, May 4, 1837.

4. Ibid., February 6, 1839. At this meeting the consistory noted that although Prague's services were only occasional, it was well to continue his financial aid.

5. Tableau of state-salaried rabbis, 1861, in A.N. F^{19}* 1821. Cf. Tableau du mouvement qui a eu lieu depuis 1830, dans le corps des rabbins français, 1860, in Arch. CC, 3 G 1, which says that there were fifty-seven rabbinic posts in France.

6. By 1860 thirty-eight of the ninety-eight rabbis had died; one had

entered a mental institution; one had been dismissed from the rabbinate; and one had voluntarily left the rabbinate for another career. Alexandre Séligmann of Nîmes was dismissed by the central consistory on the request of the Marseille consistory (Arch. CC, 1 B 5, November 15, 1859). For a list of all the rabbis from 1830 to 1860, see Tableau du mouvement (1860), Arch. CC, 3 G 1, and Jules Bauer, *L'Ecole rabbinique de France* (Paris, 1930), p. 113.

7. Bauer, *L'Ecole rabbinique*, p. 4. Cf. Robert Anchel, *Napoléon et les Juifs* (Paris, 1928), pp. 540–541, who says that as early as 1809 the central consistory had asked for permission to open a faculty of theology. After some hesitation, permission was denied in 1812. It is unclear from Anchel's account whether the central consistory had proposed a modernization of the rabbinic studies as early as 1809.

8. Arch. M.C., in A.D. Moselle, 17 J 72.

9. Ibid., 17 J 39, minutes, meeting of *notables*, November 18, 1820.

10. Ibid., December 10, 1820.

11. Ibid., draft of letter from Metz *notables* to the central consistory, February 5, 1823. Cf. Bauer, *L'Ecole rabbinique*, p. 4, who mistakenly reports that the Metz school never opened due to financial problems.

12. Tsarphati [Olry Terquem], *Sixième lettre d'un israélite français à ses coreligionnaires* (Paris, 1824), p. 13.

13. Ibid., p. 14.

14. Bauer, *L'Ecole rabbinique*, p. 4.

15. Ibid., pp. 8, 16.

16. When the school moved to Paris, the new *règlement* required that rabbinic students obtain the *bachelier* within one year of their entrance into the seminary. Again, however, this was not applied, and it was much later (in the twentieth century) that such preparation became the norm for rabbinic students. Bauer, *L'Ecole rabbinique*, p. 145.

17. Ibid., p. 39, central consistory to Metz consistory, February 8, 1831.

18. Ibid., pp. 49–51, citing A.N. F^{19} 11025.

19. Arch. CC, 1 B 4, December 6, 1846.

20. Central consistory to Paris consistory, April 10, 1841, in Arch. P.C., B 22.

21. Arch. CC, 1 B 4, November 10, 1844.

22. Ibid., May 28, 1846.

23. Arch. M.C., in A.D. Moselle, 17 J 40, September 4, 1846, and Arch. CC, 1 B 4, December 6, 1846.

24. Arch. CC, 1 B 4, December 6, 1846.

25. Ibid., December 27, 1846.

26. Ibid., January 17, 1847, and Arch. M.C., in A.D. Moselle, 17 J 40, March 14, 1847. This is a level of achievement approximately equal to graduation from an American high school today.

27. Bauer, *L'Ecole rabbinique*, p. 67.

28. Arch. CC, 1 B 4, January 17, 1847.

29. Ibid., 1 B 5, December 3, 1848, and January 11, 1849.

30. Ibid., April 9, 1850.

31. Abraham Créhange, *Almanach religieux et moral pour l'an du monde 5611 (1850–1851) à l'usage des Israélites* (Paris, 1850).

32. Arch. CC, 1 B 5, November 16, 1850, and May 11 and June 5, 1851.

33. Ibid., June 11, 1851.

34. Arch. P.C., AA 4, January 12, 1854, and Bauer, *L'Ecole rabbinique*, p. 67.

35. Arch. M.C., in A.D. Moselle, 17 J 40, March 18, 1855.

36. Abraham Créhange, *Annuaire Parisien du culte israélite* (Paris, 1856).

37. *U.I.* (1857), p. 248.

38. Arch. CC, 1 B 5, March 29, 1856.

39. Ibid., June 12, 1856.

40. Ibid., October 2, 1856.

41. S.C. minutes, uncatalogued, March 11 and April 22, 1857. Cf. Bauer, *L'Ecole rabbinique*, pp. 101–102. It is interesting to note that this opinion came from a member of the University and not from the Jewish community. Although the consistories were anxious to foster the kind of dispersion of the Jews into the general population that existed in Paris, government officials were not as quick to condemn the existence of an identifiable Jewish community.

42. Arch. CC, 1 B 5, November 2, 1857.

43. Ibid., February 22, 1858.

44. Ibid., April 12, 1858.

45. Decree of July 1, 1859, authorizing moving the school to Paris, in Bauer, *L'Ecole rabbinique*, p. 110.

46. Abraham Créhange, *Annuaire parisien du culte israélite pour 5626 (1865–1866)* (Paris, 1865).

47. Samuel Cahen, in *A.I.*, 1 (1840), 49.

48. Bauer, *L'Ecole rabbinique*, pp. 80–81.

49. Ibid., pp. 148–149.

50. Ibid., p. 113, quoting *U.I.* (1860), p. 164.

51. B. Lipman was elected grand rabbi in Metz in 1863. It was 1867 when Grand Rabbi S. Klein of Colmar died. Strasbourg had been annexed by Germany for many years before Grand Rabbi A. Aron was replaced by Isaac Weill (1889). Bayonne received its first rabbinic school graduate as grand rabbi in 1887 (A. Astruc).

52. Tableau des ministres du culte du consistoire israélite de Nancy, January 13, 1856, in Arch. P.C., I^{CC} 31.

53. Bauer, *L'Ecole rabbinique*, p. 44.

54. Arch. CC, 1 B 4, April 25, 1847.

55. *U.I.*, 12 (1857), 420.

56. Colmar consistory to central consistory, November 1, 1857, in A.N. F^{19} 11037.

57. Arch. CC, 1 B 5, October 20, 1857.

58. Arch. S.C., minutes, uncatalogued, June 7, 1860.

59. Adolphe Franck rose from a very humble family background to a brilliant career in the university and in Jewish affairs. Curiously, he had originally hoped to become a rabbi, but was refused a scholarship to the rabbinic school.

60. In towns of less than 5000 people the rates were: 300 francs for a Jewish population between 200 and 600, 400 francs for a Jewish population between 601 and 1000, and 600 francs when the Jewish population exceeded 1000. In towns with a general population of more than 5000 people, the respective salaries were 400, 500, and 700 francs.

61. Strasbourg consistory to central consistory, April 5, 1843, in Arch. P.C., I^{CC} 15.

62. Arch. CC, 1 B 4, May 28, 1846.

63. Ibid., 1 B 5, March 4, 1849.

64. Georges Duveau, *La vie ouvrière en France sous le second empire* (Paris, 1946), passim.

65. Ibid.

66. Deutz to central consistory, July 1828.

67. Paris consistory to central consistory, December 20, 1844, in Arch. CC, 2 G 1.

68. Central consistory to Paris consistory, May 19, 1845, in Arch. P.C., B 25.

69. The decision to establish such an emergency fund for the rabbis had been suggested as early as 1852 by the Rothschilds. The rabbis in 1856 may have been inspired by Louis Napoleon's creation of a fund for retiring aged priests. Cf. John Wolf, *France 1814–1919* (New York, 1963), p. 269.

70. Bauer, *L'Ecole rabbinique*, p. 18.

71. Ibid., p. 113.

72. Ibid., p. 108.

73. Arch. P.C., AA 3, April 18, 1844, and Paris consistory to minister, reacting to the March, 1844, draft of the 1844 *ordonnance*, in A.N. F^{19} 11015.

74. Baron, *Jewish Community*, Vol. 2, p. 87. Baron thus describes the general situation in the Jewish communities of Europe from the fifteenth to the nineteenth centuries.

75. Central consistory to Grand Maître de l'Université impériale, October 16, 1809, in A.N. F^{19} 11028.

76. Arch. S.C., minutes, uncatalogued, November 3, 1853.

77. Arch. M.C., in A.D. Moselle, 17 J 40, June 8, 1853.

78. Salomon Ulmann, pastoral letter, in *U.I.*, 9 (1853-54), 203 ff.

79. Bayonne consistory to central consistory, September 22, 1864, in Arch. P.C., I^{CC} 19.

80. It is of no small interest to note that Terquem, generally considered the most radical of the early French reformers, supported for the post a man who had rejected Abraham Geiger's radicalism and who had published a condemnation of the German rabbinical conferences.

81. Bauer, *L'Ecole rabbinique*, pp. 61-64.

82. *U.I.*, 8 (1853), 289-295.

83. Bloch, in *U.I.*, 8 (1853), 385-391. Similar views were expressed by others, especially Rabbi Samuel Dreyfus of Mulhouse, who also published in *U.I.*

84. Arch. S.C., minutes, uncatalogued, November 3, 1853.

85. Lettre pastorale adressée par M. le grand rabbin du consistoire central à MM les grand rabbins, rabbins communaux et ses coreligionnaires de France, December 11, 1853, in A.D. Bas-Rhin, SHIAL, Boite I, A 22.

86. Ibid.

87. Ibid.

88. Benoît Lévy, *Les droits et les devoirs du Grand Rabbin* (Paris, 1865).

89. Olry Terquem, *Cinquième lettre d'un israélite français à ses coreligionnaires* (Paris, 1824).

90. Anchel, *Napoléon*, p. 492.

91. Arch. P.C., 1 B 4, November 14, 1847.

92. Benjamin Gradis to central consistory, "Deuxième lettre sur la réforme électorale," 1856, in Arch. JTS.

93. Arch. M.C., in A.D. Moselle, 17 J 40, January 11, February 8, 1846. The Metz consistory checked the accounts of the synagogues submitted by the rabbi. The grand rabbi was authorized to pay, from the revenues of the temple, a sum of 87^{F}50 owed to M. Mayer, printer.

94. Strasbourg consistory to central consistory, July 20, 1842, in Arch. P.C., I^{CC} 15.

95. Benjamin Wahl, *Résponses à la deuxième lettre de M. Samuel Dreyfus, rabbin à Mulhouse* (Altkirch, 1845).

96. Arch. S.C., minutes, uncatalogued, November 29, 1855.

97. Ibid., passim.

98. Metz consistory to central consistory, January 17, 1858, in Arch. P.C., I^{CC} 18.

99. Isaac Noah Mannheimer was a nineteenth-century Viennese Jewish preacher and a moderate reformer.

100. Wahl, *Réponses*.

101. On the function of the rabbis as preachers, see also Strasbourg consistory to central consistory, July 20, 1842, in Arch. P.C., I^{CC} 15 (on a salary increase for Benjamin Roos); Arch. S.C., minutes, uncatalogued, November 29, 1855 (on an assistant for Grand Rabbi Aron); Metz consistory to central consistory, January 17, 1858, in Arch. P.C., I^{CC} 18 (on an assistant for Grand Rabbi Lambert).

102. Strasbourg consistory to central consistory, July 20, 1842, in Arch. P.C., I^{CC} 15, and Arch. P.C., AA 4, July 23, 1851.

103. Arch. P.C., AA 4, July 23, 1851; Arch. S.C., minutes, uncatalogued,

November 29, 1855; Metz consistory to central consistory, January 17, 1858, in Arch. P.C., I^CC 18.

104. *U.I.*, 9 (1854), 277.

105. Arch. S.C., minutes, uncatalogued, July 21, 1859.

106. Grand Rabbi Wittersheim to Schwab (lay member of the Metz consistory), April 5, 1822, in Arch. M.C., in A.D. Moselle, 17 J 71.

107. Charleville was protesting that his modest 900 francs salary was not raised, despite repeated requests. Charleville to Paris consistory, April 19, 1855, in Arch. P.C., B 32.

108. Dreyfus, in *Le Lien d'Israél* (1855), p. 380.

109. Arch. S.C., minutes, uncatalogued, November 20, 1856.

110. S. Bloch, in *U.I.* February 1857, p. 243.

111. Arch. B.C., 2 A 6, May 12, 1853.

112. *U.I.*, 8 (1853), 203–205.

113. Arch. P.C., AA 2, December 3, 1829.

114. The Paris consistory members favored Rabbi Mayer Charleville, communal rabbi in Dijon, because he had a reputation for being very liberal. A large number of Parisian *notables,* under the influence of Crémieux, favored Rabbi Lazare Isidor of Phalsbourg, who had become well known because of his refusal to administer an oath *more judaïco.* At his successful court battle he was defended by Crémieux. The ideological dispute that underlay the competition between the two factions ran like a continuous thread throughout nineteenth-century French Jewish history. The consistory was interested in ceremonial reforms and modernization, and accommodation of the Jewish population to French society. Crémieux was an ardent and principled liberal who fought for the right of Jews to be accepted on their own terms in a secular, liberal France. It is interesting to note that in 1847, when this election campaign was being waged, Crémieux had been out of the consistory for two years. His resignation in 1845 is generally attributed to the conversion to Christianity of his wife and children, but I am of the opinion that if this was a factor in Crémieux's resignation, it was not the only one. Crémieux's liberal principles had already caused him several conflicts with his consistory colleagues. In the case of the Parisian Jewish cemeteries, Crémieux alone, of the consistory, had defended the idea that Jewish usage should prevail in Jewish cemeteries. In the case of the oath *more judaïco,* Crémieux had argued against *any* form of the oath and not only against the highly offensive one sworn in the synagogue with the Torah scrolls in hand. The consistory, on the other hand, favored a modern "inoffensive" form of the oath, which Crémieux found to be inconsistent with the concept of total equality of all citizens in the eyes of the law.

115. Nancy consistory to central consistory, January 28, 1854, in Arch. P.C., I^CC 31, and *U.I.*, 9 (1854), 328.

116. The Assembly of Notables, in reply to the question of how the rabbis are named, replied that everything regarding the rabbis was now uncertain. Since the Revolution, they said, the system had not been uniform, but in general rabbis were named by a majority vote of the heads of households.

117. Arch. CC, 1 B 5, November 10, 1850; Arch. M.C., in A.D. Moselle, 17 J 40, November 20, 1850, and February 17, 1851; Metz consistory to central consistory, November 25, 1850, in Arch. P.C., I^CC 18.

118. A.D. Bas-Rhin, SHIAL, Boite 1, No. A 19; Colmar consistory to central consistory, October 13, 1852, in Arch. P.C., I^CC 11; Arch. CC, 1 B 5, October 27, 1852; *U.I.*, 8 (1852), 107–109, 145–147.

119. *U.I.*, 8 (1852), 65–66.

120. *U.I.*, 8 (1853), 203–205.

121. Ibid., pp. 272–273.

122. Rough draft of minutes of M.C., October 2, 1837, in Arch. M.C., A.D. Moselle, 17 J 42.

123. Arch. CC, 1 B 4, March 21, 1841; Arch. P.C., AA 3, April 15, 1841; Nathan Netter, *Vingt siècles,* p. 373.

124. Arch. P.C., I^{CC} 69, Metz consistory to *Préfet de la Moselle*, March, 1842.

125. Ibid., Ministry to central consistory, April 4, 1842.

126. Arch. P.C., B 23, CC circular of July 7, 1843.

127. Grand Rabbi Ulmann's report to the central consistory on the results of the rabbinic conference, in Arch. CC, 1 B 5, June 4, 1856.

128. Bauer, *L'Ecole rabbinique*, p. 171.

129. The minutes of the Bordeaux consistory, Arch. B.C., 2 A 6, for February 5, 1852, record the decision that M. Fereyra, *ministre officiant* at the temple, would begin to instruct the cantorial students. The grand rabbi was charged with directing the courses and with periodic examinations of the students.

130. The sources describe Fereyra as *chantre*. I assume that he was supported by the Bordeaux community, in contrast to Castro, who received a state salary.

131. Arch. B.C., 2 A 6, November 15, 1853.

132. Arch. B.C., 4 A 7, B.C. circular of November 22, 1853.

133. A. D. Gironde, 1 V Culte israélite, No. 1.

134. *Le lien d'Israél*, 7 (1861), 265.

135. A.D. Bas-Rhin, V 523.

136. Several such minutes are preserved in A.D. Haut-Rhin, 1 V 92.

137. A.N. F^{19}* 1821.

138. Ibid., F^{19} 11024.

139. Ibid., F^{19}* 1821. There were at least fifty-seven *ministres officiants* according to this 1861 document. Unfortunately our copy of the document lacks two pages which would probably show another four to ten *ministres officiants*, or a total of sixty-one to sixty-seven.

Chapter X: Lay-Rabbinic Struggle

1. Good summaries of the history of the rabbinate and the development of the lay-rabbinic struggle in the early modern period are found in Baron, *Jewish Community*, Vol. 2, chapter 11, "Lay and Ecclesiastical Officers"; Katz, *Tradition and Crisis*, chapters 9, 10, "The Kehilla Organization" and "The Kehilla's Range of Activity"; and Hertzberg, *The French Enlightenment*, chapter 7, "The Jewish Community."

2. Baron, *Jewish Community*, Vol. 2, p. 89.

3. Hertzberg, *The French Enlightenment*, p. 241.

4. Baron, p. 89. Cf. p. 75, where Baron speaks of Italian Jewish "'spiritual judges' in charge of religious affairs," who were "members of mixed lay and rabbinic tribunals." Unfortunately, Baron does not elaborate on this phenomenon, and it is not clear what he means by "religious" affairs. They were probably not issues of ritual but questions that were religious then and would today be called civil (such as weddings and divorces). Cf. Hertzberg, p. 245, who, in his discussion of the Sephardi communities of southern France, argues that an intrusion of lay influence into the realm of ritual decisions had already begun in the eighteenth century. As proof he cites a 1738 dispute between the Bordeaux *parnassim* and Rabbi Jacob Haim Athias, which occurred after the rabbi dismissed a ritual slaughterer without first seeking the approval of the *parnassim*. Noting that the *parnassim* countermanded the rabbi's order, Hertzberg takes this as evidence of lay interference with ritual decisions, but I disagree with this interpretation. The regulation that Athias had violated concerned the making of public statements and posting notices in the synagogue without the approval of the *syndics* and the *parnassim* (Georges Cirot, *Recherches sur les juifs espagnols et portugais à Bordeaux*, Bordeaux, 1908, p. 81). This kind of regulation was routine and was practiced in Metz also (Anchel, *Napoléon*, pp. 491–492). Therefore, the fact that Athias was overruled is not clear evidence that Sephardi leader-

ship had lost respect for the rabbis as ritual authorities. In fact, Hertzberg himself notes (p. 206) that during a similar dispute between Athias and the *parnassim* several years later, Rabbi Hayyim Joseph David Azulai, who was in Bordeaux at the time, was asked to intervene and render judgement. It was only after Azulai judged in favor of the *parnassim* that Rabbi Athias was overruled; the elders had not taken it upon themselves to make a ritual decision, and this shows that the principle of rabbinic authority in ritual matters was still intact.

5.   Hertzberg, p. 245.

6.   In further support of his argument about the diminished prestige of eighteenth-century rabbis in the south of France, Hertzberg quotes a letter from the Bordeaux community to the prefect, in response to a question about the Bordeaux rabbis. The letter says that there is only one rabbi among them, that he has no authority, but is simply a casuist. It adds that rabbis should not take part in political meetings. Ibid., p. 245n. (The document itself is in A.D. Gironde, 1 V Culte israélite, No. 2, and not V 13 as reported by Hertzberg.) Hertzberg dates this letter at about 1790, but in my opinion it was written in 1806 and refers to the impending Assembly of Notables. Hertzberg interprets this letter as evidence of a poor lay opinion of rabbis among the Sephardim, but to me such an interpretation is not warranted. Although the word "casuist" in English is often used in a deprecating sense, this was not the case with the nineteenth-century French use of the term. The writers of the letter were simply saying that the role of the rabbi is limited to handling matters of religion and conscience, through theological interpretation, and that they should not take part in the Assembly of Notables, which was about to be convened. That Bordeaux Jewish leaders spoke of the lack of *autorité* of the rabbi meant simply that the rabbi had no right or power to *impose* obedience—i.e., no means of compulsion. This is an accurate reflection of his lack of civil jurisdiction.

7.   Benjamin Rodrigues to central consistory, August 24, 1825, in Arch. P.C., I^{CC} 58.

8.   Hertzberg, pp. 244, 246.

9.   Cirot, *Recherches,* pp. 77–82.

10.   Katz, *Tradition,* p. 89.

11.   Napoleon's original idea, as expressed in his note of August 23, 1806, was for the establishment in Paris of "un conseil de rabbins dont les membres seront les députés, les supérieurs, les surveillants des Juifs." Anchel, *Napoléon,* p. 230. The April 7, 1807, report to Napoleon by his three delegates (*commissaires*) recommended the addition of laymen who could enlighten and supervise the rabbis and carefully watch out for any secret plotting among them to increase their power. A.N., AF^{1V} pl. 2150, No. 62 et 2151, No. 119, cited by Anchel, *Napoléon,* p. 234.

12.   S. Bloch, *U.I.* (May 1857), p. 387.

13.   When the consistory system was first described in the 1806 *règlement,* the law did not assign the central consistory rabbis any ritualistic functions. They were not expected to preach in any synagogue, render ritual decisions, or teach. They were, however, to name and supervise the other rabbis, and to perform several purely administrative (civil) functions.

14.   S. Bloch, *U.I.,* 5 (1849–1850), 151–155.

15.   Arch. S.C., minutes, uncatalogued, October 22, 1857.

16.   *La Sentinelle,* troisième livraison, septième lettre, p. 6.

17.   Arch. S.C., minutes, uncatalogued, passim.

18.   A.N. F^{19} 11038.

19.   Arch. P.C., AA 2, March 26 and May 27, 1834.

20.   Paris consistory to central consistory, April 25, 1844, Arch. P.C., I^{CC} 34.

21.   Arch. CC, 1 B 4, September 19, 1844.

22.   Arch. P.C., AA 3, February 17, 19, 1847.

23.   *Le Lien d'Israél* (1855), p. 101.

24.   *U.I.,* 9 (1854), 349–352.

25. Arch. S.C., minutes, uncatalogued, November 19, 1857; Arch. P.C., AA 4, August 14, 1850; Arch. M.C., in A.D. Moselle, August 16, 1850.

26. Arch. CC, 1 B 5, June 4, 1850.

27. Bloch had held a secretarial post in the central consistory, from which he was fired because he expressed dissenting opinions in his journal, *Univers Israélite*. Although Bloch had been in a position to know and to expose consistorial secrets, his revelations cannot be accepted unquestioningly in view of his bitterness.

28. Bloch, in *U.I.*, 12 (February 1857), 245.

29. Ibid.

30. Arch. CC, 1 B 5, December 6, 1852.

31. Wormser, *Français israélites*, p. 35.

32. A.N. F^{19} 11038; cf. Szajkowski, "Simon Deutz," pp. 53–67.

33. Arch. CC, 1 B 4, June 17, 1833. The student was Alex Brunschwig, and he was expelled because of negligence in his studies and insubordination and infraction of the rules. The central consistory acted on the request to expel him, which was transmitted, according to the rules, by the Metz consistory, and because it judged that Brunschwig would set a bad example for the school.

34. Ibid.; the four rabbis ordained were Michel David Cahen, June 25, 1833; Arnaud Aron, August 21, 1833; Louis Morhange, September 25, 1833; Salomon Ulmann, May 12, 1834. The eleven rabbis whose appointments were confirmed were: Samuel Dreyfus, rabbi of Mulhouse, December 10, 1833; Salomon Ulmann, rabbi of Lauterbourg, June 5, 1834; Josué Wahl, rabbi of Sierentz, July 9, 1834; Moïse Weil, rabbi at the prison of Ensisheim, August 20, 1834; Moïse Nordmann, rabbi of Hegenheim, September 15, 1834; Simon Loeb, rabbi of Soultzmatt, September 15, 1834; David Halbronn, rabbi of Pfastatt, September 15, 1834; Nathan Strauss, rabbi of Darmbach, June 5, 1835; J. Lévy, rabbi of Niedernai, May 3, 1835; M. Durckheim, rabbi of Vosges and Haut-Marne, May 31, 1835.

35. Arch. P.C., AA 4, December 26, 1842.

36. Deutz to the Ministry of Cults, October 18, 1833, in A.N. F^{19} 11038.

37. Arch. P.C., AA 2, October 15, 1829.

38. Arch. CC, 1 B 4, July 26 and November 5, 1843.

39. Arch. P.C., AA 2, October 7, 1829.

40. Arch. M.C., in A.D. Moselle, 17 J 40, December 8, 1850.

41. The school was created in 1853 and run by Klein and the Colmar consistory (see above, pp. 254–255).

42. Colmar consistory to central consistory, November 1, 1857, in A.N. F^{19} 11037; Arch. CC, 1 B 5, March 27 and April 12, 1858; several documents in the collection of Arch. JTS, notably: printed circular by Klein, August 31, 1857; Extrait des registres des arrêtés du consistoire [de Colmar], May 27, 1858; Grand Rabbi Klein to Grand Rabbi Ulmann, undated; central consistory to Minister of Cults, undated but probably from June 1858; Cerfberr to central consistory, July 19, 1858.

43. Arch. CC, 1 B 5, September 8, 1856.

44. Grand Rabbi Wittersheim to Schwab of the Metz consistory, April 5, 1822, in Arch. M.C., in A.D. Moselle, 17 J 71.

45. Metz consistory to central consistory, March 13, 1840, in Arch. P.C., I^{CC} 18.

46. Grand Rabbi Lambert to Metz consistory, May 19, 1846, in Arch. JTS.

47. "Arrêté du ministre de la justice, chargé de l'administration des cultes, du 15 octobre 1832," in Halphen, *Recueil*, pp. 100–103.

48. *U.I.*, 12 (February 1857), 244.

49. Lettre No. 5806 in Arch. CC, 1 C 8, *Copie de Lettres*.

50. The entire text of this letter will be found below, pp. 385–386.

51. While this volume was in press I discovered Grand Rabbi Ennery's response in the archives of the Leo Baeck Institute (Alsace-Lorraine

collection), and Rabbi Dreyfus' reply in the Jewish Theological Seminary's French collection (Box Nº18).

52. Benjamin Gradis to the delegates named to elect the grand rabbi of the central consistory, no date, in Arch. JTS.

53. Arch. CC, 1 B 4, January 31, 1847.

54. Arch. P.C., AA 3, March 10, 1847.

55. Arch. P.C., AA 4, June 24, July 5, August 9 and 30, September 13, October 9 and 12, 1847.

56. Ibid., June 24, 1847.

57. Ibid., July 5, 1847. Unfortunately, none of the written replies has been found.

58. Ibid., September 13, 1847.

59. Ibid., October 9, 1847.

60. Ibid., August 30, 1847.

61. Ibid., October 12, 1847.

62. Arch. CC, 1 B 5, April 5 and May 17, 1853.

Summary and Conclusions

1. See, in this regard, Marshall Sklare, *Conservative Judaism* (New York, 1972), p. 66, who finds that decreased Jewish density is a factor in the breakdown of traditional community structure and leads to institutional and religious reforms. Although Sklare regards densities of 10–15 percent in a neighborhood as low and conducive to acculturation, while in France densities of 2–8 percent are "high," the argument in general seems transferable. We have not been able to plot density on a more local level than the town, but it is known that the Jews tended to live in close proximity within towns.

2. Fear of the poor seems to parallel the general nineteenth-century French development of the notion that the poor were dangerous, and that crowded urban conditions were responsible for the increase of crime. See Louis Chevalier, *Classes laborieuses, classes dangeureuses* (Paris, 1958).

3. Thus, Rabbi Dreyfus, in *Le Lien d'Israél*, 1 (1855), p. 101: "We will never forget that rabbis have purely religious function and the consistories have administrative functions."

4. The 1844 *ordonnance* charged the central consistory with ". . . la haute surveillance des intérêts du culte israélite. . . ."

5. Central consistory to Colmar consistory, June 25, 1837, in Arch. P.C., I^{CC} 11.

6. Arch. CC, 1 B 4, August 28, 1837. The planned measure probably prohibited householders from giving charity to migrant Jews, a traditional practice which the consistories claimed attracted foreigners to France.

7. Prefect of Haut-Rhin to Ministry of Cults, January 20, 1861, in A.D. Haut-Rhin, 1 V 91.

8. Described by Hertzberg in *The French Enlightenment*, pp. 235-236.

9. Katz, *Tradition and Crisis*, p. 130.

10. Arch. P.C., AA 2, March 26, 1834.

11. The loss of the right to tax proved to be a great problem for the Paris consistory in 1837, when that consistory saw no way to repay the temple debt by voluntary contributions. Both the Paris and the central consistories supported the reinstitution of a special Jewish tax, enforced by the state, for this purpose, but the government refused to allow it. Arch. P.C., AA 2, June 6, 1837. In 1847 the central consistory ruled that the Colmar consistory could not collect a tax to support the *école de travail de Mulhouse*. Arch. CC, 1 B 4, July 26, 1847. In 1849 the Metz consistory told the community of Tragny that no tax for support of its school was permissible. Arch. M.C., in A.D. Moselle, 17 J 40, May 23, 1849. In 1851 the Paris consistory warned the Reims community that any tax would have to be voluntary. Arch. P.C., AA 4, April 2, 1851.

12.   These factors included the emancipated status of French Jews, the low educational level achieved by the French rabbis and the general intellectual climate in France, where intellectuals were not religious. These conditions were responsible for the fact that French Jews who were disenchanted with the synagogue tended to abandon it rather than to reform it.

Appendix B

1.   The irregular and inconsistent orthography and capitalizations used in the texts that follow have been maintained in their original form.

Appendix C

1.   The questions were to be asked by the departmental consistories of candidates for the post of grand rabbi of the central consistory. Arch. CC, 1 C 8, Copie des lettres, 12 mars 1846.

INDEX